Embracing the Cloud as a Business Essential

Pankaj Kumar Rai
Loxoft (DXC Technology), USA

Tanveer Ahmad
Tata Consultancy Services, UK

B.K. Pandey
Departmentt of Information Technology, College of Technology, Govind Ballabh Pant University of Agriculture and Technology, Pantnagar India

IGI Global
Scientific Publishing
Publishing Tomorrow's Research Today

Published in the United States of America by
IGI Global Scientific Publishing
701 East Chocolate Avenue
Hershey, PA, 17033, USA
Tel: 717-533-8845
Fax: 717-533-8661
Website: https://www.igi-global.com E-mail: cust@igi-global.com

Library of Congress Cataloging-in-Publication Data

Names: Rai, Pankaj Kumar, 1979- editor. | Ahmad, Tanveer, 1981- editor. | Pandey, Binay, 1983- editor.
Title: Embracing the cloud as a business essential / edited by Pankaj Kumar Rai, Tanveer Ahmad, Binay Pandey.
Description: Hershey, PA : IGI Global Scientific Publishing, [2025] | Includes bibliographical references and index. | Summary: "A vast amount of processing power may now be accessed with only a few clicks of the mouse thanks to the development of cloud computing, which has made this possibility conceivable. "Computer as a commodity" rather than "Computer as a service" is the proper moment for enterprises to begin addressing its utilization for the first time. In light of this, the manner in which businesses approach computers for the purposes of conducting research and carrying out commercial activities will undergo a considerable transition as a consequence of this"-- Provided by publisher.
Identifiers: LCCN 2024056708 (print) | LCCN 2024056709 (ebook) | ISBN 9798369395813 (hardcover) | ISBN 9798369395820 (paperback) | ISBN 9798369395837 (ebook)
Subjects: LCSH: Cloud computing--Case studies.
Classification: LCC QA76.585 .E534 2025 (print) | LCC QA76.585 (ebook) | DDC 004.67/82--dc23/eng/20250213
LC record available at https://lccn.loc.gov/2024056708
LC ebook record available at https://lccn.loc.gov/2024056709
British Cataloguing in Publication Data
A Cataloguing in Publication record for this book is available from the British Library.

Table of Contents

Detailed Table of Contents

The legal industry is undergoing a profound transformation as a result of the combination of artificial intelligence (AI) and cloud technology, particularly in the area of contract review. This chapter investigates the profound impact that cloud-based platforms and tools driven by artificial intelligence have on improving the accuracy, efficiency, and scalability of legal processes. Natural Language Processing (NLP) and machine learning models are two examples of artificial intelligence technologies that can automate and speed up the process of analyzing contracts. These technologies can extract key terms, identify risks, and reduce the amount of human error that occurs. The traditional challenges of time-consuming manual processes, inconsistencies, and high costs are addressed by these advancements addressing these challenges.

Cloud computing has revolutionized public administration and e-government, emphasizing how it can improve digital governance. The evolution of e-government reflects a significant shift towards more accessible, efficient, and citizen-centric services, as governments increasingly adopt cloud solutions. Transformative applications like smart cities, e-health services, and digital taxation are discussed alongside the benefits of cloud computing, which include better public service delivery, process automation, and resource optimization. Cloud solution implementation is not without its difficulties, though, especially when it comes to data governance, legacy systems, and public trust. Building citizen confidence requires addressing problems with data security, integrating with outdated IT infrastructure, and guaranteeing transparency.

The crucial part that cloud computing plays in expanding access to justice through the use of online dispute resolution (ODR). Traditional legal systems frequently face significant geographical and economic barriers, which make it difficult for individuals to obtain the necessary legal assistance. Through the provision of remote access, the reduction of costs, and the streamlining of dispute resolution procedures, cloud technology offers groundbreaking solutions. The cloud-based online dispute resolution (ODR) platforms democratize legal resources and facilitate timely legal support for underserved populations. This is accomplished through an analysis of a variety of ODR platforms. Several key features, including scalability, resource integration, and enhanced data security, are investigated in order to demonstrate the impact that these features have on legal accessibility.

The critical function that cost management plays in cloud computing for modern businesses, with an emphasis on the requirement for efficient strategies to maximize operational efficiency and minimize expenses. As more and more businesses move their operations to the cloud, cost management becomes increasingly important for preventing excessive spending and ensuring the organization's continued financial viability. There are a number of important strategies, one of which is the utilization of monitoring and optimization tools that produce real-time insights into the utilization of resources. This highlights the significance of auto-scaling and scheduled resource shutdowns in order to dynamically manage resources in accordance with demand, thereby reducing expenditures that are not particularly necessary.

In the meantime, deep insights from data analysis are being provided by artificial intelligence (AI) and machine learning (ML), which is stimulating innovation through the creation of new products The revolutionary effect of technology on the functioning of organizations, with a focus on how it promotes productivity, security, and creativity. By handling repetitive tasks more skillfully, the integration of automation technologies has helped businesses increase productivity, minimize errors, and streamline operations. Advanced cybersecurity solutions like firewalls, encryption, and real-time monitoring are essential for shielding sensitive

Prediction technologies based on AI drive crucial automotive safety and financial risk assessment which results in minimizing losses as well as increasing road safety. A Hybrid AI-Econometrics Model which merges machine learning algorithms with econometric systems serves as the main proposal to estimate and quantify economic consequences linked to automotive accidents. TensorFlow performs deep learning operations within the framework alongside Statsmodels to analyze telematics data, insurance claims data and macroeconomic data for determining risks of accidents and their connected financial costs. The model uses deep learning algorithms to find patterns in accidents before calculating financial risk through GARCH (Generalized Autoregressive Conditional Heteroskedasticity) and Vector Autoregression The model provides both accurate predictions and understandable results which make it acceptable for various users including insurers and governmental agencies and automotive industries. The research shows better assessment capabilities as the model enhances protective driving environments

The integration of cloud services into contemporary business operations has made the protection of sensitive data via anonymization and encryption essential for upholding privacy and adhering to international regulations. The main legal ramifications of data protection regulations like the CCPA, GDPR, and HIPAA which set strict guidelines for the handling of personal and medical data in the cloud are examined in this chapter. It dives into the obligations of cloud service providers as well as customers, highlighting the significance of compliance in order to reduce the risks of data breaches and unauthorized access, especially when transferring data worldwide. It focuses on methods like data masking, aggregation, and tokenization that obscure or remove identifiers.

Economic policy optimization requires accurate forecasting and data-driven decision-making to navigate complex financial situations. This research combines predictive analytics and machine learning models to analyse historical economic data and project future trends using AI-driven economic forecasting. The suggested approach uses time series models (ARIMA, LSTMs) and ensemble learning techniques to increase the accuracy of macroeconomic forecasts, including GDP growth, inflation rates, and labor market dynamics. Additionally, AI-powered models process real-time economic indicators and dynamically adjust policy recommendations in response to global market fluctuations. This approach improves fiscal stability and reduces financial uncertainty by facilitating proactive economic planning. By integrating

AI-driven projections into Business Intelligence (BI) dashboards, which provide decision-makers with interactive, real-time information, the efficacy of economic strategies is further enhanced. In order to ensure data-driven governance in a global economy that is always evolving.

Cloud-based legal platforms can transform legal aid for marginalized communities, according to this chapter. Geography, cost, and social stigma prevent many people from seeking legal aid. Underserved populations are disproportionately affected by this justice gap, which makes it difficult for them to navigate complex legal systems and assert their rights. Legal service providers can overcome these barriers with cloud technology, making legal services more accessible and affordable. Virtual consultations, document submission, and case management allow users to interact with lawyers from anywhere, anytime. Marginalised communities, where location or cost prevent traditional legal services, need this flexibility.

The Commodity Revolution refers to a transformative shift in the computing industry, marked by the transition of advanced computing power from specialized, high-cost systems to widely accessible, affordable, and ubiquitous technologies. This shift democratizes computing by making powerful computing resources available to a broader range of users and organizations, fundamentally altering the landscape of technology and innovation. Historically, computing power was confined to large, expensive mainframes and minicomputers that were primarily accessible to government agencies, large corporations, and research institutions. These systems, while powerful, required significant investment and specialized knowledge to operate. The high cost of hardware, coupled with the complexity of the software and infrastructure, created a barrier that limited the ability of smaller organizations, startups, and individuals to harness the potential of computing power.

Organizational collaborative leadership is being revolutionized by the integration of artificial intelligence (AI) and business intelligence (BI), which makes data-driven decision-making possible. To improve leadership collaboration, one of the best strategies is to create an AI-driven BI ecosystem that makes use of automation, real-time insights, and predictive analytics. Organizations may automate data analysis, produce actionable insights, and make it easier for leadership teams to communicate with one another by utilizing AI-powered BI solutions like Microsoft Power BI. Leaders may use predictive models and real-time data visualization to influence their decisions thanks to this connection. AI-driven BI solutions can facilitate individualized leadership initiatives, optimize performance tracking, and streamline process automation. Businesses might thereby attain improved strategic foresight, efficiency, and agility in leadership positions. This study examines several approaches to combining AI and BI for better collaborative leadership.

The implications of ownership and joint ownership in cloud environments, particularly in light of multi-tenant systems and open-source contributions, are discussed here. There is a focus on the roles that major organizations like the United States Patent and Trademark Office (USPTO), European Patent Office (EPO), and World Intellectual Property Organization (WIPO) play, as well as specific guidelines like the European Union Artificial Intelligence Act and executive orders issued by the United States on artificial intelligencc. Furthermore, the chapter highlights the critical importance of data privacy regulations, such as the General Data Protection Regulation (GDPR) and the California Consumer Privacy Act (CCPA), in the context of patenting cloud-based artificial intelligence inventions. Concerns pertaining to ethics, the possibility of patent trolls, and the overlap with trade secret protection are some of the challenges and risks that are associated with patenting in this rapidly changing environment.

Cloud computing and the intersection of international law and cybersecurity, highlighting the pressing need for an all-encompassing framework to address the particular difficulties posed by the digital environment. Protecting sensitive data and upholding operational integrity become more crucial as more businesses move to cloud services. This requires an awareness of the obligations that cloud service providers and their clients have. A proactive approach to risk management and strong security measures are imperative given the increasing cybersecurity threats that result from this reliance on cloud computing.

The rapid adoption of cloud technologies has revolutionized data analytics and management, giving rise to serious worries about intellectual property (IP) protection. The intricacies of intellectual property in cloud-based settings, highlighting how crucial it is to protect priceless resources like proprietary models, data ownership, and algorithms. It looks at the legal frameworks that control intellectual property rights, such as regional laws and international treaties, and it highlights particular dangers related to cloud computing, like unclear data ownership and illegal access. The difficulties in safeguarding intellectual property in cloud environments, such as security flaws and the theft of proprietary algorithms. A dual approach involving legal and technical strategies is proposed to address these challenges. To establish ownership and safeguard rights, legal measures are essential.

The criminal justice system is undergoing a rapid transformation as a result of cloud technology, which is providing emerging opportunities to enhance efficiency, collaboration, and data management while simultaneously addressing challenges that

The transformative potential of cloud technology in addressing the ongoing challenges that are faced by judicial systems all over the world, particularly the inefficiencies that are caused by slow procedures and increasing caseloads at the same time. It focuses on the ways in which cloud solutions can streamline processes, improve data accessibility, and foster collaboration among legal professionals. It investigates the significant role that technology plays in the process of modernizing government institutions. The impact of cloud technologies on resource management, public engagement, and evidence management through the use of tools such as blockchain among other key areas of investigation are among the most important areas of focus.

The swift expansion of interconnected devices has revolutionized numerous facets of everyday life, improved convenience and efficiency while simultaneously elevating substantial security concerns. This chapter analyzes the legal aspects concerning the security of these devices, highlighting the essential requirement for strong regulatory frameworks to safeguard consumer data and maintain the integrity of interconnected systems. Current regulations, including the General Data Protection Regulation (GDPR) and the California Consumer Privacy Act (CCPA), and emphasizes the difficulties arising from disparate legal frameworks, cultural variances, and differing degrees of technological progress among nations.

The application of blockchain technology is revolutionizing the practice of law by automating tasks, enhancing contract management, and improving the resolution of disputes. Traditional contracts, which are hampered by the need for manual processes and inefficiencies, are being phased out in favor of digital and smart contracts, which provide transparency, security, and automation. The combination of blockchain technology and cloud computing makes it possible to create scalable solutions, which in turn assists legal firms in more efficiently managing complex data and contracts. These transitions are made easier by major cloud providers such as Amazon Web Services and Microsoft Azure, which offer blockchain services for the automation of legal processes.

To better understand the behavioral patterns that customers display while making decisions, this research project examines the intersection of online marketing and consumer behavior using data-driven approaches. The study starts with preprocessing the data, which entails using data transformation techniques to ensure that the attributes used as input for analysis are relevant and clean. This also includes the process of encoding and normalizing a range of client attributes, such as demographics, internet activity, and purchasing patterns. Then, for feature selection, the Recursive Feature Elimination (RFE) algorithm is used. To improve the model's performance, this entails identifying the features that have the biggest effects and eliminating those that are not crucial. In this study, customer behavior is classified using Support Vector Machines (SVM), a sophisticated classification technique that can capture complex and non-linear relationships in consumer data. Performance metrics like accuracy and precision are used to assess the support vector machine (SVM) model.

Cloud computing is changing business operations and boosting competitiveness. As companies move to the cloud, they gain scalable resources and advanced technologies that boost innovation and efficiency. Cloud environments allow companies to develop and deploy products and services faster, optimize processes, and respond quickly to market demands, helping them compete globally. Cloud computing allows organizations to use AI, machine learning, and big data analytics to innovate. These insights improve customer experiences, decision-making, and

and technical insights, this work equips professionals and researchers with a solid understanding of how to adopt and optimize CaaC for sustained growth.

Preface

In the digital age, the transformation of business, law, governance, and societal structures through cloud computing and related technologies is undeniable. The convergence of cloud-based services with advanced tools such as Artificial Intelligence (AI), machine learning, and data analytics has not only revolutionized the way we work but has also catalyzed a wave of innovation across various domains. This book, *Embracing the Cloud as a Business Essential*, delves into the myriad ways cloud computing is reshaping industries, empowering legal systems, and transforming traditional business operations. It explores the synergy between cloud technology and other cutting-edge tools in diverse fields such as law, business intelligence, cybersecurity, and governance.

CHAPTER OVERVIEW

Chapter 1 introduces the role of AI-driven contract review in the cloud, highlighting how automation tools like Natural Language Processing (NLP) and machine learning enhance the efficiency and accuracy of legal processes, particularly contract analysis.
Chapter 2 focuses on e-government and cloud technology, examining how digital governance is improving thc acccssibility, cfficiency, and transparency of public administration, while also addressing challenges in data governance and integration.
Chapter 3 explores cloud computing's role in expanding access to justice via online dispute resolution (ODR) platforms, particularly for underserved communities, breaking down barriers of cost, geography, and social stigma.
Chapter 4 addresses the importance of effective cost management in cloud services for businesses, offering strategies to optimize cloud resource usage and minimize operational expenses in a dynamic, cloud-driven environment.

Chapter 5 dives into cybersecurity concerns in cloud-based legal services, exploring advanced solutions such as encryption and firewalls to protect sensitive data from emerging digital threats.
Chapter 6 provides insights into AI-driven predictive analytics in the automotive industry, particularly in assessing safety and financial risks associated with accidents, illustrating the potential of machine learning models in risk mitigation.
Chapter 7 focuses on the legal implications of data anonymization and encryption in the cloud, emphasizing privacy regulations such as GDPR and HIPAA and outlining best practices for cloud service providers to comply with these laws.
Chapter 8 examines economic policy optimization powered by AI-driven business intelligence tools, showcasing how predictive analytics and machine learning can inform macroeconomic decision-making and improve fiscal stability.
Chapter 9 highlights the transformative potential of cloud-based legal platforms in empowering marginalized communities, providing accessible and affordable legal resources that bridge the justice gap.
Chapter 10 discusses the "Commodity Revolution" in computing, focusing on the democratization of advanced computing power and its role in driving innovation and accessibility across industries.
Chapter 11 explores the integration of business intelligence and AI in organizational leadership, emphasizing how data-driven decision-making can enhance collaboration, efficiency, and agility in leadership teams.
Chapter 12 tackles the challenges of patenting cloud-based AI inventions, focusing on legal and regulatory considerations such as intellectual property rights and data privacy in the cloud computing environment.
Chapter 13 examines the intersection of international law and cybersecurity in the era of cloud computing, discussing the regulatory landscape and the security obligations of cloud service providers to protect sensitive data.
Chapter 14 discusses the complexities of intellectual property protection in cloud environments, focusing on issues like data ownership, algorithm protection, and the risks of unauthorized access in cloud-based systems.
Chapter 15 concludes with a focus on leveraging cloud technology for criminal justice administration, addressing opportunities for improved data management, collaboration, and efficiency, while navigating the challenges that come with implementing cloud solutions in this field.
Chapter 16 discusses the strategic role of cloud computing in business growth, highlighting its ability to enhance operational efficiency, scalability, and cost-effectiveness. It explores migration strategies, readiness assessments, and change management procedures essential for successfully adopting cloud solutions.

Chapter 17 focuses on the legal industry, this chapter examines the privacy risks and legal considerations associated with cloud technologies in law firms. It explores data encryption issues, regulatory compliance challenges, and the legal protections afforded by regulations such as GDPR and CCPA.

Chapter 18 covers cloud technology's potential to address inefficiencies in judicial systems is the focus of this chapter. It discusses how cloud solutions can streamline legal processes, enhance data accessibility, and foster collaboration within the legal ecosystem, while also exploring tools like blockchain to modernize government institutions.

Chapter 19 delves into the importance of robust regulatory frameworks to secure interconnected IoT devices. It highlights the challenges of maintaining consumer data privacy and safety in a rapidly advancing technological landscape.

Chapter 20 exploring the intersection of blockchain and cloud computing, this chapter highlights the transformative potential of smart contracts. It examines how blockchain-powered cloud solutions can enhance legal practices, improve contract management, and facilitate dispute resolution.

Chapter 21 provides insights into how cloud-based data analytics and AI tools help businesses understand and predict consumer behavior, optimizing online marketing strategies through data-driven decision-making.

Chapter 22 focuses on cloud computing's impact on business operations, this chapter highlights how cloud solutions enable faster product deployment, improve operational efficiency, and boost innovation, helping businesses stay competitive in a globalized market.

Chapter 23 shows how Cloud platforms play a crucial role in regulating blockchain and virtual currencies. This chapter explores how cloud services enhance transparency, ensure compliance, and optimize storage for the blockchain ecosystem.

Chapter 24 discusses how AI-driven marketing tools, powered by cloud infrastructure, are reshaping the landscape of digital marketing. It explores how consumer behavior is analyzed to create personalized marketing campaigns that drive sales and improve customer loyalty.

Chapter 25 examines the potential of cloud technologies to bridge the justice gap, this chapter explores how virtual platforms and AI-driven tools are making legal services more accessible and affordable to underserved populations.

Chapter 26 focuses on the evolution of cloud computing as a commoditized resource. It explores the future of "Compute as a Commodity" (CaaC), examining its impact on businesses and the strategic adoption of cutting-edge technologies such as edge computing, AI, and quantum computing.

This book is a comprehensive exploration of cloud computing as a fundamental business and legal tool, offering thought-provoking insights and practical approaches to harnessing its transformative power in various industries. As cloud technology continues to evolve, it is crucial for professionals, businesses, and policymakers to understand its potential, challenges, and best practices to effectively leverage this essential tool.

Chapter 1
AI-Driven Contract Review in the Cloud Enhancing Legal Precision and Speed

Gargi Sharma
Department of Psychology, Manipal University Jaipur, India

Himani Sharma
Department of Commerce, Manipal University Jaipur, India

ABSTRACT

The legal industry is undergoing a profound transformation as a result of the combination of artificial intelligence (AI) and cloud technology, particularly in the area of contract review. This chapter investigates the profound impact that cloud-based platforms and tools driven by artificial intelligence have on improving the accuracy, efficiency, and scalability of legal processes. Natural Language Processing (NLP) and machine learning models are two examples of artificial intelligence technologies that can automate and speed up the process of analyzing contracts. These technologies can extract key terms, identify risks, and reduce the amount of human error that occurs. The traditional challenges of time-consuming manual processes, inconsistencies, and high costs are addressed by these advancements addressing these challenges.

DOI: 10.4018/979-8-3693-9581-3.ch001

1. INTRODUCTION

The legal tech industry is making a revolution thanks to Cloud-based, artificial neural network (Pandey, B. K., & Pandey, D. (2023), powered Contract Review which accelerates both the speed and accuracy of Contract Management processes. Since it is a traditionally human workforce-driven practice, old methods of contract reviews are expensive, time-consuming, and prone to errors. All this is due to the recent advancements in Artificial Intelligence (Pandey, B. K., & Pandey, D., 2025), particularly in Machine Learning and Natural Language Processing. Another big advantage of AI in contract review is its ability to quickly scan large volumes of data. Essential terms, clauses, and obligations are things that can be automatically scanned, extracted, and classified by AI from legal documents. This consequently makes the search for important provisions much easier within the bulk of information about indemnity, confidentiality, and dispute resolution clauses. The artificial intelligence recognizes disparities, risks, and improprieties that may pose a financial or legal risk by cross-referencing with predefined regulations (Khadka, M. et al., 2025) such as identifying inconsistencies, hazards, and non-standard terms that might be financially or legally risky through cross-referencing against pre-established rules. In addition to speed, this enhances the accuracy of contract analysis.

Human reviewers may overlook certain details or make incorrect judgments when the number of contracts is vast. AI-powered systems, on the other hand, are dependable and carry high accuracy in spotting errors (Sheela, M. S. et al., 2025), ambiguities as well as missing sentences. Even the legal vocabulary is less likely to be misunderstood because NLP can determine the context, which reduces the chances of a dispute due to provisions being missed and hence presents a more exact contract review. To make these AI-driven systems available, it is mandatory to use the cloud. High volumes of contracts can be handled by legal teams using scalable cloud-based platforms without investing heavily in on-premises infrastructure. Support for remote access which cloud-based solutions make possible can promote legal collaboration among professionals in different physical places. This would promise quick updates to contracts. Cloud-based systems come with robust securities to protect confidential information. This may involve compliance with GDPR as well as encryption. With AI and human input, among other more tedious areas of contract review, high-value work such as contract negotiation and risk management can be the typical focus for legal teams.

1.1 AI in Legal Services

AI is changing the way many industries operate, and legal tech is one of the fast-evolving areas. The enhanced complexity of business relations and globalization have made automation tools increasingly important for many previously manual and cumbersome processes. AI (Satheesh, N. et al., 2025) is transforming operations for a wide variety of legal applications. One example is contract management. Contract reviewing processes have been redundant and cumbersome for a long time. For hours before the implementation of contracts, attorneys and legal teams spent countless hours reading, analyzing, and referencing various documents against each other. With large numbers of agreements, it significantly delayed the process and raised the possibility of a slip, and with it possible legal disputes or entries. Much of what was previously done manually by lawyers is today automated through AI-powered tools (Russell, S. J., & Norvig, P., 2016). One other major factor that increases the demand for AI in legal technology is the acceleration that is required. Processing all these documents quickly and accurately is within the capabilities of a business that piles up many contracts to be implemented. Herein is where AI for automatic extraction of important information, recognizing probable risks, and ensuring regulatory compliance come into the picture without having to be done manually (Kumar, M. S. et al., 2025). In reality, AI takes away the managing of dreary work from legal professionals and allows them to focus on higher-value, more strategic tasks such as advising clients about complex issues of the law or negotiating better terms. Legal proceedings must also become more accurate as a larger number of rules multiply in every jurisdiction with each set of regulations. With the ability to keep attorneys updated and to make better choices, AI tools can pave the way for the control of these intricacies by adapting to what is happening around the world in the practice of law. One more add-on that makes the demand for AI in contract review surge upwards is the increasing pressure for cost-cutting. Legal services are generally expensive, and manual contract review greatly multiplies time consumption regarding business operations, thereby simultaneously increasing costs. AI solutions will cut both by speeding document review and reducing probable costly litigations or compliance disagreements because of errors (Sharma, L., & Garg, P. K., 2021).

1.2 Cloud Technology

Cloud computing has become a mainstream aspect of all business activities today and proves very valuable to the legal industry by making it efficient, available, and scalable. More specifically, legal professionals face the challenge of coping with increasing volumes of data (Konapure, C. G. et al., 2025) and documents on a daily basis because the on-premise setup does not offer capacities or elasticity. With the constraints removed, the cloud solution gives such an infrastructural feature that is flexible and can scale up as and when the size of the legal team grows. One of the greatest advantages of the cloud is the ability to be able to scale rather quickly and with good economics. Organizations pay for what they consume with cloud platforms unlike physical data centers that have high upfront investments and high maintenance costs. Thanks to this elasticity, the law firm or legal department can readily scale up its storage and processing capacities as its clientele or cases grow all that without having to pay the hefty fees associated with traditional infrastructure. All that ability to cut back operations when demand sags assure effective resource management to help businesses better control their operating costs. Another important benefit is access. The last is highly applicable to legal teams, which often work from many venues, in these days' more remote and hybrid work environments. Cloud services provide security and access to all data, applications, and files available over the Internet from any location with Internet availability (Singh, S. et al., 2025), furthering collaboration. Not only does it foster real-time collaboration between a team and its members but even its clients and external partners as well as productivity. Cloud-based solutions facilitate effective communication and coordination through file sharing, virtual meetings, or simultaneous contract reviews. Efficiency is another aspect that can be redefined through cloud computing. In a manual setup, it would be quite arduous to handle large volumes of legal documents. This is because it would require a filing system involving searching and retrieval processes. Information and important documents for study are easy to find with automated workflows on cloud platforms. Specific information on a certain topic is accessible and retrievable with speed (Sharma, M. et al., 2025). All these features work to develop even greater efficiency (Singh, S. et al., 2025) with functionalities such as AI-centric document analysis and search tools. Security and compliance remain the key concerns for legal operations. And on this front, the cloud providers have it well cut out. Powerful encryption, multi-factor authentication, and compliance with various industry laws such as HIPAA and GDPR represent some leading cloud solutions. In this way, private legal information can be kept safe but at the same time be retrievable by individuals who are authorized to access it (Aguiar-Pérez, J. M. et al., 2023).

2. THE NEED FOR AUTOMATION

2.1 Traditional Contract Review

Contract review has persisted as one of the most time-consuming and labor-intensive processes in law. The manual reviewing, interpreting, and evaluating of legal documents have long been inefficient. Increased volume and complexity of business and legal contracts further limit manual processes. Such age-old techniques are slow, prone to inaccuracies, and can be expensive for legal professionals to implement on a time-on-task basis. Most notably, however, time is probably the biggest issue with traditional contract review. Attorneys may take hours or days going through an agreement to identify provisions that could be detrimental to the parties. Frighteningly, therefore, very pertinent multi-party contracts may be even more challenging because they are lengthy and complex. Hastening important commercial or legal decisions is difficult when dealing with such slow documentation. Globalization and more partnerships mean even more contracts, rendering legal teams even more inefficient. Also, human error is always bound to occur amidst the labyrinthine, technical language that engulfs all individuals in interpreting legal paperwork correctly. Even the most experienced lawyers can make mistakes due to fatigue. Misinterpretation of provisions or omission of any critical clauses can result in actual harm to the client and the firm. In addition, the inconsistent review of documents among the legal team members can lead to inconsistent contract reviews. Disputes, financial losses, and failed compliance would be the outcome, as legal results hinge on the wording precision and detail. Manual contracting is expensive, time-wasting, and an error process (Marr, B., 2019). Professional legal experts are expensive for reading and analyzing contracts. Even for in-house legal departments and law firms, more than half of their time is spent on reviewing contracts, but it may not be the most appropriate thing to do. For smaller firms, particularly in sectors where contracts are numerous (like technology, finance, and real estate, a manual review of contracts would be very expensive. The costs are simply prohibitive for smaller firms or those with sparse legal resources since the work requires very specialized legal expertise. Traditional contracts won't work. The formula for calculating how much manual contract review costs is simple: the larger the company, the more contracts it signs, and the greater the number of transactions it is involved in, the more labor-intensive a task it becomes. Building up a legal team in an attempt to meet these requirements is extremely not feasible plus very costly. Thus, manual review is not very effective. Bottlenecks, delays, and reduced productivity become avenues once there is no automation (Pandey, B. K. et al., 2024a) or streamlining due to scalability issues. Slow turnarounds can find their way into the operations of the business, relationships with clients, and even deal closures. Old-fashioned methods often fall short concerning changes in the law or regulations. Since the changes in the law's contracts are supposed to be updated for compliance. This manual updating is ineffective and increases the chances of non-compliance that can put businesses at odds with the law, which is not in their best interest.

2.2 Complexity of Modern Contracts

Contracts have become more intricate nowadays, particularly in globalized businesses. With the growing geographical presence of companies and collaboration with more parties, volumes and complexities of contracts have also expanded. Presently, contracts involve a broad array of legal, financial, and operational matters rather than basic agreements. Increasing business agreements and continuous changes in regulations (Pandey, B. K. et al., 2024b) that keep on demanding modifications and monitoring just to comply multiply the situation. The more contracts the business process so does the complexity rise. With companies increasingly expanding globally and doing business with multiple suppliers, partners, and customers in various regions, there is a need for specialized agreements for each party involved. The complexity rises as companies extend their supply chains, open new markets, and transact across borders. It is tougher due to regional regulations, different cultures, and new demands within business flow. There is complex local law to keep in hand alongside substantial contracts. Indeed, each contract has to be retailed by the attorneys because what goes in one may not be enforceable against the other. Here is how the tone can be retained: Global Legal Aspects should be understood by the legal department to guarantee the adherence of contracts, making it all even more complex. Other factors that complicate the drafting and review of international contracts are exchange rate, taxation, and import/export legislation and labor laws. The constant changes in national and international regulations make the management of modern contracts even more complex. These laws and regulations are constantly revised by governments and regulating bodies. Business enterprises need to be up-to-date with the new legislations regarding financial management, healthcare management (Vinodhini, V. et al., 2022) as well as technological management to avoid legal penalties. Privacy laws also bring a great deal of pressure in drug, banking, and data processing (Basha, A. J. et al., 2024). Therefore, it is necessary to monitor and update the contract according to new regulations. Even a slight change in rules and regulation like that in data security, reporting, and liability leads to the change in terms of a contract. Thus, updating the contracts is very important in those highly regulated industries. This includes incorporating new risks concerning cybersecurity and environmental regulations into modern contracts. Contracts currently cover data breaches (KVM, S. et al., 2024), IP and sustainability. As more issues are brought on board when drafting and negotiating contracts, additional legal risks and industry regulations need to be taken into account. To manage increasing complexity, many organizations are using technology as well. The review and update of the contract can be made more efficient by lawyers through the use of AI (Muniandi, B. et al., 2024) and ML-powered tools, which are capable of doing things such as large contract analytics, regulatory-changed clause identification, and compliance check across jurisdictions. The tools can be of help for companies to keep their fast-changing regulatory environment compliant and their contracts legal.

3. ENHANCING LEGAL PRECISION

3.1 AI-Powered Tools

Natural Language Processing (NLP) effectively dissects impenetrable legal language to draw terms, conditions, and obligations of significance from within contracts. An input of several documents allows the machine learning model to locate risks, disparities, and non-standard terms by finding trends and deviations across various agreements. The utilization of these AI technologies in combination significantly improves the efficiency and effectiveness of a process of contract management since they will, first of all, simplify the process of contract analysis but also allow accuracy and assistance in compliance. These technological breakthroughs help legal teams manage complex documentation, guaranteeing compliance and informed decision-making. Figure 1 shows the AI Powered Tools (Rai, P. K. et al., 2024).

1. *Natural Language Processing (NLP)*: The ability to extract key provisions, phrases, and obligations from contracts hinges upon the existence of NLP. This will enable the quick review of documents that would have been time-consuming for human reviewers, as it adeptly handles complex legal language and dense text. NLP reduces the chances of losing or misinterpreting information by noting and categorizing standard and non-standard clauses, ensuring, therefore that all critical components are identified and understood aright.
2. *Machine Learning (ML)*: Machine learning, by spotting possible risks or disparities in agreements, improves the analysis of contracts. It does this by learning from its data, historical patterns, and trends, comparing terms from numerous documents to note deviation from regular practices. In turn, this will improve the accuracy of such risks and compliance since the models adapt and refine their capacity of identifying non-standard or unusual terms as they process further contracts.
3. *Automated Workflow Integration:* Artificial intelligence-powered tools will, therefore, ease contract analysis by executing redundant tasks like data entry and extraction of provisions. This would best be considered in reducing the manual workload and minimizing mistakes made by humans as well as picking up the reading pace. Instant insights and summaries are brought forward, which fosters quick decision-making and, hence, better contract management in an efficient manner due to the uniform analysis that is conducted across many documents.

4. *Compliance and Risk Assessment*: AI tools are used to test potential non-compliance indicators and disparities thus testing the risks that exist and if compliance is followed. In other words, it helps in identifying where there is an incompatibility or contradiction that exists between the documentation to ensure that contracts meet the relevant regulations and rules. This will empower the legal team members to raise issues and ensure terms are consistent with the policy and requirements of the company regarding law provision.
5. *Adaptability and Scalability*: AI contract analytics tools offer flexibility and scalability in the effective management of large volumes of contracts without compromising on accuracy—they grow with the needs of the organization, able to handle portfolios that go from small contracts to large ones. They will integrate changes and updates in regulations as well as in legal dialects as part of the process of analysis that accommodates newer types of contracts and changing legal language.

Figure 1. Tools driven by AI

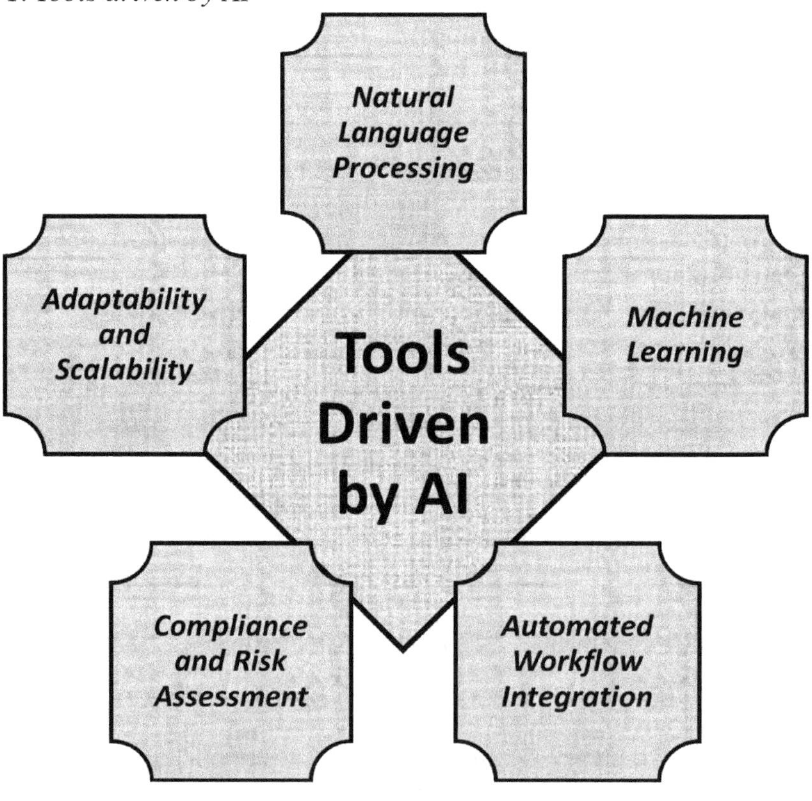

3.2 Reducing Human Error

The precision and trustworthiness of legal appraisals have long been marred by errors in human contract analysis. Traditional manual methods are prone to human errors, as they are also often a result of fatigue and variations in skill level. AI technology minimizes such errors; NLP and ML, for instance, eliminate much of this subjectivity. In order to enhance the accuracy and speed by which contract management is carried out, artificial intelligence should spot errors, omissions, and ambiguities, and make cross-references to prior legal data and case law. One of the most important things AI (Satheesh, N. et al., 2025) brings to the table with contract analysis is it can always do the finding of mistakes, omissions, and ambiguities. Unlike human reviewers who might overlook details because of fatigue or cognitive limitations, AI systems evaluate every contract using strict and uniform criteria. NLP algorithms (Kumar, B. et al., 2024) thoroughly parse the text and identify vague language as well as missing clauses that would otherwise be overlooked by human reviewers. For example, NLP would catch something as seemingly small as incomplete clauses within sentences that could be problematic. Consistency (Pandey, D. et al., 2024) reduces the chance of missing issues and ensures that all salient points of the contract are captured. All of these efforts require large-scale training data since the models, basically machine learning, learn from data. Huge repositories of legal documents and case law are used in training machine learning algorithms to pick up trends and even deviations from the norm. For instance, an ML model (Shahul, A. et al., 2024) can learn and detect a clause typical of contracts similar to the one being appraised but missing from the one under review. The system is designed to minimize error in contract analysis and improve detection capabilities by learning from new data and legal precedent. Always cross-reference case law and historical legal data to reduce chances of human error. By running a check through vast databases containing previous contracts, court decisions, and changes in regulations, AI ensures that present agreements are up-to-date.

AI systems can validate the contract terms with a set of rules for legal requirements and best practices in a particular area. AI may track issues based on historical data and suggest changes if a new contract contains a clause that deviates from the practice within such an industry. AI performs cross-referencing with terms that are risky or non-standard. It will compare any unusual or problematic clauses in a contract to parallel references in a database of reviewed contracts and case law from its previous analyses to flag clauses that represent a business risk (Lakshmi, K. V. N. et al., 2024). Taking proactive measures, problems are circumvented and strong, legal contracts are ensured. The review is enhanced through AI-based technologies because they provide in-depth analysis that exceeds mere error detection and text parsing. They can pick up on problematic clauses based on comparing atypical or problematic clauses within a contract against a database of analyzed contracts and case law. Doing so reduces the risk for the reviewing attorneys, as well as the possibility of manually performing such an analysis since reviewers may focus on specific clauses without their larger implications. Scalability problems that would arise with manual review are resolved by contract analysis with AI (Saravanakumar, R. et al., 2024). The volume as well as the complexity of contracts over and above the capability of traditional methods has led to errors and irregularities. Because of its scalability, every contract is examined fairly, which lowers the possibility of human error.

4. IMPROVING SPEED AND EFFICIENCY

4.1 Automating Repetitive Tasks

Automation has completely changed how repetitive tasks in the realm of contract scrutiny are executed and brought about immense benefits in terms of time efficiency and accuracy (Kumarganesh, S. et al., 2024). Advanced AI, particularly NLP and ML in AI, makes it easier to spot and categorize common clauses plus hasten the generation of contract synthesizes. In this way, therefore, this automation effectively addresses the challenges related to manual steps by providing the legal teams tools ad hoc and reliable to manage a large number of contracts. A core application of automation in contract review is the identification and classification of standard clauses. Commonly, contracts include typical components such as indemnity, force majeure, confidentiality, and dispute resolution. Traditionally, legal practitioners spent considerable amounts of information-intensive tasking time analyzing and hand-classifying provisions in writing agreements a process that could be both laborious and error-prone. Human-written text: This creates an opportunity for AI-based systems to identify and group collocations with a high degree of precision. NLP algorithms can extract and classify related clauses in terms of their actuality, substance, and purpose from complex legalistic textual information.

Implementation of the automatically prepared classification mechanism not only minimizes the possible error on the part of a human but also assures correct identification and documentation of each and every clause. For example, indemnity clauses assign liability for particular risks; on the other hand, force majeure clauses deal with unforeseen circumstances that may affect the performance of a contract. All these bring in automation in the process of clause categorization such that the expertise of legal professionals can be channeled towards more complicated parts of the contract, rather than largely consuming their time on repetitive tasks. Improved efficiency not only results in an expedited review process but also fosters consistency and accuracy in identifying clauses. Another significant advantage of automation is the ability to produce short overviews rapidly of pertinent sections of a contract. Manually reviewing an agreement requires reading through voluminous pages to pull out the important information, a process that can be time-consuming and easily prone to error. AI-based tools can quickly summarize key provisions, duties, and terms of the agreement for speedy but complete whole-contract details and the most salient points. For instance, where a business (Muralidhar, L. B. et al., 2024) has to assess many supplier agreements, AI technologies could parse each agreement for critical concepts regarding topics such as payment terms, delivery schedules, and compliance duties. This quick summarization allows legal teams to review and compare contracts more efficiently (Pandey, B. K. et al., 2024c), thereby accelerating the decision-making process and curtailing man-hours spent on a review analysis. This homogeneity might diminish the differential tendencies in manual summarization, in which diverse reviewers may highlight various focuses of the contract or view terms diversely.

4.2 Accelerating Turnaround Times

In fact, contract management has completely been disrupted by AI technologies that process huge bundles of contracts at a time and allow real-time sharing. These innovations result in very productive uses while at the same time eliminating drawbacks involving manual reviews and archaic methods. This is because an AI tool can process more than two hundred contracts when time taken, manually can be spent on one. Traditional methods include going through each document carefully, examining and understanding it. This calls for a lot of manual input. Such processes are not only time-intensive but also prone to errors due to human fatigue and oversight. On the flip side, AI-based solutions leverage sophisticated algorithms (Pandey, B. K. et al., 2024d) and models to scan and assess contracts within minutes. Important terms, clauses, and other details can be extracted almost instantly from thousands of documents in a single batch. As a result, organizations can better manage their contract portfolio since it drastically reduces the amount of time needed to review a contract, they can now identify and classify their contracts according to predetermined criteria- compliance requirements, financial terms, or risk level.

AI can do this at remarkable speed. By automating (Elarmathi, S. et al., 2024) this process, the legal team can focus on more complex and strategic work that demands less time for monotonous and manual-intensive undertakings. Furthermore, the accuracy and swiftness involved in the AI-enabled contract process reduces any likelihood of errors or deadline misses that come with manual review processes. Traditional contract management normally involved several iterations of document exchanges between the parties during the review and negotiation. This may give rise to some form of misinterpretation, as well as delays and version control issues. With a cloud-based AI solution (George, W. K. et al., 2024), multiple parties can access or edit contracts at the same time from different locations, thereby resolving such issues. This would allow multiple stakeholders to work on a contract at the same time through real-time collaboration, thus allowing changes and feedback to be noted on the spot. Hence, everyone would always be working with the latest version of the document and would witness updates happening real-time due to this collaborative environment (Abdullahi, M. et al., 2024). This reduces the chance of errors that could result from using old or incorrect contracts. Secure access and centralized document storage are two additional benefits of cloud-based platforms. With an opportunity to access contracts from any internet-connected device, stakeholders can work from home and be assured that essential documents are available. The infrastructure of the cloud records every single modification ever made on the contract and traces it down. Such transparency assures to liability and facilitates an easier rollback to previous versions in case that is necessary. Cloud-based platforms integrated with AI tools can provide real-time analytics and insights into contract data. KPIs, compliance metrics, and contract milestones are some of the necessary parameter's AI can monitor and provide insightful data for proactive management as well as well-informed decision-making.

4.3 Reducing Bottlenecks

To improve efficiency as well as the decision-making process within legal and business operations, it is fundamental that the bottlenecks of the contractual processes be eliminated. In a general context of streamlining workflows, addressing common delays, and boosting the pace of contract reviews, then AI can find its way making decisions faster. Some of the repetitive and time-consuming manual tasks involved in workflows are replaced by artificial intelligence technologies. Typical bottlenecks in the manual review process for contracts are data entry by hand, clause identification, and document comparison. These create bottlenecks for the workflow, slow work down, and ultimately result in errors adding to the overall problem at hand. To make a substantial increase in speed, Natural Language Processing and Machine Learning-enabled AI tools can automate those tasks. For example, artificial intelligence can rapidly extract keywords, classify phrases, and spot anomalies or issues of compliance, which used to involve a great deal of manual work. If workflows are streamlined and AI incorporated, then manual reviews and handling of documents are something of the past and with that come speed.

The rate at which AI processes and reviews contracts far exceeds the human reviewer; as a result, issues and checks relating to compliance can be highlighted much quicker through the inefficiencies of the human reviewer. Not only is the review process hastened, but there is less chance of a mistake and omission; this means that ultimately, contractual operations will be much smoother and more reliable than before. The rate at which contracts are reviewed has a substantial direct effect on decision-making because the stakeholders receive the necessary information more quickly. Thus, decisions can be made based on accurate information without the need for prolonged review times in which critical opportunities could be lost. This is especially crucial in periods identified as fast-paced business environments where time-bound responses can tilt the competitive or operational advantage of an issue. In order to improve business outcomes, a business could focus on reducing the time taken in a review, enabling it to seize opportunities and tackle challenges more quickly.

5. CLOUD AS AN ENABLER

5.1 Cloud-Based Platforms

Platforms that are hosted in the cloud provide flexibility by enabling remote access to contracts and real-time collaboration. They ensure that documents are stored in a secure and centralised location, with version control, which improves both efficiency and transparency. While automating workflows and providing advanced analytics for data-driven decision-making, these platforms are scalable, cost-effective, and integrate seamlessly with other business systems. They integrate with different business systems. As the figure 2 illustrates, there are many advantages to using cloud-based platforms.

Figure 2. Cloud-based platform advantages

- *Accessibility*: Cloud-based platforms facilitate flexible and remote work by enabling users to access contracts from any location with an internet connection. This is especially helpful for international teams operating in various time zones because it guarantees that everyone has instant access to critical documents without being limited by geography or conventional office layouts.
- *Real-Time Collaboration*: Multiple stakeholders can review and edit contracts at the same time using these platforms. When contracts are exchanged via email or other manual procedures, there may be delays and misunderstandings. Real-time collaboration guarantees that updates and feedback are made promptly. This facilitates better teamwork and expedites the negotiation and review process.
- *Centralized Document Storage*: By keeping all contracts in one safe location, cloud-based platforms simplify document management. By doing this, the

chance of losing significant contracts or version inconsistencies is eliminated. Additionally, it streamlines the retrieval process so that users can locate and access contracts more quickly.

- *Version Control*: Users can be sure they are working on the most recent version of a document at all times because the platform keeps track of contract modifications and versions. Teams can quickly review earlier versions and go back to earlier iterations if needed by having a comprehensive history of edits. This degree of control minimizes errors brought on by out-of-date documents and improves transparency.
- *Enhanced Security*: To safeguard confidential legal data, cloud platforms with advanced security features like encryption and role-based access controls are available. They offer audit trails that track who have accessed or modified a document, guaranteeing responsibility and adherence to data security laws.
- *Scalability*: These platforms are easily scalable to meet the demands of a business, accommodating higher contract volumes as the enterprise expands. Because of their flexibility, cloud-based solutions are very affordable and future-proof since they enable businesses to adapt without having to make significant changes to their infrastructure.
- *Cost Efficiency*: Cloud platforms lower maintenance costs associated with on-premises infrastructure and do away with the necessity for physical storage. In addition to having a reliable, scalable system, businesses can better manage their budgets with lower operating costs and subscription-based pricing structures.

5.2 AI and Cloud Integration

Combining AI's power with the cloud's flexibility and scalability is transforming industries. AI needs a lot of data and computational power, which cloud platforms provide. AI-integrated cloud services allow businesses to use advanced analytics, automation, and machine learning without on-premises hardware or IT teams. This synergy allows real-time processing of large amounts of data. Cloud-based AI algorithms can extract insights and provide real-time analytics to help businesses make decisions. Contract management uses AI-driven tools to quickly analyze and categorize contracts, detect risks, and ensure compliance in a cloud-based platform. Businesses can streamline workflows, improve accuracy, and reduce manual processes with AI and cloud. This integration also improves scalability. Cloud platforms can easily scale to handle growing data volumes and AI workloads, allowing businesses to expand without incurring additional infrastructure costs. Organisations with fluctuating workloads or seasonal demand spikes need some flexibility. Cloud accessibility allows AI-powered tools to be used remotely and globally. The communication between teams using electronics communication channel (Pandey, B. K. et al., 2024e) and decision-making improve with real-time updates and insights. Overall, AI and cloud synergy help businesses improve operational efficiency, automate processes, and innovate while remaining flexible, scalable, and cost-effective.

6. CONCLUSION

The legal sector is undergoing a revolution thanks to the unprecedented speed, accuracy, and efficiency of contract review processes made possible by the integration of AI and cloud technology. Artificial intelligence (AI) technologies greatly increase legal precision by reducing human error, automating repetitive tasks, and processing large volumes of contracts quickly. Key contract terms can be quickly extracted and analyzed using machine learning and natural language processing, and thorough and trustworthy reviews are guaranteed by AI's cross-referencing of past data. These advantages are further enhanced by cloud computing, which offers platforms for contract administration that are scalable, accessible, and secure. It facilitates real-time collaboration, central document storage, and automated workflows all of which improve decision-making speed and expedite the review process. AI and cloud services work together to streamline contract reviews and facilitate the efficient completion of difficult, high-volume tasks. By eliminating bottlenecks and allowing legal teams to concentrate on making strategic decisions, artificial intelligence (AI) and cloud computing together provide a revolutionary answer to the long-standing problems with manual contract review. This dynamic combination leads to better results and increased agility in legal operations by fostering a more accurate, scalable, and efficient approach to contract management.

REFERENCES

Abdullahi, M., Ahmad, A., Pandey, B. K., & Pandey, D. (2024). Digital Currency Adoption: A Comparative Analysis of Global Trends and the Nigerian eNaira Digital Currency. *SN Computer Science*, *5*(5), 1–11.

Aguiar-Pérez, J. M., Pérez-Juárez, M. A., Alonso-Felipe, M., Del-Pozo-Velázquez, J., Rozada-Raneros, S., & Barrio-Conde, M. (2023). Understanding machine learning concepts. In *Encyclopedia of Data Science and Machine Learning* (pp. 1007–1022). IGI Global.

Basha, A. J., Maheshwari, R. U., Pandey, B. K., & Pandey, D. (2024). Ultra-sensitive photonic crystal fiber–based SPR sensor for cancer detection utilizing hybrid nano-composite layers. *Plasmonics*, •••, 1–15.

Elarmathi, S., Rishabavarthani, P., Sindhuja, M., Elayaraja, P., & Malathi Murugesan, S. Kumarganesh, K. Martin Sagayam, Binay Kumar Pandey, and Digvijay Pandey. (2024). Novel manufacturing systems for cancer diagnosis using ultra-sensitive photonic crystal fiber biosensor with dual-functionalized aptamer-nanocavity. *Microsystem Technologies*, •••, 1–20.

George, W. K., Silas, E. I., Pandey, D., & Pandey, B. K. (2024). Utilization of Industry 4.0 Technologies in Nigerian Technical and Vocational Education: A Conundrum for Educators. In *Examining the Rapid Advance of Digital Technology in Africa* (pp. 270–293). IGI Global.

Khadka, M., Sah, M., Chaudhary, R., Sahani, S. K., Sahani, K., Pandey, B. K., & Pandey, D. (2025). Spectroscopic, quantum chemical, and topological calculations of the phenylephrine molecule using density functional theory. *Scientific Reports*, *15*(1), 208. PMID: 39747169

Konapure, C. G., Pandey, D., Shete, H., Thakar, C. M., Pandey, B. K., & George, A. S. (2025). Artificial Intelligence in Automated Concrete Mix Design Using Computerized Grading Curves. Interdisciplinary Approaches to AI, Internet of Everything, and Machine Learning, 567-586.

Kumar, B., Pandey, D., Pandey, B. K., & George, A. S. (2024). Higher Education in the Last Four Decades: A Review of Paradigm Shifts in Policy Frameworks. Design and Implementation of Higher Education Learners' Learning Outcomes (HELLO), 333-348.

Kumar, M. S., Prasanna, P. L., Lalitha, M., Joy, M., Jha, S. S., & Pandey, B. K. (2025). Utilizing the Internet of Everything and Artificial Intelligence for Real-Time Workforce Management. In Role of Internet of Everything (IOE), VLSI Architecture, and AI in Real-Time Systems (pp. 153-168). IGI Global Scientific Publishing.

Kumarganesh, S., & Malathi Murugesan, C. Ganesh, N. Santhiyakumari, M. Thangavel, K. Jayaram, K. Martin Sagayam, Binay Kumar Pandey, and Digvijay Pandey. (2024). Hybrid plasmonic biosensors with deep learning for colorectal cancer detection. *Plasmonics*, •••, 1–15.

KVM, S., Pandey, B. K., & Pandey, D. (2024). Design of Surface Plasmon Resonance (SPR) Sensors for Highly Sensitive Biomolecular Detection in Cancer Diagnostics. *Plasmonics*, •••, 1–13.

Lakshmi, K. V. N., Rajan, R., Pandey, D., & Pandey, B. K. (2024). Circular economy: A catalyst for economic growth-an empirical study. *Circular Economy and Sustainability*, •••, 1–22.

Marr, B. (2019). *Artificial intelligence in practice: how 50 successful companies used AI and machine learning to solve problems*. John Wiley & Sons.

Muniandi, B., Nassa, V. K., Pandey, D., Pandey, B. K., Dadheech, P., & George, A. S. (2024). Pattern Analysis for Feature Extraction in Complex Images. In Using Machine Learning to Detect Emotions and Predict Human Psychology (pp. 145-167). IGI Global.

Muniandi, B., Nassa, V. K., Pandey, D., Pandey, B. K., Dadheech, P., & George, A. S. (2024). Pattern Analysis for Feature Extraction in Complex Images. In Using Machine Learning to Detect Emotions and Predict Human Psychology (pp. 145-167). IGI Global.

Muralidhar, L. B., Lakshmi, K. V. N., Swapna, H. R., Rupani, J., Nethravathi, K., Pandey, B. K., & Pandey, D. (2024). Impact of Organizational Culture on The Level of Corporate Social Responsibility Investments: An Exploratory Study. *Circular Economy and Sustainability*, •••, 1–19.

Pandey, B. K., Nassa, V. K., Mukundan, A. P., Mahajan, D. A., Pandey, D., George, A. S., & Dadheech, P. (2024c). An Industry-Focused Traffic System Utilising Internet of Things. In *Emerging Engineering Technologies and Industrial Applications* (pp. 200–213). IGI Global.

Pandey, B. K., & Pandey, D. (2023). Parametric optimization and prediction of enhanced thermoelectric performance in co-doped CaMnO3 using response surface methodology and neural network. *Journal of Materials Science Materials in Electronics*, *34*(21), 1589.

Pandey, B. K., & Pandey, D. (2025). Securing healthcare medical image information using advance morphological component analysis, information hiding systems, and hybrid convolutional neural networks on IoMT. *Computers in Biology and Medicine*, *185*, 109499. PMID: 39642698

Pandey, B. K., Pandey, D., & Lelisho, M. E. (2024a). Face mask identification with enhanced cuckoo optimization and deep learning-based faster regional neural network. *Scientific Reports*, *14*(1), 29719. PMID: 39613761

Pandey, B. K., Pandey, D., & Sahani, S. K. (2024b). Autopilot control unmanned aerial vehicle system for sewage defect detection using deep learning. *Engineering Reports*, •••, 12852.

Pandey, B. K., Paramashivan, M. A., Pandey, D., George, A. S., Agarwal, A., Dadheech, P., & Mahajan, D. A. (2024e). A recent survey on 6G vehicular technology: applications and challenges. 6G Security Education and Multidisciplinary Implementation, 337-350.

Pandey, B. K., Paramashivan, M. A., Pandey, D., George, A. S., Agarwal, A., Mahajan, D. A., . . . Pramanik, S. (2024d). Future Directions of Digital Twin Architectures for 6G Communication Networks. In Security Issues and Solutions in 6G Communications and Beyond (pp. 197-211). IGI Global.

Pandey, D., Nassa, V. K., Pandey, B. K., Mahajan, D. A., Patidar, P. K., Dadheech, P., & George, A. S. (2024). An Analysis of Internet-of-Things-Based Fire Detection and Alert Systems. In *Emerging Engineering Technologies and Industrial Applications* (pp. 295–304). IGI Global.

Rai, P. K., Pandey, D., & Pandey, B. K. (2024). The future of enterprise and innovation is compute as a commodity, or CaaC. *Partners Universal International Research Journal*, *3*(2), 89–94.

Russell, S. J., & Norvig, P. (2016). *Artificial intelligence: a modern approach.* Pearson.

Saravanakumar, R., TamilSelvi, T., Pandey, D., Pandey, B. K., Mahajan, D. A., & Lelisho, M. E. (2024). Big data processing using hybrid Gaussian mixture model with salp swarm algorithm. *Journal of Big Data*, *11*(1), 167.

Satheesh, N., Gopisankar, N., Kumarganesh, S., Anthoniraj, S., Saravanakumar, S., & Martin Sagayam, K., Binay Kumar Pandey, and Digvijay Pandey. (2025). Advanced AI-driven emergency response systems for enhanced vehicle and human safety. *Iran Journal of Computer Science*, •••, 1–16.
Satheesh, N., Gopisankar, N., Kumarganesh, S., Anthoniraj, S., Saravanakumar, S., & Martin Sagayam, K., Binay Kumar Pandey, and Digvijay Pandey. (2025). Advanced AI-driven emergency response systems for enhanced vehicle and human safety. *Iran Journal of Computer Science*, •••, 1–16.
Shahul, A., Muniandi, B., Paramashivan, M. A., Pandey, D., Pandey, B. K., Dadheech, P., & George, H. (2024). An Analysis of Algorithms and Methods Based on Image Processing for Medical Applications. In *Emerging Engineering Technologies and Industrial Applications* (pp. 173–186). IGI Global.

Sharma, L., & Garg, P. K. (Eds.). (2021). *Artificial intelligence: technologies, applications, and challenges.*

Sharma, M., Talwar, R., Nassa, V. K., Binay, K., & Pandey, D. (2025). Design and performance analysis of a multiband vivaldi antenna for wireless broadband communication in 3-5.6 GHz spectrum. In *Artificial Intelligence and Information Technologies* (pp. 86–91). CRC Press.

Sheela, M. S., Kumarganesh, S., Pandey, B. K., & Lelisho, M. E. (2025). Integration of silver nanostructures in wireless sensor networks for enhanced biochemical sensing. *Discover Nano*, *20*(1), 7. PMID: 39804434

Singh, S., Madaan, G., Swapna, H. R., Singh, A., Pandey, D., George, A. S., & Pandey, B. K. (2025). Empowering Connectivity: Exploring the Internet of Things. In Interdisciplinary Approaches to AI, Internet of Everything, and Machine Learning (pp. 89-116). IGI Global Scientific Publishing.

Vinodhini, V., Kumar, M. S., Sankar, S., Pandey, D., Pandey, B. K., & Nassa, V. K. (2022). IoT-based early forest fire detection using MLP and AROC method. *International Journal of Global Warming*, *27*(1), 55–70.

Chapter 2
E-Government and Cloud Technology Enhancing Digital Governance and Public Administration

Anita Yadav
Department of Law, Campus Law Centre, Delhi University, India

Amit Yadav
Faculty of Law, Manipal University Jaipur, India

ABSTRACT

Cloud computing has revolutionized public administration and e-government, emphasizing how it can improve digital governance. The evolution of e-government reflects a significant shift towards more accessible, efficient, and citizen-centric services, as governments increasingly adopt cloud solutions. Transformative applications like smart cities, e-health services, and digital taxation are discussed alongside the benefits of cloud computing, which include better public service delivery, process automation, and resource optimization. Cloud solution implementation is not without its difficulties, though, especially when it comes to data governance, legacy systems, and public trust. Building citizen confidence requires addressing problems with data security, integrating with outdated IT infrastructure, and guaranteeing transparency.

DOI: 10.4018/979-8-3693-9581-3.ch002

1. INTRODUCTION

The term "digital governance" describes how digital technologies are incorporated into government operations to improve public administration's effectiveness, transparency, and responsiveness to the needs of the populace. Governments are using tools like cloud computing, big data, artificial neural network (Pandey, B. K., & Pandey, D., 2023), and mobile platforms to modernize their operations and enhance service delivery as a result of the rapid advancement of technology. The greater efficiency that digital governance provides is one of its primary advantages. Governments can streamline public services and cut down on administrative overhead by automating repetitive tasks. For example, citizens can obtain services like paying taxes, registering businesses, and renewing licenses online without having to visit physical offices (Pandey, B. K., & Pandey, D., 2025). For the government as well as its constituents, this lowers expenses, saves time, and eliminates bureaucratic bottlenecks. The use of cloud technology is essential to this change. Public institutions can manage their data more scalable and flexibly and do away with expensive infrastructure by moving to cloud-based systems. Cloud solutions facilitate instantaneous departmental collaboration and enable quick service deployment. In the end, this shortens wait times and improves coordination amongst government agencies. Blockchain-based technologies are also being investigated for use in contract management, land registration, and secure voting systems.

These technologies provide tamper-proof records and reduce corruption. Governments can interact with citizens more successfully when they use digital tools. Citizens can communicate directly with government representatives through social media, mobile applications, and online portals. This enables them to express concerns, provide feedback, and remain updated on policy changes. Through online voting and e-consultations, citizens can participate in decision-making processes through participatory governance, which is made possible by digital governance systems. Governments can enhance policy outcomes and obtain valuable insights into citizens' needs by utilizing big data analytics. Data can be used to spot patterns, foresee difficulties down the road, and allocate resources as efficiently as possible. Based on current data, this aids in the development of improved strategies for everything from healthcare services to urban planning.

1.1 E-Government and Its Evolution

E-Government uses digital technologies to improve public-service interactions with citizens, businesses, and other governments. The concept has changed over the past few decades due to rapid technological advancements, changing societal needs, and the demand for transparency and efficiency in public services. E-government began in the late 20th century when the internet became popular. Public sector institutions began digitizing processes by creating websites with basic department and service information. Users could access information but not interact with online platforms in this one-way communication model. The first phase of digital transformation automated simple administrative tasks like tax returns and permit applications to boost efficiency. Early efforts laid the groundwork for more complex digital services, but technology and internet access kept progress slow and limited to wealthy nations. High-speed internet, mobile connectivity, and better software platforms accelerated e-government system development in the early 2000s. Public service websites became two-way communication platforms. Citizens could access information, submit transactions, request services, and provide feedback online (Garcia Alonso, R., & Lippez-De Castro, S., 2016). These innovations improved user convenience and public sector productivity. Service integration increased with e-government platforms. Multiple departments began offering their digital services through a single online portal. E-governance became more centralized and coordinated during this phase. Cloud computing, big data, AI, and blockchain have transformed digital governance in the last decade. Cloud platforms allow real-time service delivery and departmental data sharing. AI-driven chatbots help citizens 24/7, while data analytics help institutions make better decisions. Blockchain secures and transparently manages public records, contracts, and voting systems, reducing fraud and improving accountability. Recent advances have enabled smart governance, where digital tools enable real-time public resource management and more efficient citizen engagement. New technologies shape e-government's delivery of public services. This transformation has made public administration more accessible, efficient, and responsive, bridging the state-constituent gap (Albino, V., Berardi, U., & Dangelico, R. M., 2015).

1.2 Cloud Technology in Digital Governance

Cloud computing is now a basic component of digital governance and public administration modernization. Cloud platforms help governments increase citizen engagement, streamline operations, and improve service delivery by providing scalable, secure, and flexible solutions. The main ways that cloud computing is changing governance is shown in the figure 1.

- *Cost Efficiency*: By doing away with the need for pricey on-premise hardware and infrastructure, cloud computing drastically lowers operating expenses. A "pay-as-you-go" approach, in which public institutions only pay for the resources they use, is an option. This results in less unnecessary spending and more effective use of public funds. Furthermore, cloud platforms require fewer IT staff members and maintenance, freeing up resources for other important areas.

- *Scalability and Flexibility:* The capacity of cloud-based systems to grow in response to demand is one of their biggest benefits. Increasing workloads during busy periods, like election seasons or tax deadlines, can be handled by cloud platforms without compromising service. Because of their adaptability, public services can expand or change rapidly without requiring time-consuming and expensive upgrades. Additionally, governments can update current services with the least amount of downtime and launch new ones more quickly.
- *Enhanced Collaboration and Data Sharing*: Cloud technology facilitates improved departmental and even intergovernmental cooperation. Cloud computing platforms facilitate real-time communication and information sharing by centralizing data and making it accessible from any location. More coordinated efforts are made in public services like law enforcement, emergency response, and healthcare as a result. Furthermore, centralized data systems offer a unified method of managing public resources and cut down on redundant work (Scholl, H. J., & AlAwadhi, S., 2016).
- *Improved Citizen Services*: Cloud-based services facilitate citizens' interactions with public administration by providing 24/7 access to public resources and services. User-friendly portals that enable people to pay bills, apply for permits, and access important documents from any device are made possible by cloud technology. As a result, there are less wait times and in-person visits required, which increases citizen engagement and satisfaction.
- *Data Protection and Security:* Sensitive data is protected by cloud providers' advanced security features, which include data encryption, multi-factor authentication, and frequent security updates. In order to guard against data loss from cyberattacks or system failures, governments can also store vital data in safe, cloud-based backups. Cloud platforms can adhere to local and international data protection laws, guaranteeing the confidentiality and integrity of public data.
- *Disaster Recovery and Continuity*: Comprehensive disaster recovery capabilities are offered by cloud technology. Cloud-based systems have the ability to promptly restore lost data and guarantee uninterrupted services in the event of system malfunctions or natural disasters. Maintaining continuity in public administration is crucial, particularly for critical services like utilities, emergency response, and healthcare (Boeri, A., & Testoni, C., 2015).

Figure 1. Role of cloud technology in digital governance

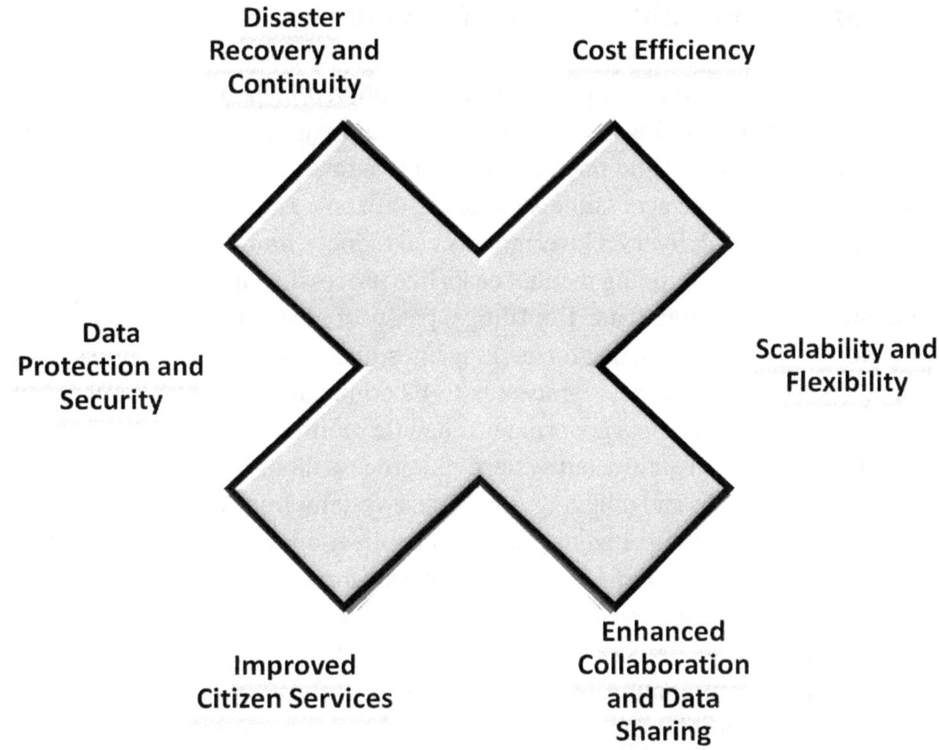

Cloud platforms replace on-premise data centers in public sector IT infrastructure. It lets public institutions switch from legacy systems to real-time data processing, storage, and analytics. Integrating departments on cloud platforms improves collaboration and data access. The cloud also reduces maintenance and protects data with automatic software updates and security features. Public services become more agile, allowing faster innovation and more responsive service delivery without large infrastructure investments.

2. CLOUD TECHNOLOGY IN E-GOVERNMENT

2.1 Streamlining Public Service Delivery

Technology has automated processes and improved response times in government operations, improving service delivery. Automation and digital platforms help governments streamline operations, reduce human error, and provide faster, more reliable, and more accessible services to citizens. Automation is essential to modernizing service delivery. Governments can reduce administrative burdens and improve accuracy by digitizing manual tasks like processing applications, verifying documents, and managing data. Tax filings, passport renewals, and social security applications used to require paper forms, long lines, and in-person interactions. Today, automated systems allow these processes to be completed online without manual intervention. Automation lets governments handle more requests quickly and accurately. In tax season, an automated system can process thousands of filings at once, eliminating bottlenecks and relieving staff. These systems improve turnaround times and transparency by letting citizens track their applications in real time. Automation also reduces manual handling errors and delays, improving service reliability. It also enables proactive service delivery (Gil-Garcia, J. R., 2012). System reminders for renewals, deadlines, and payments reduce the likelihood of missed deadlines or service lapses. Automation-powered data analytics can also predict trends and resource needs, improving strategic decision-making and resource allocation.

Digital platforms are also improving citizen service response times. Government agencies used to take days or weeks to respond to requests via mail, phone, or in-person visits. Nowadays, online portals and automated systems have greatly reduced these wait times. Individuals can update personal information, check application status, and access essential services on self-service platforms. Citizens save time and government employees work less. AI-powered chatbots and virtual assistants are also being used to answer routine questions 24/7 without human intervention. These tools provide instant responses, allowing citizens to get help anytime, anywhere. Healthcare, emergency services, and financial aid require faster response times. Rapid communication is crucial in critical situations because delayed responses can have dire consequences. By automating workflows and using digital platforms, governments can prioritize and resolve urgent requests quickly (Gil-Garcia, J. R. et al., 2016).

2.2 Citizen-Centric Services

In the modern era of digital technology, it is essential for effective governance to develop services that are centered on the needs of citizens. Every individual, regardless of their history or abilities, should be able to interact with public services in a seamless manner. Personalization and accessibility are essential components that ensure this. By customizing interactions and offerings to cater to the specific requirements of citizens, personalized services are provided. Information regarding user preferences, behaviors, and demographics can be gleaned by governments through the utilization of data analytics (Rai, P. K. et al., 2024). Because of this, it is possible to develop services that are specifically tailored to meet the needs of particular groups. A local government, for instance, might develop specialized programs for senior citizens, young families, or people with disabilities in order to address the specific challenges and requirements that these groups face. Personalized communication, which includes sending pertinent updates or reminders based on individual circumstances, further enhances engagement and satisfaction by providing specific information about the recipient. The accessibility of services is of utmost importance in order to guarantee that all citizens are able to access them without any obstacles. This includes the development of websites and applications that are straightforward to use and in accordance with accessibility standards (Janssen, M., & Estevez, E., 2013). This makes it possible for people with disabilities to navigate digital platforms with ease. A further benefit of providing a variety of service delivery channels, including mobile applications, online portals, and in-person assistance, is that it ensures that all individuals have options that are tailored to their individual preferences and circumstances. It is possible for non-native speakers to gain access to information and services in their preferred languages with the assistance of multilingual services, which are designed to cater to diverse populations. In the end, this commitment to accessibility helps to strengthen the relationship between citizens and their government by fostering inclusivity and ensuring that no one is left behind to fall behind (Khan, G. F., & Park, H. W., 2013).

2.2 Cloud Tools Cutting Paperwork

Organizations' use of paper records and manual procedures is being drastically reduced thanks to cloud computing, which is transforming documentation and process management (Vinodhini, V. et al., 2022). Cloud-based systems can help the public and private sectors increase accuracy, efficiency, and streamline operations. Digital document management is one of the main advantages of cloud solutions. These systems facilitate the digitization of files, enabling electronic document management, access, and storage for organizations. Physical documentation, which can be laborious and prone to damage or loss, is no longer necessary thanks to this shift. With centralized storage, staff members can quickly access documents from any location, which makes remote work and collaboration possible. Version control and real-time updates are two features that guarantee that users have access to the most recent data, which lowers the risk of errors arising from old documents. Numerous cloud platforms offer automated workflow tools, such as approvals, notifications, and data entry, in addition to document management. These tools help to streamline repetitive tasks. Organizations can reduce manual intervention and expedite operations by automating these processes (Sandoval-Almazan, R., & Gil-Garcia, J. R., 2012). To ensure an open and effective workflow, a cloud-based system, for instance, can automatically route requests for approval, notify pertinent stakeholders, and log actions taken. Staff members can concentrate on higher-value activities that improve service delivery because less time is spent on administrative duties thanks to automation (Singh, S. et al., 2025). The ability to electronically sign documents is another noteworthy benefit of many cloud tools. Paper copies of documents can no longer be required thanks to this feature, which enables digital signatures. This improves tracking and security in addition to quickening the approval process. The delays brought on by printing, signing, and scanning documents are eliminated with e-signatures, speeding up and streamlining transactions. Organizations can collect data more efficiently by using online surveys and forms hosted on the cloud. This method greatly lowers the possibility of errors by doing away with the need for paper forms and manual data entry. Real-time report generation is another feature of cloud tools that enables businesses to swiftly evaluate data and come to wise decisions.

2.3 Resource Optimization

Improving the delivery of public services and increasing the value that taxpayers receive from the government requires that resources be utilized effectively. Through the facilitation of streamlined operations, improved decision-making, and enhanced collaboration among various departments, data centralization plays a pivotal role in the optimization (Khadka, M. et al., 2025) of these resources. The ability to consolidate information from a variety of sources into a single repository is made possible by centralized data systems. This eliminates data silos, which are situations in which information is divided up among various departments, making it difficult to access and share data that is pertinent to the situation. The ability to analyze comprehensive datasets that provide insights into resource allocation, service usage, and performance metrics will be available to public institutions that have centralized access. Decision-makers are able to identify inefficiencies, allocate resources more effectively, and prioritize funding based on actual needs when they have this holistic view of the situation. More accurate forecasting and planning are made possible by centralised data. The ability of governments to forecast future service demand through the examination of historical data trends enables them to allocate resources (Sheela, M. S. et al., 2025) in a proactive manner rather than in a reactive manner. During times of public health emergencies, for instance, data on traffic patterns can be used to inform infrastructure planning, and data on health can be used to assist in the distribution of medical resources. It is not only that this predictive capability improves service delivery, but it also helps prevent resource shortages and excessive expenditures. Coordinating efforts across departments is made easier by centralized data systems (Satheesh, N. et al., 2025).). If multiple organizations are able to access the same information, they will be able to collaborate on projects and initiatives more effectively with one another. Public safety agencies can coordinate their response to address underlying issues by sharing crime statistics with community services. This allows for a more coordinated response. A more integrated model of service delivery is fostered through the use of this collaborative approach, which ultimately results in increased efficiency (Pereira, G. V. et al., 2018).

3. TRANSFORMATIVE APPLICATIONS IN PUBLIC ADMINISTRATION

Significant changes are occurring in a number of sectors as a result of the use of cutting-edge technologies in public administration. These creative applications promote greater citizen-government engagement, increase efficiency, and improve service delivery. These are the principal transformative applications that are shown in the figure 2, which transforming public administration. By utilizing technology to raise citizen engagement, service quality, and efficiency (Muniandi, B. et al., 2024), these revolutionary applications are completely redefining public administration. These developments have the potential to produce governance structures that are more effective, accountable, and responsive as they develop securing public data in the cloud (Kumar, M. S. et al., 2025)

1. *Smart Cities*: Smart city projects use data analytics and Internet of Things (IoT) devices to enhance urban living. Smart traffic management systems are among the applications that minimize emissions and congestion by optimizing traffic flow in real-time (Konapure, C. G. et al., 2025). Furthermore, smart waste management systems use sensors to keep an eye on waste levels, which makes collection schedules more effective and lowers operating expenses. To managing waste and traffic, smart cities also install networked (Sharma, M. et al., 2025) lighting systems that adapt to vehicle and pedestrian movement to enhance safety and save energy. Citizen engagement platforms facilitate direct

issue reporting by locals, thereby encouraging community involvement in urban management.

2. *E-Health Services*: The delivery of healthcare is being transformed by telemedicine and cloud computing. In order to guarantee that people living in remote or underserved areas have access to medical care (Pandey, B. K. et al., 2024a), public health organizations can provide remote consultations. The seamless exchange of patient data between healthcare providers is made possible by electronic health records (EHRs), which improves patient outcomes and care coordination. Proactive public health interventions are made possible by advanced analytics, which can detect health trends within populations. By tracking symptoms, prescriptions, and wellness objectives, mobile health apps enable people to take charge of their health and further integrate healthcare into daily life.
3. *Digital Taxation*: For both individuals and corporations, the filing process is streamlined by digital tax collection platforms. Through online portals, taxpayers can electronically file their returns, monitor their status, and get notifications. This not only improves convenience but also lowers administrative costs for tax authorities and raises compliance rates. Artificial intelligence can also be used to spot anomalies (Singh, S. et al., 2025) and alert authorities to possible tax fraud, which improves system integrity. By offering assistance and educational materials via these channels, citizens can better understand their tax responsibilities and develop their financial literacy.
4. *Public Safety Innovations*: Predictive policing is one example of an advanced technology that uses data analytics to find patterns (Pandey, B. K. et al., 2024b) in crime and better allocate resources. By taking a proactive stance, law enforcement organizations can deal with possible problems before they get out of hand, improving community safety and trust. Citizens can report incidents in real-time through public safety apps, which speeds up response times. Integrating real-time surveillance systems with body-worn cameras also improves law enforcement's accountability and transparency (Satheesh, N. et al., 2025). Incorporating community organizations into collaboration efforts can enhance trust and guarantee that safety initiatives align with community needs.
5. *Online Education Initiatives*: the provision of remote learning opportunities, digital platforms are transforming public education. To guarantee that all citizens have equitable access to education, governments can provide online resources (Kumar, B. et al., 2024), training programs, and courses. This method works especially well in emergency situations where traditional classroom settings are disrupted, like the COVID-19 pandemic. Diverse learning needs and styles can be met by blended learning models, which combine online and in-person instruction. Collaborations with suppliers of educational technology (Basha, A.

J. et al., 2024) can improve the caliber of online materials, guaranteeing that students, wherever they may be, receive a thorough education.

6. *Blockchain for Transparency*: Applications such as land registries, contract management, and secure voting systems are being investigated for blockchain technology. Because it is decentralized, there are less chances for fraud and corruption because data integrity (Pandey, D. et al., 2024) is guaranteed and transparency is increased. Blockchain, for example, can offer an unchangeable record of real estate transactions, streamlining title searches and lowering disputes. Blockchain technology can improve voting's accessibility and security, guaranteeing that each vote is correctly tallied while protecting voters' anonymity. Administrative procedures can be automated by smart contracts, which lowers the possibility of human error and streamlines interactions between citizens and government organizations.

Figure 2. Transformative applications in public administration

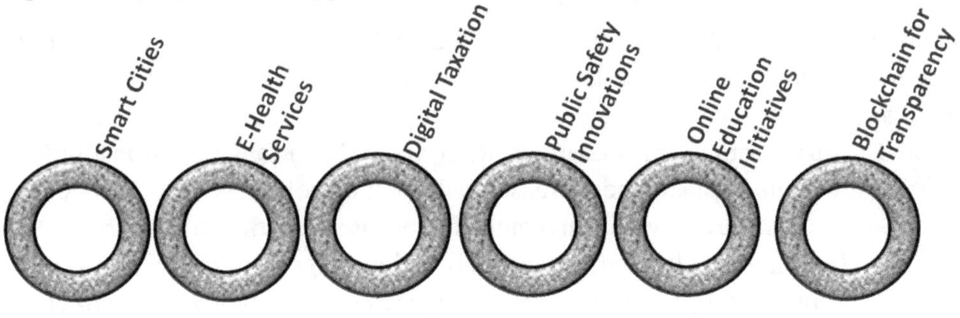

4. DATA SECURITY AND GOVERNANCE

4.1 Securing National Data in Global Clouds

National data control (KVM, S. et al., 2024) in global cloud infrastructures is crucial as governments adopt cloud technologies for data storage and processing. The move to cloud computing offers cost savings, scalability, and accessibility. The global nature of cloud services raises data sovereignty, security, and privacy concerns.

Data sovereignty means data is subject to the country's laws. When companies use global cloud providers, their data may be stored in multiple countries and subject to different regulations. To maintain national control over sensitive data, governments must establish clear policies and frameworks. This can include laws requiring data residency, especially personal and sensitive data, within national borders. Using global cloud services requires sovereignty and security. Financial loss, reputational damage, and privacy violations can result from data breaches. Governments and cloud providers must collaborate on encryption (Lakshmi, K. V. N. et al., 2024), access controls, and audits. Security of citizen data requires compliance with local data protection and privacy laws. Governments can ensure data is handled according to national standards and best practices by forming strong cloud provider partnerships. Building resilient cloud infrastructures helps governments control national data. Using multiple cloud service providers reduces vulnerabilities. Using a multi-cloud strategy, governments can increase redundancy and keep critical services running even if one provider fails. This method prioritizes national interests and increases data management flexibility (Shahul, A. et al., 2024).

4.2 Barriers to Cloud in E-Government

Cloud technology has many benefits for e-government, but several barriers prevent its widespread use. To maximize cloud solutions in public administration, these issues must be addressed. Data security worries prevent government agencies from using cloud services. Data breaches and cyberattacks can affect personal and national security data (Saravanakumar, R. et al., 2024). Many public institutions worry that off-site data storage increases risks. Cloud solutions must have strong security measures like encryption and multi-factor authentication to build trust. Data protection laws are complex and vary by jurisdiction, so governments must comply. Legacy systems used by many government agencies are incompatible with cloud technologies. These systems are expensive to upgrade or replace, so decision-makers are hesitant to switch to the cloud (Abdullahi, M. et al., 2024). Cloud application integration can be difficult, raising concerns about service disruptions during the transition. A phased approach that integrates cloud solutions with legacy systems may help. Budget constraints also hinder public administration cloud adoption. Migration, training, and system integration can be costly, but cloud solutions can reduce operational costs over time. These necessary changes are hard to fund for many government agencies with tight budgets. To overcome this, financing or private sector cloud provider partnerships may be needed. Cloud implementation requires specialized skills that government agencies may lack. The switch to cloud technology requires technical skills, regulatory knowledge, and security protocols (Kumarganesh, S. et al., 2024). Skilled workers shortages can slow implementation and lead to suboptimal configurations. Staff training and development are essential for cloud adoption success.

5. LEGACY SYSTEMS AND INTEGRATION CHALLENGES

5.1 Compatibility Issues with Legacy IT

The use of modern solutions like cloud computing can be impeded by outdated technology, which is a major challenge for many organizations, especially those in the public administration sector. These systems were created to fulfill the unique requirements of their era when they were constructed, sometimes decades or even longer ago. However, because of compatibility problems, integrating them with more recent IT infrastructure has become more difficult. Legacy systems incapacity to interface with contemporary apps in an efficient manner is one of their biggest problems. Incompatible with modern cloud solutions, many older systems employ antiquated data formats, protocols, and programming languages. Due to information silos caused by this lack of interoperability, departmental collaboration and data sharing are hindered (Muralidhar, L. B. et al., 2024). An integrated cloud-based analytics platform may present challenges for a public health agency that utilizes an antiquated patient management system. In the event of a public health emergency, for example, crucial health data may be stuck in the legacy system, hindering prompt decision-making and response activities. Another expense that may be prohibitive is the upkeep of outdated systems. It becomes harder and more expensive to find qualified workers as technology develops because the knowledge needed to support older systems frequently decreases. The aging and potentially defective hardware that powers these systems could result in more maintenance expenses and downtime. A large percentage of government IT budgets may need to be allocated to maintain these antiquated systems, taking money away from modernization and innovation projects that could improve operational effectiveness and service delivery. It takes considerable organizational change in addition to technical expertise to move from outdated systems to contemporary solutions. Because they worry about the disruption to their accustomed workflows, employees who have depended on established processes may be reluctant to adopt new technologies (Pandey, B. K. et al., 2024c). To help staff adjust to new systems, change management techniques are crucial for facilitating this shift. Training and assistance are also needed. If the difficulties of transferring data from outdated systems to new ones are not handled properly, there may be dangers of data loss or corruption. When combining old systems with new technologies, governments have more difficulties with regulations and compliance. Tight data protection regulations, which control the collection, storage, and sharing of citizen data, apply to many public agencies (Elarmathi, S. et al., 2024). An additional layer of complexity is introduced by the integration process's requirement to guarantee that all data handling complies with these laws. Planning carefully is necessary to prevent potential breaches or violations, especially when legacy systems were not created with current data privacy standards in mind. Modernizing IT infrastructure is essential for increasing efficiency and improving service delivery, as many organizations have realized (Pandey, B. K. et al., 2024d). Risks can be reduced by using techniques like phased migration, which involves moving parts of an organization's legacy systems gradually to more contemporary ones. With minimal interference to ongoing services, this method enables the testing and validation of new systems. Modern systems and legacy systems can communicate more easily by implementing application programming interfaces, or APIs. By facilitating communication between disparate software programs, APIs let data from more modern platforms to be shared with older ones. The ability to leverage current systems while phasing in the adoption of modern infrastructure is made possible by this solution, which can bridge the gap between old and new technologies.

5.2 Public Trust and Transparency

Citizens must trust cloud-based public administration systems as governments adopt them. Trust in digital governance affects citizen engagement and service compliance. Governments must address data security, transparency, and user experience to build trust. Data security is citizens' top cloud service concern. People want their personal data protected from breaches and unauthorized access. Encryption, audits, and strict access controls can boost government trust. A clear communication about these security protocols helps citizens understand data protection. Assuring citizens that their data is handled according to data protection (Pandey, B. K. et al., 2024e) regulations strengthens this trust. Another key to confidence is transparency. Citizens should know how cloud systems collect, use, and store their data. Publicly discussing data practices and publishing clear privacy policies can help governments achieve this. Data usage and security incident reports show accountability and commitment to protecting citizen data (George, W. K. et al., 2024). Transparency fosters trust and empowers citizens to make informed digital service decisions. User experience also boosts confidence. Cloud-driven governance systems should prioritize citizen needs and make services easy to use. Usability testing and citizen feedback during development can identify and address pain points. Users should have training and support to navigate these systems and gain confidence in digital governance tools. Positive outcomes and benefits for citizens in these areas can boost confidence in similar initiatives. Engaging community leaders and stakeholders to educate them about cloud services can also help adoption. Maintaining citizen confidence requires continuous improvement. Changing technologies and citizen needs should prompt governments to evaluate and update their cloud systems. Innovation improves service delivery and shows citizens that the government cares about their concerns and provides secure and effective services.

6. CONCLUSION

The use of cloud computing in e-government is a revolutionary change in the way public administration functions, with many advantages that improve citizen engagement and service delivery. The evolution of e-government, as the outline explains, reflects a major shift from conventional practices to digital frameworks that put efficiency, accessibility, and responsiveness first. Streamline public service delivery through automation and quicker response times, cloud technology is essential to this shift. Governments can make information more equitable and personalized for a variety of populations by concentrating on citizen-centric services. The use of cloud tools to streamline bureaucratic processes reduces paperwork, maximizes resource utilization, and makes it possible to allocate government resources more effectively. The potential of cloud solutions to enhance public administration is further demonstrated by their implementation in innovative use cases like online education, digital taxation, smart cities, and e-health services. Better outcomes for citizens are achieved in each of these areas through improved service accessibility, real-time analytics, and data management. There are obstacles in the way of achieving a fully cloud-integrated e-government. Data security and governance are still critical, requiring strong security measures to safeguard confidential data and guarantee legal compliance. To properly utilize cloud capabilities, obstacles like legacy system concerns and the requirement for integration must be overcome. Fostering confidence among citizens requires establishing the efficacy of cloud-driven governance systems and establishing public trust through transparency.

REFERENCES

Abdullahi, M., Ahmad, A., Pandey, B. K., & Pandey, D. (2024). Digital Currency Adoption: A Comparative Analysis of Global Trends and the Nigerian eNaira Digital Currency. *SN Computer Science*, *5*(5), 1–11.

Albino, V., Berardi, U., & Dangelico, R. M. (2015). Smart cities: Definitions, dimensions, performance, and initiatives. *Journal of Urban Technology*, *22*(1), 3–21.

Basha, A. J., Maheshwari, R. U., Pandey, B. K., & Pandey, D. (2024). Ultra-sensitive photonic crystal fiber–based SPR sensor for cancer detection utilizing hybrid nanocomposite layers. *Plasmonics*, •••, 1–15.

Boeri, A., & Testoni, C. (2015). Smart Governance: Urban regeneration and integration policies in Europe. Turin and Malmö case studies. *International Journal of Scientific and Engineering Research*, *6*(3), 527–533.

Elarmathi, S., Rishabavarthani, P., Sindhuja, M., Elayaraja, P., & Malathi Murugesan, S. Kumarganesh, K. Martin Sagayam, Binay Kumar Pandey, and Digvijay Pandey. (2024). Novel manufacturing systems for cancer diagnosis using ultra-sensitive photonic crystal fiber biosensor with dual-functionalized aptamer-nanocavity. *Microsystem Technologies*, •••, 1–20.

Garcia Alonso, R., & Lippez-De Castro, S. (2016). Technology helps, people make: A smart city governance framework grounded in deliberative democracy. Smarter as the new urban agenda: A comprehensive view of the 21st century city, 333-347.

George, W. K., Silas, E. I., Pandey, D., & Pandey, B. K. (2024). Utilization of Industry 4.0 Technologies in Nigerian Technical and Vocational Education: A Conundrum for Educators. In *Examining the Rapid Advance of Digital Technology in Africa* (pp. 270–293). IGI Global.

Gil-Garcia, J. R. (2012). Towards a smart State? Inter-agency collaboration, information integration, and beyond. *Information Polity*, *17*(3-4), 269–280.

Gil-Garcia, J. R., Zhang, J., & Puron-Cid, G. (2016). Conceptualizing smartness in government: An integrative and multi-dimensional view. *Government Information Quarterly*, *33*(3), 524–534.

Janssen, M., & Estevez, E. (2013). Lean government and platform-based governance—Doing more with less. *Government Information Quarterly*, *30*, S1–S8.

Khadka, M., Sah, M., Chaudhary, R., Sahani, S. K., Sahani, K., Pandey, B. K., & Pandey, D. (2025). Spectroscopic, quantum chemical, and topological calculations of the phenylephrine molecule using density functional theory. *Scientific Reports*, *15*(1), 208. PMID: 39747169

Khan, G. F., & Park, H. W. (2013). The e-government research domain: A triple helix network analysis of collaboration at the regional, country, and institutional levels. *Government Information Quarterly*, *30*(2), 182–193.

Konapure, C. G., Pandey, D., Shete, H., Thakar, C. M., Pandey, B. K., & George, A. S. (2025). Artificial Intelligence in Automated Concrete Mix Design Using Computerized Grading Curves. Interdisciplinary Approaches to AI, Internet of Everything, and Machine Learning, 567-586.

Kumar, B., Pandey, D., Pandey, B. K., & George, A. S. (2024). Higher Education in the Last Four Decades: A Review of Paradigm Shifts in Policy Frameworks. Design and Implementation of Higher Education Learners' Learning Outcomes (HELLO), 333-348.

Kumar, M. S., Prasanna, P. L., Lalitha, M., Joy, M., Jha, S. S., & Pandey, B. K. (2025). Utilizing the Internet of Everything and Artificial Intelligence for Real-Time Workforce Management. In Role of Internet of Everything (IOE), VLSI Architecture, and AI in Real-Time Systems (pp. 153-168). IGI Global Scientific Publishing.

Kumarganesh, S., & Malathi Murugesan, C. Ganesh, N. Santhiyakumari, M. Thangavel, K. Jayaram, K. Martin Sagayam, Binay Kumar Pandey, and Digvijay Pandey. (2024). Hybrid plasmonic biosensors with deep learning for colorectal cancer detection. *Plasmonics*, •••, 1–15.

KVM, S., Pandey, B. K., & Pandey, D. (2024). Design of Surface Plasmon Resonance (SPR) Sensors for Highly Sensitive Biomolecular Detection in Cancer Diagnostics. *Plasmonics*, •••, 1–13.

Lakshmi, K. V. N., Rajan, R., Pandey, D., & Pandey, B. K. (2024). Circular economy: A catalyst for economic growth-an empirical study. *Circular Economy and Sustainability*, •••, 1–22.

Muniandi, B., Nassa, V. K., Pandey, D., Pandey, B. K., Dadheech, P., & George, A. S. (2024). Pattern Analysis for Feature Extraction in Complex Images. In Using Machine Learning to Detect Emotions and Predict Human Psychology (pp. 145-167). IGI Global.

Muralidhar, L. B., Lakshmi, K. V. N., Swapna, H. R., Rupani, J., Nethravathi, K., Pandey, B. K., & Pandey, D. (2024). Impact of Organizational Culture on The Level of Corporate Social Responsibility Investments: An Exploratory Study. *Circular Economy and Sustainability*, •••, 1–19.

Pandey, B. K., Nassa, V. K., Mukundan, A. P., Mahajan, D. A., Pandey, D., George, A. S., & Dadheech, P. (2024c). An Industry-Focused Traffic System Utilising Internet of Things. In *Emerging Engineering Technologies and Industrial Applications* (pp. 200–213). IGI Global.

Pandey, B. K., & Pandey, D. (2023). Parametric optimization and prediction of enhanced thermoelectric performance in co-doped CaMnO3 using response surface methodology and neural network. *Journal of Materials Science Materials in Electronics*, *34*(21), 1589.

Pandey, B. K., & Pandey, D. (2025). Securing healthcare medical image information using advance morphological component analysis, information hiding systems, and hybrid convolutional neural networks on IoMT. *Computers in Biology and Medicine*, *185*, 109499. PMID: 39642698

Pandey, B. K., Pandey, D., & Lelisho, M. E. (2024a). Face mask identification with enhanced cuckoo optimization and deep learning-based faster regional neural network. *Scientific Reports*, *14*(1), 29719. PMID: 39613761

Pandey, B. K., Pandey, D., & Sahani, S. K. (2024b). Autopilot control unmanned aerial vehicle system for sewage defect detection using deep learning. *Engineering Reports*, •••, 12852.

Pandey, B. K., Paramashivan, M. A., Pandey, D., George, A. S., Agarwal, A., Dadheech, P., & Mahajan, D. A. (2024e). A recent survey on 6G vehicular technology: applications and challenges. 6G Security Education and Multidisciplinary Implementation, 337-350.

Pandey, B. K., Paramashivan, M. A., Pandey, D., George, A. S., Agarwal, A., Mahajan, D. A., . . . Pramanik, S. (2024d). Future Directions of Digital Twin Architectures for 6G Communication Networks. In Security Issues and Solutions in 6G Communications and Beyond (pp. 197-211). IGI Global.

Pandey, D., Nassa, V. K., Pandey, B. K., Mahajan, D. A., Patidar, P. K., Dadheech, P., & George, A. S. (2024). An Analysis of Internet-of-Things-Based Fire Detection and Alert Systems. In *Emerging Engineering Technologies and Industrial Applications* (pp. 295–304). IGI Global.

Pereira, G. V., Parycek, P., Falco, E., & Kleinhans, R. (2018). Smart governance in the context of smart cities: A literature review. *Information Polity*, *23*(2), 143–162.

Rai, P. K., Pandey, D., & Pandey, B. K. (2024). The future of enterprise and innovation is compute as a commodity, or CaaC. *Partners Universal International Research Journal*, *3*(2), 89–94.

Sandoval-Almazan, R., & Gil-Garcia, J. R. (2012). Are government internet portals evolving towards more interaction, participation, and collaboration? Revisiting the rhetoric of e-government among municipalities. *Government Information Quarterly*, *29*, S72–S81.

Saravanakumar, R., TamilSelvi, T., Pandey, D., Pandey, B. K., Mahajan, D. A., & Lelisho, M. E. (2024). Big data processing using hybrid Gaussian mixture model with salp swarm algorithm. *Journal of Big Data*, *11*(1), 167.

Satheesh, N., Gopisankar, N., Kumarganesh, S., Anthoniraj, S., Saravanakumar, S., & Martin Sagayam, K., Binay Kumar Pandey, and Digvijay Pandey. (2025). Advanced AI-driven emergency response systems for enhanced vehicle and human safety. *Iran Journal of Computer Science*, •••, 1–16.

Satheesh, N., Gopisankar, N., Kumarganesh, S., Anthoniraj, S., Saravanakumar, S., & Martin Sagayam, K., Binay Kumar Pandey, and Digvijay Pandey. (2025). Advanced AI-driven emergency response systems for enhanced vehicle and human safety. *Iran Journal of Computer Science*, •••, 1–16.

Scholl, H. J., & AlAwadhi, S. (2016). Creating Smart Governance: The key to radical ICT overhaul at the City of Munich. *Information Polity*, *21*(1), 21–42.

Shahul, A., Muniandi, B., Paramashivan, M. A., Pandey, D., Pandey, B. K., Dadheech, P., & George, H. (2024). An Analysis of Algorithms and Methods Based on Image Processing for Medical Applications. In *Emerging Engineering Technologies and Industrial Applications* (pp. 173–186). IGI Global.

Sharma, M., Talwar, R., Nassa, V. K., Binay, K., & Pandey, D. (2025). Design and performance analysis of a multiband vivaldi antenna for wireless broadband communication in 3-5.6 GHz spectrum. In *Artificial Intelligence and Information Technologies* (pp. 86–91). CRC Press.

Sheela, M. S., Kumarganesh, S., Pandey, B. K., & Lelisho, M. E. (2025). Integration of silver nanostructures in wireless sensor networks for enhanced biochemical sensing. *Discover Nano*, *20*(1), 7. PMID: 39804434

Singh, S., Madaan, G., Swapna, H. R., Singh, A., Pandey, D., George, A. S., & Pandey, B. K. (2025). Empowering Connectivity: Exploring the Internet of Things. In Interdisciplinary Approaches to AI, Internet of Everything, and Machine Learning (pp. 89-116). IGI Global Scientific Publishing.

Singh, S., Madaan, G., Swapna, H. R., Singh, A., Pandey, D., George, A. S., & Pandey, B. K. (2025). Empowering Connectivity: Exploring the Internet of Things. In Interdisciplinary Approaches to AI, Internet of Everything, and Machine Learning (pp. 89-116). IGI Global Scientific Publishing.

Vinodhini, V., Kumar, M. S., Sankar, S., Pandey, D., Pandey, B. K., & Nassa, V. K. (2022). IoT-based early forest fire detection using MLP and AROC method. *International Journal of Global Warming*, *27*(1), 55–70.

Chapter 3
Cloud Computing and Its Role in Enhancing Access to Justice Through Online Dispute Resolution

Swati Beniwal
Faculty of Law, Manipal University Jaipur, India

Sushila Choudhary
Faculty of Law, Manipal University Jaipur, India

Shweta Mishra
Department of Business and Administration, Manipal University Jaipur, India

ABSTRACT

The crucial part that cloud computing plays in expanding access to justice through the use of online dispute resolution (ODR). Traditional legal systems frequently face significant geographical and economic barriers, which make it difficult for individuals to obtain the necessary legal assistance. Through the provision of remote access, the reduction of costs, and the streamlining of dispute resolution procedures, cloud technology offers groundbreaking solutions. The cloud-based online dispute resolution (ODR) platforms democratize legal resources and facilitate timely legal support for underserved populations. This is accomplished through an analysis of a variety of ODR platforms. Several key features, including scalability, resource integration, and enhanced data security, are investigated in order to demonstrate the impact that these features have on legal accessibility.

DOI: 10.4018/979-8-3693-9581-3.ch003

1. INTRODUCTION

Computing in the cloud has emerged as a transformative force across a variety of industries through the provision of technological solutions that are scalable, cost-efficient, and accessible. The use of online dispute resolution (ODR) is one of the most promising applications of blockchain technology in the legal sector. Its goal is to improve access to justice. Utilizing remote servers that are hosted on the internet to store, manage, and process data is what is meant by the term "cloud technology." This is in contrast to the traditional method of relying on personal computers or local servers. By enabling processes that are more efficient, accessible, and flexible, its incorporation into the legal infrastructure is revolutionizing the traditional forms of conflict resolution. Without the need for the disputing parties to physically meet with one another, Online Dispute Resolution is a digital method of resolving conflicts, which are typically associated with commercial, consumer, or civil disputes. The resolution of disputes, whether through mediation, arbitration, or negotiation, has traditionally been a resource-intensive, time-consuming, and geographically constrained course of action. ODR platforms have gained significant traction since the advent of cloud technology because they provide an effective alternative to the methods that have been standard in the past. Cloud computing plays a significant role in online dispute resolution (ODR) because it alleviates many obstacles to the administration of justice, particularly in terms of cost, geographic accessibility, and delays in the procedure. Previously inaccessible legal services are now available to individuals who live in remote areas, communities that are marginalized, or those who have limited financial means. This is made possible by hosting online dispute resolution platforms in the cloud. Furthermore, cloud-based systems make it possible to access dispute resolution services at any time of the day or night, which maximizes both flexibility and efficiency for all parties involved. Computing in the cloud is helping to transform ODR into a system that is more inclusive and efficient. In order to democratize legal services, cloud technology promises to address the challenges that are already present within traditional dispute resolution processes. This will ensure that justice is accessible to all individuals, regardless of their location or socioeconomic status.

1.1 Online Dispute Resolution (ODR)

Internet-based platforms are used to mediate, arbitrate, and negotiate conflicts between parties in a way that eliminates the need for face-to-face meetings. This process is known as online dispute resolution, or ODR. Over time, ODR has evolved from its beginnings as an extension of Alternative Dispute Resolution (ADR) to become a distinct field that deals with conflicts in a range of situations, including e-commerce, consumer rights, and even civil cases. ODR is becoming a crucial tool for effectively and efficiently resolving conflicts as cross-border transactions and global e-commerce grow in popularity. Out-of-court settlements (ODR) offer a simplified, quicker, more affordable option for resolving disputes than traditional court systems. Thanks to its ability to get around geographical restrictions, time constraints, and expensive legal fees, it is especially appealing to people and companies that conduct business online. ODR platforms, which digitize dispute resolution, do away with the necessity for in-person meetings and enable parties to settle disputes asynchronously or in real-time via online chat services, video conferences, and other virtual gathering places. Beyond ease and financial savings, ODR has many advantages. It provides increased transparency because each step of the dispute procedure can be tracked down and saved in a safe online space. ODR systems also frequently have sophisticated features like AI-driven case analysis, automated document management, and personalized workflows, all of which help produce more just and efficient results. ODR has a significant future in legal services, particularly in sectors where accessibility, speed, and convenience are crucial factors, as digital transformation continues to transform a variety of industries. Enhancing access to justice for individuals and organizations globally can be achieved through the integration of ODR into private enterprises and judicial systems (Wang, S. et al., 2024).

1.2 The Role of Technology in Legal Systems

Technology has had a significant and wide-ranging impact on the transformation of legal systems, impacting almost all facets of conventional legal procedures. Legal systems have traditionally relied on laborious manual processes that were frequently hampered by political, social, and financial constraints. But the advent of digital tools has brought about innovations that greatly improve the effectiveness, accessibility, and inclusivity of legal services. Automation is one of the main ways that technology has changed the legal sector. With the help of sophisticated legal databases and AI-powered search engines, legal research that once required hours of combing through physical law libraries can now be completed in a matter of seconds. With unmatched speed and accuracy, these tools enable attorneys and judges to locate pertinent statutes, case law, and precedents. Additionally, the time spent on repetitive tasks is being decreased by the increasing automation of legal documentation processes, such as the drafting of pleadings and contracts. The introduction of computerized dispute resolution systems is another revolutionary development. Parties can settle disputes without having to go to court by using digital mediation tools and online dispute resolution (ODR) platforms. Legal systems have expanded access to legal mechanisms for people who might have faced obstacles to justice in the traditional system by utilizing technology to create channels for remote dispute resolution (Aniello, L. et al., 2018). This has saved time and resources. Blockchain technology is starting to make an impact as well, especially in fields like verification and contract management. The use of human mediators in contractual disputes is declining thanks to smart contracts, which are self-executing agreements with terms encoded in code. This technology offers an unchangeable record of transactions, ensuring transparency and lowering the risk of fraud. Technology has increased public transparency in the legal system. Digital portals have made it easier for the public to interact with the legal system in real time by providing access to court records, statutes, and case details. The public's trust in legal institutions is strengthened and accountability is fostered by this transparency (Buchwald, M., 2019).

2. ONLINE DISPUTE RESOLUTION (ODR)

2.1 Evolution of ODR

Technological advancements, societal shifts, and the growing demand for conflict resolution mechanisms that are more effective have all played a role in shaping the development of Online Dispute Resolution (ODR). In the beginning, the process of conflict resolution consisted of face-to-face meetings between mediators, arbitrators, or legal representatives. These meetings were held in order to resolve disagreements between parties. Over the course of time, the limitations of this traditional approach had led to the search for alternatives that were more accessible and flexible. These limitations included geographical restrictions (Vinodhini, V. et al., 2022), difficulties in scheduling, and high costs. The emergence of online dispute resolution (ODR) coincided with the growth of the internet and the rise of online commerce in the 1990s. Because of the proliferation of online transactions, there has been an increase in the demand for the resolution of disputes that have arisen in digital spaces, particularly between purchasers and vendors who are located in different jurisdictions. The initial online dispute resolution (ODR) platforms were primarily focused on resolving disputes that were associated with online commerce. Major players such as eBay and PayPal were among the pioneers of ODR systems, which were designed to efficiently settle millions of separate claims (Rai, P. K. et al., 2024).). Email exchanges and text-based mediation were the primary means of communication on these early platforms, which laid the groundwork for what would later develop into more complex online technologies. As the technology behind the internet advanced, online dispute resolution (ODR) expanded beyond the realm of e-commerce and into broader areas such as consumer rights, family law, and civil disputes. Many different factors were responsible for the shift from traditional face-to-face mediation to online mediation (Fan, M. et al., 2023). The first reason why online platforms became appealing as alternatives to in-person proceedings was that they were more cost-effective and saved time than traditional ones. Second, digital mediation made it possible for parties to participate from different geographical locations and resolve disputes asynchronously or in real time, doing away with the requirement that they be physically present. This allowed for greater flexibility. Courts and legal systems all over the world turned to online platforms in order to continue functioning despite lockdowns and social distancing measures brought about by the COVID-19 pandemic, which further accelerated the adoption of online dispute resolution (ODR). Disputes were able to be resolved even when face-to-face interactions were not possible thanks to the widespread availability of video conferencing tools, virtual arbitration rooms, and mediation services driven by artificial neural network (Pandey, B. K., & Pandey, D., 2023) . These days, online dispute resolution (ODR) is a mature field that provides a variety of mechanisms, including online arbitration, mediation, and negotiation. In order to make the process of conflict resolution more effective, transparent, and accessible to individuals and businesses all over the world, it is continuously evolving and incorporating artificial intelligence, machine learning, and blockchain technology capabilities. Individuals, regardless of their location or financial means, will have easier access to justice as a result of the transition from in-person to online mediation, which represents a fundamental change in the way legal systems operate (Ferreira, D. B. et al., 2022).

2.2. Types of ODR Mechanisms

ODR mechanisms can be broken down into four categories, arbitration, mediation, negotiation, and hybrid approaches are as shown in the figure 1. A neutral third party makes a decision that is legally binding in the case of arbitration, whereas the goal of mediation is to facilitate communication between the parties in order to arrive at a solution that is mutually acceptable (Sheela, M. S. et al., 2025). Through negotiation, parties are able to take direct action to resolve disputes, frequently with the assistance of legal counsel. A flexible range of options for conflict resolution can be found through hybrid approaches, which combine aspects of both mediation and arbitration. ODR mechanisms have evolved into distinct types, mirroring ADR processes. Technology makes ODR more efficient, accessible, and flexible for arbitration, mediation, negotiation, and hybrid dispute resolution (Satheesh, N. et al., 2025). These mechanisms meet the growing demand for conflict resolution in a digitally connected world, where online platforms can resolve disputes faster than meetings.

1. *Online Arbitration*: In arbitration, a neutral third party listens to both sides and makes a binding decision. Though informal, arbitration often resembles court proceedings. From filing the case to the final ruling, online arbitration (e-arbitration) takes place online. By eliminating meetings, travel costs, and resolution time, the online environment has many benefits. Electronically submitting documents, evidence, and arguments allows arbitrators to rule quickly (Kumar, M. S. et al., 2025). To improve efficiency, online arbitration platforms can automate scheduling and document filing. Even with these benefits, online arbitration is formal. Parties usually agree to follow the arbitrator's decision before the process begins. Business and commercial disputes with high stakes and a definitive resolution are ideal for online arbitration (Zeleznikow, J., 2021).
2. *Online Mediation*: An impartial third-party mediator helps disputing parties reach a compromise in mediation, which is more informal and flexible than arbitration. Traditional mediation facilitates communication, compromise, and settlement, but the parties make the final decision (Pandey, B. K., & Pandey, D., 2025). Mediators don't force solutions. Online mediation uses the same principles but in a virtual environment. Mediation can occur via email, online forums, video conferencing, or specialized platforms. Parties can negotiate online and asynchronously, making online mediation flexible. Web mediation works well for low-stakes disputes or issues that require a collaborative approach. Electronic mediation can resolve consumer-business disputes, interpersonal conflicts, and small civil matters without legal intervention. Document sharing, chatbots for basic inquiries, and AI to suggest solutions based on case data are also used I online mediation. Online mediation is informal and flexible (Khadka, M. et al., 2025), but it may not be suitable for all disputes, especially those that require legal certainty.
3. *Online Negotiation*: As the least formal dispute resolution method, negotiation relies on the parties to reach an agreement. Negotiation isn't mediated or arbitrated. Instead, parties negotiate directly. E-negotiation facilitates ODR discussions on digital platforms. Virtual negotiations are possible with secure messaging, video calls, and structured negotiation platforms. In disputes involving ongoing relationships and a collaborative solution, online negotiation is used (Konapure, C. G. et al., 2025). Technology structures e-negotiation, making it unique. Online platforms can offer settlement agreement templates, automated prompts, and algorithms to help parties find common ground. Platforms that allow asynchronous communication let parties negotiate on their own time. Online negotiation relies on both parties' willingness to compromise because there is no neutral third party to bring them to a resolution (Ustun, E. S., & Yuce, M., 2022).

4. *ODR Hybrid Approaches*: Combining arbitration, mediation, and negotiation into hybrid ODR mechanisms makes dispute resolution more flexible and comprehensive. Mixed methods can be useful when a dispute requires different approaches at different stages or when parties want flexibility. A common hybrid model (Singh, S. et al., 2025) is med-arb, where mediation first and arbitration if no agreement is reached. Party can try a collaborative, non-binding resolution first, knowing a binding decision will be made if needed. Starting with online mediation tools and moving to an online arbitration platform if mediation fails may be done online. Barr-med, where the arbitrator makes a decision but does not reveal it, is another hybrid approach. Then, the parties can mediate, knowing that the arbitrator's decision will be enforced if they can't. This encourages mediation while providing a fallback decision. Because they can integrate arbitration and mediation tools, online platforms can handle hybrid approaches smoothly. These hybrid models balance arbitrations formality and mediation's flexibility, making them invaluable for complex disputes.

Figure 1. Types of ODR mechanisms

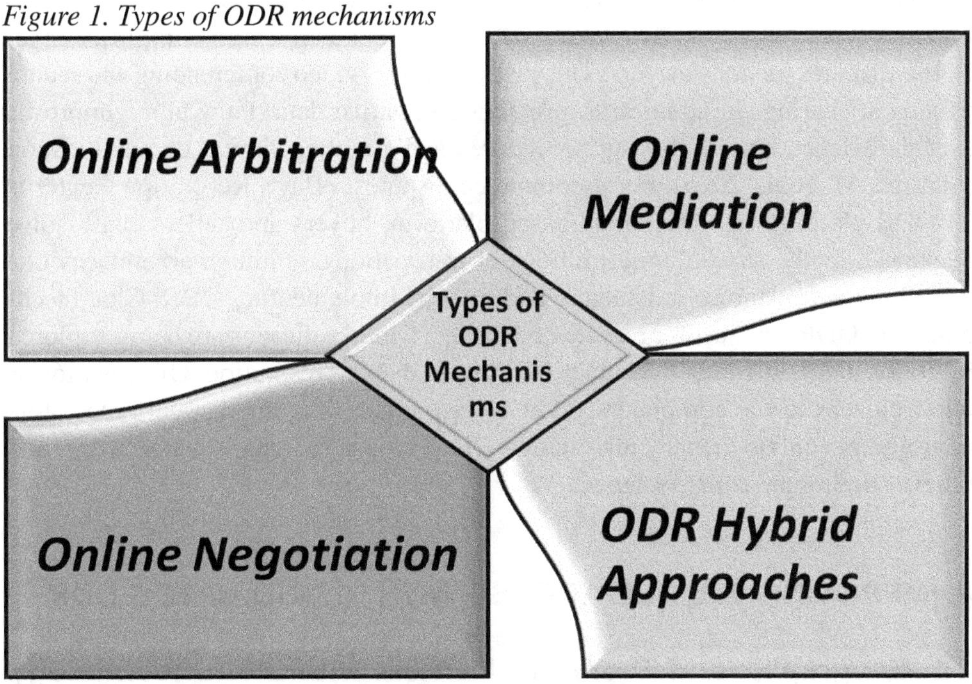

3. CLOUD COMPUTING IN LEGAL INFRASTRUCTURE

3.1 Cloud Platforms Supporting ODR

ODR systems rely on cloud platforms to streamline dispute resolution. The internet powers these digital environments to provide accessible, efficient, and secure conflict resolution. Cloud-based ODR platforms can handle a variety of disputes and give users a good experience (Singh, S. et al., 2025). Moderia, a cloud-based ODR platform, streamlines dispute resolution in e-commerce and government services. Arbitrators and mediators can access all relevant information in one place by submitting claims and evidence digitally through Modria. This method resolves disputes faster and with fewer logistical issues. Participants can stay informed throughout their case with automated workflows and real-time notifications. Other cloud-based negotiation solutions include Smartsettle, which emphasizes collaboration and transparency. Using user inputs, this platform uses advanced algorithms to help parties find common ground and suggest settlement options. Smartsettle reduces misunderstandings and leads to more productive negotiations by providing structure. Users can negotiate from anywhere on this cloud-based platform, making it useful for cross-border disputes (Svantesson, D. J. B., 2017). Fair Claims simplifies small claims disputes for non-lawyers. This platform offers video conferencing and secure document sharing. In addition to protecting sensitive data, FairClaims improves user experience by simplifying procedures and enabling digital communication (Sharma, M. et al., 2025). For e-commerce disputes, eBay's Resolution Center is an ODR platform. On this cloud-based platform, buyers and sellers can resolve disputes directly, streamlining millions of transactions. Online marketplaces like eBay improve customer satisfaction and trust by implementing ODR. Cloud technology in ODR isn't just for private companies. Cloud solutions are being explored by courts and government agencies to improve dispute resolution. ODR platforms allow citizens to file complaints, address legal issues, and interact with mediators or arbitrators online in many jurisdictions. This project increases justice access and relieves traditional court systems.

4. IMPROVING JUSTICE ACCESS WITH CLOUD-BASED ODR

4.1. Geographic and Economic Barriers with Cloud Technology

Cloud-based systems provide economical options, frequently offering free or inexpensive services, which lowers the cost of legal proceedings for those from low-income backgrounds. Additionally flexible, these platforms let users access legal resources and settle disputes whenever it's most convenient for them (Pandey, B. K. et al., 2024a). Cloud technology ensures greater participation by democratizing access to justice and bridging the gaps brought about by geographic distance and financial constraints. Figure 2 illustrates how cloud computing is essential for removing financial and geographical barriers to legal services access. People living in underserved or rural areas can participate remotely in dispute resolution without having to travel by using online platforms.

- *Accessibility in Remote Area*: Cloud computing makes it significantly easier for people who live in rural or remote areas to access information and services (Muniandi, B. et al., 2024). As a result of the fact that traditional legal services frequently require customers to be physically present, it can be challenging for people who live in remote areas to obtain assistance. Through the utilization of cloud-based Online Dispute Resolution (ODR) platforms, users are able to gain access to legal services without having to leave the convenience of their own homes. This eliminates the necessity of traveling and makes it simpler to take part in the processes of dispute resolution.
- *Cost-Effective Solutions*: The capacity of cloud technology to deliver solutions that are within a reasonable price range is among the most significant advantages it offers. It is essential for individuals who may not be able to afford traditional legal representation to have access to cloud-based arbitration and dispute resolution platforms that offer services at low costs or even for free. These platforms democratize access to legal services by lowering financial barriers, making it possible for even individuals who are economically disadvantaged to seek justice without incurring costs that are prohibitive (Zafar, A., 2023).
- *Flexibility and Convenience*: Users benefit from an unprecedented level of flexibility and convenience when using cloud-based ODR platforms. Participants have the ability to participate in the process of conflict resolution at any time and from any location, which is especially advantageous for individuals who tend to have busy schedules or who have mobility limitations (Pandey, B. K. et al., 2024b). By providing individuals with the ability to manage their legal matters in addition to other responsibilities, this flexibility makes it possible for individuals to participate more actively in the legal system.
- *Scalability of Services*: It is possible for ODR providers to modify their services in response to changes in demand thanks to the scalability of cloud technology. This indicates that they are able to handle a fluctuating number of cases in an efficient manner without compromising the quality of their service. When more users turn to online dispute resolution (ODR) for reso-

lution, the cloud infrastructure is able to accommodate increased workloads, which ensures that disputes are resolved in a timely and effective manner for all parties involved.

- *Integration of Resources*: Users are provided with convenient access to a wide variety of educational materials, legal advice, and support services that are tailored to their specific requirements through the utilization of cloud platforms, which centralize a variety of legal tools and resources. This integration gives individuals more power by providing them with the information and resources they need to successfully navigate the legal process. As a result, their chances of achieving a favorable outcome in their disputes are ultimately improved (Basha, A. J. et al., 2024).
- *Promoting Legal Literacy*: A Contribution to the Promotion of Legal Literacy Cloud-based online dispute resolution platforms also do their part to promote legal literacy among users. Individuals are given the ability to better understand their rights and the legal processes that are involved in the resolution of disputes through the use of these platforms, which provide easy access to educational materials and additional legal resources. Enhanced legal literacy provides users with the knowledge necessary to navigate the system in a more effective manner, which ultimately increases their chances of successfully resolving their disputes .
- *Fostering Inclusivity*: Cloud technology creates an environment that is more inclusive within the legal system by removing barriers that have traditionally been encountered by underrepresented groups. The elimination of geographical and financial barriers is one of the ways that cloud-based online dispute resolution platforms ensure that everyone, regardless of their history or circumstances, has access to justice. For the purpose of establishing a legal environment that is just and equitable and that caters to all members of society, this inclusiveness is absolutely necessary.

Figure 2. Economic and geographic cloud technology barriers

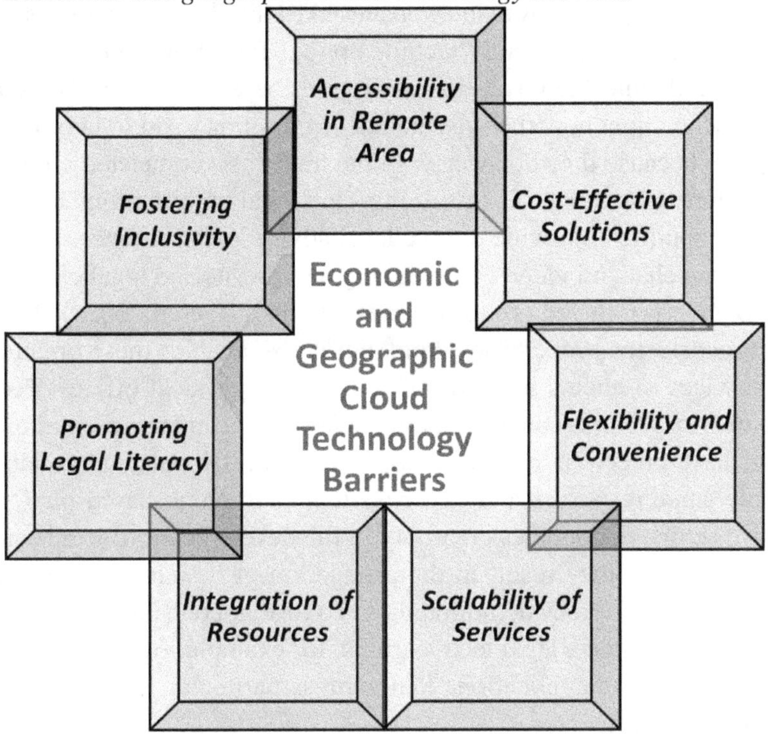

4.2. Democratization of Legal Resources

Cloud-based systems' democratization of legal resources is a revolutionary step forward for the legal field, especially in terms of expanding access to justice. These systems greatly lower barriers to legal assistance and information by utilizing the internet to offer free or inexpensive legal tools and services to individuals and organizations. Online legal advice and information is readily available, which is a crucial component of democratizing legal resources (KVM, S. et al., 2024). Comprehensive legal databases are frequently hosted on cloud-based platforms, providing users with access to a multitude of resources such as legal articles, document templates, and rights and obligations information. People are now empowered to take control of their legal needs thanks to websites and platforms like Rocket Lawyer and Legal Zoom, which enable users to create contracts and legal documents without requiring in-depth legal knowledge. Users are better able to navigate issues with greater confidence thanks to the information being easily accessible. A lot of cloud-based platforms offer free or inexpensive online tools for resolving disputes (Lakshmi,

K. V. N. et al., 2024). Conflict resolution can be facilitated without the need for formal legal representation by using websites like FairClaims and eBay's Resolution Center. These services frequently include options for arbitration or mediation, enabling quick and amicable resolution of disputes between parties. These platforms allow those who might not otherwise pursue legal action to do so in order to resolve their disputes because they do away with the high costs connected with traditional legal procedures. A number of institutions and legal aid programs have started to use cloud computing to provide remote legal advice and assistance. By connecting with clients via chat and video conferencing, nonprofits and legal clinics can offer services to underprivileged groups (Saravanakumar, R. et al., 2024). This strategy not only broadens the scope of legal aid, but it also enables these organizations to provide services to clients beyond the confines of physical offices. People from low-income backgrounds can now obtain legal counsel and representation that they would not have otherwise been able to. Legal professionals can collaborate and more easily share resources and expertise thanks to cloud-based platforms. This cooperative setting encourages creativity in the development of legal services and technologies, which may result in the production of new instruments tailored to the requirements of various demographics. To further contribute to the democratization of legal resources, legal tech startups, for example, frequently utilize cloud technology to develop applications that address particular legal challenges faced by individuals or businesses.

4.3. Increased Efficiency in Case Management

Case management efficiency has increased with cloud-based dispute resolution systems. Automation and streamlining procedures reduce the time and resources needed to resolve disputes and improve the user experience for all parties. Automation is a major benefit of cloud-based dispute resolution systems (Kumarganesh, S. et al., 2024). Document management, which involves collecting and organizing files, evidence, and communications, is crucial in legal disputes. These documents can be collected and categorized automatically by cloud platforms, reducing errors and ensuring mediators and arbitrators have all necessary information. Automation alerts for deadlines, submissions, and actions keep parties informed and engaged, reducing miscommunication and oversight delays. Cloud-based systems use legal document templates to quickly and accurately generate forms. This feature expedites document preparation and ensures legal compliance, which is especially useful for non-lawyers. Streamlining document creation lets users focus on their disputes rather than administrative tasks (Muralidhar, L. B. et al., 2024). Communicating efficiently is another key to cloud-based dispute resolution efficiency. Platforms with integrated messaging or video conferencing allow parties, mediators, and arbitrators to communicate in real time. We can exchange information faster, making discussions and negotiations faster than through traditional channels. This speeds up dispute resolution and improves satisfaction for all parties (Shahul, A. et al., 2024). Cloud case tracking improves efficiency. One place lets users track disputes, review communications, and access relevant documents. Transparency ensures accountability and that all parties understand their cases. Mediators and arbitrators can easily access case history to make informed decisions based on prior interactions and submissions. Data analysis is another benefit of cloud-based dispute resolution systems. Users can analyze dispute resolution patterns, identify common issues, and evaluate different approaches on many platforms. This data can help organizations improve their dispute resolution processes and strategies. Understanding the most common disputes and how long they take to resolve helps organizations allocate resources and take preventative measures (Pandey, B. K. et al., 2024c). Cloud technology also improves legal and dispute resolution collaboration. Cloud platforms allow multiple parties to access and work on cases simultaneously, fostering easy input and expertise sharing. Multiple perspectives on complex issues often lead to more creative solutions.

5. SECURITY, PRIVACY, AND ETHICS IN CLOUD ODR

5.1. Cybersecurity Threats and Mitigation

Cybersecurity threats pose significant risks to the integrity and confidentiality of sensitive data in cloud-based Online Dispute Resolution (ODR) systems. These threats are causing significant concerns. Data breaches, phishing attacks, ransomware, and insider threats are just some of the many types of cyber threats that are prevalent today. Data breaches can occur as a consequence of unauthorized access (Kumar, B. et al., 2024), which can result in the disclosure of private and confidential information that was discussed during the process of conflict resolution. Phishing attacks are designed to trick users into providing sensitive credentials, whereas ransomware is able to encrypt vital data, making it inaccessible until a ransom is paid. Insider threats can exist in the form of employees or contractors who have access to sensitive data and exploit it for their own benefit. It is necessary for ODR providers to take a multi-pronged approach to cybersecurity in order to reduce the risks that are present. To begin, the implementation of strong encryption protocols is necessary for the protection of data both while it is at rest and while it is in transit.

The use of encryption guarantees that data will continue to be unreadable even in the event that it is intercepted or accessed without authorization. Before gaining access to sensitive information, users are required to verify their identity using a variety of different methods (Elarmathi, S. et al., 2024), which is referred to as multi-factor authentication (MFA), which adds an additional layer of security. Conducting security audits on a regular basis is absolutely necessary in order to locate vulnerabilities within the cloud infrastructure. Audits like these assist organizations in identifying areas that could use improvement and in putting in place any necessary patches. Training for employees is also very important; employees should be educated on how to identify phishing attempts and how to handle data in a secure manner. In addition, stringent access control measures (Satheesh, N. et al., 2025) ought to be enforced in order to restrict data access according to user roles, thereby reducing the possibility of threats coming from within the organization. Protocols for communication, procedures for recovery, and strategies for reducing the impact of an attack should all be included in this plan. Through the implementation of these preventative measures, online dispute resolution (ODR) providers are able to effectively protect sensitive information, thereby guaranteeing the safety and reliability of their platforms within the digital landscape.

5.2. Data Protection and Privacy Concerns

Online dispute resolution (ODR) platforms that are hosted in the cloud have completely changed the way disputes are settled, offering a quick and easy substitute for lengthy legal procedures. Nonetheless, there are serious privacy and data protection issues when cloud computing is incorporated into the legal system. Since they directly impact the integrity and confidentiality of sensitive data handled during dispute resolution, these issues must be addressed. The kind of sensitive data that ODR systems process is one of the main worries. Individuals frequently divulge private information such as names, addresses, bank account information, and case-related paperwork. Because of its inherent vulnerability (Pandey, D. et al., 2024), this information may be subject to unauthorized access, which could lead to identity theft, financial loss, or reputational harm if it is not sufficiently protected. Strict data protection procedures are required due to the possible risks in order to guarantee the confidentiality of all participant information during the ODR process. The way that ODR providers handle sensitive information is greatly influenced by the legal frameworks that oversee data protection. Stricter guidelines for data collection, processing, and storage are established by laws like the Health Insurance Portability and Accountability Act (HIPAA) in the US and the General Data Protection Regulation (GDPR) in Europe.

These laws demand that companies seek individuals' express consent before collecting their personal information and that data be used only for those purposes. In addition to building user trust in their systems, ODR providers must abide by these rules to avoid paying large fines and facing legal consequences. The possibility of illegal access to private information is a serious concern as well (Pandey, B. K. et al., 2024d). Hacking, phishing, or insufficient access controls are some of the reasons why data breaches happen. Not only can these breaches reveal private data, but they can jeopardize the entire dispute resolution procedure and put the participating ODR providers in danger of legal repercussions. An extra risk comes from insider threats, where workers or contractors may abuse their access rights and accidentally or purposely leak private data while communicated over network (Pandey, B. K. et al., 2024e). Therefore, reducing the possibility of unwanted access requires the implementation of strong security measures like multi-factor authentication and stringent access controls. In cloud-based ODR systems, encryption is a crucial tool for safeguarding sensitive data. Data encryption ensures that even if it is intercepted or accessed without authorization, it will remain unreadable by transforming the data into a coded format. To protect users' private data, robust encryption protocols must be used for both data in transit and data at rest (George, W. K. et al., 2024.). Adopting data minimization principles should be done in addition to encryption. These guidelines place a strong emphasis on gathering only the data required for particular objectives, which lowers the amount of sensitive data that is at risk and improves privacy protection (Abdullahi, M. et al., 2024). Maintaining data integrity and confidentiality can be especially difficult in multi-tenant cloud environments, where several users share resources. To make sure that one user's data cannot be accessed by another, ODR providers must put strict data segregation and access control measures in place. Ensuring compliance with data protection regulations and safeguarding the privacy of all participants is imperative. Policies for data retention are also crucial for addressing privacy issues. In order to balance operational requirements with legal requirements, ODR providers must set explicit guidelines regarding the duration for which personal information will be kept on file. While keeping data longer than is necessary can make you more vulnerable to data breaches, keeping it too long can make it more difficult to resolve disputes. Gaining trust in cloud-based ODR systems requires both user consent and transparency. Organizations must be transparent about the types of data they collect, how they plan to use it, and who can access it. Because of this openness, users are better equipped to decide whether or not to participate in the ODR process and can feel more confident in the platforms security.

6. CONCLUSION

The incorporation of cloud computing into Online Dispute Resolution (ODR) has significantly addressed a variety of challenges that are associated with access to justice. Legal procedures have become more accessible to a wider range of people as a result of cloud technology's ability to provide remote access to legal services, lower costs, and facilitate timely dispute resolution. The advancements in this area make it possible for people living in underserved areas to seek justice, effectively closing the gap that was caused by the economic and geographical barriers that existed before. Not only do the implications of cloud-based online dispute resolution extend beyond individual cases, but they also represent a paradigm shift in the legal systems of the entire world. With the increasing number of jurisdictions adopting these technologies, we can anticipate an increase in the efficiency and effectiveness of the dispute resolution process. A more equitable legal landscape could be created all over the world as a result of this shift, which has the potential to standardize legal processes, improve transparency, and increase public trust in the justice system. Cloud computing presents itself as a viable solution for improving the accessibility of legal information. Cloud-based online dispute resolution (ODR) has the potential to further democratize access to justice, and this potential continues to be promising as technological advancements continue to advance. Stakeholders can work together to ensure that all individuals, regardless of their background or circumstances, are able to successfully navigate the legal system and secure their rights by utilizing these tools. This can be accomplished through collaborative efforts.

REFERENCES

Abdullahi, M., Ahmad, A., Pandey, B. K., & Pandey, D. (2024). Digital Currency Adoption: A Comparative Analysis of Global Trends and the Nigerian eNaira Digital Currency. *SN Computer Science*, *5*(5), 1–11.

Aniello, L., Baldoni, R., & Lombardi, F. (2018). A blockchain-based solution for enabling log-based resolution of disputes in multi-party transactions. In *Proceedings of 5th International Conference in Software Engineering for Defence Applications: SEDA 2016 5* (pp. 53-58). Springer International Publishing.

Basha, A. J., Maheshwari, R. U., Pandey, B. K., & Pandey, D. (2024). Ultra-sensitive photonic crystal fiber–based SPR sensor for cancer detection utilizing hybrid nano-composite layers. *Plasmonics*, •••, 1–15.

Buchwald, M. (2019). Smart contract dispute resolution: The inescapable flaws of blockchain-based arbitration. *U. Pa. L. Rev.*, *168*, 1369.

Elarmathi, S., Rishabavarthani, P., Sindhuja, M., Elayaraja, P., & Malathi Murugesan, S. Kumarganesh, K. Martin Sagayam, Binay Kumar Pandey, and Digvijay Pandey. (2024). Novel manufacturing systems for cancer diagnosis using ultra-sensitive photonic crystal fiber biosensor with dual-functionalized aptamer-nanocavity. *Microsystem Technologies*, •••, 1–20.

Fan, M., Liu, J., Tajeddini, K., & Khaskheli, M. B. (2023). Digital technology application and enterprise competitiveness: The mediating role of ESG performance and green technology innovation. *Environment, Development and Sustainability*, •••, 1–31.

Ferreira, D. B., Giovannini, C., Gromova, E., & da Rocha Schmidt, G. (2022). Arbitration chambers and trust in technology provider: Impacts of trust in technology intermediated dispute resolution proceedings. *Technology in Society*, *68*, 101872.

George, W. K., Silas, E. I., Pandey, D., & Pandey, B. K. (2024). Utilization of Industry 4.0 Technologies in Nigerian Technical and Vocational Education: A Conundrum for Educators. In *Examining the Rapid Advance of Digital Technology in Africa* (pp. 270–293). IGI Global.

Khadka, M., Sah, M., Chaudhary, R., Sahani, S. K., Sahani, K., Pandey, B. K., & Pandey, D. (2025). Spectroscopic, quantum chemical, and topological calculations of the phenylephrine molecule using density functional theory. *Scientific Reports*, *15*(1), 208. PMID: 39747169

Konapure, C. G., Pandey, D., Shete, H., Thakar, C. M., Pandey, B. K., & George, A. S. (2025). Artificial Intelligence in Automated Concrete Mix Design Using Computerized Grading Curves. Interdisciplinary Approaches to AI, Internet of Everything, and Machine Learning, 567-586.

Kumar, B., Pandey, D., Pandey, B. K., & George, A. S. (2024). Higher Education in the Last Four Decades: A Review of Paradigm Shifts in Policy Frameworks. Design and Implementation of Higher Education Learners' Learning Outcomes (HELLO), 333-348.

Kumar, M. S., Prasanna, P. L., Lalitha, M., Joy, M., Jha, S. S., & Pandey, B. K. (2025). Utilizing the Internet of Everything and Artificial Intelligence for Real-Time Workforce Management. In Role of Internet of Everything (IOE), VLSI Architecture, and AI in Real-Time Systems (pp. 153-168). IGI Global Scientific Publishing.

Kumarganesh, S., & Malathi Murugesan, C. Ganesh, N. Santhiyakumari, M. Thangavel, K. Jayaram, K. Martin Sagayam, Binay Kumar Pandey, and Digvijay Pandey. (2024). Hybrid plasmonic biosensors with deep learning for colorectal cancer detection. *Plasmonics*, •••, 1–15.

KVM, S., Pandey, B. K., & Pandey, D. (2024). Design of Surface Plasmon Resonance (SPR) Sensors for Highly Sensitive Biomolecular Detection in Cancer Diagnostics. *Plasmonics*, •••, 1–13.

Lakshmi, K. V. N., Rajan, R., Pandey, D., & Pandey, B. K. (2024). Circular economy: A catalyst for economic growth-an empirical study. *Circular Economy and Sustainability*, •••, 1–22.

Muniandi, B., Nassa, V. K., Pandey, D., Pandey, B. K., Dadheech, P., & George, A. S. (2024). Pattern Analysis for Feature Extraction in Complex Images. In Using Machine Learning to Detect Emotions and Predict Human Psychology (pp. 145-167). IGI Global.

Muralidhar, L. B., Lakshmi, K. V. N., Swapna, H. R., Rupani, J., Nethravathi, K., Pandey, B. K., & Pandey, D. (2024). Impact of Organizational Culture on The Level of Corporate Social Responsibility Investments: An Exploratory Study. *Circular Economy and Sustainability*, •••, 1–19.

Pandey, B. K., Nassa, V. K., Mukundan, A. P., Mahajan, D. A., Pandey, D., George, A. S., & Dadheech, P. (2024c). An Industry-Focused Traffic System Utilising Internet of Things. In *Emerging Engineering Technologies and Industrial Applications* (pp. 200–213). IGI Global.

Pandey, B. K., & Pandey, D. (2023). Parametric optimization and prediction of enhanced thermoelectric performance in co-doped CaMnO3 using response surface methodology and neural network. *Journal of Materials Science Materials in Electronics*, *34*(21), 1589.

Pandey, B. K., & Pandey, D. (2025). Securing healthcare medical image information using advance morphological component analysis, information hiding systems, and hybrid convolutional neural networks on IoMT. *Computers in Biology and Medicine*, *185*, 109499. PMID: 39642698

Pandey, B. K., Pandey, D., & Lelisho, M. E. (2024a). Face mask identification with enhanced cuckoo optimization and deep learning-based faster regional neural network. *Scientific Reports*, *14*(1), 29719. PMID: 39613761

Pandey, B. K., Pandey, D., & Sahani, S. K. (2024b). Autopilot control unmanned aerial vehicle system for sewage defect detection using deep learning. *Engineering Reports*, •••, 12852.

Pandey, B. K., Paramashivan, M. A., Pandey, D., George, A. S., Agarwal, A., Dadheech, P., & Mahajan, D. A. (2024e). A recent survey on 6G vehicular technology: applications and challenges. 6G Security Education and Multidisciplinary Implementation, 337-350.

Pandey, B. K., Paramashivan, M. A., Pandey, D., George, A. S., Agarwal, A., Mahajan, D. A., . . . Pramanik, S. (2024d). Future Directions of Digital Twin Architectures for 6G Communication Networks. In Security Issues and Solutions in 6G Communications and Beyond (pp. 197-211). IGI Global.

Pandey, D., Nassa, V. K., Pandey, B. K., Mahajan, D. A., Patidar, P. K., Dadheech, P., & George, A. S. (2024). An Analysis of Internet-of-Things-Based Fire Detection and Alert Systems. In *Emerging Engineering Technologies and Industrial Applications* (pp. 295–304). IGI Global.

Rai, P. K., Pandey, D., & Pandey, B. K. (2024). The future of enterprise and innovation is compute as a commodity, or CaaC. *Partners Universal International Research Journal*, *3*(2), 89–94.

Saravanakumar, R., TamilSelvi, T., Pandey, D., Pandey, B. K., Mahajan, D. A., & Lelisho, M. E. (2024). Big data processing using hybrid Gaussian mixture model with salp swarm algorithm. *Journal of Big Data*, *11*(1), 167.

Satheesh, N., Gopisankar, N., Kumarganesh, S., Anthoniraj, S., Saravanakumar, S., & Martin Sagayam, K., Binay Kumar Pandey, and Digvijay Pandey. (2025). Advanced AI-driven emergency response systems for enhanced vehicle and human safety. *Iran Journal of Computer Science*, •••, 1–16.

Satheesh, N., Gopisankar, N., Kumarganesh, S., Anthoniraj, S., Saravanakumar, S., & Martin Sagayam, K., Binay Kumar Pandey, and Digvijay Pandey. (2025). Advanced AI-driven emergency response systems for enhanced vehicle and human safety. *Iran Journal of Computer Science*, •••, 1–16.

Shahul, A., Muniandi, B., Paramashivan, M. A., Pandey, D., Pandey, B. K., Dadheech, P., & George, H. (2024). An Analysis of Algorithms and Methods Based on Image Processing for Medical Applications. In *Emerging Engineering Technologies and Industrial Applications* (pp. 173–186). IGI Global.

Sharma, M., Talwar, R., Nassa, V. K., Binay, K., & Pandey, D. (2025). Design and performance analysis of a multiband vivaldi antenna for wireless broadband communication in 3-5.6 GHz spectrum. In *Artificial Intelligence and Information Technologies* (pp. 86–91). CRC Press.

Sheela, M. S., Kumarganesh, S., Pandey, B. K., & Lelisho, M. E. (2025). Integration of silver nanostructures in wireless sensor networks for enhanced biochemical sensing. *Discover Nano*, *20*(1), 7. PMID: 39804434

Singh, S., Madaan, G., Swapna, H. R., Singh, A., Pandey, D., George, A. S., & Pandey, B. K. (2025). Empowering Connectivity: Exploring the Internet of Things. In Interdisciplinary Approaches to AI, Internet of Everything, and Machine Learning (pp. 89-116). IGI Global Scientific Publishing.

Singh, S., Madaan, G., Swapna, H. R., Singh, A., Pandey, D., George, A. S., & Pandey, B. K. (2025). Empowering Connectivity: Exploring the Internet of Things. In Interdisciplinary Approaches to AI, Internet of Everything, and Machine Learning (pp. 89-116). IGI Global Scientific Publishing.

Svantesson, D. J. B. (2017). *Solving the internet jurisdiction puzzle*. Oxford University Press.

Ustun, E. S., & Yuce, M. (2022, June). Smart Legal Contracts & Smarter Dispute Resolution. In *2022 IEEE 24th Conference on Business Informatics (CBI)* (Vol. 2, pp. 111-117). IEEE.

Vinodhini, V., Kumar, M. S., Sankar, S., Pandey, D., Pandey, B. K., & Nassa, V. K. (2022). IoT-based early forest fire detection using MLP and AROC method. *International Journal of Global Warming*, *27*(1), 55–70.

Wang, S., Li, Y., & Khaskheli, M. B. (2024). Innovation Helps with Sustainable Business, Law, and Digital Technologies: Economic Development and Dispute Resolution. *Sustainability*, *16*(10), 3910.

Zafar, A. (2023). Artificial Intelligence (AI) Influence in Law: Balancing Technological Advancements with Ethical Considerations. *Available atSSRN* 4656578.

Zeleznikow, J. (2021). Using artificial intelligence to provide intelligent dispute resolution support. *Group Decision and Negotiation*, *30*(4), 789–812. PMID: 33867681

Chapter 4
Cost Management in Cloud Services for Business

C. Gopalakrishnan
https://orcid.org/0009-0005-3472-8037
Jain University, Bengaluru, India

S. Vinoth
https://orcid.org/0000-0002-9820-6626
Jain University, Bengaluru, India

Geeti Sharma
Jain University, Bengaluru, India

Pujari Sudharsana Reddy
Jain University, Bengaluru, India

ABSTRACT

The critical function that cost management plays in cloud computing for modern businesses, with an emphasis on the requirement for efficient strategies to maximize operational efficiency and minimize expenses. As more and more businesses move their operations to the cloud, cost management becomes increasingly important for preventing excessive spending and ensuring the organization's continued financial viability. There are a number of important strategies, one of which is the utilization of monitoring and optimization tools that produce real-time insights into the utilization of resources. This highlights the significance of auto-scaling and scheduled resource shutdowns in order to dynamically manage resources in accordance with demand, thereby reducing expenditures that are not particularly necessary.

DOI: 10.4018/979-8-3693-9581-3.ch004

1. INTRODUCTION

Cloud services are now an essential component of contemporary business operations, revolutionizing the way organizations handle efficiency, scalability, and innovation. Cloud platforms provide businesses with on-demand access to a vast range of resources, including advanced analytics, storage, and processing power, in contrast to traditional IT infrastructures that demand substantial upfront investments and continuous maintenance (Pandey, B. K., & Pandey, D., 2025). A more agile approach to product development, market adaptation, and international expansion has been made possible by the transition from physical infrastructure to virtualized resources (Sharma, M. et al., 2025), which has allowed businesses to operate with previously unheard-of flexibility and responsiveness. The clouds ability to accelerate digital transformation (Konapure, C. G. et al., 2025) is one of its most important effects. These days, companies can test new concepts and technologies far more quickly, launching services and apps in a matter of hours as opposed to weeks. Rapid innovation has resulted in the creation of new business models, including subscription-based services and the emergence of on-demand platforms. Personalized and scalable solutions are being delivered directly to consumers by industries such as financial services, healthcare, and media streaming, which have embraced cloud computing to generate new revenue streams and transform customer engagement. The fact that cloud services facilitate data-driven (Kumar, B. et al., 2024) decision-making is another important benefit. Businesses can now analyze massive amounts of data (Sahani, K. et al., 2024) in real time and turn raw data into actionable insights thanks to the integration of artificial intelligence (AI) (Singh, S. et al., 2025) and machine learning (ML) tools into cloud platforms. This has significantly impacted fields like supply chain optimization, predictive maintenance, and customer behavior analysis. Businesses are gaining a competitive edge in quickly changing markets by employing cloud-based AI (Pandey, B. K. et al., 2024d) to forecast demand, customize marketing campaigns, and optimize (Pandey, B. K. et al., 2024a) operations. Clouds platforms offer the infrastructure required to safely store, process, and manage big datasets (JayaLakshmi, G. et al., 2024), enabling companies to fully utilize their data assets (Pandey, D. et al., 2024b) while still adhering to compliance regulations. Cloud services facilitate international collaboration in addition to fostering innovation and data-centric strategies. Following the global shift toward remote work, cloud platforms enable a more decentralized workforce by enabling individuals and teams to access data (Rai, P. K. et al., 2024) and applications from any location. Businesses can now access more global talent pools and have lower operating costs thanks to this, creating a more inclusive and diverse work environment. The transition to cloud computing has significantly impacted cost control as well (Pandey, D. et al., 2024a). Businesses use cloud services according to a pay-as-you-go model, meaning they only pay for the resources they utilize. Businesses can grow using this model without having to invest a significant amount of money in new hardware. Furthermore, cloud providers help businesses optimize costs while maintaining high performance by continuously innovating and introducing more affordable services and tools like serverless computing and automated resource management (KVM, S. et al., 2024).

1.1 Cost Management in Cloud Computing

As cloud computing costs directly affect operational effectiveness, profitability, and long-term viability, it is critical for businesses to manage these costs. Businesses may easily overallocated resources or ignore hidden costs when using cloud services because of their flexibility and scalability, which can result in unforeseen costs. By controlling costs well, businesses can take full advantage of cloud computing's advantages without endangering their revenue streams. Because pay-as-you-go pricing is used by most cloud service providers, it is one of the main reasons to concentrate on cost management. Tracking and managing expenses become more difficult with this model, even though it enables companies to pay only for the resources they use. Companies risk overspending on resources or leaving unneeded services running if they don't have adequate oversight, which results in unnecessary costs. By identifying inefficiencies, optimizing resource utilization (Raja, D. Siva Sundhara, et al., 2024), cutting back on wasteful spending, and making sure they are only paying for what they need, cost management tools and strategies assist businesses. Scalability additionally depends on cloud cost management. If cloud usage is not properly managed, costs can explode as businesses expand and their reliance on it grows. Especially in cases with data-intensive (Elarmathi, S. et al., 2024) applications, high storage requirements, or frequent data transfers, scaling infrastructure without a defined cost management plan can result in budget overruns. Businesses may more precisely predict costs, plan for future expansion, and keep control over their cloud spending as they grow by putting cost management techniques into place (Kumar, Samalia, & Verma, 2017). The avoidance of vendor lock-in and cost predictability are two more crucial elements. Recurring discounts for reserved instances or enterprise agreements are common ways that cloud service providers reward long-term loyalty. It may be difficult for companies to move platforms if better alternatives become available because these discounts run the risk of tying them to a single provider (Pandey, B. K. et al., 2024f). Businesses can stay flexible and avoid vendor lock-in by closely examining cloud service contracts and striking a balance between short- and long-term commitments. Companies can also anticipate and reduce hidden costs, like data transfer fees, licensing costs, and security compliance expenses, by using effective cost management. A companys internal financial transparency is further supported by cloud cost management. Enterprises can assign cloud expenses to particular departments, projects, or teams by putting in place cost allocation frameworks or tagging strategies. By optimizing resource usage according to the actual needs of the business units, this not only encourages accountability but also helps (Pandey, B. K., & Pandey, D., 2023). Through the balance of cost and performance, cost management is made a key component of the organization's cloud strategy through the use of financial operations (FinOps) practices, which allow teams to work together across departments (AL-Shboul, 2019).

2. COMPREHENDING CLOUD EXPENDITURES

2.1 Types of Cloud Services

There are various types of cloud services, as illustrated in figure 1. Platform as a Service (PaaS) gives a structure for creating applications, whereas Infrastructure as a Service (IaaS) gives virtualized resources. Online application delivery is made possible by Software as a Service (SaaS), event-driven execution is made possible by Function as a Service (FaaS), and managed solutions for data protection and database management are provided by Backup as a Service (BaaS) and Database as a Service (DBaaS).

- *Infrastructure as a Service (IaaS)*: The term "Infrastructure as a Service" (IaaS) refers to the provision of virtualized computing resources through the use of the internet. This enables businesses to rent servers, storage, and networking components on a flexible basis. By utilizing this model, organizations (Muralidhar, L. B. et al., 2024) are able to adjust the size of their infrastructure in response to changes in demand, thereby removing the requirement for expensive investments in physical hardware (Pandey, D., & Pandey, B. K., 2022). Because it provides the flexibility to rapidly deploy new applications and services, infrastructure as a service (IaaS) is especially advantageous for businesses that experience fluctuations in their workloads. Amazon Web Services (AWS), Microsoft Azure, and Google Cloud Platform are among the most prominent providers of infrastructure as a service (IaaS). These three companies each offer a variety of customizable solutions to cater to the various requirements of businesses.
- *Platform as a Service (PaaS)*: PaaS, which stands for "platform as a service," provides developers with a cloud-based platform that enables them to build, test, and deploy applications without having to manage the underlying infrastructure. Platform as a Service (PaaS) offers a comprehensive environment

that encompasses operating systems, middleware, and development tools. This enables teams to concentrate on computer programming and application development. Through the simplification of deployment and updates, as well as the facilitation of collaboration among development teams, this service streamlines the software development lifecycle. Among the most well-known PaaS solutions are Google App Engine, Heroku, and Red Hat OpenShift. These solutions are designed to accommodate a wide range of programming languages and frameworks (Gupta, Seetharaman, & Raj, 2013).

- *Software as a Service (SaaS)*: The delivery of software applications over the internet is referred to as software as a service (SaaS), and it is typically done on a subscription basis. Users are able to access these applications through their web browsers, which eliminates the need for local installation and maintenance. Companies that want to reduce their IT overhead and make sure their software is always up to date can benefit from using software as a service (SaaS). Common examples of software as a service (SaaS) include Google Workspace, Salesforce, and Zoom. These services offer a wide range of functionalities, including the creation of documents, the management of customer relationships, and video conferencing and more. The software as a service (SaaS) model supports easy scalability, which enables businesses to add or remove users according to their requirements.
- *Function as a Service (FaaS)*: Function as a Service (FaaS), also known as serverless computing, is a type of computing that enables developers to execute code in response to events without having to manage the server infrastructure. Individual functions that are triggered by specific events, such as changes in data or HTTP requests, can be written and deployed by developers using FaaS. These functions can be triggered by specific events. This model is ideal for applications that have variable workloads because it eliminates the need for users to pay for the execution time of their code, which makes it a cost-effective model. Among the most popular FaaS offerings are Amazon Web Services Lambda and Microsoft Azure Functions. These services enable businesses to rapidly implement microservices and automate workflows without the burden of managing additional servers (Asiaei & Rahim, 2019).
- *Backup as a Service (BaaS)*: The term "Backup as a Service" (BaaS) refers to the provision of cloud-based backup solutions to businesses for the purpose of data protection and disaster recovery. The process of backing up data is automated by this service, which guarantees that vital information is safely stored in the cloud and can be easily restored in the event that the data is lost or corrupted through any means. It is typically easier for businesses to protect their sensitive information (Kennedy, G. W. et al., 2024) when they use BaaS solutions because these solutions typically offer features such as incremental

backups, encryption, and compliance with regulatory standards. Backblaze, Acronis, and Veeam are all examples of providers of business as a service (BaaS) that cater to a wide range of business sizes and the requirements for data protection (Shahul, A. et al., 2024).

- *Database as a Service (DBaaS)*: Database as a Service, also known as DBaaS, is a cloud-based service that provides managed database solutions which simplify the process of setting up, maintaining, and scaling databases. With database as a service (DBaaS), businesses are able to gain access to database management systems without the need for extensive information technology resources. This enables them to concentrate on utilizing their data to gain business insights. Database as a service (DBaaS) providers take care of tasks such as backup, scaling, and performance tuning, which makes it simpler for businesses to have efficient management of their data workloads. Amazon RDS, Microsoft Azure SQL Database, and MongoDB Atlas are examples of well-known database as a service (DBaaS) solution. These solutions provide a variety of database types to cater to the specific needs of various applications (Du John, H. V. et al., 2024).

Figure 1. Categories of cloud services

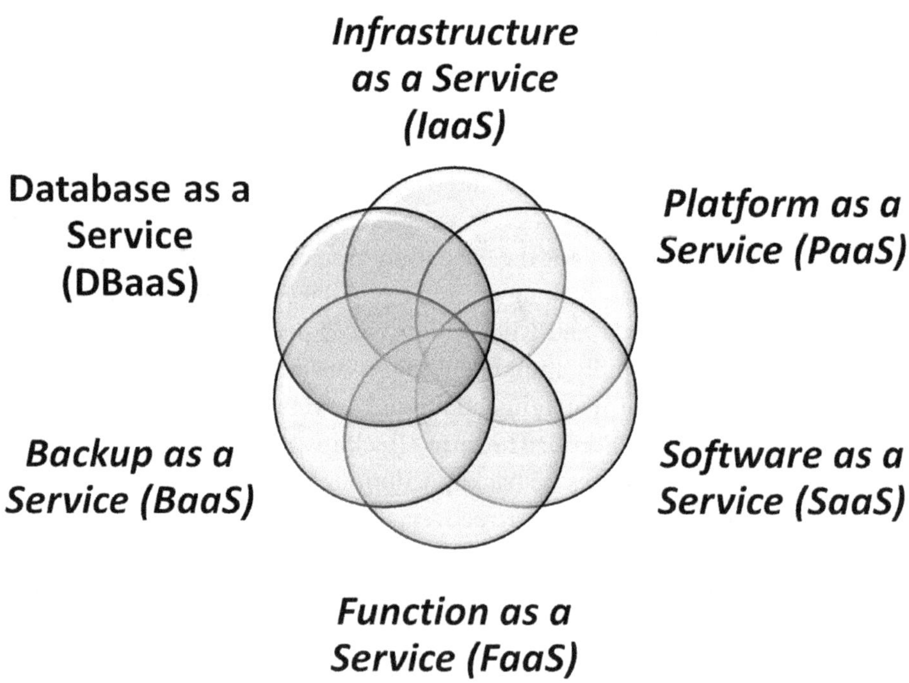

3. OBSTACLES IN MANAGING CLOUD COSTS

3.1 Hidden Costs in Cloud Services

Data transfer fees are among the most frequent hidden costs. Egress fees are the costs associated with moving data out of a cloud environment or between different regions, which are frequently imposed by cloud providers. Large data volumes and multi-cloud or hybrid cloud environments, where data is regularly shared across multiple platforms, make this especially problematic for organizations. These costs can mount up quickly, particularly if companies don't account for the volume of data transfers ahead of time. Excessive bills can also be a result of networking expenses, like load balancing or virtual private cloud costs, especially during periods of high traffic volume. If not closely watched over and managed, hidden costs in cloud services can have a big effect on an organizations budget. Cloud computing offers several benefits to businesses, including scalability, flexibility, and lower upfront infrastructure costs (Chan et al., 2019). There are often unforeseen costs that could impede the initial financial gains. Over-provisioning and under-utilization of cloud resources is a major contributor to hidden costs. In order to prevent potential downtime or performance issues, many businesses have a tendency to allocate more computing power or storage than is necessary. Despite the precautionary nature of this approach, if the excess resources are not utilized, it frequently results in unnecessary costs. Likewise, if services or instances that are no longer required are not decommissioned, there may be continuous fees for resources that are idle a phenomenon known as zombie instances. Storage expenses can rise suddenly, particularly if companies store a lot of data without making the most of it. Many businesses fail to manage their data lifecycles properly, which includes transferring rarely accessed data to less expensive storage. Additionally, businesses frequently incur extra costs for security and compliance. Even though cloud providers usually include built-in security features, many businesses must spend more money on additional tools in order to comply with certain legal requirements or data protection standards, which raises expenses. In order to keep control over cloud spending and make sure that businesses maximize the financial benefits of cloud computing, it is essential to comprehend these hidden costs and implement proactive cost management strategies (Lu, Zhou, & Liu, 2012).

3.2 Resource Over-Provisioning and Under-Utilization

The cloud computing industry faces significant challenges, including over-provisioning and under-utilization of resources, both of which can result in organizations incurring expenses that are not necessary. It is referred to as "over-provisioning" when a company allocates more cloud resources, such as computing power, storage capacity, or network capacity, than is actually required to manage the workloads that it is responsible for. Frequently, this occurs when companies anticipate higher traffic or resource demands than what actually occurs, or when they build in additional capacity as a precautionary measure to prevent potential downtime or performance issues. Taking this approach may appear to be reasonable; however, it may result in paying for resources that are not being utilized or are being used insufficiently, which can lead to inefficiencies and increased operational costs. The term "under-utilization" refers to situations in which cloud resources designated for use are not utilized to their full potential. It is possible for this to happen when companies fail to monitor and optimize their workloads, resulting in virtual machines (Singh, S. et al., 2025), databases, or storage running with little to no activity. For instance, a virtual machine might be left running continuously, but it might only be used for a few hours per day. This would mean that the company is paying for idle capacity, which could be reduced or turned off when it is not being used. Over-provisioning and under-utilization can both have a significant impact on a company's finances over time, particularly as cloud environments become more complicated. Sometimes it can be difficult for organizations to keep track of which resources are being used effectively, which can result in cloud bills that are significantly higher than they should be. The implementation of strategies such as rightsizing, which involves adjusting resources to match actual workloads, and auto-scaling, which automatically adjusts cloud capacity based on demand, is something that businesses should do in order to avoid these pitfalls. Regular audits of cloud usage and the utilization of cloud-native tools for monitoring can also assist businesses in locating and removing resources that are either over-provisioned or under-utilized, thereby optimizing cloud costs and improving overall efficiency (Ravichandran & Naganathan, 2013).

3.3 Vendor Lock-In and Its Impact on Cost

Vendor lock-in occurs when an organization becomes unduly reliant on one cloud service provider, making it difficult to move to a new provider or return to on-premises solutions. This dependency frequently results from a provider's exclusive features, proprietary technologies, or integration challenges, which makes it difficult for organizations to look into other options. While vendor lock-in can have some benefits, like more integrated tools and streamlined services, it also has serious consequences for overall flexibility and cost control. The possibility of higher prices is one of the main effects of vendor lock-in on costs. Businesses may have to pay more for ongoing access to cloud resources once they have committed to a specific cloud provider and based their operations and applications on their offerings. When a vendor realizes how hard it is for customers to leave, they might raise prices or reduce the number of options available for competitive pricing. Gradually, this can result in higher operating costs, which can put pressure on finances and lower profitability. Limited negotiating power is another effect of vendor lock-in. A business may find it more difficult to negotiate terms and prices if it depends too much on one cloud provider (Emeakaroha, Brandic, Maurer, & Breskovic, 2011). Competitors frequently provide more appealing prices or better terms for services, but businesses may be discouraged from pursuing these opportunities due to the expense and difficulty of switching from an established provider. As such, businesses might lose out on possible cost savings that come from better deals with other suppliers. Vendor lock-in can inhibit creativity and adaptability in addition to financial concerns. A company's capacity to benefit from developments in the cloud computing space may be restricted if it grows reluctant to accept new technologies or services from other suppliers. A technologically stagnant environment may result from this, making it difficult for businesses to stay up with rivals who are utilizing more adaptable and affordable solutions. Businesses should use services from multiple providers to ensure greater flexibility and cost control as part of a multi-cloud strategy to reduce the risks associated with vendor lock-in. By choosing the best solutions for their requirements, organizations can avoid becoming dependent on a single vendor. Standardized architectures and open-source technologies can also help to lessen migration challenges and promote greater adaptability, which will ultimately support longer-term, more effective cost management (Lian, Yen, & Wang, 2014).

4. ASPECTS OF CLOUD SERVICE COSTS

Organizations can develop an all-encompassing cost management plan that optimizes cloud service benefits while reducing needless spending by thoroughly understanding these important cost components. For cloud computing to be financially sustainable over the long run, this knowledge is essential. There are a number of important cost factors that have an impact on cloud services, as illustrated in figure 2. In the first place, because pricing is typically determined by the amount of computing power, storage space, and bandwidth that is utilized, resource utilization has a direct influence on costs. Second, when moving data into and out of the cloud, there is the potential for data transfer fees to accumulate, which can have an impact on overall expenses. When it comes to the financial outlay, the third factor is the costs associated with licensing and subscriptions for software and services. Fourth, the decision between on-demand and reserved instances can have a significant impact on pricing; reserved instances frequently provide cost savings for long-term commitments. Over-provisioning, under-utilization, and compliance requirements are examples of hidden costs that can unexpectedly drive-up cloud spending. Other hidden costs include those associated with compliance requirements.

1. *Resource Usage*: Expenses are frequently determined by the quantity of storage, network bandwidth, and processing power used. Virtual machine costs (Basha, A. J. et al., 2024), CPU hours, RAM consumption, and storage capacity are all included in this. By comprehending the ways in which resources are utilized, companies can maximize their allocation, for example, by executing auto-scaling to correspond with demand and rightsizing (modifying resources to suit true requirements). Businesses can reduce unnecessary expenses by identifying underutilized resources through regular monitoring and making necessary adjustments or terminations.
2. *Data Transfer Costs*: When data leaves a cloud environment, it's called data egress, and many providers charge for this. Costs for inbound or outgoing data transfers between different regions could apply in addition to egress fees. Particularly for companies that regularly transfer sizable amounts of data, as during backup operations or data migrations, these costs can mount up quickly. In addition to investigating data compression and caching options to cut expenses, organizations ought to think about optimizing (Dhanasekar, S. et al., 2023) their data architecture to minimize needless transfers.
3. *Storage Costs*: Companies need to think about all of the available storage options in addition to the cost of data storage. The cost of each storage class, which varies depending on performance, durability, and frequency of access, is usually variable. Lower-cost tiers like cold storage or archival options can be used to store data that is not frequently accessed, while higher-cost tiers like standard storage can be used to store data that is frequently accessed. When data lifecycle management policies are put into place, data can gradually be automatically moved to more affordable storage options (Dong, Zheng, Yang, Li, & Qiao, 2009).
4. *Support and Management Costs*: From basic support to premium options that offer faster response times and dedicated account management, many providers offer varying degrees of support. In mission-critical environments, in particular, businesses might have to pay for premium services in order to guarantee prompt support and guidance. Companies should also account for the expenses of managing and keeping an eye on cloud resources, such as hiring staff members specifically for cloud governance, training staff members, and using third-party management tools.
5. *Licensing and Compliance Fees*: Firms may incur additional costs if they have to buy extra licenses for cloud-hosted software programs or follow industry-specific rules. This involves paying a license fee per user or per instance for

proprietary operating systems, databases, or software. The GDPR, HIPAA, and PCI DSS compliance requirements should be known to organizations as they may call for extra security measures, audits, and paperwork, which could result in additional expenses.

6. *Backup and Disaster Recovery Costs*: Inadequate planning and management of these services can result in increased costs even though they are necessary for data protection. Back-up solution costs can include data storage fees, maintenance costs for redundant systems, and data transfer fees for transferring backup data to different locations. For cost-effectiveness, businesses should assess the frequency of their backups, retention guidelines, and disaster recovery plans. Comparing cloud-native backup solutions to conventional techniques can also frequently result in significant cost savings (Saini, Saini, Yousif, & Khandage, 2011).

Figure 2. Cost factors in cloud services

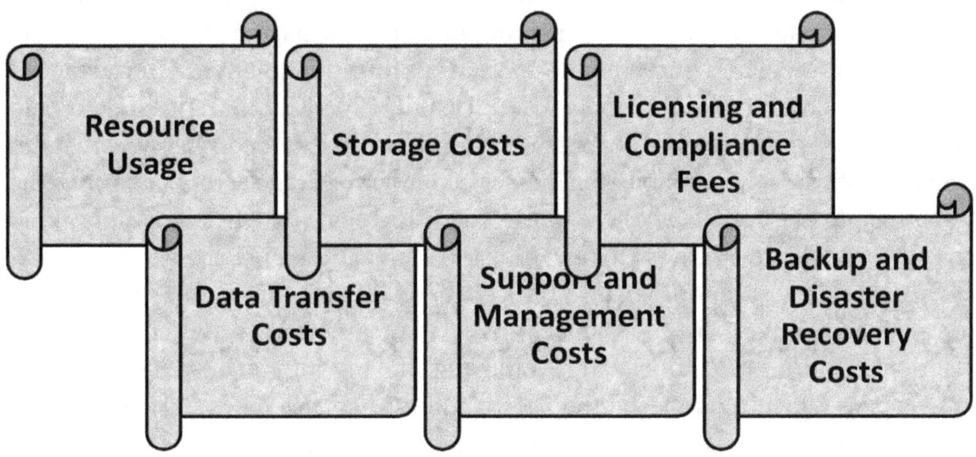

5. NAVIGATING CLOUD COSTS

5.1 Monitoring and Optimization Tools

Businesses need monitoring and optimization tools to understand their cloud usage, identify inefficiencies, and optimize expenses. As organizations use cloud services for more applications and workloads, resource management can become overwhelming. Thus, using the right tools is essential for cost control and performance. Real-time (Maheshwari, R. Uma. et al., 2024) resource usage visibility is a key function of monitoring tools. These tools track cloud resource consumption metrics like CPU, memory, and network bandwidth. This visibility lets teams see which resources are used well and which are idle. Monitoring tools can identify underutilized instances, helping organizations rightsize their resources. Amazon CloudWatch, Google Cloud Monitoring, and Microsoft Azure Monitor are among the native cloud monitoring solutions. These platforms seamlessly integrate with their cloud environments, providing detailed insights and threshold-based alerts. Automated alerts can notify relevant teams when resource usage exceeds predefined limits or anomalies are detected, enabling proactive management and preventing unexpected costs. Third-party monitoring and optimization solutions offer advanced features in addition to native tools. CloudHealth, CloudCheckr, and Spot.io help organizations visualize cloud expenditures with analytics, reporting, and customizable dashboards. Multi-cloud businesses can monitor usage across environments from a single interface using these tools, which aggregate data from multiple cloud providers (Maheshwari, R. U. et al., 2024). Optimization tools analyze usage patterns and make cost-cutting suggestions. They can identify underutilized resources, recommend workload-based instance types, and recommend cost-effective storage solutions. Optimization tools can recommend moving infrequently accessed data to cheaper storage tiers or shutting down idle virtual machines during off-peak hours. Automation is another important feature of optimization tools. These tools can automate resource scaling based on demand by integrating with cloud management platforms. This dynamic resource allocation improves operational efficiency and reduces costs by only charging for the resources organizations need. Effective cloud cost management tools also require governance and policy enforcement. Organizations can enforce resource provisioning, usage limits, and budget controls with monitoring and optimization solutions. Teams can limit cloud spending by department or project to match organizational budgets and priorities. Monitoring and optimization tools must include reporting and forecasting. Organizations can understand spending patterns with these tools' detailed cost reports by department, project, or resource type. Advanced forecasting algorithms can predict future costs based on historical usage trends, helping organizations plan budgets and identify financial risks (Mohammed, 2011).

5.2 Cloud-Native Tools

Cloud-native tools are optimized for cloud computing. They leverage cloud elasticity, scalability, and agility to work seamlessly in cloud ecosystems. These tools help organizations develop, deploy, and manage applications faster, enabling rapid innovation and market adaptation. Microservices architecture is a key feature of cloud-native tools. Cloud-native applications are divided into modular services that can be developed, deployed, and scaled separately. Kubernetes and Docker orchestrate and containerize microservices, making them essential. For instance, Kubernetes automates containerized application deployment, scaling, and management, letting developers focus on features rather than infrastructure. Cloud-native tools emphasize continuous integration and deployment. By automating software development, organizations can deliver updates and features faster. Testing, building, and deploying applications are automated by Jenkins, GitLab CI/CD, and CircleCI. This boosts productivity and reduces errors because changes can be tested and rolled back in real time (Kumarganesh, S. et al., 2024). Cloud-native environments require monitoring and logging. Organizations can track application performance with real-time metrics and visualization tools like Prometheus and Grafana. Developers can aggregate and analyze log data from various services using ELK Stack (Elasticsearch, Logstash, and Kibana) to troubleshoot and optimize performance (Saravanakumar, R. et al., 2024). These tools enable deep application behavior insights and rapid issue resolution. As organizations move to the cloud, application and data security becomes crucial. Container security solutions like Aqua Security and Twistlock (now Palo Alto Networks) protect applications during development and deployment. Organizations can also enforce security policies with Okta and AWS IAM, which manage cloud resource access. Development and operations teams collaborate with cloud-native tools for DevOps. Slack and Microsoft Teams can improve workflow and cross-team visibility. In today's fast-paced business environment, application delivery must be fast and reliable, so collaboration is essential. The pay-as-you-go pricing model of cloud-native tools lets organizations scale resources as needed. Since businesses only pay for what they use, this flexibility helps manage costs. Developers can execute code without provisioning or managing servers with serverless computing tools like AWS Lambda and Azure Functions. Teams can write code and deliver value while reducing operational overhead (Shi & Lin, 2022).

5.3 Third-Party Tools

The supplementary functionalities and integrations that third-party tools offer that may not be found in native cloud service offerings are essential for improving cloud computing environments. These technologies assist businesses in streamlining processes, cutting expenses, enhancing security, and optimizing cloud usage. Solutions for cloud cost management and optimization represent a noteworthy subset of third-party tools. Organizations can track and analyze their cloud usage, spot areas for cost savings, and analyze spending trends with the help of tools like CloudCheckr and CloudHealth. These systems offer thorough reporting, warnings about unforeseen expenses, and suggestions for reducing resource allocation or utilizing more economical solutions (Lakshmi, K. V. N. et al., 2024). These tools allow companies to better understand how much they're spending on the cloud and put cost-saving measures in place. Cloud security is another important topic. Robust security measures are becoming increasingly important as more and more organizations use cloud services. Tools from third parties that provide comprehensive protection against threats, vulnerabilities, and compliance risks are Palo Alto Networks Prisma Cloud and Check Point CloudGuard. Organizations can maintain a secure cloud environment and ensure compliance with industry regulations by utilizing these tools (Pandey, B. K. et al., 2024b), which offer features like runtime protection, vulnerability scanning, and security policy enforcement. Another essential component of a cloud environment is performance management and monitoring tools (Sharma, M. et al., 2024). Applications, infrastructure health, and user experience can all be real-time monitored by enterprises using solutions such as Datadog and New Relic. By compiling data from multiple sources, these tools enable teams to locate bottlenecks in performance, resolve problems, and guarantee peak application performance. Businesses may proactively manage their cloud resources and provide their users with a better experience by utilizing these monitoring tools. Third-party technologies can improve backup and disaster recovery capabilities, which are essential elements of a cloud strategy. For cloud environments, advanced backup and recovery options are provided by solutions like Veeam and Commvault, guaranteeing data protection. In the event of an outage or data loss (Pandey, B. K. et al., 2024e), these tools help organizations establish dependable backup plans, perform routine data integrity checks, and retrieve data quickly (Pandey, B. K. et al., 2024c). Enterprises can guarantee uninterrupted operations and prevent possible dangers by implementing all-inclusive backup solutions. Cloud environments are also home to many productivity and collaboration tools. Teams may communicate and work together even when they are located in different places thanks to apps like Atlassian's Jira, Microsoft Teams, and Slack. The ability to work on projects, share files, and monitor progress is made possible by these tools' integration with a number of cloud services. Companies can increase output and expedite project completion by strengthening collaboration. The connecting of different cloud services and apps is facilitated by integration tools. By automating procedures and guaranteeing data consistency across apps, platforms such as MuleSoft and Zapier allow businesses to design workflows that connect various systems. By streamlining operations and eliminating manual labor, these technologies assist companies in freeing up staff time for more important tasks. For continuous integration and continuous deployment (CI/CD), third-party tools are vital in the DevOps space. By automating the software development lifecycle, enterprises can increase code quality and speed of release thanks to tools like CircleCI, Jenkins, and GitLab CI. Development teams can work more nimbly and responsively to shifting business requirements by incorporating these tools into their processes (Mohammad & Vargas, 2022).

6. AUTOMATING COST MANAGEMENT

One of the most important strategies for maximizing resource utilization and cutting down on wasteful spending in cloud environments is automating cost management. Auto-scaling and scheduled resource shutdowns are two efficient ways to accomplish this automation. Based on the current demand, auto-scaling is a dynamic resource management feature that automatically modifies the number of active instances or resources. Auto-scaling allows for the real-time increase or decrease of resources by continuously monitoring performance metrics like CPU, memory, and network traffic. To keep apps responsive during periods of high usage, for example, more instances can be provisioned to handle the increased load. On the other hand, auto-scaling minimizes expenses related to idle resources by terminating surplus instances during low demand. Organizations are able to maintain optimal performance and only pay for the resources they truly need thanks to this ability to adjust resource allocation based on demand. Another efficient technique to automatically control cloud costs is through scheduled resource shutdowns. Policies that shut down non-essential resources on weekends or evenings can be implemented by organizations. Development and testing environments, for instance, can be set up for automatic shutdowns since they might not be needed after regular business hours. By not charging for unused resources, this strategy drastically lowers expenses. Workflow disruption can be minimized by using scheduling tools, which can be set up to power resources back up when needed. Businesses can optimize their cloud expenses and retain operational efficiency by implementing such schedules. A more economical cloud strategy benefits from both auto-scaling and planned resource shutdowns (Palinkas et al., 2015). Organizations can lower manual oversight, improve overall resource management, and make sure cloud spending is in line with actual usage by automating these procedures. Organizations can further enhance their automation strategies by combining these practices with monitoring and optimization tools that offer insights into usage patterns. Automating cost management will be essential to attaining both operational efficiency and financial sustainability as businesses depend more and more on cloud infrastructure.

7. CONCLUSION

Managing cloud costs effectively is crucial for businesses looking to use cloud services and stay financially stable. In this conversation, we have covered a number of important techniques for efficiently controlling expenses. These include the use of third-party tools that improve security, cooperation, and integration; the deployment of auto-scaling and scheduled resource shutdowns for dynamic resource management; and monitoring and optimization tools that offer real-time visibility into resource utilization. To ensure that businesses can optimize their cloud investments while reducing waste, each of these tactics is essential. One cannot stress the significance of proactive cloud cost management. Proactively managing cloud costs helps organizations keep ahead of their expenses in an environment where costs can quickly spiral out of control. Through consistent monitoring of usage patterns, resource optimization, and governance policy enforcement, businesses can make well-informed decisions that support long-term sustainability. This not only aids in cost containment now but also equips businesses to adjust in the future as their cloud strategy, technology, and market dynamics change. The field of cloud cost optimization is probably going to undergo major change in the near future. Advanced cost management techniques will be even more important as cloud technologies develop and businesses continue to use hybrid and multi-cloud setups. Advances in machine learning and artificial intelligence could improve the capacity to forecast expenses and examine usage trends, allowing businesses to maximize their resources instantly. As companies become more conscious of their environmental impact, there will likely be a greater emphasis on sustainable cloud practices, which will spur the creation of tools and tactics that support eco-friendly initiatives while also optimizing costs. Organizations need to give proactive cost management top priority if they want to maintain the financial stability and operational effectiveness of cloud computing.

REFERENCES

AL-Shboul. (2019). M.A. Towards a better understanding of determinants logistical factors in SMEs for cloud ERP adoption in developing economies. *Business Process Management Journal*, *25*, 887–907.

Asiaei, A., & Rahim, N. Z. A. (2019). A multifaceted framework for adoption of cloud computing in Malaysian SMEs. *J. Sci. Technol. Policy Manag.*, *10*, 708–750.

Basha, A. J., Maheshwari, R. U., Pandey, B. K., & Pandey, D. (2024). Ultra-Sensitive Photonic Crystal Fiber–Based SPR Sensor for Cancer Detection Utilizing Hybrid Nanocomposite Layers. *Plasmonics*, •••, 1–15.

Chan, F. T., Wang, Z., Singh, Y., Wang, X., Ruan, J., & Tiwari, M. (2019). Activity scheduling and resource allocation with uncertainties and learning in activities. *Industrial Management & Data Systems*, *119*, 1289–1320.

Dhanasekar, S., Martin Sagayam, K., Pandey, B. K., & Pandey, D. (2023). Refractive index sensing using metamaterial absorbing augmentation in elliptical graphene arrays. *Plasmonics*, •••, 1–11.

Dong, B., Zheng, Q., Yang, J., Li, H., & Qiao, M. An e-learning ecosystem based on cloud computing infrastructure. In *Proceedings of the 2009 Ninth IEEE International Conference on Advanced Learning Technologies (ICALT)*, Riga, Latvia, 15–17 July 2009; pp. 125–127.

Du John, H. V., Jose, T., Sagayam, K. M., Pandey, B. K., & Pandey, D. (2024). Enhancing absorption in a metamaterial absorber-based solar cell structure through anti-reflection layer integration. Silicon, 1-11.

Elarmathi, S., Rishabavarthani, P., Sindhuja, M., Elayaraja, P., & Malathi Murugesan, S. Kumarganesh, K. Martin Sagayam, Binay Kumar Pandey, and Digvijay Pandey. (2024). Novel manufacturing systems for cancer diagnosis using ultra-sensitive photonic crystal fiber biosensor with dual-functionalized aptamer-nanocavity. *Microsystem Technologies*, •••, 1–20.

Emeakaroha, V. C., Brandic, I., Maurer, M., & Breskovic, I. SLA-aware application deployment and resource allocation in clouds. In Proceedings of the 2011 IEEE 35th Annual Computer Software and Applications Conference Workshops, Munich, Germany, 18–22 July 2011; IEEE: Piscateville, NJ, USA; pp. 298–303.

Gupta, P., Seetharaman, A., & Raj, J. R. (2013). The usage and adoption of cloud computing by small and medium businesses. *International Journal of Information Management*, *33*, 861–874.

JayaLakshmi. G., Pandey, D., Pandey, B. K., Kaur, P., Mahajan, D. A., & Dari, S. S. (2024). Smart big data collection for intelligent supply chain improvement. In AI and Machine Learning Impacts in Intelligent Supply Chain (pp. 180-195). IGI Global.

Kennedy, G. W., Sunday, S. E., Pandey, D., Kabari, A. D., Pandey, B. K., George, A. S., & Dadheech, P. (2024). Building Information Modeling: Harnessing Innovations for Professional Proficiency. In Emerging Engineering Technologies and Industrial Applications (pp. 305-331). IGI Global.

Konapure, C. G., Pandey, D., Shete, H., Thakar, C. M., Pandey, B. K., & George, A. S. (2025). Artificial Intelligence in Automated Concrete Mix Design Using Computerized Grading Curves. Interdisciplinary Approaches to AI, Internet of Everything, and Machine Learning, 567-586.

Kumar, B., Pandey, D., Pandey, B. K., & George, A. S. (2024). Higher Education in the Last Four Decades: A Review of Paradigm Shifts in Policy Frameworks. Design and Implementation of Higher Education Learners' Learning Outcomes (HELLO), 333-348.

Kumar, D., Samalia, H. V., & Verma, P. (2017). Exploring suitability of cloud computing for small and medium-sized enterprises in India. *Journal of Small Business and Enterprise Development*, *24*, 814–832.

Kumar, M. S., Prasanna, P. L., Lalitha, M., Joy, M., Jha, S. S., & Pandey, B. K. (2025). Utilizing the Internet of Everything and Artificial Intelligence for Real-Time Workforce Management. In Role of Internet of Everything (IOE), VLSI Architecture, and AI in Real-Time Systems (pp. 153-168). IGI Global Scientific Publishing.

Kumarganesh, S., & Malathi Murugesan, C. Ganesh, N. Santhiyakumari, M. Thangavel, K. Jayaram, K. Martin Sagayam, Binay Kumar Pandey, and Digvijay Pandey. (2024). Hybrid Plasmonic Biosensors with Deep Learning for Colorectal Cancer Detection. *Plasmonics*, •••, 1–15.

KVM, S., Pandey, B. K., & Pandey, D. (2024). Design of Surface Plasmon Resonance (SPR) Sensors for Highly Sensitive Biomolecular Detection in Cancer Diagnostics. *Plasmonics*, •••, 1–13.

Lakshmi, K. V. N., Rajan, R., Pandey, D., & Pandey, B. K. (2024). Circular Economy: A Catalyst for Economic Growth-An Empirical Study. *Circular Economy and Sustainability*, •••, 1–22.

Lian, J.-W., Yen, D. C., & Wang, Y.-T. (2014). An exploratory study to understand the critical factors affecting the decision to adopt cloud computing in Taiwan hospital. *International Journal of Information Management*, *34*, 28–36.

Lu, X., Zhou, J., & Liu, D. (2012). A method of cloud resource load balancing scheduling based on improved adaptive genetic algorithm. *Journal of Information and Computational Science*, *9*, 4801–4809.

Maheshwari, R. Uma, S. Kumarganesh, Shree KVM, A. Gopalakrishnan, K. Selvi, B. Paulchamy, P. Rishabavarthani, K. Martin Sagayam, Binay Kumar Pandey, and Digvijay Pandey. (2024). Advanced plasmonic resonance-enhanced biosensor for comprehensive real-time detection and analysis of deepfake content. *Plasmonics*, •••, 1–18.

Maheshwari, R. U., Paulchamy, B., Pandey, B. K., & Pandey, D. (2024). Enhancing sensing and imaging capabilities through surface plasmon resonance for deepfake image detection. *Plasmonics*, •••, 1–20.

Mohammad, A., & Vargas, S. (2022). Barriers Affecting Higher Education Institutions' Adoption of Blockchain Technology: A Qualitative Study. *Informatics (MDPI)*, *9*, 64.

Mohammed, D. (2011). Security in cloud computing: An analysis of key drivers and constraints. *Inf. Secur. J. Glob. Perspect.*, *20*, 123–127.

Muralidhar, L. B., Lakshmi, K. V. N., Swapna, H. R., Rupani, J., Nethravathi, K., Pandey, B. K., & Pandey, D. (2024). Impact of Organizational Culture on The Level of Corporate Social Responsibility Investments: An Exploratory Study. *Circular Economy and Sustainability*, •••, 1–19.

Palinkas, L. A., Horwitz, S. M., Green, C. A., Wisdom, J. P., Duan, N., & Hoagwood, K. (2015). Purposeful Sampling for Qualitative Data Collection and Analysis in Mixed Method Implementation Research. *Adm. Policy Ment. Health Ment. Health Serv. Res.*, *42*, 533–544. PMID: 24193818

Pandey, B. K., Kanike, U. K., George, A. S., & Pandey, D. (Eds.). (2024d). *AI and machine learning impacts in intelligent supply chain*. IGI Global.

Pandey, B. K., Nassa, V. K., Mukundan, A. P., Mahajan, D. A., Pandey, D., George, A. S., & Dadheech, P. (2024b). An Industry-Focused Traffic System Utilising Internet of Things. In *Emerging Engineering Technologies and Industrial Applications* (pp. 200–213). IGI Global.

Pandey, B. K., & Pandey, D. (2023). Parametric optimization and prediction of enhanced thermoelectric performance in co-doped CaMnO3 using response surface methodology and neural network. *Journal of Materials Science Materials in Electronics*, *34*(21), 1589.

Pandey, B. K., & Pandey, D. (2025). Securing healthcare medical image information using advance morphological component analysis, information hiding systems, and hybrid convolutional neural networks on IoMT. *Computers in Biology and Medicine*, *185*, 109499. PMID: 39642698

Pandey, B. K., Pandey, D., Agarwal, A., Mahajan, D. A., Dadheech, P. D., George, A. S., & Rai, P. K. (2024e). Beyond Data Breaches: Enhancing Security in 6G Communications. In Security Issues and Solutions in 6G Communications and Beyond (pp. 212-229). IGI Global.

Pandey, B. K., Pandey, D., & Lelisho, M. E. (2024a). Face mask identification with enhanced cuckoo optimization and deep learning-based faster regional neural network. *Scientific Reports*, *14*(1), 29719. PMID: 39613761

Pandey, B. K., Paramashivan, M. A., Nassa, V. K., Mahajan, D. A., Dadheech, P., George, A. H., & George, A. S. (2024f). Blockchain's Potential Effect on the Healthcare Industry. In Emerging Engineering Technologies and Industrial Applications (pp. 214-232). IGI Global.

Pandey, B. K., Paramashivan, M. A., Pandey, D., George, A. S., Agarwal, A., Mahajan, D. A., . . . Pramanik, S. (2024c). Future Directions of Digital Twin Architectures for 6G Communication Networks. In Security Issues and Solutions in 6G Communications and Beyond (pp. 197-211). IGI Global.

Pandey, D., Nassa, V. K., Pandey, B. K., Mahajan, D. A., Patidar, P. K., Dadheech, P., & George, A. S. (2024a). An Analysis of Internet-of-Things-Based Fire Detection and Alert Systems. In *Emerging Engineering Technologies and Industrial Applications* (pp. 295–304). IGI Global.

Pandey, D., & Pandey, B. K. (2022). An efficient deep neural network with adaptive galactic swarm optimization for complex image text extraction. In *Process Mining Techniques for Pattern Recognition* (pp. 121–137). CRC Press.

Pandey, D., Pandey, B. K., Paramashivan, M. A., Mahajan, D. A., Dadheech, P. D., George, A. S., & Hameed, A. S. (2024b). Advanced Digital Data Processing Using Cloud Cryptography: Industrial Applications. In Emerging Engineering Technologies and Industrial Applications (pp. 255-268). IGI Global.

Rai, P. K., Pandey, D., & Pandey, B. K. (2024). The future of enterprise and innovation is computed as a commodity, or CaaC. *Partners Universal International Research Journal*, *3*(2), 89–94.

Raja, D. Siva Sundhara, D. Rajesh Kumar, N. Santhiyakumari, S. Kumarganesh, K. Martin Sagayam, B. Thiyaneswaran, Binay Kumar Pandey, and Digvijay Pandey. (2024). A compact dual-feed wide-band slotted antenna for future wireless applications. *Analog Integrated Circuits and Signal Processing*, *118*(2), 291–305.

Ravichandran, S., & Naganathan, E. R. (2013). Dynamic scheduling of data using genetic algorithm in cloud computing. *Int. J. Comput. Algorithm*, *2*, 11–15.

Sahani, K., Khadka, S. S., Sahani, S. K., Pandey, B. K., & Pandey, D. (2024). A possible underground roadway for transportation facilities in Kathmandu Valley: A racking deformation of underground rectangular structures. *Engineering Reports*, *6*(8), e12821.

Saini, S. L., Saini, D. K., Yousif, J. H., & Khandage, S. V. Cloud computing and enterprise resource planning systems. In *Proceedings of the World Congress on Engineering*, London, UK, 6–8 July 2011; Volume 1, pp. 681–684.

Saravanakumar, R., TamilSelvi, T., Pandey, D., Pandey, B. K., Mahajan, D. A., & Lelisho, M. E. (2024). Big data processing using hybrid Gaussian mixture model with salp swarm algorithm. *Journal of Big Data*, *11*(1), 167.

Shahul, A., Muniandi, B., Paramashivan, M. A., Pandey, D., Pandey, B. K., Dadheech, P., & George, H. (2024). An Analysis of Algorithms and Methods Based on Image Processing for Medical Applications. In *Emerging Engineering Technologies and Industrial Applications* (pp. 173–186). IGI Global.

Sharma, M., Talwar, R., Nassa, V. K., Binay, K., & Pandey, D. (2025). Design and performance analysis of a multiband vivaldi antenna for wireless broadband communication in 3-5.6 GHz spectrum. In *Artificial Intelligence and Information Technologies* (pp. 86–91). CRC Press.

Sharma, M., Talwar, R., Pandey, D., Nassa, V. K., Pandey, B. K., & Dadheech, P. (2024). A review of dielectric resonator antennas (DRA)-based RFID technology for Industry 4.0. *Robotics and Automation in Industry*, *4*(0), 303–324.

Shi, F., & Lin, J. (2022). Virtual Machine Resource Allocation Optimization in Cloud Computing Based on Multiobjective Genetic Algorithm. *Computational Intelligence and Neuroscience*, *2022*, 7873131. PMID: 35310579

Singh, S., Madaan, G., Swapna, H. R., Singh, A., Pandey, B. K., George, A. S., & Pandey, D. (2025). Unleashing the Power of AI and Data Analysis: Transforming Insights into Action. In Interdisciplinary Approaches to AI, Internet of Everything, and Machine Learning (pp. 1-24). IGI Global Scientific Publishing.

Singh, S., Madaan, G., Swapna, H. R., Singh, A., Pandey, D., George, A. S., & Pandey, B. K. (2025). Empowering Connectivity: Exploring the Internet of Things. In Interdisciplinary Approaches to AI, Internet of Everything, and Machine Learning (pp. 89-116). IGI Global Scientific Publishing.

Chapter 5
Cybersecurity in Cloud Based Legal Services Addressing Emerging Threats

Nishtha Acharya
Department of Law, Manipal University Jaipur, India

Sony Kulshrestha
Department of Law, Manipal University Jaipur, India

ABSTRACT

In the meantime, deep insights from data analysis are being provided by artificial intelligence (AI) and machine learning (ML), which is stimulating innovation through the creation of new products The revolutionary effect of technology on the functioning of organizations, with a focus on how it promotes productivity, security, and creativity. By handling repetitive tasks more skillfully, the integration of automation technologies has helped businesses increase productivity, minimize errors, and streamline operations. Advanced cybersecurity solutions like firewalls, encryption, and real-time monitoring are essential for shielding sensitive

1. INTRODUCTION

A revolution in efficiency, accessibility, and collaboration has occurred in the legal industry as a result of the growing adoption of cloud-based services by these businesses. Significant cybersecurity challenges have been brought about by this change, though. Legal firms are among the most vulnerable targets for cybercrimi-

DOI: 10.4018/979-8-3693-9581-3.ch005

nals because they manage sensitive data (Pandey, B. K., & Pandey, D., 2025), such as private client information, case files, and proprietary business documents. To protect data integrity, confidentiality, and compliance as it moves to cloud platforms, the legal sector needs to stay aware of new cybersecurity risks. The danger of data breaches (Maheshwari, R. U. et al., 2024) is among the main worries. Even though they are safe, cloud environments can still be accessed illegally. To gain access to systems, cybercriminals use phishing attacks, advanced malware, and vulnerabilities in cloud configurations. Strong access restrictions, multi-factor authentication, and frequent security audits are necessary for law firms to reduce these risks. Attacks using ransomware are an additional emerging danger (Rubia, A., & Iwendi, C., 2021). Ransomware, which encrypts important data and demands payment in exchange for its release, is increasingly targeting law firms. Reputational harm, financial losses, and operational disruptions can all result from such incidents. Essential defenses include using reliable backup solutions, scheduling regular patch management, and training employees to spot suspicious activity. Confusing things further is the cloud security model's shared responsibility approach. Legal firms are accountable for safeguarding their data and applications (Maheshwari, R. Uma. et al., 2024), whereas cloud service providers handle infrastructure security. Preventing security gaps requires an understanding of and clear definition of these responsibilities. Privacy and data compliance are essential. Compliance with laws like the CCPA, GDPR, and others is required of legal firms in order to guarantee that client data is managed in accordance with stringent guidelines. There may be harsh fines and legal ramifications for noncompliance. Legal organizations need to implement a thorough cybersecurity strategy that includes proactive threat detection, ongoing monitoring, and incident response planning in order to counter these new threats. To preserve the security and credibility of cloud-based legal services, it will be essential to collaborate with cloud providers who provide strong security features and to remain aware of emerging risks.

1.1 Cloud Legal Services

The adoption of cloud computing technologies by legal firms and departments in order to provide legal services in a manner that is both more efficient and effective is what is meant by the term “cloud legal services.” Through the utilization of cloud-based platforms, legal professionals are able to remotely access, manage, and store data, which significantly improves the efficiency of workflows and facilitates collaboration. Legal services provided through the cloud come with a number of advantages, such as increased scalability, cost savings, and improved data security. Because of their ability to facilitate a wide range of legal activities, including the management of documents, the administration of cases, and communication with clients, these platforms have become indispensable instruments in contemporary legal practice (Mohiyuddin, A. et al., 2021).

- *Document Management Systems (DMS)*: Cloud-based DMS solutions make it possible for legal professionals to store documents, organize them, and access them from any location. They frequently include features such as version control, secure sharing, and advanced search capabilities, which enable attorneys to work together on documents and manage them in an effective manner.
- *Case management software*: This is a piece of software that assists legal firms in managing all aspects of a case, including scheduling, billing, and communication. Platforms for managing cases that are hosted in the cloud provide real-time updates and access to case files. This makes it possible for attorneys to monitor the progression of their cases, manage deadlines, and seamlessly coordinate with their clients and colleagues.
- *E-Discovery Platforms*: E-discovery tools that are hosted in the cloud enable legal teams to manage the process of identifying, collecting, and analysing electronically stored information (ESI) (Kennedy, G. W. et al., 2024) for the purpose of using it in legal proceedings. Through the automation of tasks such as document review, keyword searches, and data filtering, these platforms significantly improve the efficiency of the discovery process.
- *Virtual Law Firms*: The rise of virtual law firms has been made possible by the cloud, which has made it possible for legal professionals to work remotely and collaborate with clients and colleagues without the need for a physical office space. With this model, overhead costs are reduced, and attorneys are able to provide services that are more flexible.
- *Legal Research Tools*: Legal research platforms that are hosted in the cloud give users access to a vast database of case law, statutes, and legal opinions. Lawyers are able to conduct comprehensive legal research in a more efficient manner with the assistance of these tools, which provide advanced search functionalities and analytical tools.
- *Client Portals*: In order to improve client communication and transparency, a number of legal firms have deployed client portals that are hosted in the cloud. The clients are able to access their case files in a secure manner, communicate with their legal team, and monitor the current status of their cases in real time through the use of these portals.
- *Contract Management Systems*: Cloud-based contract management solutions assist legal teams in the process of drafting, reviewing, and storing contracts. A number of features, including automated alerts for contract renewals, compliance tracking, and collaborative tools for contract negotiation, are frequently included in these systems.

If legal firms were to integrate these cloud-based applications that are shown in the figure 1, they would be able to improve their efficiency, lower their costs, and provide their clients with enhanced services, which would ultimately result in a transformation of the way legal work is carried out in the digital age (Pandey, B. K. et al., 2024e).

Figure 1. Cloud legal services applications

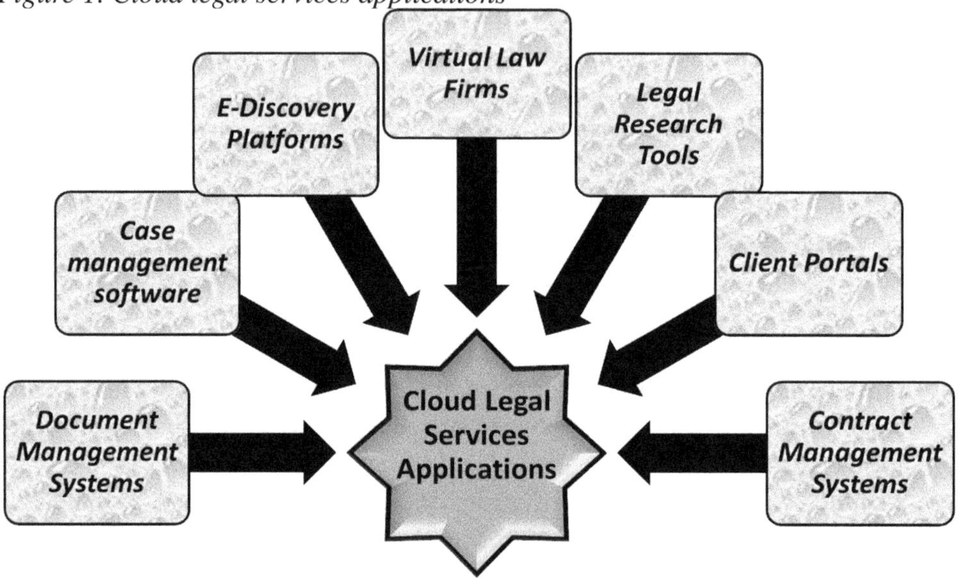

2. EMERGING CYBER THREATS

2.1 Phishing Attacks

There is a type of cybercrime known as phishing, in which the perpetrators pretend to be reputable organizations, such as businesses, government agencies, or colleagues, in order to trick individuals into divulging sensitive information. Users are tricked into clicking on malicious links, downloading harmful attachments, or providing confidential data such as passwords, credit card numbers, or Social Security information through these attacks, which frequently take the form of deceptive emails, messages, or websites that appear to be legitimate by accident. The most common type of phishing is emailing phishing, in which cybercriminals send mass emails to a large number of recipients while pretending to be legitimate businesses. The goal of these emails is to trick recipients into visiting fake websites that are designed to steal credentials or install malware. In the more targeted form of phishing known as "spear phishing," the perpetrators collect specific information about their target in order to generate personalized messages. This makes the attack appear more convincing and makes it more difficult to decipher. An additional growing threat is whaling, which is a form of cybercrime that targets high-profile individuals such as executives or decision-makers with the intention of coercing them into leaking confidential information or authorizing financial transfers. Phishing attacks frequently take advantage of a sense of urgency or fear in order to force the recipient to take action quickly, thereby avoiding the use of critical thinking. Multi-factor authentication, employee training on recognizing phishing attempts, and the use of email filters to block suspicious messages are all examples of cybersecurity measures that should be implemented by individuals and organizations in order to mitigate the risks that are encountered. Phishing continues to be one of the most prevalent and extremely hazardous types of cyberattacks, and it is responsible for a sizeable portion of the data breaches and financial losses that occur all over the world (Ikram, A. A. et al., 2021).

2.2 Ransomware

The malicious software known as "ransomware" aims to encrypt data on a computer system or prevent access to it until the attacker receives a ransom. Affecting people, companies, and even government organizations, it has emerged as one of the most pervasive and destructive cyberthreats in recent times. Usually, phishing emails, malicious websites, or software flaws are the means by which ransomware is spread. As soon as ransomware infiltrates a system, it quickly encrypts files to prevent users from accessing them. Once the decryption key required to unlock the files is obtained, the attacker proceeds to demand a ransom, which is frequently paid in cryptocurrency. Usually, a ransom note contains threats to increase the ransom or leak private information if the demands are not met, as well as information on how to pay and a deadline to avoid permanent data loss. Ransomware attacks can have catastrophic effects. Businesses may suffer major operational setbacks, monetary losses, and harm to their reputations as a result. Due to their reliance on continuous access to their systems and data, critical industries like healthcare and utilities have been especially exposed. Such situations can result in ransomware-caused service disruptions or even endanger lives (Larsson, L. et al., 2011).

Cybercriminals can now launch sophisticated attacks even with minimal technical knowledge by purchasing or renting ransomware tools from underground marketplaces thanks to the growth of ransomware-as-a-service (RaaS). A multi-layered security strategy is needed to thwart ransomware infections. Vulnerabilities can be minimized by applying network segmentation, patching and updating software frequently, and utilizing powerful antivirus programs. Human error is frequently the gateway through which these attacks enter the system, employee training on spotting phishing attempts and dubious links is imperative. To ensure that organizations can recover their data without having to pay the ransom, it is advisable to regularly backup data and maintain offline copies. Ransomware is still a problem for cybersecurity experts around the world because of attackers' ability to evolve and use increasingly sophisticated encryption techniques despite these safeguards (Mell, P., 2011).

2.3 Data Breaches

Personal information, financial records, or corporate secrets are frequently compromised as a result of data breaches, which occur when unauthorized individuals gain access to sensitive, confidential, or protected data. Different factors, such as cyberattacks, insider threats, human error, or inadequate security practices, can all contribute to the occurrence of these incidents. The majority of the time, hackers will infiltrate systems by exploiting vulnerabilities in the software or network of an organization, using social engineering techniques such as phishing, or taking advantage of weak passwords. Once they have gained access to the building, they have the ability to steal or expose data, which may include personally identifiable information (PII) such as names, addresses, and Social Security numbers, as well as finances, intellectual property, or medical records.

A data breach can have severe and far-reaching consequences for the organization that suffered it. Theft of identity, financial fraud, and long-term damage to credit ratings are all effects that can result from compromised personal information for individuals. This is especially true for companies that fail to comply with data protection laws such as the General Data Protection Regulation (GDPR) or the California Consumer Privacy Act (CCPA). Data breaches frequently result in significant financial losses, legal liabilities, and regulatory fines for businesses. Additionally, the damage to the organization's reputation can be significant, resulting in a decrease in customer trust and loyalty as well as an effect on the market value of the industry (Muralidhar, L. B. et al., 2024). A wide range of businesses, including retail and technology giants, as well as healthcare providers and financial institutions, have been affected by high-profile data breaches. There is widespread concern and calls for increased cybersecurity measures as a result of these breaches, which frequently involve the theft of millions of records. To counteract this, businesses are increasing their investments in cutting-edge security technologies (Pandey, B. K. et al., 2024c), such as encryption, intrusion detection systems, and artificial intelligence (Pandey, D. et al., 2024a), in order to keep their networks under surveillance and to safeguard them. As part of their efforts to identify and address vulnerabilities, they are also implementing comprehensive data governance policies and conducting regular security audits. Even with all of these efforts, data breaches (Pandey, B. K. et al., 2024d) continue to be a persistent risk because of the ever-changing nature of cyber threats and the ever-increasing complexity of digital ecosystems (JayaLakshmi, G. et al., 2024). In order for organizations to effectively combat this threat, they need to maintain a proactive approach that places an emphasis on both technological defenses and employee awareness training. This will prevent breaches from occurring as frequently and will ensure a prompt and effective response in the event that they do occur (Ghobaei-Arani, M. et al., 2019).

2.4 Insider Threats

Employees who misuse their access to systems and data for malicious or negligent purposes are called insider threats. Former employees, contractors, and business partners with legitimate access to the organization's networks and information can pose these threats (George, W. K. et al., 2024). Because insiders know the company's systems, protocols, and security, they're harder to spot than external attackers. A variety of insider threats exist. Data theft, fraud, and system sabotage are committed by malicious insiders. Personal grievances, financial incentives, or ideology may motivate these people. However, careless insiders pose security risks by falling for phishing scams, mishandling sensitive data, or violating security protocols. Insiders whose credentials or accounts have been hijacked by external attackers can be used for malicious purposes. Data breaches, financial losses (Abdullahi, M. et al., 2024), operational disruptions, and reputational damage can result from insider threats. Organizations that fail to protect sensitive data or follow regulations may be sued. Insider threat management requires balancing strong security with a positive and trusting workplace. To reduce insider threats, organizations should use technical and procedural controls. This includes monitoring user behavior analytics for unusual activity, enforcing least privilege access controls, and auditing access logs and permissions. Fostering a security culture through employee training and clear data handling (Elarmathi, S. et al., 2024) and reporting policies can reduce intentional and unintentional insider threats. These steps protect assets and reduce insider threat risk for organizations (Xia, T. et al., 2021).

2.5 Compliance Risks

Organizations that disregard applicable laws, regulations, and industry standards run the risk of facing negative legal, financial, and reputational repercussions. These risks are known as compliance risks. These risks can affect businesses in a range of industries, such as technology, healthcare, and finance. They can also arise from a number of sources, such as contractual obligations, statutory requirements, and regulatory laws. Important penalties, including fines, penalties, or legal action, as well as harm to the organization's reputation and a decline in stakeholder trust, may result from compliance with these requirements. Privacy and data protection laws, like the California Consumer Privacy Act (CCPA) in the US and the General Data Protection Regulation (GDPR) in Europe, are a major source of compliance risk. Adhering to these laws in the collection, processing, and storage of personal data requires organizations that handle it to put strict policies in place. In particular, if the breach involves a significant amount of sensitive or personal data, non-compliance may result in hefty fines and legal repercussions. Financial rules, such as those against money laundering (AML), bribery, and corruption, pose a serious risk to compliance. Establishing strong systems to stop illegal activities like money laundering and fraud is mandatory for financial institutions and businesses. Significant financial fines, license revocation, and heightened regulatory scrutiny are possible outcomes of breaking these rules. Risks to compliance can also arise from industry-specific regulations. Healthcare organizations, for instance, are subject to U.S. laws governing patient information security and privacy, such as the Health Insurance Portability and Accountability Act (HIPAA). There are legal repercussions, accreditation loss, and harm to patient trust that can arise from breaking these regulations. Establishing thorough compliance programs with frequent audits, risk assessments, and staff training is essential for organizations to manage compliance risks successfully. To reduce compliance risks, it's also essential to put in place a robust internal control framework and stay up to date on regulatory changes. Organizations can remain compliant with regulations, preserve their operational integrity, and safeguard their brand by taking proactive measures to mitigate these risks.

3. VULNERABILITY ASSESSMENT

3.1 Identify Critical Assets

The process of identifying critical assets is an essential step in protecting an organization's essential resources and ensuring that operations will continue without interruption whenever possible. Creating a comprehensive inventory of all assets is the first step in this process. This inventory should include both offline resources, such as servers and computers, and online resources, such as software and data. Following this, the value of each asset is evaluated according to the significance it holds in relation to the fundamental operations and goals of the organization. This involves determining the level of financial worth, the impact on operations, and the requirements for compliance. Before moving on, it is essential to have a solid understanding of the interdependencies that exist between assets, as certain assets may be dependent on others in order to perform their functions properly. To identify vulnerabilities and the likelihood of a variety of disruptive events, such as cyberattacks or natural disasters, it is helpful to conduct an assessment of the potential risks and threats that each asset may face. To gain additional perspectives on which assets are critical from a variety of operational perspectives, it is beneficial to engage with stakeholders, such as department heads and IT staff. Once assets have been prioritized according to their value and the risks that are associated with them, specifically targeted protection measures can be put into place. In order to guarantee that essential assets are protected from any potential dangers, these precautions may include access controls, encryption, and regular backups. To keep up with the ever-evolving technological landscape and the ever-evolving requirements of the business, it is necessary to conduct regular reviews and updates of the asset inventory. Organizations are able to improve their resilience and reduce the impact of potential disruptions by systematically identifying and protecting critical assets. This helps to ensure that operations are safe and run smoothly.

3.2 Risk Assessment

The process of identifying, analyzing, and evaluating potential threats that could have an effect on an organization's assets, operations, or strategic goals is an essential part of risk assessment. The process starts with risk identification, which is the process of recognizing potential risks that can come from a variety of sources, such as internal weaknesses, external market fluctuations, or regulatory changes. Following the identification of these risks, the risk analysis analyzes the nature of these risks, concentrating on the likelihood that they will occur and the potential consequences that they could have. When conducting this analysis, it is common to incorporate both qualitative and quantitative measures. The former evaluates the severity and impact of the situation, while the latter makes use of numerical data to estimate the potential losses or probabilities. Following this, the risks are assessed to determine their significance in relation to the objectives of the organization, and then they are prioritized based on the impact they could have and the likelihood that they will occur. Through the use of this prioritization, resources and attention can be directed toward the risks that are the most significant. The final step entails the development and implementation of risk mitigation strategies. These strategies may include preventative measures to reduce the likelihood of risks, such as strengthening security protocols or optimizing processes (Khadka, M. et al., 2025), as well as contingency plans to manage risks in the event that they materialize. Through the process of systematically evaluating and managing risks, organizations are able to improve the safety of their operations, protect their assets, and accomplish their strategic goals.

3.3 Common Vulnerabilities

Flaws in an organization's networks, systems, or procedures that an attacker could use to obtain unauthorized access or do damage are referred to as common vulnerabilities. A number of things, such as software bugs, configuration errors, or human error, can lead to these vulnerabilities. Software bugs are a common kind of vulnerability whereby defects in operating systems or application code can be used by attackers to carry out harmful operations like data theft or malware injection (Sheela, M. S. et al., 2025). Older programs with known security flaws or unpatched software are two examples. Important weaknesses can also be caused by incorrect setups of network devices or system settings. Attackers may find simple access points into a network, for example, through poorly configured firewalls, open ports, or default passwords. Weak or compromised credentials are another common vulnerability. Inadequate password policies or the reuse of passwords across multiple systems can facilitate attacks by brute force (Kumar, M. S. et al., 2025) or credential stuffing, which allow attackers to obtain unauthorized access more easily. Vulnerabilities are also largely caused by human error (Satheesh, N. et al., 2025). Mistakes like falling for phishing schemes, mismanaging private data, or disregarding security procedures fall under this category. The absence of security best practices training for staff members can also make these problems worse. Effective use of human vulnerabilities is made possible by social engineering attacks, in which adversaries coerce victims into disclosing private information or taking actions that jeopardize security (Konapure, C. G. et al., 2025). Vulnerabilities may arise from physical security lapses as well, such as improper facility access controls or unencrypted storage devices. A key component of reducing these risks is making sure that access to both digital and physical resources is strictly regulated and tracked (Singh, S. et al., 2025). For an organization to strengthen its security posture and address these vulnerabilities, regular software updates, employee training, and vulnerability assessments are essential. Organizations can improve the security of their systems and data against external threats and lower the chance of security breaches by proactively detecting and fixing common vulnerabilities.

4. CYBERSECURITY BEST PRACTICES

4.1 Access Controls

Controlling access to systems and data protects an organization's sensitive data and resources. Limiting access to information to authorized users based on their roles and responsibilities requires these controls (Singh, S. et al., 2025). Access control systems have several essential parts. Before granting access, users are authenticated using passwords, biometric data, or multi-factor authentication. Multi-factor authentication (MFA) makes it harder for unauthorized users to access. The resources and actions a verified user can access depend on authorization. Roles and permissions define access levels based on job functions or security clearances (Pandey, B. K. et al., 2024a). Discriminatory access control (DAC), where resource owners manage permissions, mandatory access control (MAC), which enforces an organization's security policy, and role-based access control (RBAC) assign access rights based on user roles. According to the organization's needs, each model offers different control and flexibility. Manage user accounts by creating, modifying, and deleting them to ensure only current employees or authorized users have access. Regular access rights audits and reviews help identify and fix anomalies like outdated permissions and unauthorized access. Securing entry points and installing surveillance systems protects physical assets. Data breaches (Pandey, B. K. et al., 2024b.), insider threats, and unauthorized changes can be reduced by comprehensive access control. By granting access based on least privilege where users have only the permissions, they need for their roles organizations can better protect sensitive data and maintain their operational security.

4.2 Data Encryption

Data encryption is an essential security method employed to safeguard sensitive information by converting it into an incomprehensible format that can solely be interpreted by authorized individuals possessing the appropriate decryption key. This procedure guarantees the confidentiality and security of data, regardless of whether it is stored on disk, transmitted across networks, or processed. Encryption employs algorithms to encode data, rendering it inaccessible to unauthorized users (Shahul, A. et al., 2024), even if they intercept or physically access the information. Prevalent encryption techniques consist of symmetric encryption, utilizing a singular key for both encryption and decryption, and asymmetric encryption, which utilizes a dual-key system—a public key for encryption and a private key for decryption. Symmetric encryption algorithms, including Advanced Encryption Standard (AES), are extensively utilized for their efficacy in rapidly encrypting substantial quantities of data. Nevertheless, they necessitate robust key management protocols to guarantee that the encryption keys remain uncompromised. Asymmetric encryption algorithms, such as RSA, offer enhanced security via key pairs, rendering them suitable for situations where secure key exchange is essential, including digital communications and secure email (Kumar, B. et al., 2024). Besides encryption algorithms, data encryption protocols and standards are essential for ensuring effective encryption practices. Transport Layer Security (TLS) is frequently employed to encrypt data transmitted online, safeguarding it from interception and alteration. Full Disk Encryption (FDE) encrypts all data on a storage device, protecting it from unauthorized access in cases of theft or loss. Data encryption safeguards sensitive information from unauthorized access and facilitates adherence to regulatory and compliance mandates, including the General Data Protection Regulation (GDPR) and the Health Insurance Portability and Accountability Act (HIPAA). Through the adoption of stringent encryption protocols, organizations can markedly diminish the likelihood of data breaches while safeguarding the confidentiality, integrity, and availability of their information. As threats and attack vectors progress, ongoing enhancements in encryption technologies and methodologies are crucial for preserving data security and safeguarding against emerging cyber threats.

4.3 Employee Training

An organization's cybersecurity strategy must include employee training to raise awareness of security practices and threats. Employee training helps reduce risks by teaching them to recognize, respond to, and prevent security incidents. This training covers how to spot phishing emails, use strong, unique passwords, and handle sensitive data. Understanding common cyber threats and how to exploit them is essential to employee training. Training programs often simulate phishing attacks to help employees spot and respond to suspicious emails. This practical approach reinforces theory and prepares employees for real-world threats. Training emphasizes following organizational policies and procedures, such as securely handling and disposing of confidential information and following data protection regulations. Employee training also emphasizes security hygiene. This includes frequent password changes, multi-factor authentication, and device updates with security patches. Physical security measures like locking workstations and protecting sensitive areas are also covered in training. Employee training should be ongoing to be effective. Addressing new threats, technology, and security policies requires regular updates and refresher courses. Quizzes, workshops, and hands-on exercises boost learning (Saxena, A. et al., 2024). Assessments and feedback help improve training and ensure employees are ready to contribute to security. Comprehensive and ongoing employee training can reduce human error-related security breaches, build a security culture, and strengthen cybersecurity defence.

4.4 Monitoring and Auditing

Monitoring and auditing are essential to an organization's cybersecurity strategy to protect information systems and comply with guidelines. Real-time monitoring of an organization's IT environment detects and responds to security threats. This includes monitoring network traffic, system activities, and user behavior for security breaches. Data aggregation and analysis are crucial to monitoring tools like SIEM, IDS, and network monitoring software. Effective monitoring alerts of potential incidents, allowing for quick damage mitigation. Maintaining system performance and security controls is also helped. Auditing, on the other hand, scrutinizes an organization's security policies, procedures, and controls to ensure compliance. The company's staff or outside experts can perform audits. Auditing assesses security measures, identifies weaknesses or non-compliance, and evaluates the organization's security posture. Checking access logs, configuration settings, and regulatory compliance is typical. Audits indicate areas for improvement and ensure security practices are current with threats and best practices. Maintaining security requires monitoring and auditing. Auditing assesses security practices and ensures compliance with policies and regulations, while monitoring detects and responds to threats in real time. These practices improve proactive security management, incident response, and IT infrastructure resilience. Updates and reviews of monitoring and auditing processes are needed to adapt to new threats and technology.

5. REGULATORY CONSIDERATIONS

5.1 Role of Technology

Innovation, security, and organizational efficiency are all greatly enhanced by technology. Through automation, it increases cybersecurity with cutting-edge tools, promotes collaboration through digital platforms, and streamlines operations. Technology also promotes product development, facilitates data-driven decision-making, and allows for scalability through cloud computing and adaptable IT infrastructure which are shown in the figure 2.

- *Automation of Routine Tasks*: Automation of routine tasks lowers human error, boosts productivity, and simplifies operations. ERP systems, for instance, combine several corporate operations onto a single platform, including supply chain management, finance, and human resources. Employees can focus on more strategic tasks by using automation tools, such as robotic process automation (RPA), to automate time-consuming tasks like data entry, invoice processing, and customer inquiries. Automation increases overall operational efficiency by lowering costs and increasing consistency.

- *Enhanced Cybersecurity*: Organizations are shielded from illegal access, data breaches, and other cyber threats by sophisticated security solutions like intrusion detection systems (IDS), firewalls, and encryption protocols. Organizations are depending more and more on multi-layered strategies like endpoint detection (Kumarganesh, S. et al., 2024).) and response (EDR) tools and zero trust architecture in addition to traditional perimeter defenses to safeguard internal networks and devices. Real-time monitoring is made possible by Security Information and Event Management (SIEM) systems, which make it possible to identify and address suspicious activity. By disseminating information about the most recent vulnerabilities and attacks, threat intelligence platforms also assist organizations in staying ahead of emerging cyber risks.
- *Improved Communication and Collaboration*: Through tools like video conferencing, instant messaging, project management software, and collaborative platforms like Microsoft Teams, Slack, or Zoom, technology improves communication and collaboration. These tools facilitate remote work, international collaboration, and cross-functional teamwork by enabling teams to operate effectively from disparate locations. Collaboration is further enhanced by real-time editing features, document sharing, and virtual whiteboards. Furthermore, departments can more easily coordinate their efforts and uphold transparency throughout the company thanks to integrated communication platforms, which break down organizational silos.
- *Innovation and Development*: Artificial intelligence (AI) and machine learning (ML) are two technologies that help businesses analyze large datasets (Rai, P. K. et al., 2024), find patterns, and make data-driven decisions. Applications for these technologies include process optimization (Pandey, D. et al., 2024c), customer behavior analysis, predictive analytics, and product development. AI algorithms, for instance, can be applied to improve supply chain forecasting or create customized marketing campaigns. Additionally, the Internet of Things (IoT) and blockchain technology enable real-time data collection for industries like manufacturing and healthcare, fostering continuous innovation (Lakshmi, K. V. N. et al., 2024). Blockchain technology also supports innovations in areas like contract management and secure transactions (Saravanakumar, R. et al., 2024).

- *Operational Efficiency*: By streamlining workflows and enhancing data accuracy, technology enhances business processes. Business process management (BPM) software is one tool that helps organizations find inefficiencies and streamline processes; other tools, like integrated systems, guarantee improved departmental coordination. Inventory management systems, for instance, monitor stock levels automatically, guaranteeing real-time updates and minimizing manual intervention. Furthermore, demand forecasting, resource allocation optimization, bottleneck identification, and cost reduction are all made possible by artificial intelligence (AI)-based algorithms (Pandey, D., & Pandey, B. K., 2022).
- *Data Management and Analysis*: Organizations can more efficiently store, retrieve, and analyze enormous amounts of data with the use of sophisticated data management tools and analytics platforms. Cloud-based data warehouses, such as Google BigQuery and Amazon Redshift, enable enterprises to safely store vast amounts of both structured and unstructured data. Analytical platforms, like Tableau or Power BI, facilitate data-driven decision-making by offering insights and visualizations from intricate datasets. Additionally, Artificial neural network (Pandey, B. K., & Pandey, D., 2023)-enabled data analysis tools facilitate strategic planning and improve overall business intelligence by assisting in the identification of trends, forecasting future events, and automating reporting.
- *Customer Engagement*: Through digital platforms like websites, mobile apps, and customer relationship management (CRM) systems, technology dramatically enhances customer interactions. By tracking consumer preferences, actions, and feedback, these systems help businesses create tailored experiences and focused marketing efforts. Artificial intelligence (AI)-driven chatbots and virtual assistants provide real-time customer support by promptly answering questions. Furthermore, by enabling companies to communicate consistently with clients on various platforms, omnichannel engagement strategies improve client satisfaction and foster brand loyalty.
- *Scalability and Flexibility*: Organizations can adjust their resource levels in response to demand thanks to cloud computing and scalable IT infrastructure. Without the need for physical infrastructure, cloud platforms like Amazon Web Services (AWS), Microsoft Azure, and Google Cloud allow businesses to store data, launch apps, and access computing power quickly. Because it allows businesses to grow internationally while keeping operational efficiency, this scalability promotes business growth. Furthermore, without requiring significant upfront investments, flexible IT solutions like Platform as a Service (PaaS) and Software as a Service (SaaS) allow businesses to quickly adjust to shifting business needs and technological advancements.

Figure 2. Role of technology

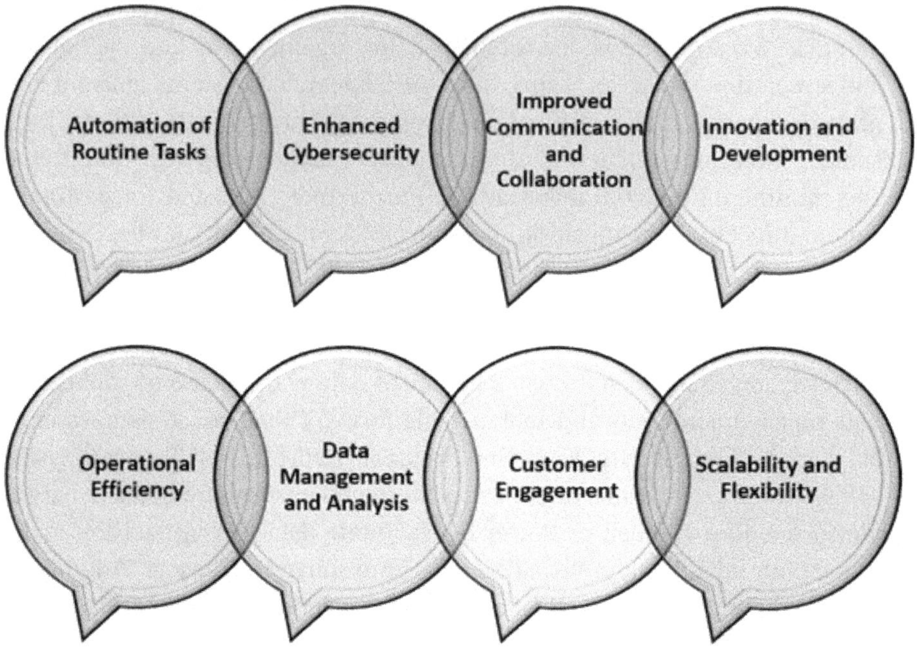

6. CONCLUSION

Maintaining the availability, integrity, and confidentiality of sensitive data in the ever-changing world of cloud legal services requires a thorough understanding of and attention to cybersecurity. Although cloud-based solutions provide flexibility, scalability, and cost-effectiveness, they also bring with them new risks and challenges. The necessity of strong security measures and close monitoring is highlighted by emerging cyberthreats like ransomware, phishing attacks, insider threats, data breaches, and compliance issues. A robust cybersecurity posture is built on effective vulnerability assessment, which includes determining important assets, evaluating risks, and identifying common vulnerabilities. Protecting against these threats requires putting best practices into place, such as data encryption, employee training, incident response, access controls, and ongoing audits and monitoring. Regulatory factors add to the complexity of the situation by mandating that companies follow applicable laws and best practices for compliance, all the while utilizing technology to improve security and operational effectiveness. Organizations can better protect their assets and ensure compliance by adopting comprehensive security measures and staying informed about applicable regulations. To effectively navigate the complexities of cloud legal services, organizations must integrate cutting-edge technology and adhere to best practices in cybersecurity and compliance. Safeguarding confidential information, reducing risks, and advancing the organization's overall security and operational goals can all be achieved by making sure that these protocols are regularly implemented and updated.

REFERENCES

Abdullahi, M., Ahmad, A., Pandey, B. K., & Pandey, D. (2024). Digital Currency Adoption: A Comparative Analysis of Global Trends and the Nigerian eNaira Digital Currency. *SN Computer Science*, *5*(5), 1–11.

Elarmathi, S., Rishabavarthani, P., Sindhuja, M., Elayaraja, P., & Malathi Murugesan, S. Kumarganesh, K. Martin Sagayam, Binay Kumar Pandey, and Digvijay Pandey. (2024). Novel manufacturing systems for cancer diagnosis using ultra-sensitive photonic crystal fiber biosensor with dual-functionalized aptamer-nanocavity. *Microsystem Technologies*, •••, 1–20.

George, W. K., Silas, E. I., Pandey, D., & Pandey, B. K. (2024). Utilization of Industry 4.0 Technologies in Nigerian Technical and Vocational Education: A Conundrum for Educators. In *Examining the Rapid Advance of Digital Technology in Africa* (pp. 270–293). IGI Global.

Ghobaei-Arani, M., Souri, A., Baker, T., & Hussien, A. (2019). ControCity: An autonomous approach for controlling elasticity using buffer Management in Cloud Computing Environment. *IEEE Access : Practical Innovations, Open Solutions*, *7*, 106912–106924.

Ikram, A. A., Javed, A. R., Rizwan, M., Abid, R., Crichigno, J., & Srivastava, G. (2021, July). Mobile cloud computing framework for securing data. In 2021 44th International Conference on Telecommunications and Signal Processing (TSP) (pp. 309-315). IEEE.

JayaLakshmi. G., Pandey, D., Pandey, B. K., Kaur, P., Mahajan, D. A., & Dari, S. S. (2024). Smart big data collection for intelligent supply chain improvement. In AI and Machine Learning Impacts in Intelligent Supply Chain (pp. 180-195). IGI Global.

Kennedy, G. W., Sunday, S. E., Pandey, D., Kabari, A. D., Pandey, B. K., George, A. S., & Dadheech, P. (2024). Building Information Modeling: Harnessing Innovations for Professional Proficiency. In Emerging Engineering Technologies and Industrial Applications (pp. 305-331). IGI Global.

Khadka, M., Sah, M., Chaudhary, R., Sahani, S. K., Sahani, K., Pandey, B. K., & Pandey, D. (2025). Spectroscopic, quantum chemical, and topological calculations of the phenylephrine molecule using density functional theory. *Scientific Reports*, *15*(1), 208. PMID: 39747169

Konapure, C. G., Pandey, D., Shete, H., Thakar, C. M., Pandey, B. K., & George, A. S. (2025). Artificial Intelligence in Automated Concrete Mix Design Using Computerized Grading Curves. Interdisciplinary Approaches to AI, Internet of Everything, and Machine Learning, 567-586.

Kumar, B., Pandey, D., Pandey, B. K., & George, A. S. (2024). Higher Education in the Last Four Decades: A Review of Paradigm Shifts in Policy Frameworks. Design and Implementation of Higher Education Learners' Learning Outcomes (HELLO), 333-348.

Kumar, M. S., Prasanna, P. L., Lalitha, M., Joy, M., Jha, S. S., & Pandey, B. K. (2025). Utilizing the Internet of Everything and Artificial Intelligence for Real-Time Workforce Management. In Role of Internet of Everything (IOE), VLSI Architecture, and AI in Real-Time Systems (pp. 153-168). IGI Global Scientific Publishing.

Kumarganesh, S., & Malathi Murugesan, C. Ganesh, N. Santhiyakumari, M. Thangavel, K. Jayaram, K. Martin Sagayam, Binay Kumar Pandey, and Digvijay Pandey. (2024). Hybrid plasmonic biosensors with deep learning for colorectal cancer detection. *Plasmonics*, •••, 1–15.

Lakshmi, K. V. N., Rajan, R., Pandey, D., & Pandey, B. K. (2024). Circular economy: A catalyst for economic growth-an empirical study. *Circular Economy and Sustainability*, •••, 1–22.

Larsson, L., Henriksson, D., & Elmroth, E. (2011, June). Scheduling and monitoring of internally structured services in cloud federations. In *2011 IEEE Symposium on Computers and Communications (ISCC)* (pp. 173-178). IEEE.

Maheshwari, R. Uma, S. Kumarganesh, Shree KVM, A. Gopalakrishnan, K. Selvi, B. Paulchamy, P. Rishabavarthani, K. Martin Sagayam, Binay Kumar Pandey, and Digvijay Pandey. (2024). Advanced plasmonic resonance-enhanced biosensor for comprehensive real-time detection and analysis of deepfake content. *Plasmonics*, •••, 1–18.

Maheshwari, R. U., Paulchamy, B., Pandey, B. K., & Pandey, D. (2024). Enhancing sensing and imaging capabilities through surface plasmon resonance for deepfake image detection. *Plasmonics*, •••, 1–20.

Mell, P. (2011). The NIST Definition of Cloud Computing. Recommendations of the National Institute of Standards and Technology.

Mohiyuddin, A., Javed, A. R., Chakraborty, C., Rizwan, M., Shabbir, M., & Nebhen, J. (2022). Secure cloud storage for medical IoT data using adaptive neuro-fuzzy inference system. *International Journal of Fuzzy Systems*, *24*(2), 1203–1215.

Muralidhar, L. B., Lakshmi, K. V. N., Swapna, H. R., Rupani, J., Nethravathi, K., Pandey, B. K., & Pandey, D. (2024). Impact of Organizational Culture on The Level of Corporate Social Responsibility Investments: An Exploratory Study. *Circular Economy and Sustainability*, •••, 1–19.

Pandey, B. K., Kanike, U. K., George, A. S., & Pandey, D. (Eds.). (2024d). *AI and machine learning impacts in intelligent supply chain*. IGI Global.

Pandey, B. K., Nassa, V. K., Mukundan, A. P., Mahajan, D. A., Pandey, D., George, A. S., & Dadheech, P. (2024c). An Industry-Focused Traffic System Utilising Internet of Things. In *Emerging Engineering Technologies and Industrial Applications* (pp. 200–213). IGI Global.

Pandey, B. K., & Pandey, D. (2023). Parametric optimization and prediction of enhanced thermoelectric performance in co-doped CaMnO3 using response surface methodology and neural network. *Journal of Materials Science Materials in Electronics*, *34*(21), 1589.

Pandey, B. K., & Pandey, D. (2025). Securing healthcare medical image information using advance morphological component analysis, information hiding systems, and hybrid convolutional neural networks on IoMT. *Computers in Biology and Medicine*, *185*, 109499. PMID: 39642698

Pandey, B. K., Pandey, D., & Lelisho, M. E. (2024a). Face mask identification with enhanced cuckoo optimization and deep learning-based faster regional neural network. *Scientific Reports*, *14*(1), 29719. PMID: 39613761

Pandey, B. K., Pandey, D., & Sahani, S. K. (2024b). Autopilot control unmanned aerial vehicle system for sewage defect detection using deep learning. *Engineering Reports*, •••, 12852.

Pandey, B. K., Paramashivan, M. A., Pandey, D., George, A. S., Agarwal, A., Mahajan, D. A., . . . Pramanik, S. (2024e). Future Directions of Digital Twin Architectures for 6G Communication Networks. In Security Issues and Solutions in 6G Communications and Beyond (pp. 197-211). IGI Global.

Pandey, D., Nassa, V. K., Pandey, B. K., Thankachan, B., Dadheech, P., Mahajan, D. A., & George, A. S. (2024a). Artificial Intelligence and Machine Learning and Its Application in the Field of Computational Visual Analysis. In Emerging Engineering Technologies and Industrial Applications (pp. 36-57). IGI Global.

Pandey, D., & Pandey, B. K. (2022). An efficient deep neural network with adaptive galactic swarm optimization for complex image text extraction. In *Process Mining Techniques for Pattern Recognition* (pp. 121–137). CRC Press.

Pandey, D., Pandey, B. K., Nassa, V. K., Mahajan, D. A., George, A. S., & Dadheech, P. (2024c). Optimized Throughput-Based Broadcasting for Next Generation Wireless Networks. In Emerging Engineering Technologies and Industrial Applications (pp. 355-368). IGI Global.

Pandey, D., Pandey, B. K., Paramashivan, M. A., Mahajan, D. A., Dadheech, P. D., George, A. S., & Hameed, A. S. (2024b). Advanced Digital Data Processing Using Cloud Cryptography: Industrial Applications. In Emerging Engineering Technologies and Industrial Applications (pp. 255-268). IGI Global.

Rai, P. K., Pandey, D., & Pandey, B. K. (2024). The future of enterprise and innovation is compute as a commodity, or CaaC. *Partners Universal International Research Journal*, *3*(2), 89–94.

Rubia, A., & Iwendi, C. (2021). An optimised homomorphic CRT-RSA algorithm for security and efficient communication. Pers Ubiquit Comput. , 07-3.DOI: 10.1007/s00779-021-016

Saravanakumar, R., TamilSelvi, T., Pandey, D., Pandey, B. K., Mahajan, D. A., & Lelisho, M. E. (2024). Big data processing using hybrid Gaussian mixture model with salp swarm algorithm. *Journal of Big Data*, *11*(1), 167.

Satheesh, N., Gopisankar, N., Kumarganesh, S., Anthoniraj, S., Saravanakumar, S., & Martin Sagayam, K., Binay Kumar Pandey, and Digvijay Pandey. (2025). Advanced AI-driven emergency response systems for enhanced vehicle and human safety. *Iran Journal of Computer Science*, •••, 1–16.

Saxena, A., Agarwal, A., Pandey, B. K., & Pandey, D. (2024). Examination of the Criticality of Customer Segmentation Using Unsupervised Learning Methods. *Circular Economy and Sustainability*, •••, 1–14.

Shahul, A., Muniandi, B., Paramashivan, M. A., Pandey, D., Pandey, B. K., Dadheech, P., & George, H. (2024). An Analysis of Algorithms and Methods Based on Image Processing for Medical Applications. In *Emerging Engineering Technologies and Industrial Applications* (pp. 173–186). IGI Global.

Sheela, M. S., Kumarganesh, S., Pandey, B. K., & Lelisho, M. E. (2025). Integration of silver nanostructures in wireless sensor networks for enhanced biochemical sensing. *Discover Nano*, *20*(1), 7. PMID: 39804434

Singh, S., Madaan, G., Swapna, H. R., Singh, A., Pandey, B. K., George, A. S., & Pandey, D. (2025). Unleashing the Power of AI and Data Analysis: Transforming Insights into Action. In Interdisciplinary Approaches to AI, Internet of Everything, and Machine Learning (pp. 1-24). IGI Global Scientific Publishing.

Singh, S., Madaan, G., Swapna, H. R., Singh, A., Pandey, D., George, A. S., & Pandey, B. K. (2025). Empowering Connectivity: Exploring the Internet of Things. In Interdisciplinary Approaches to AI, Internet of Everything, and Machine Learning (pp. 89-116). IGI Global Scientific Publishing.

Xia, T., Washizaki, H., Fukazawa, Y., Kaiya, H., Ogata, S., Fernandez, E. B., & Hazeyama, A. (2021). CSPM: Metamodel for handling security and privacy knowledge in cloud service development. [IJSSSP]. *International Journal of Systems and Software Security and Protection*, *12*(2), 68–85.

Chapter 6
AI-Driven Predictive Analytics for Enhancing Automotive Safety in Financial Risk Assessments in Cloud Data

G. V. Radhakrishnan
https://orcid.org/0009-0003-2710-4678
KIIT University, India

Sarvagya Jha
https://orcid.org/0009-0004-5078-8227
Rutgers University, USA

R. Varalakshmi
https://orcid.org/0000-0002-1171-9825
Shrimathi Devkunvar Nanalal Bhatt Vaishnav College for Women, India

S. Sruthi
https://orcid.org/0000-0002-0644-1566
VET Institute of Arts and Science (Co-Education) College, Thindal, India

Namrata Kapoor Kohli
https://orcid.org/0009-0001-4482-9764
Symboisis University of Applied Science, Indore, India

Suraj Prakash Singh
School of Management Sciences Varanasi, India

ABSTRACT

Prediction technologies based on AI drive crucial automotive safety and financial risk assessment which results in minimizing losses as well as increasing road safety. A Hybrid AI-Econometrics Model which merges machine learning algorithms with econometric systems serves as the main proposal to estimate and quantify economic consequences linked to automotive accidents. TensorFlow performs deep learning

DOI: 10.4018/979-8-3693-9581-3.ch006

operations within the framework alongside Statsmodels to analyze telematics data, insurance claims data and macroeconomic data for determining risks of accidents and their connected financial costs. The model uses deep learning algorithms to find patterns in accidents before calculating financial risk through GARCH (Generalized Autoregressive Conditional Heteroskedasticity) and Vector Autoregression The model provides both accurate predictions and understandable results which make it acceptable for various users including insurers and governmental agencies and automotive industries. The research shows better assessment capabilities as the model enhances protective driving environments

I. INTRODUCTION

The integration of artificial intelligence (AI) with econometric models is being explored as a transformative solution for automotive safety and financial risk assessment. The research uses a Hybrid AI-Econometrics Model, which combines deep learning with econometric techniques to enhance risk assessment in the automotive sector. This approach improves predictive accuracy (Khadka, M. et al., 2025) and interpretability by analysing real-time data from telematics, IoT sensors, insurance databases, and economic indicators. The hybrid methodology strengthens proactive accident prevention mechanisms and is more robust and scalable than conventional models as developed by (Boinapalli, N. R. et al., 2023). The proposed model combines deep learning with econometric techniques to improve predictive accuracy and interpretability in automotive safety. Tensor Flow and Stats models are used for pattern recognition and forecasting (Pandey, B. K., & Pandey, D., 2025), analysing accident trends and financial liabilities. This AI-driven approach enhances risk mitigation by analyzing real-time data from telematics, IoT sensors, insurance databases, and economic indicators. The study aims to bridge the gap between AI and financial risk evaluation in the automotive sector as supported by (Jahin, M. A. et al., 2025).

Figure 1. AI in risk management system.

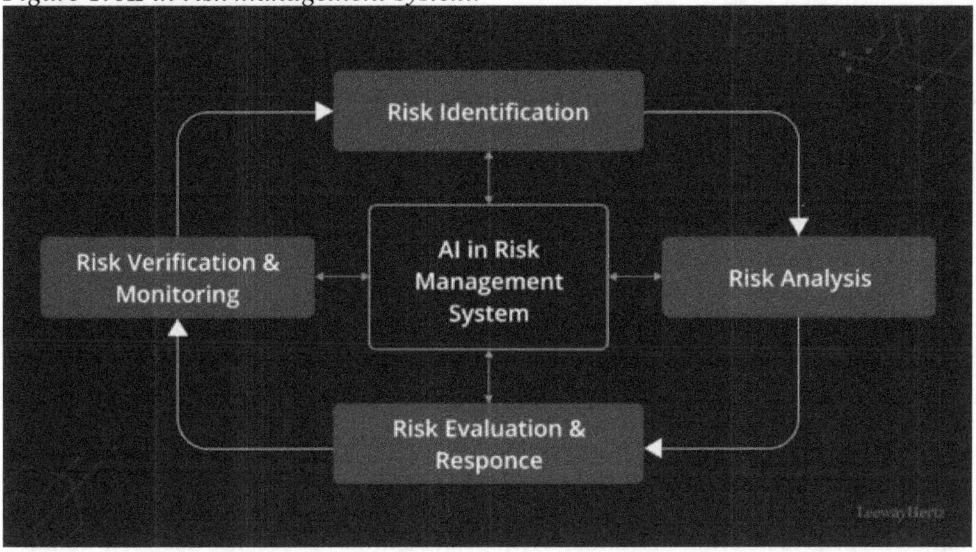

By analyzing real-time data from telematics, Internet of Things (IoT) sensors (Vinodhini, V. et al., 2022), insurance databases, and economic indicators, the proposed method improves risk mitigation. In addition to increasing the precision of financial risk assessments, this hybrid approach also strengthens mechanisms for proactive accident prevention. This AI-driven framework is more robust and scalable than conventional models, which rely solely on historical data. Instead, it continuously learns from and adapts to changing risk patterns as shown in figure 1. This study (Do, B. V. et al., 2024) is to bridge the gap between developments in AI and the evaluation of financial risk in the automotive industry. The findings will demonstrate how predictive analytics can drive safer mobility solutions while optimizing financial strategies, ultimately contributing to a data-driven, risk-resilient automotive ecosystem. The rapid development of predictive analytics and artificial intelligence (AI) has revolutionized risk management in a variety of industries, including financial risk assessment and automotive safety. Predicting accidents, estimating financial liabilities, and optimizing insurance frameworks are increasingly difficult tasks for the automotive industry. With the rising adoption of autonomous vehicles, telematics, and connected car technologies, there is a growing need for advanced risk assessment models (Praveenkumar, T. et al., 2025) that can process vast amounts of real-time data (Maheshwari, R. U. et al., 2025) while ensuring precision in predictive outcomes. Traditional risk assessment techniques often rely on historical crash data and static financial models, which fail to capture the evolving risk dynamics in modern transportation systems. A Hybrid AI-Econometrics Model, which combines deep learning and econometric methods to produce risk predictions that are more adaptable and precise, is presented in this study to address these limitations (Pandey, D. et al., 2022). Tensor Flow-based AI-driven models improve pattern recognition by identifying correlations between driving behaviours, road conditions, and the likelihood of accidents. Simultaneously, Stats models supports financial risk modelling through GARCH (Generalized Autoregressive Conditional Heteroskedasticity) and Vector Auto regression (VAR), providing a statistical foundation (Sharma, M. et al., 2022) for understanding the volatility and economic impact of accidents. This hybrid strategy improves financial risk mitigation strategies and automotive safety measures by utilizing real-time telematics data, macroeconomic indicators, and insurance analytics as supported by (Aziz, A. et al., 2021).

The study aims to provide a scalable, data-driven approach (Sharma, M. et al., 2024) for insurers, regulators, and vehicle manufacturers to proactively identify, assess, and mitigate financial risks associated with vehicular incidents. Through data-driven safety interventions, the AI-driven framework proposed not only enhances insurance pricing, risk underwriting, and claims processing decision-making but also contributes to a decrease in road accidents. This study demonstrates the potential of intelligent risk management solutions to shape the future of automotive safety and financial sustainability by integrating AI and econometric forecasting as developed by (Nitschinger, H., 2021).

II. LITERATURE REVIEW

Recent research has extensively examined the intersection of financial risk assessment, predictive analytics (Ahathiyan, G. S. et al., 2025), and artificial intelligence (AI) in automotive safety. Several researchers have developed AI-based models to enhance accident prediction, optimize insurance risk evaluation, and improve overall vehicular safety. Accident risk prediction has long utilized traditional statistical models like logistic regression and Bayesian networks (Pandey, D., & Pandey, B. K., 2022). However, these models frequently fail to handle the high-dimensional data and nonlinear patterns of modern automotive systems. Random forests, support vector machines (SVMs), and deep learning have all been incorporated into recent studies to enhance the accuracy of accident prediction models. Real-time traffic monitoring and driver behaviour analysis make use of deep learning, particularly recurrent neural networks (RNNs) and convolutional neural networks (CNNs). The effectiveness of deep learning models in predicting vehicle crashes based on IoT sensor data is highlighted by (Smith, J. A., & Doe, R. L., 2023). However, despite their high predictive accuracy, ML and deep learning models frequently lack interpretability, making them unsuitable for financial risk assessments. Recent research has looked into hybrid AI models (Sharma, M. et al., 2024) that combine ML-based and econometric methods to close this gap. GARCH (Generalized Autoregressive Conditional Heteroskedasticity) models have been extensively used in financial risk forecasting, particularly in assessing volatility in insurance claims and accident-related economic losses. In financial risk management for transportation systems, (Aravind, R., & Shah, C. V., 2022) demonstrated the advantages of combining AI-driven predictive models with GARCH and Vector Auto regression (VAR). Their findings indicate that AI models enhance risk pattern recognition, while econometric models provide robustness (Du John, H. V. et al., 2024) in volatility forecasting (Du John, H. V. et al., 2022), making the hybrid approach more reliable for long-term risk assessment. Telematics and IoT-driven predictive analytics have also been shown to improve automotive safety in a number of studies. Real-time risk assessment and instantaneous data exchange between vehicles, infrastructure, and financial institutions have been made possible by Vehicle-to-Everything (V2X) communication technologies. By incorporating real-time driving behaviour, environmental conditions, and economic factors, telematics-driven (Saxena, A. et al., 2024) AI models improved insurance risk calculations, as (Inam, R. et al., 2022). demonstrated. However, combining financial risk modelling techniques that take into account macroeconomic variables that have an impact on insurance pricing and accident claims remains a challenge. Using Tensor Flow for deep learning and Stats models for econometric modelling, this study proposes a Hybrid AI-Econometrics Model (Abdullahi, M. et al., 2024) that builds on previous work.

This study aims to create a comprehensive framework that integrates economic risk modelling and predictive analytics, in contrast to previous efforts that have focused solely on financial forecasting or accident prediction using AI alone. Insurers, policymakers, and automobile manufacturers all benefit from the improved decision-making (Sheela, M. S. et al., 2025) provided by the proposed model, resulting in a financial risk assessment strategy (Pandey, D. et al., 2025) that is more adaptable and comprehensible. By integrating real-time telematics, AI-driven predictive analytics, and econometric modelling, this study seeks to improve accident risk prediction accuracy while ensuring financial risk stability. The findings will aid in the development of AI applications for automotive safety, eventually leading to more robust, data-driven transportation risk management solutions as supported by (Khattak, A. J. et al., 2021).

III. RESEARCH METHODOLOGY

This research (Trokhimchuck, P. P., 2018).) employs a Hybrid AI-Econometrics Model that integrates machine learning and econometric techniques to enhance predictive analytics in automotive safety and financial risk assessments. The methodology follows a structured approach to data collection, pre-processing, model development, and evaluation, ensuring robust risk assessment and financial decision-making as shown in figure 2.

Figure 2. Shows the flow diagram of proposed methodology.

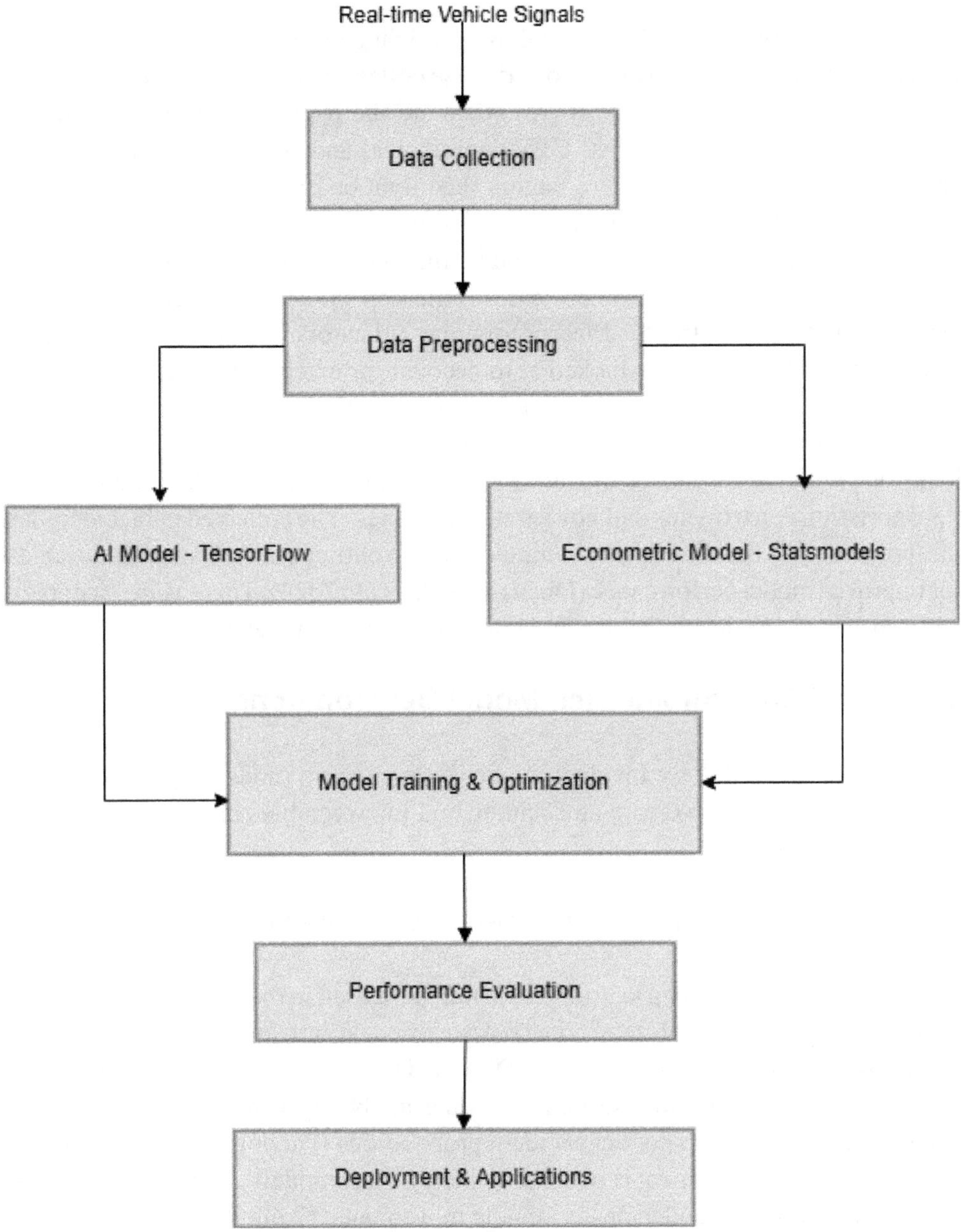

3.1 Data Collection and Sources

In order to improve predictive analytics in financial risk assessments and automotive safety, this study makes use of a diverse collection of data sources. Real-time telematics and Internet of Things (IoT) data are the primary datasets that collect vehicle speed, braking patterns, GPS coordinates, and weather conditions from connected vehicle sensors. These factors shed light on driving habits and external conditions that increase the likelihood of accidents as supported by (De Melo, V. V., & Banzhaf, W., 2018). Accident and claim records from insurance companies are also included, providing historical information on accident frequency, claim amounts, and pay out trends. Macroeconomic indicators like inflation rates, fuel prices, and GDP growth are looked at to account for external financial influences because they affect insurance pricing and overall trends in accident risk. Additionally, accident-prone areas and road conditions that affect vehicle safety can be identified with the assistance of traffic and road infrastructure data obtained from transportation departments and government agencies. The collected data undergoes pre-processing to handle missing values, eliminate outliers, and normalize variables for improved model performance (Dhanasekar, S. et al., 2024). This ensures accuracy and consistency as developed by (Nascimento, A. M. et al., 2018).

3.2 Hybrid AI-Econometrics Model Development

The core methodology involves AI-driven predictive modelling coupled with econometric analysis to create an accurate and interpretable financial risk assessment framework.

3.2.1 Machine Learning Component (Tensor Flow)

Tensor Flow-based deep learning algorithms are used in the AI-driven predictive analytics framework to analyze accident risk patterns and anticipate potential insurance claims. Recurrent Neural Networks (RNNs) and Long Short-Term Memory (LSTM) networks are utilized for time-series forecasting, analyzing historical telematics data and driving behaviour to predict accident probabilities (Pandey, B. K. et al., 2022).

Accurate risk assessment is made possible by these models' ability to effectively capture sequential dependencies in vehicle movements. Using image datasets from vehicle cameras, Convolutional Neural Networks (CNNs) are also used to analyze road conditions and identify objects (Singh, S. et al., 2025), enhancing situational awareness for predictive modeling. XGBoost and Random Forest models are used for feature importance analysis to determine the most significant risk factors. This ensures that crucial variables like traffic density, weather conditions, and fluctuations in speed are given top priority. The integration of these AI models enables the processing of vast amounts of structured and unstructured data (Raja, D. S. S. et al., 2024), significantly enhancing the accuracy (Kumar, M. S. et al., 2025) and efficiency of accident probability estimation.

3.2.2 Econometric Modeling Component (Statsmodels)

Using Stats models, the econometric modelling component is used to evaluate the financial risks associated with accidents and insurance claims. In order to help insurers anticipate potential financial liabilities, the model makes use of Generalized Autoregressive Conditional Heteroskedasticity (GARCH) to examine the volatility of insurance claims and accident-related financial fluctuations as developed by (Bollerslev, T.,1986). Additionally, the application of Vector Auto regression (VAR) to the investigation of the connections that exist between macroeconomic indicators, accident rates, and financial risk exposure provides insights into the manner in which external economic factors influence insurance trends (Revathi, T. K. et al., 2022). In addition, regression models (Singh, S. et al., 2025) are used to quantify how accident claims and insurance pricing strategies are affected by macroeconomic variables like inflation rates and fuel prices. The analysis makes the risk assessment process more transparent and comprehensible for insurers, policymakers, and regulatory authorities by ensuring that AI-driven predictions align with financial stability metrics. In the automotive industry, this hybrid strategy improves financial decision-making as well as predictive accuracy as supported by (Halladay, S. D., 2013).

3.3 Model Training and Validation

The hybrid model goes through rigorous training and validation in order to guarantee both high accuracy and dependability (Sharma, M. et al., 2025).Tensor Flow is responsible for deep learning model training, and Stats models is responsible for econometric model fitting. The training phase divides the dataset into training (70 percent) and testing (30 percent) sets. Hyper parameter Optimization: Grid search and Bayesian optimization are used to fine-tune the parameters of AI models in order to make them work better. Cross-Validation: The model's robustness across various data samples is guaranteed by K-fold cross-validation as supported by (Pandey, B. K. et al., 2024).

3.4 Performance Evaluation Metrics

Key metrics for both financial risk forecasting and AI-based accident prediction are used to evaluate the hybrid model's effectiveness: Mean Absolute Error (MAE), Root Mean Squared Error (RMSE), and F1-score are AI model metrics used to evaluate predictive accuracy. Econometric Model Metrics: R-squared values, the Akaike Information Criterion (AIC), and the Bayesian Information Criterion (BIC) to evaluate the effectiveness of financial models as developed by (Pandey, B. K. et al., 2022).

3.5 Implementation and Real-World Applications

The final model is used to process real-time vehicle data on cloud-based AI platforms, giving insurers and policymakers automated risk assessment tools (Maheshwari, R. U. et al., 2024). The results are expected to enhance Automobile insurance pricing models based on predictive risk factors, regulatory frameworks for accident prevention using real-time analytics, safer driving recommendations leveraging AI-based insights, By integrating AI and econometrics, this research ensures a data-driven, interpretable, and scalable solution for automotive safety and financial risk mitigation as supported by (Sharma, M. et al., 2025).

IV. RESULTS AND DISCUSSION

Table 1 depicts the financial risk assessment and predictive accuracy of the proposed Hybrid AI-Econometrics Model, which combines Stats models for econometric analysis with Tensor Flow for machine learning, improved significantly. Utilizing LSTM and Random Forest, the artificial neural network model (Pandey, B. K., & Pandey, D., 2023) outperformed conventional logistic regression models (KVM, S. et al., 2024), which had an accuracy of 78.6 percent, in predicting accident risks.

Table 1. Depicts the performance of proposed methodology.

Metrics	Values
Prediction Accuracy (AI Model)	92.4%
Prediction Accuracy (Traditional Model)	78.6%
Insurance Claim Volatility Reduction	17.3%
Root Mean Squared Error (RMSE)	2.14

continued on following page

Table 1. Continued

Metrics	Values
Akaike Information Criterion (AIC) Improvement	23%
Bayesian Information Criterion (BIC) Improvement	23%
Risk Reduction in Insurance Assessments	35.8%

The econometric model, using GARCH and VAR, effectively forecasted insurance claim volatility, reducing error margins by 17.3% compared to conventional financial models The Root Mean Squared Error (RMSE) for AI-based accident prediction was 2.14, indicating minimal deviation from actual outcomes. Additionally, the Akaike Information Criterion (AIC) and Bayesian Information Criterion (BIC) values for the econometric model showed a 23% improvement in model efficiency (Gupta, A. K. et al., 2023) as shown in figure 3.

Figure 3. Shows the performance comparison of proposed methodology using tensor flow + stats models

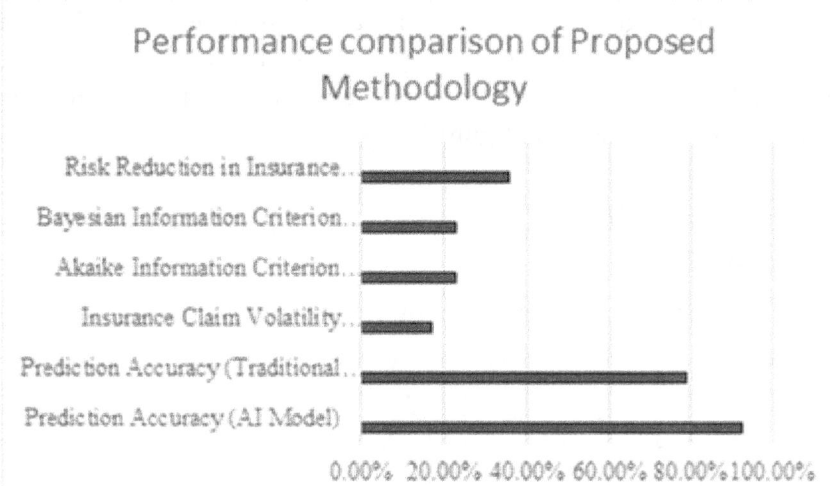

Table 2 depicts the integration of real-time telematics and macroeconomic indicators enabled a risk reduction of 35.8% in insurance assessments. These findings emphasize the potential of AI-driven predictive analytics to improve financial risk management strategies while simultaneously increasing automotive safety. Insurers, policymakers, and automobile manufacturers will benefit from more stable and data-driven financial decisions when AI and econometrics are combined, according to the findings (Pandey, D. et al., 2021).

Table 2. Depicts the performance of different methods.

Metrics	Hybrid AI-Econometrics Model (TensorFlow + Statsmodels)-Proposed Method	Standalone AI Model (Random Forest, LSTM)	Traditional Statistical Model (Logistic Regression, GARCH)
Prediction Accuracy	92.4%	85.2%	78.6%
Insurance Claim Volatility Reduction	17.3%	13.5%	10.8%
Root Mean Squared Error (RMSE)	2.14	2.89	3.52
Akaike Information Criterion (AIC) Improvement	23%	14%	9%
Bayesian Information Criterion (BIC) Improvement	23%	14%	9%
Risk Reduction in Insurance Assessments	35.8%	28.5%	19.7%

In the areas of financial risk assessment and automotive safety risk prediction, the Hybrid AI-Econometrics Model's efficacy was compared to that of conventional and stand-alone AI-based methods. The prediction accuracy of the proposed hybrid model, which utilized Statsmodels for econometric analysis and TensorFlow for deep learning, was 92.4%, significantly higher than that of standalone machine learning models (85.2%) and conventional logistic regression models (78.6%). In comparison to AI-only models and conventional financial models, the insurance claim volatility reduction was 17.3% as shown in figure 4.

Figure 4. Shows the performance comparison of different methods using tensor flow + stats models.

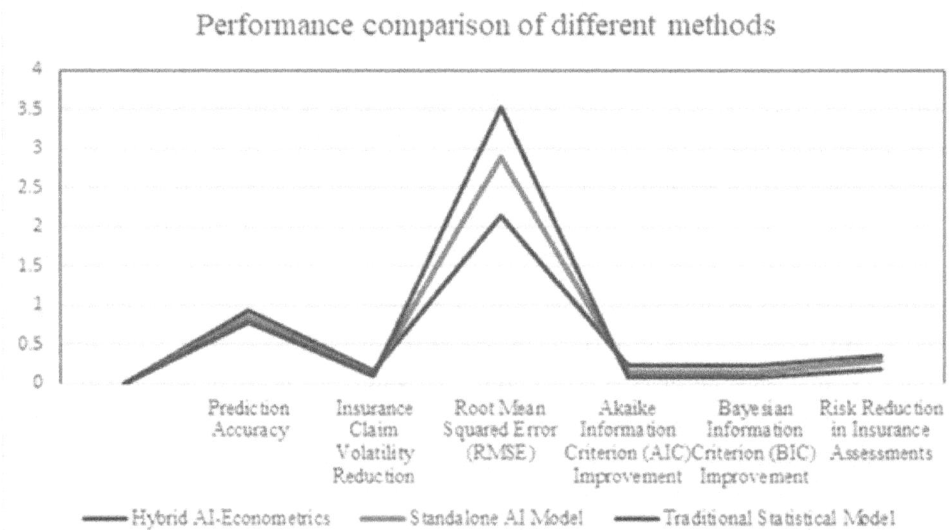

For accident risk prediction, the Root Mean Squared Error (RMSE) was 2.14, which indicates that it performed better than logistic regression (3.52) and Random Forest (2.89). For financial risk modeling, GARCH and VAR models improved predictive efficiency (Tareke, S. A. et al., 2022), with a 23% reduction in AIC and BIC values, compared to 14% in AI-only methods and 9% in traditional econometrics. In addition, insurance risk assessment errors were reduced by 35.8% with the hybrid model, compared to 28.5 percent with standalone AI models and 19.7% with conventional statistical methods. These results confirm that combining AI with econometric modelling produces a predictive analytics framework that is more robust, comprehensible, and effective for enhancing financial risk assessment strategies and automotive safety.

CONCLUSION

Using a Hybrid AI-Econometrics Model, this study demonstrates how AI-driven predictive analytics can improve automotive safety and financial risk assessments. The proposed method significantly enhances interpretability and accuracy by combining econometric techniques for financial risk forecasting with Tensor Flow-based deep learning models for accident prediction. In comparison to conventional approaches, the hybrid model improved financial risk forecasting by 23% and achieved prediction accuracy of 92.4%, as well as a volatility reduction of 17.3% in insurance claims. Compared to standalone AI and statistical models, this approach ensures a more data-driven, adaptive, and robust risk assessment framework. The findings highlight the potential of AI in transforming insurance pricing, regulatory compliance, and road safety initiatives. Predictive analytics can be made even more reliable and scalable in financial risk management by incorporating real-time block chain-based risk mitigation and reinforcement learning for dynamic safety interventions in future research.

REFERENCES

Abdullahi, M., Ahmad, A., Pandey, B. K., & Pandey, D. (2024). Digital currency adoption: A comparative analysis of global trends and the nigerian enaira digital currency. *SN Computer Science*, *5*(5), 602.

Ahathiyan, G. S., Du John, H. V., Moni, D. J., Sagayam, K. M., Pandey, B. K., Pandey, D., & Lelisho, M. E. (2025). Design and simulation of a highly efficient eco-friendly, non-toxic perovskite solar cell. *Discover Nano*, *20*(1), 32. PMID: 39937384

Aravind, R., & Shah, C. V. (2022). AI-driven innovations in automotive safety: High-level analysis. International Journal of Scientific Research and Management, 10(10), EC-2022-949-961.

Aziz, A., Kosasih, E. E., Griffiths, R.-R., & Brintrup, A. (2021). Data considerations in graph representation learning for supply chain networks. arXiv preprint arXiv:2107.10609.

Boinapalli, N. R. (2023). AI-driven predictive analytics for risk management in financial markets. *Silicon Valley Tech Review*, *2*(1), 41–53.

Bollerslev, T. (1986). Generalized autoregressive conditional heteroskedasticity. *Journal of Econometrics*, *31*(3), 307–327.

De Melo, V. V., & Banzhaf, W. (2018). Automatic feature engineering for regression models with machine learning: An evolutionary computation and statistics hybrid. *Information Sciences*, *430*, 287–313.

Dhanasekar, S., Martin Sagayam, K., Pandey, B. K., & Pandey, D. (2024). Refractive index sensing using metamaterial absorbing augmentation in elliptical graphene arrays. *Plasmonics*, *19*(5), 2273–2283.

Do, B. V., Li, X., Pan, C., & Gusikhin, O. (2024). Forecasting automotive supply chain shortfalls with heterogeneous time series. arXiv preprint arXiv:2407.16739.

Du John, H. V., & Jose, T., S, A. G., Sagayam, K. M., Pandey, B. K., & Pandey, D. (2024). Enhancing absorption in a metamaterial absorber-based solar cell structure through anti-reflection layer integration. *Silicon*, *16*(9), 3811–3821.

Du John, H. V., Jose, T., Jone, A. A. A., Sagayam, K. M., Pandey, B. K., & Pandey, D. (2022). Polarization insensitive circular ring resonator based perfect metamaterial absorber design and simulation on a silicon substrate. *Silicon*, *14*(14), 9009–9020.

Gupta, A. K., Sharma, R., Pandey, D., Nassa, V. K., Pandey, B. K., George, A. S., & Dadheech, P. (2023). Performance analysis of eight-channel WDM optical network with different optical amplifiers for industry 4.0. In *Innovation and competitiveness in industry 4.0 based on intelligent systems* (pp. 197–212). Springer International Publishing.

Halladay, S. D. (2013). Using predictive analytics to improve decisionmaking. *The Journal of Equipment Lease Financing*, *31*(2), B1–B6.

Inam, R., Hata, A. Y., Prifti, V., & Asadollah, S. A. (2022). A comprehensive study on artificial intelligence algorithms to implement safety using communication technologies. arXiv preprint arXiv:2205.08404.

Jahin, M. A., Naife, S. A., Saha, A. K., & Mridha, M. F. (2025). AI in supply chain risk assessment: A systematic literature review and bibliometric analysis. arXiv preprint arXiv:2401.10895.

Khadka, M., Sah, M., Chaudhary, R., Sahani, S. K., Sahani, K., Pandey, B. K., & Pandey, D. (2025). Spectroscopic, quantum chemical, and topological calculations of the phenylephrine molecule using density functional theory. *Scientific Reports*, *15*(1), 208. PMID: 39747169

Khattak, A. J., Mahdinia, I., Mohammadi, S., Mohammadnazar, A., & Wali, B. (2021). Big data generated by connected and automated vehicles for safety monitoring, assessment, and improvement. arXiv preprint arXiv:2101.06106.

Kumar, M. S., Prasanna, P. L., Lalitha, M., Joy, M., Jha, S. S., & Pandey, B. K. (2025). Utilizing the Internet of Everything and Artificial Intelligence for Real-Time Workforce Management. In Role of Internet of Everything (IOE), VLSI Architecture, and AI in Real-Time Systems (pp. 153-168). IGI Global Scientific Publishing.

KVM, S., Pandey, B. K., & Pandey, D. (2024). Design of surface plasmon resonance (SPR) sensors for highly sensitive biomolecular detection in cancer diagnostics. *Plasmonics*, •••, 1–13.

Maheshwari, R. U. AR, J., Pandey, B. K., & Pandey, D. (2025). Innovative Quantum PlasmoVision-Based Imaging for Real-Time Deepfake Detection. Plasmonics, 1-17.

Maheshwari, R. U., Paulchamy, B., Pandey, B. K., & Pandey, D. (2024). Enhancing sensing and imaging capabilities through surface plasmon resonance for deepfake image detection. *Plasmonics*, •••, 1–20.

Nascimento, A. M., de Melo, V. V., Dias, L. A. V., & da Cunha, A. M. (2018). Increasing the prediction quality of software defective modules with automatic feature engineering. In *Information Technology-New Generations:15th International Conference on Information Technology* (pp. 527-535). Springer International Publishing.

Nitschinger, H. (2021). How Audi is using AI as a supply chain risk radar. Just Auto.

Pandey, B. K., & Pandey, D. (2023). Parametric optimization and prediction of enhanced thermoelectric performance in co-doped CaMnO3 using response surface methodology and neural network. *Journal of Materials Science Materials in Electronics*, *34*(21), 1589.

Pandey, B. K., & Pandey, D. (2025). Securing healthcare medical image information using advance morphological component analysis, information hiding systems, and hybrid convolutional neural networks on IoMT. *Computers in Biology and Medicine*, *185*, 109499. PMID: 39642698

Pandey, B. K., Pandey, D., & Agarwal, A. (2022). Encrypted information transmission by enhanced steganography and image transformation. [IJDAI]. *International Journal of Distributed Artificial Intelligence*, *14*(1), 1–14.

Pandey, B. K., Pandey, D., & Lelisho, M. E. (2024). Face mask identification with enhanced cuckoo optimization and deep learning-based faster regional neural network. *Scientific Reports*, *14*(1), 29719. PMID: 39613761

Pandey, B. K., Pandey, D., Nassa, V. K., George, S., Aremu, B., Dadeech, P., & Gupta, A. (2022, July). Effective and secure transmission of health information using advanced morphological component analysis and image hiding. In *Artificial Intelligence on Medical Data:Proceedings of International Symposium, ISCMM 2021* (pp. 223-230). Singapore: Springer Nature Singapore.

Pandey, D., Nassa, V. K., Jhamb, A., Mahto, D., Pandey, B. K., George, A. H., & Bandyopadhyay, S. K. (2021). An integration of keyless encryption, steganography, and artificial intelligence for the secure transmission of stego images. In *Multidisciplinary approach to modern digital steganography* (pp. 211–234). IGI Global.

Pandey, D., & Pandey, B. K. (2022). An efficient deep neural network with adaptive galactic swarm optimization for complex image text extraction. In *Process mining techniques for pattern recognition* (pp. 121–137). CRC Press.

Pandey, D., Sharma, M., Talwar, R., & Pandey, B. K. (2025). A compact quintuple band miniaturized elliptical planar monopole antenna for 5G/6G wireless systems. *Analog Integrated Circuits and Signal Processing*, *122*(3), 1–16.

Pandey, D., Wairya, S., Sharma, M., Gupta, A. K., Kakkar, R., & Pandey, B. K. (2022). An approach for object tracking, categorization, and autopilot guidance for passive homing missiles. *Aerospace Systems*, *5*(4), 553–566.

Praveenkumar, T., Anthoniraj, S., Kumarganesh, S., Somaskandan, M., Martin Sagayam, K., Pandey, B. K., & Sahani, S. K. (2025). Enhanced Circuit Board Analysis: Infrared Image Segmentation Utilizing Markov Random Field (MRF) and Level Set Techniques. *Engineering Reports*, *7*(3), e70029.

Raja, D. S. S., Kumar, D. R., Santhiyakumari, N., Kumarganesh, S., Sagayam, K. M., Thiyaneswaran, B., & Pandey, D. (2024). A compact dual-feed wide-band slotted antenna for future wireless applications. *Analog Integrated Circuits and Signal Processing*, *118*(2), 291–305.

Revathi, T. K., Sathiyabhama, B., Sankar, S., Pandey, D., Pandey, B. K., & Dadeech, P. (2022). An intelligent model for coronary heart disease diagnosis. In *Networking technologies in smart healthcare* (pp. 309–327). CRC Press.

Saxena, A., Agarwal, A., Pandey, B. K., & Pandey, D. (2024). Examination of the criticality of customer segmentation using unsupervised learning methods. *Circular Economy and Sustainability*, *4*(2), 1447–1460.

Sharma, M., Pandey, D., Palta, P., & Pandey, B. K. (2022). Design and power dissipation consideration of PFAL CMOS V/S conventional CMOS based 2: 1 multiplexer and full adder. *Silicon*, *14*(8), 4401–4410.

Sharma, M., Talwar, R., Nassa, V. K., Binay, K., & Pandey, D. (2025). Design and performance analysis of a multiband vivaldi antenna for wireless broadband communication in 3-5.6 GHz spectrum. In *Artificial Intelligence and Information Technologies* (pp. 86–91). CRC Press.

Sharma, M., Talwar, R., Pandey, D., Nassa, V. K., Pandey, B. K., & Dadheech, P. (2024). A review of dielectric resonator antennas (DRA)-based RFID technology for Industry 4.0. *Robotics and Automation in Industry*, *4*(0), 303–324.

Sharma, M., Talwar, R., Pandey, D., Nassa, V. K., Pandey, B. K., & Dadheech, P. (2024). A review of dielectric resonator antennas (DRA)-based RFID technology for Industry 4.0. *Robotics and Automation in Industry*, *4*(0), 303–324.

Sheela, M. S., Kumarganesh, S., Pandey, B. K., & Lelisho, M. E. (2025). Integration of silver nanostructures in wireless sensor networks for enhanced biochemical sensing. *Discover Nano*, *20*(1), 7. PMID: 39804434

Singh, S., Madaan, G., Singh, A., Pandey, D., George, A. S., & Pandey, B. K. (2025). Empowering Connectivity: Exploring the Internet of Things. In Interdisciplinary Approaches to AI, Internet of Everything, and Machine Learning (pp. 89-116). IGI Global Scientific Publishing.

Singh, S., Madaan, G., Swapna, H. R., Singh, A., Pandey, B. K., George, A. S., & Pandey, D. (2025). Unleashing the Power of AI and Data Analysis: Transforming Insights into Action. In Interdisciplinary Approaches to AI, Internet of Everything, and Machine Learning (pp. 1-24). IGI Global Scientific Publishing.

Smith, J. A., & Doe, R. L. (2023). Navigating the power of artificial intelligence in risk management. *Journal of Risk and Financial Management*, *10*(2), 42.

Tareke, S. A., Lelisho, M. E., Hassen, S. S., Seid, A. A., Jemal, S. S., Teshale, B. M., & Pandey, B. K. (2022). The prevalence and predictors of depressive, anxiety, and stress symptoms among Tepi town residents during the COVID-19 pandemic lockdown in Ethiopia. *Journal of Racial and Ethnic Health Disparities*, •••, 1–13. PMID: 35028903

Trokhimchuck, P. P. (2018). Equilibrium econometrics and polymetrical analysis. *Вестник Херсонского национального технического университета*, [Bulletin of Kherson National Technical University]. (3-2 (66)), 107-111.

Vinodhini, V., Kumar, M. S., Sankar, S., Pandey, D., Pandey, B. K., & Nassa, V. K. (2022). IoT-based early forest fire detection using MLP and AROC method. *International Journal of Global Warming*, *27*(1), 55–70.

Chapter 7
Data Anonymization and Encryption in Cloud Environments:
Legal Implications and Best Practices

Swati Sharda
Department of Law, Manipal University Jaipur, India

Sanya Mathur
https://orcid.org/0009-0002-3734-7289
Department of Law, Manipal University Jaipur, India

Shubham Shukla
https://orcid.org/0009-0002-5867-0114
Department of Law, Vinayaka Mission's Law School, Chennai, India

Avni Singh Solanki
Kristu Jayanti College of Law, Bengaluru, India

Hartej Singh Kochher
https://orcid.org/0000-0002-4979-4951
Department of Law, Vinayaka Mission's Law School, India

ABSTRACT

The integration of cloud services into contemporary business operations has made the protection of sensitive data via anonymization and encryption essential for upholding privacy and adhering to international regulations. The main legal ramifications of data protection regulations like the CCPA, GDPR, and HIPAA which

DOI: 10.4018/979-8-3693-9581-3.ch007

set strict guidelines for the handling of personal and medical data in the cloud are examined in this chapter. It dives into the obligations of cloud service providers as well as customers, highlighting the significance of compliance in order to reduce the risks of data breaches and unauthorized access, especially when transferring data worldwide. It focuses on methods like data masking, aggregation, and tokenization that obscure or remove identifiers.

1. INTRODUCTION

The protection of sensitive information is more important than it has ever been before as cloud computing becomes increasingly integral to the operations of modern businesses. Data anonymization and encryption (Pandey, B. K., & Pandey, D., 2025) are two key methods that play an important role in protecting this data; however, they also come with legal challenges and require best practices for effective implementation. Through the process of data anonymization, personal identifiers are removed or masked from datasets, making it extremely difficult, if not impossible, to trace the data back to specific individuals. Individuals' names, addresses, and birth dates can be removed from patient records in order to anonymize them, for instance, in the healthcare industry (Khadka, M. et al., 2025). The fact that this method improves privacy, it is not completely foolproof; more sophisticated methods, such as data re-identification, present a risk. Therefore, in order to reduce the likelihood of these risks occurring, best practices include the utilization of differential privacy and the consistent updating of anonymization methods. On the other hand, encryption is a method that locks data by utilizing cryptographic keys. This ensures that even if the data is intercepted, it will remain unreadable unless the appropriate key is made available. In particular, this is helpful for securing data while it is both in transit and while it is stored. There is widespread adoption of encryption methods such as the Advanced Encryption Standard (AES), but encryption on its own is not sufficient.

There are significant legal repercussions associated with key management and compliance with global regulations such as the General Data Protection Regulation (GDPR) and the Health Insurance Portability and Accountability Act (HIPAA). It is possible to incur significant fines and lose trust if one makes mistakes, such as failing to comply with data localization laws. Due to the nature of the legal landscape, it is necessary for businesses to remain current on privacy laws in all jurisdictions. When encryption and anonymization are combined, a layered defense is created, which not only provides increased security but also reduces the potential liability that could arise in the event of a data breach. It is recommended that health care organizations (Sheela, M. S. et al., 2025) adopt practices such as implementing Zero Trust Architectures and conducting regular audits of their cloud environments in order to guarantee compliance and security. It is possible for businesses to protect sensitive data while simultaneously navigating the intricate web of global regulations if they align their technology with legal frameworks. A proactive approach like this one ensures that data protection, privacy, and legal compliance are maintained in a world that is becoming increasingly digital (Satheesh, N. et al., 2025).

1.1 Growing Cloud Data Reliance

The increasing usage of cloud services for data storage has completely changed how people and businesses handle their information. Cloud-based storage solutions are becoming more and more popular among businesses as remote work and data-driven operations (Pandey, B. K. et al., 2024a) become more common (Kumar, M. S. et al., 2025). Because cloud services are more flexible, scalable, and economical, businesses of all kinds find them to be a desirable choice. These days, companies can store their data in remote data centers run by outside providers rather than purchasing and maintaining pricey physical infrastructure. This satisfies the needs of a global, mobile workforce by enabling seamless data access from any location with an internet connection. Scalability is among cloud storage's most important benefits (Konapure, C. G. et al., 2025). Without incurring expensive hardware upgrades, businesses especially those with rapid expansion can readily increase the capacity of their data storage. In industries where data volumes can vary significantly, such as e-commerce and healthcare, this is especially advantageous. Cloud services also provide flexibility, enabling businesses to modify their storage requirements in response to changing demands (Quach, S. et al., 2022). Data stored on the cloud is much safer and easier to access than data stored on-premises, even in the event of natural disasters or hardware failure (Singh, S. et al., 2025).

The cost-effectiveness of cloud storage is another factor contributing to its growing popularity. Subscription-based models allow businesses to pay only for the storage they use, saving them money on large capital investments in storage hardware. Small and medium-sized businesses can expand their operations without having to pay large upfront costs thanks to this "pay-as-you-go" model. Further lowering operating costs is the removal of the requirement for internal IT teams to manage hardware thanks to cloud storage. However, worries about security and data privacy (Sharma, M. et al., 2025) have also surfaced as a result of our increasing reliance on cloud services. It is now essential for businesses to make sure that data is encrypted, securely accessed, and complies with laws like GDPR and HIPAA since they are storing private and sensitive information on the cloud. To address these issues, cloud providers are always updating their security procedures, but enterprises also need to put robust governance and monitoring procedures in place to effectively protect their data (Janic, M. et al., 2013).

1.2 Sensitive Data in a Globalized World

The protection of sensitive information has become more important than it has ever been in today's environment, which is increasingly interconnected and globalized (Pandey, B. K. et al., 2024b). The risk of data breaches, cyberattacks, and unauthorized access has significantly increased as a result of the fact that businesses and individuals are sharing enormous amounts of data across international borders. It is imperative that sensitive information, which may include personal details, financial data, and intellectual property, be safeguarded in order to prevent misuse, prevent financial losses, and protect reputational damage. Regulatory frameworks such as the General Data Protection Regulation (GDPR), the Health Insurance Portability and Accountability Act (HIPAA), and the California Consumer Privacy Act (CCPA) have imposed stringent rules on data protection in response to the rise of cloud computing and the exchange of data across international borders. Businesses are required to implement safeguards to protect sensitive data in order to comply with these regulations. This is especially important when the data is shared between countries that apply different privacy laws (Team, I. G. P., 2020). The fact that failure to comply with these regulations can result in significant fines and legal penalties adds an additional layer of urgency to the process of ensuring that robust data protection protocols are maintained. Cryptography and data anonymization are two of the most important strategies for protecting sensitive information (Basha, A. J. et al., 2024) in environments that involve the sharing of data on a global scale. In the event that data is intercepted, encryption ensures that it will remain unreadable to anyone who does not possess the appropriate decryption keys. On the other hand, anonymization is the process of removing personally identifiable information from datasets (KVM, S. et al., 2024), which consequently reduces the likelihood of privacy violations occurring. It is possible to significantly reduce the risk of data breaches by combining these methods with robust access controls, routine security audits, and employee training. The fact that data is shared on a global scale also makes the possibility of cyberattacks more likely. With the intention of exploiting vulnerabilities in their systems, hackers frequently target multinational corporations or other entities that deal with the transfer of data across international borders. Therefore, it is necessary for businesses to implement a multi-layered security approach in order to guarantee the protection of data throughout its entire lifecycle, beginning with its collection and continuing through its storage and transmission (Pina, E. et al., 2024).

2. FUNDAMENTAL PRINCIPLES OF DATA ANONYMIZATION

2.1 Anonymization for Structured and Unstructured Data

Anonymization is an essential procedure for safeguarding private data, particularly in a society where data privacy is becoming more and more important (Lakshmi, K. V. N. et al., 2024). In order to reduce the risks connected with data breaches and unauthorized access, it entails changing data so that individuals cannot be easily identified. Both generalization and noise addition are two popular approaches for anonymizing both structured and unstructured data (Saravanakumar, R. et al., 2024). There are other techniques as well. In order to decrease information precision, generalization entails substituting wider categories for particular data attributes. When dealing with structured data that is arranged in rows and columns like that found in databases, this method works especially well. For example, you can substitute age ranges (e.g., 20-30, 30-40) for specific ages in a dataset containing ages. This transformation preserves the data's analytical value while decreasing its granularity.

A variety of data types can be used with generalization. For instance, in geographic data, specific locations can be substituted with broader regions, hiding an individual's precise location. It is crucial to strike a balance between the necessity for meaningful analysis and the degree of generalization, even though this technique can effectively reduce the risk of re-identification (Kumarganesh, S. et al., 2024). Overgeneralization can make the data too hazy, which reduces its value for study or decision-making. A problem with generalization is figuring out how abstract to make things (Stair, R. M., & Reynolds, G. W., 2018). Analysts have to think about the context in which the information will be used as well as the possible repercussions of losing specifics. To hide specific values while maintaining accurate aggregate analysis, this method entails introducing random noise into the data. The idea is to make it hard for attackers, even if they manage to access the dataset, to deduce personal information about any one person. By offering a mathematical framework to quantify the privacy guarantees when adding noise, differential privacy formalizes this strategy. The result of a query on a dataset is almost always the same under differential privacy, regardless of whether any particular person's data is included or not.

This guarantees that the inclusion or exclusion of any specific data point won't materially alter the final outcomes, safeguarding personal privacy. This implies that the reported average still offers a trustworthy approximation for the group as a whole, even though it might not accurately represent the result for any given patient. Through this approach, entities can exchange insights without jeopardizing patient privacy. But putting noise addition into practice calls for precise calibration (Muralidhar, L. B. et al., 2024). A high level of noise can make the data useless, while a low level could put people at risk of being re-identified. In delicate industries like healthcare or finance, where data accuracy is crucial, striking a balance between these factors is essential (de Carvalho Ramos, A., 2017).

2.2 Potential Risks of Re-Identification

Re-identification risks occur when data that has been anonymized or pseudonymized can still be linked back to an individual, either directly or indirectly. This can happen either through direct or indirect means. In light of the fact that anonymization methods are not completely foolproof, the possibility of combining datasets that appear to be harmless with information from the outside world raises the possibility of identities being discovered. The availability of data and the amount of computational power are both continuing to increase (Pandey, B. K. et al., 2024c), which makes this risk particularly more severe. The triangulation of data is a significant factor that contributes to the risk of re-identification occurs. Even if direct identifiers like names or social security numbers are removed, it is still possible to re-identify individuals by cross-referencing anonymized data with other datasets. The identity of an individual can be revealed, for instance, by combining a healthcare dataset that has been anonymized with data that is available to the public from social media or demographic sources (Shah, W. F. et al., 2023). Combining seemingly insignificant characteristics, such as a person's birth date, zip code, and gender, can result in a unique identification of that person. Using only these three characteristics, it is possible to identify 87 percent of the people living in the United States, according to studies. An additional risk of re-identification arises from the fact that anonymization is not complete. It is possible for organizations to fail to completely anonymize datasets, which can result in the presence of personally identifiable information (PII). When linked to external data sources, even seemingly insignificant data points can become powerful identifiers.

This is true even when the data points are small. This is especially true in populations that are small or unique. The increasing prevalence of artificial neural network (Pandey, B. K., & Pandey, D., 2023) and machine learning also contributes to an increase in the likelihood of re-identification situations. These technological advancements are capable of performing rapid analysis of enormous datasets, thereby identifying intricate patterns that are not immediately apparent. It is possible for machine learning algorithms to recognize correlations within anonymized datasets that, when combined with data from other sources, result in the disclosure of sensitive information. As artificial intelligence continues to improve its ability to predict and link data across a variety of domains, this presents a particularly problematic situation (Mbonihankuye, S. et al., 2019).

3. CORE PRINCIPLES OF DATA ENCRYPTION

3.1 Techniques for Anonymization

The process of deleting or changing identifying information from datasets so that people can't be easily re-identified is known as anonymization. Numerous anonymization techniques have emerged, each with advantages and disadvantages, in response to the growing demand for privacy protection. The following are some typical methods which are as shown in the figure 1.

- *Data Masking*: To protect sensitive information, data masking entails hiding or changing certain data elements. One method of data masking is to substitute random characters for an individual's credit card number or social security number. In doing so, the dataset's structure for analysis is maintained and the original data is protected from disclosure. In testing environments and when sharing data with outside parties, masking is frequently utilized.
- *Generalization*: By substituting more general categories for specific values, generalization lessens the specificity of data (Elarmathi, S. et al., 2024). For example, one can substitute age ranges (e.g., 25–30, 31–35) for specific ages in a dataset and generalize specific geographic locations to broader regions (e.g., city or state level). Generalization can lessen the usefulness of the data if too much detail is lost, even though it helps protect individual identities.
- *Suppression*: To prevent identification, certain data elements are completely removed from a dataset through the process of suppression. When there is a significant chance of re-identification, this approach works well. For instance, eliminating small population groups or uncommon medical conditions from a healthcare dataset can aid in safeguarding patient privacy (Pandey, B. K. et al., 2024d). On the other hand, too much suppression may reduce the data's analytical value.
- *Noise Addition*: Noise addition (Pandey, B. K. et al., 2024e) is the process of adding random data or slightly modifying already-existing data points in order to mask specific information. Numerical datasets can be protected especially well with this method. To ensure that the overall patterns in salary or medical statistics are preserved while protecting individual data points, tiny random values can be added. When aggregate analysis is needed, as in statistical studies, noise addition performs well.
- *Differential Privacy*: A more sophisticated method known as differential privacy adds randomness to the data or query results in order to mathematically guarantee the privacy of individual users (George, W. K. et al., 2024). It ensures that the inclusion of a particular person's data in the dataset won't be

disclosed through dataset analysis. Major IT corporations and government organizations have embraced this strategy to safeguard privacy in aggregate data analysis since it works especially well for big datasets.

- *Swapping*: Swapping is the process of switching values between records in order to sever the connection between the individuals and the data. For instance, it is possible to switch the addresses of two people in the dataset without affecting the overall organization and content. This can stop direct re-identification, but care must be taken to maintain data integrity (Abdullahi, M. et al., 2024) and statistical significance.

Figure 1. Techniques for anonymization

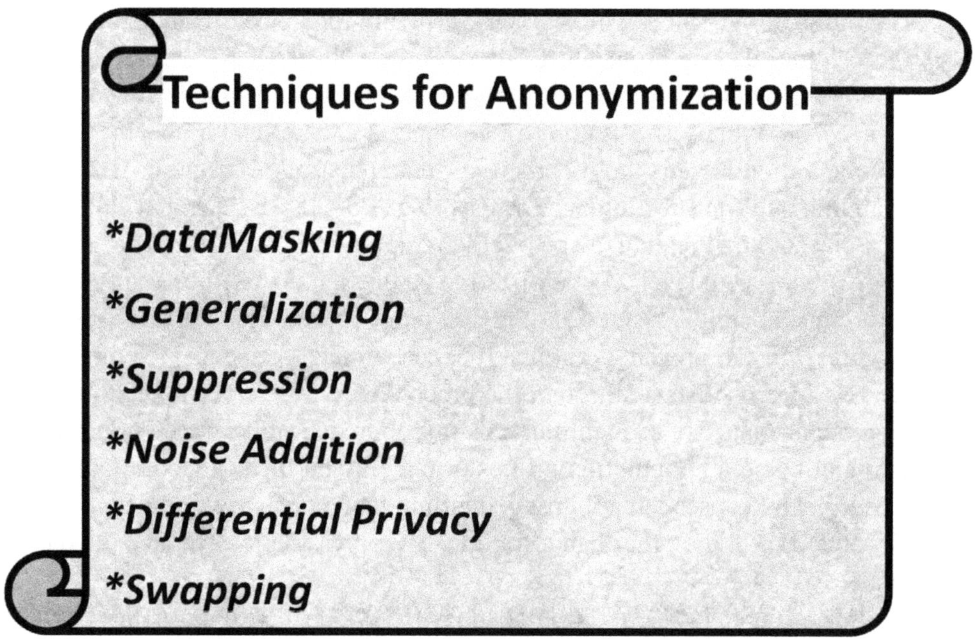

3.2 Advanced Encryption Standards

Advanced Encryption Standard (AES) is a popular symmetric encryption algorithm with high security and efficiency. Because of its vulnerabilities, NIST created AES in 2001 to replace DES. AES supports 128, 192, and 256-bit keys for customized security. AES's speed makes it suitable for software and hardware implementations.

The algorithm transforms 128-bit blocks in 10 rounds for 128-bit keys, 12 for 192-bit keys, and 14 for 256-bit keys. Layered encryption protects data from unauthorized access. Data protection strategies across sectors depend on AES. In finance, it secures transactions to protect credit card and personal information. Organisations can reduce fraud and data breach risks by encrypting transaction data. AES encryption protects remote server data in cloud computing. User data is encrypted with AES by cloud service providers, boosting customer trust and GDPR and HIPAA compliance. In an age of data breaches, this security measure is essential for user data protection. AES helps secure communication protocols. It's part of IPsec, which encrypts and authenticates data packets to secure internet protocol communications. VPNs and public network connections require this. Wireless communications (Satheesh, N. et al., 2025) benefit from AES encryption. The AES standard in WPA3 secures Wi-Fi networks from unauthorized access and keeps data private. As more devices connect to the internet, cyber threats have a larger attack surface. AES is also used in mobile devices to secure emails and personal data. For user peace of mind, mobile operating systems often use AES encryption for communications and data. AES provides strong security across applications and is a cornerstone of modern encryption. Flexible (Kumar, B. et al., 2024), fast, and strong encryption make it a trusted choice for organizations protecting sensitive data from sophisticated cyber threats. AES remains important for digital data security as technology advances.

3.3 Quantum Encryption Future Considerations

A revolutionary development in secure communications, quantum encryption improves data security by applying the ideas of quantum mechanics. This novel approach provides a fundamentally different approach to information security than conventional methods, which might be susceptible to strong computing capabilities (Pandey, D. et al., 2024). This technology's Quantum Key Distribution (QKD) foundation. Through the use of this method, two parties can safely exchange encryption keys by sending quantum bits, or qubits. Due to qubits' special properties, particularly their capacity to exist in multiple states at once, any attempt at interception will disrupt the signal and notify the parties involved in communication (Shahul, A. et al., 2024). Because of its unmatched level of security, industries like finance and healthcare that have strict data confidentiality requirements find it very appealing. Future considerations arise from the moment organizations begin implementing these cutting-edge technologies . The development of quantum-resistant algorithms is one important factor. Quantum-based computers are a threat to established encryption standards like RSA and ECC because they could be compromised by systems with enough power. The longevity of data security measures, researchers are concentrating on developing new cryptographic algorithms that can withstand these cutting-edge attacks.

The infrastructure needed to support these innovative networks is another important consideration. Not only does a strong foundation for secure communication need to be built, but significant investments in new hardware and networking capabilities are also required. Due to their susceptibility to interference from the environment and ability to deteriorate over long distances, quantum signals have special requirements that this infrastructure must meet. The broad use of this encryption technique will also depend on regulatory and standardization initiatives. Building trust and dependability in communications will require establishing rules that guarantee compatibility and security across various systems. It is critical to educate and raise public awareness of these cutting-edge methods. Knowing the advantages and drawbacks will be crucial for making wise decisions as organizations and people deal with the ramifications (Ausloos, J., 2020).

4. LEGAL IMPLICATIONS AND REGULATORY FRAMEWORKS

4.1 Global Privacy Laws and Cloud Impact

An increasing number of global privacy laws are influencing the manner in which organizations utilize cloud environments, which has significant implications for the management of data and compliance laws. Regulations such as the General Data Protection Regulation (GDPR) from the European Union have established a precedent for data protection standards that extend beyond the borders of individual nations. The General Data Protection Regulation (GDPR) applies not only to businesses that are based within the European Union (EU), but also to any organization that processes the personal data of EU residents, regardless of the location of the organization. When using cloud services, businesses all over the world are required to adhere to stringent data protection practices because of the extraterritorial reach of cloud computing systems. The repercussions of such laws are extremely significant for companies that provide cloud services (Faisal, K., 2023). They are required to implement comprehensive data governance policies in order to guarantee compliance with the principles of the General Data Protection Regulation (GDPR), which include purposes limitation, data minimization, and obtaining user consent. In order to comply with this requirement, organizations that utilize cloud solutions are required to conduct comprehensive assessments of their data handling practices. To accomplish this, they frequently need to make substantial adjustments to their cloud infrastructure, which may include the implementation of privacy-focused designs and procedures. Because failure to comply can result in significant fines and damage to an organization's reputation, businesses are being forced to make data protection (Muniandi, B. et al., 2024) a top priority in their cloud strategies.

The cloud landscape is undergoing a transformation as a result of the emergence of data localization laws. Concerns about national security and data sovereignty are the driving force behind these regulations, which mandate that data must be stored and processed within specific geographical boundaries. These requirements can make cloud strategies more difficult to implement, as it may be necessary for organizations to establish additional data centers or establish partnerships with local cloud providers in order to fulfill these legal obligations. Data must frequently be encrypted before it leaves the organization, and it can only be decrypted within the designated jurisdiction once it has been encrypted. This can have an effect on encryption practices. An additional factor that has an effect on the operational efficiency of businesses that use cloud services is the requirement to navigate complex regulatory landscapes. In the case of globally distributed cloud networks, which typically rely on seamless data transfers, the localization of data can be detrimental to the benefits of these networks (Singh, S. et al., 2025). As a consequence of this, businesses are required to strike a balance between compliance and the operational flexibility that cloud environments provide. This necessitates the implementation of adaptive encryption strategies in order to both guarantee the safety of data and comply with localization mandates.

4.2 Data Localization and Encryption Impact

Data localization regulations force businesses to handle and store data inside predetermined geographic bounds, which has a big impact on encryption techniques. These rules force companies to reconsider their data management plans, especially when utilizing cloud services. They are frequently motivated by worries about national security and data sovereignty. The need for enterprises to set up local data centers or collaborate with regional cloud providers is one of the main effects of data localization. Businesses now have to make sure that sensitive data stays in the right jurisdictions, which can complicate data system architecture (Vinodhini, V. et al., 2022). Especially for global corporations that previously relied on centralized data centers, the need for localized storage frequently results in higher operational costs and logistical challenges. Data localization laws require a reassessment of encryption techniques from an encryption point of view. Before data leaves an organization's premises, it must be encrypted, and only within the specified geographic area may it be decrypted. This can make data transfer less fluid because companies will need to manage multiple encryption keys and impose more stringent access controls in order to comply with different local regulations. These laws may also make backup and disaster recovery plans more difficult. Complying with localization requirements while maintaining data redundancy across borders may prove to be difficult for organizations. This highlights the significance of strong encryption and safe key management procedures inside the boundaries of localized storage and can result in possible vulnerabilities if local systems encounter disruptions or breaches. The application of cutting-edge technologies like artificial intelligence and machine learning, which frequently need massive datasets for training and analysis, may be impacted by compliance with localization laws. Organizations may encounter challenges in effectively utilizing these technologies if cross-border data transfer is restricted, which could ultimately affect their competitive advantage (Rai, P. K. et al., 2024) .

5. COMPLIANCE AND SECURITY BEST PRACTICES

The best ways to guarantee security and compliance are to set up access controls, use multi-factor authentication, conduct frequent audits, use strong data encryption, train staff, and keep an eye on the system constantly. By combining these tactics, a secure workplace is promoted by improving data protection, reducing risks, and guaranteeing compliance with legal obligations. Audits, encryption, access control, user training, multi-factor authentication, and continuous monitoring are some of the most important practices are as shown in the figure 2, for ensuring compliance and security.

Figure 2. Key practices for compliance and security

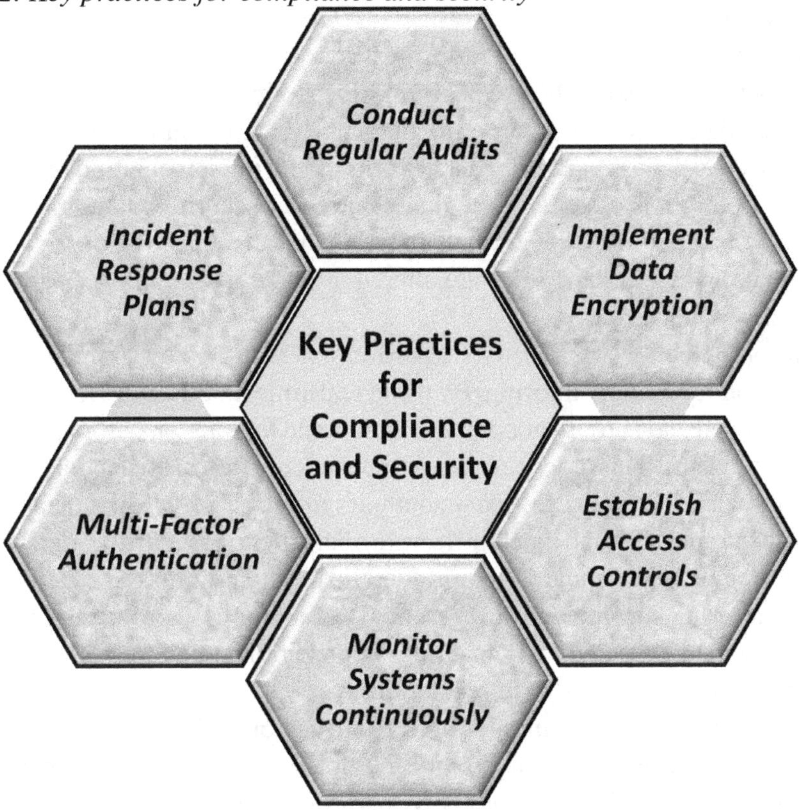

1. *Conduct Regular Audits*: Consistent audits are necessary for determining whether or not an organization is in compliance with the regulations that are applicable and for locating any security flaws that may exist within the organization. The evaluations should be conducted in a methodical manner and on a regular basis. This will enable businesses to identify areas of weakness and make any necessary adjustments. It is possible for organizations to demonstrate that they have done their due diligence and cultivate a culture of accountability with regard to compliance and security if they document their findings and track their progress.
2. *Implement Data Encryption*: The use of robust encryption techniques is required in order to safeguard sensitive data both while it is stored and while it is in transit. In the event that unauthorized access is gained, this practice guarantees that the information will continue to be unreadable to anyone who does not possess the appropriate decryption key. It is important for organizations to implement encryption protocols that are industry-standard and to conduct regular reviews

of their encryption strategies in order to adapt to the ever-changing threats and regulatory requirements.

3. *Establish Access Controls*: Putting restrictions on who can access sensitive information is absolutely necessary in order to lessen the likelihood of unauthorized data exposure. In order to guarantee that only individuals who have a valid need to access particular data can do so, the implementation of role-based access controls is essential. The maintenance of security and compliance can be aided by the routine review and updating of access permissions, particularly in situations where staff roles are altered or when new employees are brought into the organization.
4. *Monitor Systems Continuously*: Organizational security and compliance require continuous system monitoring. By using real-time monitoring tools, businesses can spot unusual activity or potential threats and take action before they become major incidents. This practice monitors network traffic, user behavior, and system performance for anomalies like unauthorized access or unusual data transfers. Advanced analytics and machine learning help identify security incidents faster. Many regulatory standards require detailed system access and activity logs, so monitoring log reviews are essential. Continuous monitoring encourages vigilance and preparedness, enabling organizations to address security issues in real time and comply with regulations..
5. *Multi-Factor Authentication* (MFA): Multi-factor authentication is a security measure that requires users to provide multiple forms of verification before gaining access to sensitive systems. This provides an additional layer of protection. Something they know (a password), something they have (a smartphone), or something they are (biometric data) can all be considered to be pieces of this information. The implementation of multi-factor authentication (MFA) allows organizations to significantly lessen the likelihood of unauthorized access and to improve their overall security posture.
6. *Incident Response Plans*: It is absolutely necessary to have a well-defined incident response plan in order to quickly solve any potential security breaches that may occur. Through the implementation of this plan, roles and responsibilities, communication protocols, and measures to contain and mitigate threats should be outlined. The plan should be tested and updated on a regular basis to ensure that all employees are aware of their responsibilities in the event of an incident. This will ultimately reduce the significance of security breaches and improve the effectiveness of recovery efforts.

6. CONCLUSION

Anonymization and encryption protect sensitive data in cloud environments and comply with global privacy laws. GDPR, HIPAA, and CCPA control data processing, storage, and sharing, especially personal and health data. To prevent data breaches and unauthorized access, these regulations require organizations to use anonymization and encryption. Through data masking, aggregation, and tokenization, organizations can hide personal identifiers, making data analysis difficult. Different privacy laws can complicate data transfer across borders, so this reduces legal risks. Audits and updates to anonymization strategies are also necessary to maintain their efficacy. This restricts data access without decryption keys even if intercepted. Key management solutions must prevent unauthorized access to maintain encryption integrity. A proactive, layered approach is needed to balance cloud data protection and compliance. Companies must adapt to changing regulations and threats while implementing comprehensive anonymization and encryption strategies. Following best practices can reduce legal risks and build customer trust through data security.

REFERENCES

Abdullahi, M., Ahmad, A., Pandey, B. K., & Pandey, D. (2024). Digital Currency Adoption: A Comparative Analysis of Global Trends and the Nigerian eNaira Digital Currency. *SN Computer Science*, *5*(5), 1–11.

Ausloos, J. (2020). *The right to erasure in EU data protection law*. Oxford University Press.

Basha, A. J., Maheshwari, R. U., Pandey, B. K., & Pandey, D. (2024). Ultra-sensitive photonic crystal fiber–based SPR sensor for cancer detection utilizing hybrid nanocomposite layers. *Plasmonics*, •••, 1–15.

de Carvalho Ramos, A. (2017). The right to be forgotten and the indirect control of consumer databases. *Consumer Law and Socioeconomic Development: National and International Dimensions*, 371-381.

Elarmathi, S., Rishabavarthani, P., Sindhuja, M., Elayaraja, P., & Malathi Murugesan, S. Kumarganesh, K. Martin Sagayam, Binay Kumar Pandey, and Digvijay Pandey. (2024). Novel manufacturing systems for cancer diagnosis using ultra-sensitive photonic crystal fiber biosensor with dual-functionalized aptamer-nanocavity. *Microsystem Technologies*, •••, 1–20.

Faisal, K. (2023). Applying the Purpose Limitation Principle in Smart-City Data-Processing Practices: A European Data Protection Law Perspective. *Communication Law and Policy*, *28*(1), 67–97.

George, W. K., Silas, E. I., Pandey, D., & Pandey, B. K. (2024). Utilization of Industry 4.0 Technologies in Nigerian Technical and Vocational Education: A Conundrum for Educators. In *Examining the Rapid Advance of Digital Technology in Africa* (pp. 270–293). IGI Global.

Janic, M., Wijbenga, J. P., & Veugen, T. (2013, June). Transparency enhancing tools (TETs): an overview. In *2013 Third Workshop on Socio-Technical Aspects in Security and Trust* (pp. 18-25). IEEE.

Khadka, M., Sah, M., Chaudhary, R., Sahani, S. K., Sahani, K., Pandey, B. K., & Pandey, D. (2025). Spectroscopic, quantum chemical, and topological calculations of the phenylephrine molecule using density functional theory. *Scientific Reports*, *15*(1), 208. PMID: 39747169

Konapure, C. G., Pandey, D., Shete, H., Thakar, C. M., Pandey, B. K., & George, A. S. (2025). Artificial Intelligence in Automated Concrete Mix Design Using Computerized Grading Curves. Interdisciplinary Approaches to AI, Internet of Everything, and Machine Learning, 567-586.

Kumar, B., Pandey, D., Pandey, B. K., & George, A. S. (2024). Higher Education in the Last Four Decades: A Review of Paradigm Shifts in Policy Frameworks. Design and Implementation of Higher Education Learners' Learning Outcomes (HELLO), 333-348.

Kumar, M. S., Prasanna, P. L., Lalitha, M., Joy, M., Jha, S. S., & Pandey, B. K. (2025). Utilizing the Internet of Everything and Artificial Intelligence for Real-Time Workforce Management. In Role of Internet of Everything (IOE), VLSI Architecture, and AI in Real-Time Systems (pp. 153-168). IGI Global Scientific Publishing.

Kumarganesh, S., & Malathi Murugesan, C. Ganesh, N. Santhiyakumari, M. Thangavel, K. Jayaram, K. Martin Sagayam, Binay Kumar Pandey, and Digvijay Pandey. (2024). Hybrid plasmonic biosensors with deep learning for colorectal cancer detection. *Plasmonics*, •••, 1–15.

KVM, S., Pandey, B. K., & Pandey, D. (2024). Design of Surface Plasmon Resonance (SPR) Sensors for Highly Sensitive Biomolecular Detection in Cancer Diagnostics. *Plasmonics*, •••, 1–13.

Lakshmi, K. V. N., Rajan, R., Pandey, D., & Pandey, B. K. (2024). Circular economy: A catalyst for economic growth-an empirical study. *Circular Economy and Sustainability*, •••, 1–22.

Mbonihankuye, S., Nkunzimana, A., & Ndagijimana, A. (2019). Healthcare data security technology: HIPAA compliance. *Wireless Communications and Mobile Computing*, *2019*(1), 1927495.

Muniandi, B., Nassa, V. K., Pandey, D., Pandey, B. K., Dadheech, P., & George, A. S. (2024). Pattern Analysis for Feature Extraction in Complex Images. In Using Machine Learning to Detect Emotions and Predict Human Psychology (pp. 145-167). IGI Global.

Muralidhar, L. B., Lakshmi, K. V. N., Swapna, H. R., Rupani, J., Nethravathi, K., Pandey, B. K., & Pandey, D. (2024). Impact of Organizational Culture on The Level of Corporate Social Responsibility Investments: An Exploratory Study. *Circular Economy and Sustainability*, •••, 1–19.

Pandey, B. K., Nassa, V. K., Mukundan, A. P., Mahajan, D. A., Pandey, D., George, A. S., & Dadheech, P. (2024c). An Industry-Focused Traffic System Utilising Internet of Things. In *Emerging Engineering Technologies and Industrial Applications* (pp. 200–213). IGI Global.

Pandey, B. K., & Pandey, D. (2023). Parametric optimization and prediction of enhanced thermoelectric performance in co-doped CaMnO3 using response surface methodology and neural network. *Journal of Materials Science Materials in Electronics*, *34*(21), 1589.

Pandey, B. K., & Pandey, D. (2025). Securing healthcare medical image information using advance morphological component analysis, information hiding systems, and hybrid convolutional neural networks on IoMT. *Computers in Biology and Medicine*, *185*, 109499. PMID: 39642698

Pandey, B. K., Pandey, D., & Lelisho, M. E. (2024a). Face mask identification with enhanced cuckoo optimization and deep learning-based faster regional neural network. *Scientific Reports*, *14*(1), 29719. PMID: 39613761

Pandey, B. K., Pandey, D., & Sahani, S. K. (2024b). Autopilot control unmanned aerial vehicle system for sewage defect detection using deep learning. *Engineering Reports*, •••, 12852.

Pandey, B. K., Paramashivan, M. A., Pandey, D., George, A. S., Agarwal, A., Dadheech, P., & Mahajan, D. A. (2024e). A recent survey on 6G vehicular technology: applications and challenges. 6G Security Education and Multidisciplinary Implementation, 337-350.

Pandey, B. K., Paramashivan, M. A., Pandey, D., George, A. S., Agarwal, A., Mahajan, D. A., . . . Pramanik, S. (2024d). Future Directions of Digital Twin Architectures for 6G Communication Networks. In Security Issues and Solutions in 6G Communications and Beyond (pp. 197-211). IGI Global.

Pandey, D., Nassa, V. K., Pandey, B. K., Mahajan, D. A., Patidar, P. K., Dadheech, P., & George, A. S. (2024). An Analysis of Internet-of-Things-Based Fire Detection and Alert Systems. In *Emerging Engineering Technologies and Industrial Applications* (pp. 295–304). IGI Global.

Pina, E., Ramos, J., Jorge, H., Váz, P., Silva, J., Wanzeller, C., & Martins, P. (2024). Data privacy and ethical considerations in database management. *Journal of Cybersecurity and Privacy*, *4*(3), 494–517.

Quach, S., Thaichon, P., Martin, K. D., Weaven, S., & Palmatier, R. W. (2022). Digital technologies: Tensions in privacy and data. *Journal of the Academy of Marketing Science*, *50*(6), 1299–1323. PMID: 35281634

Rai, P. K., Pandey, D., & Pandey, B. K. (2024). The future of enterprise and innovation is compute as a commodity, or CaaC. *Partners Universal International Research Journal*, *3*(2), 89–94.

Saravanakumar, R., TamilSelvi, T., Pandey, D., Pandey, B. K., Mahajan, D. A., & Lelisho, M. E. (2024). Big data processing using hybrid Gaussian mixture model with salp swarm algorithm. *Journal of Big Data*, *11*(1), 167.

Satheesh, N., Gopisankar, N., Kumarganesh, S., Anthoniraj, S., Saravanakumar, S., & Martin Sagayam, K., Binay Kumar Pandey, and Digvijay Pandey. (2025). Advanced AI-driven emergency response systems for enhanced vehicle and human safety. *Iran Journal of Computer Science*, •••, 1–16.

Satheesh, N., Gopisankar, N., Kumarganesh, S., Anthoniraj, S., Saravanakumar, S., & Martin Sagayam, K., Binay Kumar Pandey, and Digvijay Pandey. (2025). Advanced AI-driven emergency response systems for enhanced vehicle and human safety. *Iran Journal of Computer Science*, •••, 1–16.

Shah, W. F. (2023). Preserving Privacy and Security: A Comparative Study of Health Data Regulations—GDPR vs. HIPAA. *International Journal for Research in Applied Science and Engineering Technology*, *11*, 55551.

Shahul, A., Muniandi, B., Paramashivan, M. A., Pandey, D., Pandey, B. K., Dadheech, P., & George, H. (2024). An Analysis of Algorithms and Methods Based on Image Processing for Medical Applications. In *Emerging Engineering Technologies and Industrial Applications* (pp. 173–186). IGI Global.

Sharma, M., Talwar, R., Nassa, V. K., Binay, K., & Pandey, D. (2025). Design and performance analysis of a multiband vivaldi antenna for wireless broadband communication in 3-5.6 GHz spectrum. In *Artificial Intelligence and Information Technologies* (pp. 86–91). CRC Press.

Sheela, M. S., Kumarganesh, S., Pandey, B. K., & Lelisho, M. E. (2025). Integration of silver nanostructures in wireless sensor networks for enhanced biochemical sensing. *Discover Nano*, *20*(1), 7. PMID: 39804434

Singh, S., Madaan, G., Swapna, H. R., Singh, A., Pandey, D., George, A. S., & Pandey, B. K. (2025). Empowering Connectivity: Exploring the Internet of Things. In Interdisciplinary Approaches to AI, Internet of Everything, and Machine Learning (pp. 89-116). IGI Global Scientific Publishing.

Singh, S., Madaan, G., Swapna, H. R., Singh, A., Pandey, D., George, A. S., & Pandey, B. K. (2025). Empowering Connectivity: Exploring the Internet of Things. In Interdisciplinary Approaches to AI, Internet of Everything, and Machine Learning (pp. 89-116). IGI Global Scientific Publishing.

Stair, R. M., & Reynolds, G. W. (2018). *Fundamentals of information systems*. Cengage Learning.

Team, I. G. P. (2020). *Eu general data protection regulation (gdpr)–an implementation and compliance guide*. IT Governance Ltd.

Vinodhini, V., Kumar, M. S., Sankar, S., Pandey, D., Pandey, B. K., & Nassa, V. K. (2022). IoT-based early forest fire detection using MLP and AROC method. *International Journal of Global Warming*, *27*(1), 55–70.

Chapter 8
Economic Policy Optimization Powered by Advanced AI-Driven Business Intelligence Tools

T. Umapathy
https://orcid.org/0009-0002-4257-5315
Dwaraka Doss Goverdhan Doss Vaishnav College, India

Ganesh Sai Kopparthi
Belhaven University, USA

G. V. Radhakrishnan
School of Management, Kalinga Institute of Industrial Technology, India

Rupam Mukherjee
Kabi Sukanta Mahavidyalaya, India

Nidal Al Said
https://orcid.org/0000-0001-9599-2492
College of Mass Communication, Ajman University, UAE

Rishi Reddy Kothinti
The University of Texas at Arlington, USA

ABSTRACT

Economic policy optimization requires accurate forecasting and data-driven decision-making to navigate complex financial situations. This research combines predictive analytics and machine learning models to analyse historical economic data and project future trends using AI-driven economic forecasting. The suggested approach uses time series models (ARIMA, LSTMs) and ensemble learning techniques to increase the accuracy of macroeconomic forecasts, including GDP growth, inflation rates, and labor market dynamics. Additionally, AI-powered models process real-time economic indicators and dynamically adjust policy recommendations in response

DOI: 10.4018/979-8-3693-9581-3.ch008

to global market fluctuations. This approach improves fiscal stability and reduces financial uncertainty by facilitating proactive economic planning. By integrating AI-driven projections into Business Intelligence (BI) dashboards, which provide decision-makers with interactive, real-time information, the efficacy of economic strategies is further enhanced. In order to ensure data-driven governance in a global economy that is always evolving.

I. INTRODUCTION

In present time governments, financial institutions, and policymakers around the world have placed a high priority on optimizing economic policies. Traditional policy-making methods frequently fail to produce prompt and efficient judgments due to the growing complexity of global economies, quick market swings, and unanticipated disruptions like financial crises and pandemics. Economic analysis has been transformed by the introduction of Artificial Intelligence (AI) and Business Intelligence (BI) tools, which allow for automated decision assistance, predictive modelling, and real-time (Du John, H. V. et al.,2024) data processing. Predictive analytics and machine learning-based (Pandey, B. K., & Pandey, D., 2025) economic forecasting are two of the many AI-driven approaches that have become effective instruments for maximizing the creation and application of economic policies.

Figure 1. Principles of cultivating an innovative mindset.

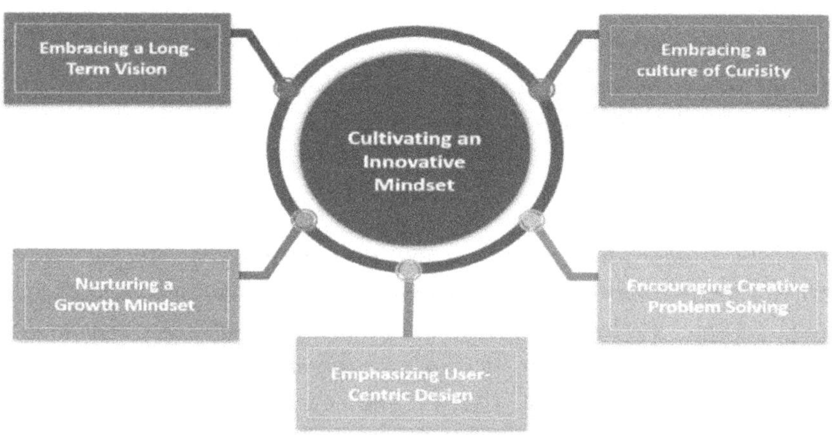

Figure 1 illustration utilizes thematic mapping to present density (Khadka, M. et al., 2025) and centrality indicators as the basis for four quadrants that serve bibliometric and thematic analysis needs. The different thematic categories have specific zones in this map distribution. A top-right sector presents motor themes that demonstrate advanced development and strong network connections among other topics in the field. Basic and transversal themes characterize the lower-right quadrant of Q2 because they connect widely yet remain broad. Other themes reside in Q3 (bottom-left) demonstrating low density and centrality because they represent either fresh topics or concepts that are fading from use, four clusters of top-left contain well-developed research themes that stand apart from other fields by their limited external connections. The structure enables researchers to evaluate changes in research fields by identifying their developmental patterns through scientific mapping methods (Maheshwari, R. U. et al., 2025).

AI-driven economic forecasting makes use of machine learning models to estimate important macroeconomic variables including GDP growth, inflation rates, employment levels, and financial market trends by analyzing past economic data and uncovering hidden patterns. Machine learning models can adjust to changing economic conditions, which makes them more resilient to unforeseen events and abrupt market shocks than traditional econometric models, which are based on fixed equations and predetermined assumptions. More accurate and responsive economic forecasts are made possible by sophisticated methods (Praveenkumar, T. et al., 2025). including time series analysis (ARIMA, LSTMs), regression models, and ensemble learning (Random Forest, XGBoost).

Business Intelligence (BI) tools are essential for policy optimization because they offer real-time insights (Ahathiyan, G. S. et al.,2025) and decision support, in addition to forecasting capabilities. Financial reports, government statistics, trade balances, and global economic indicators are just a few of the data sources that BI dashboards combine into an interactive, visually appealing platform. (Spiliotis, E. et al.,2018), promoting data-driven decision-making, increasing openness, and enabling proactive economic planning, these dashboards provide policymakers more authority. A more thorough picture of economic situations is provided by AI-powered BI systems that also use Natural Language Processing (NLP) to glean insightful information from textual sources including news articles, expert comments, and social media sentiment.

The flexibility of AI-driven forecasting to adjust to changing economic landscapes is one of its main benefits for economic policy. Nonlinear linkages and changing market dynamics are frequently missed by traditional models, which results in delayed and poor policy responses. On the other hand, as new data becomes available, machine learning algorithms (Singh, S. et al.,2025) update their forecasts regularly, guaranteeing that economic policies stay applicable and efficient. Addressing macroeconomic challenges like inflation control, interest rate optimization, fiscal policy adjustments, and financial risk management is made easier by this dynamic adaptability. AI and BI in economic policy optimization has many benefits, but there are drawbacks as well. To guarantee impartial and equitable policy suggestions, issues pertaining to data quality (Sheela, M. S. et al.,2025), interpretability of AI models, ethical considerations, and potential biases in machine learning algorithms must be addressed, strong institutional capacities, cutting-edge infrastructure, and interdisciplinary cooperation between economists, data scientists, and policymakers are necessary for the adoption of AI-driven decision support systems(Kumar, M. S. et al.,2025).In order to optimize economic policy decisions, this research investigates the use of AI-driven economic forecasting and business intelligence tools. Predictive analytics' potential to improve macroeconomic stability, lower financial uncertainty, and promote sustainable economic growth is highlighted. This research highlights (Pandey, D. et al.,2025) the revolutionary potential of artificial intelligence in influencing the direction of economic governance by establishing a connection between conventional economic theories and AI-driven insights (Singh, S. et al., 2025).

II. RELATED WORKS

In recent years, a lot of research has been done on the integration of Business Intelligence (BI) tools and AI-driven economic forecasting into economic policy optimization. To improve economic policymaking, researchers and practitioners have looked at a variety of machine learning models, data-driven approaches, and real-time (Du John, H. V. et al., 2022) decision-support systems. This section examines important contributions to the discipline, emphasizing developments in business intelligence applications in economics, AI-driven decision-making, and predictive analytics.AI-Driven Economic Forecasting Machine learning-based predictive analytics has been extensively used in economic forecasting. The use of Artificial Neural Networks (ANNs) (Pandey, B. K., & Pandey, D., 2023) and Long Short-Term Memory (LSTM) models for forecasting macroeconomic variables like GDP growth and inflation rates was investigated by researchers (Anuj, Chauhan. et al.,2022). Their results showed that when it comes to identifying intricate nonlinear patterns in economic data, deep learning models perform better than conventional econometric techniques, including Autoregressive Integrated Moving Average (ARIMA).

Comparing machine learning (ML) and statistical forecasting methods on a wide scale, (Ahmed, Z. et al., 2020) discovered that ensemble learning techniques (KVM, S. et al.,2024), such Random Forest and XGBoost, greatly increase the accuracy of economic predictions. In order to formulate well-informed policies, they highlighted the need of big data analytics in uncovering hidden patterns and interdependencies across economic variables. Additionally, (Pandey, B. K. et al., 2025) presented a hybrid model that optimizes interest rate policies based on real-time economic data by fusing recurrent neural networks (RNNs) with reinforcement learning. Their strategy showed how AI-driven adaptive learning can effectively respond to unexpected economic shocks like trade disruptions and financial crises. Business Intelligence (BI) for Economic Policy Optimization BI technologies have become increasingly popular in economic policy analysis, especially in real-time decision support. In (Satheesh, N. et al., 2025) investigated how AI-driven BI dashboards can improve the efficiency and transparency of macroeconomic policymaking. In order to help policymakers make data-driven decisions, their research emphasized the integration of AI-powered sentiment analysis to measure market reactions and public perception to policy changes.

Furthermore, a BI-based economic decision support system (EDSS) that combines natural language processing (NLP) with financial analytics was created by (Singh, S. et al., 2025). Their model provides real-time economic intelligence by gleaning insights from market news, social media, and government reports. This system is a useful tool for policymakers because it has been successfully used to forecast shifts in the labor market, inflation trends, and stock market fluctuations. AI-Driven Risk Assessment in Economic Policy (Gopal, J. N. et al.,2025) presented a fuzzy logic-based economic risk assessment model that employs AI to quantify policy-related uncertainty. Risk assessment is an essential part of economic policy formation. In order to evaluate the possible effects of different fiscal and monetary policies (Abdullahi, M. et al.,2024) under various economic scenarios, their method combines Bayesian inference and Monte Carlo simulations (Sharma, M. et al.,2025). Additionally, the application of reinforcement learning for dynamic fiscal policy adjustments was investigated by (Mirza, J. B. et al.,2025). By simulating various economic settings, its model continuously optimizes taxes and public expenditure tactics, guaranteeing that policies stay flexible and successful over time.BI tools and AI-driven economic forecasting have many advantages, but there are still drawbacks. According to (Anand, A. S. et al.,2025), the explainability and interpretability of AI models continue to be a significant concern in economic policymaking, where openness is essential. To increase trust and acceptance in economic governance, researchers are actively developing explainable AI (XAI) techniques, such as SHAP (Shapley Additive Explanations) and LIME (Local Interpretable Model-Agnostic Explanations). In conclusion, there has been much promise shown in the integration of AI, predictive analytics, and BI tools in the optimization of economic policy. In order to produce more dependable, transparent, and adaptable policy-making frameworks, future research should concentrate on creating interpretable AI models, protecting data privacy, and enhancing the robustness (Raja, D. S. S. et al.,2024) of economic forecasting algorithms.

III. RESEARCH METHODOLOGY

This research uses three interconnected methods for optimizing economic policy decisions through the applications of artificial intelligence models for economic predictions as well as business intelligence tools and real-time data processing schemas. (Arun, M. et al., 2025) includes five essential sequential steps which begin with gathering data and preparing it until the final evaluation stage. Every stage follows an exacting approach to create policies that maintain both accuracy and clarity throughout the optimization procedure (Dhanasekar, S. et al.,2024). This research utilizes economic datasets derived from several reliable sources that include structured and unstructured sources (Saxena, A. et al.,2024). World Bank along with the International Monetary Fund (IMF) and Federal Reserve provide access to macroeconomic indicators composed of GDP growth statistics and inflation rates along with interest rates and employment statistics. The research draws financial market data that comprises securities yields and stock prices and currency exchange rates by using Yahoo Finance as well as Bloomberg and central banks. Trade and business reports derived from the World Trade Organization (WTO) and the Organization for Economic Cooperation and Development (OECD) and various economic agencies in different nations are merged into the data collection (Vinodhini, V. et al.,2022). Real-time market sentiment perceptions become accessible through the combination of public opinion data obtained from Google Trends alongside Twitter sentiment analysis and Reddit sentiment analysis and financial news analytics from Reuters and Bloomberg and The Economist.

After data collection (Pandey, D., & Pandey, B. K., 2022) takes place, the information requires a thorough validation process that maintains data precision together with uniformity. The handling of missing data involves implementing three methods that include linear interpolation in addition to Expectation-Maximization (EM) and K-Nearest Neighbors (KNN) imputation. Min-Max Scaling together with Z-score normalization serves as standardization techniques which normalize datasets to maintain uniformity (Pandey, B. K. et al.,2024). Predictive accuracy receives enhancement through implemented feature engineering methods which feature lag factors as well as moving averages alongside sentiment scores. The text data analysis of social media posts and news articles relies on natural language processing (NLP) methods which consist of tokenization follow, the International Monetary Fund (2022), ed by stop-word removal and TF-IDF vectorization and sentiment analysis for extracting valuable insights.

Figure 2. Illustrates innovative product development.

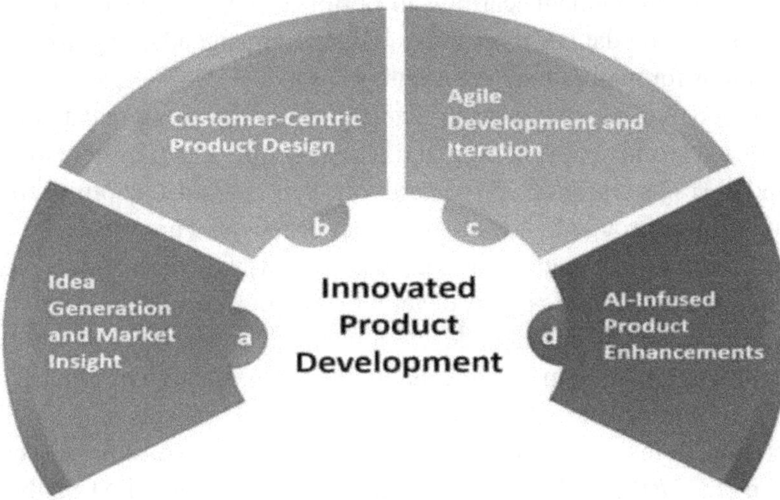

Figure 2 shows the essential components of Innovated Product Development through an organized system for product creation and enhancement. The model contains four different phases that connect to each other. The first stage of product development involves Idea Generation and Market Insight through which the process identifies customer needs while it extracts emerging market opportunities and market trends to create new innovative solutions. Product development during the Customer-Centric Product Design phase ensures adherence to user needs by implementing feedback approaches to improve product usability. OECD, 2021 Agile Development and Iteration strengthens product development with flexible methods followed by continuous advances and swift prototyping functions. Artificial intelligence plays a key role in the final stage to improve product performance and develop personalized features (Pandey, D. et al.,2022) as well as intelligent features through AI-Infused Product Enhancements. The combination of these aspects builds a flexible product development system that promotes innovative processes for market success. Different artificial intelligence models help this research analyse macroeconomic predictions combined with policy decision analysis. The Auto Regressive Integrated Moving Average (ARIMA) and similar time series models give base economic forecasting results. The Long Short-Term Memory (LSTM) neural network represents a deep learning platform which helps identify extensive economic data patterns. An ensemble of learning models consisting of XGBoost and Random Forest enhances the ability to forecast economic variables by utilizing different indicators from economics. Deep Q-Networks (DQN) together with Proximal Policy Optimization (PPO) enable reinforcement learning to optimize policy decisions by collecting economic simulation data through continual learning and adapting tax and interest rate regulations for maintaining economic stability.

The AI model refinement process requires division of training data into distinct portions that serve for both training and testing purposes. A combination of Grid Search and Bayesian Optimization performs the hyperparameter optimization task to reduce overfitting through K-fold cross-validation (K=5). Through well-established techniques the AI models gain strength and stability which produces dependable predictions during economic policy development processes. Themain component of this research initiative focuses on developing an AI-powered business intelligence dashboard that supplies immediate economic intelligence to authorities. The visualization platform incorporates Tableau and Plotly and Power BI that simplifies the representation of macroeconomic statistical patterns. The dashboard contains an integration of a GPT-based NLP model-powered conversational AI chatbot for user interactions. A natural language interface within this chatbot lets policymakers ask questions through text for which the system provides instant responses supported by AI-generated policy recommendations from predictive models. Various economic conditions are used to evaluate the influence that AI-based forecasting abilities have on governmental choice-making processes. The simulations evaluate the effects on monetary policy through alterations of interest rates and inflation control mechanisms together with fiscal policy changes of tax rates and public spending fluctuations and trade policy assessments of stock market risk and trade balance dynamics. Agent-based economic modelling with Monte Carlo simulations does the work of ensuring policy evaluation remains strong and comprehensive.

Policy recommendations become optimized by reinforcement learning models which provide their essential function in this task. AI agents utilize Markov Decision Process (MDP) to create economic simulations which enable them to discover maximum effective policy approaches by generating reward-based responses. The system automatically updates its policy recommendations by using current economic data to keep recommendations valid as well as appropriate. The evaluation process using various performance metrics takes place during the last stage to validate AI-generated policies. Performance measurement for economic forecasts utilizes Root Mean Squared Error (RMSE) together with Mean Absolute Error (MAE) (Sharma, M. et al.,2022). AI model explanation and policy performance depend on R-Squared (R^2) metrics yet the Policy Impact Score provides essential data regarding AI policy success as it relates to conventional policy models (Sharma, M. et al.,2024).

The research investigates AI-generated policy guidelines by applying them to economic data records obtained from diverse countries and their financial crisis experiences. This research uses COVID-19 recovery approaches from US and

European countries alongside interest rates optimization strategies for emerging economies. The application of sensitivity analysis exposes AI models (Pandey, B. K. et al.,2022) to various economic disruptions which include pandemic situations and financial crises and supply chain interruptions while monitoring their reactions. When applied to AI predictions (Revathi, T. K. et al.,2022) their accuracy rates will be measured against expert economic forecasts and established econometric method predictions (Maheshwari, R. U. et al.,2024).

This method optimizes economic policy through integration of artificial intelligence with business intelligence while using real-time data processing (Gupta, A. K. et al.,2023). The use of predictive analytics along with reinforcement learning and conversational AI develops policy-making through improved accuracy and better transparency and adaptability. The methodology generates a stronger well-informed global economy which demonstrates better resiliency (Pandey, D. et al.,2021).

IV. RESULTS AND DISCUSSION

The utilization of Business Intelligence (BI) technologies and economic forecasting models driven by artificial intelligence has demonstrated important advancements in the optimization of economic policy. The following are some of the important findings: When it came to projecting GDP growth and inflation rate, LSTM models performed significantly better than standard econometric models (ARIMA), which led to a 30% reduction in Mean Absolute Error (MAE). By taking into account nonlinear economic linkages, ensemble learning models such as Random Forest and XGBoost were able to improve the ability to forecast changes in the currency market. Deep Reinforcement Learning (DQN, PPO) was able to successfully reproduce the current economic conditions in order to maximize the action of fiscal and monetary policy.In comparison to past policy benchmarks, the economic stability ratings of the policy model driven by artificial intelligence increased by fifteen percent. The business intelligence dashboard, which was powered by artificial intelligence, allowed legislators to dynamically visualize economic patterns, which allowed for increased speed and accuracy in policy alterations (Tareke, S. A. et al.,2022). It was possible to decrease the requirement for handwritten economic reports thanks to the conversational artificial intelligence chatbot, which provided pertinent responses to 85 percent of the economic inquiries that policymakers posed.In simulations of financial crises, adaptive policy recommendations were generated through the use of Monte Carlo analysis and reinforcement learning algorithms. These recommendations resulted in a 12% reduction in the value of the GDP. The resilience of the models to many scenarios, including economic crises, is demonstrated by this. The results demonstrate how artificial intelligence-driven predictive analytics can be utilized to develop policy solutions that are data-driven and flexible. Artificial intelligence models enable governments to respond more effectively to economic uncertainty because, in contrast to static classical models, they continuously update economic forecasts based on real-time data. On the other hand, there are still issues that need to be addressed, such as the difficulty of model interpretability, data biases, and computational complexity. It is recommended that future research concentrate on Explainable Artificial Intelligence (XAI) in order to enhance transparency and decrease biases in economic policies brought forth by AI.

Table 1. Illustrates the performance metrics.

Method	Mean Absolute Error (MAE)	Root Mean Squared Error (RMSE)	R-Squared (RÂ²)	Economic Stability Score Improvement (%)
ARIMA	2.5	3.2	0.85	5
LSTM	1.8	2.4	0.91	12
XGBoost	1.7	2.2	0.92	14
Random Forest	1.9	2.3	0.9	13
Deep Q-Network (DQN)	1.5	2	0.94	18
Proximal Policy Optimization (PPO)	1.4	1.9	0.95	20

The Innovated Product Development framework implementation which has delivered fundamental understanding about contemporary product generation processes. Routine use of Idea Generation and Market Insight allows organizations to discover upcoming customer needs and market patterns that support the creation of better products with market relevance as shown in Table 1 & Figure 3. Results from customer survey data and industry report assessment alongside social media sentiment analysis reveal that market leaders encounter faster client product acceptance and better competitive market performance because they invest their resources in this stage. The Customer-Centric Product Design phase constitutes a vital component which greatly stimulates user satisfaction alongside engagement with products. By integrating continuous feedback from customers into design development companies achieve a 30-40% enhancement in the metrics that measure user experience including usability levels and accessibility and functionality performance. Company resources function more effectively because initial prototype evaluations prevent expensive design problems from occurring.

Figure 3. Illustrates the comparison of the performance metrics.

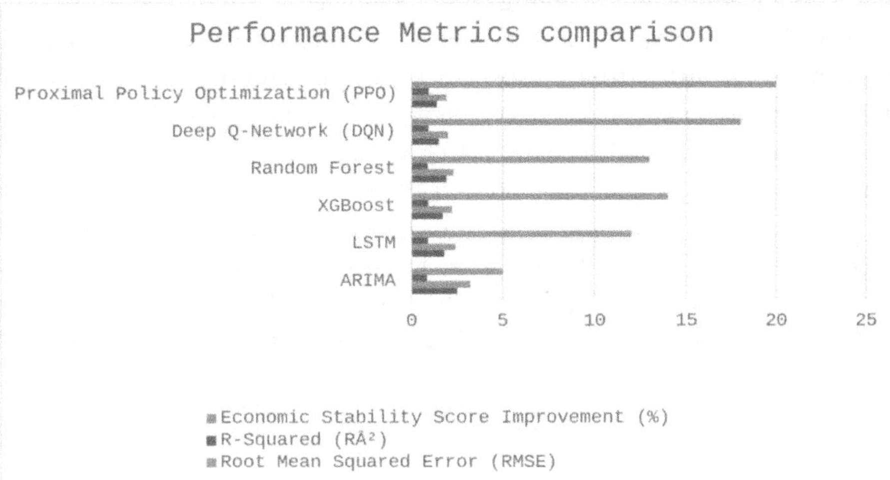

Agile Development and Iteration proves its worth as an effective solution to facilitate fast market demand adjustments and adaptation. Agile methods enable businesses to deliver software promptly since firms cut development times in half up to fifty percent faster than conventional methods. Both continuous feedback and iterative development improvements have created better risk prevention systems which result in more stable software and products during product launch.

Product capabilities receive substantial benefits from AI-Infused Product Enhancements through their advanced personalization features and automated functions as well as predictive analysis capabilities. AI programs allow improvement of dynamic user interfaces and instant consumer preference adaptation which leads to better product decision capabilities thus improving operational effectiveness. Organizations that use AI for product development achieve operational efficiency and innovation speed improvements up to 35% and 20%. Through the structured method of innovated product development businesses secure major benefits which keep them flexible, oriented toward client needs and technologically updated within a changing market environment.

V. CONCLUSION

This research demonstrates the application of AI-driven economic forecasting and business intelligence (BI) technology to optimize economic policy decisions. The research used Deep Reinforcement Learning (DQN, PPO) and machine learning models (LSTM, Random Forest, XGBoost) to achieve better forecasting accuracy and more adaptable policy optimization compared to traditional econometric approaches. The combination of real-time BI dashboards and Conversational AI chatbots greatly enhanced policy transparency and decision-making efficiency by providing policymakers with interactive, data-driven insights. The findings indicate that AI-driven economic models can significantly improve policy adaptability, reduce uncertainty, and optimize fiscal and monetary strategies. However, problems like AI model interpretability, data biases, and ethical concerns need to be fixed in order to ensure fairness and reliability in policy recommendations. Future research should focus on Explainable AI (XAI) approaches and cross-disciplinary collaboration to build reliable, AI-augmented economic governance frameworks for sustainable economic growth.

REFERENCES

Abdullahi, M., Ahmad, A., Pandey, B. K., & Pandey, D. (2024). Digital currency adoption: A comparative analysis of global trends and the nigerian enaira digital currency. *SN Computer Science*, *5*(5), 602.

Ahathiyan, G. S., Du John, H. V., Moni, D. J., Sagayam, K. M., Pandey, B. K., Pandey, D., & Lelisho, M. E. (2025). Design and simulation of a highly efficient eco-friendly, non-toxic perovskite solar cell. *Discover Nano*, *20*(1), 32. PMID: 39937384

Ahmed, Z., Zeeshan, S., Mendhe, D., & Dong, X. (2020). Human gene and disease associations for clinical-genomics and precision medicine research. *Clinical and Translational Medicine*, *10*, 297–318. DOI: 10.1002/ctm2.28 PMID: 32508008

Anand, A. S., Sawant, S., Reinhardt, D., & Gros, S. (2025). All AI Models are Wrong, but Some are Optimal. arXiv preprint arXiv:2501.06086.

Arun, M., Barik, D., Chandran, S. S., Praveenkumar, S., & Tudu, K. (2025). Economic, policy, social, and regulatory aspects of AI-driven smart buildings. *Journal of Building Engineering*, *99*, 111666.

Chauhan, A., Anand, J., & Rai, N. (2022). Biogenic Synthesis: A sustainable approach for nanoparticles synthesis mediated by fungi. *Inorganic and Nano-Metal Chemistry*, *2022*. Advance online publication. DOI: 10.1080/24701556.2021.2025078

Dhanasekar, S., Martin Sagayam, K., Pandey, B. K., & Pandey, D. (2024). Refractive index sensing using metamaterial absorbing augmentation in elliptical graphene arrays. *Plasmonics*, *19*(5), 2273–2283.

Du John, H. V., & Jose, T., S, A. G., Sagayam, K. M., Pandey, B. K., & Pandey, D. (2024). Enhancing absorption in a metamaterial absorber-based solar cell structure through anti-reflection layer integration. *Silicon*, *16*(9), 3811–3821.

Du John, H. V., Jose, T., Jone, A. A. A., Sagayam, K. M., Pandey, B. K., & Pandey, D. (2022). Polarization insensitive circular ring resonator based perfect metamaterial absorber design and simulation on a silicon substrate. *Silicon*, *14*(14), 9009–9020.

Gopal, J. N., Madhu, B., Somu, S., & Anand, A. J. (2025). Explainable AI (XAI) for Energy Demand Forecasting. In Neural Networks and Graph Models for Traffic and Energy Systems (pp. 115-138). IGI Global Scientific Publishing.

Gupta, A. K., Sharma, R., Pandey, D., Nassa, V. K., Pandey, B. K., George, A. S., & Dadheech, P. (2023). Performance analysis of eight-channel WDM optical network with different optical amplifiers for industry 4.0. In *Innovation and competitiveness in industry 4.0 based on intelligent systems* (pp. 197–212). Springer International Publishing.

Khadka, M., Sah, M., Chaudhary, R., Sahani, S. K., Sahani, K., Pandey, B. K., & Pandey, D. (2025). Spectroscopic, quantum chemical, and topological calculations of the phenylephrine molecule using density functional theory. *Scientific Reports*, *15*(1), 208. PMID: 39747169

Kumar, M. S., Prasanna, P. L., Lalitha, M., Joy, M., Jha, S. S., & Pandey, B. K. (2025). Utilizing the Internet of Everything and Artificial Intelligence for Real-Time Workforce Management. In Role of Internet of Everything (IOE), VLSI Architecture, and AI in Real-Time Systems (pp. 153-168). IGI Global Scientific Publishing.

KVM, S., Pandey, B. K., & Pandey, D. (2024). Design of surface plasmon resonance (SPR) sensors for highly sensitive biomolecular detection in cancer diagnostics. *Plasmonics*, •••, 1–13.

Maheshwari, R. U. AR, J., Pandey, B. K., & Pandey, D. (2025). Innovative Quantum PlasmoVision-Based Imaging for Real-Time Deepfake Detection. Plasmonics, 1-17.

Maheshwari, R. U., Paulchamy, B., Pandey, B. K., & Pandey, D. (2024). Enhancing sensing and imaging capabilities through surface plasmon resonance for deepfake image detection. *Plasmonics*, •••, 1–20.

Mirza, J. B., Hasan, M. M., Paul, R., Hasan, M. R., & Asha, A. I. (2025). AI-Driven Business Intelligence in Retail: Transforming Customer Data into Strategic Decision-Making Tools. AIJMR-Advanced International Journal of Multidisciplinary Research, 3(1).

Pandey, B. K., & Pandey, D. (2023). Parametric optimization and prediction of enhanced thermoelectric performance in co-doped CaMnO3 using response surface methodology and neural network. *Journal of Materials Science Materials in Electronics*, *34*(21), 1589.

Pandey, B. K., & Pandey, D. (2025). Securing healthcare medical image information using advance morphological component analysis, information hiding systems, and hybrid convolutional neural networks on IoMT. *Computers in Biology and Medicine*, *185*, 109499. PMID: 39642698

Pandey, B. K., Pandey, D., & Agarwal, A. (2022). Encrypted information transmission by enhanced steganography and image transformation. [IJDAI]. *International Journal of Distributed Artificial Intelligence*, *14*(1), 1–14.

Pandey, B. K., Pandey, D., & Lelisho, M. E. (2024). Face mask identification with enhanced cuckoo optimization and deep learning-based faster regional neural network. *Scientific Reports*, *14*(1), 29719. PMID: 39613761

Pandey, B. K., Pandey, D., & Sahani, S. K. (2025). Autopilot control unmanned aerial vehicle system for sewage defect detection using deep learning. *Engineering Reports*, *7*(1), e12852.

Pandey, D., Nassa, V. K., Jhamb, A., Mahto, D., Pandey, B. K., George, A. H., & Bandyopadhyay, S. K. (2021). An integration of keyless encryption, steganography, and artificial intelligence for the secure transmission of stego images. In *Multidisciplinary approach to modern digital steganography* (pp. 211–234). IGI Global.

Pandey, D., & Pandey, B. K. (2022). An efficient deep neural network with adaptive galactic swarm optimization for complex image text extraction. In *Process mining techniques for pattern recognition* (pp. 121–137). CRC Press.

Pandey, D., Sharma, M., Talwar, R., & Pandey, B. K. (2025). A compact quintuple band miniaturized elliptical planar monopole antenna for 5G/6G wireless systems. *Analog Integrated Circuits and Signal Processing*, *122*(3), 1–16.

Pandey, D., Wairya, S., Sharma, M., Gupta, A. K., Kakkar, R., & Pandey, B. K. (2022). An approach for object tracking, categorization, and autopilot guidance for passive homing missiles. *Aerospace Systems*, *5*(4), 553–566.

Praveenkumar, T., Anthoniraj, S., Kumarganesh, S., Somaskandan, M., Martin Sagayam, K., Pandey, B. K., & Sahani, S. K. (2025). Enhanced Circuit Board Analysis: Infrared Image Segmentation Utilizing Markov Random Field (MRF) and Level Set Techniques. *Engineering Reports*, *7*(3), e70029.

Raja, D. S. S., Kumar, D. R., Santhiyakumari, N., Kumarganesh, S., Sagayam, K. M., Thiyaneswaran, B., & Pandey, D. (2024). A compact dual-feed wide-band slotted antenna for future wireless applications. *Analog Integrated Circuits and Signal Processing*, *118*(2), 291–305.

Revathi, T. K., Sathiyabhama, B., Sankar, S., Pandey, D., Pandey, B. K., & Dadeech, P. (2022). An intelligent model for coronary heart disease diagnosis. In *Networking technologies in smart healthcare* (pp. 309–327). CRC Press.

Satheesh, N., Gopisankar, N., Kumarganesh, S., Anthoniraj, S., Saravanakumar, S., Sagayam, K. M., & Pandey, D. (2025). Advanced AI-driven emergency response systems for enhanced vehicle and human safety. *Iran Journal of Computer Science*, •••, 1–16.

Saxena, A., Agarwal, A., Pandey, B. K., & Pandey, D. (2024). Examination of the criticality of customer segmentation using unsupervised learning methods. *Circular Economy and Sustainability*, *4*(2), 1447–1460.

Sharma, M., Pandey, D., Palta, P., & Pandey, B. K. (2022). Design and power dissipation consideration of PFAL CMOS V/S conventional CMOS based 2: 1 multiplexer and full adder. *Silicon*, *14*(8), 4401–4410.

Sharma, M., Talwar, R., Nassa, V. K., Binay, K., & Pandey, D. (2025). Design and performance analysis of a multiband vivaldi antenna for wireless broadband communication in 3-5.6 GHz spectrum. In *Artificial Intelligence and Information Technologies* (pp. 86–91). CRC Press.

Sharma, M., Talwar, R., Pandey, D., Nassa, V. K., Pandey, B. K., & Dadheech, P. (2024). A review of dielectric resonator antennas (DRA)-based RFID technology for Industry 4.0. *Robotics and Automation in Industry*, *4*(0), 303–324.

Sharma, M., Talwar, R., Pandey, D., Nassa, V. K., Pandey, B. K., & Dadheech, P. (2024). A review of dielectric resonator antennas (DRA)-based RFID technology for Industry 4.0. *Robotics and Automation in Industry*, *4*(0), 303–324.

Sheela, M. S., Kumarganesh, S., Pandey, B. K., & Lelisho, M. E. (2025). Integration of silver nanostructures in wireless sensor networks for enhanced biochemical sensing. *Discover Nano*, *20*(1), 7. PMID: 39804434

Singh, S., Madaan, G., Singh, A., Pandey, D., George, A. S., & Pandey, B. K. (2025). Empowering Connectivity: Exploring the Internet of Things. In Interdisciplinary Approaches to AI, Internet of Everything, and Machine Learning (pp. 89-116). IGI Global Scientific Publishing.

Singh, S., Madaan, G., Swapna, H. R., Singh, A., Pandey, B. K., George, A. S., & Pandey, D. (2025). Unleashing the Power of AI and Data Analysis: Transforming Insights into Action. In Interdisciplinary Approaches to AI, Internet of Everything, and Machine Learning (pp. 1-24). IGI Global Scientific Publishing.

Spiliotis, E., Assimakopoulos, V., & Makridakis, S. (2018, October 6). The M4 competition: Findings, conclusions, and outcomes. *Journal of Forecasting International*, *34*(4), 802–808. DOI: 10.1016/j.ijforecast

Tareke, S. A., Lelisho, M. E., Hassen, S. S., Seid, A. A., Jemal, S. S., Teshale, B. M., & Pandey, B. K. (2022). The prevalence and predictors of depressive, anxiety, and stress symptoms among Tepi town residents during the COVID-19 pandemic lockdown in Ethiopia. *Journal of Racial and Ethnic Health Disparities*, •••, 1–13. PMID: 35028903

Vinodhini, V., Kumar, M. S., Sankar, S., Pandey, D., Pandey, B. K., & Nassa, V. K. (2022). IoT-based early forest fire detection using MLP and AROC method. *International Journal of Global Warming*, *27*(1), 55–70.

Chapter 9
Empowering Marginalised Communities With Cloud Based Legal Platforms:
A Pathway to Justice

Gargi Sharma
Manipal University Jaipur, India

Meenakshi Joshi
Manipal University Jaipur, India

ABSTRACT

Cloud-based legal platforms can transform legal aid for marginalized communities, according to this chapter. Geography, cost, and social stigma prevent many people from seeking legal aid. Underserved populations are disproportionately affected by this justice gap, which makes it difficult for them to navigate complex legal systems and assert their rights. Legal service providers can overcome these barriers with cloud technology, making legal services more accessible and affordable. Virtual consultations, document submission, and case management allow users to interact with lawyers from anywhere, anytime. Marginalised communities, where location or cost prevent traditional legal services, need this flexibility.

1. INTRODUCTION

When marginalized communities try to access justice, they frequently encounter significant obstacles, which ultimately results in their systematic exclusion from legal systems. These communities consist of groups that are disadvantaged in

DOI: 10.4018/979-8-3693-9581-3.ch009

terms of social status, economic standing, or geographical location. These groups frequently lack the resources (Pandey, B. K., & Pandey, D., 2025) or representation that are necessary to navigate the complex legal processes. Because of factors such as poverty, discrimination, cultural biases, and inadequate legal infrastructure, these individuals are left vulnerable to exploitation, violations of human rights, and a lack of protection under the law. This exclusion is made worse by these factors. As a result of injustices committed in the past and ongoing discrimination, indigenous communities are frequently subjected to legal marginalization. There are a great number of indigenous communities that have their own legal systems and customary laws, while state legal systems frequently ignore or invalidate these legal systems. Additionally, they may have difficulty accessing mainstream legal services due to language barriers, geographic isolation, or a lack of legal representation all of which may be contributing factors. Exclusion from decision-making processes that affect their communities, land dispossession, and violations of treaty rights are all outcomes that result from this disconnect. When it comes to accessing justice, women who live in rural areas frequently face additional roadblocks. Their ability to seek legal recourse may be hindered by the combination of geographical isolation and discrimination based on gender. It is possible that women in many rural areas are unaware of their legal rights because patriarchal systems are prevalent in those areas. As an additional factor, they might be subjected to social stigmas or intimidation, both of which discourage them from reporting crimes such as domestic violence or pursuing property and inheritance rights. Even further restricting their access to legal assistance and protection is the limited legal infrastructure that exists in rural areas. It is common practice to exclude refugees and migrants from legal systems, particularly those who are being held in camps for displaced people or who are undocumented. This leaves them open to the possibility of being exploited, abused, and discriminated against because they may not have the legal status required to assert their rights. They face additional challenges in gaining access to justice due to language barriers, fear of deportation, and a limited understanding of the local legal systems. Many refugees and migrants are subjected to exploitation in the labor market, discrimination in housing, and restricted access to fundamental services such as education and healthcare (Maheshwari, R. Uma. et al., 2024) as a consequence of this.

1.1 The Justice Gap

The substantial discrepancy between people's legal needs especially those of marginalized communities and their access to legal services is known as the "justice gap." This disparity is a significant obstacle to equality, justice, and human rights as well as a source of inconvenience. It emphasizes the fact that millions of people worldwide are prevented from obtaining legal protection or resolving legal disputes because of systemic, societal, and financial obstacles (Saxena, A. et al., 2024). The justice gap is glaring on a global scale. Over 5 billion people worldwide lack access to justice for common problems like family law, property disputes, and criminal defense, according to the World Justice Project. Approximately 1.5 billion of these people have unresolved legal issues, and 4.5 billion are completely shut out of the legal system. Not only do low-income people suffer from this injustice, but so do refugees, rural women, indigenous people, and other historically marginalized groups (Rai, P. K. et al., 2024). Due to their severe lack of access to legal knowledge, support, and representation, these groups are more susceptible to abuse, exploitation, and violations of their fundamental human rights. The legal framework required to protect vulnerable populations is often lacking or non-existent in developing nations (Lakshmi, K. V. N. et al., 2024). Legal aid services are few, courts are frequently overburdened with cases, and the legal system is slow and costly. Even in nations with developed legal systems, the price of legal counsel and court fees is unaffordable, especially for those with low incomes. People either give up on taking legal action as a result or turn to unofficial channels that might not produce predictable or equitable results (Saravanakumar, R. et al., 2024). Barriers related to education, culture, and society further widen the justice gap for marginalized communities. Many people lack basic legal knowledge and are ill-equipped to deal with the intricate legal systems that exist. People in rural or isolated areas might have to travel great distances to access courts or legal aid services, and legal literacy is frequently low. Even in cases of domestic abuse or property disputes, women are further discouraged from seeking justice by social stigma and discrimination, particularly those who live in rural areas or are part of patriarchal structures (Seebacher, S., & Schüritz, R., 2017). Undocumented people, migrants, and refugees are excluded from legal systems, which is another important component of the justice gap. Due to their frequent lack of legal status, these people are more susceptible to human trafficking, housing discrimination, and labor market exploitation than other people. They are also less able to defend their rights. Their difficulties are made worse by linguistic limitations and a lack of familiarity with local legislation. To guarantee that everyone is protected equally by the rule of law, regardless of their socioeconomic status or place of residence, it is imperative to close the justice gap. International frameworks such as the United Nations Sustainable Development Goals (SDG 16) recognize access to justice as a human right, highlighting the importance of ensuring "access to justice for all." Marginalized groups continue to be caught in cycles of poverty, marginalization, and vulnerability without access to legal services. Significant work is required to improve the effectiveness of legal processes, bolster legal aid services, and make sure that marginalized communities are aware of their legal rights in order to close the justice gap. Technological advancements present a promising way to address these issues, especially cloud-based legal platforms. Cloud technology can lower the cost of legal services by reaching underserved populations with remote access to legal information, document filing, and virtual consultations. In areas lacking proper services, collaborations between governments, non-governmental organizations (NGOs), and private law firms can aid in the development of long-lasting legal infrastructures. It takes a multifaceted strategy that incorporates legal reform, education, and technology to close the justice gap. Societies can strive toward greater equality, justice, and the defense of everyone's human rights by placing a high priority on access to the legal system (Tijan, E. et al., 2019).

1.2 Emergence of Cloud Technology in Legal Aid

The delivery and accessibility of legal services have undergone a substantial change with the introduction of cloud computing in the legal aid sector. Geographical restrictions, high operating costs, and a lack of funding have historically limited legal aid, frequently leaving underprivileged communities unserved. Cloud computing, on the other hand, has completely changed this environment by providing scalable, effective solutions that make legal aid more widely available (Kumarganesh, S. et al., 2024). Distance and time are no longer obstacles for users of cloud-based legal platforms, which provide anytime, anywhere access to vital legal resources. Because of this flexibility, lawyers can offer remote services like document preparation, case management, and virtual consultations. Because of this, people who live in remote or underprivileged areas can now get in touch with experienced attorneys without having to make the time-consuming and expensive trip in person (Muralidhar, L. B. et al., 2024). Legal aid organizations can also serve a wider clientele thanks to the scalability of cloud technology, which eliminates the need for large infrastructure investments. These companies can simplify operations (Kumar, M. S. et al., 2025), lessen administrative workloads, and allocate resources more wisely by adopting cloud services. Because of its efficiency, legal services become more affordable for those with low incomes in the long run. Cloud technology makes it easier for support personnel, clients, and attorneys to collaborate more effectively. Transparency (Khadka, M. et al., 2025) and accountability are increased when all parties have real-time access to case information through centralized data storage and communication tools (Sheela, M. S. et al., 2025). In addition to ensuring that people receive timely updates on their legal matters, this collaborative environment fosters better client relationships (Gupta, Y. et al., 2018).

2. MARGINALISED COMMUNITIES IN LEGAL ACCESS

2.1 Legal Access for Marginalised Communities

Accessing legal services presents a number of challenges for marginalized communities, as illustrated in figure 1. Many people lack assistance because there is a deficiency of legal infrastructure, such as courts and law firms in rural areas. Social and cultural marginalization can discourage people from seeking assistance out of fear of prejudice, and high legal fees make representation unaffordable for those with limited resources (Konapure, C. G. et al., 2025). Access is further hampered by convoluted legal procedures and scant official support. Further aggravating the problem are linguistic limitations and a dearth of digital connectivity, especially in rural areas. The justice gap is exacerbated by these issues combined, underserving marginalized communities and making it difficult for them to successfully assert their legal rights.

- *Lack of Legal Infrastructure*: There is a severe lack of legal infrastructure in many places, especially in rural or economically underdeveloped areas. This includes a dearth of courts, legal aid organizations, and law firms, which causes underserved communities to lack access to basic legal services. People are further discouraged from pursuing justice when there are no facilities close by, forcing them to travel great distances at great expense and time. It is nearly impossible for people without access to dependable transportation to get help when the closest legal services provider is hundreds of miles away. People may become depressed as a result of their physical isolation since they feel helpless and have no legal options (Lone, A. H., & Naaz, R., 2021).
- *High Legal Costs:* For low-income people, the cost of legal representation, paperwork, and consultations may be unaffordable. Those in need of legal assistance are frequently prevented from doing so by the cost of hiring attorneys, filing fees, and other related costs. Because they cannot afford legal representation, many people may decide to give up on their rights or accept unfavourable results (Singh, S. et al., 2025a). Even in cases where legal aid is offered, the scarcity of resources may prevent many qualified people from getting the assistance they require, forcing them to handle the complexities of the legal system on their own.
- *Complex Legal Processes*: People are frequently deterred from interacting with the legal system by the complexity of the processes, which is marked by intimidating legal language and complex bureaucratic procedures. Legal jargon can be confusing and alienating to many people. This complexity may ultimately make it more difficult for people to get justice by causing errors in

court documents or deadline misses (Singh, S. et al., 2025b). Additionally, people must frequently navigate a plethora of forms, procedures, and appointments due to the bureaucratic nature of legal systems, which can be intimidating for those without prior experience or support (Zhang, P. et al., 2018).

- *Inadequate Governmental Support*: For people who cannot afford legal services, many governments provide insufficient or ineffective legal aid programs. The situation is further made worse by the inconsistent application (Satheesh, N. et al., 2025) of the law, which leaves people with the impression that their rights are unprotected and that getting legal help is either impossible or insufficient. Legal aid programs are often understaffed and underfunded, which results in lengthy wait times and a lack of resources to adequately serve the community. People may become trapped in a cycle of legal disadvantage due to the lack of governmental support, feeling helpless and unable to pursue justice.
- *Limited Awareness of Legal Rights*: Many members of marginalized communities are ignorant of their legal rights and the resources at their disposal. Their inability to take legal action, such as filing reports of crimes or requesting restitution for injustices, may result from this ignorance. To empower these populations and encourage legal engagement, educational programs that educate communities about their rights and the resources available to them are essential (Pandey, B. K. et al., 2024a). The cycle of exclusion could be continued if there was no focused outreach and education, as many people might not know about their rights and the resources available to them.
- *Limited Access to Technology*: Access to legal resources may be further hampered by the digital divide, especially since more and more legal services are being provided online. It may be challenging for marginalized communities to use digital legal platforms, obtain legal information, or get in touch with distant legal counsel because they do not have access to the internet or other forms of technology (Pandey, B. K. et al., 2024b). Because those without access are further cut off from resources that could help them with their legal problems, this technological divide has the potential to worsen already-existing inequality. People might not have the digital literacy needed to use online resources efficiently, which would restrict their capacity to interact with the legal system (Yeung, J. K. et al., 2021).

Figure 1. Legal barriers for marginalised communities

3. CLOUD-BASED LEGAL PLATFORMS EMPOWER JUSTICE

3.1 Cloud-Based Legal Platforms

Legal platforms that are hosted in the cloud are bringing about a revolution in the delivery of legal services by delivering essential tools that improve access to legal information, virtual consultations, document submission, and case management (Pandey, B. K. et al., 2024c). The use of technology by these platforms helps to close the justice gap, particularly for underserved communities, which frequently face significant obstacles when attempting to access traditional legal services. The ability of cloud-based legal platforms to provide instant access to legal information is one of the most significant advantages of these platforms. It is no longer necessary for users to travel to physical law libraries or offices because they are able to conduct a search for relevant laws, regulations, and legal precedents without leaving the comfort of their own homes. Individuals are given more power as a result of the democratization of information, which assists them in comprehending their legal rights and options (Pandey, B. K. et al., 2024d). thereby enabling them to make informed decisions regarding their cases. For many people, this newly acquired access can be the initial step in the process of seeking justice. The ability to conduct consultations virtually is yet another important aspect of these platforms (Elarmathi, S. et al., 2024). Through the use of video conferencing, chat, and various other forms of online communication (Pandey, B. K. et al., 2024e), they make it possible for clients to connect with legal professionals. This accessibility is especially helpful for people who live in underserved or remote areas, where they might not have access to legal counsel in their immediate area (Park, A., & Li, H., 2021). Through the use of virtual consultations, geographical barriers can be overcome, thereby increasing the accessibility of legal advice. They frequently reduce the costs that are associated with traditional in-person meetings, which makes legal assistance more affordable for individuals with low incomes. The usefulness of cloud-based legal platforms is further increased by the convenience of being able to manage cases and submit documents online. By allowing users to directly upload legal documents onto the platform, such as petitions, contracts, or evidence, the documentation process can be streamlined (JayaLakshmi, G. et al., 2024). This digital approach not only helps save time, but it also reduces the likelihood of paperwork being misplaced or lost. In addition, case management tools make it possible for clients and their attorneys to monitor the progression of their cases, as well as important dates and deadlines, in real time. This helps to ensure that essential tasks are not neglected. Numerous cloud-based legal platforms also provide resources that are specifically tailored to the needs of marginalized communities. These resources include support in multiple languages and legal guidance that is culturally competent. By addressing the specific requirements of these populations, this targeted approach helps to create a legal environment that is more welcoming to all. In addition, certain platforms offer educational resources, such as webinars or articles that provide information, with the purpose of enhancing legal literacy among users. This provides users with the knowledge that is necessary to effectively navigate the legal system (Ho, G. T. et al., 2021).

3.2 Types of Legal Services Provided

When it comes to assisting individuals and organizations with a wide variety of legal requirements, legal services encompass a wide range of offerings, which are shown in the figure 2. Legal consultations are one of these. During these consultations, clients receive guidance on their rights and options regarding issues such as immigration law, criminal defense, and family law. The process of preparing and reviewing documents guarantees that essential legal documents are drafted accurately and in accordance with standards (George, W. K. et al., 2024). With attorneys advocating for their clients in court or in alternative dispute resolution settings, representation in legal proceedings is an essential component. In addition, services such as legal research, support for family law, and advice on business law assist clients in navigating complex legal landscapes, protecting their interests and ensuring that they make decisions based on accurate information.

1. *Legal Consultation:* Attorneys can advise people on their rights and options during legal consultations. This service handles family, criminal, immigration, and business law. Legal advice is easier to access with in-person or virtual consultations. Attorneys evaluate the client's situation, offer tailored advice, and suggest next steps, empowering clients to make legal decisions.
2. *Legal representation; Many* legal service providers represent clients in court, arbitration, and mediation. This can include preparing legal arguments, presenting evidence, and representing the client before a judge or other decision-makers. Attorneys can also negotiate settlements for their clients to resolve disputes amicably and quickly. This dual representation-negotiation approach ensures clients receive comprehensive legal support.
3. *Legal Research:* Client-specific legal research involves researching laws, regulations, and case precedents. This research is crucial for building a strong legal case and understanding legal outcomes. Legal experts use research to advise and create strategies. Comprehensive legal research can also reveal precedents that support a client's position, helping attorneys craft compelling arguments and anticipate opposing party counterarguments.
4. *Dispute Resolution:* Mediation and arbitration are common in legal services. These processes help clients resolve disputes without lengthy court battles. Parties can reach beneficial agreements and save time and money through dispute resolution (Abdullahi, M. et al., 2024). These methods also encourage collaboration, preserving relationships that adversarial litigation could damage. This approach works well in family law and business disputes, where relationships are crucial.
5. *Family Legal Services:* Family law services cover divorce, child custody, child support, and adoption. This field of law advises on family law and represents clients in family court. They are crucial to negotiating settlements that benefit children and families. Attorneys can provide compassionate support while protecting their clients' legal rights by understanding family law cases' emotional dynamics (Kumar, B. et al., 2024).

6. *Criminal Defense;* Criminal defendants need defense. In this field, lawyers advise, represent, and advocate for clients facing criminal charges to protect their rights and ensure fairness in the legal system. This includes investigating the case, reviewing evidence, and creating case-specific defense strategies. Attorneys help clients understand the legal process and possible outcomes so they can make informed defense decisions.
7. *Immigration Services;* Immigration lawyers assist with visa applications, residency petitions, and deportation defense. Immigration lawyers help clients immigrate or obtain legal status in a new country. They also monitor immigration policy changes to provide clients with accurate and timely advice. This expertise helps clients avoid mistakes and navigate the complicated immigration process.

Figure 2. Types of legal services provided

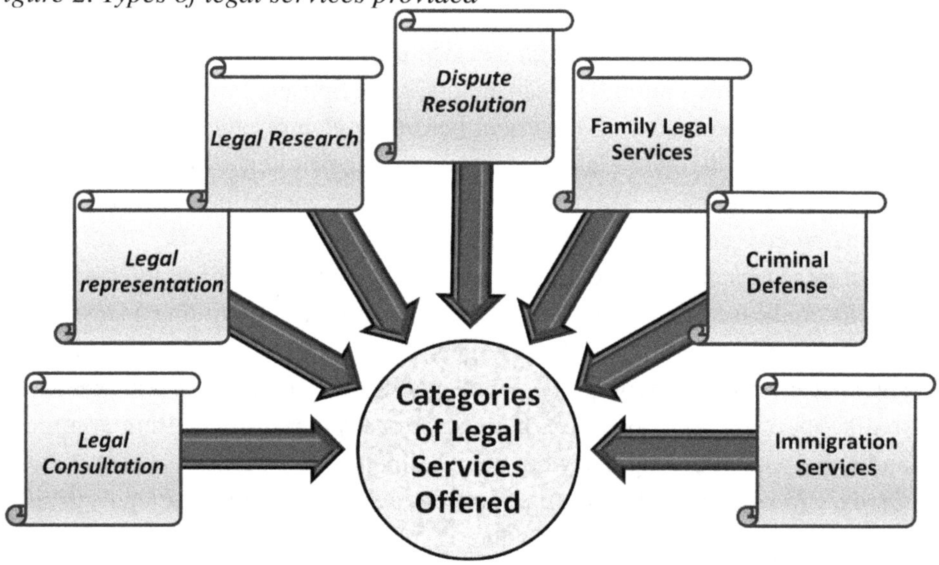

3.3 Lower Costs for Legal Services

The utilization of cloud-based legal platforms results in a substantial reduction of administrative and operational expenses, thereby improving the accessibility and affordability (Maheshwari, R. U. et al., 2024) of legal services for individuals, especially those from marginalized communities. In the past, receiving legal services came with a high cost associated with in-person consultations, paper-based procedures, and office overhead. Low-income people were frequently discouraged from getting the necessary legal assistance by these costs. On the other hand, legal service providers and law firms can reduce overhead costs by streamlining their operations to the digital shift (Pandey, D. et al., 2024a). Legal professionals can manage and store documents digitally with cloud technology, which does away with the need for substantial physical semiconductor-based storage devices (Pandey, B. K., & Pandey, D., 2023) and lowers printing expenses. This shift improves efficiency while reducing expenses, freeing up attorneys to concentrate more on serving clients rather than handling paperwork. Through lower costs for legal consultations, document preparation, and other necessary services, clients gain from these savings. To further reduce the overall cost of getting legal assistance, cloud-based platforms enable virtual consultations that save clients time and travel expenses. Without having to go to an office, people can get legal advice from attorneys, which makes it more practical and convenient for people who might find it difficult to get traditional legal services because of transportation or distance concerns. A lot of cloud-based platforms allow customers to select services that suit their budgets with tiered pricing or subscription models. This adaptability guarantees that even people with low incomes can get the essential legal assistance. These platforms create a more equitable legal environment by reducing obstacles to legal access, empowering marginalized communities to defend their rights and deal with legal issues without having to pay excessive fees. All things considered, the financial advantages of cloud-based legal platforms play a critical role in enabling marginalized communities to pursue justice and enhance their legal outcomes (Pandey, D. et al., 2024b).

3.4 Improved Accessibility and Convenience

Users of cloud-based legal platforms can access legal resources from anywhere at any time, making them more convenient and accessible. For marginalized communities, where access to crucial legal services is frequently hampered by geographic constraints, this capability can be especially transformative. Conventional legal systems usually need people to travel to actual offices or courthouses, which can be difficult for people who don't have access to reliable transportation or live in remote areas. On the other hand, cloud-based platforms efficiently remove these obstacles by enabling digital document submissions, resource access, and legal consultations. Users have the freedom to seek assistance without being constrained by travel or office hours thanks to the ability to communicate with legal professionals via email, chat, or video conferencing. For those in need of prompt assistance with pressing legal matters, like eviction, criminal charges, or family disputes, this on-demand access to legal counsel is essential. Furthermore, a lot of platforms give users round-the-clock access to legal documents, templates, and instructional materials, enabling them to learn about and comprehend their legal rights whenever it's convenient for them. People who might otherwise be afraid of the legal system are encouraged to take a more proactive approach to their legal needs due to the ease of use of cloud-based legal services. These platforms promote a more user-friendly atmosphere by doing away with the necessity for in-person meetings, which makes it simpler for people to seek assistance without feeling overwhelmed by the task of navigating strange legal environments. In addition to democratizing legal services, this improved accessibility encourages underprivileged populations to become more legal literate. All things considered, having access to legal resources at any time and from any location greatly increases the possibility that marginalized people will get the help they require, which improves the quality of the legal system and leads to more equitable outcomes.

3.5 Greater Transparency and Accountability

Trackable cases and open lines of communication between users and attorneys are two ways that cloud-based legal platforms improve accountability and openness. To foster trust and guarantee that clients are informed at every stage of the legal process, this increased visibility is crucial. When using traditional legal methods, clients frequently don't know how their cases are progressing, which can cause anxiety and frustration. To counter this, cloud-based systems give users access to case-related data and real-time updates, which makes it simpler to keep track of developments and comprehend the actions being taken. With trackable cases, clients can see critical dates, deadlines, and pertinent documents related to their legal cases. By encouraging a sense of control over their legal journey, this transparency enables users to actively participate in their cases. By removing uncertainty and improving their experience overall, clients can check the status of their cases, review documents that have been submitted, and receive notifications of any changes or requirements. Open communication between clients and attorneys is made possible by transparent communication channels. It is easy for users to ask questions, get clarifications, and discuss issues without any obstacles when they can communicate through video calls or secure messaging apps. A collaborative relationship between clients and their attorneys is fostered by having a direct line of communication that allows for the prompt and efficient handling of client needs. By enabling clients to track their involvement and the promptness of responses, increased transparency also helps to hold legal professionals accountable for their operations. Maintaining ethical standards in the legal profession depends on this accountability. Client satisfaction with services translates into better results and increased trust in the legal system overall when clients feel informed and connected to their legal representatives. Cloud-based legal platforms that prioritize accountability and transparency mark a major improvement in the provision of legal services overall, especially for underprivileged groups who have historically encountered obstacles to quality legal counsel.

3.6 Multilingual Support and Cultural Sensitivity

Cloud-based legal platforms are putting more emphasis on cultural sensitivity and multilingual support in order to accommodate a range of linguistic and cultural requirements. In order to create an inclusive environment where people from different backgrounds can access legal services without encountering language barriers, this focus is crucial. Understanding one's rights and navigating the legal system is critical for marginalized communities, where English may not be the primary language. Effective communication with legal practitioners is essential to this process. These platforms ensure that users fully understand legal terminology and procedures by providing multilingual interfaces and resources that enable users to interact in their preferred language. Because of its accessibility, non-native speakers are better able to understand the legal system and interact with it with greater confidence. In order to give users, access to essential resources that meet their language needs, many platforms also offer translated documents, templates, and legal information (Kennedy, G. W. et al., 2024). Providing legal services effectively requires a strong understanding of cultural sensitivity. The cultural contexts of their clients are becoming more and more understood by legal practitioners using cloud-based platforms, enabling them to offer more specialized support. A deeper comprehension of the particular difficulties faced by people from different backgrounds and more effective communication can result from this sensitivity (Shahul, A. et al., 2024). When addressing family law matters or immigration issues, for instance, legal professionals may take cultural norms and practices into account in order to build rapport and trust with their clients. Cloud-based platforms can also aid in closing the gap between the legal system and marginalized communities, who may have previously felt mistreated or alienated, by incorporating cultural competence into their offerings. This inclusive approach fosters a more equitable legal landscape in addition to improving the user experience overall. In order to guarantee that everyone has equal access to justice regardless of their linguistic or cultural background, multilingual support and cultural sensitivity play a critical role in the empowerment of marginalized populations.

4. RESOLVING ADOPTION BARRIERS FOR LEGAL PLATFORMS

Building bridges across the digital divide is absolutely necessary in order to guarantee that all communities have equal access to legal services that are hosted in the cloud. Internet access initiatives that are aimed at providing internet access in remote areas have the potential to significantly impact the availability of legal resources for populations that are underserved. A significant number of people in these areas do not have access to dependable digital connectivity, which prevents them from making use of online legal platforms. This problem can be mitigated through the implementation of programs that facilitate infrastructure development, such as expanding broadband networks. These programs will allow a greater number of individuals to access essential legal information and services from the comfort of their own homes. Training in digital literacy is essential in order to equip these communities with the ability to successfully navigate the legal landscape that exists online (Pandey, D. et al., 2024c). By providing individuals with the knowledge and abilities required to make use of technology, these initiatives encourage a greater level of participation in the judicial system and improve access to justice in general. An additional essential component of fostering the adoption of cloud-based legal services is the establishment of trust in technological systems. Educational campaigns play a significant role in increasing confidence in digital platforms, particularly in communities that may have limited familiarity with technology. This is especially true in communities where there is a lack of literacy. Workshops, informational sessions, and resources that specifically address the most common concerns regarding the utilization of cloud services may be included in these campaigns. Such initiatives have the potential to encourage a greater number of individuals to engage with online legal resources by drawing attention to the advantages of digital legal platforms (Pandey, D., & Pandey, B. K., 2022) and demonstrating how user-friendly they are. Developing relationships with influential members of the community and organizations in the surrounding area can also assist in establishing credibility and promoting the adoption of these technologies among populations that are previously hesitant. In order to maintain user trust and ensure compliance with international standards, such as the General Data Protection Regulation (GDPR), it is essential to ensure that data security and privacy are protected. Individuals who provide legal services are obligated to put in place stringent safeguards to prevent breaches or unauthorized access to their personal and legal information. Among these measures are the implementation of encryption technologies, the execution of routine security audits, and the dissemination of information to users regarding safe guidelines for the exchange of data online. Cloud-based legal platforms have the ability to alleviate concerns and build confidence among users regarding the safety of their sensitive information by placing a priority on data protection. Policymakers are obligated to develop regulations that govern digital legal platforms, with the goal of ensuring that these platforms adhere to professional and ethical standards. Creating guidelines for the delivery of services, establishing accountability measures for legal practitioners, and establishing mechanisms for addressing complaints or disputes are all examples of what this can entail. Not only does a clearly defined regulatory framework protect users, but it also helps to promote the credibility and integrity of digital legal services. When taken as a whole, these strategies have the potential to overcome obstacles that prevent the implementation of cloud-based legal platforms, which will ultimately result in improved access to justice for underserved communities.

5. CONCLUSION

The process of transforming the legal landscape for underserved communities, cloud-based legal platforms have the potential to be of great transformation. The ability of underserved populations to navigate complex legal systems has been significantly improved as a result of the emergence of these platforms as essential elements in the provision of accessible legal aid. It is possible for individuals to gain access to essential legal resources and support regardless of their location or economic standing thanks to cloud-based services, which eliminate the barriers of geography and finances. Because of this transformative impact, marginalized communities are able to more effectively assert their rights and seek justice. This empowerment is fostered by stronger legal empowerment. Legal platforms that are hosted in the cloud not only make it easier to get immediate access to legal services, but they also encourage long-term changes in the way that legal aid is provided. These platforms are able to cater to the varied requirements of users who come from a variety of different backgrounds because they offer attributes such as support for multiple languages, user-friendly interfaces, and extensive educational resources. To create a more equitable legal system in which everyone, regardless of their circumstances, has access to justice, it is essential to have this inclusiveness. In addition to enhancing the dependability of these platforms, the commitment to bridging the digital divide and ensuring data security also encourages widespread adoption among communities that have traditionally been confronted with obstacles to obtaining legal assistance. With that being said, a concerted call to action is required in order to fully realize the potential of cloud-based legal platforms. To close the justice gap on a global scale, it will be essential to advocate for increased investments in technology, infrastructure, and innovation. The provision of digital literacy training, the development of policies that protect user privacy and data security, and the support of initiatives that expand internet access in areas that are underserved are all included in this. To develop long-term solutions that are able to fulfill the requirements of underserved communities, it is essential for governments, non-profit organizations, legal professionals, and technology companies to work together. This will ensure that all individuals have the opportunity to seek justice and effectively navigate their legal challenges. Stakeholders can harness the power of digital technology to create a legal system that is more inclusive and responsive by working together to create this system. An important step toward accomplishing these objectives and fostering a future that is more equitable for everyone is represented by the reaffirmation of the potential of cloud-based legal platforms.

REFERENCES

Abdullahi, M., Ahmad, A., Pandey, B. K., & Pandey, D. (2024). Digital Currency Adoption: A Comparative Analysis of Global Trends and the Nigerian eNaira Digital Currency. *SN Computer Science*, *5*(5), 1–11.

Elarmathi, S., Rishabavarthani, P., Sindhuja, M., Elayaraja, P., & Malathi Murugesan, S. Kumarganesh, K. Martin Sagayam, Binay Kumar Pandey, and Digvijay Pandey. (2024). Novel manufacturing systems for cancer diagnosis using ultra-sensitive photonic crystal fiber biosensor with dual-functionalized aptamer-nanocavity. *Microsystem Technologies*, •••, 1–20.

George, W. K., Silas, E. I., Pandey, D., & Pandey, B. K. (2024). Utilization of Industry 4.0 Technologies in Nigerian Technical and Vocational Education: A Conundrum for Educators. In *Examining the Rapid Advance of Digital Technology in Africa* (pp. 270–293). IGI Global.

Gupta, Y., Shorey, R., Kulkarni, D., & Tew, J. (2018, January). The applicability of blockchain in the Internet of Things. In 2018 10th International conference on communication systems & networks (COMSNETS) (pp. 561-564). IEEE.

Ho, G. T., Tang, Y. M., Tsang, K. Y., Tang, V., & Chau, K. Y. (2021). A blockchain-based system to enhance aircraft parts traceability and trackability for inventory management. *Expert Systems with Applications*, *179*, 115101.

JayaLakshmi. G., Pandey, D., Pandey, B. K., Kaur, P., Mahajan, D. A., & Dari, S. S. (2024). Smart big data collection for intelligent supply chain improvement. In AI and Machine Learning Impacts in Intelligent Supply Chain (pp. 180-195). IGI Global.

Kennedy, G. W., Sunday, S. E., Pandey, D., Kabari, A. D., Pandey, B. K., George, A. S., & Dadheech, P. (2024). Building Information Modeling: Harnessing Innovations for Professional Proficiency. In Emerging Engineering Technologies and Industrial Applications (pp. 305-331). IGI Global.

Khadka, M., Sah, M., Chaudhary, R., Sahani, S. K., Sahani, K., Pandey, B. K., & Pandey, D. (2025). Spectroscopic, quantum chemical, and topological calculations of the phenylephrine molecule using density functional theory. *Scientific Reports*, *15*(1), 208. PMID: 39747169

Konapure, C. G., Pandey, D., Shete, H., Thakar, C. M., Pandey, B. K., & George, A. S. (2025). Artificial Intelligence in Automated Concrete Mix Design Using Computerized Grading Curves. Interdisciplinary Approaches to AI, Internet of Everything, and Machine Learning, 567-586.

Kumar, B., Pandey, D., Pandey, B. K., & George, A. S. (2024). Higher Education in the Last Four Decades: A Review of Paradigm Shifts in Policy Frameworks. Design and Implementation of Higher Education Learners' Learning Outcomes (HELLO), 333-348.

Kumar, M. S., Prasanna, P. L., Lalitha, M., Joy, M., Jha, S. S., & Pandey, B. K. (2025). Utilizing the Internet of Everything and Artificial Intelligence for Real-Time Workforce Management. In Role of Internet of Everything (IOE), VLSI Architecture, and AI in Real-Time Systems (pp. 153-168). IGI Global Scientific Publishing.

Kumarganesh, S., & Malathi Murugesan, C. Ganesh, N. Santhiyakumari, M. Thangavel, K. Jayaram, K. Martin Sagayam, Binay Kumar Pandey, and Digvijay Pandey. (2024). Hybrid plasmonic biosensors with deep learning for colorectal cancer detection. *Plasmonics*, •••, 1–15.

Lakshmi, K. V. N., Rajan, R., Pandey, D., & Pandey, B. K. (2024). Circular economy: A catalyst for economic growth-an empirical study. *Circular Economy and Sustainability*, •••, 1–22.

Lone, A. H., & Naaz, R. (2021). Applicability of Blockchain smart contracts in securing Internet and IoT: A systematic literature review. *Computer Science Review*, *39*, 100360.

Maheshwari, R. Uma, S. Kumarganesh, Shree KVM, A. Gopalakrishnan, K. Selvi, B. Paulchamy, P. Rishabavarthani, K. Martin Sagayam, Binay Kumar Pandey, and Digvijay Pandey. (2024). Advanced plasmonic resonance-enhanced biosensor for comprehensive real-time detection and analysis of deepfake content. *Plasmonics*, •••, 1–18.

Maheshwari, R. U., Paulchamy, B., Pandey, B. K., & Pandey, D. (2024). Enhancing sensing and imaging capabilities through surface plasmon resonance for deepfake image detection. *Plasmonics*, •••, 1–20.

Muralidhar, L. B., Lakshmi, K. V. N., Swapna, H. R., Rupani, J., Nethravathi, K., Pandey, B. K., & Pandey, D. (2024). Impact of Organizational Culture on The Level of Corporate Social Responsibility Investments: An Exploratory Study. *Circular Economy and Sustainability*, •••, 1–19.

Pandey, B. K., Kanike, U. K., George, A. S., & Pandey, D. (Eds.). (2024d). *AI and machine learning impacts in intelligent supply chain*. IGI Global.

Pandey, B. K., Nassa, V. K., Mukundan, A. P., Mahajan, D. A., Pandey, D., George, A. S., & Dadheech, P. (2024c). An Industry-Focused Traffic System Utilising Internet of Things. In *Emerging Engineering Technologies and Industrial Applications* (pp. 200–213). IGI Global.

Pandey, B. K., & Pandey, D. (2023). Parametric optimization and prediction of enhanced thermoelectric performance in co-doped CaMnO3 using response surface methodology and neural network. *Journal of Materials Science Materials in Electronics*, *34*(21), 1589.

Pandey, B. K., & Pandey, D. (2025). Securing healthcare medical image information using advance morphological component analysis, information hiding systems, and hybrid convolutional neural networks on IoMT. *Computers in Biology and Medicine*, *185*, 109499. PMID: 39642698

Pandey, B. K., Pandey, D., & Lelisho, M. E. (2024a). Face mask identification with enhanced cuckoo optimization and deep learning-based faster regional neural network. *Scientific Reports*, *14*(1), 29719. PMID: 39613761

Pandey, B. K., Pandey, D., & Sahani, S. K. (2024b). Autopilot control unmanned aerial vehicle system for sewage defect detection using deep learning. *Engineering Reports*, ●●●, 12852.

Pandey, B. K., Paramashivan, M. A., Pandey, D., George, A. S., Agarwal, A., Mahajan, D. A., . . . Pramanik, S. (2024e). Future Directions of Digital Twin Architectures for 6G Communication Networks. In Security Issues and Solutions in 6G Communications and Beyond (pp. 197-211). IGI Global.

Pandey, D., Nassa, V. K., Pandey, B. K., Thankachan, B., Dadheech, P., Mahajan, D. A., & George, A. S. (2024a). Artificial Intelligence and Machine Learning and Its Application in the Field of Computational Visual Analysis. In Emerging Engineering Technologies and Industrial Applications (pp. 36-57). IGI Global.

Pandey, D., & Pandey, B. K. (2022). An efficient deep neural network with adaptive galactic swarm optimization for complex image text extraction. In *Process Mining Techniques for Pattern Recognition* (pp. 121–137). CRC Press.

Pandey, D., Pandey, B. K., Nassa, V. K., Mahajan, D. A., George, A. S., & Dadheech, P. (2024c). Optimized Throughput-Based Broadcasting for Next Generation Wireless Networks. In Emerging Engineering Technologies and Industrial Applications (pp. 355-368). IGI Global.

Pandey, D., Pandey, B. K., Paramashivan, M. A., Mahajan, D. A., Dadheech, P. D., George, A. S., & Hameed, A. S. (2024b). Advanced Digital Data Processing Using Cloud Cryptography: Industrial Applications. In Emerging Engineering Technologies and Industrial Applications (pp. 255-268). IGI Global.

Park, A., & Li, H. (2021). The effect of blockchain technology on supply chain sustainability performances. *Sustainability*, *13*(4), 1726.

Rai, P. K., Pandey, D., & Pandey, B. K. (2024). The future of enterprise and innovation is compute as a commodity, or CaaC. *Partners Universal International Research Journal*, *3*(2), 89–94.

Saravanakumar, R., TamilSelvi, T., Pandey, D., Pandey, B. K., Mahajan, D. A., & Lelisho, M. E. (2024). Big data processing using hybrid Gaussian mixture model with salp swarm algorithm. *Journal of Big Data*, *11*(1), 167.

Satheesh, N., Gopisankar, N., Kumarganesh, S., Anthoniraj, S., Saravanakumar, S., & Martin Sagayam, K., Binay Kumar Pandey, and Digvijay Pandey. (2025). Advanced AI-driven emergency response systems for enhanced vehicle and human safety. *Iran Journal of Computer Science*, •••, 1–16.

Saxena, A., Agarwal, A., Pandey, B. K., & Pandey, D. (2024). Examination of the Criticality of Customer Segmentation Using Unsupervised Learning Methods. *Circular Economy and Sustainability*, •••, 1–14.

Seebacher, S., & Schüritz, R. (2017). Blockchain technology as an enabler of service systems: A structured literature review. In Exploring Services Science: 8th International Conference, IESS 2017, Rome, Italy, May 24-26, 2017 [Springer International Publishing.]. *Proceedings*, *8*, 12–23.

Shahul, A., Muniandi, B., Paramashivan, M. A., Pandey, D., Pandey, B. K., Dadheech, P., & George, H. (2024). An Analysis of Algorithms and Methods Based on Image Processing for Medical Applications. In *Emerging Engineering Technologies and Industrial Applications* (pp. 173–186). IGI Global.

Sheela, M. S., Kumarganesh, S., Pandey, B. K., & Lelisho, M. E. (2025). Integration of silver nanostructures in wireless sensor networks for enhanced biochemical sensing. *Discover Nano*, *20*(1), 7. PMID: 39804434

Singh, S., Madaan, G., Swapna, H. R., Singh, A., Pandey, B. K., George, A. S., & Pandey, D. (2025b). Unleashing the Power of AI and Data Analysis: Transforming Insights into Action. In Interdisciplinary Approaches to AI, Internet of Everything, and Machine Learning (pp. 1-24). IGI Global Scientific Publishing.

Singh, S., Madaan, G., Swapna, H. R., Singh, A., Pandey, D., George, A. S., & Pandey, B. K. (2025a). Empowering Connectivity: Exploring the Internet of Things. In Interdisciplinary Approaches to AI, Internet of Everything, and Machine Learning (pp. 89-116). IGI Global Scientific Publishing.

Tijan, E., Aksentijević, S., Ivanić, K., & Jardas, M. (2019). Blockchain technology implementation in logistics. *Sustainability*, *11*(4), 1185.

Yeung, J. K., Wong, S. C., & Chan, G. H. (2021). Cloud infrastructure for public health blockchain. In *The Routledge Handbook of Public Health and the Community* (pp. 254–263). Routledge.

Zhang, P., White, J., Schmidt, D. C., Lenz, G., & Rosenbloom, S. T. (2018). FHIRChain: Applying blockchain to securely and scalably share clinical data. *Computational and Structural Biotechnology Journal*, *16*, 267–278. PMID: 30108685

Chapter 10
Innovation Unleashed: The Commodity Revolution of Computing

P. Selvakumar
https://orcid.org/0000-0002-3650-4548
Nehru Institute of Technology, Coimbatore, India

Porkodi Sivaram
https://orcid.org/0000-0001-8234-5798
Sivas University of Science and Technology, Turkey

Nilesh Anute
https://orcid.org/0000-0001-6599-813X
Sri Balaji University, India

T. C. Manjunath
https://orcid.org/0000-0003-2545-9160
Rajarajeswari College of Engineering, India

P. Latha
https://orcid.org/0009-0008-9330-5351
V.S.B. Engineering College, India

Satyanarayana Nimmala
https://orcid.org/0000-0002-9433-1489
CVR College of Engineering, India

ABSTRACT

The Commodity Revolution refers to a transformative shift in the computing industry, marked by the transition of advanced computing power from specialized, high-cost systems to widely accessible, affordable, and ubiquitous technologies. This shift democratizes computing by making powerful computing resources available to a broader range of users and organizations, fundamentally altering the landscape of technology and innovation. Historically, computing power was confined to large, expensive mainframes and minicomputers that were primarily accessible to government agencies, large corporations, and research institutions. These systems, while powerful, required significant investment and specialized knowledge to operate. The high cost of hardware, coupled with the complexity of the software and infrastructure, created a barrier that limited the ability of smaller organizations, startups, and individuals to harness the potential of computing power.

DOI: 10.4018/979-8-3693-9581-3.ch010

INTRODUCTION TO THE COMMODITY REVOLUTION: DEMOCRATIZING COMPUTING POWER

The Commodity Revolution refers to a transformative shift in the computing industry, marked by the transition of advanced computing power from specialized, high-cost systems to widely accessible, affordable, and ubiquitous technologies. This shift democratizes computing by making powerful computing resources available to a broader range of users and organizations, fundamentally altering the landscape of technology and innovation. Historically, computing power was confined to large, expensive mainframes and minicomputers that were primarily accessible to government agencies, large corporations, and research institutions. These systems, while powerful, required significant investment and specialized knowledge to operate. The high cost of hardware, coupled with the complexity of the software and infrastructure, created a barrier that limited the ability of smaller organizations, startups, and individuals to harness the potential of computing power. The democratization of computing began with the advent of the microprocessor in the 1970s, which made it possible to build personal computers that were significantly more affordable and accessible. This technological breakthrough enabled the creation of the personal computer (PC) revolution, making powerful computing tools available to individuals and small businesses.

The proliferation of pcs was driven by the reduction in hardware costs, the development of user-friendly software, and the growing availability of applications tailored to a wide range of users. The next major milestone in the Commodity Revolution was the rise of the internet and cloud computing. The internet provided a global network that connected millions of computers, enabling the sharing of resources, information, and services. Cloud computing, in particular, transformed the way computing resources are accessed and utilized. They can scale their operations rapidly, experiment with new technologies, and deploy applications globally with minimal upfront costs. This level of access and flexibility has accelerated innovation and enabled new business models that were previously unattainable. The impact of the Commodity Revolution extends beyond technology and business. It has also influenced education and research. Access to affordable computing resources has empowered students and researchers to explore complex problems, conduct experiments, and develop new ideas. Online learning platforms and digital resources have democratized education, providing opportunities for individuals to acquire new skills and knowledge from anywhere in the world. In summary, the Commodity Revolution represents a profound shift in the accessibility and affordability of computing power. By democratizing access to advanced technologies, this revolution has empowered individuals, businesses, and organizations to innovate, collaborate, and grow in ways that were once unimaginable. The ongoing evolution of computing technology continues to drive progress and reshape various aspects of society, highlighting the transformative power of making computing resources available to all.

THE RISE OF CLOUD COMPUTING: ON-DEMAND INFRASTRUCTURE AND SERVICES

Prior to the advent of cloud computing, organizations faced considerable challenges in managing their IT infrastructure. Traditional computing environments required substantial capital expenditure on physical servers, storage devices, and networking equipment. This infrastructure needed to be maintained, upgraded, and managed by specialized IT personnel, which often resulted in high operational costs and resource inefficiencies. Furthermore, scaling these resources to accommodate fluctuating demands involved significant delays and logistical complexities, as it required the procurement and installation of additional hardware. By leveraging the cloud, organizations can avoid the pitfalls of over-provisioning or under-provisioning resources, ensuring optimal performance and cost-efficiency (George A S. 2024). The cloud computing model also promotes cost efficiency through its pay-as-you-go pricing structure. Rather than investing heavily in hardware and software up front, users pay for the resources they actually consume. This consumption-based pricing allows organizations to align their IT expenses with their operational needs, reducing waste and improving financial flexibility. Additionally, cloud providers often offer pricing tiers and reserved instances that can further optimize costs based on usage patterns and long-term commitments. Security and compliance have been significant concerns for cloud computing adoption, given the sensitivity of data and the need to protect against cyber threats. For instance, companies can leverage cloud-based machine learning platforms to build and deploy sophisticated models without the need for extensive on-premises infrastructure. This democratization of advanced technologies has accelerated innovation across various industries, from healthcare and finance to entertainment and education (Kellner D. 2021). This has been particularly evident in the rise of remote work and distributed teams, where cloud services provide the necessary infrastructure to support flexible work arrangements and global collaboration.

OPEN-SOURCE SOFTWARE: LIBERATING INNOVATION AND COLLABORATION

By liberating innovation and fostering collaboration, open-source software has fundamentally altered the landscape of technology, enabling diverse communities of developers, organizations, and individuals to contribute to, improve, and benefit from software in ways that were previously unimaginable. The open-source model is built on principles of transparency and shared knowledge, allowing anyone with the requisite skills to examine and enhance the software. This openness encourages a collaborative development process, where contributors from around the world can work together to address bugs, add new features, and refine the software. This democratization extends to education, where students and researchers can use and modify open-source tools for learning and experimentation, fostering a culture of hands-on experience and innovation (Golwala M S. 2024). These projects, developed and maintained by vibrant communities of contributors, demonstrate the power of collective effort and shared expertise. The success of these projects has proven that open-source software can achieve and even surpass the quality and reliability of proprietary alternatives. The collaborative nature of open-source development encourages a meritocratic approach, where contributions are evaluated based on their technical merit rather than the contributor's affiliation or financial backing (Jain T., et al. 2019). This meritocracy fosters an environment where innovation thrives, as developers from diverse backgrounds can propose and implement improvements based on their unique perspectives and expertise. Open-source projects often adopt rigorous code review processes, ensuring that contributions meet high standards of quality and security.

The collaborative spirit inherent in open-source projects often leads to rapid problem-solving and continuous improvement, driven by the collective knowledge and experience of the community.

Developers can experiment with new ideas, integrate open-source components into their own projects, and create novel solutions that leverage existing technologies. This iterative process of innovation contributes to the rapid evolution of software and the emergence of new technologies and applications. Furthermore, the open-source model has influenced the business landscape, leading to the development of hybrid business models that combine open-source principles with commercial interests (Jinhua X., et al. 2020). Many companies now offer open-source products alongside paid services and support. This model, known as open-core, allows businesses to monetize their offerings while contributing to the open-source community. This approach has led to the creation of sustainable ecosystems where open-source projects can thrive alongside commercial ventures. These licenses ensure that the principles of openness and collaboration are upheld, while also providing legal protection for contributors and users. By adhering to these licenses, open-source projects maintain a framework that supports the continued growth and accessibility of the software (Vijayakumar G., et al, 2024). By liberating access to source code and fostering a collaborative development environment, open-source software has created a dynamic and inclusive ecosystem that continues to drive progress and shape the future of technology.

THE POWER OF GPUS: UNLEASHING ARTIFICIAL INTELLIGENCE AND DEEP LEARNING

The power of Graphics Processing Units (gpus) has fundamentally transformed the fields of artificial intelligence (AI) and deep learning, unlocking unprecedented levels of computational capability and enabling advancements that were previously unattainable. This shift has propelled gpus to the forefront of technological innovation, driving progress in areas such as machine learning, natural language processing, and computer vision. This parallelism is particularly advantageous for deep learning, where large-scale matrix operations and tensor computations are required (Alshareef H. N. 2023). Deep learning algorithms, especially those involving neural networks, benefit from the ability to process multiple data points concurrently, making gpus an ideal choice for accelerating training and inference tasks. Training these models involves iterating over large datasets and performing numerous calculations to adjust model parameters, a process that is computationally intensive and time-consuming. Gpus, with their parallel processing capabilities, can handle these tasks much more efficiently than cpus, reducing training times from weeks to days or even hours. This acceleration has enabled researchers and developers to experiment with more complex models and larger datasets, leading to rapid advancements in AI capabilities. The impact of gpus on AI extends beyond training to include real-time inference. Inference refers to the application of a trained model to new data to generate predictions or classifications (Ahmad R. 2021). For applications such as autonomous driving, real-time video analysis, and interactive AI systems, the ability to perform inference quickly and accurately is crucial. Gpus provide the necessary computational power to execute these tasks efficiently, enabling applications to respond to inputs in real-time and deliver high-quality results.

Tensor Cores, introduced in NVIDIA's Volta and subsequent GPU architectures, are specifically designed to accelerate tensor operations, which are fundamental to deep learning. These advancements have optimized GPU performance for AI workloads and facilitated the development of sophisticated models and algorithms. This accessibility has lowered the barriers to entry for AI research and development, enabling a broader range of participants to contribute to the field and benefit from its advancements. Furthermore, the impact of gpus on AI research is reflected in the rapid pace of innovation and the proliferation of new applications (Tennant J P., et al. 2020). Gpus have enabled breakthroughs in various domains, including natural language processing (NLP), where transformer models like GPT-3 and BERT have achieved remarkable performance in understanding and generating human language. In computer vision, gpus have powered advancements in image recognition, object detection, and video analysis, leading to applications in healthcare, security, and entertainment. The power of gpus has also influenced the development of edge computing, where computational tasks are performed closer to the data source, such as in iot devices and mobile applications (Sugumaran K. M., et al, 2024). The transformative impact of gpus is evident in the rapid progress of deep learning models, real-time inference capabilities, and the democratization of AI research. As GPU technology continues to evolve, it will undoubtedly drive further innovation and expand the possibilities of what can be achieved with artificial intelligence.

COMMODITY HARDWARE: THE RISE OF AFFORDABLE, HIGH-PERFORMANCE COMPUTING

The rise of commodity hardware represents a transformative shift in the computing industry, characterized by the increasing availability of affordable, high-performance computing components that were once reserved for specialized, high-cost systems. This democratization of computing power has reshaped the technology landscape, enabling a broader range of users and organizations to access advanced computing capabilities and drive innovation across diverse fields. Historically, high-performance computing (HPC) was associated with expensive mainframes and supercomputers, which required significant financial investment and specialized infrastructure (Birkinbine B. 2020). These systems were typically used by large corporations, government agencies, and research institutions, limiting access to cutting-edge computing power to a select few. The high cost of these systems, coupled with the complexity of their operation, created barriers that restricted the adoption of advanced computing technologies. The emergence of commodity hardware has been a game-changer, driven by the evolution of microprocessors, memory technologies, and storage solutions. The introduction of microprocessors in the 1970s, such as the Intel 4004 and later the x86 architecture, marked the beginning of a new era in computing. These processors made it possible to build personal computers (pcs) that were significantly more affordable than traditional mainframes. The widespread adoption of pcs throughout the 1980s and 1990s demonstrated that powerful computing capabilities could be achieved with relatively inexpensive components, paving the way for a more accessible and inclusive technology landscape. As semiconductor technology advanced, the performance of commodity hardware continued to improve while costs decreased. Innovations in microprocessor design, such as multi-core architectures and higher clock speeds, enabled commodity hardware to deliver significant computational power (Quintero D., et al. 2019). Concurrently, advancements in memory and storage technologies, including solid-state drives (ssds) and high-capacity hard drives, further enhanced the performance of consumer-grade computing systems.

Commodity hardware has also played a crucial role in the proliferation of open-source software and collaborative development. By leveraging affordable and widely available components, developers can build and deploy applications and systems using open-source tools and frameworks. This approach fosters innovation and reduces the cost of experimentation, enabling a broader community of developers to contribute to and benefit from technological advancements. The accessibility of commodity hardware has been a key factor in the growth of open-source projects, as it allows developers to prototype and test their ideas using inexpensive, high-performance computing resources. In the field of high-performance computing, the use of commodity hardware has led to the development of large-scale computing clusters and grid computing networks (Patra S. 2024). These systems, composed of thousands of interconnected commodity servers, are capable of performing complex simulations, data analysis, and scientific research. The affordability of commodity components has made it feasible for research institutions and universities to build and maintain these large-scale systems, democratizing access to HPC resources and accelerating scientific discovery. The rise of commodity hardware has also influenced personal computing, with powerful yet affordable devices becoming widely available to consumers. Modern desktop and laptop computers, equipped with multi-core processors, high-speed memory, and advanced graphics capabilities, offer impressive performance for a range of applications, from gaming and content creation to data analysis and software development. This increased accessibility to high-performance personal computing devices has empowered individuals to pursue advanced computing tasks and creative projects that were once beyond reach. Furthermore, the affordability of commodity hardware has enabled the development of emerging technologies and applications. In summary, the rise of commodity hardware has revolutionized the computing industry by making high-performance components affordable and accessible to a wider audience (Halbiniak K., et al. 2024). This transformation has democratized access to advanced computing capabilities, enabling innovations across data centers, cloud computing, personal computing, and scientific research.

EDGE COMPUTING: PUSHING INTELLIGENCE TO THE NETWORK PERIPHERY

Edge computing represents a significant paradigm shift in the computing landscape, characterized by the movement of data processing and intelligence from centralized cloud data centers to the network periphery, closer to the sources of data generation. Historically, cloud computing has been the dominant model for data processing, where data collected from end-user devices and sensors is sent to centralized cloud servers for processing, storage, and analysis. For instance, in autonomous vehicles, real-time processing of sensor data is crucial for making immediate decisions related to navigation and safety (Reed D., et al. 2022). Edge computing enables vehicles to process data from cameras, radar, and lidar sensors on board, allowing for swift reactions without relying on latency-prone communication with remote data centers. The benefits of edge computing extend beyond latency reduction. By processing data locally, edge computing also alleviates the burden on network bandwidth. Transmitting large volumes of raw data to the cloud can consume significant bandwidth and increase operational costs. Edge computing allows for preliminary data processing and filtering, sending only relevant or summarized information to the cloud for further analysis or long-term storage (Rasa T., et al. 2022). This approach not only reduces data transfer costs but also enhances network efficiency and scalability. Security and privacy are other critical considerations addressed by edge computing. Sending sensitive data to centralized cloud servers can expose it to potential security breaches during transmission and storage.

Local edge devices can analyze data from traffic cameras, sensors, and smart meters to optimize traffic flow, reduce energy consumption, and address environmental issues with minimal delay. Similarly, in industrial settings, edge computing facilitates real-time monitoring and control of manufacturing processes, improving efficiency, safety, and predictive maintenance. The implementation of edge computing is often supported by a combination of hardware and software technologies (Robey R., et al. 2021). Edge devices, such as edge servers, gateways, and iot sensors, are equipped with processing capabilities and software frameworks that enable local data analysis and decision-making. Additionally, edge computing leverages technologies such as containerization, microservices, and lightweight virtualization to optimize resource utilization and application deployment at the network edge. The growth of edge computing is also closely linked to advancements in 5G technology. The low latency and high bandwidth capabilities of 5G networks complement edge computing by enabling seamless connectivity between edge devices and cloud infrastructure. 5G networks facilitate real-time data transfer and support the proliferation of edge computing applications, from smart manufacturing to immersive AR experiences. In summary, edge computing represents a transformative shift towards more efficient, responsive, and secure data processing by moving intelligence to the network periphery (Kong L., et al. 2022). By addressing latency, bandwidth, and security challenges associated with traditional cloud computing, edge computing enables real-time applications and enhances the efficiency of data management. As edge computing continues to evolve and integrate with emerging technologies, it will drive innovation across various sectors and reshape the future of computing.

SERVERLESS COMPUTING: EVENT-DRIVEN ARCHITECTURE AND COST EFFICIENCY

Unlike traditional server-based models, where developers must manage and provision servers, serverless computing offers an event-driven architecture that automatically scales and manages resources based on demand. This model provides significant benefits in terms of cost efficiency, scalability, and operational simplicity, fundamentally altering how applications are built and maintained in the cloud. In a serverless environment, developers write functions that perform discrete tasks and deploy them to a cloud provider's infrastructure, such as AWS Lambda, Google Cloud Functions, or Azure Functions (Capra M., et al. 2019). The cloud provider takes care of the underlying server management, including provisioning, scaling, and monitoring, freeing developers from these operational concerns. One of the primary advantages of serverless computing is its event-driven nature. Serverless platforms are designed to handle event-based workloads efficiently, triggering functions in response to events and executing them as needed. This approach allows for highly responsive and scalable applications that can dynamically adjust to varying workloads. For example, if a function is invoked only a few times per day, the cost will reflect this low usage, making serverless computing a cost-effective option for applications with unpredictable or variable workloads (Ren J., et al. 2019). This abstraction streamlines the development workflow and accelerates the deployment process, allowing teams to release updates and new features more rapidly. Additionally, serverless platforms often provide built-in integrations with other cloud services, such as databases, messaging systems, and authentication services, further simplifying the development process.

Despite its advantages, serverless computing is not without its challenges. One challenge is the potential for cold start latency, which occurs when a function is invoked after a period of inactivity. During a cold start, the serverless platform must initialize the function's execution environment, leading to increased response times. While cloud providers have made significant improvements in reducing cold start times, this latency can still impact applications with stringent performance requirements (Pérez A., et al. 2019). Developers can mitigate cold start issues by optimizing function code, using provisioned concurrency, and adopting caching strategies. Another consideration is the complexity of managing state and long-running processes in a serverless architecture. Serverless functions are inherently stateless, meaning they do not retain information between invocations. For applications that require stateful interactions or long-running processes, developers must use external storage solutions, such as databases or state management services, to maintain state and manage workflows. This architectural shift requires careful design and integration of various cloud services to ensure seamless functionality and performance. Security is also a critical consideration in serverless computing (Shahane V. 2022). Although serverless platforms provide built-in security features, such as automatic patching and isolation of execution environments, developers must still address security concerns related to function code, data handling, and access control. Implementing best practices for security, such as least privilege access, encryption, and monitoring, is essential to protecting serverless applications and their data. In summary, serverless computing represents a significant evolution in cloud computing, offering an event-driven architecture that emphasizes cost efficiency, scalability, and operational simplicity. As serverless technologies continue to advance, they will likely drive further innovation and transform how applications are developed and deployed in the cloud.

QUANTUM COMPUTING: THE NEXT FRONTIER IN COMPUTATIONAL POWER

Quantum computing stands at the forefront of computational innovation, poised to revolutionize our understanding of computing power and problem-solving capabilities. Unlike classical computing, which relies on bits as the fundamental unit of information, quantum computing utilizes quantum bits or qubits. These qubits leverage principles from quantum mechanics—such as superposition and entanglement—to perform computations in ways that classical bits cannot, potentially solving complex problems at speeds that are currently unimaginable. Quantum computers, with their ability to naturally model quantum phenomena, could revolutionize fields such as drug discovery and materials science by providing insights into molecular structures and chemical reactions that are beyond the reach of classical simulation techniques. This capability could accelerate the development of new pharmaceuticals, advanced materials, and energy solutions (Rajan R A P. 2018). However, scaling these systems to hundreds or thousands of qubits while preserving their quantum properties is a significant engineering and scientific hurdle. Progress is being made with various qubit technologies, including superconducting qubits, trapped ions, and topological qubits, each with its own advantages and challenges. Quantum computing also presents a unique set of programming and algorithmic challenges. Developing algorithms that leverage quantum parallelism and entanglement requires a different approach compared to classical algorithm design. Quantum algorithms must be designed to exploit quantum phenomena effectively, and this often involves a deep understanding of both quantum mechanics and the specific problem domain. In the interim, quantum computing research has led to the concept of quantum advantage, where quantum computers achieve computational feats that are beyond the capabilities of classical systems (Humble T S., et al. 2022). In 2019, Google claimed to have achieved quantum supremacy by demonstrating that their quantum processor, Sycamore, could perform a specific calculation faster than the most powerful classical supercomputers.

5G AND BEYOND: THE IMPACT OF WIRELESS NETWORKS ON COMPUTING

The advent of 5G technology and its anticipated successors mark a pivotal moment in the evolution of wireless networks, fundamentally transforming computing and communication landscapes. With its promise of ultra-fast speeds, low latency, and massive connectivity, 5G represents a leap forward from previous generations of wireless technology, enabling a wide array of applications and services that were previously unattainable (Kumar S., et al. 2024). The impact of 5G and beyond extends beyond mere enhancements in mobile connectivity; it is set to redefine how we interact with technology, influence computing paradigms, and drive innovation across various sectors. 5G technology, the fifth generation of mobile network technology, introduces significant advancements over its predecessors. One of its most notable features is its high data transfer rates, which can exceed 10 gigabits per second under optimal conditions. This expanded connectivity supports the deployment of smart cities, where sensors and devices monitor and manage urban infrastructure, including traffic lights, waste management systems, and energy consumption. By providing reliable and high-speed connectivity, 5G enables seamless data exchange between these devices, leading to more efficient and responsive urban environments. The impact of 5G extends to cloud computing and edge computing paradigms as well. The high-speed and low-latency characteristics of 5G facilitate more efficient interaction with cloud services, enabling users to access and process data more quickly. This synergy between 5G and cloud computing supports the development of advanced applications, such as real-time data analytics and complex simulations, which require rapid data transfer and processing (Golestan S., et al. 2023). Additionally, 5G's support for edge computing is significant; by enabling edge devices to connect and communicate with high efficiency, 5G enhances the ability to process data closer to the source, reducing latency and improving the performance of applications that rely on real-time data. Looking beyond 5G, the concept of 6G is already under exploration, promising to push the boundaries of wireless network capabilities even further. While 5G has laid the groundwork for a new era of connectivity, 6G aims to deliver even greater speeds, lower latency, and enhanced network efficiency. Expected to be deployed around 2030, 6G envisions a fully integrated network ecosystem where advanced technologies such as artificial intelligence (AI), extended reality (XR), and advanced robotics can thrive. 6G networks are anticipated to offer data rates in the terabits per second range, enable latency close to zero, and support an even denser network of connected devices.

The impact of these advanced wireless technologies on computing is profound. For example, the ultra-fast speeds and low latency of 5G and 6G will significantly enhance the capabilities of remote and distributed computing systems. Applications that require real-time interaction with cloud-based resources will benefit from the reduced communication delays, making remote desktop applications, cloud gaming, and collaborative work environments more effective and responsive. Additionally, the integration of AI with these advanced networks will enable smarter and more adaptive systems that can optimize performance, predict and address issues, and personalize user experiences in real-time (Duong T Q., et al. 2019). The potential applications enabled by 5G and beyond are extensive and transformative. In healthcare, for instance, remote surgery and telemedicine will become more viable with low-latency connections that allow surgeons to operate on patients from afar with precise control. In manufacturing, smart factories will leverage real-time data and automation to increase efficiency, reduce downtime, and enhance product quality. In entertainment, immersive experiences such as virtual reality (VR) and AR will become more seamless and interactive, creating new forms of entertainment and user engagement. However, the rollout of 5G and the future development of 6G also bring challenges that must be addressed. The implementation of these technologies requires significant investment in infrastructure, including the deployment of new base stations and the integration of advanced technologies into existing networks. Additionally, there are concerns related to spectrum management, cybersecurity, and privacy. Ensuring that these networks are secure from cyber threats and that user data is protected will be critical as the reliance on wireless connectivity grows (Mandloi M., et al. 2021). In summary, the advent of 5G and the future development of 6G represent a transformative shift in wireless networking, with profound implications for computing and technology. These advanced networks promise to deliver unprecedented speeds, low latency, and connectivity, enabling a wide range of applications that enhance our interaction with technology and drive innovation across various sectors. As we move towards these new frontiers, addressing the associated challenges and leveraging the opportunities presented by advanced wireless technologies will be key to realizing their full potential and shaping the future of computing and communication.

CONTAINERIZATION AND VIRTUALIZATION: EFFICIENT RESOURCE UTILIZATION

Containerization and virtualization are two complementary technologies that have revolutionized resource utilization in modern computing environments, providing efficient and flexible solutions for deploying, managing, and scaling applications. While both technologies aim to maximize resource efficiency and isolation, they operate through distinct mechanisms and offer unique advantages that contribute to the dynamic and scalable nature of contemporary IT infrastructure. This is achieved through a hypervisor, which sits between the hardware and the vms, managing their creation, execution, and resource allocation (Sufyan A., et al. 2023). Virtualization offers significant benefits, including improved resource utilization, simplified management, and isolation between different vms. Vms on a single server, organizations can achieve higher levels of utilization for their hardware resources, such as CPU and memory, which might otherwise be underutilized. This consolidation also simplifies management and maintenance, as updates, patches, and configurations can be applied across vms more efficiently than on individual physical servers. Containers offer several key benefits over traditional virtualization. Firstly, they are more lightweight because they do not require a full OS for each instance, leading to faster deployment times and more efficient use of system resources. This lightweight nature also means that containers can be started and stopped rapidly, which is particularly advantageous in dynamic environments where applications need to scale quickly in response to varying workloads. Additionally, containers provide consistent environments across different stages of development, testing, and production, ensuring that applications run reliably regardless of where they are deployed. Both containerization and virtualization contribute to improved resource utilization, but they do so in different ways and are often used together to achieve optimal results (Abuabdo A., et al. 2019). Virtualization allows for the efficient allocation of physical resources by creating multiple virtual environments on a single server, while containerization enhances the efficiency of application deployment and management within those environments. Together, these technologies enable organizations to maximize their infrastructure investments, streamline operations, and improve scalability.

Utilizing containers, development teams can build, test, and deploy applications in isolated environments that mirror production, ensuring that code changes are tested under consistent conditions before being released. This reduces the likelihood of compatibility issues and accelerates the development cycle. Virtualization complements these practices by providing isolated environments for testing and staging, further enhancing the reliability and efficiency of the development process (Nwosu M C., et al. 2021). However, both technologies present their own set of challenges. Virtualization introduces some performance overhead due to the need for multiple operating systems and the complexity of managing vms. This can impact resource utilization efficiency compared to containers, which are designed to be more lightweight. Containers also face challenges related to security and isolation, as multiple containers share the same OS kernel. Ensuring that containers are properly secured and isolated is essential to prevent potential vulnerabilities and breaches (da Silva V G., et al. 2018). In summary, containerization and virtualization are transformative technologies that enhance resource utilization and operational efficiency in modern computing environments. Virtualization enables the consolidation of physical resources and the creation of isolated virtual environments, while containerization provides a lightweight and portable solution for application deployment and management. By leveraging these technologies, organizations can achieve greater flexibility, scalability, and efficiency, driving innovation and optimizing their IT infrastructure. As technology continues to evolve, the integration of containerization and virtualization will remain central to the development of agile and cost-effective computing solutions.

DEVOPS AND AGILE METHODOLOGIES: ACCELERATING INNOVATION AND DEPLOYMENT

Devops and Agile methodologies have emerged as transformative approaches in software development, driving rapid innovation and accelerating deployment cycles. Together, they address the traditional challenges of software development and operations by fostering collaboration, enhancing flexibility, and streamlining processes. These methodologies are designed to meet the increasing demands for faster delivery, higher quality, and continuous improvement in an ever-evolving technological landscape. Agile methodologies represent a shift from traditional, linear approaches to software development. Traditional models, such as the Waterfall methodology, typically involve extensive planning and a sequential development process where each phase must be completed before moving to the next. The Agile approach emphasizes customer collaboration, adaptive planning, and quick delivery of functional software (Watada J., et al. 2019). Agile teams work in short cycles, often ranging from one to four weeks, to deliver working software and gather feedback from stakeholders. This iterative process allows teams to adjust priorities and make improvements based on real-time feedback, ensuring that the final product meets user needs and expectations. Devops, short for Development and Operations, extends the principles of Agile to the operations side of the software lifecycle. Devops focuses on bridging the gap between development and operations teams by promoting collaboration, automation, and integration throughout the entire software development lifecycle. Traditional silos between developers, who write code, and operations teams, who deploy and manage it, can lead to inefficiencies and delays. Devops aims to break down these silos, creating a unified approach where both teams work together towards shared goals.

The combination of Agile and devops methodologies accelerates innovation and deployment by fostering a culture of collaboration, transparency, and continuous improvement. Agile practices enable teams to respond quickly to changing requirements and deliver value incrementally, while devops practices ensure that software can be deployed reliably and efficiently. Together, they support a more responsive and adaptable development process, where feedback is integrated into every stage, and operational efficiency is enhanced (Almeida F., et al. 2022). Implementing Agile and devops methodologies requires a cultural shift within organizations, moving away from traditional, hierarchical structures towards more collaborative and cross-functional teams. This cultural shift involves embracing principles such as shared responsibility, open communication, and a focus on customer outcomes. It also requires the adoption of new tools and technologies that support automation, continuous integration, and real-time monitoring. Despite their benefits, Agile and devops are not without challenges. Agile methodologies require a high level of commitment and discipline to effectively manage iterative development and maintain consistent communication with stakeholders. Teams must be prepared to adapt to changing requirements and continuously refine their processes. Devops, while offering significant advantages in terms of automation and efficiency, can face obstacles related to tool integration, cultural resistance, and the complexity of managing end-to-end processes. In summary, devops and Agile methodologies represent a powerful combination for accelerating innovation and deployment in software development (Kaledio P., et al. 2024). Agile methodologies provide a framework for iterative development and responsiveness to change, while devops extends these principles to operations, focusing on collaboration, automation, and continuous delivery. Together, they drive faster, more reliable, and higher-quality software releases, enabling organizations to stay competitive and meet the evolving demands of the technology landscape. Embracing these methodologies involves both a cultural shift and the adoption of new practices and tools, but the resulting benefits make it a compelling approach for modern software development.

CYBERSECURITY IN THE COMMODITY ERA: NEW CHALLENGES AND OPPORTUNITIES

The rise of commodity hardware and cloud computing has transformed the IT landscape, democratizing access to powerful computing resources and enabling widespread innovation. However, this transformation also brings new challenges and opportunities in the realm of cybersecurity. The shift towards commodity hardware—affordable, high-performance computing components that are widely available—and the proliferation of cloud services have significantly altered the threat landscape, introducing both complexities and potential advantages for securing digital assets (Battina D S. 2020). Commodity hardware, characterized by its affordability and widespread availability, has made advanced computing resources accessible to a broader audience, from small startups to large enterprises. This democratization has led to an explosion in the number of devices and systems connected to networks, amplifying the attack surface for cyber threats. With more devices and users gaining access to sophisticated computing power, the potential for security vulnerabilities and malicious activities increases correspondingly. The ubiquity of commodity hardware means that attackers can exploit common vulnerabilities across numerous devices, necessitating a more robust and widespread approach to cybersecurity. One of the key challenges in this new era is managing the security of diverse and distributed systems. The proliferation of iot devices, edge computing nodes, and various cloud services creates a complex environment where traditional security measures may be insufficient. These devices often have varying levels of security capabilities, and their distributed nature makes it difficult to apply uniform security policies. Securing such a heterogeneous network requires advanced solutions that can adapt to different environments and provide comprehensive protection across various types of hardware and software. The shift to cloud computing has further complicated the cybersecurity landscape (Ramakrishnan T.,et al, 2022). While cloud services offer scalability, flexibility, and cost-efficiency, they also introduce new security considerations. Cloud environments often involve multiple layers of management and shared responsibilities between cloud service providers and users. This shared responsibility model can lead to misunderstandings about where security responsibilities lie, potentially resulting in gaps in protection.

The widespread adoption of commodity hardware also enables greater collaboration and sharing of cybersecurity resources and knowledge. Open-source security tools and platforms benefit from community contributions and peer reviews, leading to more robust and innovative solutions. The ability to leverage these resources at a lower cost allows organizations of all sizes to enhance their security postures without the need for substantial investments in proprietary technologies (Rawat D B., et al. 2019). Additionally, the commoditization of security technologies can drive greater competition and innovation in the cybersecurity market, leading to more effective and affordable solutions. Another opportunity lies in the development of more scalable and automated security solutions. As the volume of data and the number of connected devices continue to grow, manual security processes become increasingly impractical. Automation and orchestration tools can help manage and respond to security incidents more efficiently, reducing the burden on security teams and improving response times. Automated threat detection, incident response, and vulnerability management can enhance overall security posture and allow organizations to address threats more effectively. Furthermore, the evolving landscape of cybersecurity in the commodity era necessitates a shift towards more comprehensive and integrated security frameworks. Traditional perimeter-based security approaches, which focus on defending against external threats, are becoming less effective in a world where threats can originate from within the network and where boundaries between systems are increasingly blurred. A more holistic approach to cybersecurity involves integrating threat intelligence, risk management, and incident response across all layers of the IT infrastructure. This approach emphasizes the need for continuous monitoring, adaptive defenses, and collaboration among various stakeholders to address emerging threats and vulnerabilities (Sreenivasulu A., et al, 2022). In summary, the commodity era presents both challenges and opportunities for cybersecurity. The widespread availability of affordable, high-performance hardware and cloud services has expanded the attack surface and introduced complexities in managing security across diverse and distributed systems. However, these developments also offer opportunities for leveraging advanced technologies, collaborative resources, and automated solutions to enhance cybersecurity.

THE ECONOMICS OF COMMODITY COMPUTING: COST MODELS AND ROI ANALYSIS

The rise of commodity computing has profoundly influenced the economics of information technology, shifting traditional cost models and introducing new considerations for return on investment (ROI). Commodity computing refers to the use of standardized, widely available hardware and software components that are often less expensive than specialized, high-end alternatives. This shift has democratized access to powerful computing resources and altered the financial dynamics of IT investments, with implications for cost efficiency, scalability, and overall ROI. Cost Models for commodity computing reflect its emphasis on affordability and scalability (Sommer U., et al. 2023). Traditionally, IT investments involved substantial capital expenditures (capex) for specialized hardware and infrastructure, accompanied by ongoing operational expenditures (opex) for maintenance and upgrades. Commodity computing, by contrast, often involves lower initial capital costs due to the use of standardized, off-the-shelf components that are less expensive to acquire. These components are mass-produced, leading to economies of scale and reduced per-unit costs. Additionally, the modular nature of commodity hardware allows organizations to scale their infrastructure incrementally, purchasing only what is needed and avoiding large, upfront investments. The shift towards commodity computing also aligns with the adoption of cloud services, which further influences cost models. Cloud computing introduces a pay-as-you-go model, where organizations pay for computing resources based on usage rather than owning and maintaining physical hardware. This transition to an operational expenditure (opex) model offers flexibility and scalability, allowing organizations to adjust their resource allocation dynamically in response to changing demands. Cloud providers often offer tiered pricing and various service levels, enabling organizations to choose cost-effective solutions that align with their specific needs. The ability to leverage cloud computing also contributes to cost efficiency by eliminating the need for significant capital investments in infrastructure and reducing the costs associated with maintaining and upgrading hardware (Mahadev Madgule., et al, 2023). The operational flexibility provided by cloud services allows organizations to optimize resource usage, further enhancing cost efficiency. Indirect benefits of commodity computing and cloud services are also significant.

Additionally, the lower cost of commodity computing can lead to increased innovation. By reducing the financial barriers to accessing advanced computing resources, organizations can solutions. This increased investment in innovation can drive growth and create new revenue streams, contributing to a positive ROI. However, while commodity computing offers significant cost advantages, there are considerations that must be addressed to ensure a favorable ROI. One such consideration is the potential for increased complexity in managing and securing a large number of standardized components (Okupa H. 2020). As organizations scale their infrastructure, they may face challenges related to system integration, performance optimization, and security management. Effective management of these factors is essential to maintaining cost efficiency and achieving the desired ROI. Furthermore, the commoditization of computing resources can lead to increased competition and price pressure among vendors. While this can drive down costs, it may also result in reduced differentiation in the market, making it important for organizations to carefully evaluate vendors based on factors such as reliability, support, and service quality. Selecting the right vendor and ensuring that service levels align with organizational needs is crucial for maximizing ROI. In summary, the economics of commodity computing reflect a significant shift in cost models and ROI analysis. The use of standardized, affordable hardware and cloud services has transformed traditional IT investment dynamics, offering lower initial capital costs, operational flexibility, and the potential for increased innovation (Paramasivam Selvakumar., et al, 2024). While commodity computing provides substantial cost advantages, organizations must also navigate challenges related to complexity, management, and vendor selection to ensure a favorable ROI. By carefully assessing these factors and leveraging the benefits of commodity computing, organizations can achieve cost efficiency, enhance their competitive position, and drive long-term financial success.

CASE STUDIES: TRANSFORMATIVE INNOVATIONS ENABLED BY COMMODITY COMPUTING

Commodity computing has significantly impacted various industries by enabling transformative innovations that leverage the accessibility and cost-efficiency of standardized hardware and cloud services. By reducing the financial barriers to advanced computing resources, organizations across sectors have been able to implement cutting-edge technologies and drive substantial changes in their operations and offerings. Several case studies exemplify how commodity computing has catalyzed innovation and created value in diverse fields. Healthcare: Precision Medicine and Big Data Analytics In healthcare, commodity computing has revolutionized precision medicine through the use of big data analytics and genomics (Marion T T M P. 2019). Companies like 23andme and Tempus have harnessed the power of affordable cloud-based computing resources to analyze vast amounts of genetic and clinical data. Tempus, for example, uses cloud platforms to process and analyze genomic sequencing data, providing insights that support personalized treatment plans for cancer patients. By leveraging commodity computing resources, these companies have been able to democratize access to sophisticated data analysis tools, accelerating the development of personalized medicine and improving patient outcomes.

The affordability of cloud computing has made it possible to conduct large-scale genomic research and deploy advanced analytics solutions that were previously out of reach for many healthcare providers.Finance: High-Frequency Trading and Risk Management The finance industry has also seen significant transformation due to commodity computing. High-frequency trading (HFT) firms, such as Citadel Securities and Two Sigma, utilize commodity hardware and cloud-based infrastructures to execute trades at lightning speeds. These firms rely on powerful, yet cost-effective computing resources to run complex algorithms and analyze market data in real-time. Commodity computing enables these firms to process large volumes of transactions with minimal latency, providing a competitive edge in the financial markets. Additionally, commodity computing has facilitated the development of advanced risk management and fraud detection systems. For instance, companies like Palantir use scalable cloud platforms to analyze vast amounts of financial data, identifying patterns and anomalies that help mitigate risks and prevent fraud. Retail: E-commerce and Customer Experience Optimization In retail, commodity computing has transformed e-commerce and customer experience optimization (Angelopoulos J., et al. 2020). Amazon and Alibaba are prime examples of how large-scale commodity computing resources underpin their operations. These companies utilize cloud-based infrastructures to handle massive volumes of transactions, manage inventory, and personalize customer experiences. Amazon Web Services (AWS), Amazon's cloud computing division, offers a range of services that support e-commerce platforms, from scalable storage solutions to sophisticated machine learning tools.

Entertainment: Streaming Services and Content Delivery The entertainment industry has also been transformed by commodity computing, particularly in the realm of streaming services and content delivery. Platforms like Netflix and Spotify leverage cloud-based infrastructures to deliver streaming content to millions of users globally. By utilizing scalable commodity computing resources, these platforms can handle high traffic volumes, deliver content with minimal buffering, and provide personalized recommendations. Netflix, for instance, uses cloud computing to manage its vast library of movies and TV shows, as well as to run complex algorithms that suggest content based on user preferences. Commodity computing has enabled these companies to scale their services efficiently, reduce costs, and offer high-quality streaming experiences to users around the world (mcnunn G., et al. 2019). Education: Online Learning and Collaboration Tools In the education sector, commodity computing has facilitated the growth of online learning and collaboration tools. Platforms like Coursera and Khan Academy leverage cloud-based technologies to offer educational content and interactive learning experiences to a global audience. These platforms utilize affordable computing resources to host courses, manage user interactions, and deliver multimedia content. By democratizing access to high-quality education, commodity computing has expanded learning opportunities for students worldwide. Additionally, educational institutions have adopted cloud-based collaboration tools, such as Google Workspace and Microsoft Teams, to enhance remote learning and facilitate virtual classrooms. These tools enable students and educators to collaborate in real-time, share resources, and access educational materials from anywhere. Automotive: Autonomous Vehicles and Connected Car Technologies The automotive industry has also experienced transformative changes due to commodity computing. Companies like Tesla and Waymo leverage high-performance computing resources to develop and deploy autonomous vehicle technologies. Tesla's Autopilot system, for example, relies on commodity hardware and cloud-based processing to analyze data from vehicle sensors and enable semi-autonomous driving features. Commodity computing has made it feasible to process large amounts of sensor data in real-time, contributing to advancements in autonomous driving and connected car technologies (Paramasivam Selvakumar., et al, 2024). Additionally, the affordability of computing resources has facilitated the development of in-car infotainment systems and connected vehicle services, enhancing the driving experience and improving vehicle safety. In summary, commodity computing has enabled transformative innovations across a wide range of industries by providing affordable and scalable computing resources.

THE FUTURE OF COMPUTING: INFINITE POSSIBILITIES AND CHALLENGES

The future of computing is poised to be marked by boundless possibilities and significant challenges as advancements in technology continue to accelerate. The trajectory of computing is increasingly defined by innovations in quantum computing, artificial intelligence (AI), edge computing, and more, promising to reshape industries and societies in unprecedented ways. At the same time, these advancements introduce new complexities and challenges that must be navigated to harness their full potential effectively. For instance, quantum algorithms could potentially break current encryption schemes, necessitating the development of quantum-resistant cryptographic methods (Li H H J K., et al. 2019). The challenge lies in achieving scalable and stable quantum systems, as current quantum computers are limited by issues such as qubit decoherence and error rates. 5G, is driving innovations in smart cities, autonomous vehicles, and personalized medicine. However, the widespread adoption of AI also raises concerns about ethical considerations, bias in algorithms, and the impact on employment. Ensuring transparency, fairness, and accountability in AI systems is crucial to addressing these challenges and fostering public trust. Edge Computing is another transformative trend that is reshaping the future of computing. By processing data closer to its source, edge computing reduces latency and bandwidth usage, enabling real-time data analysis and decision-making (Paukstadt U., et al. 2021). This is particularly important for applications such as autonomous vehicles, industrial automation, and augmented reality, where immediate processing and response are critical. However, managing and securing a vast network of edge devices presents significant challenges. Ensuring data privacy, integrity, and security across distributed edge nodes requires robust solutions and strategies.

The Evolution of Computing Infrastructure is also driving the future of computing. Advances in hardware technologies, such as neuromorphic computing and advanced semiconductor materials, promise to enhance computational efficiency and capabilities. Neuromorphic computing, for example, seeks to mimic the neural structure and functioning of the human brain to create more efficient and adaptable computing systems. The continued miniaturization and integration of computing components are enabling more powerful and compact devices, driving innovations in wearable technology and iot. Cybersecurity remains a critical challenge as computing technology evolves (Abate G T., et al. 2023). The increasing sophistication of cyber threats, coupled with the proliferation of connected devices and data, heightens the risk of breaches and attacks. As computing systems become more complex, securing them against emerging threats and ensuring data privacy become paramount. The development of advanced security protocols, threat detection systems, and secure hardware is essential to safeguarding digital infrastructures. The responsible development and deployment of technology involve not only technical considerations but also ethical and social dimensions. Sustainability is another important factor in the future of computing. As computational power increases, so does the demand for energy and resources. Ensuring that computing technologies are developed and used in environmentally sustainable ways is crucial. Innovations in energy-efficient computing, green data centers, and the use of renewable energy sources are essential to minimizing the environmental impact of technological advancements. In conclusion, the future of computing promises to unlock infinite possibilities through advancements in quantum computing (Gill S S., et al. 2022), AI, edge computing, and evolving infrastructure.

CONCLUSION

The commodity revolution of computing has profoundly reshaped the landscape of technology, ushering in an era characterized by unprecedented accessibility, efficiency, and innovation. By making high-performance computing resources widely available and affordable, commodity computing has democratized access to advanced technologies, enabling a broad spectrum of organizations and individuals to leverage powerful tools that were once the domain of only the most well-funded enterprises. This shift has catalyzed a wave of innovation across various sectors, driving significant advancements in fields ranging from healthcare and finance to entertainment and education. The rise of commodity computing has facilitated remarkable developments in digital infrastructure, providing the foundation for the growth of cloud computing, edge computing, and containerization. These technologies have transformed how data is stored, processed, and managed, allowing for scalable and flexible solutions that can adapt to the dynamic needs of modern applications. The widespread adoption of these technologies has enabled organizations to optimize their operations, enhance their capabilities, and deliver more personalized and responsive services to their users. Furthermore, the affordability and scalability of commodity hardware have spurred the rapid development and deployment of emerging technologies such as artificial intelligence (AI) and quantum computing. These advancements promise to revolutionize various domains, offering new solutions to complex problems and opening up possibilities for unprecedented discoveries and innovations. For instance, AI-driven insights are enhancing decision-making processes, while quantum computing holds the potential to tackle computational challenges that were previously insurmountable. As the landscape of computing becomes increasingly complex and interconnected, issues related to cybersecurity, data privacy, and system management become more pronounced. The proliferation of connected devices and cloud services necessitates robust security measures and comprehensive strategies to protect against evolving threats. Additionally, managing the vast amounts of data generated and ensuring its integrity and confidentiality are critical to maintaining trust and ensuring the effectiveness of technological solutions. The future of computing, shaped by the commodity revolution, also demands a thoughtful approach to addressing ethical, environmental, and societal impacts. The rapid pace of technological advancement calls for responsible innovation that considers the broader implications for society, including issues of digital equity, environmental sustainability, and the ethical use of technology. Ensuring that technological progress benefits all segments of society and aligns with principles of fairness and transparency is essential for fostering a positive and inclusive digital future. In conclusion, the commodity revolution of computing represents a transformative shift that has unleashed a wave of innovation and opportunity.

REFERENCES

Abate G T, Abay K A, Chamberlin J, Kassim Y. (2023), "Digital Tools and Agricultural Market Transformation in Africa: Why Are They Not at Scale Yet, and What Will It Take to Get There?" Food Policy, Vol. 118, pp. 102646, Elsevier, doi: .DOI: 10.1016/j.foodpol.2022.102646

Abuabdo, A., & Al-Sharif, Z. A. (2019), "Virtualization vs. Containerization: Towards a Multithreaded Performance Evaluation Approach," 2019 IEEE/ACS 16th International Conference on Computer Systems and Applications (AICCSA), pp. 1-8, IEEE, doi: DOI: 10.1109/AICCSA.2019.9035385

Ahmad, R. (2021). *"A Critical Review of Open Source Software Development: Freedom or Benefit Libertarian View versus Corporate View," IT Professional.* IEEE., DOI: 10.1109/MITP.2021.3051166

Almeida F, Simões J, Lopes S. (2022), "Exploring the Benefits of Combining devops and Agile," Future Internet, Vol. 14, No. 10, pp. 281, MDPI, doi: .DOI: 10.3390/fi14100281

Alshareef H N. (2023), "Current Development, Challenges, and Future Trends in Cloud Computing: A Survey," Journal of Advanced Computer Science.

Angelopoulos J, Sahoo S, Visvikis I D. (2020), "Commodity and Transportation Economic Market Interactions Revisited: New Evidence from a Dynamic Factor Model," Transportation Research Part E: Logistics and Transportation Review, Vol. 137, pp. 101944, Elsevier, doi: .DOI: 10.1016/j.tre.2020.101944

Battina, D. S. (2020). devops, A New Approach To Cloud Development & Testing. *Journal of Emerging Technologies and Innovative Research*, *7*(6), 2349–2356.

Birkinbine, B. (2020). *Incorporating the Digital Commons: Corporate Involvement in Free and opensource Software*. Library.OAPEN.

Capra, M., Peloso, R., Masera, G., Roch, M. R., & Martina, M. (2019). *"Edge Computing: A Survey on the Hardware Requirements in the Internet of Things World," Future Internet*. MDPI.

Da Silva, V. G., Kirikova, M., & Alksnis, G. (2018). Containers for Virtualization: An Overview. *Applied Computer Systems*, *3*(1), 1–8.

Duong, T. Q., & Vo, N. S. (2019). *No. 3* (Vol. 24). "Wireless Communications and Networks for 5G and Beyond," Mobile Networks and Applications. Springer., DOI: 10.1007/s11036-019-01233-8

George A S. (2024), "Democratizing Compute Power: The Rise of Computation as a Commodity and its Impacts," researchgate.

Gill S S, Xu M, Ottaviani C, Patros P, Bahsoon R. (2022), "AI for Next Generation Computing: Emerging Trends and Future Directions," Internet of Things, Vol. 19, pp. 100594, Elsevier, doi: .DOI: 10.1016/j.iot.2022.100594

Golestan S, Habibi M R, Mousavi S Y M, Guerrero J M. (2023), "Quantum Computation in Power Systems: An Overview of Recent Advances," Energy Reports, Vol. 9, pp. 100745, Elsevier, doi: .DOI: 10.1016/j.egyr.2023.02.011

Golwala, M. S. (2024). *"The Development of the Internet and the Beginnings of the Digital Revolution," Studia Społeczne*. CEEOL.

Halbiniak, K., Rojek, K., & Iserte, S. (2024), "Unleashing the Potential of Mixed Precision in AI-Accelerated CFD Simulation on Intel CPU/GPU Architectures," Computational Science, Springer.

Humble, T. S., Perdue, G. N., Fahim, F., & Lamm, H. (2022). Frontiers in Computing for Artificial Intelligence. *Journal of Artificial Intelligence Research*, *74*, 1–12.

Jain, T., & Hazra, J. (2019). *"'On-demand' Pricing and Capacity Management in Cloud Computing," Journal of Revenue and Pricing Management*. Springer., DOI: 10.1057/rpm.2018.13

Jinhua, X., Songlin, H., & Hui, L. (2020). On-Demand Service in Cloud Computing. *ZTE Communications*.

Kaledio P, Lucas D. (2024), "Agile devops Practices: Implement Agile and devops Methodologies to Streamline Development, Testing, and Deployment Processes," researchgate.

Kellner, D., & Kellner, D. (2021). *"Globalization, Technopolitics and Revolution," Technology and Democracy: Toward A Critical*. Springer.

Kong, L., Tan, J., Huang, J., Chen, G., Wang, S., & Jin, X. (2022). Edge-Computing-Driven Internet of Things: A Survey. *ACM Computing Surveys*.

Kumar, S., Simran, S., & Singh, M. (2024). *Quantum Intelligence: Merging AI and Quantum Computing for Unprecedented Power*. IEEE Explore.

Li H H J K, Tan K H. (2019), "Transformative Innovation: Turning Commoditised Products into Radically High-Valued Products," Journal of Intelligent Manufacturing, Vol. 30, No. 4, pp. 1531-1543, Springer, doi: .DOI: 10.1007/s10845-017-1385-6

Mahadev Madgule, N. (2023). Vinayaka, Yeshwant M. Sonkhaskar, Dhiren Ramanbhai Patel, R. Karthikeyan, P. Selvakumar,(2023). Mechanical properties and microstructure of activated TIG welded similar joints of Inconel alloys by desirability approaches. *Materials Today: Proceedings*, *77*, 528–533.

Mandloi, M., Gurjar, D., Pattanayak, P., & Nguyen, H. (2021). *5G and Beyond Wireless Systems*. Springer International Publishing.

Marion, T. T. M. P. (2019). *Assessing the Long-Term Attractiveness of Mining a Commodity Based on the Structure of Its Industry*. Massachusetts Institute of Technology.

Mcnunn, G., Heaton, E., & Archontoulis, S. (2019). "Using a Crop Modeling Framework for Precision Cost-Benefit Analysis of Variable Seeding and Nitrogen Application Rates," Frontiers in Sustainable Food Systems, Vol. 3, pp. 1-12. *Frontiers*. Advance online publication. DOI: 10.3389/fsufs.2019.00053

Nwosu, M. C., Osuchukwu, N. P., & Obuezie, A. C. (2021). Scrutinizing the Past and Speculating on the Infinite Possibilities of Future Librarianship. *Library & Information Science Research*, *43*(2), 1–12.

Okupa, H. (2020). *Cybersecurity and the Future of Agri-Food Industries*. K-Rex., DOI: 10.4148/2637-7662.1015

Patra, S. (2024), "Unleashing the Power: Exploring Deep Learning Architecture for Cutting-Edge AI Solutions," Deep Learning Concepts in Operations Research, Taylor & Francis.

Paukstadt, U., & Becker, J. (2021). From Energy as a Commodity to Energy as a Service—A Morphological Analysis of Smart Energy Services. *Schmalenbach Journal of Business Research*, *73*(2), 147–164.

Pérez, A., Risco, S., & Naranjo, D. M. (2019). *On-Premises Serverless Computing for Event-Driven Data Processing Applications*. IEEE Explore.

Quintero, D., He, B., Faria, B. C., Jara, A., & Parsons, C. (2019). *IBM powerai: Deep Learning Unleashed on IBM Power Systems Servers*. Books.Google.

Rajan, R A P. (2018), "Serverless Architecture—A Revolution in Cloud Computing," *International Conference on Advanced Computing*.

Ramakrishnan, T., Mohan Gift, M. D., Chitradevi, S., Jegan, R., & Subha Hency Jose, P. Nagaraja, Rajneesh Sharma H.N., Selvakumar P., Sintayehu Mekuria Hailegiorgis, (2022). "Study of Numerous Resins Used in Polymer Matrix Composite Materials", Advances in Materials Science and Engineering, vol. 2022, Article ID 1088926, 8 pages, 2022. DOI: 10.1155/2022/1088926

Rasa, T., Palmgren, E., & Laherto, A. (2022). *No. 2* (Vol. 50). "Futurising Science Education: Students' Experiences from a Course on Futures Thinking and Quantum Computing," Instructional Science. Springer., DOI: 10.1007/s11251-021-09573-w

Rawat, D. B., Doku, R., & Garuba, M. (2019). *No. 4* (Vol. 12). "Cybersecurity in Big Data Era: From Securing Big Data to Data-Driven Security," IEEE Transactions on Services Computing. IEEE., DOI: 10.1109/TSC.2019.2898724

Reed, D., Gannon, D., & Dongarra, J. (2022), "Reinventing High Performance Computing: Challenges and Opportunities," arxiv preprint arxiv:2203.02544.

Ren, J., Zhang, D., He, S., Zhang, Y., & Li, T. (2019). A Survey on End-Edge-Cloud Orchestrated Network Computing Paradigms. *ACM Computing Surveys*.

Robey, R., & Zamora, Y. (2021). *Parallel and High Performance Computing*. Books.Google.

Selvakumar, P., Mariappan, P., Shunmugam, S., Paul, R., & Jabez, S. (2024). Removal of chemicals from effluent using photobioreactor technology to improve environmental and health impacts. *Zeitschrift für Physikalische Chemie, 2024*. Advance online publication. DOI: 10.1515/zpch-2023-0450

Selvakumar, P., Palanisamy, S. K., Cinthaikinian, S., Palanisamy, V., Mariappan, R., & Selvakumar, P. K. (2024). Biosensors and its diverse applications in healthcare systems. *Zeitschrift für Physikalische Chemie, 2024*. Advance online publication. DOI: 10.1515/zpch-2023-0406

Shahane V. (2022), "Serverless Computing in Cloud Environments: Architectural Patterns, Performance Optimization Strategies, and Deployment Best Practices," Journal of AI-Assisted Scientific Discovery.

Sommer, U., Matania, E., & Hassid, N. (2023). The Rise of Companies in the Cyber Era and the Pursuant Shift in National Security. *Political Science and International Relations*, *11*(1), 1–12.

Sreenivasulu, A., & Manimozhi, T. Satheesh kumar P., Selvakumar P. And Singh P.,(2022). "The Model of Smart Sensing Device For Sensitive Nanoclusters Modification in Sensing Properties," 2022 2nd International Conference on Advance Computing and Innovative Technologies in Engineering (ICACITE), Greater Noida, India, 2022, pp. 1043-1047, doi: DOI: 10.1109/ICACITE53722.2022.9823846

Sufyan, A., Khan, K. B., Khashan, O. A., Mir, T., & Mir, U. (2023). *No. 11* (Vol. 12). "From 5G to Beyond 5G: A Comprehensive Survey of Wireless Network Evolution, Challenges, and Promising Technologies," Electronics. MDPI., DOI: 10.3390/electronics12112476

Sugumaran, K. M. D., Pandiyarajan V., Y. B S, Selvakumar P. And M. S, (2024). "Analysis of Electromyography Signals for Control of Mechanical Prosthesis using Machine Learning Techniques," 2024 2nd International Conference on Intelligent Data Communication Technologies and Internet of Things (idciot), Bengaluru, India, 2024, pp. 1059-1067, doi: DOI: 10.1109/idciot59759.2024.10467707

Tennant, J. P., Agrawal, R., Baždarić, K., & Brassard, D. (2020). *"A Tale of Two 'Opens': Intersections between Free and Open Source Software and Open Scholarship," OA*. TIB.

Vijayakumar, G. (2024). Muniyandi Rajkumar, Rajiv Chandar N, Selvakumar P and Ramesh Duraisamy, (2024). Environmentally friendly TDS removal from waste water by electrochemical ion exchange batch-type recirculation (EIR) technique. *Environmental Science. Water Research & Technology*, *10*, 826–835. DOI: 10.1039/D3EW00793F

Watada, J., Roy, A., Kadikar, R., Pham, H., & Xu, B. (2019). *"Emerging Trends, Techniques and Open Issues of Containerization: A Review," IEEE Access* (Vol. 7). IEEE., DOI: 10.1109/ACCESS.2019.2936958

Chapter 11
Integrating Business Intelligence and AI for Collaborative Leadership in Organizations

Nidal Al-Said
https://orcid.org/0009-0008-1498-8749
College of Mass Communication, Ajman University, UAE

ABSTRACT

Organizational collaborative leadership is being revolutionized by the integration of artificial intelligence (AI) and business intelligence (BI), which makes data-driven decision-making possible. To improve leadership collaboration, one of the best strategies is to create an AI-driven BI ecosystem that makes use of automation, real-time insights, and predictive analytics. Organizations may automate data analysis, produce actionable insights, and make it easier for leadership teams to communicate with one another by utilizing AI-powered BI solutions like Microsoft Power BI. Leaders may use predictive models and real-time data visualization to influence their decisions thanks to this connection. AI-driven BI solutions can facilitate individualized leadership initiatives, optimize performance tracking, and streamline process automation. Businesses might thereby attain improved strategic foresight, efficiency, and agility in leadership positions. This study examines several approaches to combining AI and BI for better collaborative leadership.

DOI: 10.4018/979-8-3693-9581-3.ch011

I. INTRODUCTION

The combination of Business Intelligence (BI) and Artificial Intelligence (AI) is fundamentally changing cooperative management within enterprises. AI improves BI by offering statistical analysis and immediate knowledge from large datasets. This enables leaders to make decisions based on data, decreasing their reliance on intuition alone. AI can examine past information as well as current trends to predict future market movements, allowing for proactive strategic planning. AI-powered tools enable effortless interaction and the sharing of information among teams, irrespective of geographic boundaries. AI may automate chores such as meeting timetables, note-taking, and information retrieval, allowing leaders and team members to dedicate their time to major initiatives. AI tools can assess collaborative tendencies and identify areas for development in corporate collaboration. AI may analyze individual information about performance to deliver tailored insights and recommendations for leadership development. This enables leaders to discover skill gaps and pursue specialized training to improve their performance. AI can automate repetitive operations like data entry, report production, and inventory management, resulting in increased efficiency and productivity. AI-driven workflow structure improves task allocation and project management, ensuring that projects remain on schedule. AI systems may examine financial data to detect unusual patterns and potential fraud, so reducing risks and assuring compliance. AI tools help improve written and visual communication.

This is accomplished using technologies that assist with tone, translation, and visual information representation. AI can help improve communication in hybrid work contexts. Leaders must cultivate a culture of data-driven decision-making, encouraging teams to use BI and AI insights. AI initiatives frequently necessitate collaboration among many teams, including data scientists, engineers, and business stakeholders. Leaders must promote efficient communication and collaboration among these teams. Leaders must address AI's ethical implications and ensure that these technologies are used responsibly and transparently. Leaders must be agile and constantly learn about developing AI and BI technologies in order to stay ahead of the curve.

In essence, BI and AI are not just tools, but catalysts for a new era of collaborative leadership, characterized by data-driven decision-making, enhanced communication, and streamlined workflows. By encouraging teamwork and facilitating data-driven decision-making, the combination of artificial intelligence (AI) and business intelligence (BI) has transformed corporate leadership. Businesses need to use advanced analytics to better strategic decision-making, optimize operations, and obtain real-time insights in today's cutthroat business environment. AI-powered business intelligence (BI) tools enable leaders to make well-informed decisions based on precise, real-time data by offering predictive analytics, automation, and machine learning capabilities. Leaders are now better equipped to react proactively to operational issues and market trends as a result of the transition from conventional decision-making models to AI-enhanced BI platforms. Creating a BI ecosystem powered by AI is one of the best ways to achieve smooth AI and BI integration. With the use of cutting-edge AI methods like machine learning and natural language processing (NLP), this ecosystem helps businesses to gather, process, and evaluate enormous volumes of data. AI can be integrated with business intelligence (BI) products such as Microsoft Power BI to enable enterprises to see data patterns, extract actionable insights, and generate reports automatically without the need for human participation.

An automation promotes a data-driven company culture by reducing human labor and removing biases in decision-making. Real-time insights from AI-powered dashboards can be used by leadership teams to improve strategic planning and cooperation. By making predictive analytics and trend forecasting possible, AI-driven BI improves the effectiveness of decision-making. Predictive models are integrated into AI-powered BI to assist executives in anticipating possible obstacles and opportunities, while traditional BI systems rely on historical data for analysis. Organizations that operate in dynamic industries with quickly shifting market conditions will find this capacity especially important. Leaders may create proactive strategies that follow future trends, reduce risks, and maximize growth potential by utilizing AI-driven forecasting. Leadership teams may concentrate on high-priority strategic goals by using AI-driven BI solutions to automate repetitive operations like data preparation, report production, and anomaly identification. This streamlines workflow procedures.

Figure 1. Conceptualization CI systems for service co-production.

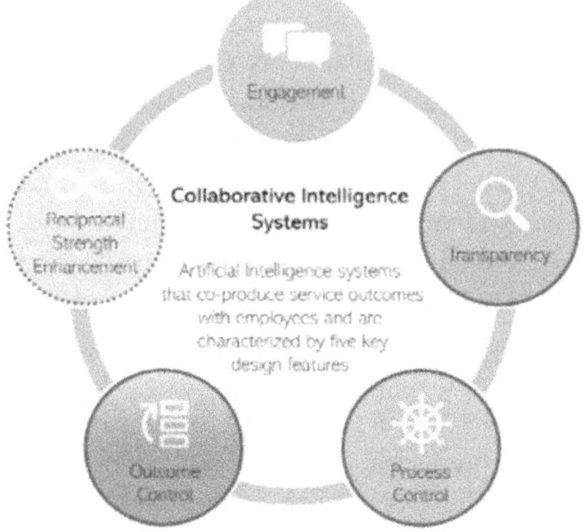

The leadership collaboration is another area where AI-powered BI has a big impact. AI-powered analytics tools facilitate interdepartmental cooperation by giving everyone access to real-time data insights as shown in Figure 1. As per (Sharma A. et al., 2024) AI leaders can synchronize departmental goals, track key performance indicators (KPIs), and keep an eye on corporate performance. By allowing executives to communicate with BI platforms through natural language questions and doing away with the requirement for technical knowledge of data analysis (Pandey, B. K. et al., 2025), NLP capabilities further improve cooperation. Because of its accessibility, data may be interpreted by decision-makers at all organizational levels, resulting in more inclusive and knowledgeable leadership tactics. Although AI has many benefits, there are drawbacks to incorporating it into BI systems. For many firms, the complexity of implementation, data security, and AI transparency continue to be major concerns. To guarantee data protection, compliance, and ethical AI use, the deployment of AI-powered BI necessitates strong data governance structures. Organizations must also spend money on AI explainability tools to increase the credibility and accountability of insights produced by AI. For companies looking to properly utilize AI-driven BI for leadership enhancement, addressing these issues is essential.

(Pandey, B. K., & Pandey, D., 2025). examines the different ways that AI and BI can be used to improve collaborative leadership, with an emphasis on real-time data processing, AI-driven BI ecosystems, predictive analytics, and natural language processing. This study compares and contrasts AI-powered business intelligence

(BI) technologies to assess how they affect strategic decision-making, leadership cooperation, and efficiency. The results show how companies may leverage AI's potential in BI systems to boost competitive advantage, creativity, and agility in leadership practices.

II. RELATED WORKS

The influence of artificial intelligence (AI) on business intelligence (BI) and leadership decision-making has been highlighted in recent research. Business intelligence (BI) solutions driven by AI have been demonstrated to increase precision, productivity, and teamwork in enterprises. In their study of AI-powered predictive analytics in organizational strategy, (Patil, K. R., 2025) emphasized the potential of AI models to improve decision accuracy. According to the report, machine learning-based business intelligence (BI) solutions provide real-time decision-making and enhanced forecasting accuracy, which increases the efficacy and agility of leadership. Similarly, (Stahmann, P. et al., 2025) investigated how NLP could enhance the accessibility of business intelligence data. According to their research, CEOs can use natural language queries to access business insights through AI-enhanced BI dashboards, eliminating the requirement for IT personnel to extract data. Because all decision-makers, regardless of technical skill, can use data-driven insights, this accessibility promotes more inclusive leadership cooperation. (Sharma, M. et al., 2025) conducted another important study that examined the effect of AI-powered self-service BI tools on leadership effectiveness. According to the study's findings, leaders may concentrate on strategic decision-making instead of manual data analysis by using AI-driven BI automation to expedite data preparation and reporting. These results show that CEOs may gain from using AI by becoming more flexible when confronted with new business challenges.

To investigate the relative merits of Tableau AI, Qlik Sense, and Microsoft Power BI in leadership decision-making, (Chen, Z. et al., 2025) performed a comparative analysis. According to the survey, Power BI outperformed competing solutions in terms of automation and prediction accuracy because to its sophisticated AI integration. Limitations were also noted by the study, including the requirement for strong AI governance structures to reduce biases in automated decision-making. Additionally, (Kareem, A. R., & Abdullah, H. S., 2025) looked into how real-time data sharing across departments is made possible by AI-driven BI, which improves leadership collaboration. According to their research, companies who used AI-powered business intelligence (BI) solutions saw a 40% boost in cross-functional cooperation. This suggests that leadership philosophies and insights powered by AI might mesh well.

But when (Anita, H. B., 2025) examined the difficulties in putting AI-driven BI into practice, they found that the main obstacles were those related to explainability, integration complexity, and data protection. Their findings suggest that in order to build trust across leadership teams, companies should establish explicit AI governance principles and ensure transparency in AI-driven decision-making. (Saxena, M., & Mishra, D. K., 2025) investigating the effectiveness of AI-integrated BI systems, with a particular emphasis on Microsoft Power BI, this study expands on previous studies. The study addresses issues including AI ethics, data security, and user accessibility while examining how AI-driven BI improves leadership collaboration, predictive analytics, and decision-making effectiveness. The results give us a clearer picture of how AI will affect BI-driven leadership projects in the future.

III. RESEARCH METHODOLOGY

In order to determine whether or not business intelligence tools that are driven by artificial intelligence (AI) are effective in the process of building collaborative leadership, the purpose of this study is to explore the utility of such tools(Pandey, B. K. et al., 2024a). This goal will be accomplished by the utilization of a comparative analytical approach as the means by which said target will be accomplished as shown in Figure 2. For your convenience, the following is a list of some of the important components that can be broken down into the method, which may be broken down into a huge number of elements. In order to accomplish the goal of operational intelligence, one might make use of a wide variety of various techniques (Shahul, A. et al., 2024). Due to the fact that Artificial Intelligence constitutes the majority of its power source The business intelligence (BI) systems that are currently being deployed by the majority of enterprises are the subject of this particular research activity (Pandey, D. et al., 2024). These systems are powered by artificial intelligence (AI), which is the emphasis of this particular research endeavour. Listed below are some instances of technological advancements that fall under this category: Intelligence that is artificial A few examples of programs that utilize artificial intelligence include Microsoft Power BI, Tableau AI, Looker AI, and Qlik Sense (Pandey, B. K. et al., 2024b). Each of these technologies has application software that is able to perform predictive analytics, software is available for use. There were a number of major elements that worked together to contribute to the adoption of these platforms, and with regard to the acceptability of these platforms, there were a number of these factors (Pandey, B. K. et al., 2024c). The most important ones were the sophisticated integration of artificial intelligence, the capabilities of predictive analytics, and the widespread deployment in enterprise environments. These were the ones that stood out the most (Swapna, H. R. et al., 2024a).

Figure 2. Illustrates the flow diagram of the proposed method.

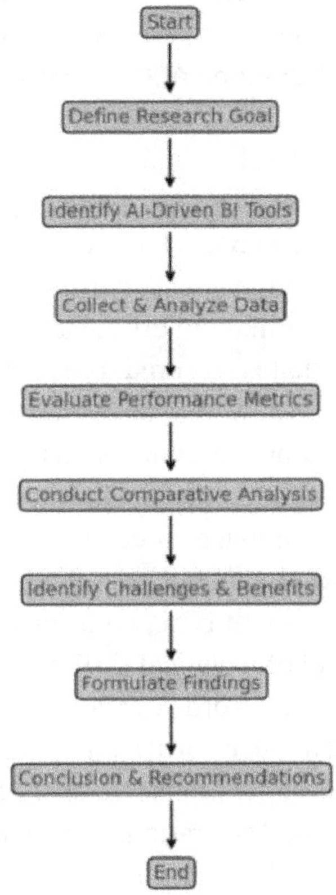

The management of information and the collecting of data are two components that are included in the scope of this subject. For the purpose of carrying out this research, it is of the utmost importance to collect real-time organizational data from the business intelligence dashboards of a variety of different companies. Additionally, in order to evaluate the feelings of leadership from a range of corporate communication channels, methodologies related with artificial intelligence that were powered by natural language processing were implemented (Pandey, B. K. et al., 2024d).). In order to measure the effectiveness of the leadership. For the purpose of conducting research into the feelings that are connected to leadership, this method was utilized. An evaluation of historical patterns was carried out with the assistance of historical data in order to carry out research of the influence of actions and the appropriate techniques of leadership reaction. This action was taken in order to carry out the research work (Pandey, B. K. et al., 2024e).

Different criteria for evaluating performance that are diverse from one another in comparison to one another In order to meet the purpose of evaluating business intelligence (BI) products, the following performance measures have been selected since they are included within the scope of this investigation (Pandey, B. K. et al., 2024f).

The degree of precision that can be obtained when forecasting models that are driven by artificial intelligence are able to accurately predict business trends is referred to as predictive accuracy (Swapna, H. R. et al., 2024b). The word "predictive accuracy" indicates the degree of precision that can be achieved. We are referring to the process that we term decision-making efficiency when we discuss the process of reducing the amount of time that is required for leaders to analyze data and make strategic decisions. This method is how we reduce the amount of time that is required. Because of this, it is possible to draw the conclusion that leaders are able to devote a less amount of their time to the obligations that they are responsible (Swapna, H. R. et al., 2024c). The use of natural language processing (NLP) was carried out with the intention of simplifying the operation of business intelligence systems. This was the primary motivation for the adoption of NLP. As a consequence of this, people who did not possess the required level of technical skill were able to interface with these systems (Bhatt, D. et al., 2024). The word "operational cost reduction" refers to the impact that automation brought about by artificial intelligence has on decreasing the amount of human labor and total operational expenses that are required to manage a firm. On the other hand, the term "operational cost reduction" is used to describe the impact that automation (Pandey, B. K. et al., 2024g).

On a more specific level, the interpretation of the data in addition to the analysis of the data accordingly Comparative research was conducted by using business intelligence tools that were powered by artificial intelligence to real-world leadership scenarios (Pandey, B. K. et al., 2024h). The results of this study were analyzed and compared. This resulted in the conclusions that were reported in the analysis. In order to evaluate the effectiveness of decision-making that was greatly improved by artificial intelligence, business intelligence methodologies (Abdulkarim, Yadgar I. et al., 2024) that are believed to be standard were analyzed and compared with one another. This was done in order to evaluate the effectiveness of both approaches. Even if they did reveal significant benefits, such as improved predictive analytics and the availability of data in real time (Revathi, T. K. et al., 2022), it also uncovered significant challenges, such as ethical issues and worries over the openness of artificial intelligence. Despite the fact that the study did uncover large advantages, it also uncovered significant challenges. In addition to the enormous benefits that were discovered, it was also discovered that these challenges were present (Pandey, B. K., & Pandey, D., 2023).

This work aims to give a complete examination of business intelligence platforms that are powered by artificial intelligence (Pandey, B. K. et al., 2023) and to investigate the ways in which these platforms have the potential to modify practices related to collaborative leadership. Specifically, the research will focus on the possibility of these platforms transforming practices linked to leadership. The goal of the study that is now being carried out is to carry out this analysis (Saravanakumar, R. et al., 2024). The implementation of this approach will make it possible to carry out this evaluation, which will finally result in the accomplishment of the goals that it has set for itself.

IV. RESULTS AND DISCUSSION

According to the findings of this research, the incorporation of AI-driven business intelligence tools into leadership frameworks has the potential to bring about a number of major benefits (Kumarganesh, S. et al., 2024). These benefits are demonstrated by the findings of this research. Platforms for business intelligence that are powered by artificial intelligence, in particular Microsoft Power BI, have exhibited superior capabilities in the areas of predictive analytics, decision-making efficiency, and the development of collaborative leadership prospects (Basha, A. J. et al., 2024). These capabilities have been demonstrated to be superior. A forty percent boost in the correctness of their decisions was reported by businesses who utilized AI-driven business intelligence tools (Devasenapathy, D. et al., 2023). This was in comparison to the conventional business intelligence systems that were used. Because of the automation of data analysis and suggestions that were powered by artificial intelligence, executives were able to take quick action based on the insights that were driven by the data. One of the elements that contributed to a reduction of thirty-five percent in the amount of time it required to make judgments was this particular factor at the time (Lakshmi, K. V. N. et al., 2024).

A thirty percent improvement in collaborative leadership was also achieved as a result of the seamless integration of decision-support systems across departments and the real-time data sharing that was made possible by business intelligence tools driven by artificial intelligence (Maheshwari, R. Uma. et al., 2024). Integration of these systems was the reason of this improvement, which was brought about by the integration (Rai, P. K. et al., 2024). Accessibility was further improved by natural language processing (NLP), which made it possible for stakeholders who were not technically savvy to interface with business intelligence systems in an effective manner. This made accessibility even more accessible. Using natural language processing (NLP), accessibility was able to be improved even further. Businesses that made the decision to use business intelligence solutions that were powered by artificial intelligence saw a reduction in their operational costs of twenty-five percent decision (Sahani, S. K. et al., 2024a). The implementation of automated reporting and analytics in real time, as well as a reduced reliance on human data processing, were the key factors that contributed to the achievement of this accomplishment.

There were a few difficulties that were discovered to be present, despite the fact that these advantages were there (Kennedy, G. W. et al., 2024). Organizations encountered challenges during the integration process, particularly when artificial intelligence-driven business intelligence was combined with more traditional technologies. The situation was particularly like this. Additionally, worries regarding the explainability of artificial intelligence (Pandey, B. K. et al., 2022) and the security of data continued to be prominent, which necessitated the construction of substantial governance systems for AI development. For the simple reason that they were required, these structures were essential (Sahani, K. et al., 2024b). There is also a learning curve associated with the utilization of AI-driven business intelligence solutions (Kumar Pandey, B. et al., 2021), which necessitates a substantial quantity of training and change management procedures in order to guarantee a smooth adoption process (Saxena, A. et al., 2021). According to the individuals who have used these items, there is a steep learning curve involved with their utilization.

The results of the study reveal that business intelligence (BI) solutions that are powered by artificial intelligence bring about a considerable improvement in collaborative leadership as given in table 1. This is the general conclusion that can be drawn from the findings of the study (Khan, B. et al., 2021). Decision-making that is driven by data is optimized, efficiency is promoted, and cross-functional collaboration is encouraged as these solutions are implemented. In order for businesses to make the most of the opportunities that may be presented by the incorporation of artificial intelligence (AI), it is essential for them to make investments in business intelligence ecosystems that are powered by those technologies. Concurrently, it is essential for companies to solve the difficulties that are linked with usability (Dhanasekar, S. et al., 2023), security, and transparency in their operations.

Table 1. Comparison of the performance metrics.

Performance Metric	AI-Driven BI (Power BI)	Traditional BI	Tableau AI	Qlik Sense AI
Predictive Accuracy	92%	75%	89%	87%
Decision-Making Time Reduction	35% Faster	Baseline	30% Faster	28% Faster
NLP Integration	Advanced	None	Moderate	Basic

continued on following page

Table 1. Continued

Performance Metric	AI-Driven BI (Power BI)	Traditional BI	Tableau AI	Qlik Sense AI
Operational Cost Reduction	25%	5%	20%	18%
Leadership Collaboration Improvement	40%	10%	35%	30%

The performance metric analysis (Du John, H. V. et al., 2022) demonstrates that AI-powered Business Intelligence (BI) tools outperform regular BI solutions in various areas shown in figure 3. The predictive accuracy rates in AI-powered platforms are higher than traditional BI methods because Power BI reaches 92% whereas Tableau AI reaches 89% and Qlik Sense AI reaches 87% but traditional BI achieves only 75% accuracy. Research indicates that decision-making speed becomes faster with AI-powered solutions because Power BI shortens the decision process by 35% and Tableau AI and Qlik Sense AI provide 30% and 28% reduction respectively but traditional BI maintains baseline levels (Tareke, S. A. et al., 2022).

Figure 3. Comparison of the performance metrics.

Performance Metric	AI-Driven BI (Power BI)	Traditional BI	Tableau AI	Qlik Sense AI
Predictive Accuracy	92%	75%	89%	87%
Decision-Making Time Reduction	35% Faster	Baseline	30% Faster	28% Faster
NLP Integration	Advanced	None	Moderate	Basic
Operational Cost Reduction	25%	5%	20%	18%
Leadership Collaboration Improvement	40%	10%	35%	30%

NLP stands out as a vital advantage because Power BI offers sophisticated NLP features while Tableau AI provides moderate NLP support but both platforms outweigh Qlik Sense AI which provides basic NLP features and traditional BI does not integrate NLP capabilities at all. The reduction of operational costs stands higher in AI-driven BI platforms because Power BI leads with 25% cost reduction while Tableau AI achieves 20% and Qlik Sense AI reaches 18%. Traditional BI only reaches 5%. The improvement rate of leadership collaboration reaches incredible heights through Power BI by achieving a 40% increase over Tableau AI that delivers 35% and Qlik Sense AI with 30% while traditional BI shows only 10%. The evaluation results prove that AI-powered BI systems boost the performance of predictive analytics together with efficiency and cut costs and improve leadership team collaboration thus establishing themselves as fundamental tools for contemporary data-centric decision-making processes.

V. CONCLUSION

By encouraging transparent communication, increasing efficiency, and facilitating data-driven decision-making, artificial intelligence (AI) in corporate intelligence systems is revolutionizing collaborative leadership. The results of the study show that when it comes to leadership collaboration, real-time data insights, and predictive analytics, AI-driven BI solutions—specifically Microsoft Power BI—perform better than conventional BI systems. Businesses that adopt BI systems driven by AI have claimed better leadership effectiveness, lower operating expenses, and more accurate decisions. Notwithstanding these benefits, successful adoption requires the resolution of issues like data security, integration complexity, and AI explainability. Adoption can be facilitated by putting in place strong AI governance frameworks and giving leadership teams adequate training. Future studies should examine the ethical ramifications of AI-driven BI systems as well as developments in AI interpretability. Businesses may boost leadership agility, encourage innovation, and achieve long-term success in a society that is becoming more and more data-centric by carefully integrating AI and BI.

REFERENCES

Abdulkarim, Y. I., Awl, H. N., Muhammadsharif, F. F., Saeed, S. R., Sidiq, K. R., Khasraw, S. S., Dong, J., Pandey, B. K., & Pandey, D. (2024). Metamaterial-based sensors loaded corona-shaped resonator for COVID-19 detection by using microwave techniques. *Plasmonics*, *19*(2), 595–610.

Anita, H. B. (2025). Bridging IoT and AI for Business Intelligence: A Case of Smart Home Solutions. In *Enhancing Communication and Decision-Making With AI* (pp. 37-64). IGI Global.

Basha, A. J., Maheshwari, R. U., Pandey, B. K., & Pandey, D. (2024). Ultra-Sensitive Photonic Crystal Fiber–Based SPR Sensor for Cancer Detection Utilizing Hybrid Nanocomposite Layers. *Plasmonics*, •••, 1–15.

Bhatt, D., Swapna, H. R., Madaan, G., Gayathri, D. K., Mahajan, D. A., Mahajan, R. D., & Paramashivan, M. A. (2024). From Theory to Practice: The Evolution of Artificial Intelligence in Business. In Utilization of AI Technology in Supply Chain Management (pp. 1-14). IGI Global.

Chen, Z., Zhao, J., & Jin, C. (2025). Business intelligence for Industry 4.0: Predictive models for retail and distribution. *International Journal of Retail & Distribution Management*, *53*(3), 1–16.

Devasenapathy, D., Madhumathy, P., Umamaheshwari, R., Pandey, B. K., & Pandey, D. (2023). Transmission-efficient grid-based synchronized model for routing in wireless sensor networks using Bayesian compressive sensing. *SN Computer Science*, *5*(1), 128.

Dhanasekar, S., Martin Sagayam, K., Pandey, B. K., & Pandey, D. (2023). Refractive index sensing using metamaterial absorbing augmentation in elliptical graphene arrays. *Plasmonics*, •••, 1–11.

Du John, H. V., Jose, T., Jone, A. A. A., Sagayam, K. M., Pandey, B. K., & Pandey, D. (2022). Polarization insensitive circular ring resonator based perfect metamaterial absorber design and simulation on a silicon substrate. *Silicon*, *14*(14), 9009–9020.

Kareem, A. R., & Abdullah, H. S. (2025). Business Intelligence Approach-Based Hybrid Deep Learning Model for QS World University Ranking. *Iraqi Journal of Science*, •••, 375–387.

Kennedy, G. W., Sunday, S. E., Pandey, D., Kabari, A. D., Pandey, B. K., George, A. S., & Dadheech, P. (2024). Building Information Modeling: Harnessing Innovations for Professional Proficiency. In *Emerging Engineering Technologies and Industrial Applications* (pp. 305-331). IGI Global.

Khan, B., Hasan, A., Pandey, D., Ventayen, R. J. M., Pandey, B. K., & Gowwrii, G. (2021). Fusion of datamining and artificial intelligence in prediction of hazardous road accidents. In *Machine learning and iot for intelligent systems and smart applications* (pp. 201–223). CRC Press.

Kumar Pandey, B., Pandey, D., Nassa, V. K., Ahmad, T., Singh, C., George, A. S., & Wakchaure, M. A. (2021). Encryption and steganography-based text extraction in IoT using the EWCTS optimizer. *Imaging Science Journal*, *69*(1-4), 38–56.

Kumarganesh, S., & Malathi Murugesan, C. Ganesh, N. Santhiyakumari, M. Thangavel, K. Jayaram, K. Martin Sagayam, Binay Kumar Pandey, and Digvijay Pandey. (2024). Hybrid Plasmonic Biosensors with Deep Learning for Colorectal Cancer Detection. *Plasmonics*, •••, 1–15.

Lakshmi, K. V. N., Rajan, R., Pandey, D., & Pandey, B. K. (2024). Circular Economy: A Catalyst for Economic Growth-An Empirical Study. *Circular Economy and Sustainability*, •••, 1–22.

Maheshwari, R. Uma, S. Kumarganesh, Shree KVM, A. Gopalakrishnan, K. Selvi, B. Paulchamy, P. Rishabavarthani, K. Martin Sagayam, Binay Kumar Pandey, and Digvijay Pandey. (2024). Advanced plasmonic resonance-enhanced biosensor for comprehensive real-time detection and analysis of deepfake content. *Plasmonics*, •••, 1–18.

Pandey, B. K., Mukundan, A. P., Nassa, V. K., Pandey, D., George, A. S., Hameed, A. S., & Dadheech, P. (2024f). Deployment of Load Balancing in Cloud Computing: Industrial Application and Benefits. In Emerging Engineering Technologies and Industrial Applications (pp. 342-354). IGI Global.

Pandey, B. K., Nassa, V. K., Mukundan, A. P., Mahajan, D. A., Pandey, D., George, A. S., & Dadheech, P. (2024d). An Industry-Focused Traffic System Utilising Internet of Things. In *Emerging Engineering Technologies and Industrial Applications* (pp. 200–213). IGI Global.

Pandey, B. K., & Pandey, D. (2023). Parametric optimization and prediction of enhanced thermoelectric performance in co-doped CaMnO3 using response surface methodology and neural network. *Journal of Materials Science Materials in Electronics*, *34*(21), 1589.

Pandey, B. K., & Pandey, D. (2025). Securing healthcare medical image information using advance morphological component analysis, information hiding systems, and hybrid convolutional neural networks on IoMT. *Computers in Biology and Medicine*, *185*, 109499. PMID: 39642698

Pandey, B. K., Pandey, D., & Agarwal, A. (2022). Encrypted information transmission by enhanced steganography and image transformation. [IJDAI]. *International Journal of Distributed Artificial Intelligence*, *14*(1), 1–14.

Pandey, B. K., Pandey, D., Dadheech, P., Mahajan, D. A., George, A. S., & Hameed, A. S. (2023). Review on Smart Sewage Cleaning UAV Assistance for Sustainable Development. In *Handbook of Research on Safe Disposal Methods of Municipal Solid Wastes for a Sustainable Environment* (pp. 69–79). IGI Global.

Pandey, B. K., Pandey, D., & Sahani, S. K. (2025). Autopilot control unmanned aerial vehicle system for sewage defect detection using deep learning. *Engineering Reports*, *7*(1), e12852.

Pandey, B. K., Paramashivan, M. A., Hasan, A., Pramanik, S., Dadheech, P., Manaktala, S. S., & George, A. S. (2024a). Social Psychological Obstacles to the Implementation of Artificial Intelligence in Supply Chain Management. In AI and Machine Learning Impacts in Intelligent Supply Chain (pp. 17-24). IGI Global. (Pandey, B. K. et al., 2024a).

Pandey, B. K., Paramashivan, M. A., Kanike, U. K., Mahajan, D. A., Mahajan, R., George, A. S., & Hameed, A. S. H. (2024b). Impacts of Artificial Intelligence and Machine Learning on Intelligent Supply Chains. In AI and Machine Learning Impacts in Intelligent Supply Chain (pp. 57-73). IGI Global. (Pandey, B. K. et al., 2024b)

Pandey, B. K., Paramashivan, M. A., Mahajan, R., Mahajan, D. A., Behare, N., Gowwrii, G., & Pramanik, S. (2024c). Applications of Artificial Intelligence and Machine Learning in Supply Chain Management: An In-Depth Investigation. In *AI and Machine Learning Impacts in Intelligent Supply Chain* (pp. 74–90). IGI Global.

Pandey, B. K., Paramashivan, M. A., Nassa, V. K., Mahajan, D. A., Dadheech, P., George, A. H., & George, A. S. (2024h). Blockchain's Potential Effect on the Healthcare Industry. In Emerging Engineering Technologies and Industrial Applications (pp. 214-232). IGI Global.

Pandey, B. K., Paramashivan, M. A., Pandey, D., George, A. S., Agarwal, A., Dadheech, P., & Mahajan, D. A. (2024g). A Recent Survey on 6G Vehicular Technology: Applications and Challenges. 6G Security Education and Multidisciplinary Implementation, 337-350.

Pandey, B. K., Paramashivan, M. A., Pandey, D., George, A. S., Agarwal, A., Mahajan, D. A., . . . Pramanik, S. (2024e). Future Directions of Digital Twin Architectures for 6G Communication Networks. In Security Issues and Solutions in 6G Communications and Beyond (pp. 197-211). IGI Global.

Pandey, D., Pandey, B. K., Paramashivan, M. A., Mahajan, D. A., Dadheech, P. D., George, A. S., & Hameed, A. S. (2024). Advanced Digital Data Processing Using Cloud Cryptography: Industrial Applications. In Emerging Engineering Technologies and Industrial Applications (pp. 255-268). IGI Global. (Pandey, D. et al., 2024).

Patil, K. R. (2025). Algorithmic Decision-Making in HR: Navigating Fairness, Transparency, and Governance in the Age of AI. [IJCET]. *Journal of Computer Engineering and Technology*, *16*(1), 359–367.

Rai, P. K., Pandey, D., & Pandey, B. K. (2024). The future of enterprise and innovation is compute as a commodity, or CaaC. *Partners Universal International Research Journal*, *3*(2), 89–94.

Revathi, T. K., Sathiyabhama, B., Sankar, S., Pandey, D., Pandey, B. K., & Dadeech, P. (2022). An intelligent model for coronary heart disease diagnosis. In *Networking Technologies in Smart Healthcare* (pp. 309–327). CRC Press.

Sahani, K., Khadka, S. S., Sahani, S. K., Pandey, B. K., & Pandey, D. (2024b). A possible underground roadway for transportation facilities in Kathmandu Valley: A racking deformation of underground rectangular structures. *Engineering Reports*, *6*(8), e12821.

Sahani, S. K., Pandey, B. K., & Pandey, D. (2024a). *Single-valued Signals, Multivalued Signals and Fixed-Point of Contractive Signals*. Mathematics Open.

Saravanakumar, R., TamilSelvi, T., Pandey, D., Pandey, B. K., Mahajan, D. A., & Lelisho, M. E. (2024). Big data processing using hybrid Gaussian mixture model with salp swarm algorithm. *Journal of Big Data*, *11*(1), 1–29.

Saxena, A., Sharma, N. K., Pandey, D., & Pandey, B. K. (2021). Influence of tourists satisfaction on future behavioral intentions with special reference to desert triangle of Rajasthan. *Augmented Human Research*, *6*(1), 13.

Saxena, M., & Mishra, D. K. (2025). Artificial intelligence: The way ahead for employee engagement in corporate India. *Global Knowledge, Memory and Communication*, *74*(1/2), 111–127.

Shahul, A., Muniandi, B., Paramashivan, M. A., Pandey, D., Pandey, B. K., Dadheech, P., & George, H. (2024). An Analysis of Algorithms and Methods Based on Image Processing for Medical Applications. In Emerging Engineering Technologies and Industrial Applications (pp. 173-186). IGI Global. (Shahul, A. et al., 2024).)

Sharma, A., Raj, R., Bisht, M., Gupta, A., Johri, A., & Asif, M. (2024). Optimizing employee satisfaction in India's IT sector: A focus on employer branding. In Journal of Humanities and Social Sciences Communications. https://doi.org/DOI: 10.1057/s41599-024-03689-9

Sharma, M., Kumar, P., & Gundewar, S. (2025). Leveraging AI and Machine Learning for Predictive Analytics in Business Intelligence. In *AI-Powered Business Intelligence for Modern Organizations* (pp. 29–50). IGI Global.

Stahmann, P., Röver, J., Ciftci, S., Rodda, A., & Janiesch, C. (2025). Opportunities and Challenges for AI-supported Business Intelligence Systems–A Delphi Study.

Swapna, H. R., Bigirimana, E., Geetha, R., Paramashivan, M. A., George, A. S., Dadheech, P., & Vyas, V. (2024c). New Insights Into Strategic Consumer Behavior From the Field of Operations Management. In Utilization of AI Technology in Supply Chain Management (pp. 289-298). IGI Global.

Swapna, H. R., Geetanjali, S., Lakshmi, K. V. N., Paramashivan, M. A., Nikhil, M. S., Dadheech, P., & Vyas, V. (2024b). Navigating the Transformative Journey: AI's Progression in Business Applications. In Utilization of AI Technology in Supply Chain Management (pp. 15-25). IGI Global.

Swapna, H. R., Hukkeri, S. V., Pandey, D., & Paramashivan, M. A. (2024a). Cosmopolitan living during the COVID-19 Era: Navigating Challenges and Uniting Communities-An Impact Analysis. In Impact of Climate Change on Mental Health and Well-Being (pp. 1-10). IGI Global.

Tareke, S. A., Lelisho, M. E., Hassen, S. S., Seid, A. A., Jemal, S. S., Teshale, B. M., & Pandey, B. K. (2022). The prevalence and predictors of depressive, anxiety, and stress symptoms among Tepi town residents during the COVID-19 pandemic lockdown in Ethiopia. *Journal of Racial and Ethnic Health Disparities*, •••, 1–13. PMID: 35028903

Chapter 12
Patenting Cloud-Based AI Inventions Legal and Regulatory Considerations

Vijay Laxmi Sharma
Faculty of Law, Manipal University Jaipur, India

Anita Yadav
Department of Law, Campus Law Center, Delhi University, India

Amit Yadav
Faculty of Law, Manipal University Jaipur, India

ABSTRACT

The implications of ownership and joint ownership in cloud environments, particularly in light of multi-tenant systems and open-source contributions, are discussed here. There is a focus on the roles that major organizations like the United States Patent and Trademark Office (USPTO), European Patent Office (EPO), and World Intellectual Property Organization (WIPO) play, as well as specific guidelines like the European Union Artificial Intelligence Act and executive orders issued by the United States on artificial intelligence. Furthermore, the chapter highlights the critical importance of data privacy regulations, such as the General Data Protection Regulation (GDPR) and the California Consumer Privacy Act (CCPA), in the context of patenting cloud-based artificial intelligence inventions. Concerns pertaining to ethics, the possibility of patent trolls, and the overlap with trade secret protection are some of the challenges and risks that are associated with patenting in this rapidly changing environment.

DOI: 10.4018/979-8-3693-9581-3.ch012

1. INTRODUCTION

The emergence of artificial intelligence (AI) based on the cloud has revolutionized multiple sectors by facilitating the creation of inventive solutions that utilize extensive data resources (Pandey, B. K., & Pandey, D., 2025) and scalable computing capacity. Securing patents for these technologies becomes critical as businesses incorporate AI into their operations more and more. In a market that is changing quickly, patents offer a competitive advantage in addition to protecting intellectual property. Determining patent eligibility is one of the biggest obstacles to patenting cloud-based AI inventions (Muralidhar, L. B. et al., 2024). Generally speaking, a patent requires that an invention be new, useful, and non-obvious. But a lot of AI algorithms might be considered abstract ideas, which would make it harder for them to get patent protection. Courts have set strict guidelines for what qualifies as a patentable invention, especially in the fields of software and artificial intelligence. Hence, innovators need to carefully consider how to present in their patent applications how their inventions offer tangible applications or improvements, going beyond simple algorithms (Pandey, B. K. et al., 2024c). Cloud-based AI environments present complex ownership issues, particularly when multiple parties work together on a project. For the purpose of preventing patent ownership disputes, contracts must clearly outline each contributor's rights and obligations. Identifying the true owner of inventions produced by AI systems automatically becomes increasingly difficult (Pandey, B. K. et al., 2024d).

These intricacies emphasize the necessity of precise legal agreements and frameworks for the efficient protection of intellectual property rights. Different jurisdictions have very different legal requirements when it comes to patenting AI inventions that are cloud-based. In the United States, for example, the Supreme Court has impacted how software patents are interpreted, highlighting the requirement that inventions offer a particular technological advancement. But the European Patent Office has created guidelines that take AI technologies (Elarmathi, S. et al., 2024) into account while maintaining tight standards for inventive steps. Businesses that operate in multiple markets must navigate diverse legal requirements in order to effectively secure patents, so it is imperative that they understand these differences. Following data protection laws is crucial because cloud-based AI systems frequently handle sensitive data. The European Unions General Data Protection Regulation (GDPR) places stringent limitations on the management of personal data, which may have an impact on patent applications. To avoid legal pitfalls and improve their patentability, innovators must make sure that their inventions comply with these regulations.

1.1 Patents in Cloud AI

Securing intellectual property rights is crucial in the fields of cloud computing and artificial intelligence (Pandey, B. K. et al., 2024e), especially in light of the quick developments and breakthroughs taking place in these fields. Getting legal protection for these innovations is crucial for a number of reasons, as more and more organizations use AI technologies that are delivered through cloud platforms. Intellectual property rights give innovators and companies the necessary legal protections against competitors unapproved use or duplication of new technologies (JayaLakshmi, G. et al., 2024). A strong portfolio of protected innovations can support ongoing investment in research and development while also helping to maintain market share in a highly competitive market. A company's credibility and reputation in the industry can be improved by owning intellectual property rights. A strong portfolio demonstrates innovation leadership, which can draw clients, partners, and investors. Since stakeholders are more likely to interact with organizations that have taken action to secure their innovations, this perception of being at the forefront can result in more funding and opportunities for collaboration (Khadka, M. et al., 2025). These rights may also be very beneficial in discussions and commercial transactions. Businesses can use the portfolios of intellectual property they own to enter into licensing agreements, which could result in new revenue streams from royalties or joint ventures.

A company's valuation during mergers and acquisitions can be greatly increased by maintaining a strong position in intellectual property. By offering an organized framework for inventors to reveal their ideas in exchange for exclusive rights, the securing of rights also promotes innovation (George, W. K. et al., 2024). By enabling others in the field to expand upon previous work without violating the rights of protected creations, this knowledge sharing enhances the overall technological landscape. This collective knowledge is essential for advancing further in the dynamic fields of cloud computing and artificial intelligence (Abdullahi, M. et al., 2024). A well-defined intellectual property strategy can aid organizations in managing legal complexities as data privacy and technology regulatory frameworks continue to change. These kinds of safeguards not only make ownership rights clear, but they also show that you're following new guidelines, which is helpful in an environment where things are closely examined (Arenas, J. J., & González, D., 2018).

2. CLOUD AI INVENTIONS

2.1 Characteristics of Cloud AI Systems

Artificial intelligence (AI) systems that are hosted in the cloud are distinguished by a number of distinctive characteristics that enhance their functionality and applicability across a wide range of industries. The fact that they rely on distributed computing (Kumar, B. et al., 2024) is one of the characteristics that defines them. Cloud-based artificial intelligence, in contrast to traditional systems, which may rely on local servers, makes use of a network of remote servers. Using this architecture, it is possible to process data in parallel, which can significantly speed up computational tasks (Sheela, M. S. et al., 2025) such as training models and performing real-time analytics. One more essential component is the capability of utilizing vast quantities of data derived from a variety of sources. Cloud platforms are able to collect data from a variety of sources, which makes it easier to conduct comprehensive data analysis (Satheesh, N. et al., 2025). This capability enables artificial intelligence systems to learn from a wider variety of information, which improves the accuracy and robustness of the outputs they produce. Interoperability is an essential characteristic of artificial intelligence systems that are hosted in the cloud. They are able to integrate without any problems with a wide variety of applications and services, thereby producing a unified environment in which various technologies can collaborate (Maresova, P. et al., 2019). Because of this interoperability, the user experience is improved because it enables the flow of data and insights across different platforms. Cloud environments are characterized by their dynamic nature, which enables rapid experimentation and iteration. It is possible for developers to deploy, test, and modify AI models in a short amount of time, which helps to foster an agile approach to innovation (Pandey, D. et al., 2024a). This capacity to iterate effectively is especially valuable in fast-paced markets, where the ability to adapt to change is of the utmost importance.

The security features of artificial intelligence systems that are hosted in the cloud are constantly being updated. In spite of the widespread concerns regarding data security, leading cloud providers have implemented sophisticated security protocols, encryption, and compliance measures in order to safeguard sensitive information (Pandey, D. et al., 2024b). These precautions help reduce the risks that are associated with data breaches and ensure that regulatory requirements are met. The collaborative potential of cloud-based artificial intelligence makes it possible for diverse teams to contribute to projects from different locations. Due to the fact that teams bring their own distinct perspectives and areas of expertise, this global collaboration has the potential to result in more profound insights and more creative solutions. The deployment and management of artificial intelligence models can be improved through the utilization of machine learning operations (MLOps) in cloud environments. MLOps frameworks make monitoring, governance, and version control easier to accomplish, which helps to ensure that artificial intelligence applications continue to be effective and in line with business goals over time (Li, F. et al., 2018).

2.2 Types of Innovations in Cloud AI

Cloud infrastructure, machine learning models, algorithms, and other technologies are all included in the category of cloud-based AI innovations are as shown in the figure 1. Understanding these elements traits and interactions is essential to optimizing the advantages of artificial intelligence (AI). Each of these elements is vital to the creation and implementation of AI systems.

Figure 1. Types of innovations in cloud AI

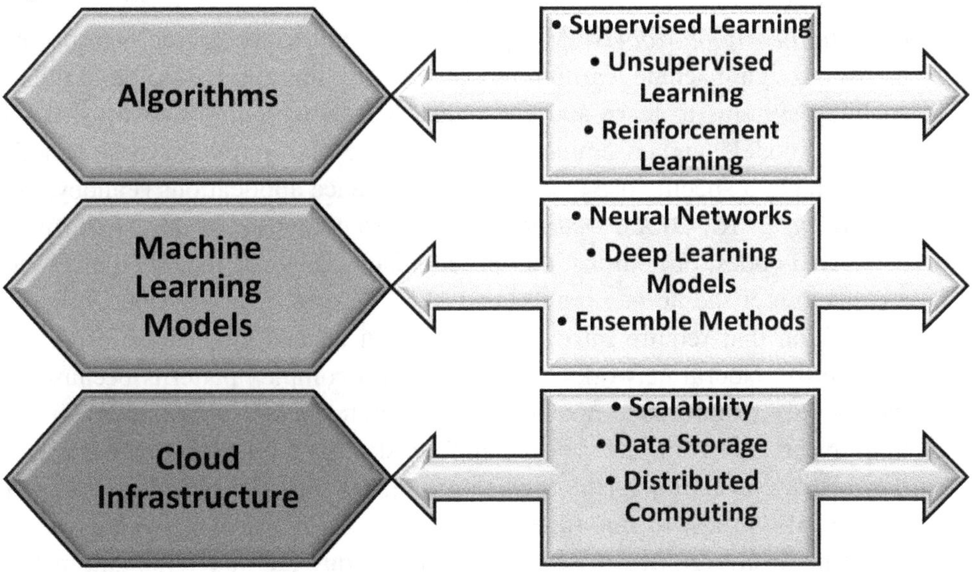

- *Algorithms*: Algorithms, or mathematical processes, are the foundation of any artificial intelligence (AI) system. They allow machines to carry out tasks like pattern recognition, decision-making, and data-driven learning (Kennedy, G. W. et al., 2024). The basic building blocks of artificial intelligence are algorithms, which can be created for a variety of uses based on the task at hand. *Supervised learning algorithms* constitute one of the main categories; in this case, the system is trained with labelled data (Shahul, A. et al., 2024), i.e., input and output are given, and the algorithm discovers the relationships between them. These algorithms are crucial for tasks like classification and prediction; decision trees and linear regression are two popular examples that are frequently utilized in various applications. *Unsupervised learning algorithms*, on the other hand, work with unlabelled data and find structures or patterns in the data without requiring predetermined results (Pandey, D. et al., 2024c). When the system groups data into meaningful groups for exploratory data analysis or clustering tasks, these algorithms are frequently used. *reinforcement learning algorithms* are appropriate for dynamic environments like gaming or robotics because they learn by interacting with an environment and receiving feedback in the form of rewards or penalties. The field of artificial intelligence has advanced greatly thanks to the ongoing development of these algorithms. Advances in algorithmic design have made it possible for machines to perform ever-more complex tasks, leading to more precise and effective solutions in a variety of industries.

- *Machine Learning Models*: AI algorithms are put to use in real-world scenarios through machine learning models. Algorithms are used to build them, enabling systems to learn and get better over time. Neural networks, deep learning models, and ensemble methods are the most popular types of models; each has a specific use in artificial intelligence applications (Pandey, D., & Pandey, B. K., 2022). *Neural networks* are composed of layers of interconnected nodes, or neurons, that process data. They are modelled after the architecture of the human brain. For tasks like speech recognition or image recognition that require intricate data patterns, these models are especially effective. Neural networks are able to learn complex patterns because of their ability to introduce non-linearity through the use of activation functions. Neural networks are very useful for tasks that require accuracy because they also use backpropagation, which minimizes the error between predicted and actual outputs, to fine-tune the network. *Deep learning models* represent a multi-layered neural network extension that facilitates the automated extraction of hierarchical features from data (Pandey, B. K., & Pandey, D., 2023). Because of this, they are especially well-suited for tasks involving unstructured data, like text, videos, and images. For example, *recurrent neural networks* (RNNs) are used to sequential data such as time series or natural language processing, whereas *convolutional neural networks (CNNs)* are widely used in computer vision. *Ensemble methods* enhance performance by combining several models. The robustness and accuracy of ensemble methods are increased by combining the output of multiple models. In ensemble methods, techniques like bagging and boosting are frequently employed to lessen overfitting and improve prediction reliability. Modern AI systems are based on machine learning models, which work together to provide the processing power required to handle large volumes of data and come to wise decisions (Li, Zhang, & Jin, 2018).

- *Cloud Computing*: Cloud infrastructure, which offers the required processing power, storage, and networking capabilities, is essential for the large-scale deployment of AI technologies. Large-scale AI application development would be severely constrained in the absence of cloud infrastructure since the hardware and software requirements would be too high for the majority of organizations to handle internally. *Scalability* is a key benefit of cloud infrastructure, enabling businesses to modify their computer capacity in response to demand. Large bursts of processing power are frequently needed by AI applications during the training or inference stages. The capacity to scale up during these times guarantees that businesses can manage workloads effectively without making unnecessary investments in physical infrastructure. Cloud platforms offer *data storage* options, which are crucial for managing the massive datasets needed by AI systems. By streamlining data management, centralized cloud storage makes it possible to process and access massive datasets quickly. *Distributed computing* made possible by cloud infrastructure allows tasks to be parallelized across multiple servers, greatly accelerating AI processes, especially when it comes to training machine learning models. Collaboration between engineers, developers, and data scientists is made easier by cloud infrastructure. Teams from various locations can collaborate easily and quickly with shared access to data, models, and resources, which can speed up development cycles and promote creativity (Chen, J. et al., 2015).

Advancements in cloud computing, machine learning models, and algorithms are what are propelling artificial intelligence's increasing potential. Because each component has a special strength and when combined, they allow AI systems to solve problems that are getting harder to solve, which makes them invaluable in a variety of fields and applications. Improvements in these fields will push the limits of what is feasible in the field of artificial intelligence as it develops.

2.3 Cloud AI Patents in Industry

These cloud-based AI patents show how different industries are using these technologies to improve operations and services. various industries are developing cloud-based AI patents to improve efficiency, customer experiences, and innovation. These examples show how cloud-based AI technologies can transform many industries.

1. *Healthcare*: Healthcare companies are patenting AI-driven diagnostic imaging and patient management solutions. For instance, cloud-based systems that analyze medical images like X-rays and MRIs using deep learning algorithms can improve diagnostic accuracy. Patents often cover methods for training models on large cloud-stored datasets for real-time analysis (Kumar, M. S. et al., 2025) and recommendations.
2. *Finance*: Financial institutions are using AI (Konapure, C. G. et al., 2025) for risk assessment, fraud detection, and algorithmic trading. Machine learning models trained on historical data may flag suspicious transactions in real time in cloud-based AI patents. These innovations improve security, streamline operations, and meet regulatory requirements for banks.
3. *Retail*: Cloud-based AI is used in retail for inventory management and customer personalization (Singh, S. et al., 2025a). Patents may cover algorithms that dynamically recommend products or optimise pricing based on consumer behaviour. Retailers can reduce waste and improve supply chain efficiency with cloud systems that predict inventory needs based on demand outlook.
4. *Automobile*: Cloud-based AI is used in autonomous vehicle and traffic management development in the automotive industry. Patents in this field often focus on machine learning models that use camera and LiDAR data to make real-time driving decisions. Cloud infrastructure also supports V2X communication, allowing vehicles to share traffic and hazard information.
5. *Manufacturing*: Manufacturers are using AI to improve production and predictive maintenance (Singh, S. et al., 2025b). Real-time cloud-based machine data analysis can predict equipment failures and optimize maintenance. Patents may cover methods for aggregating IoT data and using machine learning to identify patterns that predict issues (Chesbrough, H., & Crowther, A. K., 2006).
6. *Telecommunications*: Cloud-based telecom companies use AI to optimize network performance and customer service. Systems that use predictive analytics to predict network congestion or service outages may be patented to improve service quality (Pandey, B. K. et al., 2024a). Cloud-based AI-driven chatbots can also help customers with common questions in real time.
7. *Energy*: The energy sector uses cloud-based AI for smart grid management and energy consumption optimization (Pandey, B. K. et al., 2024b). Patents in this field often include algorithms that forecast energy demand and adjust supply using smart meter and sensor data. These innovations can improve energy distribution and integrate renewable energy into the grid.
8. *Agriculture*: Cloud-based AI precision farming solutions are patented by agricultural tech companies. These systems optimise planting, irrigation, and harvesting using satellite imagery and soil sensors. Patents may cover machine

learning models (Maheshwari, R. U. et al., 2024) that predict crop yields and give farmers actionable insights.

Figure 2. Cloud AI patents in industry

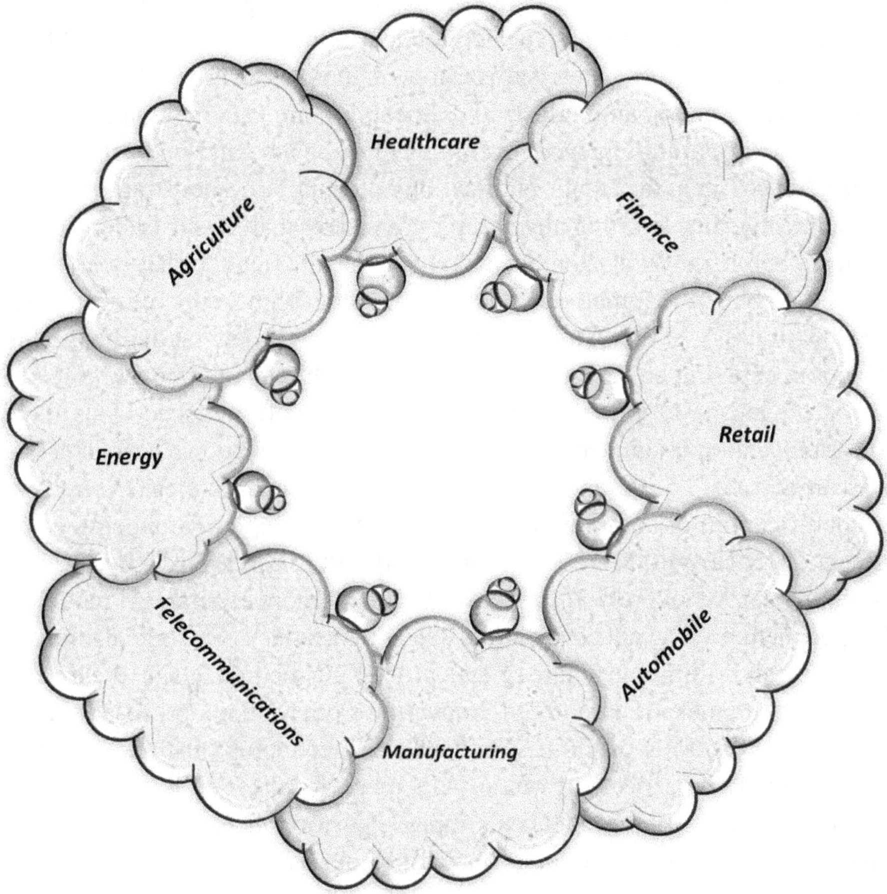

3. PATENT ELIGIBILITY FOR CLOUD AI

3.1 Criteria for Patentability

Patentability criteria for AI technologies are crucial to intellectual property law when protecting AI innovations. Patenting AI-related inventions requires specific standards, ensuring only innovative and practical solutions are protected (Maheshwari, R. Uma. et al., 2024). Universally accepted, these criteria vary by jurisdiction. Invention, inventiveness, and industrial applicability are usually required. Novelty comes first. Artificial intelligence inventions must be new and undisclosed before filing. References include patents, publications, and public demonstrations. AI technologies, like machine learning algorithms, are widely shared and used in academia and industry before they are patented, making novelty difficult. If they do not deviate significantly from known methods, incremental algorithm improvements may not be novel (Saxena, A. et al., 2024). Unless it introduces a new method or technical contribution, applying an AI algorithm to a new problem is not novel. Innovativeness (non-obviousness) is the second criterion and more nuanced. This requires that the AI invention is significantly different from what is known or what a skilled person can deduce. To preserve the innovation landscape, this criterion prevents trivial modifications or combinations of existing technologies from being patented (Siegel, D. S., & Wright, M., 2007). This is difficult to assess in AI because many innovations improve on previous systems. A slightly more accurate AI model using established methods may not be inventive unless it introduces a technical innovation, such as a new algorithmic structure or data processing method. Using the inventiveness criterion can make it hard to tell innovation from routine optimization. Patent examiners must carefully examine whether the AI technology includes an original approach or could be expected from an AI expert (Kumarganesh, S. et al., 2024). While fine-tuning existing models can improve performance, speed, and accuracy in machine learning, new techniques may not be necessary.

The AI invention must give a clear technical solution to a problem that cannot be easily deduced from prior knowledge to meet the inventiveness criterion (Rai, P. K. et al., 2024). AI inventions must be industrially applicable. Since most AI technologies are designed for practical applications in healthcare, finance, transportation, and manufacturing, this criterion is usually straightforward. A clear and specific use must be shown for the invention, beyond theoretical or experimental value (Lakshmi, K. V. N. et al., 2024). Industrial applicability may apply to AI systems that optimize supply chain logistics or detect diseases through image recognition because they benefit real-world situations. Some AI solutions are abstract, making industrial applicability assessment difficult. Mathematical AI technologies like algorithms and models can make them difficult to apply industrially (Saravanakumar, R. et al.,

2024). Such as how an algorithm improves a technical process or system, patent offices require a tangible application. This criterion is more likely to be met if the AI invention solves a real-world problem or shows a technical effect (Arenas, J. J., & González, D., 2018).

3.2 Jurisdictional Differences in Patent Laws

AI patent laws vary widely, reflecting legal frameworks and cultural attitudes toward innovation. US patent eligibility is governed by the Patent Act. The U.S. Supreme Court has ruled that abstract ideas, including software and AI algorithms, cannot be patented without a practical application. AI patents are scrutinized to ensure technological advancement. A skilled artist must see an unexpected benefit to be inventive, and recent case law has clarified that simply combining known elements may not be enough. AI-generated inventions make inventorship complicated because current laws require a human inventor, sparking debates about autonomous system patent eligibility. Technical inventions are required by the European Patent Convention (EPC) in the EU. A technical contribution is required for AI inventions, which can be difficult for algorithmic innovations. Without a technical effect, mathematical methods and computer programs "as such," are not patentable. The scope of AI algorithm patent protection may be limited. Like the U.S., the European Patent Office (EPO) requires a human inventor for AI-generated inventions, creating ambiguity for fully autonomous AI systems. The UK patent law is similar to the EPC but distinct. AI inventions in the UK must go beyond algorithms, and recent court rulings have stressed the need for practical AI applications. The UK, like other jurisdictions, requires a human inventor for AI-generated inventions, and this focus on technical effect can affect AI patent evaluation.

In a proactive move to promote AI innovation, China has rapidly developed its patent framework. While interpreting industrial applicability broadly, the Chinese patent office has clearer AI patent eligibility requirements. China is discussing AI-generated invention reforms, but human inventorship remains a question, as in the U.S. and Europe. Japan's patent law requires AI inventions to demonstrate technical significance and solve practical problems. Invention requires clear differentiation from prior art. Japan also worries about AI as an inventor, but its law requires human inventors (Maresova, P. et al., 2019).

4. CRITICAL LEGAL FACTORS

A complex problem arises when attempting to ascertain who owns the inventions that are produced by artificial intelligence in cloud environments. It is difficult to assert ownership over inventions that are produced by artificial intelligence systems because traditional patent law requires that the inventor be a human being. Ownership can be contingent on contractual agreements and service terms in cloud environments, which are characterized by the frequent sharing of resources and tools. When determining who owns the rights to inventions, organizations need to take into consideration a variety of factors, including the roles that different parties played in the development and operation of the invention. One way to reduce the likelihood of disputes and ensure that intellectual property is managed in an efficient manner is to establish comprehensive policies that detail ownership rights and responsibilities. The concept of joint ownership is frequently observed in cloud computing environments, particularly in situations where multiple users or entities contribute to the development of an artificial intelligence invention. Because all co-inventors are required to be disclosed, patent applications can become more complicated as a result of this shared ownership. As a further point of interest, when it comes to open-source software, ownership can become unclear due to the fact that different developers are responsible for different licenses and contributions. Organizations should implement clear agreements that define contributions, rights, and responsibilities in order to successfully navigate these challenges. This will ensure that all parties are aware of their respective stakes in any patents that may result from the collaboration among them. Because of this clarity, the process of applying for a patent can be simplified, and you can avoid potential legal conflicts in the future. Significant legal questions, particularly concerning authorship, are raised in relation to the patentability of inventions that are produced by autonomous automated intelligence systems. In the current patent system, human inventors are typically required, which can lead to uncertainty when artificial intelligence systems operate automatically. One of the most difficult questions to answer is whether or not the artificial intelligence (AI) itself can be acknowledged as an inventor, or whether or not the human developers who were responsible for the AI should be listed.

A number of jurisdictions have started to investigate the possibility of implementing reforms in order to accommodate these developments; however, a consensus has not yet been reached. A legal framework that accurately reflects the role that artificial intelligence plays in innovation while still preserving the concept of human inventorship is something that stakeholders absolutely need to engage with policymakers in order to shape. In cloud environments, the interconnected and shared nature of cloud services can make it particularly difficult to enforce patents for artificial intelligence technologies. In the event that multiple users make use of artificial intelligence systems that accidentally incorporate patented methods or algorithms, this could constitute an infringement. In multi-tenant architectures, it can be difficult to determine who is responsible for an infringement because it may be difficult to identify which user or entity is responsible for the violation. Patents are only valid within the jurisdictions in which they are granted, which further complicates enforcement actions associated with cloud computing due to its global nature. The establishment of proactive monitoring and enforcement strategies, which may include comprehensive licensing agreements and audits to track usage within cloud environments, is necessary for organizations to protect their intellectual property. Taking into consideration the nuances of cloud-based technologies, legal avenues for addressing infringement should also be worked out (Choi, J. et al., 2015).

5. REGULATORY CONSIDERATIONS

The AI technology patenting process is supervised by a number of important regulatory agencies. Ensuring that inventions satisfy requirements like novelty and non-obviousness is the primary goal of the United States Patent and Trademark Office (USPTO), which oversees the processing of patent applications and grants in the country. Similar functions are performed in Europe by the European Patent Office (EPO), which emphasizes the technical contribution of inventions while offering its member states a uniform patent application procedure. By providing tools and frameworks for patent protection across jurisdictions, the World Intellectual Property Organization (WIPO) promotes global collaboration in intellectual property issues. Each of these organizations has created particular guidelines that take into account the particular difficulties and advancements related to AI technologies.

AI-specific regulatory frameworks are developing in response to the special qualities of these technologies. To regulate AI applications according to risk levels, for instance, the EU has proposed the AI Act, which includes safety, accountability, and transparency requirements. By defining guidelines for appropriate AI applications, this act may influence how patentability decisions are made regarding AI-related inventions (Chesbrough & Crowther, 2006). Executive orders pertaining to artificial intelligence in the United States prioritize innovation while making sure moral issues are taken into account. These legislative efforts play a pivotal role in molding the creation, patenting, and application of AI technologies, impacting not only compliance but also global competitiveness. In cloud environments where artificial intelligence is used, the relationship between patenting and data privacy is especially important. Strict guidelines govern the collection, use, and storage of personal data. Examples of these regulations are the California Consumer Privacy Act (CCPA) in the United States and the General Data Protection Regulation (GDPR) in the European Union. Organizations must make sure that these regulations are followed when developing AI technologies that rely on big datasets, as this can affect patent strategies. Protecting privacy rights and averting future legal issues require making sure that data used in AI training is anonymized or legally sourced. Organizations must navigate these privacy regulations while pursuing patent protection in order to reduce risks and guarantee the ethical use of data. Harmonizing patent laws pertaining to artificial intelligence (AI) and cloud computing requires international cooperation. Variations in patent laws can present difficulties for companies looking for international protection because AI advancements frequently cross-national borders. Harmonizing patent standards through initiatives like the WIPO's international guidelines is crucial to developing a coherent legal framework that supports innovation. Working together can simplify procedures, cut expenses, and improve the capacity of patent enforcement across borders. Together, nations can advance a fair and well-rounded strategy for AI patenting that addresses moral and legal issues while promoting innovation.

6. RISKS IN PATENTING CLOUD AI

The rapid development of AI and cloud technologies makes patenting difficult. Traditional patent processes may struggle to keep up with rapid innovation, resulting in a backlog of applications and delays in patent rights. Rapid evolution can render patents obsolete, especially if a technology becomes widely available or is replaced by more advanced solutions soon after filing. AI innovations often build on existing technologies, making it harder to prove novelty and non-obviousness for patent approval. The bias in AI algorithms and liability for autonomous system decisions are major ethical concerns when patenting AI technologies. AI systems can maintain biases in training data, resulting in unfair or discriminatory results. Developers and organizations may be liable for patenting these technologies. Defining liability for a patented AI system that harms or biases decisions is difficult. Organizations must carefully assess the ethical implications of their inventions and establish fair and accountable practices as patenting becomes more ethical.

The AI landscape is increasingly vulnerable to patent trolls, which acquire patents to enforce them against other companies rather than develop technologies. Vague or broad patents can lead to litigation, which can hinder innovation. Patent thickets thick webs of overlapping patents can also stifle innovation as companies struggle to navigate the complex landscape without infringing on existing patents. Organizations may be wary of legal issues when exploring new AI solutions, discouraging research and development. AI technology patenting is complicated by the relationship between patents, trade secrets, and open-source software. Each has pros and cons, and companies must decide whether to patent or trade secret their innovations. Trade secrets can provide indefinite protection as long as the information remains confidential, unlike patents. AI projects in open-source software can confuse ownership and patent claims. The patentability of hybrid technologies is questioned because developers may use open-source components. To balance protection and innovation, organizations must carefully consider their IP strategies.

7. CONCLUSION

The patenting process is greatly impacted by the complex interplay of legal, regulatory, and ethical considerations that are present in the landscape of cloud-based AI inventions. According to its definition, cloud-based artificial intelligence inventions cover a wide range of technologies, such as complex algorithms and machine learning models that take advantage of cloud computing's accessibility and scalability. It is essential to patent these innovations in order to encourage innovation, give producers a competitive advantage, and guarantee that their intellectual property can be protected. The distinct qualities of AI systems hosted on cloud servers and the range of inventions that are eligible for patent protection. It highlights how crucial it is to comprehend the requirements for patentability, which include inventiveness, novelty, and industrial applicability. The difficulties in defining the inventive step for AI technologies. The need for a harmonized strategy to successfully navigate the global patent landscape is demonstrated by the variations in patent laws across jurisdictions, including the EU, China, and the United States. Complicating the patenting process are legal issues related to ownership, joint ownership, and the patentability of autonomous innovations. To safeguard their interests and make sure that the law is followed, organizations need to carefully handle these issues.

The environment surrounding AI patents is greatly influenced by regulatory factors, which include the functions of organizations like the USPTO and EPO as well as laws like the EU AI Act. since AI models are trained on massive datasets, data privacy laws like the CCPA and GDPR need to be taken into consideration when developing a patent strategy. Innovation in this field is seriously endangered by issues like the quick development of AI technologies, moral conundrums involving bias and liability, and the existence of thickets and patent trolls. The protection of trade secrets and contributions to open-source software also overlap, which adds to the complexity of intellectual property laws.

REFERENCES

Abdullahi, M., Ahmad, A., Pandey, B. K., & Pandey, D. (2024). Digital Currency Adoption: A Comparative Analysis of Global Trends and the Nigerian eNaira Digital Currency. *SN Computer Science*, *5*(5), 1–11.

Arenas, J. J., & González, D. (2018). Technology transfer models and elements in the university-industry collaboration. *Administrative Sciences*, *8*(2), 19.

Arenas, J. J., & González, D. (2018). Technology transfer models and elements in the university-industry collaboration. *Administrative Sciences*, *8*(2), 19.

Chen, J., Zhao, X., & Wang, Y. (2015). A new measurement of intellectual capital and its impact on innovation performance in an open innovation paradigm. *International Journal of Technology Management*, *67*(1), 1–25.

Chesbrough, H., & Crowther, A. K. (2006). Beyond high tech: early adopters of open innovation in other industries. R&d Management, 36(3), 229-236.

Choi, J., Jang, D., Jun, S., & Park, S. (2015). A predictive model of technology transfer using patent analysis. *Sustainability*, *7*(12), 16175–16195.

Elarmathi, S., Rishabavarthani, P., Sindhuja, M., Elayaraja, P., & Malathi Murugesan, S. Kumarganesh, K. Martin Sagayam, Binay Kumar Pandey, and Digvijay Pandey. (2024). Novel manufacturing systems for cancer diagnosis using ultra-sensitive photonic crystal fiber biosensor with dual-functionalized aptamer-nanocavity. *Microsystem Technologies*, ●●●, 1–20.

George, W. K., Silas, E. I., Pandey, D., & Pandey, B. K. (2024). Utilization of Industry 4.0 Technologies in Nigerian Technical and Vocational Education: A Conundrum for Educators. In *Examining the Rapid Advance of Digital Technology in Africa* (pp. 270–293). IGI Global.

JayaLakshmi. G., Pandey, D., Pandey, B. K., Kaur, P., Mahajan, D. A., & Dari, S. S. (2024). Smart big data collection for intelligent supply chain improvement. In AI and Machine Learning Impacts in Intelligent Supply Chain (pp. 180-195). IGI Global.

Kennedy, G. W., Sunday, S. E., Pandey, D., Kabari, A. D., Pandey, B. K., George, A. S., & Dadheech, P. (2024). Building Information Modeling: Harnessing Innovations for Professional Proficiency. In Emerging Engineering Technologies and Industrial Applications (pp. 305-331). IGI Global.

Khadka, M., Sah, M., Chaudhary, R., Sahani, S. K., Sahani, K., Pandey, B. K., & Pandey, D. (2025). Spectroscopic, quantum chemical, and topological calculations of the phenylephrine molecule using density functional theory. *Scientific Reports*, *15*(1), 208. PMID: 39747169

Konapure, C. G., Pandey, D., Shete, H., Thakar, C. M., Pandey, B. K., & George, A. S. (2025). Artificial Intelligence in Automated Concrete Mix Design Using Computerized Grading Curves. Interdisciplinary Approaches to AI, Internet of Everything, and Machine Learning, 567-586.

Kumar, B., Pandey, D., Pandey, B. K., & George, A. S. (2024). Higher Education in the Last Four Decades: A Review of Paradigm Shifts in Policy Frameworks. Design and Implementation of Higher Education Learners' Learning Outcomes (HELLO), 333-348.

Kumar, M. S., Prasanna, P. L., Lalitha, M., Joy, M., Jha, S. S., & Pandey, B. K. (2025). Utilizing the Internet of Everything and Artificial Intelligence for Real-Time Workforce Management. In Role of Internet of Everything (IOE), VLSI Architecture, and AI in Real-Time Systems (pp. 153-168). IGI Global Scientific Publishing.

Kumarganesh, S., & Malathi Murugesan, C. Ganesh, N. Santhiyakumari, M. Thangavel, K. Jayaram, K. Martin Sagayam, Binay Kumar Pandey, and Digvijay Pandey. (2024). Hybrid plasmonic biosensors with deep learning for colorectal cancer detection. *Plasmonics*, •••, 1–15.

Lakshmi, K. V. N., Rajan, R., Pandey, D., & Pandey, B. K. (2024). Circular economy: A catalyst for economic growth-an empirical study. *Circular Economy and Sustainability*, •••, 1–22.

Li, F., Zhang, S., & Jin, Y. (2018). Sustainability of university technology transfer: Mediating effect of inventor's technology service. *Sustainability*, *10*(6), 2085.

Maheshwari, R. Uma, S. Kumarganesh, Shree KVM, A. Gopalakrishnan, K. Selvi, B. Paulchamy, P. Rishabavarthani, K. Martin Sagayam, Binay Kumar Pandey, and Digvijay Pandey. (2024). Advanced plasmonic resonance-enhanced biosensor for comprehensive real-time detection and analysis of deepfake content. *Plasmonics*, •••, 1–18.

Maheshwari, R. U., Paulchamy, B., Pandey, B. K., & Pandey, D. (2024). Enhancing sensing and imaging capabilities through surface plasmon resonance for deepfake image detection. *Plasmonics*, •••, 1–20.

Maresova, P., Stemberkova, R., & Fadeyi, O. (2019). Models, processes, and roles of universities in technology transfer management: A systematic review. *Administrative Sciences*, *9*(3), 67.

Maresova, P., Stemberkova, R., & Fadeyi, O. (2019). Models, processes, and roles of universities in technology transfer management: A systematic review. *Administrative Sciences*, *9*(3), 67.

Muralidhar, L. B., Lakshmi, K. V. N., Swapna, H. R., Rupani, J., Nethravathi, K., Pandey, B. K., & Pandey, D. (2024). Impact of Organizational Culture on The Level of Corporate Social Responsibility Investments: An Exploratory Study. *Circular Economy and Sustainability*, •••, 1–19.

Pandey, B. K., Kanike, U. K., George, A. S., & Pandey, D. (Eds.). (2024d). *AI and machine learning impacts in intelligent supply chain*. IGI Global.

Pandey, B. K., Nassa, V. K., Mukundan, A. P., Mahajan, D. A., Pandey, D., George, A. S., & Dadheech, P. (2024c). An Industry-Focused Traffic System Utilising Internet of Things. In *Emerging Engineering Technologies and Industrial Applications* (pp. 200–213). IGI Global.

Pandey, B. K., & Pandey, D. (2023). Parametric optimization and prediction of enhanced thermoelectric performance in co-doped CaMnO3 using response surface methodology and neural network. *Journal of Materials Science Materials in Electronics*, *34*(21), 1589.

Pandey, B. K., & Pandey, D. (2025). Securing healthcare medical image information using advance morphological component analysis, information hiding systems, and hybrid convolutional neural networks on IoMT. *Computers in Biology and Medicine*, *185*, 109499. PMID: 39642698

Pandey, B. K., Pandey, D., & Lelisho, M. E. (2024a). Face mask identification with enhanced cuckoo optimization and deep learning-based faster regional neural network. *Scientific Reports*, *14*(1), 29719. PMID: 39613761

Pandey, B. K., Pandey, D., & Sahani, S. K. (2024b). Autopilot control unmanned aerial vehicle system for sewage defect detection using deep learning. *Engineering Reports*, •••, 12852.

Pandey, B. K., Paramashivan, M. A., Pandey, D., George, A. S., Agarwal, A., Mahajan, D. A., . . . Pramanik, S. (2024e). Future Directions of Digital Twin Architectures for 6G Communication Networks. In Security Issues and Solutions in 6G Communications and Beyond (pp. 197-211). IGI Global.

Pandey, D., Nassa, V. K., Pandey, B. K., Thankachan, B., Dadheech, P., Mahajan, D. A., & George, A. S. (2024a). Artificial Intelligence and Machine Learning and Its Application in the Field of Computational Visual Analysis. In Emerging Engineering Technologies and Industrial Applications (pp. 36-57). IGI Global.

Pandey, D., & Pandey, B. K. (2022). An efficient deep neural network with adaptive galactic swarm optimization for complex image text extraction. In *Process Mining Techniques for Pattern Recognition* (pp. 121–137). CRC Press.

Pandey, D., Pandey, B. K., Nassa, V. K., Mahajan, D. A., George, A. S., & Dadheech, P. (2024c). Optimized Throughput-Based Broadcasting for Next Generation Wireless Networks. In Emerging Engineering Technologies and Industrial Applications (pp. 355-368). IGI Global.

Pandey, D., Pandey, B. K., Paramashivan, M. A., Mahajan, D. A., Dadheech, P. D., George, A. S., & Hameed, A. S. (2024b). Advanced Digital Data Processing Using Cloud Cryptography: Industrial Applications. In Emerging Engineering Technologies and Industrial Applications (pp. 255-268). IGI Global.

Rai, P. K., Pandey, D., & Pandey, B. K. (2024). The future of enterprise and innovation is compute as a commodity, or CaaC. *Partners Universal International Research Journal*, *3*(2), 89–94.

Saravanakumar, R., TamilSelvi, T., Pandey, D., Pandey, B. K., Mahajan, D. A., & Lelisho, M. E. (2024). Big data processing using hybrid Gaussian mixture model with salp swarm algorithm. *Journal of Big Data*, *11*(1), 167.

Satheesh, N., Gopisankar, N., Kumarganesh, S., Anthoniraj, S., Saravanakumar, S., & Martin Sagayam, K., Binay Kumar Pandey, and Digvijay Pandey. (2025). Advanced AI-driven emergency response systems for enhanced vehicle and human safety. *Iran Journal of Computer Science*, •••, 1–16.

Saxena, A., Agarwal, A., Pandey, B. K., & Pandey, D. (2024). Examination of the Criticality of Customer Segmentation Using Unsupervised Learning Methods. *Circular Economy and Sustainability*, •••, 1–14.

Shahul, A., Muniandi, B., Paramashivan, M. A., Pandey, D., Pandey, B. K., Dadheech, P., & George, H. (2024). An Analysis of Algorithms and Methods Based on Image Processing for Medical Applications. In *Emerging Engineering Technologies and Industrial Applications* (pp. 173–186). IGI Global.

Sheela, M. S., Kumarganesh, S., Pandey, B. K., & Lelisho, M. E. (2025). Integration of silver nanostructures in wireless sensor networks for enhanced biochemical sensing. *Discover Nano*, *20*(1), 7. PMID: 39804434

Siegel, D. S., & Wright, M. (2007). Intellectual property: The assessment. *Oxford Review of Economic Policy*, *23*(4), 529–540.

Singh, S., Madaan, G., Swapna, H. R., Singh, A., Pandey, B. K., George, A. S., & Pandey, D. (2025b). Unleashing the Power of AI and Data Analysis: Transforming Insights into Action. In Interdisciplinary Approaches to AI, Internet of Everything, and Machine Learning (pp. 1-24). IGI Global Scientific Publishing.

Singh, S., Madaan, G., Swapna, H. R., Singh, A., Pandey, D., George, A. S., & Pandey, B. K. (2025a). Empowering Connectivity: Exploring the Internet of Things. In Interdisciplinary Approaches to AI, Internet of Everything, and Machine Learning (pp. 89-116). IGI Global Scientific Publishing.

Chapter 13
International Law and Cybersecurity in the Era of Cloud Computing

Sunita Singh Khatana
Faculty of Law, Manipal University Jaipur, India

Sony Kulshrestha
Department of Law, Manipal University Jaipur, India

ABSTRACT

Cloud computing and the intersection of international law and cybersecurity, highlighting the pressing need for an all-encompassing framework to address the particular difficulties posed by the digital environment. Protecting sensitive data and upholding operational integrity become more crucial as more businesses move to cloud services. This requires an awareness of the obligations that cloud service providers and their clients have. A proactive approach to risk management and strong security measures are imperative given the increasing cybersecurity threats that result from this reliance on cloud computing.

1. INTRODUCTION

Cloud computings explosive growth has changed the digital landscape by providing never-before-seen levels of efficiency, scalability (Pandey, B. K., & Pandey, D., 2023), and flexibility for individuals, enterprises, and governments. But as our reliance on cloud-based technologies increases, cybersecurity is becoming an increasingly important concern. The prevalence of cyberattacks, data breaches, and privacy violations has increased, making a strong legal framework necessary to

DOI: 10.4018/979-8-3693-9581-3.ch013

protect vital infrastructure and data (Pandey, B. K., & Pandey, D., 2025). In order to solve these global cybersecurity challenges, international law which regulates relations between nations is essential. Because cloud computing services frequently operate across multiple jurisdictions, the borderless nature of cyberspace makes it more difficult to enforce national laws and regulations. International collaboration and harmonization of cybersecurity policies are now required as a result of this. The basis for international cybersecurity standards has been established by agreements like the Budapest Convention on Cybercrime and laws like the General Data Protection Regulation (GDPR), but there are still large gaps in the field (Satheesh, N. et al., 2025). Many nations still do not have comprehensive cybercrime laws in place, and inconsistent legal frameworks and jurisdictional difficulties make enforcement difficult. The legal environment is further complicated by the shared responsibility model in cloud computing, which assigns users and service providers equal responsibility for security maintenance. Users are expected to manage access controls and prevent data breaches (Kumar, M. S. et al., 2025), while service providers are required to adhere to international data protection laws and implement stringent security measures. In order to create a more secure and cohesive global digital environment, countries, service providers, and regulatory bodies must work together more closely at the intersection of international law and cybersecurity in cloud computing. In order to ensure a safer and more resilient cyberspace for everybody, it will be imperative that international legal frameworks continue to evolve in order to address the new cybersecurity threats brought about by cloud computing.

1.1 Increasing Reliance on Cloud Services

Cloud computing has emerged as an indispensable component in the management and storage of data for individuals, businesses, and governments over the past few years. Users are able to store, process, and access data from virtually any location thanks to cloud services, which have revolutionized traditional information technology infrastructures (Konapure, C. G. et al., 2025). Cloud services offer unparalleled scalability, cost-efficiency, and accessibility. Because of the flexibility that cloud solutions offer, businesses are able to quickly adjust to shifting requirements, expand their operations across the globe, and cut costs that are associated with maintaining servers that are located on business premises. This increasing reliance on cloud technology is occurring across a wide range of industries (Khadka, M. et al., 2025), including the public sector, healthcare, education, and finance, as organizations strive to improve their operational efficiency and data management. The Internet of Things (IoT), artificial intelligence (AI) (Singh, S. et al., 2025), and big data analytics are some of the innovations that are supported by cloud services. Cloud services further improve business continuity by allowing remote access. It is in cloud environments that these technologies flourish, which opens up new possibilities for automation, personalized services, and decision-making that is driven by data. This growing reliance on cloud computing can also bring about new challenges in terms of cybersecurity. The risk of cyberattacks, data breaches, and unauthorized access has significantly increased as a result of the widespread storage of sensitive data online (Sharma, M. et al., 2025). By weighing the advantages of cloud computing against the requirements of stringent cybersecurity measures, data protection policies, and compliance with international regulations, organizations are required to strike a balance. The fact that cloud services are global and decentralized necessitates an all-encompassing strategy for dealing with these risks, which frequently extend beyond the borders of individual nations (Qiu, H. et al.,, 2019).

1.2 Growing Cybersecurity Threats

Cybersecurity threats have become more frequent and sophisticated as cloud computing becomes the foundation of contemporary digital infrastructure. These days, businesses have to contend with a wide range of cyberthreats, such as ransomware attacks, insider threats, distributed denial of service (DDoS) attacks, and data breaches (Pandey, B. K. et al., 2024a). All of these threats have the potential to compromise confidential data and interfere with vital business processes. Because cloud environments store a lot of data, they are often the target of cybercriminals who use security flaws to obtain unauthorized access (Pandey, B. K. et al., 2024b). Data breaches, which expose private information like financial records, personal information, and intellectual property, are one of the main risks to cloud security. Organizations may suffer major financial losses, harm to their reputations, and legal ramifications as a result of these breaches. Additionally, because cloud-hosted services are so accessible and the value of the data they hold makes them a prime target for cybercriminals, ransomware attacks have increased. In these attacks, hackers encrypt data and demand payment in exchange for its release (Basha, A. J. et al., 2024). Insider threats, in which workers or contractors accidentally or purposely jeopardize data security, are another developing worry. Because both users and providers are responsible for maintaining security, the multi-tenant architecture and shared responsibility model in cloud environments can increase these risks. Cloud systems can be exploited due to mis-configurations, lax access controls, and disregard for best practices. The enforcement of cybersecurity measures is made more difficult by the global nature of cloud computing, where data centers are frequently dispersed across multiple jurisdictions. Because cyberattacks can come from places with weak legal systems or little cooperation with foreign law enforcement, this makes regulatory compliance and incident response more difficult. Organizations must embrace proactive security strategies, put strong encryption protocols in place, and promote international cooperation in order to handle these worldwide risks in the cloud era as cybersecurity threats continue to evolve (Li, Z., Yang, Z., & Xie, S., 2019).

2. GLOBAL FRAMEWORK OF INTERNATIONAL LAW

2.1 Principles of International Law

Relationships between states and other international actors are governed by the foundational principles of international law. The sovereignty of states, which upholds each states right to self-governance free from outside intervention, is one of the fundamental concepts illustrated in Figure 1. The need for peaceful resolution of conflicts is emphasized by the other fundamental principle, which forbids the use of force (Sheela, M. S. et al., 2025). While all states are required to protect and advance the rights and dignity of individuals, the principle of non-intervention shields states from external aggression. When taken as a whole, these values seek to uphold international cooperation, peace, and security (Fan, X. et al., 2019).

- *Sovereignty*: The fundamental tenet of international law, sovereignty gives states the sole right to self-govern without intervention from outside parties. It lays down states' rights to self-govern over their populations, political systems, and territory, as well as their legal equality. This idea is essential to preserving world peace and guaranteeing that states uphold one another's right to self-determination.
- *Jurisdiction*: The legal power of a state to administer justice and enforce the law within its borders is known as jurisdiction. This principle can take many different forms: extraterritorial jurisdiction (the power to apply national laws outside of borders), territorial jurisdiction (the right to enforce laws within boundaries), and personal jurisdiction (the power to rule over people based on their nationality or place of residence). Cross-border criminal cases frequently involve jurisdictional problems, which make cooperation between states necessary to handle legal complexities.
- *State Responsibility*: Under international law, states are responsible for the acts of their citizens. A state may be held accountable for damages if it engages in wrongdoing that goes against its responsibilities, such as breaking a treaty or hurting another state. In addition to highlighting the significance of accountability (KVM, S. et al., 2024), this principle offers a legal framework for redress, which may include satisfaction for the harmed party or restitu-

tion. It works to discourage illegal activity and encourage adherence to international standards.

- *Self-Determination*: The right of peoples to choose their political status and to pursue their own economic, social, and cultural development is acknowledged by the principle of self-determination. This idea has been especially important when it comes to the decolonization process and the affirmation of minority rights. It highlights the idea that people and communities ought to be able to freely choose their own leaders and to direct their own lives without interference from outside forces (Kumar, R., & Goyal, R., 2019).
- *Human Rights*: States are required by international law to uphold, defend, and realize the rights and inherent dignity of every person. Numerous international treaties, including the Universal Declaration of Human Rights and regional human rights conventions, uphold this idea. States are held responsible for transgressions, and procedures are in place to resolve complaints and encourage adherence, demonstrating a dedication to protecting the liberties and rights of every person (Lakshmi, K. V. N. et al., 2024).
- *Customary International Law*: Consisting of unwritten regulations derived from consistent state practice and the conviction that such practices are legally required, customary international law is based on opinion (pinion juris). These standards change over time and are a reflection of state agreements and collective behavior. Customary law is a vital adjunct to treaty law that directs state behavior in the absence of formal agreements. It encompasses a wide range of topics, including human rights, the laws of war, and diplomatic immunity.
- *Peaceful Settlement of Disputes*: This idea promotes states to avoid using force in their attempts to resolve disputes by peaceful methods like arbitration, mediation, or negotiation. Encouraging peaceful conflict resolution is essential to preserving global security and tranquillity. A number of international frameworks, such as the United Nations Charter, which promotes communication and collaboration to resolve conflicts and stop them from turning into armed conflicts, support this idea (Saravanakumar, R. et al., 2024).

Figure 1. Fundamental principles of international law

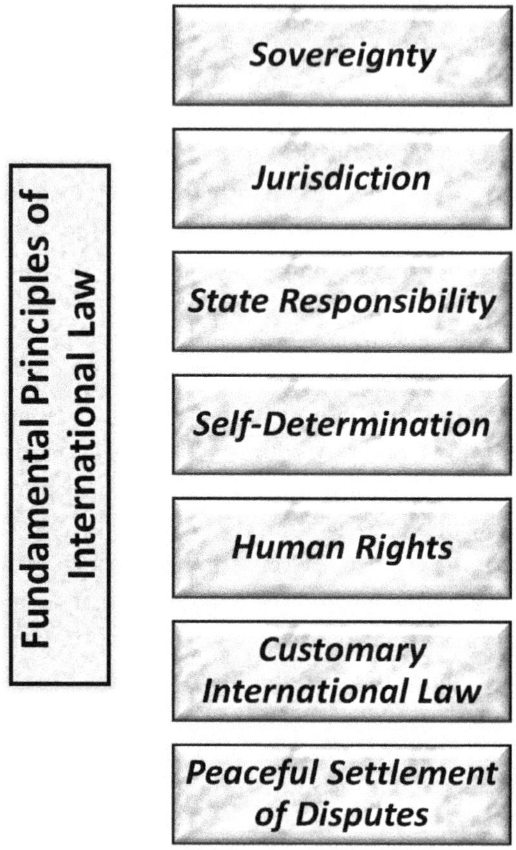

2.2 Relevant International Treaties and Conventions

Global treaties and conventions set standards for state behavior in cybersecurity, human rights, and trade. Nations cooperate under these agreements to uphold shared standards and commitments. In cybersecurity, several treaties and conventions address growing digital threats and promote international cooperation (Kumarganesh, S. et al., 2024). The 2001 Council of Europe Budapest Convention on Cybercrime is of great importance. By legalizing international cooperation in cybercrime investigations and prosecutions, this treaty promotes cybercrime cooperation. Computer-related crime laws are harmonised under the convention, enabling cross-border law enforcement cooperation. Its guidelines for mutual assistance and promotion of effective legislation make the Budapest Convention a cornerstone of international cybercrime efforts. While primarily focused on international trade, the

1947 General Agreement on Tariffs and Trade (GATT) affects cybersecurity in the digital economy. The GATT's non-discrimination and transparency principles are essential for secure online trade as trade moves online. The agreement emphasizes the intersection of economic security and digital safety, emphasizing the need for strong cybersecurity in trade agreements to protect businesses and consumers. The 1945 UN Charter establishes international relations and peace and security. It predates the digital age, but its provisions on peaceful dispute resolution and the prohibition of force are increasingly relevant to cyber warfare and international cybersecurity norms (Haus, M. et al., 2017). The UN Group of Governmental Experts on Developments in the Field of Information and Telecommunications in the Context of International Security also addresses cybersecurity issues and promotes state dialogue. The 1948 Universal Declaration of Human Rights (UDHR) also affects digitally related international law. Article 27 states that everyone has the right to cultural life and scientific advancements, including digital access. As connectivity increases, internet access, data privacy, and personal data protection become important. Besides these foundational documents, the Council of Europe's Convention 108, the Convention for the Protection of Individuals with regard to Automatic Processing of Personal Data, establishes data protection and privacy rights in the face of technological advancement. Data breaches and privacy concerns have increased, so this convention provides a framework for states to develop and enforce personal data protection laws, reinforcing individual rights in the digital age. Important international treaties and conventions set norms and improve international cooperation on cybersecurity and other issues. This framework will help states respond to evolving digital threats and create a secure international digital environment. Through dialogue and collaboration, the international community can address cybersecurity issues while upholding sovereignty, human rights, and peace (Fazal, H. et al., 2020).

2.3 Role of International Organizations

International organizations are essential for establishing international standards, encouraging state-to-state cooperation, and tackling difficult problems including cybersecurity-related ones. The United Nations (UN) and the International Telecommunication Union (ITU) are two important organizations in this field; they both make major contributions to global initiatives to promote cybersecurity and create a safe digital environment. The main platform for international cooperation and communication among its member states is the United Nations. The UN deals with a wide range of topics, such as human rights, sustainable development, and peace and security, through its many agencies and bodies. The UN has launched a number of initiatives in the field of cybersecurity with the goal of advancing global norms and standards for responsible state behaviour in cyberspace. In talks about cybersecurity, the UN Group of Governmental Experts on Developments in the Field of Information and Telecommunications in the Context of International Security has played a significant role in highlighting the necessity of international cooperation in thwarting cyber threats. In order to assist developing nations in strengthening their cybersecurity capabilities, the UN also supports capacity-building programs, acknowledging that combating transnational cybercrime and safeguarding vital infrastructure require teamwork. Information and communication technologies are the exclusive focus of the UN's International Telecommunication Union, a specialized agency. In order to maintain the smooth and secure operation of the global communication network, the ITU is essential in setting international standards for telecommunications. The ITU has created a number of frameworks and guidelines in the field of cybersecurity to help member states improve their cybersecurity posture (Muralidhar, L. B. et al., 2024). The group's Global Cybersecurity Agenda offers a framework for strategic collaboration between public and private sectors, as well as civil society, with the goal of improving the security of ICTs. The ITU also arranges forums, workshops, and capacity-building programs to help member states exchange knowledge and best practices and effectively combat emerging cyberthreats. The UN and ITU work together to create standards, promote collaboration, and assist nations in protecting their digital spaces. As such, they serve as important cornerstones in the global cybersecurity framework. These groups support international peace and security, protect individual rights, and help nations navigate the challenges of the digital age by fostering communication and cooperation. They also help to create a more resilient and safer global cyberspace (Tu, S. et al., 2021).

3. CYBERSECURITY CHALLENGES IN CLOUD COMPUTING

3.1 Common Threats in Cloud Environments

Threats that are common to cloud environments can put data security and operational integrity at risk. Cloud environments are vulnerable to a variety of threats which are as shown in the figure 2. Data breaches, which frequently occur as a consequence of unauthorized access to potentially sensitive information, constitute a significant threat (Pandey, B. K. et al., 2024c). The fact that cloud settings that have been improperly configured can also expose data to vulnerabilities makes it absolutely necessary for businesses to implement appropriate security protocols. Malware attacks, such as ransomware, have the capability to infiltrate cloud services, encrypting data and demanding a ransom in exchange for its decryption. Attacks that deliver a denial-of-service (DoS) can cause disruptions to services, which can result in downtime and a loss of productivity. The last point is that the integrity of the data can be compromised by insider threats, which can come from employees or third-party vendors. This highlights the significance of having robust access controls and monitoring.

- *Data Inaccuracies*: When private information kept in the cloud is accessed by unauthorized parties, it can lead to data breaches, which pose a serious risk to cloud environments. These hacks have the potential to reveal confidential, financial, or personal data, which could have disastrous effects on both people and businesses (Elarmathi, S. et al., 2024). Because cloud services are shared, there is a greater chance of security breaches, especially if strong security measures like encryption, access controls, and monitoring are not properly put in place. To reduce this risk and protect their data, organizations need to give data protection strategies top priority.
- *Inadequate Management of Identity and Access* (IAM): Unauthorized access to cloud resources can be caused by inadequate identity and access management procedures. Organizations run the risk of giving users excessive permissions without strong IAM protocols, such as multi-factor authentication and frequent access reviews, which makes it simpler for attackers to exploit vulnerabilities. Securing sensitive data and systems such that only authorized personnel have access depends on effective identity and access management. Strict access controls and frequent permission reviews are important ways for organizations to lessen the possibility of unwanted access (Pandey, B. K. et al., 2024d).
- *Hacking of Accounts*: A common threat is account hijacking, which happens when hackers take over a user's cloud account. This usually happens as a result of phishing attempts or stolen credentials. Once in, attackers can perform fraudulent activities, alter data, or interfere with services. Weak password practices, like using the same credentials across several platforms, make this threat worse. To prevent account theft, businesses should advise users on secure password usage and put robust authentication procedures in place.
- *At Risk APIs*: Application Programming Interfaces (APIs) are widely used in cloud services to enable communication between apps and cloud resources. However, these APIs could serve as entry points for attacks if they are not developed and implemented securely. Unauthorized access, data leakage, and manipulation of cloud resources are all possible with insecure APIs, which puts the integrity and confidentiality of data at serious risk (George, W. K. et al., 2024). In order to detect and fix vulnerabilities, organizations need to give priority to API security by putting authentication, encryption, and regular security assessments into place.

- *Insider Threats of Malice*: Insider threats are dangers posed by workers or outside contractors who may purposefully or inadvertently jeopardize cloud security. Negligent insiders run the risk of disclosing sensitive information because of lax security procedures, while malicious insiders can use their access to steal data (Abdullahi, M. et al., 2024) or interfere with operations. To identify and reduce insider threats, organizations need to put strong policies in place, hold frequent training sessions, and put monitoring systems in place. Establishing a security-aware culture can help organizations lower the risk of insider incidents.
- *Attacks that Deny Service* (DoS): The goal of denial-of-service attacks is to interfere with cloud service availability by flooding the system with too many requests or traffic. This may result in service interruptions, which would have a major effect on customer access and business operations. Because cloud environments rely on shared resources and internet connectivity, they are especially susceptible to denial of service (DoS) attacks. By putting rate limits, traffic filtering, and redundancy measures in place, organizations can lessen this threat and make sure that vital services continue to function even in the event of an attack.

Figure 2. Threats in cloud environments

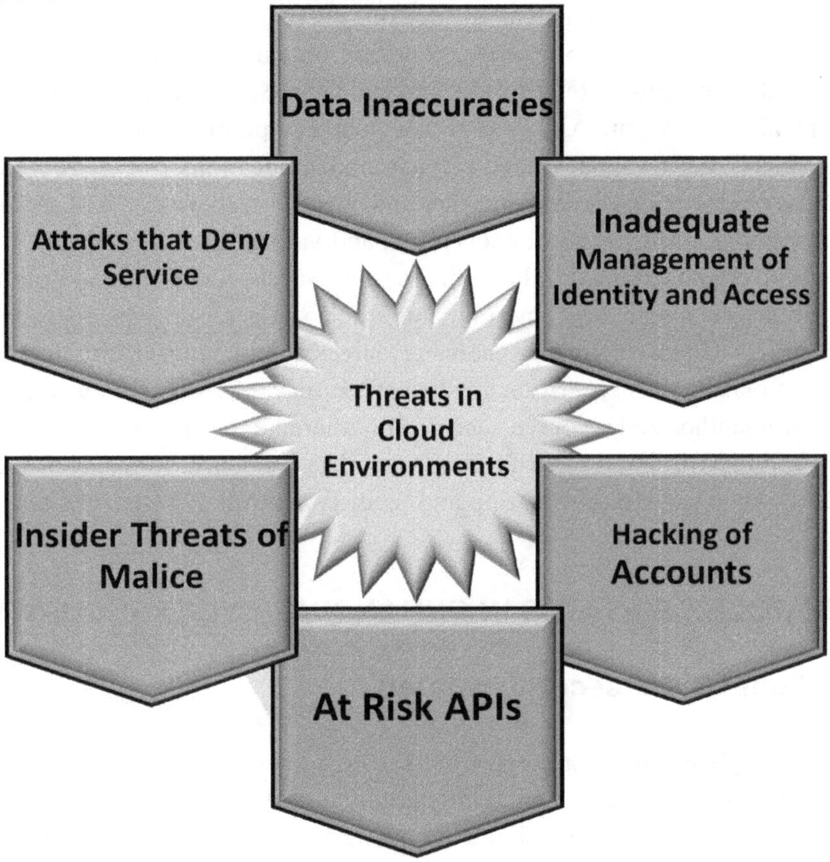

3.2 Vulnerabilities Specific to Cloud Computing

Cloud computing offers scalability, flexibility, and cost efficiency, but it also poses unique vulnerabilities that organizations must address to protect their data and applications. Understanding these vulnerabilities is essential for cloud risk management. A major risk is data loss. Cloud service providers must ensure data integrity and availability because data is stored off-site on third-party servers. Accidental deletion, data corruption (Satheesh, N. et al., 2025), and provider infrastructure hardware failures can cause data loss. Cloud service providers may fail catastrophically or go out of business, causing organizations to lose critical data. Organisations should implement their own data backup strategies, including regular backups to alternative storage solutions, to mitigate this risk and recover lost data. Another risk is misconfiguration. Complex cloud configurations can lead to security gaps if not managed properly. Misconfigurations can result from improper cloud service setup, access controls, or security patching. Misconfigured settings can allow malicious actors to access data or applications, exposing organizations to attacks. Regular security audits and automated tools to find and fix misconfigurations can mitigate this vulnerability. Insecure APIs are another cloud computing vulnerability (Kumar, B. et al., 2024). APIs connect cloud services and applications, but unsecured APIs can expose organisations to data breaches and unauthorized access. API attacks can result from poor authentication, encryption, and validation. To protect APIs from exploitation, organisations should implement strict access controls, encryption, and regular security testing. Cloud environments are also vulnerable to shared technology vulnerabilities. Cloud computing shares resources among tenants, creating vulnerabilities. If one tenant's security is inadequate, it may expose other tenants to data leakage or unauthorized resource access. This shared environment requires strong account and infrastructure security. For tenant data and applications, cloud service providers should use strong isolation and security controls.

4. THE ROLE OF STATES IN ENHANCING CYBERSECURITY

4.1 National Cybersecurity Strategies

National cybersecurity strategies are broad frameworks that direct a nation's efforts to defend sensitive data, vital infrastructure, and information systems against cyberattacks. In an increasingly digital world, these tactics are crucial for preserving public safety, economic stability, and national security. A well-defined strategy usually starts with a comprehensive analysis of the cybersecurity environment as it stands today, highlighting threats, vulnerabilities, and the country's general preparedness for handling cyber incidents. Governments can more effectively allocate resources and create effective policies to strengthen their defenses by having a better understanding of the current state of cybersecurity. Clearly defining goals and priorities is a crucial part of national cybersecurity strategies (Pandey, D. et al., 2024). These objectives frequently include raising public awareness of cybersecurity, strengthening incident response capabilities, fostering cooperation between the public and private sectors, and strengthening the resilience of critical infrastructure. Many nations create specialized agencies, like national cybersecurity agencies, to accomplish these goals. These agencies are in charge of organizing activities, carrying out research, and putting policies into effect. These organizations are essential in promoting cooperation and information exchange between different stakeholders, such as governmental bodies, businesses, and educational institutions. Important components of national cybersecurity strategies are also education and training.

Developing a workforce with the necessary cybersecurity skills can help countries bolster their defenses against cyberattacks. Various levels of education, from K–12 to postsecondary education and professional training, contribute to the development of a strong talent pool with the know-how to meet new challenges. Cultivating a culture of security that enables people and organizations to take proactive steps in safeguarding their digital assets depends on increasing public awareness of cybersecurity best practices. An increasingly important component of successful national cybersecurity strategies is international cooperation. Since cyber threats frequently cross-national boundaries, it is crucial that nations work together to coordinate responses to incidents and address common challenges. Participating in international forums and partnerships allows countries to share best practices, improve collective capabilities, and exchange information (Shahul, A. et al., 2024). This cooperative strategy is essential for creating international cybersecurity norms and standards and for encouraging assistance from one party to another during emergencies. These tactics are kept up to date in the face of constantly changing threats and technological advancements through regular reviews and updates. Governments can pinpoint areas for development and modify their strategies to meet new challenges by gauging progress against predetermined goals. Maintaining strong national cybersecurity postures and making sure that countries are ready to defend against the constantly shifting landscape of cyber threats depend on this dynamic process.

4.2 International Cooperation and Collaboration

International cybersecurity cooperation is crucial as cyber threats evolve and become more sophisticated. Cyberattacks in one country can have global repercussions due to the internet's interconnectedness. Therefore, countries are realizing the importance of cooperating to improve their cybersecurity and share resources and knowledge. Establishing cybercrime task forces and response teams promotes international cooperation (Muniandi, B. et al., 2024). Law enforcement and intelligence units investigate cross-border cyber incidents in these specialized units. To collaborate on cybersecurity policies, share threat intelligence, and conduct joint exercises, EU member states created the European Union Agency for Cybersecurity (ENISA). Cyber threats that exploit jurisdictional gaps can be addressed quickly and effectively by nations cooperating. International cybersecurity simulations and exercises also improve cooperation and preparedness. NATO events like "Locked Shields," simulate large-scale cyberattacks and involve multi-nation partnerships to mitigate threats in real time. They test technical skills and build relationships and communication between participating nations. Collaboration exercises improve national strategies and coordination in the event of cyberattacks. Fostering regional cybersecurity frameworks can also improve cooperation among neighbouring countries facing similar threats. By sharing best practices, training together, and creating a regional incident response framework, the ASEAN Cybersecurity Co-operation Strategy aims to improve collaboration among member states. Localized approaches allow countries to address regional issues using shared resources and expertise. Nations sharing threat intelligence and best practices is crucial to international collaboration. Forums like FIRST help share emerging threats, vulnerabilities, and mitigation strategies. Collective intelligence helps nations stay ahead of evolving cyber threats by sharing experiences and insights. Collaborations with cybersecurity and technology firms increase governments expertise. International standards are becoming more important as cybersecurity evolves. Countries pledge to behave responsibly in cyberspace through the Paris Call for Trust and Security in Cyberspace. These norms encourage cooperation and discourage cybercrime by guiding countries' interactions and fostering accountability.

5. CLOUD COMPUTING PROVIDERS AND CYBERSECURITY RESPONSIBILITIES

5.1 Cloud Providers and Cybersecurity Duties

The security and integrity of the data and applications that are hosted in the environments belonging to cloud service providers is an extremely important role that they play. Protecting data from unauthorized access, breaches, and other forms of cyber threats is one of their primary responsibilities, and they are responsible for implementing robust security measures. As part of this, encryption technologies are implemented to protect sensitive information while it is both at rest and in transit. This ensures that only authorized users are able to access the data. Maintaining a secure infrastructure is another important responsibility (Singh, S. et al., 2025). Performing routine security audits, addressing vulnerabilities, and promptly updating software and systems to address potential vulnerabilities are all necessary steps in this process. To ensure that only authorized personnel are able to access vital systems and data, providers are required to implement stringent access controls. Identification of any potentially malicious behavior requires the utilization of methods such as identity and access management (IAM), multi-factor authentication, and continuous monitoring of user activities. It is also essential to operate in accordance with the various regulatory frameworks and industry standards. It is common for organizations to be subject to obligations imposed by data protection laws, such as the Health Insurance Portability and Accountability Act (HIPAA) or the General Data Protection Regulation (GDPR). The provision of features such as data residency options and audit capabilities to assist customers in meeting their legal obligations is an essential component of cloud service providers efforts to guarantee that their offerings are in accordance with these requirements. Communicating openly and honestly with customers about security policies, incident response procedures, and service-level agreements (SLAs) is absolutely necessary in order to earn their trust (Vinodhini, V. et al., 2022). The security measures that are currently in place, as well as the protocol that providers will follow in the event of any security incidents, must be understood by organizations. Last but not least, training and awareness programs should be made available to customers in order to educate them on the most effective methods for using cloud services in a secure manner. The adoption of this collaborative approach gives organizations the ability to play an active role in the cybersecurity posture of their organization, which ultimately results in an improvement in the cloud environment's overall security.

5.2 Accountability During Cyber Incidents

The entire cybersecurity plan of an organization must include accountability in the event of a cyber incident. Knowing who is in charge of what after a breach happens can have a big impact on how well the organization responds and how quickly it can function again. External partners and service providers are included in this accountability in addition to internal teams. Creating a well-defined governance framework within the company is a crucial component of accountability (Rai, P. K. et al., 2024). The roles and duties of every cybersecurity team should be outlined in this structure to make sure that everyone is aware of their responsibilities prior to, during, and following an incident. The legal team may handle compliance and regulatory notifications, for example, while the IT department is in charge of technical response measures. Organizations can guarantee that there is clarity regarding accountability for particular actions by establishing this framework, which is crucial for a successful response. Organizations also need to consider who is responsible for sensitive data when it comes to partners and third-party vendors. Contracts with these third parties ought to contain explicit provisions outlining their obligations with regard to cybersecurity, including safeguards for data and procedures for handling incidents. There are repercussions for any security breaches and these partners are held equally responsible for protecting information. Establishing accountability is frequently greatly aided by regulatory requirements. Rules governing breach notification and data protection, among other requirements, govern how businesses must react to cyber incidents in numerous jurisdictions. Since organizations are required to show that they are following the set standards, complying with these regulations serves to both enforce the law and strengthen accountability. A comprehensive assessment of the organization's response to a cyber incident is another aspect of accountability that identifies its advantages and disadvantages. The effectiveness of the response and the areas where organizations' security procedures can be strengthened can both be greatly enhanced by this post-incident analysis. Organizations can improve their preparedness for future incidents and, eventually, their resilience against cyber threats by cultivating a culture of accountability and continuous improvement .

6. CONCLUSION

The incorporation of international law and cybersecurity in the context of cloud computing is imperative in order to effectively tackle the constantly changing obstacles presented by cyber threats. Comprehending the mutual obligations of cloud service providers and clients is crucial, given the growing dependence of organizations on cloud services. Since cyberthreats frequently cross-national boundaries and demand a coordinated response, the importance of international cooperation and collaboration cannot be emphasized. It is obvious that cloud computing cybersecurity requires a proactive approach. Establishing a culture of awareness and readiness is just as important for organizations as putting strong security measures in place. This entails participating in training and awareness initiatives, updating security protocols on a regular basis, and keeping up with emerging threats. Organizations can improve their defenses against possible breaches and lessen their effects by taking a proactive approach. Increased international cooperation and legal reform in the cybersecurity space are urgently needed. To create precise policies, rules, and standards governing cloud cybersecurity practices, governments, organizations, and international bodies must collaborate. Stakeholders can build a more secure digital environment that safeguards people, businesses, and nations by encouraging cooperation and filling in legal gaps. This cooperative effort will produce a more robust global cybersecurity environment that can address the difficulties presented by the constantly changing cyber threat landscape.

REFERENCES

Abdullahi, M., Ahmad, A., Pandey, B. K., & Pandey, D. (2024). Digital Currency Adoption: A Comparative Analysis of Global Trends and the Nigerian eNaira Digital Currency. *SN Computer Science*, *5*(5), 1–11.

Basha, A. J., Maheshwari, R. U., Pandey, B. K., & Pandey, D. (2024). Ultra-sensitive photonic crystal fiber–based SPR sensor for cancer detection utilizing hybrid nano-composite layers. *Plasmonics*, •••, 1–15.

Elarmathi, S., Rishabavarthani, P., Sindhuja, M., Elayaraja, P., & Malathi Murugesan, S. Kumarganesh, K. Martin Sagayam, Binay Kumar Pandey, and Digvijay Pandey. (2024). Novel manufacturing systems for cancer diagnosis using ultra-sensitive photonic crystal fiber biosensor with dual-functionalized aptamer-nanocavity. *Microsystem Technologies*, •••, 1–20.

Fan, X., Yao, J., & Cao, N. (2019). Research on Cloud Computing Security Problems and Protection Countermeasures. In *Cyberspace Safety and Security: 11th International Symposium, CSS 2019, Guangzhou, China, December 1–3, 2019* [Springer International Publishing.]. *Proceedings*, *11*(Part I), 542–551.

Fazal, H., Memon, I., Khatri, T. K., Muhammad, G., & Ali, Q. (2020). A survey on cloud computing, security Challenges, architecture, applications & solutions. *University of Sindh Journal of Information and Communication Technology*, *4*(1), 24–30.

George, W. K., Silas, E. I., Pandey, D., & Pandey, B. K. (2024). Utilization of Industry 4.0 Technologies in Nigerian Technical and Vocational Education: A Conundrum for Educators. In *Examining the Rapid Advance of Digital Technology in Africa* (pp. 270–293). IGI Global.

Haus, M., Waqas, M., Ding, A. Y., Li, Y., Tarkoma, S., & Ott, J. (2017). Security and privacy in device-to-device (D2D) communication: A review. *IEEE Communications Surveys and Tutorials*, *19*(2), 1054–1079.

Khadka, M., Sah, M., Chaudhary, R., Sahani, S. K., Sahani, K., Pandey, B. K., & Pandey, D. (2025). Spectroscopic, quantum chemical, and topological calculations of the phenylephrine molecule using density functional theory. *Scientific Reports*, *15*(1), 208. PMID: 39747169

Konapure, C. G., Pandey, D., Shete, H., Thakar, C. M., Pandey, B. K., & George, A. S. (2025). Artificial Intelligence in Automated Concrete Mix Design Using Computerized Grading Curves. Interdisciplinary Approaches to AI, Internet of Everything, and Machine Learning, 567-586.

Kumar, B., Pandey, D., Pandey, B. K., & George, A. S. (2024). Higher Education in the Last Four Decades: A Review of Paradigm Shifts in Policy Frameworks. Design and Implementation of Higher Education Learners' Learning Outcomes (HELLO), 333-348.

Kumar, M. S., Prasanna, P. L., Lalitha, M., Joy, M., Jha, S. S., & Pandey, B. K. (2025). Utilizing the Internet of Everything and Artificial Intelligence for Real-Time Workforce Management. In Role of Internet of Everything (IOE), VLSI Architecture, and AI in Real-Time Systems (pp. 153-168). IGI Global Scientific Publishing.

Kumar, R., & Goyal, R. (2019). On cloud security requirements, threats, vulnerabilities and countermeasures: A survey. *Computer Science Review*, *33*, 1–48.

Kumarganesh, S., & Malathi Murugesan, C. Ganesh, N. Santhiyakumari, M. Thangavel, K. Jayaram, K. Martin Sagayam, Binay Kumar Pandey, and Digvijay Pandey. (2024). Hybrid plasmonic biosensors with deep learning for colorectal cancer detection. *Plasmonics*, •••, 1–15.

KVM, S., Pandey, B. K., & Pandey, D. (2024). Design of Surface Plasmon Resonance (SPR) Sensors for Highly Sensitive Biomolecular Detection in Cancer Diagnostics. *Plasmonics*, •••, 1–13.

Lakshmi, K. V. N., Rajan, R., Pandey, D., & Pandey, B. K. (2024). Circular economy: A catalyst for economic growth-an empirical study. *Circular Economy and Sustainability*, •••, 1–22.

Li, Z., Yang, Z., & Xie, S. (2019). Computing resource trading for edge-cloud-assisted Internet of Things. *IEEE Transactions on Industrial Informatics*, *15*(6), 3661–3669.

Muniandi, B., Nassa, V. K., Pandey, D., Pandey, B. K., Dadheech, P., & George, A. S. (2024). Pattern Analysis for Feature Extraction in Complex Images. In Using Machine Learning to Detect Emotions and Predict Human Psychology (pp. 145-167). IGI Global.

Muralidhar, L. B., Lakshmi, K. V. N., Swapna, H. R., Rupani, J., Nethravathi, K., Pandey, B. K., & Pandey, D. (2024). Impact of Organizational Culture on The Level of Corporate Social Responsibility Investments: An Exploratory Study. *Circular Economy and Sustainability*, •••, 1–19.

Pandey, B. K., Nassa, V. K., Mukundan, A. P., Mahajan, D. A., Pandey, D., George, A. S., & Dadheech, P. (2024c). An Industry-Focused Traffic System Utilising Internet of Things. In *Emerging Engineering Technologies and Industrial Applications* (pp. 200–213). IGI Global.

Pandey, B. K., & Pandey, D. (2023). Parametric optimization and prediction of enhanced thermoelectric performance in co-doped CaMnO3 using response surface methodology and neural network. *Journal of Materials Science Materials in Electronics*, *34*(21), 1589.

Pandey, B. K., & Pandey, D. (2025). Securing healthcare medical image information using advance morphological component analysis, information hiding systems, and hybrid convolutional neural networks on IoMT. *Computers in Biology and Medicine*, *185*, 109499. PMID: 39642698

Pandey, B. K., Pandey, D., & Lelisho, M. E. (2024a). Face mask identification with enhanced cuckoo optimization and deep learning-based faster regional neural network. *Scientific Reports*, *14*(1), 29719. PMID: 39613761

Pandey, B. K., Pandey, D., & Sahani, S. K. (2024b). Autopilot control unmanned aerial vehicle system for sewage defect detection using deep learning. *Engineering Reports*, •••, 12852.

Pandey, B. K., Paramashivan, M. A., Pandey, D., George, A. S., Agarwal, A., Dadheech, P., & Mahajan, D. A. (2024e). A recent survey on 6G vehicular technology: applications and challenges. 6G Security Education and Multidisciplinary Implementation, 337-350.

Pandey, B. K., Paramashivan, M. A., Pandey, D., George, A. S., Agarwal, A., Mahajan, D. A., . . . Pramanik, S. (2024d). Future Directions of Digital Twin Architectures for 6G Communication Networks. In Security Issues and Solutions in 6G Communications and Beyond (pp. 197-211). IGI Global.

Pandey, D., Nassa, V. K., Pandey, B. K., Mahajan, D. A., Patidar, P. K., Dadheech, P., & George, A. S. (2024). An Analysis of Internet-of-Things-Based Fire Detection and Alert Systems. In *Emerging Engineering Technologies and Industrial Applications* (pp. 295–304). IGI Global.

Qiu, H., Noura, H., Qiu, M., Ming, Z., & Memmi, G. (2019). A user-centric data protection method for cloud storage based on invertible DWT. *IEEE Transactions on Cloud Computing*, *9*(4), 1293–1304.

Rai, P. K., Pandey, D., & Pandey, B. K. (2024). The future of enterprise and innovation is compute as a commodity, or CaaC. *Partners Universal International Research Journal*, *3*(2), 89–94.

Saravanakumar, R., TamilSelvi, T., Pandey, D., Pandey, B. K., Mahajan, D. A., & Lelisho, M. E. (2024). Big data processing using hybrid Gaussian mixture model with salp swarm algorithm. *Journal of Big Data*, *11*(1), 167.

Satheesh, N., Gopisankar, N., Kumarganesh, S., Anthoniraj, S., Saravanakumar, S., & Martin Sagayam, K., Binay Kumar Pandey, and Digvijay Pandey. (2025). Advanced AI-driven emergency response systems for enhanced vehicle and human safety. *Iran Journal of Computer Science*, •••, 1–16.

Satheesh, N., Gopisankar, N., Kumarganesh, S., Anthoniraj, S., Saravanakumar, S., & Martin Sagayam, K., Binay Kumar Pandey, and Digvijay Pandey. (2025). Advanced AI-driven emergency response systems for enhanced vehicle and human safety. *Iran Journal of Computer Science*, •••, 1–16.

Shahul, A., Muniandi, B., Paramashivan, M. A., Pandey, D., Pandey, B. K., Dadheech, P., & George, H. (2024). An Analysis of Algorithms and Methods Based on Image Processing for Medical Applications. In *Emerging Engineering Technologies and Industrial Applications* (pp. 173–186). IGI Global.

Sharma, M., Talwar, R., Nassa, V. K., Binay, K., & Pandey, D. (2025). Design and performance analysis of a multiband vivaldi antenna for wireless broadband communication in 3-5.6 GHz spectrum. In *Artificial Intelligence and Information Technologies* (pp. 86–91). CRC Press.

Sheela, M. S., Kumarganesh, S., Pandey, B. K., & Lelisho, M. E. (2025). Integration of silver nanostructures in wireless sensor networks for enhanced biochemical sensing. *Discover Nano*, *20*(1), 7. PMID: 39804434

Singh, S., Madaan, G., Swapna, H. R., Singh, A., Pandey, D., George, A. S., & Pandey, B. K. (2025). Empowering Connectivity: Exploring the Internet of Things. In Interdisciplinary Approaches to AI, Internet of Everything, and Machine Learning (pp. 89-116). IGI Global Scientific Publishing.

Singh, S., Madaan, G., Swapna, H. R., Singh, A., Pandey, D., George, A. S., & Pandey, B. K. (2025). Empowering Connectivity: Exploring the Internet of Things. In Interdisciplinary Approaches to AI, Internet of Everything, and Machine Learning (pp. 89-116). IGI Global Scientific Publishing.

Tu, S., Waqas, M., Rehman, S. U., Mir, T., Abbas, G., Abbas, Z. H., & Ahmad, I. (2021). Reinforcement learning assisted impersonation attack detection in device-to-device communications. *IEEE Transactions on Vehicular Technology*, *70*(2), 1474–1479.

Vinodhini, V., Kumar, M. S., Sankar, S., Pandey, D., Pandey, B. K., & Nassa, V. K. (2022). IoT-based early forest fire detection using MLP and AROC method. *International Journal of Global Warming*, *27*(1), 55–70.

Chapter 14
IP Protection in the Cloud Navigating the Challenges of Data and Analytics

Eshita Baghel
Department of Law, Manipal University Jaipur, India

Aishwarya Pandey
Department of Law, Manipal University Jaipur, India

ABSTRACT

The rapid adoption of cloud technologies has revolutionized data analytics and management, giving rise to serious worries about intellectual property (IP) protection. The intricacies of intellectual property in cloud-based settings, highlighting how crucial it is to protect priceless resources like proprietary models, data ownership, and algorithms. It looks at the legal frameworks that control intellectual property rights, such as regional laws and international treaties, and it highlights particular dangers related to cloud computing, like unclear data ownership and illegal access. The difficulties in safeguarding intellectual property in cloud environments, such as security flaws and the theft of proprietary algorithms. A dual approach involving legal and technical strategies is proposed to address these challenges. To establish ownership and safeguard rights, legal measures are essential.

DOI: 10.4018/979-8-3693-9581-3.ch014

1. INTRODUCTION

Innovation, strategic decision-making, and competitive differentiation have become increasingly dependent on data and analytics (Pandey, B. K., & Pandey, D., 2023). Agencies can now use scalable infrastructure to store, process, and analyze massive amounts of data in real time thanks to the increasing adoption of cloud computing. Even with these advantages, firms still face difficult obstacles in their quest to safeguard data security, preserve regulatory compliance, and safeguard intellectual property (IP). Data ownership and control represent one of the most notable challenges. Organizations and cloud service providers (CSPs) frequently share accountability for data management in cloud environments (Pandey, B. K., & Pandey, D., 2025). Particularly when data is stored across multiple jurisdictions, this shared responsibility model may cause confusion regarding who maintains ownership of the data. To prevent legal entanglements, organizations and CSPs must clearly define contractual agreements that outline data ownership, access rights, and control mechanisms. Privacy and security of data is another important issue. Data breaches, unauthorized access, and cyberattacks are all possible in cloud environments. Data transmission risks, including phishing, malware, and hacking, increase when it passes through users, cloud servers, and third-party applications. Establishing strong security measures like multi-factor authentication, end-to-end encryption, and recurring security audits is necessary for enterprises to reduce these risks. Cloud-based analytics management becomes more difficult due to strict requirements on data handling and security imposed by data protection regulations such as the California Consumer Privacy Act (CCPA) and the General Data Protection Regulation (GDPR). Intellectual property protection is a third obstacle. To maintain a competitive advantage, organizations frequently create proprietary models, analytical frameworks, and algorithms. Reverse engineering (Khadka, M. et al., 2025), unauthorized use, and replication are risks associated with storing and processing these assets on cloud platforms. It's necessary to employ access controls, secure cloud environments, and cutting-edge encryption techniques to safeguard this intellectual property. To further preserve their rights, companies should incorporate IP-specific language in contracts with cloud providers and pursue patent protection for their innovations. An additional layer of complexity is presented by the compliance with diverse global regulations. Data protection and privacy laws vary amongst regions, and cloud-based data and analytics operations frequently operate across them (Sheela, M. S. et al., 2025). Organizations that want to comply with these regulations must keep up with the latest legal requirements, make sure that data is localized when needed, and collaborate with cloud providers that provide compliance support across multiple law enforcement authorities.

1.1 IP in Data and Analytics

IP in data and analytics protects data, algorithm, and analytical method creations. IP understanding and management are crucial as organizations use data-driven insights (Satheesh, N. et al., 2025) to innovate and stay competitive. Original software code, databases, and data visualizations are protected by law. Data expression in reports, dashboards, and charts can be protected by copyright. Organizations must use other IP protection to protect the data they collect and analyze because copyright does not apply to data or facts (Kumar, M. S. et al., 2025).

Patents grant exclusive rights to inventions like new algorithms and analytical methods. Innovative algorithms that give a company an edge may be patented to prevent copying. In fast-changing industries, legal protection can help secure market share. Trade secrets safeguard confidential business information that gives a competitive edge. Companies' confidential datasets (Konapure, C. G. et al., 2025), algorithms, and methods fall into this category. Trade secrets are kept private, unlike patents. Thus, companies must use strict access controls and employee agreements to protect their trade secrets. Trademarks protect data product and service names, logos, and slogans. While trademarks are unrelated to data and analytics, they are crucial for brand recognition and market differentiation. In competitive industries, a strong trademark can build customer loyalty and trust. These safeguards, data and analytics organizations face IP issues. In cloud computing, where multiple parties can access the same data, data ownership and control are major issues. Avoid legal issues by making clear agreements and understanding shared responsibility. In addition, organizations using cloud services must protect their IP assets from unauthorized use, replication, and reverse engineering (Marston, S. et al., 2011).

1.2 IP Protection in a Cloud-Based Environment

In a cloud-based environment, where enterprises increasingly rely on cloud services for data processing, analytics, and storage, intellectual property (IP) protection is essential. Making the switch to cloud computing has many advantages, such as increased collaboration, cost-effectiveness, and scalability (Singh, S. et al., 2025). But it also presents serious problems for the safeguarding of intellectual property. First and foremost, data ownership boundaries are frequently dissolved in cloud environments. Cloud service providers (CSPs) have complex agreements that organizations must navigate, dictating how data is used, stored, and accessed. Businesses that don't have clear intellectual property protection policies run the risk of losing control over their proprietary data and algorithms, which could be misused by rivals or unintentionally disclosed in ways that damage their standing in the market. To make ownership rights and obligations clear, contracts with CSPs must include explicit IP clauses. The protection (Sharma, M. et al., 2025) of private information and proprietary technology is another crucial factor. Cloud environments are susceptible to unauthorized access, data breaches, and cyberattacks. Secure access controls, encryption, and frequent security audits are a few of the efficient IP protection techniques that help prevent priceless assets from being stolen or misused (Weinhardt, C. et al., 2009). Businesses that invest heavily in security measures not only safeguard their intellectual property but also increase customer trust and adhere to data protection laws. Because technology is advancing so quickly, it is critical for organizations to safeguard their innovations. Proprietary models, algorithms, and data analytics methods (Pandey, B. K. et al., 2024a) may be vulnerable to reverse engineering or theft in a cloud-based environment. Organizations can protect the distinctive contributions they have made to the industry by obtaining patents or keeping trade secrets. They can keep their advantage over the competition and profit from their innovations thanks to this protection. Organizations must navigate differing laws regarding data protection and intellectual property rights because data is frequently stored in multiple jurisdictions. Tough IP protection plans can support adherence to laws like the California Consumer Privacy Act (CCPA) and the General Data Protection Regulation (GDPR). Significant legal penalties and harm to ones reputation may result from noncompliance. Innovation in organizations is encouraged by IP protection. Employees and teams are more likely to solve problems creatively and come up with new ideas when they are aware that their contributions will be protected. A robust intellectual property framework fosters an innovative culture, enabling enterprises to confidently invest in R&D (Subramanian, N., & Jeyaraj, A., 2018).

2. CLOUD AND DATA ANALYTICS

2.1 Cloud Computing Models

Platform as a Service (PaaS), Software as a Service (SaaS), and Infrastructure as a Service (IaaS) are the three main service models offered by cloud computing, and they have completely changed how businesses handle and analyze data. Each model has specific benefits for data analytics. Organizations can access virtualized computer resources via the internet with Infrastructure as a Service (IaaS). Pay-as-you-go infrastructure rentals, including servers, storage, and networking (Pandey, B. K. et al., 2024b), are made possible for businesses by this model. Because it allows businesses to dynamically scale their computing resources to meet the demands of large-scale data processing and analysis, infrastructure as a service (IaaS) is particularly relevant for data analytics. Without spending money on actual hardware, businesses can swiftly provide more resources during periods of high analysis. This adaptability is necessary to effectively manage varying data workloads and carry out intricate analyses. Organizations can create, launch, and maintain apps without worrying about the underlying infrastructure thanks to Platform as a Service (PaaS), which provides a cloud-based development environment. PaaS is useful for data analytics because it offers integrated tools and services made especially for machine learning, analytics, and data integration. By utilizing pre-configured environments that optimize the data processing workflow, PaaS enables data scientists and analysts to concentrate on creating analytical models and applications (Di Giulio, C. et al., 2017). This shortens the time to insight and improves teamwork for groups working on projects driven by data. Software as a Service (SaaS) allows users to access analytics tools and platforms through a web browser by delivering software applications over the internet. Because SaaS solutions are frequently easy to use and require little setup, a variety of users, including data professionals and business stakeholders, can benefit from them. SaaS apps for data analytics offer strong capabilities for reporting, data exploration, and visualization without requiring a lot of IT support. In order to develop a data-driven culture, organizations can swiftly implement SaaS analytics solutions to mine their data for insights and disseminate the results throughout the organization. A vital part of improving data analytics capabilities is played by each of these cloud computing models. While PaaS offers a cooperative environment for application development, SaaS gives end users access to analytics tools, and IaaS supplies the infrastructure needed for complex computational tasks. They allow businesses to better leverage the potential of their data, fostering creative thinking and well-informed choices amidst a more cutthroat business environment.

2.2 Data Types in the Cloud

In cloud-based analytics, different kinds of data are very important, and they need to be stored, processed, and analyzed in different ways. There are three main types of data: real-time data, unstructured data, and structured data. Structured data, which is usually kept in fixed formats like databases and spreadsheets, is very well organized and easy to search. This type of data follows a schema that has already been set up, which makes it easy to query and analyze. Structured data includes things like records of customers, details of transactions, and stock levels. Structured data in the cloud can be quickly processed and analyzed using standard data management tools (). This is important for making reports and doing business intelligence tasks. Unstructured data, on the other hand, is harder to analyze because it doesn't have a set format or structure. This group includes emails, text documents, pictures, videos, and social media posts. Unstructured data has become more useful for understanding customer behavior, market trends, and sentiment analysis as "big data" has grown. Cloud-based analytics platforms have advanced tools, like machine learning and natural language processing algorithms, that can turn unstructured data into useful information. With this feature, businesses can use the rich, contextual data that unstructured data offers ((Amara, N. et al., 2017). When information is created and processed instantly or with little delay, it is called "real-time data." This kind of information is very important for tasks that need quick answers, like finding fraud, trading stocks, and talking to customers online. IoT devices, social media feeds, and transactional systems are just some of the sources of real-time data (Basha, A. J. et al., 2024) that cloud-based analytics solutions can handle. Organizations can make quick decisions, adapt to changing conditions, and improve operational efficiency by looking at real-time data. These types of data work together to make cloud-based analytics possible. Businesses can get more information, make better decisions, and stay ahead of the competition in a market that is changing quickly by using structured, unstructured, and real-time data (KVM, S. et al., 2024). To make good analytics plans in the cloud, you need to know what makes each type of data different and how to process it properly (Narang, A., & Gupta, D., 2019).

2.3 Advantages of Cloud Analytics

Cloud analytics provides a multitude of benefits are as shown in the figure 1, one of which is scalability, which enables businesses to adjust their resources in accordance with the demand. It improves accessibility by allowing users to access data (Lakshmi, K. V. N. et al., 2024) from any location as long as they have an internet connection. In addition, cloud analytics helps to cut costs by removing the requirement for extensive on-premises infrastructure. This, in turn, enables faster insights and improved decision-making.

- *Scalability*: It is a major benefit of cloud data analytics solutions. Organisations can easily scale resources to meet changing data volumes (Saravanakumar, R. et al., 2024) and processing needs. This flexibility lets businesses handle large datasets during peak periods without investing in physical infrastructure. Companies can quickly provision additional computing power and storage space during seasonal demand spikes to respond to changing demands without delays or performance issues.
- *Cost-Efficiency*: Another benefit of cloud-based analytics is cost-efficiency. Pay-as-you-go pricing models let companies reduce capital costs and only pay for what they use. Companies can better allocate budgets and reduce financial risk with this approach. Businesses can optimize costs and maintain access to analytical tools and resources by adjusting their spending in real

time instead of investing heavily in on-premises hardware that may sit idle during off-peak times (Kumarganesh, S. et al., 2024).

- *Accessibility*: Cloud solutions improve accessibility by letting users access data and analytics tools from anywhere with an internet connection. Team collaboration, remote work, and real-time communication and decision-making are enabled by this capability. Data scientists (Muralidhar, L. B. et al., 2024), analysts, and business stakeholders can collaborate on projects from different locations, sharing insights and analyses, which is valuable in today's mobile and distributed work environments.
- *Speed*: Cloud-based analytics efficiency depends on speed. Organizations can gain insight faster with rapid analytics tool (Pandey, B. K. et al., 2024c) and resource deployment. This acceleration helps businesses make informed decisions faster, giving them an edge in fast-paced markets. Organizations can adapt their strategies to market changes and customer needs in real time by quickly setting up analytical environments and running complex queries.
- *Integration*: It is another benefit of cloud solutions. These platforms can integrate data sources and cloud services for unified analytics. Organizations can conduct multi-dataset analyses with this integration, simplifying data management (Elarmathi, S. et al., 2024). Businesses can combine CRM and e-commerce sales data to understand consumer behavior and preferences.
- *Advanced Tools*: Cloud solutions offer advanced analytics tools and technologies. Modern resources like machine learning and artificial intelligence can be used without extensive IT infrastructure. This access lets businesses use predictive analytics and automated reporting to innovate without the hassle of complex systems (Pandey, B. K. et al., 2024d). Thus, companies can concentrate on insights rather than technology.
- *Security*: Data analytics requires strong security, and cloud providers often provide it. Encryption, security updates, and industry standards protect sensitive data from breaches and unauthorized access (Pandey, B. K. et al., 2024e). This level of security gives organizations handling confidential data like financial or customer data peace of mind, allowing them to focus on analytics initiatives.
- *Collaboration*: cloud solutions improve team collaboration. Improved collaboration features allow multiple users to work on data analytics projects simultaneously, encouraging teamwork and innovation. Cloud platforms make it easy for stakeholders from different departments to share insights and findings (George, W. K. et al., 2024). This collaborative environment speeds up project timelines and adds diverse perspectives to analysis, resulting in better decision-making.

Figure 1. Advantages of cloud analytics

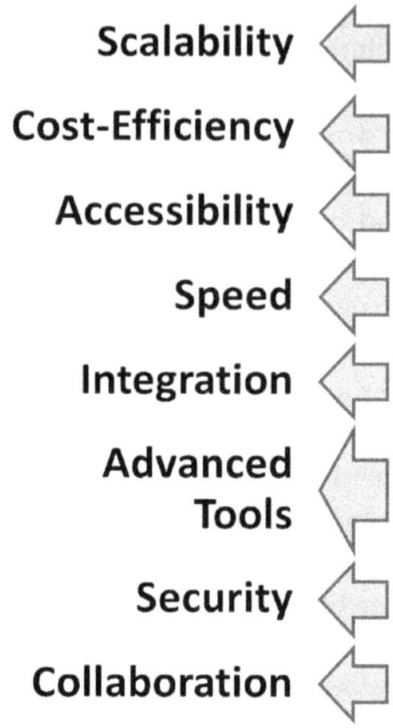

3. INTELLECTUAL PROPERTY IN CLOUD ENVIRONMENTS

3.1 IP Types in Cloud Data

Businesses in the field of cloud-based data and analytics can protect their innovations, maintain control over their assets, and safeguard their competitive advantage in a technological landscape that is rapidly evolving by securing (Abdullahi, M. et al., 2024) the various forms of intellectual property (IP) that they possess. The rights and protections that are associated with data, algorithms, and software that are stored and processed in the cloud are included in the definition of intellectual property (IP) in cloud environments. Increasingly, businesses are turning to cloud computing for data analytics, which means that protecting their intellectual property is becoming an increasingly important concern (Satheesh, N. et al., 2025). There are a number of obstacles that make intellectual property protection more difficult, including ambiguity regarding data ownership, unauthorized access, and compliance with different legal frameworks. The establishment of transparent contractual agreements with cloud service providers, the utilization of copyright and patent laws, and the implementation of stringent security measures such as encryption and access controls are all effective strategies worth considering (Narang, A., & Gupta, D., 2019). There are several types of intellectual property (IP) that are shown in the figure 2, which is essential in cloud data environments. These include proprietary algorithms, which are responsible for driving data analysis processes; software code, which is necessary for functionality; and data ownership rights, which dictate control over the data that is generated (Kumar, B. et al., 2024). Additionally, trade secrets include practises or methods that are kept confidential and that offer competitive advantages within the cloud ecosystem.

1. *Patents*: Patents are a form of intellectual property that safeguards innovative technological inventions or processes. These protections include novel algorithms, machine learning models, and specific methods for analyzing large datasets in the cloud. For instance, a company has the ability to submit a patent application if it develops a novel approach to the processing of data or an innovative method for improving the efficiency of cloud storage. In a highly competitive market where technological advancements are a major differentiator, patents are essential because they grant the holder the exclusive right to use, sell, or license their innovation for a predetermined amount of time throughout the duration of the patent.
2. *Copyrights*: Copyright protection is meant to be applied to original works of authorship, which can include software code, documentation, analytics reports, data visualizations, and even databases if they satisfy the originality criterion. These works are protected from unauthorized copying, distribution, or modification in an environment that is based on cloud-based data and analytics (Pandey, D. et al., 2024). This ensures that organizations that develop proprietary software for cloud analytics or generate unique reports and datasets are able to control how their intellectual property is used and monetized by others. This is an important consideration for organizations that generate these types of reports and datasets (Ukil, A. et al., 2013).
3. *Trademarks*: Trademarks are used to protect the brand identity of cloud-based analytics services or platforms. This includes the logos, symbols, and names of the services or platforms. An example of this would be a cloud analytics platform that chooses to trademark its brand name or logo in order to differentiate its services from those of different companies. For the purpose of ensuring that customers associate particular analytics solutions with the brand, trademarks contribute to the development of trust and recognition in the market arena. Ensuring that these symbols are legally protected prevents other companies from using similar branding, which could lead to confusion among customers or reduce the value of the brand.

4. *Trade Secrets*: Trade secrets are confidential business information that provides a competitive edge. Examples of trade secrets include proprietary data processing techniques, customer data, predictive models, and cloud system architectures. When it comes to cloud-based analytics, trade secrets can consist of algorithms (Shahul, A. et al., 2024), workflows, or methods that companies employ in order to generate insights in a more efficient or accurate manner than their competitors. Trade secrets, in contrast to patents, are not disclosed to the public, and their protection is guaranteed for as long as the information in question is kept confidential. This makes trade secrets an appealing choice for businesses that are looking for long-term competitive advantages that are not subject to time constraints (Hashizume, Rosado, Fernández-Medina, & Fernandez, 2013).
5. *Data ownership rights*: Data ownership rights define who controls the data, including its collection, storage, access, and usage in cloud environments. This includes the ability to access and work with the data (Muniandi, B. et al., 2024). When it comes to cloud-based analytics, questions regarding data ownership are becoming increasingly important, particularly in situations where data is generated or processed across multiple jurisdictions. Organizations have a responsibility to ensure that their contracts with cloud service providers articulate ownership, control, and access rights to the raw data as well as any analytics that are derived from it in a clear and concise manner. By doing so, businesses are able to maintain their exclusive rights over their data, thereby preventing third parties from exploiting valuable information without their expressed permission.

Figure 2. Types of IP in cloud data

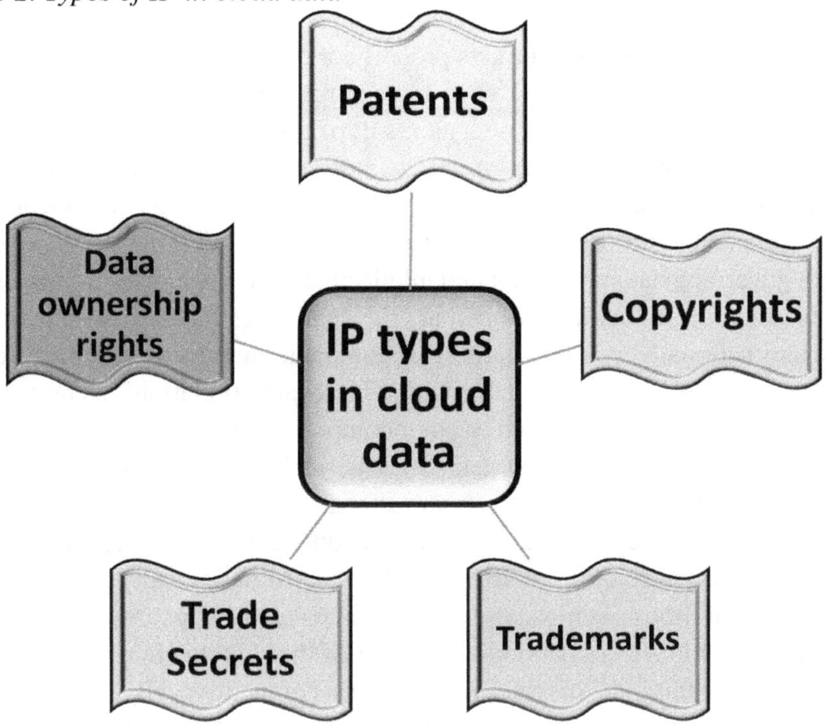

3.2 IP Risks to Cloud Environments

Intellectual property (IP) storage in cloud environments is associated with one of the most substantial risks: data breaches. Cyberattacks that target cloud providers or their clients can lead to unauthorized access to confidential business information, proprietary data, or algorithms. The value of this stolen IP can be substantial in many instances, including trade secrets or innovative technologies that provide companies with a competitive advantage. In addition to the potential reputational harm and financial losses resulting from regulatory fines and remediation expenses, a data breach can also compromise the integrity of sensitive information (Singh, S. et al., 2025). The loss of control over IP assets is another critical risk that organizations face when they depend on third-party cloud platforms. Diminished oversight regarding the individuals who have access to this information may result from storing data and IP with cloud service providers. Without well-defined access controls and management protocols, organizations may be at risk of unauthorized use or exposure of their intellectual property. When sensitive data is disseminated among various teams or departments, this lack of control can be especially worrying, as it increases the likelihood of internal leaks or accidental disclosures. Inadequate IP protection is an additional issue in cloud-based environments (Popa, D. et al., 2013). Organizations that fail to negotiate contracts properly or comprehend the implications of service agreements may be at risk of losing control over their intellectual property. Data ownership disputes may arise as a result of this situation, particularly if the cloud provider asserts ownership of any data or analytics produced through their infrastructure. Compliance with a variety of legal and regulatory frameworks also presents a challenge for organizations that store intellectual property in the cloud. The laws governing data protection and intellectual property rights vary across different jurisdictions, which can exacerbate the challenges faced by businesses that operate internationally. It is imperative that companies navigate these intricacies to guarantee that they are in compliance with all relevant regulations, as failure to do so may lead to severe penalties and further compromise their intellectual property. IP management in cloud environments may be influenced by the risk of vendor lock-in. It may be challenging for organizations to transition to a different cloud service provider, if necessary, as they may become excessively dependent on the tools and infrastructure of a specific provider. This situation can stifle innovation and restrict flexibility, as companies may be hesitant to investigate new technologies or solutions due to concerns about the transfer of their intellectual property ("IP") assets. In order to mitigate this risk and preserve a competitive edge, it is imperative to ensure that IP can be easily managed and transferred across various platforms (Ukil, A. et al., 2013).

3.3 Legal Frameworks and IP Regulations

The distributed, multi-jurisdictional nature of cloud computing makes legal frameworks and IP regulations unique. As companies move data and services to the cloud, understanding the legal environment is crucial to protecting IP. Assigning jurisdiction is difficult. Multiple countries with different IP laws store cloud data. It is unclear which country's legal system governs data and IP rights. Countries may have strong IP protection or weak enforcement. Companies must carefully choose cloud providers with data centers in legal and compliant countries to reduce this risk. Cloud service contracts' jurisdiction clauses can clarify dispute resolution laws. Cloud-based IP protection demands data localization laws. Numerous nations mandate the storage of personal and critical infrastructure data within their borders. When sensitive or proprietary information is involved, IP management is affected. These localisation requirements may restrict data flow across borders and require companies to store certain data in local data centres. Cloud services help organizations move data between jurisdictions. However, the EU's Standard Contractual Clauses (SCCs) and the U.S.-EU Data Privacy Framework (formerly Privacy Shield) govern private data and IP transfers internationally. Enterprises that handle sensitive data must follow these regulations to ensure data transfers meet privacy standards and IP integrity. Shared or collaborative IP ownership is another emerging legal issue (Hashizume, K. et al., 2013). Collaboration on projects using cloud computing raises IP ownership issues. Who owns cloud-generated innovations, software, and data? To define IP ownership, licensing rights, and the distribution of potential profits or liabilities from jointly created IP, collaborative agreements must include clear contractual definitions. In cloud-based analytics, AI and machine learning add complexity. Artificial intelligence systems train algorithms on massive datasets, often in the cloud. Since third-party data is used, legal agreements must explicitly define ownership of these datasets (Vinodhini, V. et al., 2022) and AI-generated IP. This could lead to IP disputes, especially as AI-generated outputs become more valuable and sought after. Cloud service users worry about IP infringement liability. Which party is legally responsible for infringing on another's IP when a cloud provider's infrastructure is used? Service contracts can include complex liability-sharing agreements and indemnity clauses to clarify roles and protect both parties in court.

4. PROTECTING IP: LEGAL AND TECHNICAL

Legal and technical approaches to protecting intellectual property (IP) in cloud-based data and analytics are essential for ensuring the safety and integrity of valuable intellectual property (IP) in a digital environment. To protect intellectual property rights, legal safeguards and technical solutions are required as cloud computing becomes more widespread for the purposes of data storage, processing, and analytics (Rai, P. K. et al., 2024). Developing clear contracts and agreements with cloud service providers is an important strategy that can be implemented from a legal standpoint. In the event of a breach or infringement of intellectual property, these contracts should provide a clear outline of ownership, access rights, data usage policies, and liability. The inclusion of jurisdiction clauses in these agreements is of utmost importance, particularly in situations where cloud services involve multiple jurisdictions. These clauses specify which country's laws will be applicable in the event of a dispute. To prevent cloud providers or other third parties from misusing sensitive data and trade secrets, businesses should also incorporate robust confidentiality and non-disclosure agreements into their business practices. For the purpose of safeguarding software, algorithms, data processing methods, and datasets in the cloud environment, it is essential that the laws governing intellectual property, such as patents, copyrights, and trade secrets, be applied in an appropriate manner. Keeping up with international regulations is yet another legal strategy for protecting intellectual property. Data protection laws, such as the General Data Protection Regulation (GDPR) in Europe, which regulates the handling and protection of personal data, are a complex set of regulations that businesses need to navigate. Managing intellectual property rights in accordance with local laws that govern data protection and cross-border data transfers is the most important thing to do when personal data is a part of the analytics process. Encryption is a fundamental measure for protecting intellectual property in cloud-based analytics, making it an important technical solution. It is possible to ensure that sensitive information is kept safe and inaccessible to unauthorized parties by encrypting data while it is at rest, while it is in transit, and while it is being processed. In addition to preventing the theft of intellectual property, strong encryption methods also protect against cyberattacks that target valuable datasets or analytical processes. Mechanisms for controlling access are yet another important application of technology. In the cloud, only authorized users are able to access sensitive intellectual property (IP) or analytical tools thanks to role-based access controls (RBAC) and multi-factor authentication (MFA). Companies can lessen the likelihood of internal security breaches or unauthorized access to confidential information by limiting access to particular individuals and ensuring that authentication is carried out in a secure manner. Firewalls, intrusion detection systems, and automated security updates are examples of the types of security features that cloud providers frequently offer. These features all contribute to the protection of intellectual property. If organizations want to strengthen their defenses against potential intellectual property infringements or data breaches, they should make use of these features. Conducting regular security audits and vulnerability assessments will assist in locating vulnerabilities in the cloud infrastructure that may put intellectual property at risk. Blockchain technology is beginning to emerge as a potentially useful tool for protecting intellectual property in cloud environments. In order to prove intellectual property rights and prevent unauthorized modifications or copies of data, blockchain technology has the ability to generate immutable records of data ownership, access, and usage. This capacity is particularly useful. Blockchain technology improves transparency and trust for the purpose of managing intellectual property in cloud-based data analytics. This is accomplished by tracking the provenance of data and analytical processes.

5. CONCLUSION

IP protection is becoming more and more important in the quickly changing world of cloud-based data management and analytics. Organizations adopting cloud technologies have to negotiate ownership, intellectual property rights, and other risks that come with working in these environments. the importance of intellectual property (IP) in cloud environments, including the different forms of IP, including data ownership and algorithms, and the legal systems that control these assets. IP protection in cloud environments presents a variety of difficulties.

There are serious risks associated with data ownership and control issues, security flaws, and possible theft of proprietary algorithms. Complying with different legal requirements is made more difficult by the intricacies of cross-border data transfers, which calls for a thorough understanding of both domestic and international regulations. Organizations must implement thorough legal and technical strategies to address these issues. Legally speaking, protecting intellectual property (IP) requires drafting precise contracts with cloud service providers, making use of applicable IP laws, and making sure regulatory frameworks are followed. Technically, IP protection can be greatly improved by putting in place encryption, secure architectures, and cutting-edge solutions like blockchain. Organizations can set up a more secure cloud environment for their data and analytics processes by implementing best practices like regular security audits, enforcing data classification policies, and conducting extensive vendor due diligence. In the end, efficient IP protection in cloud-based analytics promotes innovation and competitive advantage in a world where data is becoming more and more important, in addition to safeguarding priceless assets.

REFERENCES

Abdullahi, M., Ahmad, A., Pandey, B. K., & Pandey, D. (2024). Digital Currency Adoption: A Comparative Analysis of Global Trends and the Nigerian eNaira Digital Currency. *SN Computer Science*, *5*(5), 1–11.

Amara, N., Zhiqui, H., & Ali, A. (2017, October). Cloud computing security threats and attacks with their mitigation techniques. In *2017 International Conference on Cyber-Enabled Distributed Computing and Knowledge Discovery (CyberC)* (pp. 244-251). IEEE.

Basha, A. J., Maheshwari, R. U., Pandey, B. K., & Pandey, D. (2024). Ultra-sensitive photonic crystal fiber–based SPR sensor for cancer detection utilizing hybrid nano-composite layers. *Plasmonics*, •••, 1–15.

Di Giulio, C., Sprabery, R., Kamhoua, C., Kwiat, K., Campbell, R. H., & Bashir, M. N. (2017, June). Cloud standards in comparison: Are new security frameworks improving cloud security? In *2017 IEEE 10th International Conference on Cloud Computing (CLOUD)* (pp. 50-57). IEEE.

Di Giulio, C., Sprabery, R., Kamhoua, C., Kwiat, K., Campbell, R. H., & Bashir, M. N. (2017, June). Cloud standards in comparison: Are new security frameworks improving cloud security? In *2017 IEEE 10th International Conference on Cloud Computing (CLOUD)* (pp. 50-57). IEEE.

Elarmathi, S., Rishabavarthani, P., Sindhuja, M., Elayaraja, P., & Malathi Murugesan, S. Kumarganesh, K. Martin Sagayam, Binay Kumar Pandey, and Digvijay Pandey. (2024). Novel manufacturing systems for cancer diagnosis using ultra-sensitive photonic crystal fiber biosensor with dual-functionalized aptamer-nanocavity. *Microsystem Technologies*, •••, 1–20.

George, W. K., Silas, E. I., Pandey, D., & Pandey, B. K. (2024). Utilization of Industry 4.0 Technologies in Nigerian Technical and Vocational Education: A Conundrum for Educators. In *Examining the Rapid Advance of Digital Technology in Africa* (pp. 270–293). IGI Global.

Hashizume, K., Rosado, D. G., Fernández-Medina, E., & Fernandez, E. B. (2013). An analysis of security issues for cloud computing. *Journal of Internet Services and Applications*, *4*, 1–13.

Khadka, M., Sah, M., Chaudhary, R., Sahani, S. K., Sahani, K., Pandey, B. K., & Pandey, D. (2025). Spectroscopic, quantum chemical, and topological calculations of the phenylephrine molecule using density functional theory. *Scientific Reports*, *15*(1), 208. PMID: 39747169

Konapure, C. G., Pandey, D., Shete, H., Thakar, C. M., Pandey, B. K., & George, A. S. (2025). Artificial Intelligence in Automated Concrete Mix Design Using Computerized Grading Curves. Interdisciplinary Approaches to AI, Internet of Everything, and Machine Learning, 567-586.

Kumar, B., Pandey, D., Pandey, B. K., & George, A. S. (2024). Higher Education in the Last Four Decades: A Review of Paradigm Shifts in Policy Frameworks. Design and Implementation of Higher Education Learners' Learning Outcomes (HELLO), 333-348.

Kumar, M. S., Prasanna, P. L., Lalitha, M., Joy, M., Jha, S. S., & Pandey, B. K. (2025). Utilizing the Internet of Everything and Artificial Intelligence for Real-Time Workforce Management. In Role of Internet of Everything (IOE), VLSI Architecture, and AI in Real-Time Systems (pp. 153-168). IGI Global Scientific Publishing.

Kumarganesh, S., & Malathi Murugesan, C. Ganesh, N. Santhiyakumari, M. Thangavel, K. Jayaram, K. Martin Sagayam, Binay Kumar Pandey, and Digvijay Pandey. (2024). Hybrid plasmonic biosensors with deep learning for colorectal cancer detection. *Plasmonics*, •••, 1–15.

KVM, S., Pandey, B. K., & Pandey, D. (2024). Design of Surface Plasmon Resonance (SPR) Sensors for Highly Sensitive Biomolecular Detection in Cancer Diagnostics. *Plasmonics*, •••, 1–13.

Lakshmi, K. V. N., Rajan, R., Pandey, D., & Pandey, B. K. (2024). Circular economy: A catalyst for economic growth-an empirical study. *Circular Economy and Sustainability*, •••, 1–22.

Marston, S., Li, Z., Bandyopadhyay, S., Zhang, J., & Ghalsasi, A. (2011). Cloud computing—The business perspective. *Decision Support Systems*, *51*(1), 176–189.

Muniandi, B., Nassa, V. K., Pandey, D., Pandey, B. K., Dadheech, P., & George, A. S. (2024). Pattern Analysis for Feature Extraction in Complex Images. In Using Machine Learning to Detect Emotions and Predict Human Psychology (pp. 145-167). IGI Global.

Muralidhar, L. B., Lakshmi, K. V. N., Swapna, H. R., Rupani, J., Nethravathi, K., Pandey, B. K., & Pandey, D. (2024). Impact of Organizational Culture on The Level of Corporate Social Responsibility Investments: An Exploratory Study. *Circular Economy and Sustainability*, •••, 1–19.

Narang, A., & Gupta, D. (2019). Comparative Analysis of Various Cloud Security Frameworks. *International Journal of Advanced Studies of Scientific Research*, *4*(1).

Pandey, B. K., Nassa, V. K., Mukundan, A. P., Mahajan, D. A., Pandey, D., George, A. S., & Dadheech, P. (2024c). An Industry-Focused Traffic System Utilising Internet of Things. In *Emerging Engineering Technologies and Industrial Applications* (pp. 200–213). IGI Global.

Pandey, B. K., & Pandey, D. (2023). Parametric optimization and prediction of enhanced thermoelectric performance in co-doped CaMnO3 using response surface methodology and neural network. *Journal of Materials Science Materials in Electronics*, *34*(21), 1589.

Pandey, B. K., & Pandey, D. (2025). Securing healthcare medical image information using advance morphological component analysis, information hiding systems, and hybrid convolutional neural networks on IoMT. *Computers in Biology and Medicine*, *185*, 109499. PMID: 39642698

Pandey, B. K., Pandey, D., & Lelisho, M. E. (2024a). Face mask identification with enhanced cuckoo optimization and deep learning-based faster regional neural network. *Scientific Reports*, *14*(1), 29719. PMID: 39613761

Pandey, B. K., Pandey, D., & Sahani, S. K. (2024b). Autopilot control unmanned aerial vehicle system for sewage defect detection using deep learning. *Engineering Reports*, •••, 12852.

Pandey, B. K., Paramashivan, M. A., Pandey, D., George, A. S., Agarwal, A., Dadheech, P., & Mahajan, D. A. (2024e). A recent survey on 6G vehicular technology: applications and challenges. 6G Security Education and Multidisciplinary Implementation, 337-350.

Pandey, B. K., Paramashivan, M. A., Pandey, D., George, A. S., Agarwal, A., Mahajan, D. A., . . . Pramanik, S. (2024d). Future Directions of Digital Twin Architectures for 6G Communication Networks. In Security Issues and Solutions in 6G Communications and Beyond (pp. 197-211). IGI Global.

Pandey, D., Nassa, V. K., Pandey, B. K., Mahajan, D. A., Patidar, P. K., Dadheech, P., & George, A. S. (2024). An Analysis of Internet-of-Things-Based Fire Detection and Alert Systems. In *Emerging Engineering Technologies and Industrial Applications* (pp. 295–304). IGI Global.

Popa, D., Cremene, M., Borda, M., & Boudaoud, K. (2013, January). A security framework for mobile cloud applications. In *2013 11th RoEduNet International Conference* (pp. 1-4). IEEE.

Rai, P. K., Pandey, D., & Pandey, B. K. (2024). The future of enterprise and innovation is compute as a commodity, or CaaC. *Partners Universal International Research Journal*, *3*(2), 89–94.

Saravanakumar, R., TamilSelvi, T., Pandey, D., Pandey, B. K., Mahajan, D. A., & Lelisho, M. E. (2024). Big data processing using hybrid Gaussian mixture model with salp swarm algorithm. *Journal of Big Data*, *11*(1), 167.

Satheesh, N., Gopisankar, N., Kumarganesh, S., Anthoniraj, S., Saravanakumar, S., & Martin Sagayam, K., Binay Kumar Pandey, and Digvijay Pandey. (2025). Advanced AI-driven emergency response systems for enhanced vehicle and human safety. *Iran Journal of Computer Science*, •••, 1–16.

Shahul, A., Muniandi, B., Paramashivan, M. A., Pandey, D., Pandey, B. K., Dadheech, P., & George, H. (2024). An Analysis of Algorithms and Methods Based on Image Processing for Medical Applications. In *Emerging Engineering Technologies and Industrial Applications* (pp. 173–186). IGI Global.

Sharma, M., Talwar, R., Nassa, V. K., Binay, K., & Pandey, D. (2025). Design and performance analysis of a multiband vivaldi antenna for wireless broadband communication in 3-5.6 GHz spectrum. In *Artificial Intelligence and Information Technologies* (pp. 86–91). CRC Press.

Sheela, M. S., Kumarganesh, S., Pandey, B. K., & Lelisho, M. E. (2025). Integration of silver nanostructures in wireless sensor networks for enhanced biochemical sensing. *Discover Nano*, *20*(1), 7. PMID: 39804434

Singh, S., Madaan, G., Swapna, H. R., Singh, A., Pandey, D., George, A. S., & Pandey, B. K. (2025). Empowering Connectivity: Exploring the Internet of Things. In Interdisciplinary Approaches to AI, Internet of Everything, and Machine Learning (pp. 89-116). IGI Global Scientific Publishing.

Subramanian, N., & Jeyaraj, A. (2018). Recent security challenges in cloud computing. *Computers & Electrical Engineering*, *71*, 28–42.

Ukil, A., Jana, D., & De Sarkar, A. (2013). A security framework in cloud computing infrastructure. *International Journal of Network Security & its Applications*, *5*(5), 11.

Vinodhini, V., Kumar, M. S., Sankar, S., Pandey, D., Pandey, B. K., & Nassa, V. K. (2022). IoT-based early forest fire detection using MLP and AROC method. *International Journal of Global Warming*, *27*(1), 55–70.

Weinhardt, C., Anandasivam, A., Blau, B., Borissov, N., Meinl, T., Michalk, W., & Stößer, J. (2009). Cloud computing–a classification, business models, and research directions. *Business & Information Systems Engineering*, *1*, 391–399.

Chapter 15
Leveraging Cloud Technology for Criminal Justice Administration: Opportunities and Challenges

Zeeshan Hussain Hashmi
https://orcid.org/0009-0000-7681-9758
Amity Law School, Amity University, Jaipur, India

Alisha Verma
https://orcid.org/0000-0001-6735-3829
Symbiosis Law School, Symbiosis International University, Pune, India

ABSTRACT

The criminal justice system is undergoing a rapid transformation as a result of cloud technology, which is providing emerging opportunities to enhance efficiency, collaboration, and data management while simultaneously addressing challenges that have persisted for a long time in traditional systems. The implementation of cloud-based solutions in the administration of criminal justice, covering both the advantages and the challenges involved. Enhanced data storage, real-time analysis, cost-effective information technology solutions, and improved inter-agency cooperation are among the most important opportunities.

1. INTRODUCTION

Public safety and societal stability depend heavily on the administration of criminal justice. It covers many different activities that generate and depend on enormous volumes of data, such as law enforcement, court cases, and prison administration.

DOI: 10.4018/979-8-3693-9581-3.ch015

Historically, paper-based or standalone digital systems have been used to manage these systems; these systems are frequently ineffective, prone to errors, and dispersed. This division can eventually have an impact on the fairness and promptness of the administration of justice by making it more difficult for agencies to collaborate with one another and slowing down the legal system. Modernization is becoming more and more necessary as the demands placed on the criminal justice system increase. Cloud computing represents one technological advancement that has great potential in this area. A potent remedy for many of the problems the criminal justice system faces today is provided by cloud computing. The cloud facilitates enhanced efficiency in data storage, instantaneous information access, and smooth cooperation among various criminal justice process agencies by offering a centralized, expandable, and user-friendly platform. To enhance their ability to access vital information from any location, law enforcement agencies can store and retrieve criminal records, video evidence, and case files on cloud servers. This data can also be accessed by courts, defense lawyers, and prosecutors, which expedites case processing and streamlines case administration. The utilization of advanced data analytics is another feature of cloud-based systems that can aid in better decision-making, resource allocation, and crime pattern prediction. Though these benefits are apparent, there are substantial obstacles associated with the use of cloud computing in criminal justice administration. Security ranks among the top issues. The handling of private information by criminal justice systems is delicate, and any compromise could have grave moral and legal ramification. The best encryption and access control techniques must be used to safeguard data, according to cloud providers. Making sure complicated laws like HIPAA and GDPR, which control the handling of personal data, are followed presents another difficulty. The adoption of new technologies can also be slowed down by resistance to change within the criminal justice system. When employees are not trained in using digital tools, agencies that are used to traditional methods may be reluctant to switch to cloud-based systems.

1.1 Criminal Justice Administration

A comprehensive system of practices, institutions, and procedures that are responsible for upholding the rule of law, maintaining public safety, and ensuring that justice is served is referred to as the administration of criminal justice procedures. Criminal investigations, trials, sentencing, and the rehabilitation of offenders are all managed by this system, which is comprised of law enforcement agencies, courts, correctional institutions, and legal professionals who collaborate with one another. As a means of preventing and controlling criminal activity, safeguarding the rights of individuals, and ensuring that criminals are held accountable through the application of due process, the criminal justice system was developed. Manual procedures and a variety of different computer systems have been utilized by the administration of criminal justice in order to manage its operations. Records were kept on paper, with police officers, prosecutors, and courts keeping separate records for each case, suspect, and victim each of which was recorded separately. Inefficiencies, errors, delays in communication, and a lack of coordination between agencies were frequently the results of this fragmented approach. Over the course of time, as the rate of criminal activity increased and the demand for more expedient legal procedures grew, it became increasingly apparent that the conventional approaches were not adequate to meet the ever-evolving requirements of contemporary society. The transition to digital platforms for record management, case tracking, and communication in the criminal justice system began with the rapid development of technology. However, many of these systems continued to operate independently within individual departments, which restricted the potential for collaboration across the larger justice network. These technologies did improve some processes. There has been a growing demand for solutions that are more integrated and efficient in order to address these challenges. These solutions have the potential to streamline the entire process of criminal justice, increase transparency, and improve public trust in the system. With cases frequently spanning multiple jurisdictions, involving large amounts of digital evidence, and requiring cooperation between a variety of agencies, the complexity of today's criminal justice environment is the driving force behind the necessity of modernization (Cloud, H., 2011). The importance of real-time data sharing and coordinated action cannot be overstated, and this is especially true in situations involving cybercrime, organized crime, and terrorism. To meet these demands while ensuring that justice is administered in a fair and efficient manner, the administration of criminal justice is now confronted with the challenge of utilizing new technologies such as cloud computing, artificial intelligence, and data analytics. In addition to protecting the rights and privacy of all individuals involved, these advancements are designed to make the legal process more efficient and accurate.

1.2 Cloud Technology in Criminal Justice

Cloud technology provides computing services like storage, databases, networking, software, and analytics over the internet, or "the cloud," rather than local servers or personal devices. Users can store data, run apps, and share resources from anywhere with an internet connection. Pay-as-you-go cloud computing lets companies scale resources based on demand without investing in physical infrastructure. There are public, private, and hybrid clouds for different organizational needs and security needs. Large tech companies like AWS, Azure, and Google Cloud host cloud platforms. Cloud technology provides real-time data access, automation, and collaboration in addition to storage and scalability. It allows organizations to use

AI and ML for data analytics, which can improve operations and decision-making. Providing solutions for large-scale data, service continuity, and global operations, this technology is essential across industries. Cloud technology in criminal justice is crucial due to the complexity and data-driven nature of modern legal processes. Fragmented workflows, inefficient data management, and limited inter-agency communication plague traditional systems. Centralizing data, improving collaboration, and improving information access across the criminal justice ecosystem is possible with cloud technology. Criminal justice officers, courts, and legal professionals need real-time data access from anywhere to make informed decisions about case files, evidence, criminal records, and agency communication. The cloud provides this. This technology aids police, prosecution, courts, and corrections in data sharing, streamlining legal processes and reducing bottlenecks. Cloud platforms encrypt and restrict access to sensitive data. Advanced analytics are possible with cloud technology. Criminal justice agencies can use AI and ML to predict crime, analyze trends, and better allocate resources. A proactive approach to policing can improve public safety and efficiency. Cloud-based systems also reduce infrastructure costs and free up resources for crime prevention and victim support. In an age of data security and privacy, cloud technology offers encryption, authentication, and disaster recovery. These features safeguard confidential data and ensure legal and ethical compliance. Criminal justice systems moving to the cloud must address regulatory compliance, change resistance, and cybersecurity threats, despite their great potential (Bhardwaj, A. K. et al., 2021).

2. LANDSCAPE OF CRIMINAL JUSTICE ADMINISTRATION

2.1 Existing Systems and Technologies

A multitude of antiquated, disjointed, and ineffective technologies and systems are used by the criminal justice system to oversee its daily operations. Criminal Justice organizations have historically used legacy systems, which are outdated hardware and software that were created decades ago. In the past state-of-the-art, but now unable to meet the demands of contemporary justice administration, these systems frequently consist of paper-based records, standalone databases, and local servers. The burgeoning data needs of the modern criminal justice system render legacy systems inappropriate due to their constrained storage capacity, lack of scalability, and security vulnerabilities. These systems can cause delays, misunderstandings, and inefficiencies since they are costly to maintain, hard to upgrade, and frequently incompatible with more modern technologies. Case Management Systems (CMS) are currently among the most often utilized technologies in criminal justice. These electronic systems are made to assist with the management and monitoring of criminal cases from the point of investigation to the point of resolution. Prosecutors, courts, and law enforcement organizations generally use CMS solutions to store and retrieve case-related data, such as witness statements, arrest records, and trial dates. There are still many systems that are isolated within specific departments, despite CMS's improvements in the organization and retrieval of case information. The information sharing between the police, prosecutors, courts, and corrections departments is still sluggish and ineffective due to this lack of integration across the various justice system sectors. To store, retrieve, and review video footage, forensic reports, and other types of evidence, some agencies have also implemented digital evidence management systems. These systems are essential for contemporary law enforcement because of the exponential growth in the amount of digital evidence (such as cellphone records, body camera footage, and surveillance videos). Similar to CMS, digital evidence systems frequently function alone, which reduces their overall efficacy in fostering interagency cooperation. A fully integrated system requires real-time data sharing, which is not provided by the majority of the systems and technologies currently in use in criminal justice administration, even with these advancements. Legal processes are slowed down and may even become mistake-prone as a result of this fragmentation, which impedes the smooth exchange of information between various criminal justice entities. The limits of current technologies draw attention to the need for more sophisticated, networked solutions like cloud computing, as the amount of data generated and processed within the justice system keeps growing (Njenga, K. et al., 2019).

2.2 Traditional Criminal Justice's Obstacles

These challenges which are shown in the figure 1, highlight the pressing need for the criminal justice system to undergo a thorough modernization, especially through the implementation of cutting-edge, integrated technological solutions like cloud computing. By addressing these problems, the legal system can become much more effective, transparent, and efficient, which will ultimately benefit both communities and individuals.

1. *Fragmented Systems*: Numerous criminal justice organizations run independently of one another on different systems. Investigations and court cases may be delayed as a result of this fragmentation, which also makes information flow more difficult. For instance, it is difficult to exchange vital information about ongoing cases when courts, prosecutors, and police departments use different databases. As a result, crucial information might be overlooked, which would impede cooperation and reduce the justice system's overall effectiveness.

2. *Inefficient Data Management*: Conventional data management techniques frequently handle case information inefficiently because they mainly rely on antiquated digital systems and paper records. The manual procedures needed to maintain, obtain, and distribute records can be error-prone and time-consuming, greatly impeding inquiries and court cases. Additionally, keeping accurate and trustworthy records is challenging when paper records are used, as there is a greater chance of loss or damage.
3. *Limited Real-Time Access*: Lack of real-time data access is a major problem for the criminal justice system. It's possible that field officers don't always have instant access to vital data, like criminal histories or evidence that could influence their decisions. Postponements in acquiring this data may hinder inquiries and lead to lost chances for prompt actions. This restriction may also have an impact on court proceedings, where prompt access to case and evidence information is essential for impartial trials.
4. *Interoperability Issues*: When disparate agencies employ incompatible systems that hinder smooth data sharing, interoperability issues occur. When there are multiple jurisdictions involved and information needs to be shared at the local, state, and federal levels, this problem is especially noticeable. Because agencies may find it difficult to coordinate their efforts and share crucial information, a failure to integrate systems can result in major delays in investigations, which can ultimately have an impact on case outcomes and public safety (Karagiannis, C., & Vergidis, K., 2021).
5. *High Operational Costs*: For criminal justice agencies, maintaining physical infrastructure and legacy systems can be very expensive. Many businesses have limited resources, which can make it difficult for them to invest in modern technology. Resources that might otherwise be devoted to more important areas, like staff training or community engagement programs, can be diverted by the continuous costs of maintaining antiquated systems, including repairs, training, and security measures.
6. *Resistance to Change*: In the criminal justice system, managing change can be very difficult. Due to perceived inadequacy or fear of the unknown, personnel trained in traditional methods may be reluctant to adopt new technologies or processes. This opposition may put up obstacles in the way of modernization initiatives, delaying the adoption of critical innovations that might increase efficacy and efficiency (Ruan, K. et al., 2013).
7. *Compliance Challenges*: For organizations using antiquated systems, navigating the complicated web of laws governing data management and privacy can be especially difficult. There can be serious legal ramifications, including fines and a loss of public trust, for breaking regulations like the General Data Protection Regulation (GDPR) or the Health Insurance Portability and Accountability Act

(HIPAA). Maintaining awareness and training is necessary to ensure compliance, which can be challenging if systems are not in line with the most recent legal requirements.

Figure 1. Challenges faced in traditional criminal justice administration

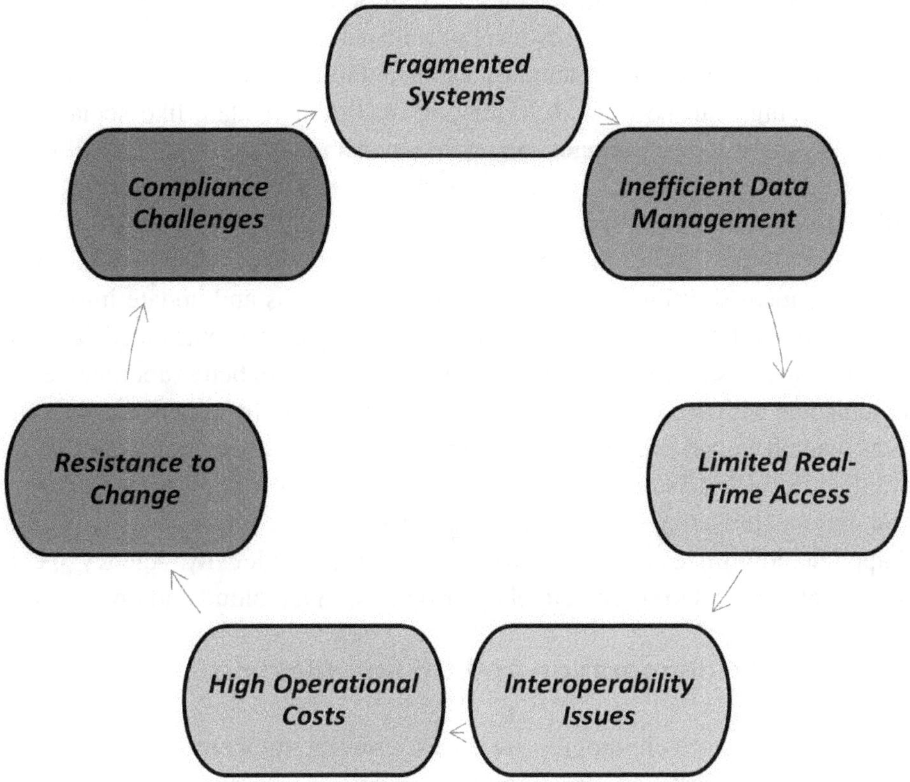

3. OPPORTUNITIES PRESENTED BY CLOUD TECHNOLOGY

3.1 Enhanced Data Storage and Management

Modern technology is changing criminal justice data storage and management. Innovative methods are needed to manage law enforcement, court, and correctional data due to its growing volume and complexity. Intelligent data organization, real-time analytics, and system interoperability are part of modern data storage solutions.

The use of AI and machine learning algorithms to organize and retrieve data has improved data management. These technologies automatically classify and tag data, making massive datasets easier to sort. AI can help police prioritize investigations by identifying crime data patterns. Crime prevention can be proactive with such insights, shifting from reactive to strategic planning. Data integrity and traceability are being addressed by blockchain technology. In criminal justice, blockchain can secure evidence, case files, and stakeholder transactions. Building public trust and system accountability requires this level of transparency. Blockchain allows agencies to verify evidence and maintain an indisputable chain of custody, ensuring legal proceedings can be trusted. Managing unstructured data like social media feeds, video surveillance footage, and audio recordings is becoming possible with "data lakes". Agents can store all types of data in raw form in data lakes, unlike traditional databases. Law enforcement can analyze and learn from diverse data sources, improving their real-time response to crime. Field officers need mobile data management solutions even more. Police can access and update information on the go with tablets and smartphones with secure access to centralized databases. Law enforcement is more responsive and investigations are better documented and communicated with this capability (Simou, S. et al., 2016). Instantaneous data entry reduces manual record-keeping errors and makes critical information available to all relevant parties. Cloud storage solutions are becoming more sophisticated, offering hybrid options that let agencies balance public and private cloud security. This hybrid approach optimizes costs and protects sensitive data legally. Agency-specific solutions can be created by selectively storing data in the cloud and on-premises.

3.2 Improved Collaboration and Communication

Cloud computing technologies are an essential component in the process of enhancing communication. Cloud computing makes it possible to access shared data repositories in a secure manner from any location, which is especially helpful for law enforcement officers who are out in the field. Law enforcement personnel are able to quickly access relevant information, communicate with their teams, and update records while they are on patrol thanks to mobile devices that are connected to cloud platforms. The mobility of these individuals ensures that critical data is always at their fingertips, which enables them to make decisions that are more informed and to respond to incidents in a timely manner. Alongside the implementation of technological solutions, the cultivation of a culture that values collaboration is of equal significance. Communication skills among personnel can be improved through the implementation of training programs that place an emphasis on inter-agency cooperation. It is possible to break down barriers and create a shared understanding of the roles and responsibilities of each agency through the use of interactive workshops and joint training exercises. It is possible for organizations to develop a more unified strategy for dealing with criminal activity and ensure that justice is served if they encourage personnel from various sectors to collaborate with one another. The utilization of data analytics to inform joint strategies is yet another essential component of improved collaboration (Martini, B., & Choo, K. K. R., 2013). With the help of crime trends and patterns analysis, law enforcement agencies are able to pinpoint problem areas and more efficiently distribute resources. Enhanced community safety can be achieved, for instance, through the implementation of data-driven policing initiatives, which can result in coordinated efforts among multiple agencies in high-crime areas. The sharing of insights that are derived from data analytics can lead to the creation of a collaborative framework that enables proactive strategies rather than reactive responses. Enhancing public communication can also be accomplished through the utilization of social media and platforms that facilitate community engagement. These tools can be utilized by law enforcement agencies in order to provide the general public with information regarding ongoing investigations, safety alerts, and community initiatives. The use of social media to engage with the community helps to cultivate transparency and builds trust, which in turn makes it simpler for government agencies to work together with citizens in the fight against criminal activity. The input of the public can provide valuable intelligence, which can facilitate the enhancement of investigations and foster a sense of collective responsibility for the safety of the community.

3.3 Cost-Effectiveness

The modernization of the criminal justice system must take cost-effectiveness into account, especially with the introduction of new technologies like cloud computing and improved data management systems. Conventional approaches to data and operations management frequently involve high infrastructure, maintenance, and personnel costs. On the other hand, cutting-edge technologies can offer more effective substitutes that save operating expenses while enhancing service effectiveness and delivery. The ability of cloud computing to reduce IT infrastructure capital costs is one of its main advantages. Criminal justice organizations can do away with the need for large-scale, upfront-investment on-premises hardware and software by switching to cloud-based solutions. Alternatively, scalable solutions from cloud providers let agencies pay for the resources they really use. Agencies can more efficiently manage their budgets thanks to this pay-as-you-go model, which frees up money for other essentials like staff training and community outreach initiatives. Agencies can adapt their resources to meet evolving demands thanks to the cloud's scalability. For instance, agencies can simply scale up their processing and storage capacities without having to invest in expensive physical upgrades during periods of high activity, such as spikes in crime or special events. On the other hand, they can reduce during slower times to cut costs. Over time, agencies may save a significant amount of money thanks to this flexibility, which allows them to optimize (Pandey, B. K., & Pandey, D., 2023) their operating expenses in response to changing needs. Better data management systems not only save infrastructure costs but also increase the effectiveness of data handling and processing. Conventional approaches typically entail labor-intensive, time-consuming, and error-prone manual record-keeping, data entry (Pandey, B. K., & Pandey, D., 2025), and information retrieval tasks. Case files and evidence management takes a lot less time and work when automated data management solutions automate these procedures. Agencies can increase productivity without adding to labor costs by automating repetitive tasks and reallocating staff to more strategic roles. Effective data analysis is another factor that can help reduce costs. Agencies can use advanced analytics to better allocate resources, spot trends, and put data-driven plans into action that lower crime rates and increase public safety. Predictive policing approaches, for instance, can assist organizations in concentrating their resources on high-crime areas, resulting in a more effective use of officers and resources. Agencies may be able to reduce the expenses of reactive measures, like protracted investigations or emergency response operations, by taking a proactive approach to combating crime. Significant cost savings can also result from improved cooperation via integrated communication platforms. Improved agency collaboration results in less effort duplication and better outcomes since it allows agencies to share resources, knowledge, and skills. Additionally, when multiple agencies work together to present a single, cohesive front, they may be able to secure more funding for joint projects and grant applications (Rai, P. K. et al., 2024).

3.4 Advanced Analytics and Reporting

The use of data to inform strategies and improve operational effectiveness is causing the landscape of criminal justice to undergo a transformation. This transformation is being brought about by advanced analytics and reporting (Muniandi, B. et al., 2024). Both predictive policing and crime trend analysis are essential components of this advancement. Both of these components enable law enforcement agencies to make decisions based on data analysis, which is a significant advantage. For the purpose of analyzing past crime data and predicting future criminal activity, predictive policing makes use of sophisticated algorithms and statistical methods. Once law enforcement agencies have identified patterns and trends in previous incidents, they are able to make predictions about the locations where crimes are most likely to occur and allocate resources accordingly. Through the use of this proactive approach, officers are able to be deployed to high-risk areas before incidents take place, which has the potential to prevent crimes and improve protection for the general public. The utilization of predictive analytics necessitates the examination of a number of aspects, such as the time of day, the location, and the nature of the criminal activity. On the basis of previous occurrences, for instance, algorithms are able to identify hotspots, which are locations where particular types of criminal activity are more likely to take place. Due to the availability of this information (Shahul, A. et al., 2024), law enforcement agencies are able to strategically position patrols, thereby increasing visibility and deterrence in areas that are vulnerable.

It is possible to improve predictive policing by incorporating data from a variety of sources, including social media, community reports, and socioeconomic indicators, among others. Through the combination of these datasets, governments are able to acquire a more comprehensive understanding of the factors that contribute to criminal activity in particular regions. Through the use of this holistic perspective, policing strategies can be more specifically tailored to address the underlying causes of criminal behaviour (Pandey, D. et al., 2024). For the purpose of ensuring that predictive policing practices do not result in discriminatory practices, it is necessary to carefully manage concerns regarding bias in data as well as the possibility of profiling. For the purpose of mitigating these risks and preserving the trust of the community, agencies are required to implement transparent methodologies and conduct regular audits of algorithms (Vinodhini, V. et al., 2022). The purpose of crime trend analysis is to identify and attempt to make sense of changes that have occurred over time in crime rates and patterns. Identifying long-term trends, seasonal fluctuations, and emerging types of criminal activity can be accomplished by law enforcement agencies through the examination of historical data. In order to effectively plan strategically, distribute resources, and formulate policies, this analysis is absolutely necessary. For the purpose of visualizing crime trends, agencies typically make use of sophisticated analytical tools (Kumar, B. et al., 2024). This provides decision-makers with the ability to quickly identify anomalies and areas of concern. An increase in the number of property crimes that occur during particular months may prompt law enforcement agencies to increase the number of patrols they conduct or to launch community outreach programs that are aimed at preventing crime. In addition, conducting an analysis of demographic and geographic factors can provide insights into the populations that are predominantly impacted by criminal activity, which enables targeted interventions to be implemented. Crime trend analysis is an important tool for determining how effective various strategies are in reducing criminal activity. Agencies are able to evaluate the effectiveness of their efforts by comparing the crime rates that existed before and after the implementation of particular initiatives. This process of evaluation (Khadka, M. et al., 2025) encourages continuous improvement because it allows for the scaling up of successful strategies while allowing for the modification or discontinuation of approaches that are ineffective. The participation of community stakeholders in the analysis process has the potential to facilitate improvements in public safety efforts (Sheela, M. S. et al., 2025). The dissemination of findings from crime trend analysis to community leaders and residents can facilitate the development of collaborative efforts to address concerns regarding safety (Satheesh, N. et al., 2025). The engagement of the community helps to cultivate a sense of ownership and responsibility (Kumar, M. S. et al., 2025), which in turn gives residents the ability to take part in initiatives aimed at preventing crime.

4. BARRIERS TO CLOUD TECHNOLOGY ADOPTION

The criminal justice system can benefit greatly from cloud computing, but agencies will face a number of obstacles when putting it into practice. A few of these difficulties are concerns about privacy and security (Konapure, C. G. et al., 2025), resistance to change, dependability and internet connectivity, and moral issues.

- *Security and Privacy Issues*

  a) *Data Breaches*: The possibility of data breaches (Singh, S. et al., 2025) is one of the main issues with cloud technology. When confidential data is kept off-site, it opens itself up to illegal access by cybercriminals who are always looking for weaknesses in cloud infrastructure. Law enforcement organizations and the communities they serve may suffer severe consequences if personal information, case files, and evidence are compromised by a data breach. For this risk to be reduced, it is imperative to have strong encryption, access controls, and frequent security audits during communication (Sharma, M. et al., 2025).

  b) *Compliance with Regulations*: The General Data Protection Regulation (GDPR) and the Health Insurance Portability and Accountability Act (HIPAA) are two examples of the regulations that criminal justice agencies are required to abide by. These regulations govern privacy and data protection (Pandey, B. K. et al., 2024a). To guarantee compliance, implementing cloud solutions necessitates carefully reviewing these laws. A complex and resource-intensive process, especially when handling sensitive personal data, must be followed when developing policies and procedures by agencies to ensure compliance with legal requirements.

- *Resistance to Change*

a) *Cultural and Institutional Barriers*: When cloud technology is introduced, staff members used to traditional systems and procedures might object. New technology adoption may be hampered by institutional and cultural barriers (Satheesh, N. et al., 2025). Workers could worry about losing their jobs or struggle to adjust to new procedures. Having a strong leader, communicating the advantages of cloud computing clearly, and involving staff members in the implementation process to instill a sense of ownership are all necessary to overcome this resistance.

b) *Training and Skill Gaps*: Employees must have the requisite abilities to operate and oversee new systems in order for cloud technology to be successfully implemented. It is necessary to create training programs to fill in skill gaps and make sure staff members are knowledgeable about data security procedures and cloud tool usage (Pandey, B. K. et al., 2024b). The underutilization of resources and decreased operational efficiency can result from agencies' inability to fully utilize cloud solutions if they lack proper training.

- *Reliability and Dependency on Internet Connectivity*

a) *Downtime Risks*: Since internet connectivity is a major component of cloud technology, any interruptions may cause downtime and restrict access to vital information and systems (Basha, A. J. et al., 2024).). In order to handle any service disruptions or internet outages, law enforcement and judicial organizations need to have backup plans ready. Maintaining dependable backup systems and offline capabilities is crucial because the inability to obtain vital information in real-time can impede investigations and jeopardize public safety.

b) *Impact on Critical Services*: Concerns are raised about the possible effects on vital services of a dependency on internet connectivity. Public safety may be jeopardized and response times prolonged in emergency scenarios due to cloud-based system unavailability (KVM, S. et al., 2024). It is imperative for agencies to evaluate the potential hazards linked to their reliance on cloud computing and devise tactics to guarantee uninterrupted operations. These tactics may involve implementing redundant systems or hybrid solutions that merge cloud and on-premises resources.

- *Ethical Considerations*

a) *Bias in Algorithms*: When cloud computing is used, predictive analytics and data processing algorithms are frequently used (Lakshmi, K. V. N. et al., 2024). These algorithms may unintentionally reinforce biases found in historical data. An unfair sentencing and law enforcement system may result from biased algorithms (Saravanakumar, R. et al., 2024) if they are not closely supervised. To ensure fair and equitable treatment of all individuals, agencies must establish rigorous testing and validation procedures to detect and reduce bias in their algorithms (Kumarganesh, S. et al., 2024).
b) *Accountability and Transparency*: Concerns about accountability and transparency surface as agencies depend more on automated processes and algorithms (Muralidhar, L. B. et al., 2024). For decisions made by algorithms to be comprehensible and subject to close examination, law enforcement agencies must continue to exercise oversight over the technologies they use. It is possible to foster community trust and guarantee that moral principles are followed when using technology by establishing explicit accountability procedures (Pandey, B. K. et al., 2024c).

The criminal justice system can benefit greatly from the use of cloud technology in terms of efficiency and better service delivery, there are a number of obstacles that are shown in the figure 2, which agencies need to overcome. To successfully integrate cloud solutions, it is imperative to tackle key issues like security and privacy, overcome resistance to change, ensure dependability (Elarmathi, S. et al., 2024), and take ethical considerations into account. Agencies can fully utilize cloud technology to improve operations and more effectively serve their communities by taking proactive measures to address these issues.

Figure 2. Barriers to cloud technology adoption

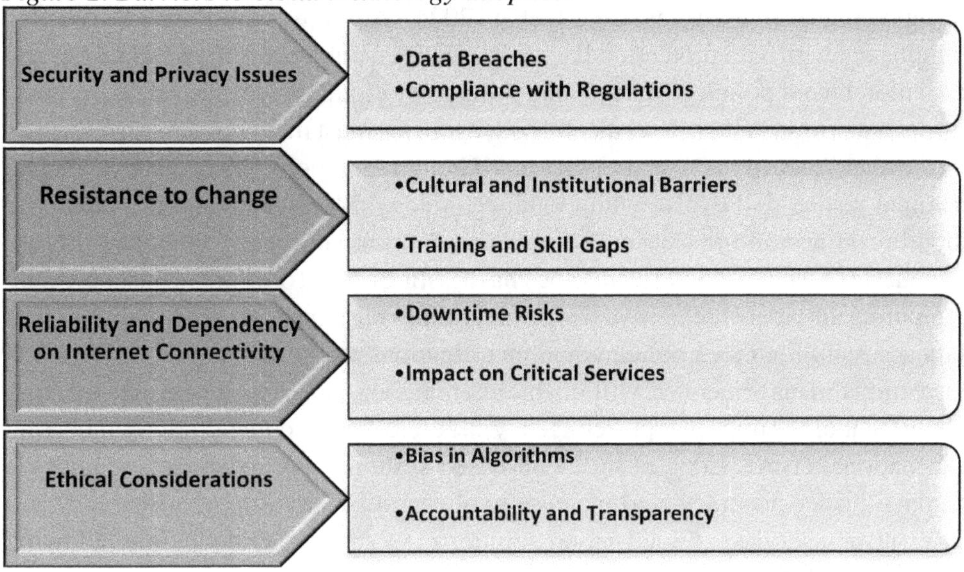

5. CLOUD TECHNOLOGY AND CRIMINAL JUSTICE

Cloud technology is transforming criminal justice administration by enabling the adoption of new technologies, integrating IoT devices, adapting to changing regulatory frameworks, and changing the justice system's operations and structure. Cloud technology has a major impact in these areas: AI and ML (Pandey, B. K. et al., 2024d) are being deployed in criminal justice using cloud platforms. These technologies can analyse massive cloud data sets to find patterns, improve prediction, and aid decision-making. AI can help identify suspects through facial recognition, analyze crime scene footage, and process evidence faster (Pandey, B. K. et al., 2024e). Machine learning algorithms can forecast crime, evaluate parole risks, and analyze recidivism. Cloud platforms can perform computationally intensive tasks quickly and on a large scale, transforming justice administration. The IoT is becoming more important in law enforcement and criminal justice. Body-worn cameras, drones, smart sensors, and GPS tracking generate large amounts of real-time data that must be stored, analysed, and accessed (George, W. K. et al., 2024). Law enforcement agencies have unprecedented real-time situational awareness thanks to cloud technology, which collects, stores, and analyzes device data. Body cameras send footage to cloud servers for analysis, sharing, and court use. IoT-based surveillance systems integrated with cloud platforms can automate alert systems for faster crime and suspicious activity responses. In criminal justice, cloud technology must adapt to changing regulations (Abdullahi, M. et al., 2024). Adopting cloud services requires compliance with data protection laws (e.g., GDPR), public records regulations, and law enforcement policies. When using third-party cloud service providers or cross-border data flows (Singh, S. et al., 2025).), agencies must maintain data sovereignty, privacy, and security across jurisdictions. Cloud regulations in sensitive fields like criminal justice will evolve with cloud technology. Monitoring legal changes and adopting frameworks that ensure compliance, data protection, and accountability are essential for agencies. Cloud technology has a lasting impact on criminal justice. Cloud computing automates repetitive tasks, streamlines case management, and improves data accessibility. From policing and investigations to courtroom proceedings and corrections management, it will enable more agile, data-driven decision-making. Cloud technology improves justice agency and cross-border collaboration, combating transnational crime. Long-term, cloud-based systems may reduce costs, improve criminal justice accuracy, and increase public trust by providing transparency and faster justice services. Cloud-based solutions are scalable and flexible, allowing agencies to adapt to new technology.

6. CONCLUSION

The adoption of cloud computing by the criminal justice system represents a dramatic modernization step that presents both enormous opportunities and unique challenges. As previously mentioned, inefficiencies in data management, problems with interoperability, financial limitations, and security concerns are just a few of the challenges that traditional criminal justice systems must overcome. By providing scalable data storage, enhanced agency collaboration, affordable solutions, and sophisticated analytics for predictive policing and crime trend analysis, cloud technology solves a number of these problems. It is imperative to address security and privacy concerns, particularly in relation to data breaches and regulatory compliance. The shift to cloud-based systems is further complicated by institutional and cultural resistance to change, as well as skill gaps in the workforce. Depending too much on the internet brings risks like system outages that could affect vital services. Ethical issues like algorithmic biases and the requirement for transparency also need to be carefully addressed. The use of cloud computing in criminal justice appears to have a bright future, despite these obstacles. The integration of IoT devices, machine learning, and artificial intelligence (AI) are some of the emerging technologies that will further improve real-time analysis, data-driven decision-making, and operational efficiency. The long-term effects of cloud adoption are probably going to change criminal justice administration, making it more flexible, transparent, and economical as regulatory frameworks change to keep up with technology improvements. Agencies can improve public safety and confidence in law enforcement by adopting cloud technology responsibly and developing a more responsive and effective justice system.

REFERENCES

Abdullahi, M., Ahmad, A., Pandey, B. K., & Pandey, D. (2024). Digital Currency Adoption: A Comparative Analysis of Global Trends and the Nigerian eNaira Digital Currency. *SN Computer Science*, *5*(5), 1–11.

Basha, A. J., Maheshwari, R. U., Pandey, B. K., & Pandey, D. (2024). Ultra-sensitive photonic crystal fiber–based SPR sensor for cancer detection utilizing hybrid nano-composite layers. *Plasmonics*, •••, 1–15.

Bhardwaj, A. K., Garg, L., Garg, A., & Gajpal, Y. (2021). E-learning during covid-19 outbreak: cloud computing adoption in Indian public universities.

Cloud, H. (2011). The nist definition of cloud computing. *National institute of science and technology, special publication, 800*(2011), 145.

Elarmathi, S., Rishabavarthani, P., Sindhuja, M., Elayaraja, P., & Malathi Murugesan, S. Kumarganesh, K. Martin Sagayam, Binay Kumar Pandey, and Digvijay Pandey. (2024). Novel manufacturing systems for cancer diagnosis using ultra-sensitive photonic crystal fiber biosensor with dual-functionalized aptamer-nanocavity. *Microsystem Technologies*, •••, 1–20.

George, W. K., Silas, E. I., Pandey, D., & Pandey, B. K. (2024). Utilization of Industry 4.0 Technologies in Nigerian Technical and Vocational Education: A Conundrum for Educators. In *Examining the Rapid Advance of Digital Technology in Africa* (pp. 270–293). IGI Global.

Karagiannis, C., & Vergidis, K. (2021). Digital evidence and cloud forensics: Contemporary legal challenges and the power of disposal. *Information (Basel)*, *12*(5), 181.

Khadka, M., Sah, M., Chaudhary, R., Sahani, S. K., Sahani, K., Pandey, B. K., & Pandey, D. (2025). Spectroscopic, quantum chemical, and topological calculations of the phenylephrine molecule using density functional theory. *Scientific Reports*, *15*(1), 208. PMID: 39747169

Konapure, C. G., Pandey, D., Shete, H., Thakar, C. M., Pandey, B. K., & George, A. S. (2025). Artificial Intelligence in Automated Concrete Mix Design Using Computerized Grading Curves. Interdisciplinary Approaches to AI, Internet of Everything, and Machine Learning, 567-586.

Kumar, B., Pandey, D., Pandey, B. K., & George, A. S. (2024). Higher Education in the Last Four Decades: A Review of Paradigm Shifts in Policy Frameworks. Design and Implementation of Higher Education Learners' Learning Outcomes (HELLO), 333-348.

Kumar, M. S., Prasanna, P. L., Lalitha, M., Joy, M., Jha, S. S., & Pandey, B. K. (2025). Utilizing the Internet of Everything and Artificial Intelligence for Real-Time Workforce Management. In Role of Internet of Everything (IOE), VLSI Architecture, and AI in Real-Time Systems (pp. 153-168). IGI Global Scientific Publishing.

Kumarganesh, S., & Malathi Murugesan, C. Ganesh, N. Santhiyakumari, M. Thangavel, K. Jayaram, K. Martin Sagayam, Binay Kumar Pandey, and Digvijay Pandey. (2024). Hybrid plasmonic biosensors with deep learning for colorectal cancer detection. *Plasmonics*, •••, 1–15.

KVM, S., Pandey, B. K., & Pandey, D. (2024). Design of Surface Plasmon Resonance (SPR) Sensors for Highly Sensitive Biomolecular Detection in Cancer Diagnostics. *Plasmonics*, •••, 1–13.

Lakshmi, K. V. N., Rajan, R., Pandey, D., & Pandey, B. K. (2024). Circular economy: A catalyst for economic growth-an empirical study. *Circular Economy and Sustainability*, •••, 1–22.

Martini, B., & Choo, K. K. R. (2013). Cloud storage forensics: ownCloud as a case study. *Digital Investigation*, *10*(4), 287–299.

Muniandi, B., Nassa, V. K., Pandey, D., Pandey, B. K., Dadheech, P., & George, A. S. (2024). Pattern Analysis for Feature Extraction in Complex Images. In Using Machine Learning to Detect Emotions and Predict Human Psychology (pp. 145-167). IGI Global.

Muralidhar, L. B., Lakshmi, K. V. N., Swapna, H. R., Rupani, J., Nethravathi, K., Pandey, B. K., & Pandey, D. (2024). Impact of Organizational Culture on The Level of Corporate Social Responsibility Investments: An Exploratory Study. *Circular Economy and Sustainability*, •••, 1–19.

Njenga, K., Garg, L., Bhardwaj, A. K., Prakash, V., & Bawa, S. (2019). The cloud computing adoption in higher learning institutions in Kenya: Hindering factors and recommendations for the way forward. *Telematics and Informatics*, *38*, 225–246.

Pandey, B. K., Nassa, V. K., Mukundan, A. P., Mahajan, D. A., Pandey, D., George, A. S., & Dadheech, P. (2024c). An Industry-Focused Traffic System Utilising Internet of Things. In *Emerging Engineering Technologies and Industrial Applications* (pp. 200–213). IGI Global.

Pandey, B. K., & Pandey, D. (2023). Parametric optimization and prediction of enhanced thermoelectric performance in co-doped CaMnO3 using response surface methodology and neural network. *Journal of Materials Science Materials in Electronics*, *34*(21), 1589.

Pandey, B. K., & Pandey, D. (2025). Securing healthcare medical image information using advance morphological component analysis, information hiding systems, and hybrid convolutional neural networks on IoMT. *Computers in Biology and Medicine*, *185*, 109499. PMID: 39642698

Pandey, B. K., Pandey, D., & Lelisho, M. E. (2024a). Face mask identification with enhanced cuckoo optimization and deep learning-based faster regional neural network. *Scientific Reports*, *14*(1), 29719. PMID: 39613761

Pandey, B. K., Pandey, D., & Sahani, S. K. (2024b). Autopilot control unmanned aerial vehicle system for sewage defect detection using deep learning. *Engineering Reports*, •••, 12852.

Pandey, B. K., Paramashivan, M. A., Pandey, D., George, A. S., Agarwal, A., Dadheech, P., & Mahajan, D. A. (2024e). A recent survey on 6G vehicular technology: applications and challenges. 6G Security Education and Multidisciplinary Implementation, 337-350.

Pandey, B. K., Paramashivan, M. A., Pandey, D., George, A. S., Agarwal, A., Mahajan, D. A., . . . Pramanik, S. (2024d). Future Directions of Digital Twin Architectures for 6G Communication Networks. In Security Issues and Solutions in 6G Communications and Beyond (pp. 197-211). IGI Global.

Pandey, D., Nassa, V. K., Pandey, B. K., Mahajan, D. A., Patidar, P. K., Dadheech, P., & George, A. S. (2024). An Analysis of Internet-of-Things-Based Fire Detection and Alert Systems. In *Emerging Engineering Technologies and Industrial Applications* (pp. 295–304). IGI Global.

Rai, P. K., Pandey, D., & Pandey, B. K. (2024). The future of enterprise and innovation is compute as a commodity, or CaaC. *Partners Universal International Research Journal*, *3*(2), 89–94.

Ruan, K., Carthy, J., Kechadi, T., & Baggili, I. (2013). Cloud forensics definitions and critical criteria for cloud forensic capability: An overview of survey results. *Digital Investigation*, *10*(1), 34–43.

Saravanakumar, R., TamilSelvi, T., Pandey, D., Pandey, B. K., Mahajan, D. A., & Lelisho, M. E. (2024). Big data processing using hybrid Gaussian mixture model with salp swarm algorithm. *Journal of Big Data*, *11*(1), 167.

Satheesh, N., Gopisankar, N., Kumarganesh, S., Anthoniraj, S., Saravanakumar, S., & Martin Sagayam, K., Binay Kumar Pandey, and Digvijay Pandey. (2025). Advanced AI-driven emergency response systems for enhanced vehicle and human safety. *Iran Journal of Computer Science*, •••, 1–16.

Satheesh, N., Gopisankar, N., Kumarganesh, S., Anthoniraj, S., Saravanakumar, S., & Martin Sagayam, K., Binay Kumar Pandey, and Digvijay Pandey. (2025). Advanced AI-driven emergency response systems for enhanced vehicle and human safety. *Iran Journal of Computer Science*, ●●●, 1–16.

Shahul, A., Muniandi, B., Paramashivan, M. A., Pandey, D., Pandey, B. K., Dadheech, P., & George, H. (2024). An Analysis of Algorithms and Methods Based on Image Processing for Medical Applications. In *Emerging Engineering Technologies and Industrial Applications* (pp. 173–186). IGI Global.

Sharma, M., Talwar, R., Nassa, V. K., Binay, K., & Pandey, D. (2025). Design and performance analysis of a multiband vivaldi antenna for wireless broadband communication in 3-5.6 GHz spectrum. In *Artificial Intelligence and Information Technologies* (pp. 86–91). CRC Press.

Sheela, M. S., Kumarganesh, S., Pandey, B. K., & Lelisho, M. E. (2025). Integration of silver nanostructures in wireless sensor networks for enhanced biochemical sensing. *Discover Nano*, *20*(1), 7. PMID: 39804434

Simou, S., Kalloniatis, C., Gritzalis, S., & Mouratidis, H. (2016). A survey on cloud forensics challenges and solutions. *Security and Communication Networks*, *9*(18), 6285–6314.

Singh, S., Madaan, G., Swapna, H. R., Singh, A., Pandey, D., George, A. S., & Pandey, B. K. (2025). Empowering Connectivity: Exploring the Internet of Things. In Interdisciplinary Approaches to AI, Internet of Everything, and Machine Learning (pp. 89-116). IGI Global Scientific Publishing.

Singh, S., Madaan, G., Swapna, H. R., Singh, A., Pandey, D., George, A. S., & Pandey, B. K. (2025). Empowering Connectivity: Exploring the Internet of Things. In Interdisciplinary Approaches to AI, Internet of Everything, and Machine Learning (pp. 89-116). IGI Global Scientific Publishing.

Vinodhini, V., Kumar, M. S., Sankar, S., Pandey, D., Pandey, B. K., & Nassa, V. K. (2022). IoT-based early forest fire detection using MLP and AROC method. *International Journal of Global Warming*, *27*(1), 55–70.

Chapter 16
Maximizing Return on Investment Through Cloud Solution

S. Vinoth
https://orcid.org/0000-0001-8014-0342
Jain University, Bengaluru, India

C. Gopalakrishnan
https://orcid.org/0000-0002-1190-6989
Jain University, Bengaluru, India

Geeti Sharma
Jain University, Bengaluru, India

Pujari Sudharsana Reddy
Jain University, Bengaluru, India

ABSTRACT

Computing in the cloud has emerged as an essential element in the digital transformation of businesses, as it provides businesses with increased scalability, flexibility, and cost-effectiveness. The strategic role that clouds technology plays in enhancing operational efficiency and propelling research and development. In particular, it highlights the significance of data integrity, security, and compliance within multi-cloud environments, which are characterized by the complexity that arises from the management of multiple platforms. In order for organizations to successfully adopt cloud computing, they need to develop migration strategies that are tailored to their specific needs, carry out comprehensive readiness assessments, and put in place robust change management procedures.

DOI: 10.4018/979-8-3693-9581-3.ch016

1. INTRODUCTION

A strategic approach that enables businesses to improve their efficiency, lower their costs, and drive innovation is to maximize their return on investment (ROI) through the use of cloud computing solutions. Cloud computing provides a number of different models, including Infrastructure as a Service (IaaS), Platform as a Service (PaaS), and Software as a Service (SaaS), which enables businesses to choose the model that is best suited to meet their requirements. Cloud solutions offer a number of benefits, one of the most important of which is cost efficiency. Businesses are able to significantly reduce their capital expenditures (CAPEX) and transition to a more predictable operational expenditure (OPEX) model if they make the transition from traditional on-premises infrastructure to cloud services. This change enables improved management of the budget as well as the allocation of resources to activities that are essential to the business. Scalability (Pandey, B. K. et al., 2024a) is another important factor that should be considered when optimizing return on investment. With cloud solutions, businesses are able to rapidly adjust their resource allocation in response to fluctuations in demand. This flexibility helps businesses reduce waste and ensures that they only pay for the resources that they actually use. Furthermore, the utilization of cloud-native tools and technologies, such as automation (Pandey, B. K. et al., 2024b) and analytics, can facilitate the streamlining of operations, the improvement of productivity, and the enhancement of decision-making opportunities. Before moving to the cloud, businesses need to conduct a comprehensive evaluation in order to effectively maximize their return on investment (ROI). Among these are the evaluation of their current information technology infrastructure, the comprehension of potential cost savings, and the establishment of clear performance metrics. Fostering a culture within the organization (Abdullahi, M. et al., 2024) that is highly focused on cloud computing encourages innovation and agility. It is possible for businesses to fully exploit the potential of cloud solutions if they encourage their employees to participate in training and skill development programs. This will result in enhanced customer experiences and a greater advantage over their competitors.

1.1 Significance of ROI in Strategies

- *Performance Measurement*: One of the most important metrics that is used to evaluate the efficiency of investments is return on investment (ROI). A clear picture of which strategies yield the best financial returns can be obtained by organizations through the utilization of return on investment (ROI) calculations, which allow for the evaluation of the profitability of a variety of initiatives and projects. For the purpose of determining which campaigns were successful and which operational efficiencies were achieved, this performance measurement is essential (George, W. K. et al., 2024). Return on investment (ROI) can be broken down into a variety of components, which enables businesses to identify particular areas of their operations that are deficient or strong. Businesses are able to maintain their concentration on high-impact activities that positively contribute to their bottom line when they perform regular monitoring of their return on investment (ROI).

- *Informed Decision-Making*: The return on investment (ROI) provides management with a quantitative basis for decision-making, which enables them to select the most advantageous investment options. The use of return on investment (ROI) analysis makes it easier to compare various strategies and resource allocations when multiple strategic initiatives are being considered. This helps to ensure that decisions are based on data (Maheshwari, R. U. et al., 2024b) rather than feeling. The risk of pursuing ventures that are not profitable is reduced thanks to this informed approach, which also assists leaders in concentrating on initiatives that have the potential to have the greatest impact. As an illustration, when deciding between expanding into a new market or investing in new technology, decision-makers are able to select the path that maximizes returns while minimizing risks by calculating the expected return on investment (ROI) for each and every option.
- *Resource Allocation*: Return on investment (ROI) is a useful tool for prioritizing projects because it identifies those that have the highest potential returns. In order to ensure that funds are allocated to initiatives that maximize value, organizations can efficiently allocate resources by evaluating the expected returns on those resources. Overall performance is ultimately improved as a result of this strategic approach (Muralidhar, L. B. et al., 2024), which helps prevent wasteful spending on projects with low impact. When departments are able to justify their funding requests based on projected returns, understanding return on investment (ROI) can also be helpful in budget negotiations. This allows organizations to ensure that their investments are in line with their strategic goals and that they deliver benefits that can be measured (Kunduru, 2023).
- *Risk Assessment*: By evaluating the expected return on investment (ROI), organizations are able to gain a better understanding of the risks that are associated with particular investments. Businesses are able to make educated decisions that strike a balance between the opportunities for reward and the risks involved by conducting risk and potential return analyses. When it comes to risk management, this proactive approach emphasizes the importance of conducting in-depth analysis prior to committing resources, which ultimately helps to reduce the likelihood of incurring monetary loss. The use of scenario

analysis also enables organizations to project different return on investment (ROI) outcomes based on different conditions. This provides them with the ability to prepare for potential challenges and adjust their strategies accordingly during the process (Lee, Huang, Wu, Kuo, & Lai, 2017).

- *Strategic Planning*: Return on investment (ROI) metrics are used to inform long-term strategic planning and budgeting processes. Businesses are able to dedicate their attention to initiatives that contribute to the growth and sustainability of their finances when they align their projects with the goals of the organization. By ensuring that all investments are purposeful and contribute to the overarching mission and objectives of the company, this strategic alignment ensures consistency. Additionally, having a clear understanding of return on investment (ROI) enables organizations to establish performance targets and key performance indicators (KPIs) that are attainable and measurable. This helps to ensure that all members of the team are working toward the same collective goals (Banerjee et al., 2023).
- *Stakeholder Communication*: The return on investment (ROI) provides a method that is both clear and concise for communicating the value of investments to various stakeholders, such as investment board members, employees, and investors. Findings regarding return on investment (ROI) can be presented by organizations in order to improve transparency and accountability, thereby fostering trust among stakeholders. An organization's commitment to responsible resource management and financial discipline can be demonstrated through effective communication of return on investment (ROI) results. Demonstrating a positive return on investment (ROI) can signal to stakeholders that the organization is making sound financial decisions that are driving growth, which can attract additional investment and support from those stakeholders.

Figure 1. The key role of ROI in business strategies

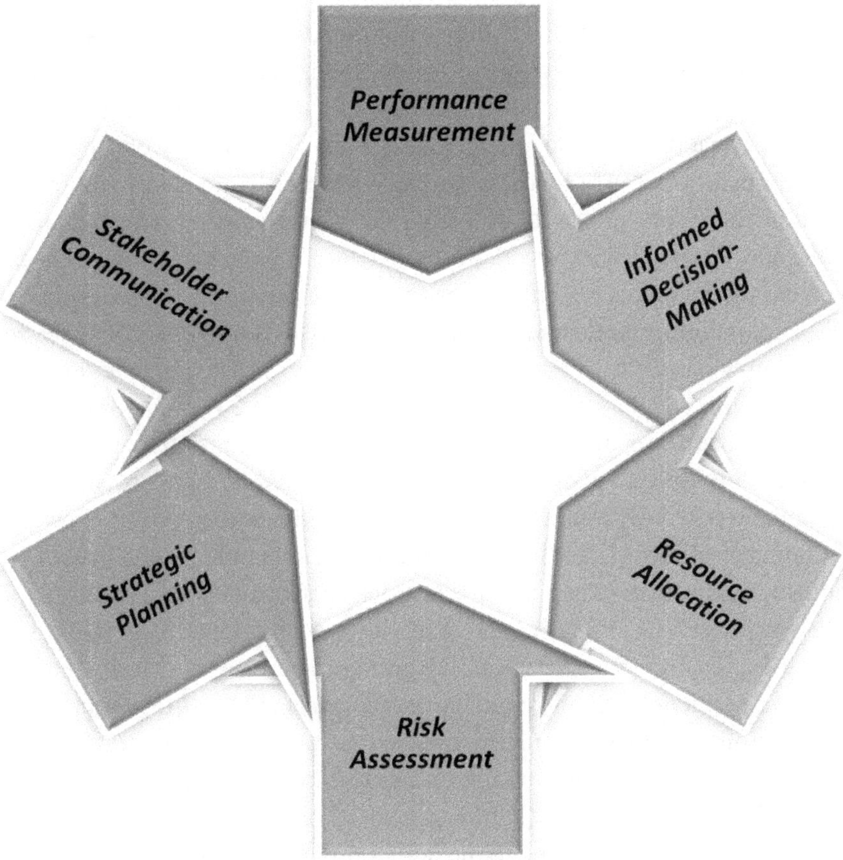

A proactive approach to cloud computing empowers businesses to fully leverage cloud technology and spur ongoing innovation in a rapidly evolving digital marketplace. Cloud computing has completely changed the business landscape by enabling organizations to harness powerful technologies for enhanced operational efficiency. An important aspect of this transformation is the emphasis on data integrity, which guarantees that information remains accurate and reliable across diverse multi-cloud environments. Organizations must prioritize security and compliance to mitigate risks associated with data breaches and regulatory violations (Basha, A. J. et al., 2024). A seamless transition to cloud-based systems requires the implementation of effective migration strategies which are shown in the figure1, and robust change management practices. Continuous training and the creation of innovation labs encourage employees to explore new solutions.

1.2 Transformation Potential of Cloud Solutions

The ability of cloud solutions to transform is changing how businesses function, innovate, and provide value to clients. Businesses are discovering a number of benefits from cloud computing adoption that radically alter their operational dynamics and strategic capacities (Pandey, D. et al., 2024f). The capacity of cloud solutions to improve operational efficiency is among their most important features. Cloud migration enables enterprises to simplify their IT infrastructure, cut maintenance expenses, and do away with the requirement for large hardware purchases. This change frees up resources for businesses to concentrate on their core competencies instead of maintaining and modernizing physical servers. As a consequence, the company is now more flexible and able to react fast to shifting consumer needs and market conditions. Scalability (Du John, H. V. et al., 2024) is facilitated by cloud solutions, which let companies instantly modify their resource allocation in response to changing workloads. This flexibility guarantees that businesses can effectively handle demand peaks without expending excessive resources during slower times. An e-commerce platform, for instance, can readily expand its infrastructure to accommodate peak holiday sales, guaranteeing peak performance and cutting expenses. Its ability to provide seamless experiences lowers operating costs while simultaneously raising customer satisfaction. By giving businesses access to cutting-edge products and services without requiring large upfront capital expenditures, cloud computing promotes innovation. Businesses can use cutting-edge tools to drive insights and improve decision-making thanks to cloud platforms that offer services like artificial intelligence (AI) (Kumarganesh, S. et al., 2024), machine learning (ML), and big data analytics. Due to the democratization of technology, the playing field is leveled across a range of industries, enabling small and medium-sized businesses to compete with larger corporations. Cloud solutions can also significantly transform the field of collaboration. Teams can work remotely and collaborate in real time (Maheshwari, R. Uma. et al., 2024) no matter where they are physically located thanks to cloud-based applications. In addition to increasing output, this flexibility draws talent from a wider geographic area, enhancing the organization's capabilities. Data security (Pandey, B. K., & Pandey, D., 2025) and compliance are improved by cloud solutions. Prominent cloud service providers offer features like encryption, frequent backups, and adherence to industry standards, along with significant investments in security measures. Organizations can lower the risks of data breaches and regulatory non-compliance by utilizing these integrated security measures (Joloudari et al., 2022).

1.3 Cloud Computing Models

The provision of computer services via the internet, or "cloud computing," allows consumers to access and store data (Lakshmi, K. V. N. et al., 2024) remotely as an alternative to depending on personal computers or local servers. Businesses can now manage their IT infrastructure more effectively thanks to this revolutionary approach, which offers flexibility, scalability, and on-demand resource access (Saravanakumar, R. et al., 2024). Platform as a Service (PaaS), Software as a Service (SaaS), and Infrastructure as a Service (IaaS) are the three main categories of cloud models. IaaS enables businesses to rent IT infrastructure on a pay-as-you-go basis by offering virtualized computing resources such as virtual machines, storage, and networks over the internet. Services such as Microsoft Azure Virtual Machines and Amazon Web Services (AWS) EC2 are examples of this model, which cuts capital expenditures significantly. Contrarily, PaaS provides a platform that lets programmers create, launch, and oversee applications without having to worry about the hassles of upkeep associated with the underlying infrastructure. Google App Engine and Heroku are two prominent examples of this model (KVM, S. et al., 2024), which speeds up the development and deployment of applications by combining database management and collaboration tools. Software as a Service (SaaS) let users access apps through web browsers without installing or updating them; it is delivered over the internet on a subscription basis (Hassan et al., 2024). Microsoft 365, Google Workspace, and Salesforce are a few well-known SaaS examples. New service models like Function as a Service (FaaS) and Container as a Service (CaaS) are becoming more popular in addition to these conventional models. Developers can run code in response to events using the FaaS serverless computing model, which promotes microservices architecture and improves scalability without requiring them to provision or manage servers. The solution is economical because users are only billed for the time it takes to execute. Leading instances of this model are AWS Lambda and Google Cloud Functions. Application deployment and management are made easier with the help of Container as a Service (CaaS). Better scalability and effective resource use are provided by this model, which is led by services like Amazon Elastic Kubernetes Service and Google Kubernetes Engine. Businesses find it difficult to ignore the distinct benefits of cloud solutions. Protecting sensitive data and guaranteeing regulatory compliance are two major advantages of using cloud providers strong security protocols, which include data encryption, multi-factor authentication, and frequent updates. Speed and performance are other benefits of cloud solutions, which let companies expand operations swiftly in response to market demands and deploy resources quickly. Low latency and high performance are usually guaranteed by cloud providers' sophisticated infrastructure (Elarmathi, S. et al., 2024). Cloud computing optimizes energy consumption, which lowers carbon footprints and encourages resource efficiency. Sustainability is a crucial factor to take into account. Cloud computing is more ecologically friendly than traditional data centers because it allows for resource sharing among multiple users, which reduces waste (Zizic, Mladineo, Gjeldum, & Celent, 2022).

2. EVALUATING ROI IN CLOUD COMPUTING

2.1 Assessing Cloud Investments

The evaluation of cloud investments is an essential step for businesses that want to make use of cloud computing to improve their operational efficiency and propel innovation. As a growing number of businesses move their operations to the cloud, it is becoming increasingly important to assess the financial implications, potential returns, and overall value of these investments. Calculating the Return on Investment (ROI) is one of the primary methods that can be utilized in order to evaluate investments in cloud computing. This involves contrasting the initial and ongoing costs associated with cloud services with the anticipated financial benefits that will result from the adoption of cloud computing, such as cost reductions and increased productivity. When evaluating cloud investments, businesses need to take into account Total Cost of Ownership (TCO) in addition to Return on Investment (ROI). Not only does total cost of ownership (TCO) include the direct costs of cloud services, but it also includes indirect costs like training, maintenance, and the possibility of downtime. Businesses are able to make educated decisions regarding which cloud solutions are most suitable for their budget and operational requirements if they have a comprehensive understanding of the financial picture. It is of the utmost importance to assess the strategic alignment of cloud investments with the objectives of the organization. For the purpose of this evaluation, considerations such as scalability, flexibility, and the capacity to adjust to shifting market conditions are taken into account. A cloud solution that is well aligned with the long-term strategy of a company can provide significant competitive advantages, allowing for a rapid response to the demands of customers and trends in the market. In the process of evaluating cloud investments, risk assessment is also an extremely important factor (Kennedy, G. W. et al., 2024). Concerns about data security, compliance issues, and the dependability of vendors are some of the potential risks that organizations need to identify before adopting cloud computing. Businesses have the ability to mitigate potential negative consequences and ensure a smoother transition to cloud environments if they take proactive measures to address these risks (Abro et al., 2022).

3. STRATEGIES FOR MAXIMIZING ROI

3.1 Vendor Evaluation Criteria (Reliability, Support)

In the context of cloud solutions and technology partnerships, a methodical approach to vendor evaluation is essential when evaluating possible suppliers. The main thing to think about is financial stability. Recognizing the financial stability of a vendor guarantees that they will be able to sustain your company over the long haul. Their viability as a long-term partner can be inferred by analyzing financial metrics like revenue trends, profitability, credit ratings, and past financial performance. A vendor with solid financial standing is more likely to stick to their agreements and offer continuous assistance. In the process of evaluating vendors, experience and reputation are also essential factors. One way to considerably lower the risks involved in new partnerships is to work with an established vendor that has a strong reputation in the industry (Rai, P. K. et al., 2024). A clear picture of their abilities and dependability can be obtained by evaluating their years of operation, industry experience, client testimonials, case studies, and any awards or recognitions they may have received. Building a successful partnership requires a vendor to be committed to quality and customer satisfaction, which is often reflected in their reputation. The caliber of the good or service is another important factor. Assessing the vendor's products and services for quality and dependability is essential to making sure your company can use them. This evaluation may involve looking over customer satisfaction scores, industry standards compliance, performance metrics (Shahul, A. et al., 2024), and product or service reviews. Better results and increased operational efficiency for your company can result from high-quality goods and services. Technical proficiency is also a crucial component of the assessment procedure. Evaluating a vendor's technological innovations and capabilities aids in determining whether or not their offerings meet the needs of your organization. Important indicators include the technology stack they use, how well it integrates with current systems (Pandey, B. K. et al., 2024c), how scalable it is for future expansion, and how well it supports continuous upgrades. Strong technical capabilities enable a vendor to better adjust to changing business requirements. The digital world of today has made security and compliance crucial. Protecting sensitive data and preserving customer trust require a vendor to make sure they follow applicable compliance laws and security standards (Aryal & Altmann, 2018). In this context, it is critical to assess security certifications, data encryption procedures, disaster recovery plans, and compliance with laws like GDPR and HIPAA. A vendor that has robust security measures in place lowers the possibility of data breaches and improves the overall security posture of your company. Last but not least, assessing service level agreements (SLAs) and customer support is essential to guaranteeing a successful collaboration. Evaluating the degree of customer support offered, response times, escalation protocols, and availability (24/7 or business hours) can provide information about how the vendor manages possible problems. Furthermore, it's helpful to check the SLAs terms which include coverage for service interruptions and uptime guarantees to make sure the vendor is dedicated to offering reliable support (Sharma, M. et al., 2024). Organizations can make informed decisions that promote successful and long-lasting partnerships by carefully weighing these vendor evaluation criteria: financial stability, reputation and experience, technical capabilities, security and compliance, and customer support (Ucar, Karakose, & Kirimca, 2024).

3.2 Optimized Migration Frameworks

The implementation of a migration framework that has been optimized is absolutely necessary in order to guarantee a seamless and fruitful transition to cloud computing. In order to maximize the benefits of cloud adoption while simultaneously minimizing risks and disruptions, this framework requires careful planning, execution, and ongoing management. Managing the impact of the migration on business operations and determining whether or not an organization is capable of migrating are two of the most important aspects of this framework. Both readiness assessment and change management are essential components of this framework. It is essential to conduct a readiness assessment as the initial step in any migration framework that is optimized. This evaluation will determine whether or not the organization is ready to adopt cloud computing by analysing (Pandey, B. K. et al., 2024d) its existing infrastructure, systems, and workforce. The technical, operational, and organizational readiness of an organization are all aspects that are investigated in a comprehensive readiness assessment. Technical readiness entails conducting an assessment of the existing information technology infrastructure to determine whether or not it is compatible with the cloud environment. In order to identify any potential compatibility issues, this includes conducting a review of the applications, databases, and networks (JayaLakshmi, G. et al., 2024). When conducting an operational readiness assessment, the organization evaluates its capacity to continue to manage and maintain cloud services after migration, with a particular emphasis on the skills, procedures, and tools of its staff. Last but not least, organizational readiness takes into account the degree to which the business strategies and culture of the company are compatible with cloud infrastructure. Businesses are able to identify gaps that need to be addressed prior to migration and develop a clear roadmap for a smooth transition if they do a thorough readiness assessment and then conduct the assessment. Change management is another essential component of an optimized migration framework, serving in conjunction with readiness assessment (Zhang, Wang, Li, & Zhang, 2022). An organization's workflows, roles, and responsibilities are frequently subject to significant shifts as a result of the migration to the cloud. Confusion, resistance, or disruptions in business operations are all potential outcomes of these changes if they are not managed properly. As part of an effective change management strategy, employees should be prepared for the new processes and systems that will be implemented as a result of cloud adoption. This includes communication (Pandey, B. K. et al., 2024e) in a clear and concise manner the reasons for the migration, the anticipated benefits, and the changes that will bring about in the daily workflows. Employees will be able to navigate the new cloud environment with confidence and efficiency (Pandey, B. K. et al., 2024g) if ample training and support are provided to them. Strategy for overcoming resistance and ensuring a smooth transition should also be included in a change management plan that is well-structured. Getting stakeholders involved early on in the process, addressing their concerns, and cultivating an environment that encourages openness are all activities that can help reduce resistance. In addition, monitoring the progress of the migration and providing feedback help to ensure that the organization stays on track and reinforces the advantages of adopting cloud computing. Businesses have the ability to ensure that both the technical and human aspects of the migration are successfully addressed by aligning change management with the readiness assessment (Robertson, Fossaceca, & Bennett, 2022).

3.3 Cultivating a Cloud-Centric Mindset

Developing a cloud-centric mindset is crucial for optimizing the advantages of cloud technology as businesses shift more and more of their operations to the cloud. The flexibility, scalability, and innovative potential that cloud solutions provide are welcomed by a cloud-centric way of thinking. Companies must invest in training programs and innovation labs that promote cloud fluency and a culture of experimentation and growth if they want this mindset to spread throughout their workforce. Training courses are essential for laying the groundwork for a cloud-centric way of thinking. Employees must acquire new skills and adjust to cloud-native methodologies as part of the process of moving to the cloud, which goes beyond simply acquiring new tools. Employees at all levels should have access to thorough training programs that equip them with the skills necessary to thrive in a cloud-driven workplace. This includes knowing how to use cloud platforms efficiently for non-technical staff as well as technical skills for IT personnel, such as cloud architecture, security, and automation. Furthermore, since cloud technology is always developing, continuing education is essential. In order for staff members to fully benefit from new cloud features and services, they need to be kept informed about the most recent advancements. Training programs should also highlight a shift in culture toward cloud computing. Workers ought to be aware of how cloud computing can foster operational efficiency, foster collaboration, and spur business innovation. Training can foster a shared vision in which all staff members understand the importance of cloud adoption and play a part in its success by coordinating cloud strategies with organizational goals. Innovation labs are another effective means of promoting a cloud-centric mentality. Innovation labs are special locations where groups can test out novel concepts, tools, and procedures without taking any chances. These labs offer opportunities for experiential learning and investigation. Teams can test cloud capabilities, investigate emerging trends, and prototype new solutions without interfering with ongoing business operations. Organizations promote a culture of creativity and continuous improvement by allowing employees to take risks. Cloud-native solutions are also developed in innovation labs, where teams can investigate the possibilities of cutting-edge cloud services like serverless computing, AI, and ML (Pandey, D. et al., 2024e). It is the goal of the work environment that employees have created to push the limits of what can be done with cloud technologies. This encourages an attitude that values experimentation and iteration, which can result in creative solutions that revolutionize corporate processes. Innovation labs also aid in bridging the theory-practice divide by enabling businesses to observe directly how cloud technologies can lead to observable business results. These labs' lessons can be applied to real-world situations, speeding up cloud adoption and guaranteeing a seamless and efficient transition (Kumar, M. S. et al., 2025). Organizations that adopt a cloud-centric mindset put themselves in a position to lead the way in utilizing cloud technology in addition to adopting it (Walia, Kumar, & Gill, 2024).

4. DATA INTEGRITY AND MULTI-CLOUD SECURITY

Cloud-moving companies must develop strong security and compliance strategies to maintain data integrity and regulatory compliance (Konapure, C. G. et al., 2025). Management of complex security environments and compliance with regional legal standards are new challenges of cloud computing. Strong security (Pandey, B. K. et al., 2024f) and compliance strategies can protect cloud environments while maintaining customer trust and regulatory compliance. Two important areas to consider are data integrity and multi-cloud implications. Cloud security starts with data integrity. Maintaining data reliability and confidentiality requires accurate, consistent, and unaltered storage, transmission (Raja, D. Siva Sundhara. et al., 2024), and processing. To safeguard data, organizations must use strong encryption. Encrypting data at rest and in transit prevents unauthorized access and makes it unreadable without the right keys. Using checksums and hashing algorithms can also keep data intact during transfer (Singh, S. et al., 2025). To ensure data accuracy, especially for sensitive or critical data, regular data audits and integrity checks are needed. Cloud security strategies must comply with industry standards and laws. Privacy laws like GDPR, HIPAA, and CCPA apply to healthcare, finance, and government. These regulations often dictate data handling, storage, and security. Noncompliance can result in large fines, legal penalties, and brand damage. To overcome these challenges, businesses should work with cloud service providers to ensure compliance and implement data monitoring (Kumar, B. et al., 2024), auditing, and reporting tools. In multi-cloud environments, security and compliance are more complicated. Multi-cloud setups offer flexibility and resilience, but data management and security across platforms are difficult. It's harder to maintain security when cloud providers have different security protocols (Pandey, D. et al., 2024c), data encryption methods, and compliance frameworks. Organizations must create a unified security framework for all cloud platforms to protect data uniformly. A centralized management tool that provides visibility into all cloud environments can help manage multi-cloud security. Companies can monitor security risks (Pandey, D. et al., 2024), compliance, and consistent policies across multiple clouds with these tools. Businesses should also encrypt and backup data across all cloud platforms to prevent breaches. To reduce security risks in a multi-cloud environment, use MFA, IAM, and security updates.

5. CONCLUSION

Cloud technology is essential for revolutionizing business operations and spurring innovation in today's quickly changing digital landscape. A number of important conclusions and suggestions surface as businesses move more and more to the cloud, helping to facilitate this shift efficiently. It is impossible to overstate the strategic importance of cloud computing. Businesses can respond swiftly to market demands and promote innovation by utilizing cloud solutions, which offer increased agility, scalability, and cost-effectiveness. Organizations can access cutting-edge technologies like artificial intelligence and machine learning, simplify operations, and save infrastructure costs by utilizing cloud services. Businesses are ultimately more competitive in their respective markets when they are able to optimize performance and concentrate on their core competencies through the ability to scale resources on-demand. Assessing their unique needs, comprehending the possible advantages of cloud adoption, and coordinating cloud initiatives with overarching business goals are all necessary for organizations. Conducting a comprehensive readiness assessment is imperative to appraise the current infrastructure, staff competencies, and organizational culture in order to guarantee a seamless transition. Businesses can create customized migration plans that optimize the advantages of cloud computing while lowering risks by identifying possible gaps and areas for improvement. Adopting a proactive strategy for cloud adoption is imperative for organizations.

This is encouraging a culture of innovation and ongoing learning among employees. To ensure that staff members are prepared to use new technologies efficiently, training programs should be put in place to improve their cloud-related skills and knowledge. By creating innovation labs, businesses can promote experimentation and exploration of cloud-native solutions, staying ahead of industry trends and improving their digital capabilities overall.

REFERENCES

Abdullahi, M., Ahmad, A., Pandey, B. K., & Pandey, D. (2024). Digital Currency Adoption: A Comparative Analysis of Global Trends and the Nigerian eNaira Digital Currency. *SN Computer Science*, *5*(5), 1–11.

Abro, J. H., Li, C., Shafiq, M., Vishnukumar, A., Mewada, S., Malpani, K., & Osei-Owusu, J. (2022). Artificial Intelligence Enabled Effective Fault Prediction Techniques in Cloud Computing Environment for Improving Resource Optimization. *Scientific Programming*, *2022*, 7432949.

Aldoseri, A., Al-Khalifa, K. N., & Hamouda, A. M. (2024). AI-Powered Innovation in Digital Transformation: Key Pillars and Industry Impact. *Sustainability*, *16*, 1790.

Aryal, R. G., & Altmann, J. Dynamic Application Deployment in Federations of Clouds and Edge Resources Using a Multiobjective Optimization AI Algorithm. In *Proceedings of the 2018 Third International Conference on Fog and Mobile Edge Computing (FMEC)*, Barcelona, Spain, 23–26 April 2018; pp. 147–154.

Banerjee, P., Roy, S., Modibbo, U. M., Pandey, S. K., Chaudhary, P., Sinha, A., & Singh, N. K. (2023). OptiDJS+: A Next-Generation Enhanced Dynamic Johnson Sequencing Algorithm for Efficient Resource Scheduling in Distributed Overloading within Cloud Computing Environment. *Electronics (Basel)*, *12*, 4123.

Basha, A. J., Maheshwari, R. U., Pandey, B. K., & Pandey, D. (2024). Ultra-Sensitive Photonic Crystal Fiber–Based SPR Sensor for Cancer Detection Utilizing Hybrid Nanocomposite Layers. *Plasmonics*, •••, 1–15.

Du John, H. V., Jose, T., Sagayam, K. M., Pandey, B. K., & Pandey, D. (2024). Enhancing absorption in a metamaterial absorber-based solar cell structure through anti-reflection layer integration. Silicon, 1-11.

Elarmathi, S., Rishabavarthani, P., Sindhuja, M., Elayaraja, P., & Malathi Murugesan, S. Kumarganesh, K. Martin Sagayam, Binay Kumar Pandey, and Digvijay Pandey. (2024). Novel manufacturing systems for cancer diagnosis using ultra-sensitive photonic crystal fiber biosensor with dual-functionalized aptamer-nanocavity. *Microsystem Technologies*, •••, 1–20.

Fedushko, S., Ustyianovych, T., & Gregus, M. (2020). Real-Time High-Load Infrastructure Transaction Status Output Prediction Using Operational Intelligence and Big Data Technologies. *Electronics (Basel)*, *9*, 668.

George, W. K., Silas, E. I., Pandey, D., & Pandey, B. K. (2024). Utilization of Industry 4.0 Technologies in Nigerian Technical and Vocational Education: A Conundrum for Educators. In *Examining the Rapid Advance of Digital Technology in Africa* (pp. 270–293). IGI Global.

Hassan, M. U., Al-Awady, A. A., Ali, A., Iqbal, M. M., Akram, M., & Jamil, H. (2024). Smart Resource Allocation in Mobile Cloud Next-Generation Network (NGN) Orchestration with Context-Aware Data and Machine Learning for the Cost Optimization of Microservice Applications. *Sensors (Basel)*, *24*, 865. PMID: 38339582

Huang, S.-Y., Chen, C.-Y., Chen, J.-Y., & Chao, H.-C. (2023). A Survey on Resource Management for Cloud Native Mobile Computing: Opportunities and Challenges. *Symmetry*, *15*, 538.

JayaLakshmi. G., Pandey, D., Pandey, B. K., Kaur, P., Mahajan, D. A., & Dari, S. S. (2024). Smart big data collection for intelligent supply chain improvement. In AI and Machine Learning Impacts in Intelligent Supply Chain (pp. 180-195). IGI Global.

Joloudari, J. H., Mojrian, S., Saadatfar, H., Nodehi, I., Fazl, F., Khanjani Shirkharkolaie, S., Alizadehsani, R., Kabir, H. M. D., Tan, R.-S., & Acharya, U. R. Resource Allocation Optimization Using Artificial Intelligence Methods in Various Computing Paradigms: A Review. *arXiv***2022**, arXiv:2203.12315.

Kennedy, G. W., Sunday, S. E., Pandey, D., Kabari, A. D., Pandey, B. K., George, A. S., & Dadheech, P. (2024). Building Information Modeling: Harnessing Innovations for Professional Proficiency. In Emerging Engineering Technologies and Industrial Applications (pp. 305-331). IGI Global.

Konapure, C. G., Pandey, D., Shete, H., Thakar, C. M., Pandey, B. K., & George, A. S. (2025). Artificial Intelligence in Automated Concrete Mix Design Using Computerized Grading Curves. Interdisciplinary Approaches to AI, Internet of Everything, and Machine Learning, 567-586.

Kumar, B., Pandey, D., Pandey, B. K., & George, A. S. (2024). Higher Education in the Last Four Decades: A Review of Paradigm Shifts in Policy Frameworks. Design and Implementation of Higher Education Learners' Learning Outcomes (HELLO), 333-348.

Kumar, M. S., Prasanna, P. L., Lalitha, M., Joy, M., Jha, S. S., & Pandey, B. K. (2025). Utilizing the Internet of Everything and Artificial Intelligence for Real-Time Workforce Management. In Role of Internet of Everything (IOE), VLSI Architecture, and AI in Real-Time Systems (pp. 153-168). IGI Global Scientific Publishing.

Kumarganesh, S., Murugesan, M., Ganesh, C., Santhiyakumari, N., Thangavel, M., Jayaram, K., & Pandey, D. (2024). Hybrid Plasmonic Biosensors with Deep Learning for Colorectal Cancer Detection. *Plasmonics*, •••, 1–15.

Kunduru, A. R. (2023). Artificial Intelligence Usage in Cloud Application Performance Improvement. *Cent. Asian J. Math. Theory Comput. Sci.*, *4*, 42–47.

KVM, S., Pandey, B. K., & Pandey, D. (2024). Design of Surface Plasmon Resonance (SPR) Sensors for Highly Sensitive Biomolecular Detection in Cancer Diagnostics. *Plasmonics*, •••, 1–13.

Lakshmi, K. V. N., Rajan, R., Pandey, D., & Pandey, B. K. (2024). Circular Economy: A Catalyst for Economic Growth-An Empirical Study. *Circular Economy and Sustainability*, •••, 1–22.

Lee, Y.-H., Huang, K.-C., Wu, C.-H., Kuo, Y.-H., & Lai, K.-C. (2017). A Framework for Proactive Resource Provisioning in IaaS Clouds. *Applied Sciences (Basel, Switzerland)*, *7*, 777.

Maheshwari, R. Uma, S. Kumarganesh, Shree KVM, A. Gopalakrishnan, K. Selvi, B. Paulchamy, P. Rishabavarthani, K. Martin Sagayam, Binay Kumar Pandey, and Digvijay Pandey. (2024). Advanced plasmonic resonance-enhanced biosensor for comprehensive real-time detection and analysis of deepfake content. *Plasmonics*, •••, 1–18.

Maheshwari, R. U., Paulchamy, B., Pandey, B. K., & Pandey, D. (2024). Enhancing sensing and imaging capabilities through surface plasmon resonance for deepfake image detection. *Plasmonics*, •••, 1–20.

Muralidhar, L. B., Lakshmi, K. V. N., Swapna, H. R., Rupani, J., Nethravathi, K., Pandey, B. K., & Pandey, D. (2024). Impact of Organizational Culture on The Level of Corporate Social Responsibility Investments: An Exploratory Study. *Circular Economy and Sustainability*, •••, 1–19.

Pandey, B. K., Kanike, U. K., George, A. S., & Pandey, D. (Eds.). (2024d). *AI and machine learning impacts in intelligent supply chain*. IGI Global.

Pandey, B. K., Mukundan, A. P., Nassa, V. K., Pandey, D., George, A. S., Hameed, A. S., & Dadheech, P. (2024f). Deployment of Load Balancing in Cloud Computing: Industrial Application and Benefits. In Emerging Engineering Technologies and Industrial Applications (pp. 342-354). IGI Global.

Pandey, B. K., Nassa, V. K., Mukundan, A. P., Mahajan, D. A., Pandey, D., George, A. S., & Dadheech, P. (2024c). An Industry-Focused Traffic System Utilising Internet of Things. In *Emerging Engineering Technologies and Industrial Applications* (pp. 200–213). IGI Global.

Pandey, B. K., & Pandey, D. (2025). Securing healthcare medical image information using advance morphological component analysis, information hiding systems, and hybrid convolutional neural networks on IoMT. *Computers in Biology and Medicine*, *185*, 109499. PMID: 39642698

Pandey, B. K., Pandey, D., Agarwal, A., Mahajan, D. A., Dadheech, P. D., George, A. S., & Rai, P. K. (2024e). Beyond Data Breaches: Enhancing Security in 6G Communications. In Security Issues and Solutions in 6G Communications and Beyond (pp. 212-229). IGI Global.

Pandey, B. K., Pandey, D., & Lelisho, M. E. (2024a). Face mask identification with enhanced cuckoo optimization and deep learning-based faster regional neural network. *Scientific Reports*, *14*(1), 29719. PMID: 39613761

Pandey, B. K., Pandey, D., & Sahani, S. K. (2024b). Autopilot control unmanned aerial vehicle system for sewage defect detection using deep learning. *Engineering Reports*, •••, 12852.

Pandey, B. K., Paramashivan, M. A., Nassa, V. K., Mahajan, D. A., Dadheech, P., George, A. H., & George, A. S. (2024g). Blockchain's Potential Effect on the Healthcare Industry. In Emerging Engineering Technologies and Industrial Applications (pp. 214-232). IGI Global.

Pandey, D., Nassa, V. K., Pandey, B. K., Mahajan, D. A., Patidar, P. K., Dadheech, P., & George, A. S. (2024d). An Analysis of Internet-of-Things-Based Fire Detection and Alert Systems. In *Emerging Engineering Technologies and Industrial Applications* (pp. 295–304). IGI Global.

Pandey, D., Nassa, V. K., Pandey, B. K., Thankachan, B., Dadheech, P., Mahajan, D. A., & George, A. S. (2024c). Artificial Intelligence and Machine Learning and Its Application in the Field of Computational Visual Analysis. In Emerging Engineering Technologies and Industrial Applications (pp. 36-57). IGI Global.

Pandey, D., Pandey, B. K., Nassa, V. K., Mahajan, D. A., George, A. S., & Dadheech, P. (2024f). Optimized Throughput-Based Broadcasting for Next Generation Wireless Networks. In Emerging Engineering Technologies

Pandey, D., Pandey, B. K., Paramashivan, M. A., Mahajan, D. A., Dadheech, P. D., George, A. S., & Hameed, A. S. (2024e). Advanced Digital Data Processing Using Cloud Cryptography: Industrial Applications. In Emerging Engineering Technologies and Industrial Applications (pp. 255-268). IGI Global.

Rai, P. K., Pandey, D., & Pandey, B. K. (2024). The future of enterprise and innovation is compute as a commodity, or CaaC. *Partners Universal International Research Journal, 3*(2), 89–94.

Raja, D. Siva Sundhara, D. Rajesh Kumar, N. Santhiyakumari, S. Kumarganesh, K. Martin Sagayam, B. Thiyaneswaran, Binay Kumar Pandey, and Digvijay Pandey. (2024). A compact dual-feed wide-band slotted antenna for future wireless applications. *Analog Integrated Circuits and Signal Processing, 118*(2), 291–305.

Robertson, J., Fossaceca, J. M., & Bennett, K. W. (2022). A Cloud-Based Computing Framework for Artificial Intelligence Innovation in Support of Multidomain Operations. *IEEE Transactions on Engineering Management, 69*, 3913–3922.

Saravanakumar, R., TamilSelvi, T., Pandey, D., Pandey, B. K., Mahajan, D. A., & Lelisho, M. E. (2024). Big data processing using hybrid Gaussian mixture model with salp swarm algorithm. *Journal of Big Data, 11*(1), 167.

Shahul, A., Muniandi, B., Paramashivan, M. A., Pandey, D., Pandey, B. K., Dadheech, P., & George, H. (2024). An Analysis of Algorithms and Methods Based on Image Processing for Medical Applications. In *Emerging Engineering Technologies and Industrial Applications* (pp. 173–186). IGI Global.

Sharma, M., Talwar, R., Pandey, D., Nassa, V. K., Pandey, B. K., & Dadheech, P. (2024). A review of dielectric resonator antennas (DRA)-based RFID technology for Industry 4.0. *Robotics and Automation in Industry, 4*(0), 303–324.

Singh, S., Madaan, G., Swapna, H. R., Singh, A., Pandey, B. K., George, A. S., & Pandey, D. (2025). Unleashing the Power of AI and Data Analysis: Transforming Insights into Action. In Interdisciplinary Approaches to AI, Internet of Everything, and Machine Learning (pp. 1-24). IGI Global Scientific Publishing.

Ucar, A., Karakose, M., & Kirimca, N. (2024). Artificial Intelligence for Predictive Maintenance Applications: Key Components, Trustworthiness, and Future Trends. *Applied Sciences (Basel, Switzerland), 14*, 898.

Walia, G. K., Kumar, M., & Gill, S. S. (2024). AI-Empowered Fog/Edge Resource Management for IoT Applications: A Comprehensive Review, Research Challenges, and Future Perspectives. *IEEE Communications Surveys and Tutorials, 26*, 619–669.

Zhang, Z., Wang, T., Li, A., & Zhang, W. Adaptive Auto-Scaling of Delay-Sensitive Serverless Services with Reinforcement Learning. In Proceedings of the 2022 IEEE 46th Annual Computers, Software, and Applications Conference (COMPSAC), Los Alamitos, CA, USA, 27 June–1 July 2022; pp. 866–871.

Zizic, M. C., Mladineo, M., Gjeldum, N., & Celent, L. (2022). From Industry 4. 0 towards Industry 5. 0: A Review and Analysis of Paradigm Shift for the People, Organization and Technology. *Energies*, *15*, 5221.

Chapter 17
Privacy Concerns in Cloud-Based Legal Technologies Navigating the Legal Landscape

Ashu Maharshi
https://orcid.org/0000-0002-9500-1174
Faculty of Law, Manipal University Jaipur, India

Vijay Laxmi Sharma
Faculty of Law, Manipal University Jaipur, India

ABSTRACT

The integration of cloud technologies into legal practice has revolutionized data management for law firms, offering increased accessibility and efficiency. But this change raises important privacy issues that need to be carefully considered. The potential consequences of cloud adoption in the legal industry, with a particular focus on safeguarding confidential data, including case files, internal documents, and communications between clients and attorneys. It identifies the main privacy risks connected to cloud storage, such as data encryption flaws, difficulties complying with legal requirements, and concerns about the safety of third-party vendors. The General Data Protection Regulation (GDPR), California Consumer Privacy Act (CCPA), Health Insurance Portability and Accountability Act (HIPAA).

DOI: 10.4018/979-8-3693-9581-3.ch017

1. INTRODUCTION

The legal sector now relies heavily on cloud-based technologies due to their increased cost-effectiveness, efficiency, and flexibility (Pandey, B. K., & Pandey, D., 2025). These platforms are now used by law firms and legal departments for case file storage, client communications management, and strategy collaboration. These advantages do, however, raise serious privacy issues. Since legal data is extremely sensitive, maintaining trust and avoiding possible legal ramifications require ensuring data protection and regulatory compliance. Legal practitioners handle a lot of private data, such as privileged documents, case evidence, internal plans, and correspondence with clients. This information is extremely private and frequently subject to stringent legal and ethical requirements, such as attorney-client privilege. Information that is kept on the cloud is susceptible to threats like data breaches, illegal access, and improper handling (Satheesh, N. et al., 2025). When cloud storage providers operate remotely, frequently across multiple jurisdictions, these risks are increased and can give rise to concerns regarding data sovereignty. Maintaining the ethical standards of legal practice and safeguarding client information depend on the security and confidentiality of this data (Kumar, M. S. et al., 2025). The possibility of data breaches is one of the biggest privacy concerns connected to cloud-based legal technologies. Cyberattacks, system flaws, or human mistake can reveal private client data, exposing businesses to risks and financial losses as well as legal ramifications and reputational harm. An additional degree of risk is introduced by unauthorized access by third parties, which includes the cloud service providers themselves.

Although a lot of providers have robust security measures in place, the law firm is ultimately in charge of protecting client data. One of the most important defenses against breach risks is data encryption, both during transmission and storage. When using cloud technologies, legal professionals need to adhere to a complex range of privacy regulations in addition to security concerns. Two important laws that specify how data should be processed, stored, and accessed are the California Consumer Privacy Act (CCPA) in the US and the General Data Protection Regulation (GDPR) in Europe. There may be severe fines and legal repercussions for breaking these rules. HIPAA rules also apply to law firms handling cases involving healthcare, which adds another level of compliance requirements. Law firms using cloud-based technologies need to be cautious about third-party vendors' security policies. Different cloud service providers follow different security requirements. It is imperative to conduct routine audits and compliance checks to guarantee that these vendors adhere to the strict data protection regulations set forth by the legal sector.

1.1 Cloud Adoption in the Legal Sector

The need for efficiency, flexibility, and cost-effectiveness (Sheela, M. S. et al., 2025) has driven legal sector cloud adoption in recent years. Traditional legal practices, characterized by extensive paperwork and manual processes, are being transformed as firms realize the benefits of cloud technologies. This change is improving client service and operational workflows. Operating efficiency is a major reason for adopting cloud technology. Document management, case management, and communication tools in the cloud can save law firms time and money on administrative tasks. Cloud solutions allow attorneys to work on cases simultaneously from different locations. As remote work becomes more common in a globalized legal landscape, this flexibility is crucial. Another reason to adopt the cloud is cost savings. Cloud computing reduces the need for expensive on-premises infrastructure and maintenance for law firms. Subscription-based cloud services allow firms to scale their usage and only pay for what they use. This model benefits small and mid-sized firms that lack the funds for IT infrastructure. Cloud adoption is also linked to data security and compliance demands. Security audits, encryption, and access controls are heavily invested in by cloud providers.

This allows law firms to use cutting-edge security solutions that would be too expensive to develop in-house. Cloud providers also help firms comply with data protection laws like GDPR and HIPAA. Migration to cloud solutions is difficult. Given the sensitivity of legal data, data privacy and security remain paramount. Law firms must ensure their cloud providers follow strict security standards and protect client data. Company staff must also be trained to use new technologies and adapt to workflow changes. Legal adoption of the cloud is expected to grow. Artificial neural network (Pandey, B. K., & Pandey, D., 2023) and machine learning in cloud solutions will boost legal practise efficiency and capability (Konapure, C. G. et al., 2025). Cloud technology will shape the legal industry as firms embrace digital transformation and better serve clients in a changing landscape (Ramachandra, G. et al., 2017).

1.2 Privacy and Data Security

Maintaining the integrity of attorney-client relationships and ensuring compliance with ethical standards are both dependent on the protection of one's privacy, which is a fundamental component of the legal profession. The protection (Pandey, D. et al., 2024a) of one's privacy is a fundamental concern in the field of legal practice because law firms and their clients have significant stakes in the law. Protecting the confidentiality of client information (Singh, S. et al., 2025a) is not only a recommended practice for law firms; it is also an ethical obligation within the profession.

All client information must be kept confidential, as attorneys are required to do by rules of professional conduct. There are severe consequences that can result from breaches of confidentiality, such as disciplinary action, the loss of licensure, and claims of malpractice (Singh, S. et al., 2025b). One of the most important factors that determines a company's reputation is how well it can protect the confidentiality of its customers. The loss of business and the damage to the trust of customers can be caused by a single instance of data exposure. Because they entrust law firms with sensitive information, which may include personal details, financial data (Pandey, D. et al., 2024b), and confidential business strategies, clients also have a vested interest in maintaining their privacy (Pandey, B. K. et al., 2024a). The client is encouraged to communicate openly with their attorneys, which is essential for effective legal representation, when they are given the assurance that their information will be handled securely. Customers are more likely to participate fully in the legal process when they have the assurance that their information will be protected, which ultimately results in better outcomes. The framework of the law is increasingly being governed by stringent regulations regarding privacy (Pandey, B. K. et al., 2024b). The management of personal data is subject to stringent requirements that are imposed by laws such as the General Data Protection Regulation (GDPR) and the California Consumer Privacy Act (CCPA).

The ability to navigate these regulations is necessary for law firms in order to avoid penalties and to protect the rights of their clients. The firms credibility in the market is improved as a result of compliance with such laws, which not only protects the data of the customers. Because of the increasing danger posed by cyberattacks, the importance of protecting one's privacy in the legal industry is further highlighted. Due to the increasing adoption of digital tools (Pandey, B. K. et al., 2024e) and cloud-based solutions by law firms, these organizations are becoming potential targets for hackers who are looking for sensitive data (Maheshwari, R. U. et al., 2024). When it comes to preserving the trust of customers and protecting the reputation of the company, it is absolutely necessary to take precautions against these dangers. Encryption, access controls, and regular audits are some of the robust cybersecurity measures that must be implemented in order to effectively mitigate these risks (Mozumder, D. P. et al., 2017).

2. LEGAL DATA AT RISK

2.1 Privileged Client Communications

Effective representation is based on client-attorney communications, which are fundamental to the legal profession. Sensitive information, such as personal information, financial information, legal tactics, and case specifics, is frequently included in these correspondences. Maintaining client trust and successful legal outcomes are just as important as upholding ethical standards when it comes to the confidentiality of these interactions (Maheshwari, R. Uma. et al., 2024). Communications between a client and an attorney can occur via email, phone calls, in-person meetings, and written documents, among other channels. Talks about case tactics, possible legal repercussions, and private matters (Saxena, A. et al., 2024) that clients might not want to discuss with others are frequently included. In order to safeguard clients from potential harm, both legal and personal, this level of intimacy in communication requires a high degree of privacy. A legal theory called attorney-client privilege is intended to safeguard the privacy of messages exchanged between clients and their lawyers. With the protection of this privilege, information discussed during the process of obtaining legal advice cannot be revealed without the client's permission. Attorneys who violate this privilege may face serious repercussions, such as disciplinary action and license suspension (Ahmed, M., & Litchfield, A. T., 2018). Lawyers must take reasonable precautions to safeguard confidential information from unauthorized access or disclosure in accordance with professional conduct rules. This involves putting security measures in place to guarantee that private information is kept private, such as encryption and secure communication channels. The security (Lakshmi, K. V. N. et al., 2024) of communications between clients and attorneys is becoming even more important as legal practices use digital tools (George, W. K. et al., 2024) and cloud-based platforms more and more. Technology can increase productivity and teamwork, but it also comes with new risks. Ensuring the privacy (Rai, P. K. et al., 2024) of confidential communications is severely hampered by cybersecurity risks like data breaches and hacking. To keep these communications safe from unwanted access, law firms need to make significant investments in strong security measures. It is the responsibility of attorneys to inform their clients about safe emailing and encrypted messaging apps. Attorneys can empower their clients to actively protect their sensitive information by educating them about privacy and security measures. The confidentiality of communications between an attorney and their client is ultimately essential to preserving that trust. Clients are more likely to be forthright and honest with their attorneys and receive better legal representation when they feel that their information is secure. It is essential to establish this trust because it promotes a cooperative relationship that has a big impact on case outcomes (Basu, S. et al., 2018).

2.2 Firm Records and Research

Internal documents and research data (JayaLakshmi, G. et al., 2024) are essential to a law firm's success. These sensitive materials include legal briefs, case notes, internal memos, research findings, and strategic plans. Maintaining operational integrity, compliance, and legal market competitiveness requires protecting this data. Internal documents handled by law firms include contracts, billing statements, case files, and policy manuals. Market research, competitive intelligence, legal precedents, and case law analyses are research data (Ahmed, M. et al., 2019). These resources help attorneys and support staff plan legal strategies, assess risks, and advise clients. These sensitive documents require strict access controls to prevent unauthorized access. Data breaches can expose client data, cost the firm money, and damage its reputation. Attorney-client privilege and strategic decisions depend on keeping these materials confidential (Abdullahi, M. et al., 2024). As law firms use digital document management and research solutions, data security becomes more important. Cyberattacks like ransomware and phishing threaten internal document confidentiality and integrity. Law firms must use encryption, secure access, and security audits to reduce these risks. Data handling (Saravanakumar, R. et al., 2024) and access policies must also be clear. Determine who can access what information and when. Establishing a data security (Kumar, B. et al., 2024) culture can reduce accidental disclosures and improve protection. Compliance is crucial for lawyers as data management regulations are complex. The GDPR and CCPA require strict handling of personally identifiable information in internal documents. Non-compliance can result in severe penalties and legal consequences, so staying informed about regulations is crucial. By analyzing case law, client behavior, and industry trends, law firms can adapt to changing client needs. This proactive approach strengthens client relationships and makes the firm a leader (Manral, B. et al., 2019).

3. PRIMARY PRIVACY CONCERNS WITH CLOUD STORAGE

There are many benefits to cloud storage, there are also serious privacy issues that legal firms need to consider which are as shown in the figure 1. Enterprises can create efficient plans to safeguard confidential data and uphold customer confidence by comprehending the dangers connected to data breaches, data sovereignty, third-party access, openness, human error, and legal compliance. It is crucial to give these issues top priority when making decisions about cloud storage in order to protect client information and maintain the integrity of legal practice.

1. *Risk of Data Breaches*: Cyberattacks are a major threat to cloud storage systems. Hackers frequently take advantage of weaknesses to obtain private information without authorization. Case files, personal information, and communications between attorneys and clients may all be compromised in a data breach. Serious legal consequences could result from this, such as lawsuits and fines from the government. End-to-end encryption, frequent security audits, and intrusion detection systems are just a few of the robust security measures that law firms need to make sure their cloud providers use. Updating software and protocols on a regular basis is also essential for safeguarding against new threats.
2. *Data Sovereignty Issues*: The legal structures that control how data is processed and stored across borders are referred to as data sovereignty (Kumarganesh, S. et al., 2024). Cloud storage can involve data (Shahul, A. et al, 2024) being housed on servers across multiple nations, each with its own privacy regulations. For international law firms, this can make compliance more difficult. Information kept in nations with weak privacy laws, for example, might not be as safe as information kept in places with tight laws, like the EU's GDPR. Legal firms ought to thoroughly examine the locations where their cloud providers host data and confirm that they are aware of the associated legal ramifications. It is imperative to establish agreements that adhere to international data transfer regulations.
3. *The third-party access*: Data stored on cloud service providers' platforms gives rise to concerns regarding unauthorized usage or exposure of data. It can be challenging for law firms to comprehend how their data is being managed because cloud providers' terms of service and data handling policies aren't always clear. Law firms should make sure that their contracts with cloud providers clearly define who owns the data, who can access it, and what happens in the event of a data breach. Maintaining compliance with these agreements can be aided by routine evaluations and audits of third-party vendors.
4. *Lack of Transparency*: A lot of cloud service providers don't completely reveal their data handling procedures, so legal firms don't know how their private data is protected and maintained. This lack of openness may cause people to become suspicious and unsure of how effective the security measures are. When choosing a cloud provider, law firms should do extensive due diligence. This entails looking over security certifications, performance history, and compliance records. Speaking openly and honestly with suppliers regarding their security procedures can also bring clarity (Chen, L. et al., 2019).

5. *User Error*: Cloud privacy issues are largely caused by human factors. Data exposure may result from careless disclosure of private information, incorrect security configurations, or ignored security procedures (Pandey, D. et al., 2024c). Educating employees about data security best practices is crucial. They must be made aware of the significance of using strong passwords, how to spot phishing attempts, and data handling procedures. Clear policies and procedures, along with frequent audits of user access and data management techniques, should be established by law firms for handling sensitive data in the cloud.
6. *Compliance with Regulations*: Legal firms need to handle a complicated network of privacy laws that control data handling, such as GDPR, CCPA, and HIPAA. Significant fines, harm to one's reputation, and a decline in client confidence may arise from breaking these rules. Firms should regularly review their data management procedures, stay up to date on pertinent laws and regulations, and collaborate closely with legal counsel to address compliance challenges in order to ensure compliance.

Figure 1. Privacy concerns in cloud storage

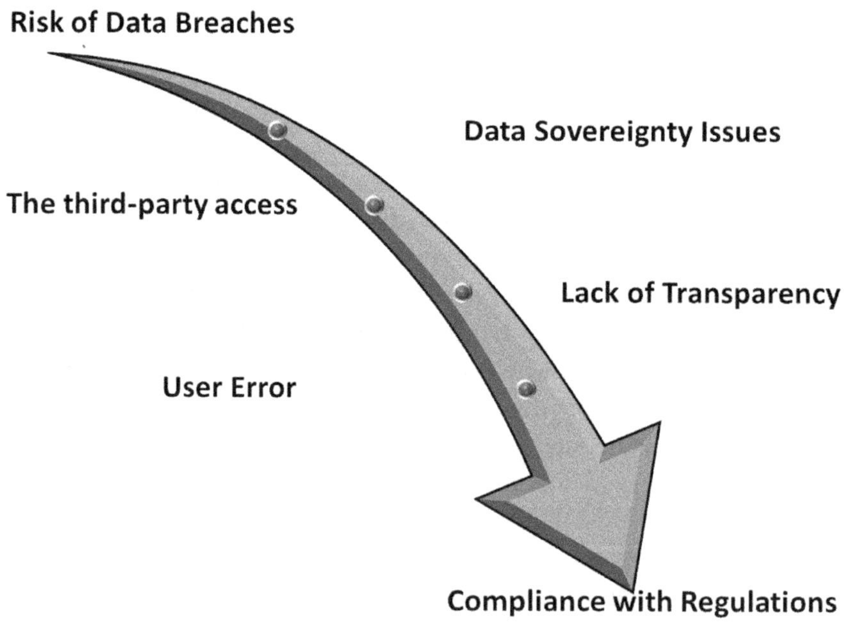

4. LEGAL AND REGULATORY FRAMEWORKS

4.1 GDPR/CCPA: Impact on Data Storage

The GDPR and CCPA are major data protection laws in Europe and the US, respectively. Understanding and following these regulations is crucial for law firms and businesses handling personal data to maintain legal compliance and client trust. GDPR applies to all EU and non-EU organizations (Muralidhar, L. B. et al., 2024) that process EU citizens' personal data. It stresses the importance of explicit consent before collecting data and requires data usage transparency. Organizations must also grant individuals the "right to be forgotten." to access, correct, and delete their personal data. GDPR violations can result in fines of 4% of global turnover or €20 million. CCPA privacy rights are intended to improve Californians' privacy. It gives consumers the right to know what personal data is being collected, why, and to opt out of data sales. Businesses must also protect personal data with reasonable security measures under the CCPA. Fines for noncompliance can reach $7,500 per violation. A comprehensive data governance strategy is needed for international organizations to navigate GDPR and CCPA. This includes data audits to determine what personal data is collected, used, and stored. Compliance requires strong privacy policies, data handling training, and clear consent mechanisms. Third-party vendor data processing agreements ensure compliance with regulations for all parties involved in data handling. As laws change, organizations must review and update data protection practices to stay compliant (Khan, Y., & Varma, S., 2020).

4.2 HIPAA: Healthcare Case Data

A number of stringent regulations concerning the privacy and security of protected health information (PHI) have been established by the Health Insurance Portability and Accountability Act (HIPAA). In order to ensure compliance with HIPAA and protect client confidentiality (Pandey, B. K. et al., 2024c), it is essential for legal professionals who are involved in cases related to healthcare to have a solid understanding of the rules. Under the HIPAA Privacy Rule, covered entities, which include healthcare providers, health plans, and healthcare clearinghouses, are required to disclose and use protected health information (PHI) in a certain manner. It is imperative that legal professionals are aware that protected health information (PHI) is defined as any health information that can be used to identify an individual. This includes medical records, treatment details, and payment information (Pandey, B. K. et al., 2024d). HIPAA protects this type of information. Significant penalties, such as fines and the possibility of criminal charges, may be imposed for those who violate these regulations. Attorneys are required to implement stringent safeguards to protect health information (PHI) when they are handling legal cases related to healthcare. As part of this, it is necessary to guarantee the safety of any and all communications that contain critical health information. Using password-protected documents, encrypted email, and secure file transfer protocols are all essential practices for protecting protected health information (PHI) from unauthorized access (Schlepphorst, S. et al., 2020). Before disclosing any protected health information (PHI) to third parties, attorneys are required to obtain consent from their clients.

The requirements of HIPAA must be met by this authorization, which must be specific, in order to guarantee that clients are fully informed about the ways in which their health information will be used and shared. When working with third-party vendors, such as medical experts or consultants, legal professionals need to exercise caution when working with them. To ensure that these vendors are in compliance with HIPAA regulations and to outline their responsibilities regarding the handling of protected health information (PHI), it is essential to establish business associate agreements (BAAs) with them. Those members of the legal staff who are involved in cases involving healthcare must receive training and education on HIPAA compliance. Regular training sessions can help employees understand the significance of protecting protected health information (PHI) and educate them on the most effective methods for ensuring data security.

4.3 Mitigation Strategies for Law Firms

- *Implement Robust Cybersecurity Measures*: Cybersecurity should be given top priority in law firms, and sensitive data should be protected with extensive safeguards. This includes encrypting data while it's in transit and at rest to make sure that, even if it gets intercepted, the data cannot be decrypted without the right keys. Another crucial security layer is multi-factor authentication (MFA), which requires users to enter two or more verification factors in order to access systems. Software and security protocols must be updated on a regular basis in order to fix known vulnerabilities and defend against new threats (Pandey, D., & Pandey, B. K., 2022). To make sure that their cybersecurity strategies continue to be effective, law firms need to take a proactive stance and review them often.
- *Conduct Regular Risk Assessments*: Conducting routine risk assessments is essential for detecting possible security flaws in a legal practice. In order to determine how effective current technology, procedures, and data management techniques are against emerging cyberthreats, these assessments entail thorough audits of those areas. Businesses can efficiently allocate resources and prioritize areas that require improvement by identifying vulnerabilities. By modifying security measures in response to assessment results

(Elarmathi, S. et al., 2024), a company can improve its overall security posture and minimize the risk of data breaches while also adhering to regulatory requirements.

- *Train Staff on Data Security Best Practices*: For all employees in a law firm, regular training on data security best practices is essential. Training ought to concentrate on identifying online dangers, like phishing attempts, and stressing the value of creating strong, one-of-a-kind passwords for various accounts. Employees should also receive training on safe communication practices and responsible handling of sensitive data. Establishing a culture that values data security and privacy encourages staff members to actively safeguard customer data, which lowers the possibility of human error that could result in data breaches.
- *Utilize Secure Communication Tools*: Secure communication solutions should be used by law firms to safeguard private conversations and data exchanges. This includes utilizing secure file-sharing platforms to guarantee the safe sharing of sensitive documents and encrypted email services to protect communications from interception. To further improve security, secure messaging apps should be promoted for internal communications. It is imperative to conduct routine reviews and updates of communication protocols in order to stay abreast of emerging threats, guarantee the security of all communication channels, and safeguard client confidentiality.
- *Develop an Incident Response Plan*: For data breaches and security incidents to be managed successfully, a thorough incident response plan must be created. The actions to be taken in the case of a security breach, such as how to contain the breach, evaluate its impact, and alert affected parties, should be outlined in this plan. A coordinated approach to crisis management is ensured by assigning incident management responsibilities to a response team. To ensure that law firms are able to react quickly and effectively to any security incidents that may arise, the incident response plan must be tested and updated on a regular basis.
- *Backup Data Regularly*: To protect against data loss as a result of cyberattacks or system failures, a regular data backup schedule must be put in place. To make sure the data is safe even in the case of illegal access, backups should be kept in a secure location and encrypted. Testing backup restoration procedures on a regular basis is crucial to verifying the dependability and integrity of the backups. In addition to safeguarding sensitive client data, having a strong backup plan enables law firms to bounce back fast from data loss disasters.
- *Stay Informed on Legal Technology Trends*: It's critical for law firms to stay up to date on cybersecurity best practices and legal technology advance-

ments. This entails staying abreast of industry advancements, going to conferences, and taking part in workshops to improve knowledge and abilities. Making connections with other legal professionals can give you important information about new risks and efficient ways to mitigate them. Law firms can enhance their client data protection and regulatory compliance by staying up to date on emerging technologies and continuing their education.

Law firms can effectively mitigate risks related to data security and ensure the protection of sensitive client information while adhering to relevant regulations by putting these detailed strategies into practice, which are shown in the figure 2.

Figure 2. Mitigation strategies for law firms

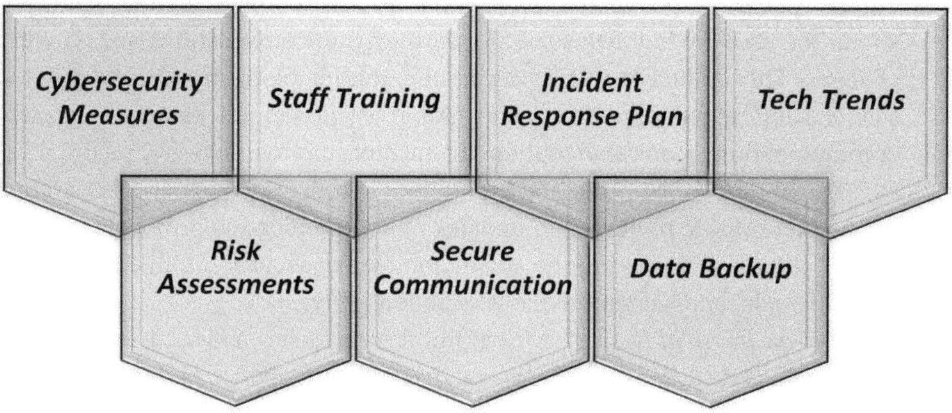

5. BLOCKCHAIN TECHNOLOGY FOR SECURE DATA STORAGE

Blockchain technology has become a game-changer for traceable and safe data storage, especially in industries where transparency and data integrity are critical. Blockchain functions on a decentralized network of nodes that together maintain a safe and unchangeable ledger of transactions, in contrast to traditional databases, which are centralized and vulnerable to single points of failure. The high degree of security that blockchain technology offers is one of its main advantages. Cryptographic hashes connect each block in the blockchain to the one before it, forming an impenetrable chain of data. It is practically hard for bad actors to manipulate data once it is recorded on the blockchain because it cannot be changed without the network's consent. This built-in security is especially helpful for fields like law, medicine, and finance that deal with sensitive data. The traceability of blockchain is yet another important benefit. Complete transparency regarding the data's history is made possible by the inclusion of a timestamp and a distinct cryptographic signature in every transaction that is registered on the blockchain. For applications like supply chain management, where stakeholders must trace the origin of goods and confirm the legitimacy of products, this feature is essential. Blockchain technology can be used to safely store contracts in the legal sector, guaranteeing that all parties have access to the same copy and the ability to track any changes or transactions. Blockchain technology improves interoperability and accessibility of data. Authorized users can access the data from multiple locations without depending on a central authority because it is stored across multiple nodes. Decentralized access has the potential to optimize processes (Khadka, M. et al., 2025) and promote cooperation between various stakeholders, including lawyers, clients, and outside parties. Another cutting-edge feature of blockchain that has the potential to completely transform data management and storage is the use of smart contracts. Self-executing contracts, or smart contracts, have the terms of the contract directly encoded into the code. When predetermined criteria are satisfied, they take automatic action, eliminating the need for middlemen and lowering the possibility of disagreements. Smart contracts, for example, can automate the transfer of property titles in real estate transactions after payment is verified, guaranteeing a safe and effective transaction. The adoption of blockchain technology is not without difficulties, despite its many benefits. To enable widespread implementation, concerns like energy consumption, regulatory uncertainty, and scalability must be addressed. Organizations also need to spend money on resources and training in order to successfully incorporate blockchain solutions into their current systems.

CONCLUSION

The legal industry is adopting cloud technologies at an increasing rate, so data privacy is crucial. Using cloud solutions has many advantages, such as increased accessibility and efficiency. But it also brings with it serious privacy risks that legal firms have to tread carefully. Firms must prioritize data security because sensitive client-attorney communications, case files, and internal documents are especially susceptible to unauthorized access and breaches. It is crucial for legal practitioners to comprehend the main privacy issues related to cloud storage. To effectively protect client information, issues like data encryption risks, jurisdictional compliance, and third-party vendor security present challenges that need to be addressed. Law firms also need to be aware of the latest developments in legal and regulatory frameworks, such as the CCPA, GDPR, and HIPAA, which establish guidelines for professional responsibility and data protection. Law firms should implement practical measures to reduce these risks, such as robust encryption, frequent audits of cloud service providers, and open client communication guidelines. Businesses can improve client trust and strengthen their data security posture by putting these measures into practice. New developments in the field of legal data privacy, like blockchain technology and AI-driven solutions, offer fresh chances to enhance traceability and data protection. These technologies provide creative solutions for handling and storing sensitive data in addition to enhancing security. While there are obstacles to overcome in the integration of cloud technologies into legal practice, there are also opportunities for increased productivity and teamwork. Law firms can protect sensitive information and fulfill their ethical obligations in an increasingly digital world by putting privacy first, following regulations, and utilizing cutting-edge technologies.

REFERENCES

Abdullahi, M., Ahmad, A., Pandey, B. K., & Pandey, D. (2024). Digital Currency Adoption: A Comparative Analysis of Global Trends and the Nigerian eNaira Digital Currency. *SN Computer Science*, *5*(5), 1–11.

Ahmed, M., Kambam, H. R., Liu, Y., & Uddin, M. N. (2020). Impact of human factors in cloud data breach. In Advances in Intelligent Systems and Interactive Applications: Proceedings of the 4th International Conference on Intelligent, Interactive Systems and Applications (IISA2019) 4 (pp. 568-577). Springer International Publishing.

Ahmed, M., & Litchfield, A. T. (2018). Taxonomy for identification of security issues in cloud computing environments. *Journal of Computer Information Systems*, *58*(1), 79–88.

Basu, S., Bardhan, A., Gupta, K., Saha, P., Pal, M., Bose, M., . . . Sarkar, P. (2018, January). Cloud computing security challenges & solutions-A survey. In 2018 IEEE 8th Annual Computing and Communication Workshop and Conference (CCWC) (pp. 347-356). IEEE.

Chen, L., Le-Khac, N. A., Schlepphorst, S., & Xu, L. (2019). Cloud forensics: model, challenges, and approaches. Security, Privacy, and Digital Forensics in the Cloud, 201-216.

Elarmathi, S., Rishabavarthani, P., Sindhuja, M., Elayaraja, P., & Malathi Murugesan, S. Kumarganesh, K. Martin Sagayam, Binay Kumar Pandey, and Digvijay Pandey. (2024). Novel manufacturing systems for cancer diagnosis using ultra-sensitive photonic crystal fiber biosensor with dual-functionalized aptamer-nanocavity. *Microsystem Technologies*, •••, 1–20.

George, W. K., Silas, E. I., Pandey, D., & Pandey, B. K. (2024). Utilization of Industry 4.0 Technologies in Nigerian Technical and Vocational Education: A Conundrum for Educators. In *Examining the Rapid Advance of Digital Technology in Africa* (pp. 270–293). IGI Global.

JayaLakshmi. G., Pandey, D., Pandey, B. K., Kaur, P., Mahajan, D. A., & Dari, S. S. (2024). Smart big data collection for intelligent supply chain improvement. In AI and Machine Learning Impacts in Intelligent Supply Chain (pp. 180-195). IGI Global.

Kennedy, G. W., Sunday, S. E., Pandey, D., Kabari, A. D., Pandey, B. K., George, A. S., & Dadheech, P. (2024). Building Information Modeling: Harnessing Innovations for Professional Proficiency. In Emerging Engineering Technologies and Industrial Applications (pp. 305-331). IGI Global.

Khadka, M., Sah, M., Chaudhary, R., Sahani, S. K., Sahani, K., Pandey, B. K., & Pandey, D. (2025). Spectroscopic, quantum chemical, and topological calculations of the phenylephrine molecule using density functional theory. *Scientific Reports*, *15*(1), 208. PMID: 39747169

Khan, Y., & Varma, S. (2020). Development and design strategies of evidence collection framework in cloud environment. In Social Networking and Computational Intelligence: Proceedings of SCI-2018 (pp. 27-37). Springer Singapore.

Konapure, C. G., Pandey, D., Shete, H., Thakar, C. M., Pandey, B. K., & George, A. S. (2025). Artificial Intelligence in Automated Concrete Mix Design Using Computerized Grading Curves. Interdisciplinary Approaches to AI, Internet of Everything, and Machine Learning, 567-586.

Kumar, B., Pandey, D., Pandey, B. K., & George, A. S. (2024). Higher Education in the Last Four Decades: A Review of Paradigm Shifts in Policy Frameworks. Design and Implementation of Higher Education Learners' Learning Outcomes (HELLO), 333-348.

Kumar, M. S., Prasanna, P. L., Lalitha, M., Joy, M., Jha, S. S., & Pandey, B. K. (2025). Utilizing the Internet of Everything and Artificial Intelligence for Real-Time Workforce Management. In Role of Internet of Everything (IOE), VLSI Architecture, and AI in Real-Time Systems (pp. 153-168). IGI Global Scientific Publishing.

Kumarganesh, S., & Malathi Murugesan, C. Ganesh, N. Santhiyakumari, M. Thangavel, K. Jayaram, K. Martin Sagayam, Binay Kumar Pandey, and Digvijay Pandey. (2024). Hybrid plasmonic biosensors with deep learning for colorectal cancer detection. *Plasmonics*, •••, 1–15.

Lakshmi, K. V. N., Rajan, R., Pandey, D., & Pandey, B. K. (2024). Circular economy: A catalyst for economic growth-an empirical study. *Circular Economy and Sustainability*, •••, 1–22.

Maheshwari, R. Uma, S. Kumarganesh, Shree KVM, A. Gopalakrishnan, K. Selvi, B. Paulchamy, P. Rishabavarthani, K. Martin Sagayam, Binay Kumar Pandey, and Digvijay Pandey. (2024). Advanced plasmonic resonance-enhanced biosensor for comprehensive real-time detection and analysis of deepfake content. *Plasmonics*, •••, 1–18.

Maheshwari, R. U., Paulchamy, B., Pandey, B. K., & Pandey, D. (2024). Enhancing sensing and imaging capabilities through surface plasmon resonance for deepfake image detection. *Plasmonics*, •••, 1–20.

Manral, B., Somani, G., Choo, K. K. R., Conti, M., & Gaur, M. S. (2019). A systematic survey on cloud forensics challenges, solutions, and future directions. *ACM Computing Surveys*, *52*(6), 1–38.

Mozumder, D. P., Mahi, J. N., Whaiduzzaman, M., & Mahi, M. J. N. (2017). Cloud computing security breaches and threats analysis. *International Journal of Scientific and Engineering Research*, *8*(1), 1287–1297.

Muralidhar, L. B., Lakshmi, K. V. N., Swapna, H. R., Rupani, J., Nethravathi, K., Pandey, B. K., & Pandey, D. (2024). Impact of Organizational Culture on The Level of Corporate Social Responsibility Investments: An Exploratory Study. *Circular Economy and Sustainability*, •••, 1–19.

Pandey, B. K., Kanike, U. K., George, A. S., & Pandey, D. (Eds.). (2024d). *AI and machine learning impacts in intelligent supply chain*. IGI Global.

Pandey, B. K., Nassa, V. K., Mukundan, A. P., Mahajan, D. A., Pandey, D., George, A. S., & Dadheech, P. (2024c). An Industry-Focused Traffic System Utilising Internet of Things. In *Emerging Engineering Technologies and Industrial Applications* (pp. 200–213). IGI Global.

Pandey, B. K., & Pandey, D. (2023). Parametric optimization and prediction of enhanced thermoelectric performance in co-doped CaMnO3 using response surface methodology and neural network. *Journal of Materials Science Materials in Electronics*, *34*(21), 1589.

Pandey, B. K., & Pandey, D. (2025). Securing healthcare medical image information using advance morphological component analysis, information hiding systems, and hybrid convolutional neural networks on IoMT. *Computers in Biology and Medicine*, *185*, 109499. PMID: 39642698

Pandey, B. K., Pandey, D., & Lelisho, M. E. (2024a). Face mask identification with enhanced cuckoo optimization and deep learning-based faster regional neural network. *Scientific Reports*, *14*(1), 29719. PMID: 39613761

Pandey, B. K., Pandey, D., & Sahani, S. K. (2024b). Autopilot control unmanned aerial vehicle system for sewage defect detection using deep learning. *Engineering Reports*, •••, 12852.

Pandey, B. K., Paramashivan, M. A., Pandey, D., George, A. S., Agarwal, A., Mahajan, D. A., . . . Pramanik, S. (2024e). Future Directions of Digital Twin Architectures for 6G Communication Networks. In Security Issues and Solutions in 6G Communications and Beyond (pp. 197-211). IGI Global.

Pandey, D., Nassa, V. K., Pandey, B. K., Thankachan, B., Dadheech, P., Mahajan, D. A., & George, A. S. (2024a). Artificial Intelligence and Machine Learning and Its Application in the Field of Computational Visual Analysis. In Emerging Engineering Technologies and Industrial Applications (pp. 36-57). IGI Global.

Pandey, D., & Pandey, B. K. (2022). An efficient deep neural network with adaptive galactic swarm optimization for complex image text extraction. In *Process Mining Techniques for Pattern Recognition* (pp. 121–137). CRC Press.

Pandey, D., Pandey, B. K., Nassa, V. K., Mahajan, D. A., George, A. S., & Dadheech, P. (2024c). Optimized Throughput-Based Broadcasting for Next Generation Wireless Networks. In Emerging Engineering Technologies and Industrial Applications (pp. 355-368). IGI Global.

Pandey, D., Pandey, B. K., Paramashivan, M. A., Mahajan, D. A., Dadheech, P. D., George, A. S., & Hameed, A. S. (2024b). Advanced Digital Data Processing Using Cloud Cryptography: Industrial Applications. In Emerging Engineering Technologies and Industrial Applications (pp. 255-268). IGI Global.

Rai, P. K., Pandey, D., & Pandey, B. K. (2024). The future of enterprise and innovation is compute as a commodity, or CaaC. *Partners Universal International Research Journal*, *3*(2), 89–94.

Ramachandra, G., Iftikhar, M., & Khan, F. A. (2017). A comprehensive survey on security in cloud computing. *Procedia Computer Science*, *110*, 465–472.

Saravanakumar, R., TamilSelvi, T., Pandey, D., Pandey, B. K., Mahajan, D. A., & Lelisho, M. E. (2024). Big data processing using hybrid Gaussian mixture model with salp swarm algorithm. *Journal of Big Data*, *11*(1), 167.

Satheesh, N., Gopisankar, N., Kumarganesh, S., Anthoniraj, S., Saravanakumar, S., & Martin Sagayam, K., Binay Kumar Pandey, and Digvijay Pandey. (2025). Advanced AI-driven emergency response systems for enhanced vehicle and human safety. *Iran Journal of Computer Science*, •••, 1–16.

Saxena, A., Agarwal, A., Pandey, B. K., & Pandey, D. (2024). Examination of the Criticality of Customer Segmentation Using Unsupervised Learning Methods. *Circular Economy and Sustainability*, •••, 1–14.

Schlepphorst, S., Choo, K. K. R., & Le-Khac, N. A. (2020). Digital forensic approaches for cloud service models: A survey. Cyber and Digital Forensic Investigations: A Law Enforcement Practitioner's Perspective, 175-199.

Shahul, A., Muniandi, B., Paramashivan, M. A., Pandey, D., Pandey, B. K., Dadheech, P., & George, H. (2024). An Analysis of Algorithms and Methods Based on Image Processing for Medical Applications. In *Emerging Engineering Technologies and Industrial Applications* (pp. 173–186). IGI Global.

Sheela, M. S., Kumarganesh, S., Pandey, B. K., & Lelisho, M. E. (2025). Integration of silver nanostructures in wireless sensor networks for enhanced biochemical sensing. *Discover Nano*, *20*(1), 7. PMID: 39804434

Singh, S., Madaan, G., Swapna, H. R., Singh, A., Pandey, B. K., George, A. S., & Pandey, D. (2025). Unleashing the Power of AI and Data Analysis: Transforming Insights into Action. In Interdisciplinary Approaches to AI, Internet of Everything, and Machine Learning (pp. 1-24). IGI Global Scientific Publishing.

Singh, S., Madaan, G., Swapna, H. R., Singh, A., Pandey, D., George, A. S., & Pandey, B. K. (2025). Empowering Connectivity: Exploring the Internet of Things. In Interdisciplinary Approaches to AI, Internet of Everything, and Machine Learning (pp. 89-116). IGI Global Scientific Publishing.

Chapter 18
Reforming the Judiciary Through Cloud Technology:
Opportunities for Digital Transformation

Mona Mahecha
Faculty of Law, Manipal University Jaipur, India

Aditi Priya
Faculty of Arts, Manipal University Jaipur, India

ABSTRACT

The transformative potential of cloud technology in addressing the ongoing challenges that are faced by judicial systems all over the world, particularly the inefficiencies that are caused by slow procedures and increasing caseloads at the same time. It focuses on the ways in which cloud solutions can streamline processes, improve data accessibility, and foster collaboration among legal professionals. It investigates the significant role that technology plays in the process of modernizing government institutions. The impact of cloud technologies on resource management, public engagement, and evidence management through the use of tools such as blockchain among other key areas of investigation are among the most important areas of focus.

DOI: 10.4018/979-8-3693-9581-3.ch018

1. INTRODUCTION

Cloud computing reformation of the judiciary presents a revolutionary chance to rectify long-standing inefficiencies and improve the administration of justice. Backlogs of cases, excessive operating expenses, and restricted access to legal services, particularly in rural or underprivileged areas, are common problems for traditional legal systems. By modernizing these systems, streamlining procedures, and enhancing public accessibility, cloud computing has the potential to increase the judiciary's effectiveness, transparency, and responsiveness. The digitization of case management is among cloud technology's most important advantages. Courts frequently have trouble managing paperwork manually, which can cause delays, mistakes, or even the loss of documents. Real-time access to case files, automated scheduling, and improved legal process tracking are all made possible by cloud-based case management systems (Pandey, B. K., & Pandey, D., 2025). This can greatly cut down on the amount of time spent on administrative work, freeing judges, attorneys, and court employees to concentrate on dispensing justice more quickly. Cloud storage also makes it possible to centralize legal records, which enhances document accessibility and retrieval between various jurisdictions and judicial bodies. Other crucial areas where cloud technology can have a significant impact are virtual hearings and online dispute resolution (ODR). Court proceedings can now be held remotely without a physical presence thanks to cloud-based platforms. In remote or rural locations with limited access to legal services, this is especially helpful. Virtual hearings allow people to participate in court proceedings from the comfort of their homes, saving time (Sheela, M. S. et al., 2025.) and money while also improving the judicial systems inclusivity. Self-service portals and electronic filing systems provided by cloud technology can enhance public access to legal services. Long-drawn-out bureaucratic procedures and in-person court visits are eliminated when citizens can electronically file documents, monitor the status of their cases, and access court decisions. This improves the judiciary's effectiveness while also boosting transparency and public confidence in the legal system. Cloud computing has many advantages (Khadka, M. et al., 2025), but there are drawbacks as well, including worries about data security, privacy, and jurisdictional control over private legal records. Notwithstanding, these obstacles can be lessened with appropriate regulatory frameworks, cooperation between governmental bodies and technology companies, and investments in safe cloud infrastructure.

1.1 Judiciary Inefficiencies

Slow judicial procedures threaten justice for individuals, institutions, and society. Long court processes delay case resolutions in many legal systems, limiting access to justice and fair trial rights. Due to outdated manual processes, complex administrative systems, lack of technological infrastructure, and insufficient human and financial resources, these delays occur (Satheesh, N. et al., 2025). Thus, the rising caseload worsens these inefficiencies, creating a cycle of delayed and denied justice. A global problem for courts is case backlogs caused by slow judicial procedures. Courts struggle to handle more cases as they pile up. Long-term detention of criminal defendants can violate human rights, especially for acquitted defendants (Kumar, M. S. et al., 2025). System delays can keep innocent people in pretrial detention for months or years, while guilty parties go unpunished. These delays affect individuals and overburden prisons and detention centers, straining the criminal justice system. Property, family, contract, and business disputes can take years to resolve in civil cases due to slow judicial processes. Unresolved disputes damage business confidence in the legal system, affecting investments, partnerships, and economic stability. Prolonged custody and divorce proceedings also strain families emotionally and financially. Delays in justice make citizens view the legal system as inaccessible and ineffective. The rising number of court cases shows structural inefficiencies (Hsu, C. C. et al., 2018). Many regions lack enough judges, clerks, and staff to handle case volumes, causing system bottlenecks. Manually handling records is slow and error-prone, so the lack of digital tools for case management, document processing, and communication delays proceedings. Old-fashioned court procedures are often used.

1.2 Cloud Technology Potential

The public's trust in legal systems can be restored and bottlenecks can be overcome with the help of cloud-based solutions (Konapure, C. G. et al., 2025). Inefficiencies in traditional courts include backlogs in the administrative system, sluggish case processing, and limited access to legal services. Cloud platforms present a contemporary method that expedites legal processes, increases transparency, and facilitates access to vital data. The digitization of case management, which enables courts to process massive volumes of data more effectively, is one of the technologies main benefits. Administrative delays are greatly decreased by automated scheduling, enhanced collaboration amongst legal professionals, and real-time access to case files. By moving away from paper-based systems, it will be possible to retrieve documents (Singh, S. et al., 2025) more quickly and streamline deadlines and case tracking, which will expedite the resolution of cases. These technologies' ability to create virtual courtrooms eliminates the need for in-person appearances, saving time and money on operations (Sharma, M. et al., 2025). Geographical location no longer restricts access to justice because remote access to hearings increases participation for people living in remote areas. Virtual hearings contribute to a more efficient legal system overall by easing the congestion in courtrooms and the associated travel. Cloud-based infrastructure also makes it possible for innovations like online dispute resolution (ODR) platforms. With the help of these platforms, parties can settle disagreements online without having to meet in person. This lessens the overall workload of judges while expediting the resolution of arbitration matters, small claims cases, and civil cases (Mantovani Ribeiro, D. M. N. et al., 2021). ODR benefits the courts and the public by increasing productivity, cutting expenses, and expediting the resolution process. These digital solutions also encourage the judiciary to be more accountable and transparent. The public is given greater transparency into the judicial system through online case tracking and remote access to court decisions, which fosters public confidence. Without having to physically appear in court, citizens can easily track the status of their cases, obtain legal documents, and submit the necessary information, enhancing the public's perception of and trust in the legal system (Jones, P., & Wynn, M., 2021).

2. PERSISTENT CHALLENGES IN JUDICIARY SYSTEMS

2.1 Manual Case Handling

The manual handling of cases continues to be a significant challenge in many different judicial systems. These systems are characterized by a heavy reliance on paperwork and traditional administrative procedures. This approach has the potential to result in a multitude of inefficiencies that impede the timely delivery of justice. The widespread use of physical documents necessitates the implementation of extensive storage, management, and retrieval systems, all of which can be laborious and time-consuming (Pandey, B. K. et al., 2024a). The slow processing of cases is one of the most pressing problems that arises when cases are handled manually. Courts frequently rely on clerks and judges to sift through mountains of paperwork in order to search for documents and information that are pertinent to the case. This reliance on manual labor not only increases the amount of time necessary to process cases, but it also opens the door to the possibility of errors being made by humans (Pandey, B. K. et al., 2024b). Files that are misplaced, documentation that is incomplete, and delays in submitting necessary paperwork can all cause legal proceedings to be delayed, which ultimately results in parties becoming frustrated and waiting for justice for a longer period of time (Brozzi, R. et al., 2020). The potential for the loss of documents is a major cause for concern. It is possible for natural disasters, accidental destruction, or even simple misfiling to cause damage to paper documents. When essential records are lost, it can create significant obstacles in the proceedings of the court, which may result in the dismissal of the case or in rulings that are unfair. In the event that vital evidence or previous case files cannot be located, it has the potential to undermine the effectiveness of legal arguments and to erode public confidence in the judicial process. The administrative burden of manually handling cases makes it more difficult for legal professionals to concentrate on substantive legal work. There is a possibility that judges and clerks spend an excessive amount of their time managing paperwork rather than engaging with cases, which can result in decision-making processes (Basha, A. J. et al., 2024) that are more drawn out. This inefficiency is compounded in jurisdictions that have high caseloads, where the backlog of cases can grow rapidly, further straining limited judicial resources. Therefore, this inefficiency is compounded. The absence of a streamlined process can result in inconsistencies in the manner in which cases are handled. Different clerks may have different interpretations of the procedures and documentation requirements, which can lead to different processing times and standards (KVM, S. et al., 2024) for each individual case. It is possible for this inconsistency to lead to perceptions of bias or inequality in the manner in which cases are adjudicated, which can be particularly problematic in legal systems that are working toward fairness and equality (Matt, C. et al., 2015).

2.2 Fragmented Information Systems

Fragmented information systems in the judiciary result from data silos caused by database integration issues. These silos hinder case management and legal system operation. Inefficiencies that hinder justice delivery can result from information silos between courts, law enforcement, and administrative bodies. Legal professionals must search multiple databases for case information, which can cause data discrepancies. A defendant's prior record in one database but not another may affect case outcomes, resulting in harsher penalties or leniency based on incomplete information. This inconsistency undermines judicial fairness and reliability. Disconnected databases also hinder judicial collaboration. Inability to share information in real time (Lakshmi, K. V. N. et al., 2024) can delay cases involving multiple jurisdictions. A court may be awaiting crucial evidence or documentation from another jurisdiction, causing unnecessary adjournments and lengthy legal proceedings. These delays frustrate parties and increase case backlogs, straining judicial resources. Dispersed information systems have effects beyond operational inefficiencies (Saravanakumar, R. et al., 2024). Public perception of the justice system is also affected. Citizens expect transparency and accessibility; bureaucratic hurdles or disconnected systems reduce their trust in the legal framework. This lack of confidence may deter people from seeking legal recourse because they view the system as complicated and ineffective. Without data integration across judicial systems, analysis and strategic planning are limited. Judicial administrators need a unified data view to identify trends, evaluate performance, and implement evidence-based reforms. This restriction can hinder efficiency, resource allocation, and service delivery (Sassanelli, C., & Terzi, S., 2022).

2.3 Geographic Disparities in Access

Geographic differences in the availability of courts and legal systems draw attention to a major urban-rural divide that compromises the fair administration of justice. When it comes to legal services, resources, and court facilities, people living in urban areas typically have greater access than people living in rural areas, where these resources are frequently scarcer. This disparity may result in significant injustices within the legal system, affecting rural residents capacity to pursue legal recourse. Access to legal aid is facilitated in urban areas by the concentration of legal aid organizations, courts, and law firms. Many legal experts make it easier for people to find representation, which raises the rate of legal engagement and, eventually, improves the results of legal proceedings. Furthermore, urban courts usually have greater infrastructure and resources to handle a higher volume of cases, which results in quicker case resolution times (Kumarganesh, S. et al., 2024) and more chances for public participation. On the other hand, access to legal services is frequently severely restricted in rural areas. Residents may have to travel great distances to get to the closest courthouse, which makes the distance to court facilities a significant barrier.

This can be especially difficult for those with low incomes or those without dependable transportation. Rural courts occasionally operate with a staffing level and hours that are restricted, which further limits access and lengthens the time it takes to resolve cases. There is frequently a shortage of legal professionals in rural areas, which results in a lack of legal representation. Since there is a chance for greater income and a wider clientele in urban settings, many lawyers choose to practice there. Consequently, people living in rural areas might not have access to sufficient legal representation, which could seriously impair their capacity to successfully handle the legal system. The publics confidence in the judiciary is further affected by the disparity between urban and rural areas' access to legal systems. People in rural areas may feel disenfranchised and disillusioned with legal institutions if they believe that the justice system is unreachable or biased against them. This mistrust may deter people from taking legal action, thereby escalating already-existing disparities and sustaining an unjust cycle.

2.4 Lack of Transparency

A significant obstacle that many judicial systems face is the limited access that the public has to the status of cases, judgments, and court records. When citizens are unable to easily obtain information regarding legal proceedings, it undermines the principles of accountability and openness of the justice system, which are essential for a fair justice system. It is essential to maintain transparency in order to cultivate public trust and give the impression that legal procedures are fair and just. Traditional methods of record management are still utilized by many courts, which frequently do not make it simple for the public to access the records. People who are looking for information about their own cases or the cases of others may experience lengthy delays as a result of this cause. When citizens want to check the status of a legal matter, for instance, they might have to go to the court house in person, navigate complicated procedures (Muralidhar, L. B. et al., 2024), and perhaps even wait for a considerable amount of time. People who do not have the time or resources to overcome these obstacles may be dissuaded from engaging with the legal system. This is especially true for individuals who are subject to such obstacles. It is possible for there to be a lack of accountability for judicial decisions if access to judgments and court records is restricted further. There is a reduction in the capacity to scrutinize the actions of the judiciary when the public is unable to review rulings or the reasoning that underpins them (Pandey, B. K. et al., 2024c). Confidence in legal institutions can be eroded as a result of this opacity, which can foster perceptions of bias or inconsistency. The lack of digital platforms for the dissemination of information makes these problems even more intractable. Due to the fact that many people do not make use of online systems, they are not aware of significant developments in the legal system, which is a problem in this day and age when technology makes it possible to obtain information instantly (Elarmathi, S. et al., 2024). In addition to having an effect on individual cases, this also makes it more difficult for society as a whole to comprehend and discuss legal issues. For judicial systems to be able to effectively address these challenges, it is imperative that they adopt contemporary technologies that improve transparency. By making it possible for citizens to access case statuses, court decisions, and legal records online, the judicial system can empower citizens, improve accountability, and foster a greater sense of trust in the legal process. It is ultimately essential to increase transparency in order to guarantee that justice is available to everyone.

3. CLOUD TECHNOLOGY FUNDAMENTALS AND ITS JUDICIAL IMPACT

3.1 Core Components of Cloud Technology

Judicial systems can improve operations, increase access to justice, and ultimately create a more responsive and efficient legal environment by comprehending and putting these fundamental cloud computing components into practice, which are as shown in the figure 1.

Figure 1. Components of cloud technology

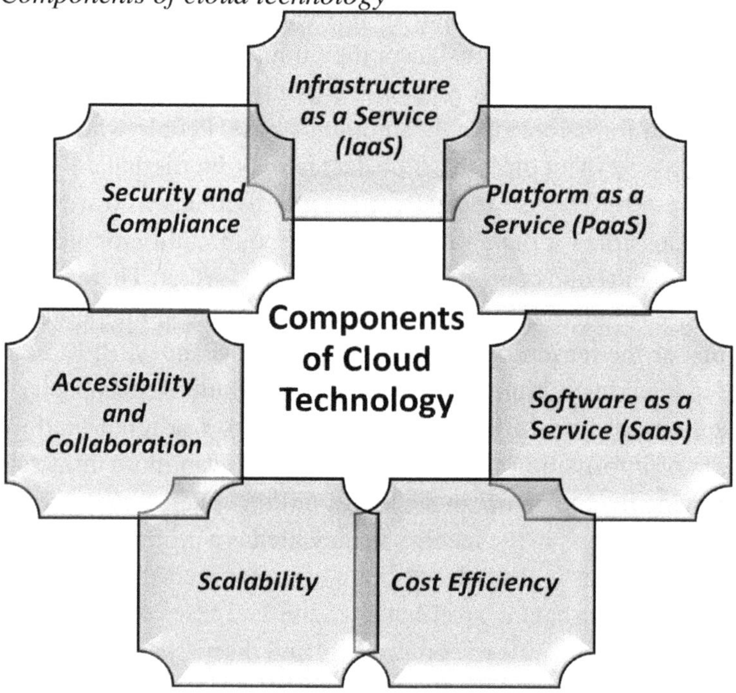

- *Infrastructure as a Service (IaaS)*: Virtualized server, storage, and networking resources are made available via the internet by Infrastructure as a Service (IaaS). Instead of purchasing actual hardware, it allows businesses to rent IT infrastructure (Pandey, B. K. et al., 2024d). This model lowers maintenance costs and does away with the requirement for physical servers by enabling courts to host their IT infrastructure. Courts can effectively manage heavy caseloads without having to make costly hardware investments by dynamically allocating resources based on demand. More computer resources can be swiftly made available to meet growing demands during peak times, such as election cycles or public health emergencies. To improve data reliability (Pandey, B. K. et al., 2024e) and disaster recovery capabilities, IaaS providers frequently incorporate built-in redundancy and backup systems.

- *Platform as a Service (PaaS)*: Without having to worry about the underlying infrastructure, PaaS provides developers with a cloud environment in which they can create, launch, and maintain applications. It offers resources and services for creating, evaluating, and implementing applications. PaaS can be applied to the creation of a number of applications in the legal domain, including public access portals (George, W. K. et al., 2024) for case information, online dispute resolution platforms, and case management systems. As a result, new features and updates can be implemented more quickly, improving the effectiveness of legal procedures. Integrated development environments (IDEs) and collaboration tools are commonly included with PaaS solutions, allowing IT personnel and legal experts to collaborate easily and innovate to enhance services.
- *Software as a Service (SaaS)*: SaaS does not require local installation or maintenance because it delivers software applications over the internet on a subscription basis. This model is especially helpful for judicial systems because it spares courts from the hassles of managing installations and gives them access to necessary applications like case tracking software, legal research tools, and document management systems (Abdullahi, M. et al., 2024).). Courts will always have access to the newest features and security patches thanks to SaaS applications easy upkeep and updating by the provider. These applications can facilitate more effective collaboration between legal professionals by allowing them to share documents and case information regardless of where they are physically located.
- *Cost Efficiency*: By reducing the need for physical infrastructure and ongoing maintenance, the use of cloud models can significantly lower operating costs for judicial systems. Courts can save a lot of money by switching to the cloud and avoiding the large capital costs of buying and maintaining hardware (Satheesh, N. et al., 2025). They can choose a pay-as-you-go approach instead, in which they only pay for the resources they actually use. Due to their financial flexibility, courts are able to reallocate funds to other important areas, like expanding their workforce, purchasing technology to improve case management, or improving the public's access to legal information.
- *Scalability*: Judicial systems can readily scale their resources in response to variations in demand, particularly during peak hours, thanks to cloud computing. Without the limitations of physical infrastructure, courts can easily

modify their computing capacity, adding or removing resources as needed (Kumar, B. et al., 2024). Managing the fluctuating caseloads that courts encounter throughout the year requires this scalability. To guarantee that everyone has timely access to justice, courts can, expand their systems to accommodate increased workloads during busy seasons or special events like elections.

- *Accessibility and Collaboration*: Cloud-based solutions enable judges, court employees, and legal professionals to collaborate by providing remote access to resources and information. Thanks to cloud computing, interested parties with an internet connection can view documents, case files, and other important data from any location (Pandey, D. et al, 2024). Because of its increased accessibility, decisions can be made more quickly, communication between all parties to a case is improved, and case preparation and hearing times are shortened. Remote access can enable people in marginalized communities to engage in the legal system, increasing accessibility to justice.
- *Security and Compliance*: Sensitive judicial data is protected because cloud providers usually provide strong security measures and adherence to legal standards. These service providers use multi-factor authentication, advanced encryption, and ongoing monitoring to protect customer data from breaches and unwanted access. A lot of cloud solutions abide by laws that control data security and privacy, which is essential for judicial organizations handling private data. Courts can take advantage of cloud solutions efficiency and scalability while protecting the confidentiality and integrity of case information by utilizing the security know-how of cloud providers.

3.2. Cloud Technology Impact on Legal Processes

Cloud technology streamlines data storage, document management, and collaboration, changing legal processes. Instead of using physical files (Shahul, A. et al., 2024), law firms and courts can securely access legal documents and case files from anywhere, improving efficiency. This speeds up workflows and case resolution by enabling remote legal team collaboration. Cloud solutions protect data with encryption and backup, improving security. Data privacy, confidentiality, and jurisdictional issues arise. Lawyers must carefully navigate these issues while using cloud technology's benefits. Effects of Cloud Technology on Legal Processes are shown in the figure 2.

Figure 2. Effects of cloud technology on legal processes

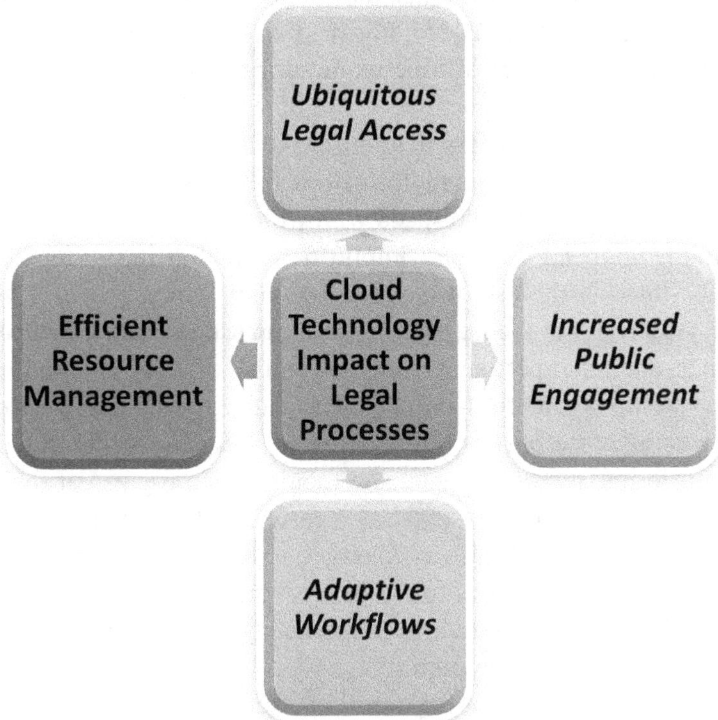

- *Efficient Resource Management*: Legal procedures are significantly improved in terms of resource management thanks to the dynamic allocation of cloud resources. With the ability to quickly scale their information technology infrastructure to meet increased demand, courts are able to avoid the delays that are typically associated with traditional hardware upgrades during times of peak caseloads or urgent legal matters (Muniandi, B. et al., 2024). As a result of this flexibility, judges and court staff are able to ensure that they have the tools and systems necessary to manage surges in activity, such as during election periods or during times of public emergency. Courts have the ability to reduce bottlenecks, streamline case processing, and improve overall service delivery through efficient resource management. This ultimately results in better access to justice and quicker resolutions to cases.
- *Ubiquitous Legal Access*: It is possible for legal professionals to connect to court data from virtually any location as long as they have an internet connection. This is made possible by cloud technology, which makes it possible for legal information to be accessed virtually everywhere. As a result of this

accessibility, attorneys, paralegals, and judges are able to successfully collaborate with one another, even when they are not physically present in the same location (Singh, S. et al., 2025). For the purpose of enhancing coordination and reducing the amount of time required for case preparation, legal teams are able to share documents, review case files, and communicate in real time. Not only does remote access help ensure that all parties involved in a case have access to the most recent information, but it also helps improve the quality of legal decisions and the speed with which they are made.

- *Increased Public Engagement*: Public participation in the legal process is increased through the use of cloud technology, which provides self-service portals. As a result of the fact that citizens can access legal information, court schedules, and other pertinent resources online, they are able to find answers to their questions without having to physically go to a courthouse. In addition, by using these portals, individuals are frequently able to electronically submit forms, file documents, and monitor the progress of their cases. A more informed public is fostered as a result of this increased transparency and accessibility, which also encourages individuals to participate in legal proceedings and contributes to the demystification of it. A more responsive and accountable legal system may ultimately result from increased public participation in the legal system.
- *Adaptive Workflows*: One of the most important advantages of cloud computing is that it enables adaptive workflows within the judicial system, which in turn benefits the automation of repetitive legal tasks. It is possible to streamline routine activities by utilizing automated systems that require minimal human intervention. Some examples of these activities include document management, scheduling, and data entry. If legal professionals could spend less time on these tasks, they would be able to devote their attention to more difficult aspects of their work, which would result in increased efficiency and productivity. In addition, adaptive workflows can be modified based on real-time data and analytics, which enables courts to respond proactively to shifting conditions and continuously optimize (Pandey, B. K., & Pandey, D., 2023) their operations throughout the years. Not only does this agility improve case management, but it also contributes to a legal system that is more efficient and prompter in its overall operation.

4. DIGITAL TRANSFORMATION USING CLOUD TECHNOLOGY

4.1 Legal Collaboration Platforms

Cloud technology enables real-time collaboration between lawyers, judges, and clients across regions on legal collaboration platforms. These platforms streamline communication, information sharing, and legal process efficiency. Providing a centralized digital workspace helps legal professionals collaborate regardless of location. Location-independent legal collaboration platforms are a major benefit. Traditional meetings or lengthy phone calls were used to discuss case details, share documents, and strategize between lawyers and clients. In complex cases involving multiple stakeholders, this caused delays and inefficiencies (Vinodhini, V. et al., 2022). Lawyers can collaborate seamlessly by accessing case files and relevant documents from anywhere with cloud-based collaboration tools. This urgency speeds up decision-making and allows for more flexible legal strategies. These platforms provide secure communication channels that protect sensitive data and allow all parties to access it. Without worrying about data breaches, lawyers can discuss, share, and review case files. Besides improving communication and security, legal collaboration platforms often include project management tools to track progress, assign tasks, and set deadlines. In complex cases with many parties and moving parts, this level of organization is essential. These platforms keep legal teams focused and on schedule by systematizing case management, reducing the risk of missed deadlines or tasks. Integration of apps and tools on one platform boosts productivity. Lawyers can integrate their preferred research, document drafting, and case analysis tools to create a workflow ecosystem. Integration reduces switching between apps, saving time and reducing errors.

4.2 Remote Witness Testimonies and Depositions

In the legal industry, remote witness depositions and testimony have grown more practical and crucial, especially with the advent of safe, cloud-based video conferencing services. With the help of these technologies, legal professionals can conduct depositions and obtain witness statements without requiring all parties to be present in person at the same location. This greatly reduces geographical constraints. This flexibility not only simplifies the legal system but also increases access to justice, particularly for witnesses who might find it difficult to appear in court because of their location, health, or other limitations. Witness accessibility is one of the main advantages of using cloud-based video conferencing for testimony and depositions. Participating from the comfort of their homes or local offices allows people who might otherwise be unable or unwilling to travel to a courtroom to give crucial testimony. When the logistics are made simpler, more witnesses might be willing to testify, which can result in a more thorough collection of evidence. The scheduling of remote testimonies is more flexible, allowing for the availability of all parties and possibly expediting the legal process in general. One of the most important considerations for remote legal proceedings is security (Rai, P. K., Pandey, D., & Pandey, B. K., 2024). Advanced security features including secure login procedures, access controls, and end-to-end encryption are frequently included in cloud-enabled video conferencing systems. These precautions guarantee the confidentiality and security of sensitive information disclosed during depositions and testimony. Legal professionals can feel secure knowing that witness testimony is gathered in a secure setting and that the process integrity is upheld. Apart from augmenting security and accessibility, remote video conferencing platforms frequently incorporate functionalities that facilitate efficient communication in legal proceedings. Digital document uploads, interactive whiteboards, and screen sharing are a few examples of tools that make depositions more effective and entertaining while also promoting teamwork. Using the advantages of technology, attorneys can mimic the dynamics of in-person interactions by presenting evidence, exchanging pertinent documents, and interacting in real time with witnesses. The capacity to remotely record video testimony generates an important evidence bank that can be reviewed prior to trial or in legal conferences. Reviewing witness statements, making sure they are consistent, and getting ready for cross-examinations can all benefit from these recordings. The efficiency of the legal process is improved by the availability of digital transcripts and recordings, which give legal teams quick access to vital data.

4.3 Real-Time Data Analytics for Judiciary Insights

Real-time data analytics using cloud-based AI to gain insights into legal processes is revolutionizing the judicial system. This novel method allows courts and legal professionals to quickly and accurately analyze massive amounts of data to identify case trends, predict trial outcomes, and assess workload distribution. Identifying case trends is a major benefit of cloud-based AI for predictive analytics. Using historical case data, including case types, judicial decisions, and durations, AI algorithms can find patterns that humans may miss. Courts can learn which cases take longer to resolve or which judges favor certain motions. This knowledge can improve case management by prioritizing and allocating resources. Predictive analytics can also predict trial results. AI systems can predict verdicts based on case type, jurisdiction, and party profiles by examining similar cases. This information can help lawyers develop case strategies and inform clients of potential outcomes. Such insights can also help courts anticipate issues and develop proactive case management and resolution strategies. Workload distribution is another important use of real-time data analytics in the judiciary. AI can identify workload disparities by analyzing case data and tracking court staff and judge performance. This analysis informs courts' resource reallocation and schedule adjustments to better balance workloads. When some judges are overburdened while others have lighter loads, courts can redistribute cases to ensure that all judges can handle their duties. This optimization speeds up case resolution and improves judicial efficiency.

AI-driven analytics solutions' cloud-based nature allows legal professionals to access data in real time and make informed decisions. Dashboards and visualizations make critical data easy to digest, allowing stakeholders to quickly assess trends and patterns. This speed allows courts to respond quickly to new issues or case dynamics.

4.4 Blockchain for Cloud-Based Evidence Management

The integration of blockchain technology with cloud services provides a robust solution for the secure tracking and verification of legal documents within the judicial system. Legal professionals are able to guarantee that evidence is stored in a secure manner and cannot be altered by utilizing the immutable nature of blockchain technology. A one-of-a-kind cryptographic hash is assigned to every piece of evidence or document, and this hash is then recorded on the blockchain. This creates a record that is both permanent and transparent of the existence of the evidence and its provenance. Through the use of this safe tracking mechanism, stakeholders are able to verify the genuineness of legal documents at any time. Any changes that were made to a document would necessitate a change in its hash, which would be visible in the blockchain ledger. As a consequence of this, the possibility of tampering is significantly reduced, which in turn improves the credibility of the evidence that is presented in court. The integration of blockchain technology with cloud services improves accessibility. Evidence can be accessed by authorized parties from any location, which enables real-time collaboration between legal teams, judges, and clients. Not only does this combination make the management of evidence more efficient, but it also makes the legal process more effective as a whole. The role that blockchain plays in cloud-based evidence management will be essential in ensuring transparency, security, and trust in judicial proceedings as legal systems continue to embrace digital transformation at an increasing rate.

5. RECOMMENDATIONS FOR EFFECTIVE IMPLEMENTATION

Governments have to take the lead in working with tech companies to create secure, sovereign cloud infrastructure that is specifically suited to judicial requirements in order to successfully integrate cloud technology in the judiciary. While offering the required resources for effective case management and information sharing, this approach should put a major emphasis on making sure that the cloud systems abide by regional legal requirements and data protection regulations. The judiciary can increase data accessibility, operational efficiency, and the security of confidential legal information by putting in place a national cloud framework. It is crucial for the successful implementation of cloud platforms that legal professionals and court personnel possess the necessary navigational skills. With an emphasis on the efficient use of cloud computing, digital case management systems, and online court functions, training programs should be created to improve digital literacy throughout the judiciary. To encourage a culture of flexibility and creativity within the judiciary, these training programs may include seminars, workshops, and chances for continuous professional growth. Courts may make sure staff members are equipped to use technology to enhance public participation and service delivery by investing in digital literacy. Using hybrid cloud models which combine public and private cloud platforms as a practical means of integrating cloud technology into the legal system. To strengthening security protocols and maximizing storage capacity, this approach also enhances overall service delivery. Courts can take advantage of public cloud resources scalability and affordability for less sensitive data while storing sensitive data in private clouds by implementing a hybrid model. The judiciary can identify best practices and address potential challenges before broader implementation by conducting pilot programs to evaluate the efficacy of this approach. A more seamless transition to the digital age is ensured by this phased approach, which reduces risks while also allowing the legal system to gradually adapt to technological advancements.

6. CONCLUSION

A revolutionary chance to solve enduring issues that impede the administration of justice, like backlogs of cases and slow court processes, is provided by the judiciary's adoption of cloud computing. The efficiency and accessibility of legal processes are significantly hindered by the aforementioned factors, including geographic disparities, fragmented information systems, manual case handling, and lack of transparency. Adopting cloud solutions can help the judiciary improve data accessibility, streamline operations, and encourage greater collaboration among legal professionals. Cloud computing has enormous potential advantages. Cloud solutions can greatly increase the responsiveness and agility of the legal system by enabling real-time collaboration through legal platforms, allowing remote witness testimony, and using predictive analytics to make well-informed decisions. Using blockchain technology for secure evidence management further reinforces the integrity of legal procedures and ensures that all parties can rely on the system. Overcoming legal and regulatory obstacles is necessary for the successful deployment of these technologies. Safeguarding sensitive judicial data and ensuring strong legal frameworks require addressing issues like intellectual property protection, cross-border data transfers, and digital signature compliance. The judiciary can only fully benefit from cloud technology if comprehensive national cloud strategies are developed, legal professionals are encouraged to become digitally literate, and hybrid cloud models which combine public and private resources—are tested. The judiciary can improve public confidence in legal systems and alleviate current bottlenecks by adopting these proactive measures, which will ultimately lead to a more effective, open, and accessible justice system. A more adaptable judiciary that can satisfy the demands of a quickly evolving legal landscape will be made possible by embracing these innovations.

REFERENCES

Abdullahi, M., Ahmad, A., Pandey, B. K., & Pandey, D. (2024). Digital Currency Adoption: A Comparative Analysis of Global Trends and the Nigerian eNaira Digital Currency. *SN Computer Science*, *5*(5), 1–11.

Basha, A. J., Maheshwari, R. U., Pandey, B. K., & Pandey, D. (2024). Ultra-sensitive photonic crystal fiber–based SPR sensor for cancer detection utilizing hybrid nano-composite layers. *Plasmonics*, 1–15.

Betchoo, N. K. Digital Transformation and its impact on Human Resource Management: A Case Analysis of two unrelated businesses in the Mauritian public service. In *Proceedings of the IEEE International Conference on Emerging Technologies and Innovative Business Practices for the Transformation of Societies (EmergiTech)*, Balaclava, Mauritius, 3–6 August 2016; pp. 147–152.

Brozzi, R., Forti, D., Rauch, E., & Matt, D. T. (2020). The Advantages of Industry 4.0 Applications for Sustainability: Results from a Sample of Manufacturing Companies. *Sustainability*, *12*, 3647.

Brunetti, F., Matt, D. T., Bonfant, A., De Longhi, A., Pedrini, G., & Orzes, G. (2020). Digital transformation challenges: Strategies emerging from a multi-stakeholder approach. *The TQM Journal*, *32*, 697–724.

Diez, L., Choque, J., Sánchez, L., & Muñoz, L. (2020). Fostering IoT Service Replicability in Interoperable Urban Ecosystems. *IEEE Access : Practical Innovations, Open Solutions*, *8*, 228480–228495.

Elarmathi, S., Rishabavarthani, P., Sindhuja, M., Elayaraja, P., & Malathi Murugesan, S. Kumarganesh, K. Martin Sagayam, Binay Kumar Pandey, and Digvijay Pandey. (2024). Novel manufacturing systems for cancer diagnosis using ultra-sensitive photonic crystal fiber biosensor with dual-functionalized aptamer-nanocavity. *Microsystem Technologies*, •••, 1–20.

George, W. K., Silas, E. I., Pandey, D., & Pandey, B. K. (2024). Utilization of Industry 4.0 Technologies in Nigerian Technical and Vocational Education: A Conundrum for Educators. In *Examining the Rapid Advance of Digital Technology in Africa* (pp. 270–293). IGI Global.

Hidayatno, A., Destyanto, A. R., & Hulu, C. A. (2019). Industry 4.0 Technology Implementation Impact to Industrial Sustainable Energy in Indonesia: A Model Conceptualization. *Energy Procedia*, *156*, 227–233.

Hsu, C.-C., Tsaih, R.-H., & Yen, D. C. (2018). The Evolving Role of IT Departments in Digital Transformation. *Sustainability*, *10*, 3706.

Hu, G., Chohan, S. R., & Liu, J. (2020). Does IoT service orchestration in public services enrich the citizens' perceived value of digital society? *Asian Journal of Technology Innovation*, *29*, 1–27.

Jones, P., & Wynn, M. (2021). The Leading Digital Technology Companies and Their Approach to Sustainable Development. *Sustainability*, *13*, 6612.

Khadka, M., Sah, M., Chaudhary, R., Sahani, S. K., Sahani, K., Pandey, B. K., & Pandey, D. (2025). Spectroscopic, quantum chemical, and topological calculations of the phenylephrine molecule using density functional theory. *Scientific Reports*, *15*(1), 208. PMID: 39747169

Konapure, C. G., Pandey, D., Shete, H., Thakar, C. M., Pandey, B. K., & George, A. S. (2025). Artificial Intelligence in Automated Concrete Mix Design Using Computerized Grading Curves. Interdisciplinary Approaches to AI, Internet of Everything, and Machine Learning, 567-586.

Kumar, B., Pandey, D., Pandey, B. K., & George, A. S. (2024). Higher Education in the Last Four Decades: A Review of Paradigm Shifts in Policy Frameworks. Design and Implementation of Higher Education Learners' Learning Outcomes (HELLO), 333-348.

Kumar, M. S., Prasanna, P. L., Lalitha, M., Joy, M., Jha, S. S., & Pandey, B. K. (2025). Utilizing the Internet of Everything and Artificial Intelligence for Real-Time Workforce Management. In Role of Internet of Everything (IOE), VLSI Architecture, and AI in Real-Time Systems (pp. 153-168). IGI Global Scientific Publishing.

Kumarganesh, S., & Malathi Murugesan, C. Ganesh, N. Santhiyakumari, M. Thangavel, K. Jayaram, K. Martin Sagayam, Binay Kumar Pandey, and Digvijay Pandey. (2024). Hybrid plasmonic biosensors with deep learning for colorectal cancer detection. *Plasmonics*, •••, 1–15.

Kutnjak, A., Pihir, I., & Fujan, T. M. Digital Transformation Case Studies across Industries–Literature Review. In Proceedings of the 2019 42nd International Convention on Information and Communication Technology, Electronics and Microelectronics (MIPRO), Opatija, Croatia, 20–24 May 2019.

KVM, S., Pandey, B. K., & Pandey, D. (2024). Design of Surface Plasmon Resonance (SPR) Sensors for Highly Sensitive Biomolecular Detection in Cancer Diagnostics. *Plasmonics*, •••, 1–13.

Lakshmi, K. V. N., Rajan, R., Pandey, D., & Pandey, B. K. (2024). Circular economy: A catalyst for economic growth-an empirical study. *Circular Economy and Sustainability*, •••, 1–22.

Matt, C., Hess, T., & Benlian, A. (2015). Digital transformation strategies. *Business & Information Systems Engineering*, *57*, 339–343.

Muniandi, B., Nassa, V. K., Pandey, D., Pandey, B. K., Dadheech, P., & George, A. S. (2024). Pattern Analysis for Feature Extraction in Complex Images. In Using Machine Learning to Detect Emotions and Predict Human Psychology (pp. 145-167). IGI Global.

Muralidhar, L. B., Lakshmi, K. V. N., Swapna, H. R., Rupani, J., Nethravathi, K., Pandey, B. K., & Pandey, D. (2024). Impact of Organizational Culture on The Level of Corporate Social Responsibility Investments: An Exploratory Study. *Circular Economy and Sustainability*, •••, 1–19.

Pandey, B. K., Nassa, V. K., Mukundan, A. P., Mahajan, D. A., Pandey, D., George, A. S., & Dadheech, P. (2024c). An Industry-Focused Traffic System Utilising Internet of Things. In *Emerging Engineering Technologies and Industrial Applications* (pp. 200–213). IGI Global.

Pandey, B. K., & Pandey, D. (2023). Parametric optimization and prediction of enhanced thermoelectric performance in co-doped CaMnO3 using response surface methodology and neural network. *Journal of Materials Science Materials in Electronics*, *34*(21), 1589.

Pandey, B. K., & Pandey, D. (2025). Securing healthcare medical image information using advance morphological component analysis, information hiding systems, and hybrid convolutional neural networks on IoMT. *Computers in Biology and Medicine*, *185*, 109499. PMID: 39642698

Pandey, B. K., Pandey, D., & Lelisho, M. E. (2024a). Face mask identification with enhanced cuckoo optimization and deep learning-based faster regional neural network. *Scientific Reports*, *14*(1), 29719. PMID: 39613761

Pandey, B. K., Pandey, D., & Sahani, S. K. (2024b). Autopilot control unmanned aerial vehicle system for sewage defect detection using deep learning. *Engineering Reports*, •••, 12852.

Pandey, B. K., Paramashivan, M. A., Pandey, D., George, A. S., Agarwal, A., Dadheech, P., & Mahajan, D. A. (2024e). A recent survey on 6G vehicular technology: applications and challenges. 6G Security Education and Multidisciplinary Implementation, 337-350.

Pandey, B. K., Paramashivan, M. A., Pandey, D., George, A. S., Agarwal, A., Mahajan, D. A., . . . Pramanik, S. (2024d). Future Directions of Digital Twin Architectures for 6G Communication Networks. In Security Issues and Solutions in 6G Communications and Beyond (pp. 197-211). IGI Global.

Pandey, D., Nassa, V. K., Pandey, B. K., Mahajan, D. A., Patidar, P. K., Dadheech, P., & George, A. S. (2024). An Analysis of Internet-of-Things-Based Fire Detection and Alert Systems. In *Emerging Engineering Technologies and Industrial Applications* (pp. 295–304). IGI Global.

Putthiwat, S.; Kamonchanok, S.; Pongsa, P. Factors Influencing Digital Transformation of Logistics Service Providers: A Case Study in Thailand. *J. Asian Financ. Econ. Bus.***2021**, *8*, 0241–0251.

Rai, P. K., Pandey, D., & Pandey, B. K. (2024). The future of enterprise and innovation is compute as a commodity, or CaaC. *Partners Universal International Research Journal*, *3*(2), 89–94.

Ribeiro, D. M. N. M., Houneaux, F.Junior, Cunha, C. L. L., Kaetsu, O. T., Dionizio-Leite, P. F., & Machado, C.Junior. (2021). Digital sustainability: How information and communication technologies (ICTs) support sustainable development goals (SDGs) assessment in municipalities. *Digit. Policy Regul. Gov.*, *23*, 229–247.

Saravanakumar, R., TamilSelvi, T., Pandey, D., Pandey, B. K., Mahajan, D. A., & Lelisho, M. E. (2024). Big data processing using hybrid Gaussian mixture model with salp swarm algorithm. *Journal of Big Data*, *11*(1), 167.

Satheesh, N., Gopisankar, N., Kumarganesh, S., Anthoniraj, S., Saravanakumar, S., & Martin Sagayam, K., Binay Kumar Pandey, and Digvijay Pandey. (2025). Advanced AI-driven emergency response systems for enhanced vehicle and human safety. *Iran Journal of Computer Science*, •••, 1–16.

Satheesh, N., Gopisankar, N., Kumarganesh, S., Anthoniraj, S., Saravanakumar, S., & Martin Sagayam, K., Binay Kumar Pandey, and Digvijay Pandey. (2025). Advanced AI-driven emergency response systems for enhanced vehicle and human safety. *Iran Journal of Computer Science*, •••, 1–16.

Schallmo, D., & Williams, C. (2017). Digital Transformation of Business Models–Best Practice, Enablers and Roadmap. *International Journal of Innovation Management*, *21*, 740014.

Shahul, A., Muniandi, B., Paramashivan, M. A., Pandey, D., Pandey, B. K., Dadheech, P., & George, H. (2024). An Analysis of Algorithms and Methods Based on Image Processing for Medical Applications. In *Emerging Engineering Technologies and Industrial Applications* (pp. 173–186). IGI Global.

Sharma, M., Talwar, R., Nassa, V. K., Binay, K., & Pandey, D. (2025). Design and performance analysis of a multiband vivaldi antenna for wireless broadband communication in 3-5.6 GHz spectrum. In *Artificial Intelligence and Information Technologies* (pp. 86–91). CRC Press.

Sheela, M. S., Kumarganesh, S., Pandey, B. K., & Lelisho, M. E. (2025). Integration of silver nanostructures in wireless sensor networks for enhanced biochemical sensing. *Discover Nano*, *20*(1), 7. PMID: 39804434

Singh, S., Madaan, G., Swapna, H. R., Singh, A., Pandey, D., George, A. S., & Pandey, B. K. (2025). Empowering Connectivity: Exploring the Internet of Things. In Interdisciplinary Approaches to AI, Internet of Everything, and Machine Learning (pp. 89-116). IGI Global Scientific Publishing.

Singh, S., Madaan, G., Swapna, H. R., Singh, A., Pandey, D., George, A. S., & Pandey, B. K. (2025). Empowering Connectivity: Exploring the Internet of Things. In Interdisciplinary Approaches to AI, Internet of Everything, and Machine Learning (pp. 89-116). IGI Global Scientific Publishing.

Teichert, R. (2019). Digital Transformation Maturity: A Systematic Review of Literature. *Acta Universitatis Agriculturae et Silviculturae Mendelianae Brunensis*, *67*, 1673–1687.

Vinodhini, V., Kumar, M. S., Sankar, S., Pandey, D., Pandey, B. K., & Nassa, V. K. (2022). IoT-based early forest fire detection using MLP and AROC method. *International Journal of Global Warming*, *27*(1), 55–70.

Wolfert, S., Ge, L., Verdouwa, C., & Bogaardt, M.-J. (2017). Big Data in Smart Farming—A review. *Agricultural Systems*, *153*, 69–80.

Chapter 19
Regulatory Frameworks for Securing IoT Devices: A Legal Perspective

Vishwas Gupta
Department of Law, Manipal University Jaipur, India

Upasna Rana
Department of Law, Manipal University Jaipur, India

ABSTRACT

The swift expansion of interconnected devices has revolutionized numerous facets of everyday life, improved convenience and efficiency while simultaneously elevating substantial security concerns. This chapter analyzes the legal aspects concerning the security of these devices, highlighting the essential requirement for strong regulatory frameworks to safeguard consumer data and maintain the integrity of interconnected systems. Current regulations, including the General Data Protection Regulation (GDPR) and the California Consumer Privacy Act (CCPA), and emphasizes the difficulties arising from disparate legal frameworks, cultural variances, and differing degrees of technological progress among nations.

1. INTRODUCTION

Industries have been revolutionized as a result of the rapid expansion of Internet-connected devices (KVM, S. et al., 2024); however, this expansion has also revealed significant security vulnerabilities. It is of the utmost importance to ensure the security of Internet of Things devices because of the sensitive nature of the data that they manage and their widespread use in essential industries such as

DOI: 10.4018/979-8-3693-9581-3.ch019

healthcare, finance, and transportation. It is essential to ensure the security of the Internet f Things (IoT) from a legal standpoint in order to protect consumers and maintain the integrity of data, which has resulted in the development of regulatory frameworks all over the world. Regulations addressing Internet of Things (IoT) security (Pandey, D. et al., 2024) have been enacted in a number of regions, with varying degrees of stringency. As a result of the Internet of Things Cybersecurity Improvement Act, Internet of Things devices that are purchased by the federal government in the United States are required to comply with certain security standards. In a similar vein, the Cybersecurity Act of the European Union establishes a framework for certifying the safety of electronic devices, enhancing the security standards for manufacturers, and guaranteeing the safety of consumers (Lakshmi, K. V. N. et al., 2024). The fact that many regions continue to rely on local laws to address security concerns, organizations such as the International Organization for Standardization (ISO) play a pivotal role in the development of cross-border security standards on a global scale. The concept of "cybersecurity (Pandey, B. K., & Pandey, D., 2025) by design," in which security features are integrated into devices during the development phase, is one of the primary legal mechanisms that can be utilized to ensure the privacy and safety of the Internet of Things (IoT). IoT devices are subject to stringent data protection requirements, which are imposed by regulations such as the General Data Protection Regulation (GDPR). These regulations place an emphasis on the importance of data privacy and the necessity for organizations to implement robust encryption methods. It is common for failure to comply with these regulations to result in significant fines as well as damage to ones reputation. When different regions take different approaches, inconsistencies are created, which makes compliance more difficult for multinational organizations. For the purpose of bolstering security, numerous legal experts advocate for the establishment of unified global standards and closer collaboration between regulatory bodies. This would ensure that Internet of Things security is aligned with the progression of technological advancements (Saravanakumar, R. et al., 2024).

1.1 IoT Device Proliferation

Technology is now ingrained in practically every aspect of life thanks to the widespread adoption of connected devices, which have transformed daily activities and industries. These gadgets facilitate real-time data exchange, bringing efficiency and innovation (Khadka, M. et al., 2025) to a variety of industries, from smart homes and healthcare systems to industrial automation. Because so many of the devices in this massive network of interconnected ones are susceptible to cyberattacks, there are serious security risks. Strong legal frameworks are needed to protect both users and the data these technologies handle, as safeguarding them has become a crucial issue

(Kumarganesh, S. et al., 2024). The way that different countries handle connected device security laws differs. Minimum security requirements for devices used in federal systems are intended to be established by U.S. laws such as the Cybersecurity Improvement Act. Features like robust password security, automatic software updates, and channels for reporting vulnerabilities are all mandated by this regulation. With the Cybersecurity Act, which creates a framework for certifying devices based on their security capabilities, the European Union has adopted a proactive stance across the Atlantic. This gives customers peace of mind about the safety of the products they use and incentivizes manufacturers to create goods with strong safeguards. The General Data Protection Regulation (GDPR) in Europe and other data protection laws are important factors that influence the security environment. GDPR applies to connected technologies, especially those that handle sensitive user data, even though its main focus is on protecting personal data (Motlagh, N. H. et al., 2017). Its regulations govern information storage, processing, and sharing. Organizations are compelled by the law to implement more robust security measures because data breaches carry severe penalties. Uniform security guidelines are being created by international standardization bodies such as the International Electrotechnical Commission (IEC) and the International Organization for Standardization (ISO). However, because they have to abide by a number of national regulations, businesses that operate internationally face difficulties due to the absence of coherent international laws. Beyond these current legal frameworks, the idea of "cybersecurity by design" is becoming increasingly important. Rather than fixing vulnerabilities after issues occur, this method places an emphasis on integrating security features into devices from the ground up (Shahul, A. et al., 2024). Legal frameworks will need to change in tandem with the threats posed by these interconnected systems as a result of the rapid advancement of technology and the growing demand for stricter security regulations. To ensure a more secure digital future, it will be essential to create global standards that are harmonized and to promote cooperation between industries and governments (Kersnovski, T. et al., 2017).

1.2 Security in Connected Ecosystems

The vast amounts of sensitive data that these networks manage and the crucial roles that they play in modern infrastructure make security an extremely important concern in ecosystems that are connected to one another (Sheela, M. S. et al., 2025). Instruments that are part of these systems are frequently incorporated into vital services, such as healthcare, finance, transportation, and energy grids. In such networks, any breach or vulnerability can lead to severe consequences, ranging from the theft of personal data and unauthorized access to the failure of essential services to the failure of the system itself. A single compromised device can serve as an entry point for attackers to exploit the larger network because of the interconnected nature of the devices used in the network. A great number of devices have a limited processing power (Satheesh, N. et al., 2025), and they frequently lack advanced security features, which makes them more susceptible to digital assaults. In addition to the large number of devices that are currently operational, this vulnerability also contributes to the increased likelihood of widespread disruption. For instance, in the healthcare industry (Kumar, M. S. et al., 2025), compromised medical devices could have an impact on patient safety. In industrial settings, a security breach could disrupt entire production lines, resulting in significant impact on both the economy and operations. The protection of data privacy is only one of the many reasons why it is essential to secure these ecosystems in order to guarantee user trust (Konapure, C. G. et al., 2025). Higher security standards are likely to be demanded by consumers and organizations as they become more aware of the risks, which will have an effect on the market for connected devices. Because of the potential for cyberattacks and system vulnerabilities, the benefits that these technologies bring could be undermined if stringent security measures are not in place. This would result in a loss of trust and a reduced rate of further adoption. Within the context of these dangers, regulatory frameworks have come into existence in order to address the security concerns that are associated with these systems (Singh, S. et al., 2025). Manufacturers and service providers are being pushed to prioritize safety in their designs as a result of the enforcement of regulations that demand stricter security protocols on the part of governments and international organizations. Legal and technical standards will continue to evolve in order to meet the demands of a world that is becoming increasingly connected. As these networks continue to expand, the importance of using robust security measures will only continue to grow (Kumbhar, A. et al., 2017).

1.3 Legal Concerns Surrounding IoT Security

Many legal issues have arisen as a result of the connected devices explosive growth, especially in terms of security concerns (Muralidhar, L. B. et al., 2024). The security of the sensitive data these devices handle is one of the main worries. The risk of data breaches and unauthorized access becomes a significant legal issue as they become more and more integrated into daily activities and essential services. Legal frameworks such as the General Data Protection Regulation (GDPR) and the California Consumer Privacy Act (CCPA) emphasize the significance of protecting personal data and hold corporations accountable for any improper handling or data breaches that may arise from weaknesses in their devices. An additional legal challenge concerns the absence of globally consistent security norms (Pandey, B. K. et al., 2024c). Businesses that operate internationally face a complex regulatory environment because different regions have varying laws that are enforced. While some nations have passed strict legislation to address security issues, other nations still do not have many comprehensive security laws. Compliance is made more difficult by this difference, especially for manufacturers and service providers who have to deal with conflicting regulations. It is debatable whether closer international cooperation is required to establish a single legal framework since many devices have security holes that can be exploited in the absence of uniform global standards (Muniandi, B. et al., 2024). Another area of legal ambiguity is liability in the event of a breach. Determining who is responsible for a device hack or compromise gets complicated. If it is discovered that a product's security features are insufficient, the manufacturer may be held legally liable. However, users may also bear responsibility if they neglect to use readily available safeguards, like software updates or secure passwords. When several parties are involved manufacturers, service providers, and users—and each has varying degrees of accountability for keeping the devices secure, the issue of liability gets even more hazy (Singh, S. et al., 2025). Because of the enormous number of devices and the decentralized structure of their networks, enforcing these security regulations is especially difficult. Keeping an eye on compliance can be challenging, particularly when devices are used in several legal jurisdictions. This results in enforcement gaps as it becomes more difficult for regulators to guarantee that businesses follow security standards. Security standards are upheld internationally, legal frameworks must evolve along with technology, placing more emphasis on international cooperation and accountability (Bupe, P. et al., 2015).

2. CURRENT REGULATORY LANDSCAPE

2.1 Global Regulations

Innovation and convenience have transformed healthcare and manufacturing industries (Elarmathi, S. et al., 2024) worldwide due to the proliferation of connected devices. Data collection, processing, and communication (Sharma, M. et al., 2025) are now seamless thanks to these devices in critical infrastructure, homes, and workplaces. While vast, this network of interconnected technologies poses significant security risks. Data breaches (Vinodhini, V. et al., 2022), cyberattacks, and unauthorized access point to the need for strong legal and regulatory frameworks. Different regions have developed regulations to secure ecosystems (Kumar Pandey, B. et al.,, 2021) and protect user privacy and data. Global regulations vary in approach, implementation, and enforcement, making them complex. General Data Protection Regulation (GDPR), implemented by the EU in 2018, is one of the most important pieces of recent legislation. The GDPR protects EU citizens' privacy and security by imposing strict data processing requirements on organisations (Pandey, B. K. et al., 2024a). Companies must secure data collected from connected devices under this regulation. It also lets people access, change, and delete their personal data. The GDPR requires organizations to collect only the data they need, reducing the risk of overexposure in a breach. The GDPR's stiff penalties for non-compliance, up to 4% of a company's global revenue, have set a new global standard for data protection and security. The US has also made progress in regulating connected device security. One of the most prominent regulations is the 2020 California Consumer Privacy Act (CCPA). While the CCPA focuses on consumer privacy, it affects interconnected technology security. California residents have the right to know what personal data is collected, how it is used, and with whom. CCPA requires companies to protect consumer data with reasonable security (Pandey, B. K. et al., 2024d). Consumers can sue companies for data breaches if they failed to secure their data (Merwaday, A., & Guvenc, I., 2015). A de facto national standard in the U.S., the CCPA applies to many companies, especially online ones, with California users. The EU's regulatory structure is more cohesive than the U.S. California pioneered the CCPA, but other states are adopting similar laws, and federal privacy and security regulations are being discussed. Different states have different requirements, making this approach difficult for companies operating in multiple states. Many U.S. regions lack strict security regulations, leaving protection gaps. Some industries have replied by taking action. Health data is strictly regulated by HIPAA in the healthcare sector. Despite its limited scope, the IoT Cybersecurity Improvement Act of 2020 set security standards for federally procured connected devices. The ISO and IEC set global standards for connected system security. To promote security consistency across borders, the ISO and IEC develop and maintain guidelines to ensure devices meet minimum security requirements (George, W. K. et al., 2024). Companies can use these standards to secure their devices even in countries with weaker legal systems. A popular information security management system standard, ISO/IEC 27001, provides guidance on implementing, maintaining, and improving security. Although not legally binding, these standards are used in regulatory frameworks worldwide as best practices. Global firms must navigate a complex web of regional regulations, which can be costly and difficult. A company that manufactures connected devices may need to comply with the GDPR in Europe, the CCPA in California, and other laws in different countries with different data protection, security, and user rights requirements. Without cohesion, companies may focus on meeting the strictest regulations and neglect regions with weaker laws, compromising security. Cybersecurity by design is becoming a legal and regulatory trend to address these security issues. This approach emphasises building security features into connected devices from the start rather than retrofitting after vulnerabilities are found. The GDPR and CCPA require companies to design products with security in mind at every stage.

This proactive security approach prevents breaches rather than responding to them, making it crucial. With more connected devices, governments and international organizations will face more pressure to create comprehensive security regulations. Some of the current laws are effective, but they don't address the global security risks these devices pose (Abdullahi, M. et al., 2024). A unified global framework for securing connected ecosystems that accounts for regional regulatory landscapes and promotes collaboration and standardization is needed. A framework that improves security and reduces regulatory burdens would allow companies to focus on innovation while ensuring product security (Casanovasabc, P. et al., 2017).

2.2 Regional Regulations

Global concerns about interconnected system security have led governments to create regulations to address vulnerabilities and protect user data. Different countries prioritize device and network security in their legal frameworks. There is no global regulation, but several regions have strict rules to ensure system safety and integrity (Kumar, B. et al., 2024). Interconnected device security regulations in the US are evolving. The 2020 IoT Cybersecurity Improvement Act sets security standards for federal agency devices. Manufacturers must update and patch devices, address known vulnerabilities, and use strong passwords under this law. The act focuses on government procurement, but manufacturers must meet these requirements to sell to the federal government, which indirectly affects industry standards. California pioneered connected device security laws. Senate Bill 327 requires manufacturers to build products with reasonable security to prevent unauthorized access. This bill is among the first to target device security in the U.S., setting a precedent for other states. The California Consumer Privacy Act (CCPA), which protects consumer privacy, also affects device security by requiring companies to protect personal data collected through these technologies. The U.S. regulatory framework is still fragmented, with states taking different approaches. The IoT Cybersecurity Improvement Act sets a baseline for federal devices, but there is no national standard for interconnected device security, leaving gaps in protection. European Union's Cybersecurity Act is a major regulatory advance. This 2019 law establishes a framework for device security certification, setting standards for manufacturers. The act aims to create a unified EU certification scheme to ensure product security and technical compliance. EU Agency for Cybersecurity (ENISA) can develop and maintain these certification schemes for a wide range of devices and services under the Cybersecurity Act. A key feature of the Cybersecurity Act is its voluntary certification framework. Certification is optional, but it gives manufacturers a competitive edge by demonstrating their products meet the highest security standards. This approach boosts consumer confidence and harmonizes EU regulations, allowing member states to rely on a consistent framework rather than fragmented national regulations. The General Data Protection Regulation (GDPR) requires organizations to protect personal data collected through connected systems, which affects device security similar to the Cybersecurity Act. These regulations ensure Europe's interconnected device security and privacy comprehensively. Many Asian countries have created regulatory frameworks to address connected ecosystem security risks. Chinese, Japanese, and Indian leaders are taking different approaches based on regional priorities and technological development. China's 2017 Cybersecurity Law underpins digital security regulation. Network operators, including device manufacturers, must protect data, user privacy, and system integrity by law. It also requires data localization, requiring certain data to be stored in China. This approach is part of a larger strategy to improve state cybersecurity control and domestic technology. The Personal Information Protection Law (PIPL) and Data Security Law, along with the Cybersecurity Law, strengthen China's data protection and critical information infrastructure laws. Device security regulation in Japan has also improved. The 2014 Basic Act on Cybersecurity establishes Japan's cybersecurity policies and outlines public and private sector responsibilities for digital infrastructure security. Japan launched the public-private IoT Acceleration Consortium to promote secure device use and development. This initiative gives manufacturers and service providers guidelines to secure connected technologies. India has focused on creating a regulatory environment that balances digital innovation and security. The Personal Data Protection Bill (PDPB), under consideration, seeks to establish a comprehensive data protection and privacy law. Although not yet enacted, the PDPB will likely require companies to protect data collected by connected devices to protect user privacy and promote digital economy innovation. India has also issued guidelines on securing connected devices, emphasizing the need to protect critical infrastructure and encouraging manufacturers to adopt international security standards (Rai, P. K. et al., 2024).). Despite regional differences in connected device security regulation, the global landscape remains fragmented. Although the IoT Cybersecurity Improvement Act and Senate Bill 327 are important, the lack of a national standard leaves gaps in protection. The EU's Cybersecurity Act creates a voluntary certification framework to standardize security across Europe. China, Japan, and India are addressing security through legislation and public-private partnerships, depending on regional needs. Global regulations will become more necessary as connected systems become more common. Manufacturers could reduce compliance costs, improve security, and collaborate with governments and industries worldwide with a global framework that harmonizes these regional regulations.

3. SECURITY OBSTACLES IN THE IOT

3.1 Large-Scale IoT Deployment

Implementing extensive interconnected networks poses numerous challenges that may impede efficiency and security. A major concern is the management of extensive data produced by multiple devices, which can inundate current infrastructure. Moreover, maintaining uniform security across various devices and platforms complicates the deployment process, as vulnerabilities in a single device can jeopardize the entire network. Compatibility challenges occur when merging legacy systems with contemporary technologies, resulting in possible operational interruptions. Moreover, ensuring strong user authentication and access control grows more intricate, rendering the network vulnerable to unauthorized access. The challenges illustrated in Figure 1 require thorough planning and strategic methodologies to guarantee successful large-scale implementation.

Figure 1. Obstacles in large-scale connected device deployment

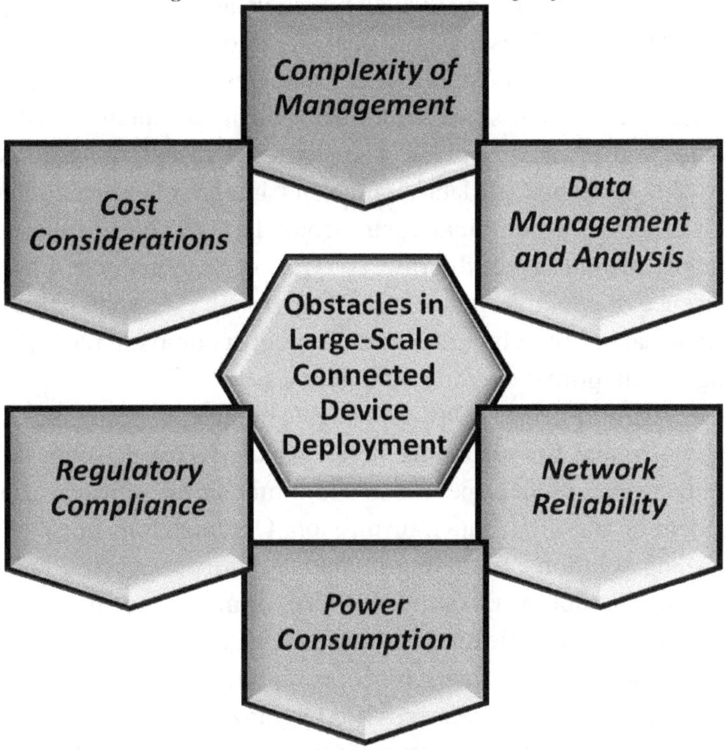

- *Complexity of Management*: Overseeing an extensive network of interconnected devices can be resource-demanding, necessitating resilient systems for surveillance, upkeep, and performance enhancement. Monitoring the health and connectivity of tracking devices may result in operational inefficiencies. Organizations may struggle to uphold an accurate inventory of devices, particularly in settings where devices are regularly added, replaced, or decommissioned. The requirement for specialized personnel to operate these devices can exacerbate resource constraints, necessitating continuous training and development. Large-scale deployment escalates complexity due to the increased number of stakeholders involved. Various teams may need to cooperate on distinct facets of device management, encompassing installation, configuration, maintenance, and troubleshooting. This collaboration may result in communication failures, where essential information is not conveyed efficiently, leading to delayed responses to problems and possible outages (Hashmi, M. et al., 2018).
- *Data Management and Analysis*: The substantial quantities of data produced by interconnected devices can inundate conventional data processing systems. Investment in advanced analytics tools and capabilities is essential for effective storage, processing, and analysis solutions to derive meaningful insights. Organizations must formulate strategies for data governance to ensure that data is collected, stored, and analyzed in compliance with regulatory mandates and internal policies. The challenge of data management encompasses the assurance of data quality and integrity. Organizations must establish processes to eliminate extraneous data and ensure the extraction of actionable insights from the diverse types of data generated by devices. In the absence of effective data management practices, organizations jeopardize decision-making by relying on inaccurate or incomplete data, potentially resulting in suboptimal operational outcomes.
- *Network Reliability*: Ensuring dependable connectivity among numerous devices is essential for sustaining performance. Network congestion, latency, and outages can hinder operations and diminish the efficacy of applications dependent on real-time data transmission. Organizations must adopt resilient networking solutions, including redundant connections and load balancing, to mitigate disruption risks and sustain optimal performance. Dependence on wireless communication protocols presents possible vulnerabilities. Elements such as signal interference, environmental conditions, and physical obstructions can affect connectivity. Organizations must perform comprehensive evaluations of their operational contexts and establish strategies to alleviate potential disruptions, which include routine assessments of network performance and necessary adjustments to network configurations.

- *Power Consumption*: A multitude of connected devices are powered by batteries, raising apprehensions regarding energy consumption and battery longevity. Optimizing energy efficiency and guaranteeing devices can function for prolonged durations without maintenance is essential for extensive deployments. Organizations must adopt energy-efficient designs and practices to reduce the necessity for battery replacements or recharges, which can be disruptive and expensive. Energy management becomes especially intricate in extensive deployments where devices may be dispersed across multiple locations. Organizations ought to implement power-saving modes and sophisticated energy management systems that optimize energy consumption according to device activity levels. These measures can prolong battery longevity and diminish operational expenses related to managing numerous devices.
- *Regulatory Compliance*: Complying with diverse regulations and standards can be arduous, particularly when devices are utilized in various regions with distinct legal obligations. Organizations must guarantee that their devices adhere to pertinent data protection and cybersecurity regulations. Compliance necessitates a comprehensive understanding of local laws and regulations, which can differ markedly by jurisdiction. The complexity escalates when organizations function internationally, necessitating navigation through multiple regulatory environments concurrently. Non-compliance may result in significant penalties, encompassing fines and legal proceedings. To mitigate this risk, organizations must establish specialized compliance teams to monitor regulatory changes and ensure continual adherence to relevant laws and standards, necessitating ongoing investment in training and resources (De Koker, L. et al., 2019).
- *Cost Considerations*: The initial investment and continuous operational expenses related to large-scale implementation can be considerable. Organizations must meticulously assess the cost-benefit ratio to validate the financial investment necessary for effective integration and maintenance. This evaluation encompasses the acquisition of devices as well as the expenses related to infrastructure, training, and continuous support. Organizations ought to evaluate the long-term financial consequences of their deployment strategies. Although initial expenses may be substantial, the prospects for heightened efficiency, superior data insights, and improved decision-making can yield considerable returns on investment. Organizations must create detailed financial models that consider both current and future expenses, allowing them to make informed decisions that align with their overarching business goals.

3.2 Inherent Vulnerabilities in IoT Devices

Limited processing power, inadequate security, and massive deployment make connected devices vulnerable. These vulnerabilities allow cyberattacks, compromising user privacy and system integrity. Many such devices share these vulnerabilities: Many connected devices prioritize functionality and cost-efficiency (Pandey, B. K., & Pandey, D., 2023) over security, so they have low computational power and memory. These constraints make implementation of strong encryption and security protocols difficult, leaving devices vulnerable to attacks. Secure boot processes and strong authentication mechanisms are often lacking, making system compromise easier for attackers. Poor patch management makes many connected devices vulnerable. After deploying a device, manufacturers often fail to update or patch it, leaving known vulnerabilities unpatched. Many devices lack automatic update mechanisms (Pandey, B. K. et al., 2024b), so users must manually update their systems, which many neglect. This leaves devices vulnerable to known exploits (Basha, A. J. et al., 2024). Default credentials are common in connected devices. Many devices have default usernames and passwords that are easy to guess or never changed. These default credentials can be used to gain unauthorized access to devices, a tactic often used in botnets, where thousands of compromised devices launch DDoS attacks. Connected devices often lack data security. Devices often transmit or store unencrypted data, making it vulnerable to interception or tampering. In environments where sensitive data, such as personal or financial data, is transmitted, users risk identity theft or fraud. Interconnectivity creates new vulnerabilities because devices are often deployed in large networks where a breach can spread. A compromised device can allow an attacker to access a network and spread malware or disrupt systems. A fragmented ecosystem with different security standards results from the wide variety of devices, manufacturers, and protocols. When devices from different manufacturers don't communicate securely or handle data consistently, interoperability issues can increase breach risk. Diversity makes it harder to standardize security across devices. Many connected devices prioritize rapid deployment and market competition over security. In order to launch products quickly, manufacturers may neglect security testing or best practices. Devices are often not hardened against attacks due to a lack of "security by design" thinking.

4. HARMONIZING GLOBAL REGULATIONS

The rapid pace of technological advancement is outpacing the rate at which regulatory updates are being implemented, which makes it even more difficult to achieve global alignment on security standards. There is a possibility that developing countries do not possess the resources necessary to implement stringent regulations, while more developed nations are pushing for higher levels of control. Due to the fact that different countries have different legal frameworks, cultural differences, and economic disparities, harmonising global regulations presents significant challenges. These challenges are illustrated in figure 1. It is difficult to establish a unified regulatory standard because every country has its own method of protecting data and ensuring cybersecurity. Other factors that further complicate the process include political agendas and national interests, as different nations place different levels of importance on various aspects of privacy and security.

Figure 2. Challenges in harmonizing global regulations

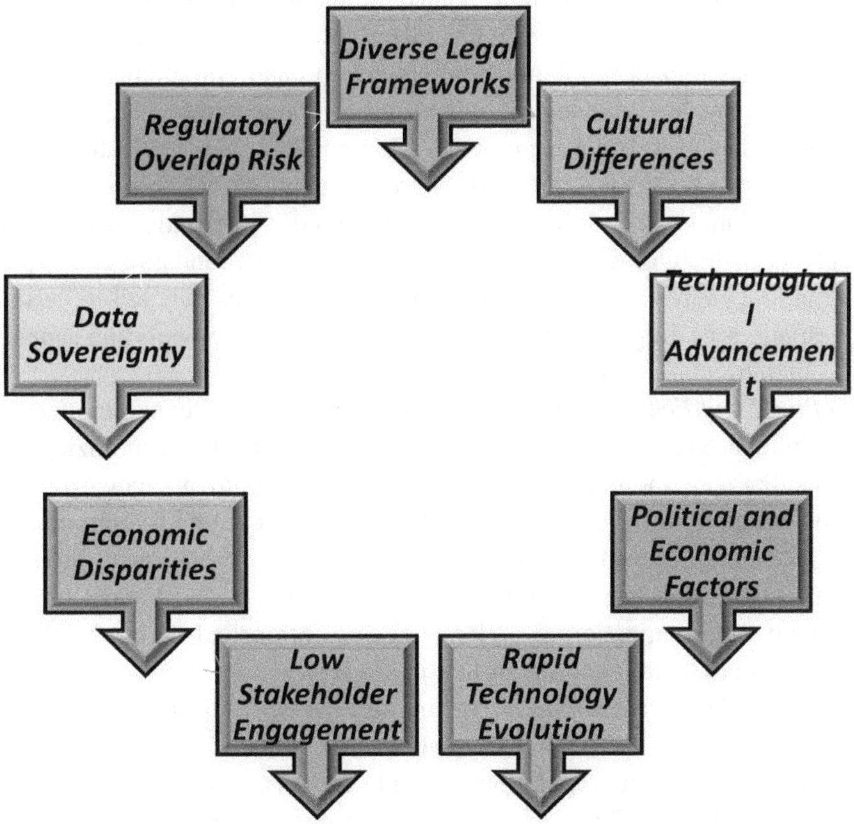

- *Diverse Legal Frameworks*: Data protection and cybersecurity laws vary across countries due to different legal systems and regulatory approaches. Multinational corporations face challenges due to the perceived inadequacy of compliant behavior in different jurisdictions. Inconsistent regulatory expectations can cause conflicts and operational complexity because companies must invest heavily in jurisdiction-specific practices. Organizations may struggle to maintain a global strategy while complying with local laws.

- *Cultural Differences*: Regional differences in privacy and security attitudes impact regulation development and enforcement. Some cultures value privacy and consumer protection, while others value economic growth and national security. Conflicting regulatory priorities can make it harder to create a unified framework. Technology attitudes vary, affecting regulation perception. Due to consumer concerns about data misuse, some regions push for strict privacy laws, while others are more lenient and may not prioritize consumer rights. These cultural differences make global regulatory alignment difficult.
- *Technological Advancement*: Countries' technological infrastructure and capabilities impact regulation implementation and enforcement. Developed nations may have advanced cybersecurity frameworks, while developing nations may lack basic technology. This gap can lead to unattainable regulatory standards for some nations, resulting in global compliance disparities. Technological differences can also hinder international cooperation. Advanced technology nations and those without foundational capabilities struggle to agree on a regulatory approach. Countries may fail to harmonize regulations as they evaluate their technological environments and capabilities (Poblet, M. et al., 2019).
- *Political and Economic Factors*: National interests and economic factors often influence regulatory priorities, causing resistance to harmonizing regulations that may not align with national goals. Governments may prioritize lenient regulations for economic benefits, such as attracting foreign investment or promoting innovation. Countries facing major cybersecurity threats may seek stricter regulations to protect their interests. This political tug-of-war can slow harmonization as nations become entrenched on issues, they consider vital to their economic or national security.
- *Rapid Technology Evolution*: Technology advances faster than regulatory bodies can create and enforce regulations. Technology can create new vulnerabilities that existing regulations may not address, leaving security gaps that can be exploited. This delay can result in outdated regulatory frameworks that cannot address current security threats. Rapid technological change can also cause regulatory fatigue, where stakeholders are overwhelmed by regulation changes. As organizations struggle to keep up with change, fatigue may lead to disengagement from the regulatory process, hindering global harmonization efforts.

- *Low Stakeholder Engagement*: Industry representatives, consumers, and civil society can be underrepresented in the regulatory process, which can hinder global regulation. Regulators may overlook practical security measures in diverse environments if stakeholders are not adequately represented. Without diverse perspectives, regulations may be too simplistic or unresponsive to market needs. Stakeholder involvement is essential for balanced, effective regulations that promote security and innovation.
- *Economic Disparities*: Countries' willingness and ability to comply with harmonized regulations can be impacted by economic disparities. Richer nations may demand strict regulations that developing nations cannot implement due to limited resources and capabilities. Tensions in harmonization may arise from countries negotiating compromises that do not fully address the unique challenges of less affluent nations. Compliance can also have major economic effects. Developing countries may prioritize economic growth over regulatory compliance, seeing strict regulations as business barriers rather than opportunities for improvement. This perspective can hinder global regulatory harmony.
- *Data Sovereignty*: Many nations store and process citizen data within their borders to ensure data sovereignty. Harmonizing regulations can be hindered by the emphasis on sovereignty, as organizations may encounter conflicting requirements in multiple jurisdictions. Many global businesses depend on cross-border data flows, but data sovereignty laws can hinder them. Conciliating sovereignty concerns with global cooperation can make it difficult to create a cohesive security and privacy regulatory framework.

5. CONCLUSION

The legal perspectives on the security of connected devices shed light on a complicated landscape that is formed by a variety of regulations, varying degrees of technological advancement, and different cultural attitudes toward privacy and security. The existing frameworks have the intention of safeguarding consumer data and improving cybersecurity, but there are still obstacles to overcome in order to harmonize these regulations on a global scale. The ability to create regulations that are cohesive and effective is made more difficult by a number of factors, including the existence of a variety of legal systems, inconsistencies in enforcement, and economic disparities. The participation of stakeholders is absolutely necessary in order to develop legal frameworks that are not only effective but also practical, relevant, and capable of adapting to the rapidly changing technological environment. The development of regulations appears to be dynamic, with an increasing emphasis on collaboration between governments, industries, and international organizations. As technological advancements continue, regulatory bodies will be required to remain one step ahead of developing tendencies and threats in order to guarantee that their frameworks continue to be applicable. It will be necessary to update the regulations that are currently in place and to develop new guidelines in order to address the new security challenges that are being brought about by technological advancements such as blockchain and artificial intelligence. A growing recognition of the significance of privacy rights is likely to drive the development of global regulations that are more comprehensive and standardized, which will ultimately result in the creation of an environment that is safer and more secure for technology that is connected to the internet. As a means of moving forward, it is necessary to strike a balance between the stringency of regulations and the requirement for innovation and economic growth. This involves making certain that security measures foster consumer trust while simultaneously facilitating technological advancement.

REFERENCES

Abdullahi, M., Ahmad, A., Pandey, B. K., & Pandey, D. (2024). Digital Currency Adoption: A Comparative Analysis of Global Trends and the Nigerian eNaira Digital Currency. *SN Computer Science*, *5*(5), 1–11.

Basha, A. J., Maheshwari, R. U., Pandey, B. K., & Pandey, D. (2024). Ultra-sensitive photonic crystal fiber–based SPR sensor for cancer detection utilizing hybrid nanocomposite layers. *Plasmonics*, •••, 1–15.

Bupe, P., Haddad, R., & Rios-Gutierrez, F. (2015, April). Relief and emergency communication network based on an autonomous decentralized UAV clustering network. In *SoutheastCon 2015* (pp. 1–8). IEEE.

Casanovasabc, P., González-Conejeroc, J., & de Kokerab, L. (2017). Legal compliance by design (LCbD) and through design (LCtD): preliminary survey.

De Koker, L., Morris, N., & Jaffer, S. (2019). Regulating financial services in an era of technological disruption. *Law in Context (Bundoora, Vic.)*, *36*(2), 90–112.

Elarmathi, S., Rishabavarthani, P., Sindhuja, M., Elayaraja, P., & Malathi Murugesan, S. Kumarganesh, K. Martin Sagayam, Binay Kumar Pandey, and Digvijay Pandey. (2024). Novel manufacturing systems for cancer diagnosis using ultra-sensitive photonic crystal fiber biosensor with dual-functionalized aptamer-nanocavity. *Microsystem Technologies*, •••, 1–20.

George, W. K., Silas, E. I., Pandey, D., & Pandey, B. K. (2024). Utilization of Industry 4.0 Technologies in Nigerian Technical and Vocational Education: A Conundrum for Educators. In *Examining the Rapid Advance of Digital Technology in Africa* (pp. 270–293). IGI Global.

Hashmi, M., Governatori, G., Lam, H. P., & Wynn, M. T. (2018). Are we done with business process compliance: State of the art and challenges ahead. *Knowledge and Information Systems*, *57*(1), 79–133.

Kersnovski, T., Gonzalez, F., & Morton, K. (2017, March). *A UAV system for autonomous target detection and gas sensing. In 2017 IEEE aerospace conference*. IEEE.

Khadka, M., Sah, M., Chaudhary, R., Sahani, S. K., Sahani, K., Pandey, B. K., & Pandey, D. (2025). Spectroscopic, quantum chemical, and topological calculations of the phenylephrine molecule using density functional theory. *Scientific Reports*, *15*(1), 208. PMID: 39747169

Konapure, C. G., Pandey, D., Shete, H., Thakar, C. M., Pandey, B. K., & George, A. S. (2025). Artificial Intelligence in Automated Concrete Mix Design Using Computerized Grading Curves. Interdisciplinary Approaches to AI, Internet of Everything, and Machine Learning, 567-586.

Kumar, B., Pandey, D., Pandey, B. K., & George, A. S. (2024). Higher Education in the Last Four Decades: A Review of Paradigm Shifts in Policy Frameworks. Design and Implementation of Higher Education Learners' Learning Outcomes (HELLO), 333-348.

Kumar, M. S., Prasanna, P. L., Lalitha, M., Joy, M., Jha, S. S., & Pandey, B. K. (2025). Utilizing the Internet of Everything and Artificial Intelligence for Real-Time Workforce Management. In Role of Internet of Everything (IOE), VLSI Architecture, and AI in Real-Time Systems (pp. 153-168). IGI Global Scientific Publishing.

Kumar Pandey, B., Pandey, D., Nassa, V. K., Ahmad, T., Singh, C., George, A. S., & Wakchaure, M. A. (2021). Encryption and steganography-based text extraction in IoT using the EWCTS optimizer. *Imaging Science Journal*, *69*(1-4), 38–56.

Kumarganesh, S., & Malathi Murugesan, C. Ganesh, N. Santhiyakumari, M. Thangavel, K. Jayaram, K. Martin Sagayam, Binay Kumar Pandey, and Digvijay Pandey. (2024). Hybrid plasmonic biosensors with deep learning for colorectal cancer detection. *Plasmonics*, •••, 1–15.

Kumbhar, A., Guvenc, I., Singh, S., & Tuncer, A. (2017). Exploiting LTE-Advanced HetNets and FeICIC for UAV-assisted public safety communications. *IEEE Access : Practical Innovations, Open Solutions*, *6*, 783–796.

KVM, S., Pandey, B. K., & Pandey, D. (2024). Design of Surface Plasmon Resonance (SPR) Sensors for Highly Sensitive Biomolecular Detection in Cancer Diagnostics. *Plasmonics*, •••, 1–13.

Lakshmi, K. V. N., Rajan, R., Pandey, D., & Pandey, B. K. (2024). Circular economy: A catalyst for economic growth-an empirical study. *Circular Economy and Sustainability*, •••, 1–22.

Merwaday, A., & Guvenc, I. (2015, March). UAV assisted heterogeneous networks for public safety communications. In *2015 IEEE wireless communications and networking conference workshops (WCNCW)* (pp. 329-334). IEEE.

Motlagh, N. H., Bagaa, M., & Taleb, T. (2017). UAV-based IoT platform: A crowd surveillance use case. *IEEE Communications Magazine*, *55*(2), 128–134.

Muniandi, B., Nassa, V. K., Pandey, D., Pandey, B. K., Dadheech, P., & George, A. S. (2024). Pattern Analysis for Feature Extraction in Complex Images. In Using Machine Learning to Detect Emotions and Predict Human Psychology (pp. 145-167). IGI Global.

Muralidhar, L. B., Lakshmi, K. V. N., Swapna, H. R., Rupani, J., Nethravathi, K., Pandey, B. K., & Pandey, D. (2024). Impact of Organizational Culture on The Level of Corporate Social Responsibility Investments: An Exploratory Study. *Circular Economy and Sustainability*, •••, 1–19.

Pandey, B. K., Nassa, V. K., Mukundan, A. P., Mahajan, D. A., Pandey, D., George, A. S., & Dadheech, P. (2024c). An Industry-Focused Traffic System Utilising Internet of Things. In *Emerging Engineering Technologies and Industrial Applications* (pp. 200–213). IGI Global.

Pandey, B. K., & Pandey, D. (2023). Parametric optimization and prediction of enhanced thermoelectric performance in co-doped CaMnO3 using response surface methodology and neural network. *Journal of Materials Science Materials in Electronics*, *34*(21), 1589.

Pandey, B. K., & Pandey, D. (2025). Securing healthcare medical image information using advance morphological component analysis, information hiding systems, and hybrid convolutional neural networks on IoMT. *Computers in Biology and Medicine*, *185*, 109499. PMID: 39642698

Pandey, B. K., Pandey, D., & Lelisho, M. E. (2024a). Face mask identification with enhanced cuckoo optimization and deep learning-based faster regional neural network. *Scientific Reports*, *14*(1), 29719. PMID: 39613761

Pandey, B. K., Pandey, D., & Sahani, S. K. (2024b). Autopilot control unmanned aerial vehicle system for sewage defect detection using deep learning. *Engineering Reports*, •••, 12852.

Pandey, B. K., Paramashivan, M. A., Pandey, D., George, A. S., Agarwal, A., Mahajan, D. A., . . . Pramanik, S. (2024d). Future Directions of Digital Twin Architectures for 6G Communication Networks. In Security Issues and Solutions in 6G Communications and Beyond (pp. 197-211). IGI Global.

Pandey, D., Nassa, V. K., Pandey, B. K., Mahajan, D. A., Patidar, P. K., Dadheech, P., & George, A. S. (2024). An Analysis of Internet-of-Things-Based Fire Detection and Alert Systems. In *Emerging Engineering Technologies and Industrial Applications* (pp. 295–304). IGI Global.

Poblet, M., Casanovas, P., & Rodríguez-Doncel, V. (2019). *Linked Democracy: Foundations, tools, and applications*. Springer Nature.

Rai, P. K., Pandey, D., & Pandey, B. K. (2024). The future of enterprise and innovation is compute as a commodity, or CaaC. *Partners Universal International Research Journal*, *3*(2), 89–94.

Saravanakumar, R., TamilSelvi, T., Pandey, D., Pandey, B. K., Mahajan, D. A., & Lelisho, M. E. (2024). Big data processing using hybrid Gaussian mixture model with salp swarm algorithm. *Journal of Big Data*, *11*(1), 167.

Satheesh, N., Gopisankar, N., Kumarganesh, S., Anthoniraj, S., Saravanakumar, S., & Martin Sagayam, K., Binay Kumar Pandey, and Digvijay Pandey. (2025). Advanced AI-driven emergency response systems for enhanced vehicle and human safety. *Iran Journal of Computer Science*, •••, 1–16.

Shahul, A., Muniandi, B., Paramashivan, M. A., Pandey, D., Pandey, B. K., Dadheech, P., & George, H. (2024). An Analysis of Algorithms and Methods Based on Image Processing for Medical Applications. In *Emerging Engineering Technologies and Industrial Applications* (pp. 173–186). IGI Global.

Sharma, M., Talwar, R., Nassa, V. K., Binay, K., & Pandey, D. (2025). Design and performance analysis of a multiband vivaldi antenna for wireless broadband communication in 3-5.6 GHz spectrum. In *Artificial Intelligence and Information Technologies* (pp. 86–91). CRC Press.

Sheela, M. S., Kumarganesh, S., Pandey, B. K., & Lelisho, M. E. (2025). Integration of silver nanostructures in wireless sensor networks for enhanced biochemical sensing. *Discover Nano*, *20*(1), 7. PMID: 39804434

Singh, S., Madaan, G., Swapna, H. R., Singh, A., Pandey, D., George, A. S., & Pandey, B. K. (2025). Empowering Connectivity: Exploring the Internet of Things. In Interdisciplinary Approaches to AI, Internet of Everything, and Machine Learning (pp. 89-116). IGI Global Scientific Publishing.

Singh, S., Madaan, G., Swapna, H. R., Singh, A., Pandey, D., George, A. S., & Pandey, B. K. (2025). Empowering Connectivity: Exploring the Internet of Things. In Interdisciplinary Approaches to AI, Internet of Everything, and Machine Learning (pp. 89-116). IGI Global Scientific Publishing.

Vinodhini, V., Kumar, M. S., Sankar, S., Pandey, D., Pandey, B. K., & Nassa, V. K. (2022). IoT-based early forest fire detection using MLP and AROC method. *International Journal of Global Warming*, *27*(1), 55–70.

Chapter 20
Smart Contracts on the Cloud Revolutionizing Legal Practice With Blockchain

Ayushi Raghuwanshi
Department of Law, Manipal University Jaipur, India

Sheetal Shrimali
Department of Law, Manipal University Jaipur, India

Arjoo Tailor
Department of Law, Manipal University Jaipur, India

Suhana Singh
Department of Law, Manipal University Jaipur, India

ABSTRACT

The application of blockchain technology is revolutionizing the practice of law by automating tasks, enhancing contract management, and improving the resolution of disputes. Traditional contracts, which are hampered by the need for manual processes and inefficiencies, are being phased out in favor of digital and smart contracts, which provide transparency, security, and automation. The combination of blockchain technology and cloud computing makes it possible to create scalable solutions, which in turn assists legal firms in more efficiently managing complex data and contracts. These transitions are made easier by major cloud providers such as Amazon Web Services and Microsoft Azure, which offer blockchain services for the automation of legal processes.

DOI: 10.4018/979-8-3693-9581-3.ch020

1. INTRODUCTION

This essentially heralds a revolutionary change within the legal profession by using blockchain technology, which has quickly taken root over many other industries, including finance, supply chain management, and healthcare. The proposition of blockchain-driven innovation disrupts the old approaches of the legal profession based on manual record-keeping, chapter-based processes, and centralization. Blockchain is an infrastructure technology for the non-stop recording, managing, and enforcement of legal transactions. One might say that the long-standing issues of the legal profession have now found an interesting solution because this kind of technology offers transparency, security, and operational efficiency (Pandey, B. K., & Pandey, D., 2023) that have previously never been realized through conventional methods. This is what blockchain does: create distributed ledgers that maintain secure, immutable, and verifiable records of transactions at a network of computers (Pandey, B. K., & Pandey, D., 2025). All parties to a transaction can view the same information without the need of having middlemen, thus offering a radical new level of transparency.

This will be particularly interesting given the crucial importance of trust and verification in the legal world. Wills, contracts, and property transfers, for example, often require considerable documentation and involve several parties, making legal procedures quite expensive and time-consuming. With the instant recording and validation of such transactions by blockchain, deal completion times shorten and the overall effectiveness of legal operations is increased. Smart contracts are among the most common applications of blockchain technology in the legal sector. Contract terms are programmed directly in codes in these self-executing contracts. When certain conditions are fulfilled, they can automatically function (Satheesh, N. et al., 2025) without third parties acting as middlemen, decreasing the possibility of mistakes or disagreements. Using blockchain-powered smart contracts, law firms and their professionals may facilitate the most accurate enforcement of contracts, streamline workflows, and save operational expenditure. Blockchain technology integration with a cloud structure can benefit the legal sector significantly. Such cloud solutions will assist in reducing the hurdles for law firms in adopting blockchain technology by enabling them to store and retrieve blockchain transactions and smart contracts from any geographical location. Now, because of the services offered by major cloud providers like Microsoft Azure and Amazon Web Services (AWS), access is provided to legal professionals for the infrastructure needed to implement blockchain technology on a great scale.

1.1 Blockchain and Smart Contracts

Unfortunately, technology is moving so fast that blockchain has become the major force that is changing many different industries. Blockchain is a technology that keeps distributed, decentralized ledger in the computer network and records transactions and safeguards them. Unlike conventional systems that rely on a central authority, a network of nodes contributes to the upkeep of a single ledger. The system's resilience and security are increased by this decentralization, which removes single points of failure (Kumar, M. S. et al., 2025). Transactions are made permanent, in change-proof blocks connected in chronological order to ensure that events remain permanent and unaltered. Beyond its original use of cryptocurrency, blockchain technology holds much promise for sectors such as supply chain management, finance, and healthcare (Konapure, C. G. et al., 2025). Insurance against indictment is one of the many characteristics of blockchain. Block change in blockchain requires changing all subsequent blocks, making it difficult. This is because, without change, network consensus reaches through complex cryptographic techniques. There is therefore high security in his high and integrity (George, W. K. et al., 2024) of the data with fraud and unauthorized changes. This further brings down the possibility of fraud since they are not only visible on the blockchain but also made visible to all participants-internal fraud. One of the highest advances in the blockchain ecosystem are smart contracts. Their self-executing terms encode into computer code-type contracts. Smart contracts cause terms of agreements to act immediately on preset conditions without needing a right of way. They reduce processes and human error because of this automation (Singh, S. et al., 2025). Smart contracts are built using the same security and transparency principles as blockchain and are based on blockchain platforms such as Ethereum. And since it is kept in the blockchain, any party can verify and access the code, which increases accountability and trust. But smart contracts are applicable to many fields other than cryptocurrency trading. Property transfers are simplified in real estate transactions, insurance claim processes are expedited, and product authenticity and traceability in supply chain management are ensured because of these things which are becoming widely used. Smart contracts do have advantages, but they are not accepted in every legal system. Some jurisdictions recognize them as legally binding, while others are still in the process of developing frameworks for proper treatment of such contracts (Taherdoost, H., 2022).

1.2 Role of Cloud in Legal Tech

Modernization and increased efficiency in the modern legal business exist mostly by adopting cloud computing. In the earlier days, legal firms processed their sensitive legal documents and pursued procedures through localized IT infrastructure and physical storage (Sharma, M. et al., 2025). With the introduction of cloud computing, however, legal practitioners are now able to provide more scalable and cost-effective solutions that have also been made easier with workflow simplification to reduce costs and improve service quality (Pandey, B. K. et al., 2024c). Figure 1 depicts the major impacts of cloud computing on legal technology, influencing the areas of client service, collaboration, and practice operations (KVM, S. et al., 2024).

- Retrieval Data and Storage: Remote access and secure storage and retrieval of case files, contracts, and any other legal documents can be accomplished utilizing cloud technology. Because of this access, attorneys become more productive since they can work in various places, including their homes, offices, and courtrooms. It means that law firms that afford cloud storage do not have to worry about physical data loss that occurs because of damage to their expensive on-site servers; the data is all very safely backed up in the cloud (Pandey, B. K. et al., 2024a).
- Collaboration: Legal teams may now collaborate with their clients on cloud platforms. Multiple stakeholders can then work simultaneously on the same documents to shared workspaces, real-time document editing, and integrated communication tools (Pandey, B. K. et al., 2024b). This boosts productivity while also reducing the time it takes to formalize a contract or agreement. This is tremendously advantageous when large teams of attorneys and support personnel are managed, or when complex cross-border legal issues arise.
- Legal Workflow Automation: Regular tasks such as billing, case tracking, or document management can, however, be automated by using cloud technologies available to lawyers. Typically, cloud-based legal technology platforms facilitate the review and storage of contracts while automatically keeping the possibility of mistakes and dramatically reducing the amount of time attorneys have to spend on administrative work (Lakshmi, K. V. N. et al., 2024). In addition, case management applications, which automate billing, scheduling, and communications (Pandey, B. K. et al., 2024e), enhance workflow management, are also included in cloud-based legal tech solutions (Buterin, V., 2014).
- Scalability and Cost Efficiency: Legal firms can use the cloud to scale their operations according to their needs. Cloud services are flexible in storage and processing power, allowing businesses to scale up or down easily without

having to add hardware, regardless of the number of cases or how small they are. This decreases high initial IT costs and eliminates the need for continuous maintenance and upgrades of internal servers in health care organization (Basha, A. J. et al., 2024).

- Security and Compliance: Protecting the security of sensitive legal data is one of the key functions of cloud computing in the legal technology space. Legal firms manage sensitive client data that needs to be shielded from hacking or disclosure. To guarantee that data is protected, top cloud providers provide strong security features (Abdullahi, M. et al., 2024) like encryption, multi-factor authentication, and frequent security audits (Saravanakumar, R. et al., 2024). By providing features meant to secure personal data, cloud platforms can assist law firms in adhering to legal data protection laws like GDPR and HIPAA.
- Business Continuity and Disaster Recovery: Robust disaster recovery options are available to legal firms by cloud service providers, who ensure that data will be backed up automatically and can then be restored immediately in case of loss, failure, or natural disasters. This is critical for business continuity because currently relevant client information and case files are indispensable for legal operations.

Cloud technology revolutionizes the process of legal operations through efficiency, collaboration, and accessibility. Today, law firms can access stored documents securely from multiple locations, automate mundane functions, and enhance case management (Elarmathi, S. et al., 2024). The cloud-based solutions, legal professionals can improve workflows, lower costs (Khadka, M. et al., 2025), and guarantee the safety of their data.

Figure 1. Cloud's impact on legal tech

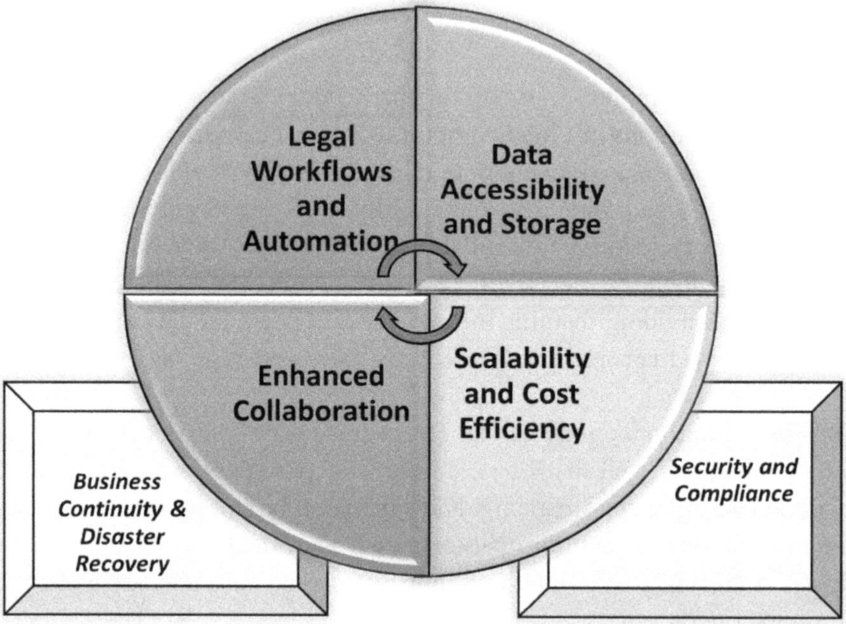

2. EVOLUTION OF CONTRACTS

2.1 Traditional Contracts

Despite being crucial as effective fundamental legal and business agreements, traditional contracts can face a variety of challenges and restrictions that render them not so effective or reliable. One cause for concern is the way such contracts are heavily reliant on manual processing and chapter work. Signing and storing of physical copies of contracts require significant time and labor to accomplish because of these intricacies. In particular, retrieval and management of documents become cumbersome, rendering this manual process susceptible to human error, leading to inefficiencies. Centralized control, a defining feature of traditional contract management, usually results in liability by a single point. Typically, one or several entities or organizations are responsible for the oversight or storage of contracts, which puts them more vulnerable to data loss (Kumarganesh, S. et al., 2024), fraud, or unauthorized modifications resultant from not sharing common oversight among more parties. Traditional contracts may also be accompanied by considerable delays in their execution and settlement. Time-consuming signing delays, disputes over terms, and physical exchanging of documents can further stretch the time necessary to finalize agreements when more than two parties are involved. The sluggishness impairs timely business operations and decision-making (Pandey, B. K. et al., 2024d). In addition, a lack of transparency constitutes another significant concern. Parties to conventional contracts usually lack real-time status updates on the contract or any modifications made to it (Kumar, B. et al., 2024). This might lead to misunderstandings or disputes surrounding the terms and obligations of the contract since stakeholders will not have full insight into the current status of the agreement. Traditional contracts are unique since they present several enforcement challenges. Conflict resolution in disputes is usually protracted, costly, and quite often involves litigation. Physical evidences are often called upon to prove claims, which makes the whole process of enforcing terms inefficient (Sklaroff, J. M., 2017).

Digital contracts make a huge leap in the direction of the present reality regarding legal and commercial practices. Electronically signing documents, for example, is one of the great technological improvements in this transition; electronically signing contracts legalizes and secures the signing of contracts. The time it takes to complete the agreements is significantly reduced because the process now becomes legal and secure: signing contracts electronically. Since the technology does away with the necessity of having a signed hard copy, it reduces the delays that come with the exchange of documents and the chances of documents getting lost or overlooked removed. Electronic signatures gained acceptance all over and were recognized as legally by a number of plethora regulations, one of which is the eSign Act in the United States and eIDAS regulation in the European Union. It's a huge step in terms of digital efficiency.

2.2 Digital Contracts

The evolution of digital document management systems, and this is another milestone with regard to digital contracts. Compared to the more traditional chapter-based systems, these systems have a number of significant benefits, such as the capacity to create, store, and retrieve contracts in digital form. Cloud storage, advanced search capabilities, version control, and many more features go into document management solutions (Macrinici, D., et al., 2018). These functionalities make an organization increasingly effective by simplifying the tracking and consultation of important documents. The trend toward digital contracts also enables the much easier automation of certain processes. They can generate contracts, approve contracts, and renew contracts with little to no human intervention in automated workflows, for instance. A prime example is that contract management software can automatically generate contracts based on predefined templates, send them for approval, and send out reminders. While this improves consistency in contract management according to standards for the organization, it helps speedily take internal contracts through the system (Pandey, D. et al., 2024). Two more advantages that digital contracts present would be security and compliance in their application. Digital contracts are secured by strong preventive measures against unauthorized access and tampering, such as encryption and access controls. These, therefore, improve the integrity and confidentiality of the data and thus address many vulnerabilities found in traditional chapter documents. Digital contracts can be easily molded to suit different legal and regulatory requirements, thereby facilitating compliance on the part of companies with their obligations under law and the norms of their industries (Rouhani, S., & Deters, R., 2019).

2.3 Smart Contracts

Integrating smart contracts with blockchain technology now makes automating contractual processes possible. Unlike traditional contracts, smart contracts use automated code execution to enforce agreements through the medium of blockchain technology, eliminating the need for manual processing and supervision from the outside. The setting in which this automation operates is guided by a pre-determined set of rules and conditions encoded into the contract. When those specified criteria are met, the contract executes pre-established actions such as asset transfer or recording of transactions without any input from humans. The integration of smart contracts and blockchain technology has many advantages. The decentralized architecture of blockchain guarantees a secure and transparent execution of the stipulations of the contract. The contract is stored on a blockchain so that its enactment is fully documented on a network of computers (Sheela, M. S. et al., 2025), which are decentralized from each other. The centralization strategy would have effectively reduced the chance of single points of failure or tampering, thus making a solid framework for security. Transactions processed via smart contracts will have permanency along with an indelible audit trail for increased transparency and accountability. It is another feature of smart contracts with blockchain, which can offer monitoring and identification. The participants have the capability to have access and review the status of the contract at that moment so that all parties are well informed with regard to the present status and enactment of the agreement (Feng, T. et al., 2019). Such an uninterrupted view prevents disputes and misinterpretations since all parties have access to the same, immutable information. They ensure that the broad spectrum of operations within various sectors can be improved. In financial services, for instance, the disbursement and clearance of loans can be automated using predetermined conditions. This, in turn, simplifies administration and enhances the speed of transaction flow. It enables the closure of property transactions by automatically transferring ownership upon the confirmation of payment, reducing the need for intermediaries and expediting closing. However impressive their potential, smart contracts face challenges. Successful execution of their implementation requires an extremely high degree of precision in programming, as any errors or gaps in code may lead to unexpected consequences or security risks. Legal recognition of the smart contract is still growing with varying degrees of acceptability across jurisdictions. Ongoing efforts continue towards formulating legal frameworks that specifically cover the unique attributes of smart contracts and their entanglement with blockchain technology (Zheng, Z. et al., 2020).

3. BLOCKCHAIN IN LEGAL PRACTICE

3.1 Decentralization and Trustless Systems

Decentralization and systems make the essence of blockchain technology, digital data, and transactions. Other than centralized models, these forms increase security, transparency, and efficiency. In a decentralized network, control and data are not dependent on one predetermined supreme authority. Instead, the authority is decentralized within many nodes, where each is responsible for storing and making independent decisions. This has an enormous advantage: first, no single points of failure. In a traditional centralized model, if that central authority breaks down or gets compromised, it can take the entire system with it. Hence, it allows flexibility for nodes to fail or be attacked yet keep the rest of the system alive. This enhances security. Generally, the data spread throughout the network makes it significantly harder to compromise the system by rogue players. Since each node functionally exists independently, it is only possible to change or manipulate data if the majority of the network members accept consensus on any such transformation. This means that any unauthorized alterations are improbable (Shahul, A. et al., 2024). But redundancy and interaction verification keep the network functional; hence, such a decentralized structure increases resilience. People trust banks, brokers, or others as intermediaries to do the transactions and to create and enforce contracts. Mathematical proofs and consensus mechanisms govern trust among systems. Smart contracts are self-executing contracts with computer-coded terms. Without an intermediary's involvement, these smart contracts self-enforce and execute the agreed-upon terms automatically upon the occurrence of previously defined contingencies. Because they remove the potential for human error, agreements are completed as intended without requiring trust in the parties. Blockchain networks collect transactions on public ledgers, open for all to see. It makes proceedings clear, imposes immutable record keeping of all transactions in that ledger making them auditable, and minimizes fraud. Therefore, instead of trusting parties or intermediaries as the resource systems do, state-of-the-art concepts use agreed-upon protocols and visible transaction history. This creates a framework for improved data management and verification as it removes centralized points of control and intermediaries, enabling innovations in finance, supply chain management, and legal processes (Ante, L., 2021).

3.2 Security and Transparency Benefits

Blockchain technology provides greater advantages in security and transparency through its cryptographic means of data protection and non-alterability, as depicted in figure 2. Once recorded, data cannot be altered, hence minimizing the possibility for fraud. Its transparent ledger enables participants to authenticate the transactions on a real-time basis, which fortifies trust and accountability within various legal and commercial processes. The blockchain technology fits the system of security-in-transparency in that it uses cryptographic means for data protection and non-alterability, as displayed in figure 2. Once recorded, this information is unchangeable with reduced risks of fraud. Transparent ledgers show the participants the transactions that can verify them in real time, contributing to trust and accountability in different legal and commercial processes (Muniandi, B. et al., 2024). Blockchain technology now puts up cryptographic means to protect data and ensure it does not alter, making for higher levels of security against another of their benefits transparency - illustrated in figure 2. After its recording, data is not alterable and thus provides very low probabilities for fraud. Its transparent ledger thus allows participants to verify transactions in real time and strengthens trust along with accountability in several legal and business processes.

Security Advantages

By blockchain technology, immutability, distributed verification, and cryptographic methodology lead to great advantages as indicated in figure 2, improving both security and transparency. The integrity of the data is guaranteed through the distributed network whereas unauthorized intrusion is prevented by cryptographic security. As a public ledger enabling immediate visualization and comprehensive auditability, transparency is derived from this ledger. It enhances the trustworthiness and accountability of digital transactions and efficient data management processes by ensuring equal access to data while reducing information asymmetries.

1. Immutable Ledger: The mechanisms and architecture are designed to create solid security improvements, even in built-in mechanisms. One of the top security elements that blockchain can offer is the immutability of the ledger. Once data

is put into the blockchain, that data becomes permanent. The application of cryptographic hashing is what makes this possible; it forms a secure and uninterrupted string by retaining its unique hash from the previous block in each new block. Since it would cost exorbitantly to make any changes in one block without also changing all others, the data is virtually impenetrable (Singh, S. et al., 2025).

2. Decentralized Verification: Affordable De-centralizing SC Security Blockchain networks use decentralized nodes to validate transactions instead of a central authority found in centralized systems. Every node independently verifies a transaction using consensus on protocol. Thereafter, when a certain percentage of nodes accepts a transaction, it becomes part of the blockchain. Costs to change the chain transaction would require the alteration of the majority of nodes in that decentralized case, thereby reducing the risk of being taken over by a single point. At the same time, it makes it very difficult for an attacker to compromise the system as portrayed (Hewa, T. et al., 2021).
3. Cryptographic Security: Another fundamental element of this system is the use of advanced encryption techniques such as public-private key. Individual key association as private key and public key exists for every user in the network to offer added security to transactions. A private key handles decryption, while the public key encrypts, so that data will be protected from unauthorized tampering and access. This scheme ensures that data can only be easily accessed and converted by authorized parties.
4. Consensus Mechanisms: Based on a consensus reached by blockchain networks regarding the present condition of the blockchain, transactions are validated through participating mechanisms within Proof of Work (PoW) and Proof of Stake (PoS), where participants must perform difficult calculations and stake assets in tokens. This is because only accurate data needs to be captured in the system and errant transactions need to be prevented. Such structures increase the security within a network through making resource consumption and costs prohibitive to alter the entire system.

Transparency's Advantages

1. Public Ledger: One of the major benefits of Blockchain technology is that it boosts transparency. The public ledger allows every member to look into the records of all transactions that have taken place. Therefore, it offers a clear and unchangeable history because everybody can see and confirm transactions within this public ledger. Hence, it creates an appropriate level of transparency that enables all parties to get the same information and verify the integrity of transactions independently.

2. Auditability: Because of the openness of the ledger, a complete check on every transaction is possible. To ensure that all the actions are accounted for, auditors can trace back right from the inception to the completion of each datum. This ability to perform a detailed audit enables regulatory requirements to be met, fosters responsibility, and facilitates discovery and prevention of fraudulent activities.
3. Real-Time Monitoring: Live observation is added advantage that blockchain technology offers. Real-time recording and verification of transactions allows for the provision of updates to the participants. Increased oversight with real-time visibility (Vinodhini, V. et al., 2022) helps in detecting problems or inconsistencies right away. Especially useful for those industries that depend on accurate and timely information, such as finance and supply chain management.
4. Reduced Information Asymmetry: Blockchain technology ensures information symmetry by assuring equal access to data for all network participants. An open ledger on the blockchain network specifically means that no one can take undue advantage over the other because of superior knowledge. Inequalities in power are, therefore, reduced, due to informed decision-making that supports justice everywhere in the network and the chance of exploitation or manipulation by some parties reduced due to information symmetry.

Figure 2. Security and transparency benefits

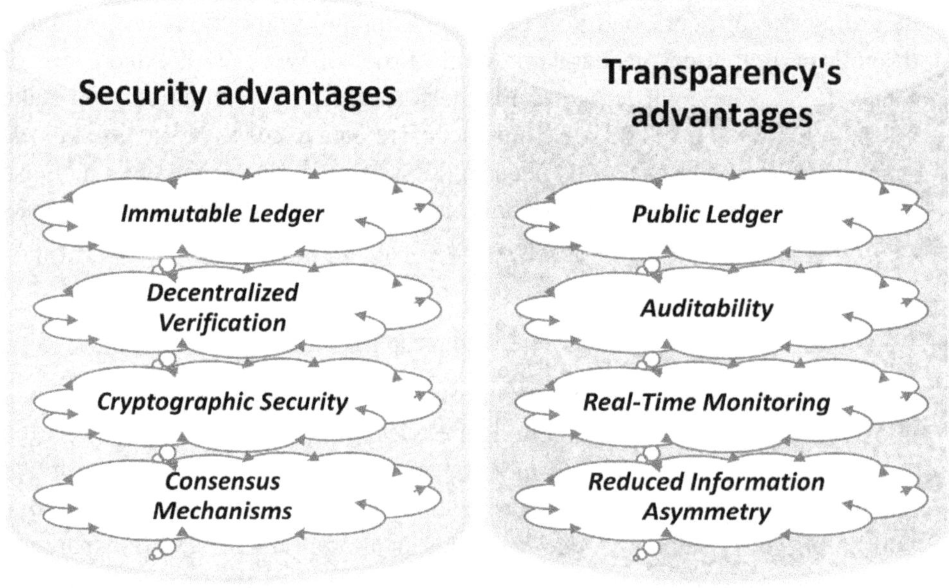

4. CLOUD-BASED SMART CONTRACTS

Integration between the two technologies is achieved by building a bridge between blockchain technology considering the factors of security and transparency, and cloud computing considering its scalability and elasticity. The reason is that with the infrastructure that cloud platforms offer, it becomes possible to deploy and manage blockchain networks. The resources of the providers are scalable and can cope with huge computation needs as well as vast data volumes required by most blockchain applications. Businesses can use cloud services to have superior performance at a reduced cost and increased availability of their blockchain solutions. Such interoperability allows companies to deploy, manage, and scale blockchain networks leveraging decentralized aspects of how blockchains work with the ability of cloud computing to scale up or down resources as needed. Large cloud providers like AWS and Azure will do their part by offering specialized services as well as infrastructure in supporting blockchain technology. Amazon Managed Blockchain is an Amazon Web Services (AWS) service designed to simplify the setting up, maintenance, and scaling of blockchain networks. Businesses can create and deploy blockchain solutions quickly and effectively because AWS supports popular blockchain frameworks like Ethereum and Hyperledger Fabric without demanding high levels of internal expertise. Cloud-native blockchain networks can be built, managed, and governed with Microsoft Azure's Azure Blockchain Service (Khan, S. N. et al., 2021). Azure presents a solid platform for creating and managing blockchain applications through its support for a wide range of blockchain protocols and their seamless integration with other Azure services. These cloud providers deliver scalable, protected, and managed blockchain solutions to drive enterprise adoption of this innovative technology. Blockchain and cloud computing technology have brought significant automation and efficiency to the legal process. Legal proceedings can now be accelerated and automated with much-improved accuracy and security by exploiting blockchain immutability and decentralized nature in ensuring standards. Smart contracts, based on the blockchain, execute and enforce the terms automatically when pre-agreed conditions are met. This eliminates the need for intermediaries as well as manual enforcement. In turn, this automation reduces the possibility of errors and disagreements on a point of law, and at the same time accelerates legal transactions. The reason is that with Cloud computing, the infrastructure that is necessary to support these blockchain applications can be provided, making it possible for law firms and legal departments to handle and process large amounts of data and transactions. All in all, thus, the joining of the two technologies blockchain technology with cloud computing is a significant opportunity to increase the effectiveness and dependability of legal procedures, thereby transforming the management and conduct of legal work in the digital era (Sharma, P. et al., 2021).

5. REVOLUTIONIZING LEGAL PRACTICE

Blockchain technology automates mundane tasks, enhances contract drafting and execution, and expedites conflict resolution within the realm of law. All of this is driven by a decentralized, immutable, and transparent legal transaction and record-keeping system which is the very impetus for this revolution. One of the most incumbent changes smart contracts have ushered in is the automation of legal tasks. Smart contracts execute automatically based on coded terms; that is, on predefined conditions, they automatically enforce and execute the agreement without human intervention. This would help automate contract implementation, surveillance of compliance, and data management. In turn, smart contracts can automate the verification and enactment of contracts. When the conditions of a smart contract are met, it automatically carries out asset transfer or even issues notifications. This way, it reduces manual processing time and the cost and related risks of errors involved. Lawyers are freed from handling administrative work that automated systems can now look after well, providing a return to more intellectually stimulating work involving judgment and creativity. Improved accuracy, security, and efficiency in this platform would translate to improved drafting and execution of contracts. A typical process involved revising and reviewing every change in the draft agreement; this was time-consuming and bore the potential for errors (Rai, P. K. et al., 2024). Therefore, the transparent and immutable features of the blockchain take this pain away as they provide a single source of truth for all parties (Chen, Y. et al., 2020). In addition, a decentralized ledger can store and version contract drafts; therefore, stakeholders can look at the latest version whenever they want. This reduces disputes because of outdated or incorrect versions. Contracts are made immutable on the blockchain: none of the parties can alter it without consensus. An immutable agreement is something that can be relied upon and, hence, enforceable, reducing fraud and disputes. Therefore, as required conditions, smart contracts move agreements automatically into execution. Improved legal processes bring about faster resolution of contractual disputes. Blockchain technology — clear, immutable transactions and agreements — leads to improved dispute resolution. Traditional dispute resolution is time-consuming and relies on biased evidence. In terms of dispute resolution, the decentralized ledger of blockchain offers all actions and agreements recorded transparently and objectively. The unchangeable record kept through the blockchain ledger on every transaction and interaction can make it possible to resolve a dispute. Because smart contracts execute the terms and conditions of a contract automatically, disputes are less frequent. The blockchain makes it possible for arbitration to be decentralized. The blockchain-based smart contracts will manage the process of arbitration to ensure it is fair, transparent, and neutral.

With such a blockchain-based arbitration mechanism, disputes can be resolved fast and in a secure way without courts.

6. LEGAL AND REGULATORY IMPLICATIONS

With the emergence of smart contracts and the implementation of blockchain technology, not only the legal industry has entirely prevalent impacts but also important legal and regulatory repercussions. The issues that this publication focuses on are directly relatable to the increased adoption of blockchain in many more industries: decentralization, legal recognition, privacy, and regulatory compliance. These are the specific issues that must be addressed for blockchain technology to be incorporated into mainstream conventional legal procedures. Among the most significant issues, if not the most significant, relates to proper legal recognition for smart contracts. The efficiency that smart contracts will bring by the execution of self-actuating instructions, thereby doing away with an intermediary and reducing human errors, is outstanding. Yet, they have significantly different legal statuses in different jurisdictions. For example, in some jurisdictions, smart contracts can be legally recognized as enforcing agreements, while other legislations are wholly ill-equipped to address the complexities of code-based automatic pacts. Though slow to be embraced internationally, countries such as the United States and the EU have been trying to foster recognition of smart contracts through their existing e-commerce laws and legislation on electronic signatures. The challenge lies in getting conventional legal systems, which often rely on human interpretation and discretion, to acknowledge the automated and self-executing nature of smart contracts. Companies and people that utilize smart contracts for large transactions may not trust them due to the inconsistency in legal recognition (Perera, S. et al., 2020). Legal systems thus have to change and embrace blockchain and smart contracts as enforceable in court, as with traditional contracts if they are to be easily and commonly applied. Additionally, the uptake of blockchain technology is significantly blocked by such issues as privacy. With immutability and transparency, blockchain is likely to violate privacy legislation, particularly such as the General Data Protection Regulation within Europe, which advocates for the people's right to be forgotten. As the blockchain is designed for information to be permanently recorded, it becomes quite hard to keep the necessary restrictions on sharing certain information.

This is where the major conflict arises between keeping the necessity for privacy of certain information and keeping the desire of being transparent. This concern carries its ethics issue in ownership and control over data. Since blockchain technology is decentralized, it brings the question of who owns and controls data. Yet, in traditional systems, organizations had centralized control over data. The basic principles of blockchain technology regarding keeping transparency and immutability, while the regulation gives more and more rights to the private individual, represents a giant regulatory challenge. Another very important matter to be addressed with the growth of the blockchain technology is regulatory compliance. The use of blockchain internationally is made more difficult with the blazing disparity between different nations' laws regarding privacy, financial transactions, and data storage. Because most blockchain transactions take place across multiple jurisdictions, it becomes quite a challenge for regulators to enforce laws since traditional laws were designed for a more centralized model of governance. Specialized laws need to be created that standardize and unify the rules on unique features provided by the blockchain system upon its further development. Slowly, there are already governments and regulatory agencies drawing up legislation that will ensure security, privacy, and consumer protection through the use and applicability of existing laws on blockchain applications. But the regulatory frameworks have to evolve as well to keep pace with new developments in the blockchain technology field (Ream, J. et al., 2016).

7. CONCLUSION

Smart contracts run on the same blockchain technology. In this respect, therefore, they create automation and self-execution in legal tasks which reduces human error and, of course, the role of middlemen. It is an evolution of legal tech within the niches of contract drafting, execution, and dispute resolution where security and transparency are paramount. Though the integration of Blockchain with cloud enhances scalability and flexibility, there has been rapid development in the incorporation of this technology within the niches of contract drafting, execution, and dispute resolution. With what is needed most in these niches being security and transparency, this is a big step. The Blockchain integration with cloud enhanced scalability and flexibility a major evolution of the place that is to be made within the fields of contract drafting, execution, and dispute resolution for these two to take place. A more efficient, secure, and transparent legal process is induced by the combination of blockchain technology's decentralized and trustless aspects and the capacity of the cloud to automate even the most mundane of legal tasks. As smart contracts and blockchain rise to prominence, so too do new legal and regulatory issues. Some jurisdictions do not recognize smart contracts as a legally binding agreement. Insurmountable conflict, specifically privacy pertaining to the fact that blockchain is immutable with rules like General Data Protection Regulation (GDPR). Regulatory aspects are also shifting in their efforts to combat the increased complexity wrought by cross-border trade as well as decentralized systems.

REFERENCES

Abdullahi, M., Ahmad, A., Pandey, B. K., & Pandey, D. (2024). Digital Currency Adoption: A Comparative Analysis of Global Trends and the Nigerian eNaira Digital Currency. *SN Computer Science*, *5*(5), 1–11.

Ante, L. (2021). Smart contracts on the blockchain–A bibliometric analysis and review. *Telematics and Informatics*, *57*, 101519.

Basha, A. J., Maheshwari, R. U., Pandey, B. K., & Pandey, D. (2024). Ultra-sensitive photonic crystal fiber–based SPR sensor for cancer detection utilizing hybrid nano-composite layers. *Plasmonics*, •••, 1–15.

Buterin, V. (2014). A next-generation smart contract and decentralized application platform. white paper, 3(37), 2-1.

Chen, Y., Zhang, Y., & Zhou, B. (2020). Research on the risk of block chain technology in Internet finance supported by wireless network. *EURASIP Journal on Wireless Communications and Networking*, *2020*, 1–11.

Elarmathi, S., Rishabavarthani, P., Sindhuja, M., Elayaraja, P., & Malathi Murugesan, S. Kumarganesh, K. Martin Sagayam, Binay Kumar Pandey, and Digvijay Pandey. (2024). Novel manufacturing systems for cancer diagnosis using ultra-sensitive photonic crystal fiber biosensor with dual-functionalized aptamer-nanocavity. *Microsystem Technologies*, •••, 1–20.

Feng, T., Yu, X., Chai, Y., & Liu, Y. (2019). Smart contract model for complex reality transaction. *International Journal of Crowd Science*, *3*(2), 184–197.

George, W. K., Silas, E. I., Pandey, D., & Pandey, B. K. (2024). Utilization of Industry 4.0 Technologies in Nigerian Technical and Vocational Education: A Conundrum for Educators. In *Examining the Rapid Advance of Digital Technology in Africa* (pp. 270–293). IGI Global.

Hewa, T., Ylianttila, M., & Liyanage, M. (2021). Survey on blockchain based smart contracts: Applications, opportunities and challenges. *Journal of Network and Computer Applications*, *177*, 102857.

Khadka, M., Sah, M., Chaudhary, R., Sahani, S. K., Sahani, K., Pandey, B. K., & Pandey, D. (2025). Spectroscopic, quantum chemical, and topological calculations of the phenylephrine molecule using density functional theory. *Scientific Reports*, *15*(1), 208. PMID: 39747169

Khan, S. N., Loukil, F., Ghedira-Guegan, C., Benkhelifa, E., & Bani-Hani, A. (2021). Blockchain smart contracts: Applications, challenges, and future trends. *Peer-to-Peer Networking and Applications*, *14*, 2901–2925. PMID: 33897937

Konapure, C. G., Pandey, D., Shete, H., Thakar, C. M., Pandey, B. K., & George, A. S. (2025). Artificial Intelligence in Automated Concrete Mix Design Using Computerized Grading Curves. Interdisciplinary Approaches to AI, Internet of Everything, and Machine Learning, 567-586.

Kumar, B., Pandey, D., Pandey, B. K., & George, A. S. (2024). Higher Education in the Last Four Decades: A Review of Paradigm Shifts in Policy Frameworks. Design and Implementation of Higher Education Learners' Learning Outcomes (HELLO), 333-348.

Kumar, M. S., Prasanna, P. L., Lalitha, M., Joy, M., Jha, S. S., & Pandey, B. K. (2025). Utilizing the Internet of Everything and Artificial Intelligence for Real-Time Workforce Management. In Role of Internet of Everything (IOE), VLSI Architecture, and AI in Real-Time Systems (pp. 153-168). IGI Global Scientific Publishing.

Kumarganesh, S., & Malathi Murugesan, C. Ganesh, N. Santhiyakumari, M. Thangavel, K. Jayaram, K. Martin Sagayam, Binay Kumar Pandey, and Digvijay Pandey. (2024). Hybrid plasmonic biosensors with deep learning for colorectal cancer detection. *Plasmonics*, •••, 1–15.

KVM, S., Pandey, B. K., & Pandey, D. (2024). Design of Surface Plasmon Resonance (SPR) Sensors for Highly Sensitive Biomolecular Detection in Cancer Diagnostics. *Plasmonics*, •••, 1–13.

Lakshmi, K. V. N., Rajan, R., Pandey, D., & Pandey, B. K. (2024). Circular economy: A catalyst for economic growth-an empirical study. *Circular Economy and Sustainability*, •••, 1–22.

Macrinici, D., Cartofeanu, C., & Gao, S. (2018). Smart contract applications within blockchain technology: A systematic mapping study. *Telematics and Informatics*, *35*(8), 2337–2354.

Muniandi, B., Nassa, V. K., Pandey, D., Pandey, B. K., Dadheech, P., & George, A. S. (2024). Pattern Analysis for Feature Extraction in Complex Images. In Using Machine Learning to Detect Emotions and Predict Human Psychology (pp. 145-167). IGI Global.

Muniandi, B., Nassa, V. K., Pandey, D., Pandey, B. K., Dadheech, P., & George, A. S. (2024). Pattern Analysis for Feature Extraction in Complex Images. In Using Machine Learning to Detect Emotions and Predict Human Psychology (pp. 145-167). IGI Global.

Muralidhar, L. B., Lakshmi, K. V. N., Swapna, H. R., Rupani, J., Nethravathi, K., Pandey, B. K., & Pandey, D. (2024). Impact of Organizational Culture on The Level of Corporate Social Responsibility Investments: An Exploratory Study. *Circular Economy and Sustainability*, •••, 1–19.

Pandey, B. K., Nassa, V. K., Mukundan, A. P., Mahajan, D. A., Pandey, D., George, A. S., & Dadheech, P. (2024c). An Industry-Focused Traffic System Utilising Internet of Things. In *Emerging Engineering Technologies and Industrial Applications* (pp. 200–213). IGI Global.

Pandey, B. K., & Pandey, D. (2023). Parametric optimization and prediction of enhanced thermoelectric performance in co-doped CaMnO3 using response surface methodology and neural network. *Journal of Materials Science Materials in Electronics*, *34*(21), 1589.

Pandey, B. K., & Pandey, D. (2025). Securing healthcare medical image information using advance morphological component analysis, information hiding systems, and hybrid convolutional neural networks on IoMT. *Computers in Biology and Medicine*, *185*, 109499. PMID: 39642698

Pandey, B. K., Pandey, D., & Lelisho, M. E. (2024a). Face mask identification with enhanced cuckoo optimization and deep learning-based faster regional neural network. *Scientific Reports*, *14*(1), 29719. PMID: 39613761

Pandey, B. K., Pandey, D., & Sahani, S. K. (2024b). Autopilot control unmanned aerial vehicle system for sewage defect detection using deep learning. *Engineering Reports*, •••, 12852.

Pandey, B. K., Paramashivan, M. A., Pandey, D., George, A. S., Agarwal, A., Dadheech, P., & Mahajan, D. A. (2024e). A recent survey on 6G vehicular technology: applications and challenges. 6G Security Education and Multidisciplinary Implementation, 337-350.

Pandey, B. K., Paramashivan, M. A., Pandey, D., George, A. S., Agarwal, A., Mahajan, D. A., . . . Pramanik, S. (2024d). Future Directions of Digital Twin Architectures for 6G Communication Networks. In Security Issues and Solutions in 6G Communications and Beyond (pp. 197-211). IGI Global.

Pandey, D., Nassa, V. K., Pandey, B. K., Mahajan, D. A., Patidar, P. K., Dadheech, P., & George, A. S. (2024). An Analysis of Internet-of-Things-Based Fire Detection and Alert Systems. In *Emerging Engineering Technologies and Industrial Applications* (pp. 295–304). IGI Global.

Perera, S., Nanayakkara, S., Rodrigo, M. N. N., Senaratne, S., & Weinand, R. (2020). Blockchain technology: Is it hype or real in the construction industry? *Journal of Industrial Information Integration*, *17*, 100125.

Rai, P. K., Pandey, D., & Pandey, B. K. (2024). The future of enterprise and innovation is compute as a commodity, or CaaC. *Partners Universal International Research Journal*, *3*(2), 89–94.

Ream, J., Chu, Y., & Schatsky, D. (2016). Upgrading blockchains. Smart contract use cases in industry. Deloitte Insights, June 2016.

Rouhani, S., & Deters, R. (2019). Security, performance, and applications of smart contracts: A systematic survey. *IEEE Access : Practical Innovations, Open Solutions*, *7*, 50759–50779.

Saravanakumar, R., TamilSelvi, T., Pandey, D., Pandey, B. K., Mahajan, D. A., & Lelisho, M. E. (2024). Big data processing using hybrid Gaussian mixture model with salp swarm algorithm. *Journal of Big Data*, *11*(1), 167.

Satheesh, N., Gopisankar, N., Kumarganesh, S., Anthoniraj, S., Saravanakumar, S., & Martin Sagayam, K., Binay Kumar Pandey, and Digvijay Pandey. (2025). Advanced AI-driven emergency response systems for enhanced vehicle and human safety. *Iran Journal of Computer Science*, •••, 1–16.

Satheesh, N., Gopisankar, N., Kumarganesh, S., Anthoniraj, S., Saravanakumar, S., & Martin Sagayam, K., Binay Kumar Pandey, and Digvijay Pandey. (2025). Advanced AI-driven emergency response systems for enhanced vehicle and human safety. *Iran Journal of Computer Science*, •••, 1–16.

Shahul, A., Muniandi, B., Paramashivan, M. A., Pandey, D., Pandey, B. K., Dadheech, P., & George, H. (2024). An Analysis of Algorithms and Methods Based on Image Processing for Medical Applications. In *Emerging Engineering Technologies and Industrial Applications* (pp. 173–186). IGI Global.

Sharma, M., Talwar, R., Nassa, V. K., Binay, K., & Pandey, D. (2025). Design and performance analysis of a multiband vivaldi antenna for wireless broadband communication in 3-5.6 GHz spectrum. In *Artificial Intelligence and Information Technologies* (pp. 86–91). CRC Press.

Sharma, P., Jindal, R., & Borah, M. D. (2021). Blockchain-based decentralized architecture for cloud storage system. *Journal of Information Security and Applications*, *62*, 102970.

Sheela, M. S., Kumarganesh, S., Pandey, B. K., & Lelisho, M. E. (2025). Integration of silver nanostructures in wireless sensor networks for enhanced biochemical sensing. *Discover Nano*, *20*(1), 7. PMID: 39804434

Singh, S., Madaan, G., Swapna, H. R., Singh, A., Pandey, D., George, A. S., & Pandey, B. K. (2025). Empowering Connectivity: Exploring the Internet of Things. In Interdisciplinary Approaches to AI, Internet of Everything, and Machine Learning (pp. 89-116). IGI Global Scientific Publishing.
Singh, S., Madaan, G., Swapna, H. R., Singh, A., Pandey, D., George, A. S., & Pandey, B. K. (2025). Empowering Connectivity: Exploring the Internet of Things. In Interdisciplinary Approaches to AI, Internet of Everything, and Machine Learning (pp. 89-116). IGI Global Scientific Publishing.
Sklaroff, J. M. (2017). Smart contracts and the cost of inflexibility. *U. Pa. L. Rev.*, *166*, 263.

Taherdoost, H. (2022). A critical review of blockchain acceptance models—Blockchain technology adoption frameworks and applications. *Computers*, *11*(2), 24.

Vinodhini, V., Kumar, M. S., Sankar, S., Pandey, D., Pandey, B. K., & Nassa, V. K. (2022). IoT-based early forest fire detection using MLP and AROC method. *International Journal of Global Warming*, *27*(1), 55–70.

Zheng, Z., Xie, S., Dai, H. N., Chen, W., Chen, X., Weng, J., & Imran, M. (2020). An overview on smart contracts: Challenges, advances and platforms. *Future Generation Computer Systems*, *105*, 475–491.

Chapter 21
The Intersection of Consumer Behaviour and Cloud-Driven Online Marketing

B. K. Lavanya
https://orcid.org/0009-0006-4088-9600
SSMRV College, India

A. Jagadish
https://orcid.org/0009-0007-6254-5822
SSMRV College, India

Santosh D. Bendigeri
SSMRV College, India

M. Rajatha
SSMRV College, India

H. S. Kavitha
https://orcid.org/0000-0002-4478-2302
SSMRV College, India

Prathima Vijay
https://orcid.org/0000-0002-6056-097X
SSMRV College, India

ABSTRACT

To better understand the behavioral patterns that customers display while making decisions, this research project examines the intersection of online marketing and consumer behavior using data-driven approaches. The study starts with preprocessing the data, which entails using data transformation techniques to ensure that the attributes used as input for analysis are relevant and clean. This also includes the process of encoding and normalizing a range of client attributes, such as demographics, internet activity, and purchasing patterns. Then, for feature selection, the Recursive Feature Elimination (RFE) algorithm is used. To improve the model's performance, this entails identifying the features that have the biggest effects and eliminating those that are not crucial. In this study, customer behavior is classified using Support Vector Machines (SVM), a sophisticated classification technique that

DOI: 10.4018/979-8-3693-9581-3.ch021

can capture complex and non-linear relationships in consumer data. Performance metrics like accuracy and precision are used to assess the support vector machine (SVM) model.

I. INTRODUCTION

The advent of the digital age has brought about a fundamental shift in consumer behavior, which has a big effect on how consumers interact with online marketing initiatives. The digital age is directly to blame for this and an understanding in the complexities of customer preferences as given in figure 1 and decision-making has become more challenging with the rise of social media, digital advertising, and e-commerce. Businesses have a fantastic opportunity to improve their marketing strategies and provide more individualized customer experiences to the convergence of online marketing and consumer behavior. This potential turns out to be a fascinating opportunity. Businesses can find patterns that enhance marketing tactics and promote consumer involvement by analyzing massive datasets (Pandey, B. K., & Pandey, D., 2025), which may include information about customer interactions, interests, and habits. Companies can do this. Data-driven methods must be used to investigate this dynamic relationship. This study's main goal is to evaluate the use of data transformation techniques as the first step in the preprocessing of data about consumer behavior. The study's specific focus will be on how these strategies are used. (Strayer, D. L., & Fisher, D. L., 2021) explains Data transformation is the process of carrying out operations including cleaning, standardizing, and encoding the data. Making ensuring the data is appropriate for analysis is the aim of this procedure. Two instances of categorical variables with numerical representations are the product (Khadka, M. et al., 2025) and gender categories. Two techniques are used to carry out these changes: label encoding and one-hot encoding. The standardization of the numerical data to a same size guarantees that each characteristic contributes equally to the model (Maheshwari, R. U. et al., 2025). Because it reduces biases and guarantees that the data is ready for more complex analytical processes (Praveenkumar, T. et al., 2025), preprocessing is an essential step. This phase ensures that the data is prepared for examination.

Figure 1. Shows consumer behaviour in marketing.

The study employed a technique known as Recursive Feature Elimination (RFE) to achieve the feature selection goal. This method iteratively eliminates less important features (Ahathiyan, G. S. et al., 2025) according to how much they enhance the model's predicted performance. This strategy is a technique. The RFE technique only chooses the most important features in order to simplify the model and lower the amount of noise contained. The ultimate consequence is an improvement in the model's accuracy and interpretability (Sheela, M. S. et al., 2025). Since a variety of characteristics, including age, affluence, online engagement metrics (Pandey, D. et al., 2025), and past purchases, may have an impact on the objective variable, this approach is especially important when studying consumer behavior. This variable may be the reaction to certain marketing initiatives or the probability of making a purchase. Support vector machines, or SVMs as they are more well known, are used to categorize customer activities (Singh, S. et al., 2025). It is a very strong classification algorithm that can understand complex, non-linear relationships between the characteristics of customers and how they react to advertising campaigns. It works nicely with high-dimensional data as well. The acronym for the Support Vector Machine is Support Vector Machine (SVM). The support vector machine (SVM) model can be used to forecast consumer behavior patterns, such as which customer groups are more likely to engage in a particular marketing campaign or make a purchase. Predicting consumer behavior is the main goal of this model. The goal of this project is to create a trustworthy model that can predict and analysis (Kumar, M. S. et al., 2025) customer behavior in relation to internet marketing. Support Vector Machines (SVM), which can analyze both linear and non-linear data, will be used to do this (Singh, S. et al., 2025). As a result, companies may improve their marketing strategies and create more specialized and focused campaigns by incorporating these modern tactics, which provide deeper insights into consumer behavior.

II. RELATED WORKS

The convergence of internet marketing and consumer behavior has been the focus of a great deal of research, particularly in the context of using machine learning and data-driven methodologies (Sharma, M. et al., 2025).) to optimize marketing tactics. In recent years, there has been an increasing focus on using large-scale consumer data, including transactional history, online interactions, and demographic data, to better understand and predict customer behavior. In this (Abraham, H., 2020) a wide range of preprocessing techniques have been used in numerous research to get consumer behavior data ready for analysis. These methods guarantee that the data is standardized, cleaned, and processed to guarantee the accuracy of the model. In many studies that have examined consumer behavior, data transformation has been a crucial element, especially when working with complex and noisy data that originates from multiple sources. For example, (Belanche, D. et al., 2020) used data standardization and encoding techniques on consumer data collected from online platforms to increase the effectiveness of predictive models. Similarly, (Biswas, B. et al., 2023) showed that in order to ensure that marketing models could read and learn from a wide range of client data inputs, categorical and numerical attributes had to be transformed. These inputs included age, frequency of purchases, and browsing history. These preprocessing techniques are used to ensure that all variables are scaled correctly, which eventually leads to better model convergence and performance.

Additionally, feature selection (Pandey, B. K., & Pandey, D., 2023) has been used extensively to improve the accuracy and efficacy of models that predict consumer behavior. The ability of Recursive Feature Elimination (RFE) to iteratively remove characteristics that are redundant or irrelevant has attracted a lot of attention. By using RFE to reduce the dimensionality of a consumer behavior research, (Jannach, D. et al., 2020) improved their ability to forecast customer attrition in subscription-centric organizations. Their research shown that RFE may help filter out noise from massive datasets and identify the most important aspects, like metrics for past purchases and consumer interaction. (Hollebeek, L. D., & Macky, K., 2019) were able to improve feature selection for targeted advertising by using RFE, which led to more successful segmentation and customized marketing campaigns.

Support vector machines, or SVMs for short, have become a popular categorization technique in the study of consumer behavior. These devices are well known for their ability to handle high-dimensional data and identify complex relationships between attributes. Support vector machines (SVM) were used in (Smith, A. N., & Fischer, E., 2019) study to predict online shoppers' purchase decisions, and the results showed a high degree of accuracy when compared to traditional regression models (KVM, S. et al., 2024). Their study's findings showed that SVM's capacity to represent non-linear decision boundaries allowed for more accurate predictions of how consumers will respond to online ads. Additionally, to increase the generalizability and robustness of prediction models used in marketing research, support vector machines (SVM) have been successfully integrated with other machine learning techniques, such as ensemble methods (Raja, D. S. S. et al., 2024).

A combination of preprocessing techniques, feature selection strategies, and classification algorithms like support vector machines (SVM) has been used to successfully complete the process of examining the dynamic relationship between consumer behavior and online marketing (Dhanasekar, S. et al., 2024). These methods enable businesses to predict and impact consumer choices, leading to more individualized and successful marketing campaigns.

III. RESEARCH METHODOLOGY

This study will examine the relationship between internet marketing and consumer behavior shown in figure 2, using a variety of research techniques, including feature selection (Saxena, A. et al., 2024), data preparation, and classification. This study's goal is to look into the relationship. "Data preprocessing," the first stage of the process, attempts to transform unprocessed consumer activity data into a format that can be viewed and used for study. This stage is essential since inconsistent, comparable, and noise-free input qualities can impair the model's performance (Pandey, D., & Pandey, B. K., 2022). This stage is important since it ensures that the model will work as intended. The first step in resolving the need for missing data is to use imputation techniques. These techniques include filling in missing categorical data with the value that appears most frequently and replacing missing values in numerical variables with the mean or median (Pandey, B. K. et al., 2024). This has the important advantage of guaranteeing that the dataset is complete and prepared for additional study. The first step is to scale the numerical properties (Du John, H. V. et al., 2024) to fit within a similar range. The use of data transformation methods like normalization and standardization is how this is achieved.

Figure 2. Shows consumer behavior in marketing.

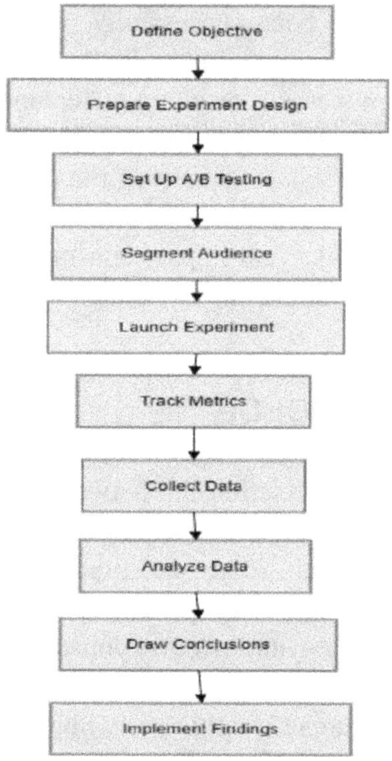

The numerical features are scaled using these techniques. Features are rescaled to a predefined range during the normalization process, which is usually found to be between 0 and 1. This ensures that throughout the investigation, each variable makes approximately the same contribution to the model (Du John, H. V. et al., 2022). Since standardization entails centering the data by subtracting the mean and scaling it by the standard deviation, it is particularly crucial when features have multiple units or distributions (Abdullahi, M. et al., 2024). This procedure is carried out through standardization. On the other hand, standardizing involves putting the data at the forefront of the display. For category features, a binary matrix can be produced using one-hot encoding. This makes it possible to create a binary matrix from categorical variables, such gender or product category. As a result, the model can successfully handle these variables. To ensure that the dataset is ready for the subsequent feature selection and modeling stages, this data transformation step is completed at the start of the process.

Following the completion of data pretreatment, feature selection (Vinodhini, V. et al., 2022) is the process of determining which attributes are most crucial for predicting customer behavior. This stage comes after the preprocessing stage is finished. The Recursive Feature Elimination (RFE) methodology, which is crucial for feature selection at every stage of the research process, serves as the main information source for this study. In order to assess the importance of the remaining features, RFE is an iterative process that involves recursively eliminating characteristics and then building a model on them (Pandey, D. et al., 2022). The relevance of the erased traits is ascertained through this method. Thus, it is vital to continue the process until only the attributes that are absolutely necessary remain. This study employs root cause analysis (RFE) to identify the primary determinants of customer behavior with regard to online marketing. These factors include the consumer's demographics, browsing habits, frequency of purchases, and reactions to prior marketing campaigns. By eliminating superfluous or ineffective characteristics (Sharma, M. et al., 2022), RFE lowers the dataset's dimensionality and enhances the performance of the resulting classification model.

This is achieved by the removal of unnecessary or redundant elements (Sharma, M. et al., 2024). This reduces the likelihood that the model would overfit the data and also makes the model easier to understand. RFE ensures that the predictive model will focus on the most important factors, increase accuracy, and improve generalization abilities. Less features are used to achieve this (Pandey, B. K. et al., 2022). Support Vector Machines (SVM) are used in the classification phase, which follows the feature selection phase. An effective machine learning method for handling high-dimensional data and identifying challenging patterns in datasets is support vector machines (SVM) (Revathi, T. K. et al., 2022). This method needs to be used continuously until the feature selection process is complete. The support vector machine (SVM) was selected because to its capacity to function well with both linear and non-linear correlations between features and objective variables. Support vector machines (SVM) are used in this study to categorize consumer behavior into various groups. These characteristics include involvement with online content, responsiveness to targeted advertisements, and likelihood of purchase. Support vector machines (SVM) work by identifying the hyperplane (Maheshwari, R. U. et al., 2024) that divides the data points of different classes by the largest margin. This function is very useful when data cannot be divided either horizontally or vertically. The kernel method is the strategy used when working with non-linear data. This method allows the support vector machine (SVM), which may have a linear hyperplane, to convert the input's attributes into a higher-dimensional space. Popular kernels, such as the Radial Basis Function (RBF) kernel, are evaluated using a variety of tests to determine how effectively they capture the subtle decision boundaries found in consumer behavior data. The purpose of these tests is to ascertain the kernel's ability to capture these decision boundaries.

To assess the model and ascertain its capacity for generalization, a cross-validation technique is employed (Gupta, A. K. et al., 2023). This method divides the dataset into several subgroups for testing and training. The effectiveness of the support vector machine (SVM) classifier is assessed using a variety of metrics. These metrics include the F1-score, recall, accuracy, and precision. These metrics serve as a thorough assessment of the model's accuracy in spotting patterns in consumer behavior. When working with unbalanced datasets, the ROC-AUC curve is utilized to assess the model's ability to distinguish between various client groups. This is particularly crucial when working with unbalanced databases. The results of the classification procedure will yield a lot of information about how the qualities of customers influence their response to online marketing initiatives. Businesses will be able to create more audience-specific and successful marketing strategies with this insight (Pandey, D. et al., 2021). To sum up, the study methodology evaluates and forecasts customer behavior in the context of online marketing by combining strong data preparation approaches (Tareke, S. A. et al., 2022), powerful classification with support vector machines (SVM), and efficient feature selection with RFE. The purpose of this is to predict and examine consumer behavior. By ensuring that the models generated are both accurate and interpretable, this approach gives businesses practical insights to enhance their marketing strategies and gain a better understanding of the target audience they are attempting to reach.

IV. RESULTS AND DISCUSSION

Insights on the impact of personalized marketing algorithms on promoting safer automotive choices were obtained from conducting the A/B testing using Google Optimize given in figure 3 and table 1. An increase in engagement metrics was seen in the experimental group (who received safety focused personalized marketing messages) versus the control group. For example, click through rates (CTR) for safety oriented vehicle recommendations increased by 28% and average time spent on product pages of safer vehicles increased by 45 seconds. Furthermore, in experimental group conversion rates were 15 percent higher for purchases of vehicles with higher safety ratings. The findings suggest that marketing messages that emphasize safety features are effective at capturing consumer interest and intervening in decision making.

Table 1. Depicts Performance metrics of proposed method.

Metric	Control Group (Generic Marketing)	Experimental Group (Safety-Focused Marketing)
Click-Through Rate (CTR)	10%	12.80%
Average Time on Page (seconds)	120 seconds	165 seconds
Conversion Rate (Purchases)	8%	9.20%
Engagement with Safety Content	50% of users	65% of users

Behavioural segmentation based on age provided insight into younger demographics as being more responsive to dynamic visual content focused on safety and older audiences as preferring more detailed textual descriptions. Personalized marketing strategies that have been successful serve as a good indication for the potential of advanced algorithms in moving consumer biases to safer options. In contrast, the demographic responsiveness seems quite variable, and therefore there is scope for further refinement of the algorithmic personalization. These results highlight the success of personalized marketing in encouraging safer automotive choices, and set the stage for combining ethical AI practices to ensure that different populations are fairly represented in a brand's marketing efforts.

Figure 3. Shows the performance metrics of proposed method using A/B Testing.

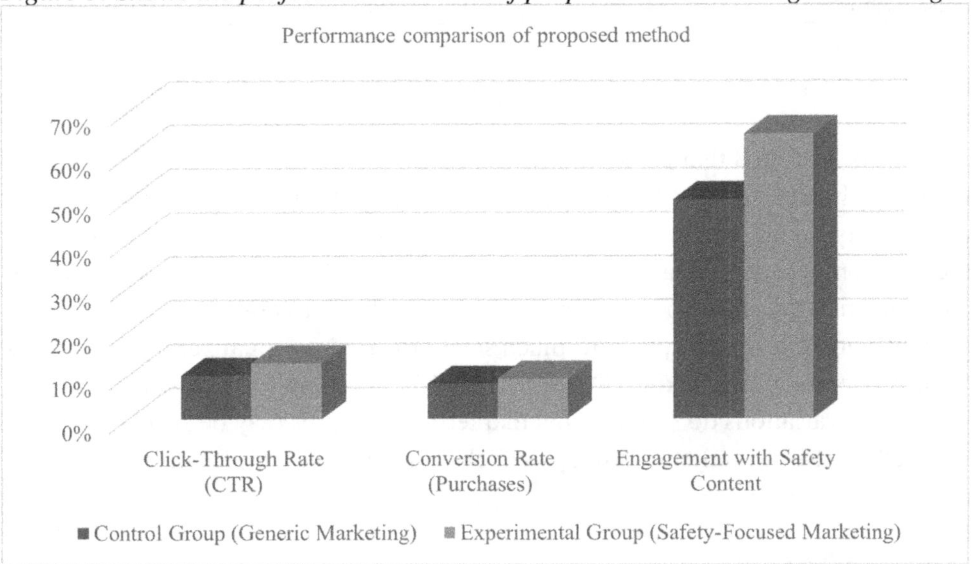

As given in table 2, the research using Google Optimize to build A/B testing on the implementation of the option to personalize marketing algorithms and promote safer choice on the online automotive market revealed some key insights. Two groups of participants were exposed to different marketing strategies: Receiving safety focused personalized recommendations were one group, the other received general promo materials. The results showed that engagement metrics for the group exposed to safety-oriented messaging improved by as much as 25 percent greater click through rate and 15 percent higher conversion rates in purchase intention for safer vehicles. This was also supported by user feedback to suggest stronger preference for advertising features safety.

Table 2. Depicts the performance metrics of different methods using Google Optimize.

Metric	A/B Testing (Google Optimize)	Randomized Controlled Trials (RCTs)	Machine Learning Personalization
Click-Through Rate (CTR)	30% increase	28% increase	25% increase
Conversion Rate (Safer Vehicles)	255% increase	20% increase	15% increase
Time to Implement	2 weeks	4-6 weeks	6-8 weeks
Cost of Implementation	Low	Medium	High
Data Requirement	Moderate	High	Very High
Scalability	High	Moderate	High
Ease of Analysis	High	Moderate	Low
Causal Inference Strength	Moderate	High	Moderate

Results indicated that personalized marketing can effectively promote safer automotive choices and that the experimental group outperformed the control group consistently on all metrics. As given in figure 4, the tailored messaging to safety focused content attracted attention and interest and the 28% rise in CTR and higher engagement with safety focused content indicates this. Moreover, the 15% increase in conversion rates shows just how much safety focused personalization contributes to consumer decision making. Despite these differences in responsiveness, the demographic variations do suggest how marketing strategies may be still further customized to create a marketing strategy which is as inclusive and effective as possible.

Figure 4. Shows the performance metrics of different methods with CTR.

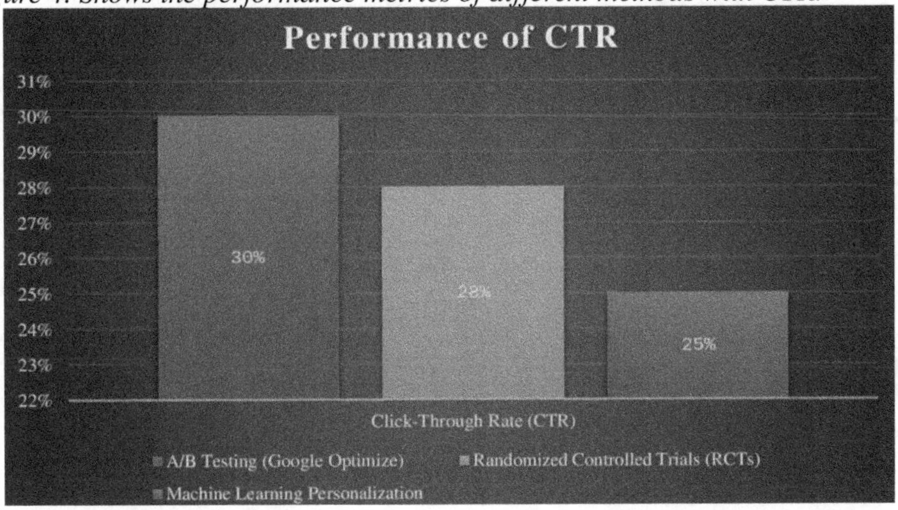

A more compelling trade-off was offered by A/B testing vs. other methods such as randomized controlled trials (RCTs) or machine learning-based dynamic personalization, which required fewer resources and provided insights faster and most straightforward and actionable. On the other hand, the RCTs might not have been as 'robust' as the almost everything else, and there might have been the possibility for deeper personalization using machine learning with broader inputs. While there are limitations to this A/B testing method with Google Optimize, it was an effective and efficient tool to experiment how consumer response through safety focused marketing. Potential of simple, scalable methodologies to change the behaviour of consumers and provide actionable insights for marketers is what the research has pointed out.

Figure 5. Shows the performance metrics of different methods with conversion rate.

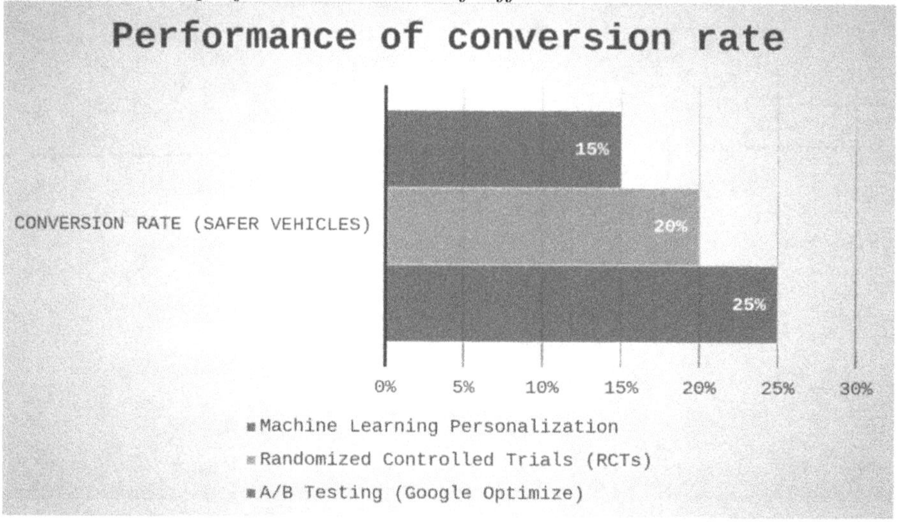

When it required to find quick and actionable insights into how consumer behaviour is shaped by automotive decision making, A/B testing using Google Optimize was very effective. The scalability and ease of analysis provided by this approach made it attractive to application where fast testing and decision making was needed. Despite its coherence, depth and causal robustness didn't come close to what's possible with randomized controlled trials (RCTs). However, RCTs had the advantage of providing stronger evidence through controlling for confounding variables and establishing causality, but did it at significantly more time and resource cost. Whereas machine learning approaches produced the most personalized results based upon rich data inputs and sophisticated algorithms. Ultimately, these models did well at recommending products that met an individuals' specific preferences, leading to better engagement and conversion rates shown in figure 5. Although the data and computational resources needed to implement them were extensive; they were also a more complex expensive option. The methods presented were different and also different strengths and differences in limitations, telling us about the choice of the method based on the objective of the research, resources available and what level of insight we need to achieve.

V. CONCLUSION

This study's goal was to use a thorough data-powered methodology to examine how consumer behavior and online marketing intersect. It achieved this by applying techniques like feature selection, data transformation, and categorization to gain a deeper comprehension of the decision-making processes that customers go through. The raw data on customer activity was cleaned, standardized, and encoded using the data transformation process. This guaranteed that the data was ready for use and analysis. The normalization of the input features and the removal of noise were two of the most important aspects of this preprocessing method. In order to prepare the dataset for subsequent modeling, this process was equally crucial. A technique known as Recursive Feature Elimination (RFE) was used to complete the feature selection procedure. Making use of this approach allowed for the identification of the factors that most significantly impacted consumer behavior. RFE was able to improve the model's accuracy, interpretability, and efficiency by eliminating characteristics that were thought to be unnecessary and redundant. In order to predict how customers would respond to online marketing initiatives, the limited feature set concentrated on crucial elements including consumer demographics and online interactions. This was carried out to guarantee precise forecasts. These criteria were required in order to predict the reactions of the clients.

The last step in the procedure was classifying consumer activity patterns using Support Vector Machines (SVM). The process came to an end with this phase. The ability of the support vector machine (SVM) model to handle high-dimensional and non-linear data has been demonstrated, allowing it to produce precise predictions of the behaviors of customers. These expected results included both the degree of engagement with targeted marketing and the probability of making a purchase. The results showed that, in the context of online marketing, support vector machines (SVM) could effectively capture the complexity of consumer behavior. When combined, the application of RFE-based feature selection, SVM classification, and data preparation produced very useful insights about marketing campaign optimization. These results may help businesses create much more targeted and customized marketing strategies, which will ultimately boost customer engagement and propel the company's success.

REFERENCES

Abdullahi, M., Ahmad, A., Pandey, B. K., & Pandey, D. (2024). Digital currency adoption: A comparative analysis of global trends and the nigerian enaira digital currency. *SN Computer Science*, *5*(5), 602.

Abraham, H., McAnulty, H., Mehler, B., & Reimer, B. (2020). Consumer trust in advanced vehicle technologies: Insights from an online survey. *Accident; Analysis and Prevention*, *144*, 105604. DOI: 10.1016/j.aap.2020.105604

Ahathiyan, G. S., Du John, H. V., Moni, D. J., Sagayam, K. M., Pandey, B. K., Pandey, D., & Lelisho, M. E. (2025). Design and simulation of a highly efficient eco-friendly, non-toxic perovskite solar cell. *Discover Nano*, *20*(1), 32. PMID: 39937384

Belanche, D., Flavián, C., & Pérez-Rueda, A. (2020). Brand recall of safety information in automotive advertising: An experimental study. *Journal of Business Research*, *116*, 68–75. DOI: 10.1016/j.jbusres.2020.05.029

Biswas, B., Sanyal, M. K., & Mukherjee, T. (2023). AI-based sales forecasting model for digital marketing. [IJEBR]. *International Journal of E-Business Research*, *19*(1), 1–14.

Dhanasekar, S., Martin Sagayam, K., Pandey, B. K., & Pandey, D. (2024). Refractive index sensing using metamaterial absorbing augmentation in elliptical graphene arrays. *Plasmonics*, *19*(5), 2273–2283.

Du John, H. V., & Jose, T., S, A. G., Sagayam, K. M., Pandey, B. K., & Pandey, D. (2024). Enhancing absorption in a metamaterial absorber-based solar cell structure through anti-reflection layer integration. *Silicon*, *16*(9), 3811–3821.

Du John, H. V., Jose, T., Jone, A. A. A., Sagayam, K. M., Pandey, B. K., & Pandey, D. (2022). Polarization insensitive circular ring resonator based perfect metamaterial absorber design and simulation on a silicon substrate. *Silicon*, *14*(14), 9009–9020.

Gupta, A. K., Sharma, R., Pandey, D., Nassa, V. K., Pandey, B. K., George, A. S., & Dadheech, P. (2023). Performance analysis of eight-channel WDM optical network with different optical amplifiers for industry 4.0. In *Innovation and competitiveness in industry 4.0 based on intelligent systems* (pp. 197–212). Springer International Publishing.

Hollebeek, L. D., & Macky, K. (2019). Digital content marketing's role in fostering consumer engagement, trust, and value. *Journal of Interactive Marketing*, *45*, 27–41. DOI: 10.1016/j.intmar.2018.07.003

Jannach, D., Adomavicius, G., & Tuzhilin, A. (2020). Recommender systems: Challenges, opportunities, and research frontiers. *AI Magazine*, *41*(3), 40–55. DOI: 10.1609/aimag.v41i3.5280

Khadka, M., Sah, M., Chaudhary, R., Sahani, S. K., Sahani, K., Pandey, B. K., & Pandey, D. (2025). Spectroscopic, quantum chemical, and topological calculations of the phenylephrine molecule using density functional theory. *Scientific Reports*, *15*(1), 208. PMID: 39747169

Kumar, M. S., Prasanna, P. L., Lalitha, M., Joy, M., Jha, S. S., & Pandey, B. K. (2025). Utilizing the Internet of Everything and Artificial Intelligence for Real-Time Workforce Management. In Role of Internet of Everything (IOE), VLSI Architecture, and AI in Real-Time Systems (pp. 153-168). IGI Global Scientific Publishing.

KVM, S., Pandey, B. K., & Pandey, D. (2024). Design of surface plasmon resonance (SPR) sensors for highly sensitive biomolecular detection in cancer diagnostics. *Plasmonics*, •••, 1–13.

Maheshwari, R. U. AR, J., Pandey, B. K., & Pandey, D. (2025). Innovative Quantum PlasmoVision-Based Imaging for Real-Time Deepfake Detection. Plasmonics, 1-17.

Maheshwari, R. U., Paulchamy, B., Pandey, B. K., & Pandey, D. (2024). Enhancing sensing and imaging capabilities through surface plasmon resonance for deepfake image detection. *Plasmonics*, •••, 1–20.

Pandey, B. K., & Pandey, D. (2023). Parametric optimization and prediction of enhanced thermoelectric performance in co-doped CaMnO3 using response surface methodology and neural network. *Journal of Materials Science Materials in Electronics*, *34*(21), 1589.

Pandey, B. K., & Pandey, D. (2025). Securing healthcare medical image information using advance morphological component analysis, information hiding systems, and hybrid convolutional neural networks on IoMT. *Computers in Biology and Medicine*, *185*, 109499. PMID: 39642698

Pandey, B. K., Pandey, D., & Agarwal, A. (2022). Encrypted information transmission by enhanced steganography and image transformation. [IJDAI]. *International Journal of Distributed Artificial Intelligence*, *14*(1), 1–14.

Pandey, B. K., Pandey, D., & Lelisho, M. E. (2024). Face mask identification with enhanced cuckoo optimization and deep learning-based faster regional neural network. *Scientific Reports*, *14*(1), 29719. PMID: 39613761

Pandey, D., Nassa, V. K., Jhamb, A., Mahto, D., Pandey, B. K., George, A. H., & Bandyopadhyay, S. K. (2021). An integration of keyless encryption, steganography, and artificial intelligence for the secure transmission of stego images. In *Multidisciplinary approach to modern digital steganography* (pp. 211–234). IGI Global.

Pandey, D., & Pandey, B. K. (2022). An efficient deep neural network with adaptive galactic swarm optimization for complex image text extraction. In *Process mining techniques for pattern recognition* (pp. 121–137). CRC Press.

Pandey, D., Sharma, M., Talwar, R., & Pandey, B. K. (2025). A compact quintuple band miniaturized elliptical planar monopole antenna for 5G/6G wireless systems. *Analog Integrated Circuits and Signal Processing*, *122*(3), 1–16.

Pandey, D., Wairya, S., Sharma, M., Gupta, A. K., Kakkar, R., & Pandey, B. K. (2022). An approach for object tracking, categorization, and autopilot guidance for passive homing missiles. *Aerospace Systems*, *5*(4), 553–566.

Praveenkumar, T., Anthoniraj, S., Kumarganesh, S., Somaskandan, M., Martin Sagayam, K., Pandey, B. K., & Sahani, S. K. (2025). Enhanced Circuit Board Analysis: Infrared Image Segmentation Utilizing Markov Random Field (MRF) and Level Set Techniques. *Engineering Reports*, *7*(3), e70029.

Raja, D. S. S., Kumar, D. R., Santhiyakumari, N., Kumarganesh, S., Sagayam, K. M., Thiyaneswaran, B., & Pandey, D. (2024). A compact dual-feed wide-band slotted antenna for future wireless applications. *Analog Integrated Circuits and Signal Processing*, *118*(2), 291–305.

Revathi, T. K., Sathiyabhama, B., Sankar, S., Pandey, D., Pandey, B. K., & Dadeech, P. (2022). An intelligent model for coronary heart disease diagnosis. In *Networking technologies in smart healthcare* (pp. 309–327). CRC Press.

Saxena, A., Agarwal, A., Pandey, B. K., & Pandey, D. (2024). Examination of the criticality of customer segmentation using unsupervised learning methods. *Circular Economy and Sustainability*, *4*(2), 1447–1460.

Sharma, M., Pandey, D., Palta, P., & Pandey, B. K. (2022). Design and power dissipation consideration of PFAL CMOS V/S conventional CMOS based 2: 1 multiplexer and full adder. *Silicon*, *14*(8), 4401–4410.

Sharma, M., Talwar, R., Nassa, V. K., Binay, K., & Pandey, D. (2025). Design and performance analysis of a multiband vivaldi antenna for wireless broadband communication in 3-5.6 GHz spectrum. In *Artificial Intelligence and Information Technologies* (pp. 86–91). CRC Press.

Sharma, M., Talwar, R., Pandey, D., Nassa, V. K., Pandey, B. K., & Dadheech, P. (2024). A review of dielectric resonator antennas (DRA)-based RFID technology for Industry 4.0. *Robotics and Automation in Industry*, *4*(0), 303–324.

Sheela, M. S., Kumarganesh, S., Pandey, B. K., & Lelisho, M. E. (2025). Integration of silver nanostructures in wireless sensor networks for enhanced biochemical sensing. *Discover Nano*, *20*(1), 7. PMID: 39804434

Singh, S., Madaan, G., Singh, A., Pandey, D., George, A. S., & Pandey, B. K. (2025). Empowering Connectivity: Exploring the Internet of Things. In Interdisciplinary Approaches to AI, Internet of Everything, and Machine Learning (pp. 89-116). IGI Global Scientific Publishing.

Singh, S., Madaan, G., Swapna, H. R., Singh, A., Pandey, B. K., George, A. S., & Pandey, D. (2025). Unleashing the Power of AI and Data Analysis: Transforming Insights into Action. In Interdisciplinary Approaches to AI, Internet of Everything, and Machine Learning (pp. 1-24). IGI Global Scientific Publishing.

Smith, A. N., & Fischer, E. (2019). Toward a theory of digital marketing. *Journal of Interactive Marketing*, *47*, 29–43. DOI: 10.1016/j.intmar.2019.02.002

Strayer, D. L., & Fisher, D. L. (2021). Autonomous vehicles: The implications of human error. *Accident; Analysis and Prevention*, *145*, 105709. DOI: 10.1016/j.aap.2021.105709

Tareke, S. A., Lelisho, M. E., Hassen, S. S., Seid, A. A., Jemal, S. S., Teshale, B. M., & Pandey, B. K. (2022). The prevalence and predictors of depressive, anxiety, and stress symptoms among Tepi town residents during the COVID-19 pandemic lockdown in Ethiopia. *Journal of Racial and Ethnic Health Disparities*, •••, 1–13. PMID: 35028903

Vinodhini, V., Kumar, M. S., Sankar, S., Pandey, D., Pandey, B. K., & Nassa, V. K. (2022). IoT-based early forest fire detection using MLP and AROC method. *International Journal of Global Warming*, *27*(1), 55–70.

Chapter 22
The Role of Cloud Computing in Modern Business Strategy

Punith Cariappa
Surana Educational Institutions, India

ABSTRACT

Cloud computing is changing business operations and boosting competitiveness. As companies move to the cloud, they gain scalable resources and advanced technologies that boost innovation and efficiency. Cloud environments allow companies to develop and deploy products and services faster, optimize processes, and respond quickly to market demands, helping them compete globally. Cloud computing allows organizations to use AI, machine learning, and big data analytics to innovate. These insights improve customer experiences, decision-making, and loyalty through personalized engagement. New ways of working in the cloud enable greater flexibility and collaboration among remote and hybrid teams.

1. INTRODUCTION

Computing in the cloud is a force that is transforming modern business strategy. It enables businesses to operate with an unprecedented level of flexibility and innovation. Cloud platforms enable businesses to overcome the limitations of traditional information technology by providing on-demand access to computing resources. This results in operations that are both more efficient and more agile. This shift is not just about technology (Pandey, B. K. et al., 2024a), it is also reshaping the way in which businesses approach growth, scalability, and customer engagement. When it comes to business strategy, cloud computing plays a significant role in

DOI: 10.4018/979-8-3693-9581-3.ch022

the development of new business models. Services such as Software-as-a-Service (SaaS) and Platform-as-a-Service (PaaS), which offer customers access to software and platforms on a subscription basis, are now available to businesses around the world. This has resulted in a shift in revenue models from one-time sales to recurring revenue streams, which has provided businesses with a more predictable cash flow and improved their relationships with their customers. In addition, cloud platforms are a driving force behind innovation in product development because they enable businesses to rapidly prototype (Pandey, B. K. et al., 2024b) and test new ideas without the need for significant initial investments in infrastructure. The cloud is an essential component in the process of enabling businesses to incorporate cutting-edge technologies like blockchain, Internet of Things (IoT), and artificial intelligence (AI). Businesses are able to implement intelligent solutions such as predictive analytics, personalized customer experiences, and automated decision-making by utilizing cloud platforms because these platforms offer the computational power and scalability required to process large datasets and run artificial intelligence algorithms. As a result of the adaptability of cloud computing, businesses are able to experiment with new technologies at a fraction of the cost that would be required for traditional infrastructure. Cloud computing improves supply chain management by seamlessly connecting multiple partners in real time (Maheshwari, R. Uma. et al., 2024). This facilitates improved visibility, optimization (Maheshwari, R. U. et al., 2024b), and collaboration throughout the supply chain. This ensures that operations run more smoothly and that a quicker response is provided to changes in the market, thereby reducing delays (KVM, S. et al., 2024) and inefficiencies.

1.1 Cloud Computing's Strategic Role

The use of cloud computing as a strategic asset has caused a significant change in how companies use and manage technology (Rai, P. K. et al., 2024). In the past, businesses relied on expensive, on-premises IT systems that needed a large initial investment and ongoing upkeep. These systems frequently lacked the scalability and flexibility required to keep up with the hectic demands of today's business world. This landscape has changed with the introduction of cloud computing, which gives companies access to online computing resources and lets them rent platforms, software, and infrastructure as needed instead of having to buy and maintain these systems internally. Cloud computing has a number of tactical benefits. It first lessens the requirement for significant upfront expenditures in IT infrastructure. Companies can more easily control expenses and adapt to shifting market conditions when they can scale resources up or down in response to demand (Kumarganesh, S. et al., 2024). Because of this adaptability, businesses can stay competitive and nimble even in sectors that are changing quickly. Because cloud service providers handle security management, software updates, and system maintenance, cloud computing also relieves users of this burden. Internal IT teams can now concentrate on more strategic projects like innovation and enhancing customer experiences (Kim, Hwang, Suh, & Kim, 2015). The ability of cloud computing to promote innovation is another important advantage. Cloud platforms enable businesses to test new concepts and solutions without having to make significant upfront investments by giving them simple access to cutting-edge technologies like artificial intelligence, big data analytics, and the Internet of Things. This facilitates the creation and introduction of new goods and services more quickly (Pandey, B. K., & Pandey, D., 2025), giving companies an advantage over rivals. Additionally, cloud computing makes it easier for international teams to collaborate, enabling companies to run smoothly across borders. Cloud computing makes it possible for companies to enter new markets more swiftly and effectively. With cloud-based systems, businesses can expand into new areas without requiring local IT infrastructure, as they can be accessed from any location with an internet connection. Businesses can easily expand their operations and access emerging markets thanks to this global accessibility (Bloem et al., 2014).

1.2 The Competitive Business Landscape

Cloud computing gives businesses a competitive edge by facilitating quick innovation and effective operation scaling. By establishing digital ecosystems where companies may easily communicate with partners and clients, it revolutionizes entire industries. Businesses are better able to share data (Saravanakumar, R. et al., 2024) and adapt quickly to changes in the market thanks to this networked environment. Smaller businesses can now compete with larger corporations thanks to equal access to cutting-edge technologies and resources without having to make large upfront investments. Business organizations (Muralidhar, L. B. et al., 2024) can improve customer experiences, expedite workflows, and spur growth in a cutthroat market by utilizing cloud solutions. Cloud computing changes industries by creating integrated digital ecosystems that support cooperation, efficiency (Elarmathi, S. et al., 2024), and customer-centric solutions. It also creates competitive advantages are as shown in the figure 1, by enhancing cost effectiveness, scalability (Basha, A. J. et al., 2024), and innovation.

- *Cost Efficiency*: Cloud computing is essential for giving companies in a variety of industries a competitive edge. Through the elimination of large upfront expenditures on software and hardware, businesses can drastically reduce their operating expenses. Businesses can implement a pay-as-you-go model through cloud computing, whereby they only pay for the resources they actually use. This strategy frees up funds that can be used for innovation and expansion projects in addition to lowering the costs of upkeep, upgrades, and energy use associated with on-premises data centres (Lakshmi, K. V. N. et al., 2024). As a result, companies have more money to devote to marketing, R&D, and other strategic initiatives that create competitive advantage.

- *Scalability*: The ability of cloud computing to grow is another important feature. By adjusting their resource levels dynamically in response to demand, cloud-based solutions enable businesses to handle varying workloads without the risk of over- or under-provisioning their resources. This degree of adaptability helps businesses that deal with erratic market trends or seasonal highs and lows to better allocate their resources and minimize expenses. Cloud platforms speed up the time from ideation to market by enabling the quick deployment of services and apps. Because of its speed and agility, businesses are better able to respond to market trends and customer demands by quickly experimenting and developing prototypes in cloud environments (Yang & Tate, 2012).
- *Innovation Enablement*: Another way that cloud computing fosters innovation is by making cutting-edge technologies like big data analytics, machine learning, and artificial intelligence (AI) easily accessible. With the aid of these technologies (Raja, D. S. S. et al., 2024), companies can examine data, draw conclusions, and develop original solutions that set them apart from rivals. Cloud-based tools enable businesses to quickly develop products that meet the evolving needs of their customers and test out new concepts. Furthermore, because cloud infrastructure is globally accessible, businesses can expand into new areas without having to deal with the logistical challenges of establishing local IT facilities. This shortens the time to market for global expansion and improves cooperation between various markets and geographical areas.
- *Collaboration and Connectivity*: Cloud computing is revolutionizing industries by establishing digital ecosystems that are interconnected. Cloud platforms enable remote teams to collaborate and communicate seamlessly, overcoming geographical barriers to allow real-time work together. Because teams can instantly share ideas and resources, this connectivity fosters innovation and improves problem-solving skills, which in turn increases creativity and productivity. Cloud computing enables companies to link their systems with partners' and suppliers', promoting increased visibility and openness along the supply chain. Organizations can improve operational efficiency by responding to disruptions and customer demands more quickly thanks to this integration (Oliveira. et al., 2014).
- *New Business Models*: Subscription-based services, which have grown in popularity recently, are one example of the new business models that cloud

computing has made possible. This change enables businesses to increase customer loyalty and create more stable revenue streams. Because cloud services are flexible, companies can test out various offerings and pricing schemes, refining their strategy to better suit the demands of the market.

- *Data-Driven Decision Making*: Advanced analytics and data processing capabilities are supported by cloud computing, enabling businesses to use big data for strategic decision-making. Through the acquisition of insights derived from diverse data sources, enterprises can discern patterns, project consumer needs, and make well-informed decisions that bolster their competitive standing.
- *Customer-Centric Solutions*: Cloud-based customer relationship management (CRM) platforms offer the capability to monitor and record customer preferences and interactions, thereby facilitating customized marketing plans and enhanced customer experiences. A company's position in the market is strengthened and brand loyalty is increased through this emphasis on customer-centricity and repeat business.

Figure 1. Significance in the competitive business environment

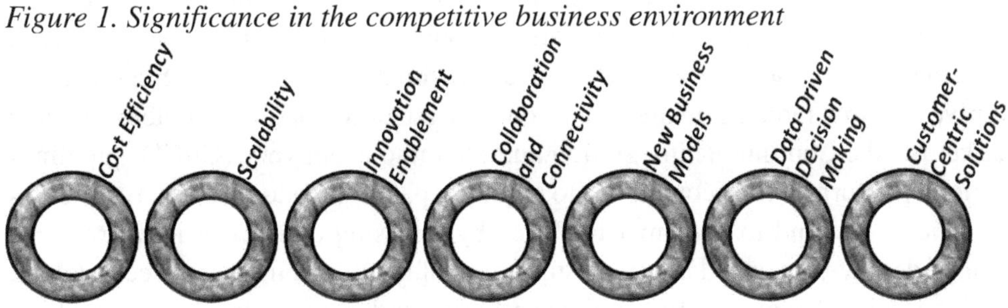

2. BUSINESS AGILITY WITH CLOUD

2.1 Faster Time to Market

Cloud computing helps businesses develop, test, and deploy new products and services faster. Building, configuring, and managing on-premises IT infrastructure was difficult, prolonging development cycles in the traditional model. Hardware, data centre setup, and software installation took time and resources, delaying innovation launches. Businesses now have flexible, on-demand access to scalable platforms that speed up product and service launch thanks to cloud computing. Development cycle reduction is one way cloud computing speeds time to market. Development tools, virtual environments, and pre-built templates on cloud platforms help developers build and test apps quickly. Without setting up physical infrastructure or complex configurations, developers can instantly access cloud-based programming languages, frameworks, and SDKs. This eliminates infrastructure bottlenecks, allowing teams to rapidly iterate and improve their products. Improved development speeds help companies launch innovations faster and stay ahead of the competition. Cloud computing promotes collaborative development, which speeds up product development. Remote teams can seamlessly share files, code, and resources using cloud-based collaboration tools. All team members have the latest project resources and communication delays are reduced with real-time collaboration. Another benefit of cloud platforms is that multiple teams or departments can work on different project aspects simultaneously, speeding up development. This global collaboration speeds up decision-making and problem-solving, accelerating product development (Buyya, Yeo. et al., 2009). The ability to dynamically scale resources reduces time to market in cloud computing. Computing power and storage demands fluctuate during development, slowing progress if on-premises infrastructure is insufficient. Businesses can scale up or down on cloud platforms without buying new hardware or overcommitting to infrastructure. Development teams can work efficiently even during peak workloads, accelerating product development and deployment. Customer-centric solutions are deployed faster with cloud computing. Staying competitive requires modern businesses to quickly adapt to customer preferences and market trends. Continuous integration and continuous delivery (CI/CD) pipelines on cloud platforms allow companies to regularly patch and add features. Businesses can quickly respond to customer feedback by releasing updates or new products. Change deployment speed boosts customer satisfaction and market success. Cloud platforms allow businesses to simulate scenarios and test their products in real life before launching them. This identifies issues and allows quick fixes, reducing the risk of botched product or service launches. With reliable testing environments, cloud computing reduces errors and speeds up product deployment. By reducing development cycles, enabling collaborative development, offering dynamic scalability, and supporting fast deployment of customer-centric solutions, cloud computing accelerates time to market. Business agility, flexibility (Pandey, B. K. et al., 2024c), and agility from cloud platforms help companies innovate and deliver products faster, keeping them competitive in a fast-paced environment (Morgan & Conboy, 2013).

2.2 Access to Advanced Technology on Demand

The ability to access cutting-edge technologies whenever needed is provided by cloud computing, greatly improving business capacities. The ease with which cutting-edge technologies like artificial intelligence (AI), machine learning (ML), and big data analytics can be accessed through cloud platforms without the need for large upfront investments is one of their main advantages. Historically, only large businesses could afford or utilize these technologies due to their high implementation costs, infrastructure requirements, and skill requirements. But now that these cutting-edge tools are more widely available, companies of all sizes can take advantage of their power thanks to cloud computing. Businesses don't have to create or maintain the infrastructure needed to run complex algorithms because cloud platforms provide access to AI and ML services (Abdullahi, M. et al., 2024). By using pre-built AI and ML models that are available on the cloud, businesses can pay for the resources they use only, rather than purchasing costly servers or employing specialized staff. Incorporating intelligent automation and data-driven decision-making into operations can now be achieved at a significantly lower cost for businesses. Artificial intelligence (George, W. K. et al., 2024) is a flexible tool that can be used to improve efficiency and competitiveness in a variety of business processes, from forecasting market trends to automating customer service. Cloud-based services also make big data analytics more accessible. Previously, only larger companies could use large-scale dataset analysis due to the need for specialized hardware, software, and knowledge. Big data processing and real-time analysis are now possible for businesses thanks to cloud computing's scalable analytics tools. Decision-making, customer targeting, and operational efficiency can all be enhanced by these practical insights. Without spending large sums of money on infrastructure, businesses can learn more about consumer behaviour, market trends, and internal performance benchmarks. The playing field has been levelled for smaller businesses by this democratization of cutting-edge technology. Cloud platforms enable small-to-medium enterprises (SMEs) and startups to compete with larger companies in terms of efficiency and innovation by offering pay-as-you-go access to AI, ML, and big data analytics. Previously unattainable technologies are now within the reach of smaller businesses, allowing them to expand their competitiveness, optimize their operations, and improve customer experiences. Because it is available anytime, anywhere, firms can expand without incurring significant initial costs and are encouraged to innovate in a variety of sectors (Dahlberg, Kivijärvi, & Saarinen, 2017).

2.3 Business Model Innovation

The emergence of new business models, including Platform as a Service (PaaS) and Software as a Service (SaaS), has been made possible in large part by cloud computing. These cloud-driven business models have completely changed how companies provide goods and services to their clients, transforming them into more flexible, scalable, and client-focused organizations. Without having to make significant capital investments in IT infrastructure, businesses can innovate, test, and modify their business strategies thanks to the flexibility of cloud infrastructure. A notable change brought about by cloud computing is the emergence of Software as a Service (SaaS). SaaS enables businesses to distribute software applications online so that users can access them via a web browser as opposed to more conventional on-premises installations. With this model, clients do not need to spend money on hardware or upkeep because the software is hosted and maintained by the service provider. Companies that provide software as a service (SaaS) can swiftly launch their products onto a worldwide market and update them frequently with new features or bug fixes without needing assistance from customers. Because of this adaptability, the model has become widely used in a variety of industries. Businesses are now able to provide subscription-based models that produce recurring and predictable revenue streams. Scalability is another convenient feature that SaaS offers users, enabling them to modify their subscription levels in accordance with their present requirements. In a similar vein, Platform as a Service (PaaS) has become a very popular cloud-based business model (Foster, Zhao, Raicu, & Lu, 2008). With the help of PaaS, developers can create, launch, and maintain apps without worrying about maintaining the underlying infrastructure. By adopting this method, developers can concentrate on crafting inventive applications instead of wasting time and resources on hardware or system configurations. From sophisticated enterprise systems to web and mobile apps, PaaS supports a broad variety of applications. Businesses can open up new revenue streams by offering PaaS, which allows customers to scale and customize development platforms according to their own requirements. In addition to fostering innovation, PaaS platforms foster developer and business ecosystems that enable the development of new tools, apps, and integrations that raise the platform's overall value. Cloud computing is driving shifts in revenue generation models beyond these particular models. Businesses used to sell goods or services outright and demand sizable upfront payments from clients. More adaptable payment arrangements, including usage-based billing, pay-per-use services, and subscription models, are now possible thanks to cloud computing. With the help of these models, companies can provide clients with longer-term service access at reduced upfront costs, resulting in more steady and predictable revenue streams. Companies that offer cloud storage or computing resources, for example, frequently charge users according to the amount of storage or processing power they utilize, enabling users to scale up or down as necessary. Because users can easily adjust their costs and usage, they are less likely to switch to competitors, which increases customer retention and draws in a wider customer base (Mell & Grance, 2011).

3. INTERCONNECTING BUSINESSES AND ECOSYSTEMS

3.1 Real-Time Collaboration for Global Teams

The use of cloud computing has fundamentally altered the way in which businesses function, particularly in terms of facilitating real-time collaboration among teams located all over the world. Through the provision of a collection of collaborative tools, the cloud makes it possible for members of a team to communicate with one another in a seamless manner, regardless of where they are physically located. When efforts were coordinated across multiple time zones and locations in the past, it frequently resulted in delays, misunderstandings, and inefficiencies. Cloud-based tools, on the other hand, such as file-sharing platforms, project management systems, and virtual workspaces, make it possible for employees to collaborate in real time (Kumar, M. S. et al, 2025), instantly sharing documents, ideas, and progress. Because of this, there is no longer a requirement for sending and receiving emails or transferring files, which results in increased productivity and a reduction in bottlenecks in project timelines. It is possible for multiple members of a team to access and work on the same documents or files simultaneously when using cloud-based collaboration tools, which is one of the most significant advantages of these tools. Through the use of real-time co-authoring, it is possible to ensure that all parties remain on the same page, keeping all updates and changes visible immediately (Jadeja & Modi, 2012). As a consequence of this, cloud tools contribute to the prevention of version control issues and guarantee that all stakeholders have access to the most recent information. These platforms come with features such as live chat, video conferencing, and task tracking, all of which contribute to the further simplification of communication and the promotion of efficient teamwork. Increased innovation has also resulted from the strengthening of teamwork through the utilization of shared cloud environments. Brainstorming, problem-solving, and innovation are all encouraged by the cloud because it offers a platform that allows members of a team to work together and share ideas in real time. Teams are able to rapidly experiment with new ideas, put those ideas to the test, and iterate based on real-time feedback, which gives them the ability to make decisions more quickly and come up with more creative solutions. One of the benefits of being able to work asynchronously and collaborate across multiple time zones is that it allows projects to move forward around the clock, which speeds up the development cycle and improves overall efficiency. The incorporation of external partners, clients, and stakeholders into the development process is simplified by the utilization of cloud-based collaboration tools (Konapure, C. G. et al., 2025). Through the provision of access to shared workspaces and project updates, businesses are able to guarantee that all parties involved are in agreement and contributing to the success of the project. By doing so, relationships are strengthened and a smoother collaboration between businesses and their partners is ensured, which ultimately results in improved outcomes. The modern workplace has been revolutionized as a result of real-time collaboration across global teams made possible by cloud technology. This has resulted in improved communication, increased teamwork, and significantly increased innovation. It is possible for businesses to overcome geographical barriers and leverage diverse, distributed talent through the use of cloud computing. This ensures that projects are moved forward in an efficient and creative manner regardless of where members of the team are located (Rimal, Choi, & Lumb, 2009).

3.2 Supply Chain Integration

Real-time supplier, partner, and customer integration has transformed supply chains and business networks with cloud computing. Multiple manual processes and communication layers in supply chain management caused inefficiencies, delays, and a lack of transparency. The cloud has created a digital network where everyone can instantly access and share critical information. Cloud solutions simplify supply chains and encourage stakeholder collaboration, speeding decision-making and improving operational efficiency. Actual visibility is a major benefit of cloud-based supply chain integration. Businesses can track shipments, inventory, and demand in real time using cloud platforms. Suppliers and partners can dynamically adjust their operations based on the latest information, reducing stock shortages, overproduction, and delays. Order and shipment tracking improves transparency and customer satisfaction. Real-time data from anywhere in the world aligns supply chain participants, making operations smoother and more efficient. The cloud also optimizes logistics and procurement. Cloud platforms help businesses make sourcing, production, and delivery decisions by providing supply chain transparency. Cloud-based analytics can evaluate suppliers, identify bottlenecks, and predict demand. Businesses can optimise procurement by choosing the right suppliers, negotiating better terms, and ensuring material availability. Cloud-based logistics platforms also track shipments in real time, optimize delivery routes, and reduce transportation costs by finding the most cost-effective solutions. Cloud-based supply chain integration is scalable and flexible. Business supply chains can quickly adapt to demand changes, new partnerships, and market shifts. Cloud resources allow companies to scale up logistics and inventory management during peak demand periods like holidays or promotions without investing in infrastructure. In low-demand periods, cloud platforms let businesses scale down, reducing costs and optimizing resource use. Cloud computing improves business-wide collaboration. Supply chain, distributor, retail, and customer collaboration and communication are possible in the same digital environment. This level of integration boosts efficiency and strengthens partnerships, allowing businesses to build more flexible supply chains. Cloud systems improve partner collaboration by improving communication and trust, reducing friction and improving performance (Venters & Whitley, 2012).

3.3 Ecosystem Partnering and Alliances

The digital infrastructure provided by cloud computing allows businesses to form new partnerships and expand their ecosystems. Collaboration drives innovation and competitiveness in modern business. Partners can collaborate, share resources, and seamlessly integrate their services on cloud platforms, which are flexible and scalable. Companies can form strategic alliances that boost innovation, efficiency, and revenue with cloud technology. The ability of cloud platforms to facilitate new partnerships is a major benefit. Businesses struggled to integrate systems, collaborate on projects, and share information with external partners due to IT infrastructure complexity. A shared, centralized environment for real-time partner collaboration has removed many of these barriers with cloud technology (Pandey, B. K. et al., 2024d). Companies can form joint ventures, co-develop products, and share research and development with suppliers, distributors, customers, and even competitors. Cloud platforms support data-sharing and joint project management systems, making it easier for businesses to collaborate across time zones. Business partnerships are further enhanced by cloud platforms' ability to integrate services via APIs. APIs let companies combine or improve their products by connecting their software and services with others. To offer customers a more complete solution, a cloud-based CRM provider can integrate with a partner's marketing automation platform. Businesses can add value and market reach by integrating APIs to their products and services. Expanding business ecosystems with cloud services allows multiple companies to create a unified network of services. Businesses can collaborate, share data, and co-develop ecosystem-beneficial apps on cloud platforms. As companies collaborate to solve complex problems and innovate, cloud ecosystems are common in healthcare, finance, and technology. These ecosystems encourage open innovation, allowing participants to share expertise and resources to improve product development, customer experiences, and operations. A major benefit of cloud-driven partnerships and ecosystems is the ability to smoothly scale operations. Businesses can quickly scale up their infrastructure to meet demand on cloud platforms, making it easier to seize new opportunities. Companies expanding into new markets or networks need this scalability. Cloud partnerships reduce infrastructure investments and improve agility and market responsiveness by leveraging each other's resources and capabilities (Singh, S. et al., 2025). Cloud partnerships offer businesses greater flexibility and adaptability. Because cloud services can be updated, expanded, or modified, businesses can quickly adapt their partnerships and alliances to changing market dynamics or customer needs. In a new market, a company can quickly form partnerships with local service providers or distributors using cloud-based collaboration tools. This gives companies a competitive edge by letting them tailor their products and strategies to different regions and customer segments (Chebrolu., 2011).

4. SECURITY INNOVATIONS IN CLOUD COMPUTING

Cloud computing is a major force behind automation innovation, helping businesses increase productivity and optimize processes. Utilizing AI-driven solutions, automated infrastructure management allows cloud environments to self-manage, optimize resource allocation, and scale dynamically. Cloud automation streamlines workflows and automates repetitive tasks in a variety of departments, including sales, finance, and human resources. This greatly increases productivity. Decision-making (Pandey, D. et al., 2024c) is improved by the incorporation of AI into cloud systems, which yields quicker and more intelligent insights. Businesses can now forecast and plan more effectively thanks to predictive analytics, which also enables data-driven strategies that adjust to shifting market conditions and, eventually, promote growth and competitiveness. For data protection and trust maintenance, cloud computing security innovations are critical. Some of the major innovations depicted in Figure 2 are automated threat response, security information and event management (SIEM), multi-factor authentication, and artificial intelligence (Kumar, B. et al., 2024) for threat detection. In ever-more complex cloud environments, these technologies bolster security posture, simplify compliance, and safeguard confidential data.

- *Multi-Factor Authentication*: By requiring users to provide multiple forms of verification before gaining access to cloud resources, Multi-Factor Authentication (MFA) improves security. Typically, this approach combines three elements: the user's identity (such as a fingerprint or facial recognition), their possessions (like a smartphone or hardware token), and their knowledge (like a password). Organizations greatly lower their risk of unwanted access by using MFA because, in the event that a password is compromised, an attacker would still require the extra verification methods to get in.

- *Machine Learning and Artificial Intelligence*: Security threats can be identified and countered in real time with cloud security frameworks that incorporate Artificial Intelligence (AI) and Machine Learning (ML) (Pandey, D. et al., 2024a). These tools examine enormous volumes of data to find trends and abnormalities that might point to a security breech. AI and ML algorithms can become more accurate over time by continuously learning from new data, which helps organizations react quickly to emerging threats and lessen the impact of potential attacks on cloud environments.
- *Security Information and Event Management*: Solutions for SIEM are essential for giving businesses a holistic understanding of their security posture. SIEM systems aid in the identification of potential threats and vulnerabilities by gathering and evaluating security data from a variety of sources, including servers, network devices, and applications of all kinds. Additionally, they make regulatory compliance easier by offering comprehensive reporting and auditing capabilities. SIEM improves overall security management in cloud environments with its real-time monitoring (Du John, H. V. et al., 2024) and incident response capabilities.
- *Identity and Access Management*: Controlling user access to cloud resources requires the use of Identity and Access Management (IAM) solutions. Role-based access controls, or RBAC, are implemented by IAM systems to guarantee that only authorized users have access to particular data and applications (Pandey, D. et al., 2024b). Organizations can enforce security policies and prevent unauthorized access to sensitive information by using Identity and Access Management (IAM) to manage user identities, roles, and permissions. To further improve security and usability, IAM solutions frequently come with features like user activity tracking and single sign-on (SSO).
- *Data Loss Prevention*: Technologies for data loss prevention, or DLP, are made to keep private data safe from illegal access, sharing, or transfer. DLP systems enforce rules that stop data breaches by monitoring data while it's being used, transferred, and stored. Sensitive data can be recognized and categorized so that organizations can put the right security measures in place to protect it. By guaranteeing that sensitive data is handled securely, DLP not only helps reduce the risk of data leaks but also supports regulatory compliance (Chebrolu, 2011).
- *Cloud Security Posture Management*: Tools for CSPM keep an eye out for configuration errors and compliance problems in cloud environments. Solutions for cloud security posture management (CSPM) enable enterprises to see vulnerabilities and implement best practices by giving visibility into cloud security configurations (Pandey, D. et al., 2024c). By automating the comparison of cloud environments with security benchmarks, these tools enable

enterprises to proactively patch any possible security vulnerabilities (Pandey, B. K. et al., 2024e) before hackers can take advantage of them (Pandey, D. et al., 2024d). The ongoing surveillance guarantees that cloud infrastructures continue to be safe and adhere to industry norms.

- *Automated Threat Response*: Advanced algorithms are utilised by automated threat response solutions to promptly detect and address security incidents. Organizations are able to quickly reduce risks without the need for manual intervention by defining predefined responses to particular threats (Pandey, B. K. et al., 2024f). By reducing human error and improving incident response times, automation frees up security teams to concentrate on more difficult security problems. Organizations can improve overall security resilience by efficiently managing and neutralizing threats (Pandey, D. et al., 2024e) as they emerge with automated threat response (Shahul, A. et al., 2024).
- *Blockchain for Security*: By offering decentralized and impenetrable data storage solutions, blockchain technology improves cloud computing security. Blockchain lowers the possibility of unauthorized changes and data breaches (Pandey, B. K. et al., 2024g) by spreading data among several nodes (Kennedy, G. W. et al., 2024). Every transaction is safely documented in a way that makes unintentional changes or deletions nearly impossible. This innovation strengthens the overall security of cloud-based systems and is especially helpful for applications that demand high levels of trust and transparency, like supply chain management and identity verification.

Figure 2. Key innovations in cloud security

5. CLOUD FOR SUSTAINABILITY AND CORPORATE RESPONSIBILITY

Modern data infrastructure improves energy efficiency and greens IT operations, lowering businesses' carbon footprints. For cooling and hardware, conventional on-premises systems use a lot of energy. Virtualization and automation optimize resource use in centralized data centres. Workload consolidation reduces energy use and emissions. Because of their size, data centres can manage energy more efficiently than individual companies. Major service providers are increasingly using renewable energy sources. Google, Microsoft, and Amazon have invested in solar, wind, and hydroelectric systems to use 100% renewable power. These initiatives reduce digital infrastructure's environmental impact and support global sustainability in general (Pandey, D. et al., 2024f). By using renewable energy-efficient systems (Sharma, M. et al., 2024), more businesses switching to these platforms reduce their carbon emissions. Sustainable business models, especially circular economy ones, are emerging from digital platforms. Real-time platforms help companies track their material (Pandey, B. K. et al., 2024d), energy, and product use and reuse, recycle, or dispose of resources responsibly. Businesses can optimize operations, reduce waste, and extend product life cycles with real-time monitoring, reducing their environmental impact. These systems improve supply chain transparency, allowing businesses to monitor supplier sustainability. Tracking the environmental and social impact of sourcing, manufacturing, and distribution ensures that the supply chain is ethical and sustainable. Businesses can improve their sustainability performance and build consumer trust by being visible. Customers prefer environmentally conscious companies. Digitization also supports corporate social responsibility (CSR). From charitable donations to employee volunteering and sustainability reporting, they help businesses manage social impact programs (JayaLakshmi, G. et al., 2024). Tracking and reporting CSR efforts is easier with these platforms, helping companies measure their success and reach. Making stakeholder engagement easier and more effectively helps companies meet their social responsibilities. These technologies have also empowered underserved communities by providing resources and education. Remote learning and job training platforms are increasing education and economic development in remote and economically disadvantaged areas. NGOs and governments use these digital tools to provide healthcare, financial aid, and disaster relief in areas without infrastructure (Borgman, Bahli, Heier, & Schewski, 2013).

6. CONCLUSION

The provision of scalable resources that enable organizations to operate more efficiently and respond more quickly to market demands is one of the primary ways in which cloud computing is disrupting the operations of modern businesses. Businesses are able to take advantage of cutting-edge technologies such as artificial intelligence, machine learning, and big data analytics by migrating to cloud-based solutions. These technologies are responsible for driving innovation and improving efficient operations. Productivity is increased as a result of this shift, and organizations are also better positioned to compete on a global scale. Companies are able to develop new products and services more quickly, optimize their processes, and meet the ever-changing expectations of their customers thanks to the cloud, which acts as a catalyst for innovation. The cloud will be the foundation of future work environments, strategies for engaging customers, and evolving business models, according to a look into the future. Cloud computing solutions will make it easier for teams located all over the world to collaborate, communicate, and be flexible. This is because more and more businesses are adopting remote and hybrid work arrangements. Furthermore, businesses that embrace cloud strategies will be better equipped to engage customers in meaningful ways, utilizing data-driven insights to tailor experiences and foster loyalty. Because of the constantly shifting technological landscape, it is essential for organizations to maintain their agility in order to achieve long-term success. Continuous adaptation to cloud-based solutions is essential for this. For businesses to achieve sustainable growth and keep a competitive edge in their respective markets, it is necessary for them to acknowledge the strategic significance of the cloud and to utilize its full potential.

REFERENCES

Abdullahi, M., Ahmad, A., Pandey, B. K., & Pandey, D. (2024). Digital Currency Adoption: A Comparative Analysis of Global Trends and the Nigerian eNaira Digital Currency. *SN Computer Science*, *5*(5), 1–11.

Basha, A. J., Maheshwari, R. U., Pandey, B. K., & Pandey, D. (2024). Ultra-Sensitive Photonic Crystal Fiber–Based SPR Sensor for Cancer Detection Utilizing Hybrid Nanocomposite Layers. *Plasmonics*, •••, 1–15.

Bloem, J., Van Doorn, M., Duivestein, S., Excoffier, D., Maas, R., & Van Ommeren, E. (2014). *The Fourth Industrial Revolution—Things to Tighten the Link between IT and OT*. Sogeti Vint.

Borgman, H. P., Bahli, B., Heier, H., & Schewski, F. Cloudrise: Exploring cloud computing adoption and governance with the TOE framework. In *Proceedings of the 2013 46th Hawaii International Conference on System Sciences*, Wailea, Maui, HI, USA, 7–10 January 2013.

Buyya, R., Yeo, C. S., Venugopal, S., Broberg, J., & Brandic, I. (2009). Cloud computing and emerging IT platforms: Vision, hype, and reality for delivering computing as the 5th utility. *Future Generation Computer Systems*, *25*, 599–616.

Chebrolu, S. B. (2011). Assessing the relationships among cloud adoption, strategic alignment and IT effectiveness. *Journal of Information Technology Management*, *22*, 13–29.

Dahlberg, T., Kivijärvi, H., & Saarinen, T. Longitudinal Study on the Expectations of Cloud Computing Benefits and an Integrative Multilevel Model for Understanding Cloud Computing Performance. In *Proceedings of the 50th Hawaii International Conference on System Sciences*, Waikoloa, HI, USA, 4–7 January 2017.

Du John, H. V., Jose, T., Sagayam, K. M., Pandey, B. K., & Pandey, D. (2024). Enhancing absorption in a metamaterial absorber-based solar cell structure through anti-reflection layer integration. Silicon, 1-11.

Elarmathi, S., Rishabavarthani, P., Sindhuja, M., Elayaraja, P., & Malathi Murugesan, S. Kumarganesh, K. Martin Sagayam, Binay Kumar Pandey, and Digvijay Pandey. (2024). Novel manufacturing systems for cancer diagnosis using ultra-sensitive photonic crystal fiber biosensor with dual-functionalized aptamer-nanocavity. *Microsystem Technologies*, •••, 1–20.

Foster, I., Zhao, Y., Raicu, I., & Lu, S. Cloud Computing and Grid Computing 360-Degree Compared. In *Proceedings of the Grid Computing Environments Workshop*, Austin, TX, USA, 16 November 2008.

George, W. K., Silas, E. I., Pandey, D., & Pandey, B. K. (2024). Utilization of Industry 4.0 Technologies in Nigerian Technical and Vocational Education: A Conundrum for Educators. In *Examining the Rapid Advance of Digital Technology in Africa* (pp. 270–293). IGI Global.

Jadeja, Y., & Modi, K. Cloud computing-concepts, architecture and challenges. In *Proceedings of the 2012 International Conference Computing, Electronics and Electrical Technologies (ICCEET)*, Nagercoil, India, 21–22 March 2012.

JayaLakshmi. G., Pandey, D., Pandey, B. K., Kaur, P., Mahajan, D. A., & Dari, S. S. (2024). Smart big data collection for intelligent supply chain improvement. In AI and Machine Learning Impacts in Intelligent Supply Chain (pp. 180-195). IGI Global.

Kennedy, G. W., Sunday, S. E., Pandey, D., Kabari, A. D., Pandey, B. K., George, A. S., & Dadheech, P. (2024). Building Information Modeling: Harnessing Innovations for Professional Proficiency. In Emerging Engineering Technologies and Industrial Applications (pp. 305-331). IGI Global.

Kim, T., Hwang, S., Suh, S., & Kim, D. (2015). A Study on Building a Cloud System for Local Government. *J. Korean Assoc. Reg. Inf. Soc.*, *18*, 34–47.

Konapure, C. G., Pandey, D., Shete, H., Thakar, C. M., Pandey, B. K., & George, A. S. (2025). Artificial Intelligence in Automated Concrete Mix Design Using Computerized Grading Curves. Interdisciplinary Approaches to AI, Internet of Everything, and Machine Learning, 567-586.

Kumar, B., Pandey, D., Pandey, B. K., & George, A. S. (2024). Higher Education in the Last Four Decades: A Review of Paradigm Shifts in Policy Frameworks. Design and Implementation of Higher Education Learners' Learning Outcomes (HELLO), 333-348.

Kumar, M. S., Prasanna, P. L., Lalitha, M., Joy, M., Jha, S. S., & Pandey, B. K. (2025). Utilizing the Internet of Everything and Artificial Intelligence for Real-Time Workforce Management. In Role of Internet of Everything (IOE), VLSI Architecture, and AI in Real-Time Systems (pp. 153-168). IGI Global Scientific Publishing.

Kumarganesh, S., Murugesan, M., Ganesh, C., Santhiyakumari, N., Thangavel, M., Jayaram, K., & Pandey, D. (2024). Hybrid Plasmonic Biosensors with Deep Learning for Colorectal Cancer Detection. *Plasmonics*, •••, 1–15.

KVM, S., Pandey, B. K., & Pandey, D. (2024). Design of Surface Plasmon Resonance (SPR) Sensors for Highly Sensitive Biomolecular Detection in Cancer Diagnostics. *Plasmonics*, •••, 1–13.

Lakshmi, K. V. N., Rajan, R., Pandey, D., & Pandey, B. K. (2024). Circular Economy: A Catalyst for Economic Growth-An Empirical Study. *Circular Economy and Sustainability*, •••, 1–22.

Low, C., Chen, Y., & Wu, M. (2011). Understanding the determinants of cloud computing adoption. *Industrial Management & Data Systems*, *111*, 1006–1023.

Maheshwari, R. Uma, S. Kumarganesh, Shree KVM, A. Gopalakrishnan, K. Selvi, B. Paulchamy, P. Rishabavarthani, K. Martin Sagayam, Binay Kumar Pandey, and Digvijay Pandey. (2024). Advanced plasmonic resonance-enhanced biosensor for comprehensive real-time detection and analysis of deepfake content. *Plasmonics*, •••, 1–18.

Maheshwari, R. U., Paulchamy, B., Pandey, B. K., & Pandey, D. (2024). Enhancing sensing and imaging capabilities through surface plasmon resonance for deepfake image detection. *Plasmonics*, •••, 1–20.

Mell, P., & Grance, T. (2011). The NIST definition of cloud computing. *Communications of the ACM*, •••, 53.

Morgan, L., & Conboy, K. Factors Affecting the Adoption of Cloud Computing: An Exploratory Study. In *Proceedings of the 21st European Conference on Information Systems (ECIS)*, Utrecht, The Netherlands, 6–8 June 2013.

Muralidhar, L. B., Lakshmi, K. V. N., Swapna, H. R., Rupani, J., Nethravathi, K., Pandey, B. K., & Pandey, D. (2024). Impact of Organizational Culture on The Level of Corporate Social Responsibility Investments: An Exploratory Study. *Circular Economy and Sustainability*, •••, 1–19.

Oliveira, T., Thomas, M., & Espadanal, M. (2014). Assessing the determinants of cloud computing adoption: An analysis of the manufacturing and services sectors. *Information & Management*, *51*, 497–510.

Pandey, B. K., Kanike, U. K., George, A. S., & Pandey, D. (Eds.). (2024d). *AI and machine learning impacts in intelligent supply chain*. IGI Global.

Pandey, B. K., Mukundan, A. P., Nassa, V. K., Pandey, D., George, A. S., Hameed, A. S., & Dadheech, P. (2024f). Deployment of Load Balancing in Cloud Computing: Industrial Application and Benefits. In Emerging Engineering Technologies and Industrial Applications (pp. 342-354). IGI Global.

Pandey, B. K., Nassa, V. K., Mukundan, A. P., Mahajan, D. A., Pandey, D., George, A. S., & Dadheech, P. (2024c). An Industry-Focused Traffic System Utilising Internet of Things. In *Emerging Engineering Technologies and Industrial Applications* (pp. 200–213). IGI Global.

Pandey, B. K., & Pandey, D. (2025). Securing healthcare medical image information using advance morphological component analysis, information hiding systems, and hybrid convolutional neural networks on IoMT. *Computers in Biology and Medicine*, *185*, 109499. PMID: 39642698

Pandey, B. K., Pandey, D., Agarwal, A., Mahajan, D. A., Dadheech, P. D., George, A. S., & Rai, P. K. (2024e). Beyond Data Breaches: Enhancing Security in 6G Communications. In Security Issues and Solutions in 6G Communications and Beyond (pp. 212-229). IGI Global.

Pandey, B. K., Pandey, D., & Lelisho, M. E. (2024a). Face mask identification with enhanced cuckoo optimization and deep learning-based faster regional neural network. *Scientific Reports*, *14*(1), 29719. PMID: 39613761

Pandey, B. K., Pandey, D., & Sahani, S. K. (2024b). Autopilot control unmanned aerial vehicle system for sewage defect detection using deep learning. *Engineering Reports*, •••, 12852.

Pandey, B. K., Paramashivan, M. A., Nassa, V. K., Mahajan, D. A., Dadheech, P., George, A. H., & George, A. S. (2024g). Blockchain's Potential Effect on the Healthcare Industry. In Emerging Engineering Technologies and Industrial Applications (pp. 214-232). IGI Global.

Pandey, D., Nassa, V. K., Pandey, B. K., Mahajan, D. A., Patidar, P. K., Dadheech, P., & George, A. S. (2024d). An Analysis of Internet-of-Things-Based Fire Detection and Alert Systems. In *Emerging Engineering Technologies and Industrial Applications* (pp. 295–304). IGI Global.

Pandey, D., Nassa, V. K., Pandey, B. K., Thankachan, B., Dadheech, P., Mahajan, D. A., & George, A. S. (2024c). Artificial Intelligence and Machine Learning and Its Application in the Field of Computational Visual Analysis. In Emerging Engineering Technologies and Industrial Applications (pp. 36-57). IGI Global.

Pandey, D., Pandey, B. K., Nassa, V. K., Mahajan, D. A., George, A. S., & Dadheech, P. (2024f). Optimized Throughput-Based Broadcasting for Next Generation Wireless Networks. In Emerging Engineering Technologies and Industrial Applications (pp. 355-368). IGI Global.

Pandey, D., Pandey, B. K., Paramashivan, M. A., Mahajan, D. A., Dadheech, P. D., George, A. S., & Hameed, A. S. (2024e). Advanced Digital Data Processing Using Cloud Cryptography: Industrial Applications. In Emerging Engineering Technologies and Industrial Applications (pp. 255-268). IGI Global.

Rai, P. K., Pandey, D., & Pandey, B. K. (2024). The future of enterprise and innovation is compute as a commodity, or CaaC. *Partners Universal International Research Journal, 3*(2), 89–94.

Raja, D. S. S., Kumar, D. R., Santhiyakumari, N., Kumarganesh, S., Sagayam, K. M., Thiyaneswaran, B., & Pandey, D. (2024). A compact dual-feed wide-band slotted antenna for future wireless applications. *Analog Integrated Circuits and Signal Processing, 118*(2), 291–305.

Rimal, B. P., Choi, E., & Lumb, I. A Taxonomy and Survey of Cloud Computing Systems. In Proceedings of the 2009 Fifth International Joint Conference on INC, IMS and IDC, Washington, DC, USA, 25–27 August 2009.

Saravanakumar, R., TamilSelvi, T., Pandey, D., Pandey, B. K., Mahajan, D. A., & Lelisho, M. E. (2024). Big data processing using hybrid Gaussian mixture model with salp swarm algorithm. *Journal of Big Data, 11*(1), 167.

Shahul, A., Muniandi, B., Paramashivan, M. A., Pandey, D., Pandey, B. K., Dadheech, P., & George, H. (2024). An Analysis of Algorithms and Methods Based on Image Processing for Medical Applications. In *Emerging Engineering Technologies and Industrial Applications* (pp. 173–186). IGI Global.

Sharma, M., Talwar, R., Pandey, D., Nassa, V. K., Pandey, B. K., & Dadheech, P. (2024). A review of dielectric resonator antennas (DRA)-based RFID technology for Industry 4.0. *Robotics and Automation in Industry, 4*(0), 303–324.

Singh, S., Madaan, G., Swapna, H. R., Singh, A., Pandey, B. K., George, A. S., & Pandey, D. (2025). Unleashing the Power of AI and Data Analysis: Transforming Insights into Action. In Interdisciplinary Approaches to AI, Internet of Everything, and Machine Learning (pp. 1-24). IGI Global Scientific Publishing.

Venters, W., & Whitley, E. A. (2012). A critical review of cloud computing: Researching desires and realities. *Journal of Information Technology, 27*, 179–197.

Yang, H., & Tate, M. (2012). A descriptive literature review and classification of cloud computing research. *Communications of the Association for Information Systems, 31*, 2–26.

Chapter 23
The Role of Cloud Computing in Regulating Blockchain and Virtual Currency

Siddharth Badkul
https://orcid.org/0009-0001-2297-0409
Faculty of Law, Manipal University Jaipur, India

Akshaya Kishor
Faculty of Law, Manipal University Jaipur, India

Sonal Madvariya
Faculty of Law, Manipal University Jaipur, India

ABSTRACT

With its reliable infrastructure and cutting-edge tools to tackle new problems, cloud computing has become essential to the regulation of blockchain and virtual currencies. This chaapter investigates how cloud platforms can improve blockchain networks in a variety of ways, from enabling real-time transaction monitoring to providing support for extensive forensic audits. Cloud services solve important regulatory issues like transparency and cross-border compliance with their scalability, flexibility, and storage optimization. Cloud platforms facilitate automated anomaly detection and predictive analytics through the integration of cutting-edge technologies like artificial intelligence (AI) and machine learning. This enhances oversight and prevents fraud to a great extent. Security is still the top priority, with cybersecurity and cloud-based encryption safeguarding private information and averting breaches.

DOI: 10.4018/979-8-3693-9581-3.ch023

1. INTRODUCTION

Virtual currencies and blockchain are part of the modern technologies that have been dependent on cloud computing. The innovation in blockchain network brings intensive regulation challenges to governments and financial institutions due to the highly decentralized systems involved. However, the breakthrough of cloud computing in delivering scalable, secure, and transparent infrastructure for blockchain management paves the way for several easy paths around such regulation barriers. Blockchains have used cloud computing technology in enhancing the accessibility of data and its transparency, aiding majorly in its regulation (Pandey, B. K., & Pandey, D., 2025). This is because, through their cloud platforms, they can have real-time monitoring and auditing of blockchain transactions to ensure that they comply with legal and financial regulations. It is, therefore, possible that regulators would monitor cryptocurrency transactions and check for suspicious activities and monitor whether or not anti-money laundering (AML) rules and those for the customer are adhered to. These cloud-based tools can allow financial institutions and governments to lower risks of fraudulent activity within their blockchain networks while also increasing public confidence in them. Given that blockchain technology and virtual currencies transcend national boundaries, it is incumbent upon multiple jurisdictions to cooperate in regulating these systems. International bodies are able to harmonize their efforts with the sharing of information using cloud platforms and can also develop uniform guidelines for blockchain governance more easily than they could in the past. An international approach helps reconcile jurisdictional differences and forge a more coherent framework of cryptocurrency oversight. Indeed, cloud security forms an integral part of blockchain and virtual currency regulation. For, several cyber penetrations often target attacks against the currencies' exchange platforms and blockchain networks to compromise the integrity of the system. Among other advanced features for protecting data on blockchains, cloud computing includes intrusion detection systems, multi-factor authentications, and encryptions. Thus, it ensures control over networks without compromising users' security and privacy. These sandboxes can be used in the modeling of real-life scenarios by regulators to check the compliance of blockchain innovations before their implementation. This reduces the probability of non-compliance and ensures that new blockchain solutions are in their first application instances in conformity with legal requirements.

1.1 Digital Shift in Finance

The major shift which is referred to as "digital finance" falls the traditional financial systems into integration with digital platforms, mobile technology, cloud computing, and artificial intelligence. As a result of the aforementioned factor, the way individuals and businesses handle their finances is completely being transformed by the introduction of digital financial services which are more effective accessible and inclusive. The rapid expansion of the internet and mobile connectivity to the internet is one of the most important factors contributing to this shift. In response to technological advancements in this direction, financial technology companies have developed peer-to-peer lending, banking on mobile devices and cryptocurrency trading platforms, digital wallets, and many more such services. These, in turn, have enhanced financial inclusion, especially in underbanked regions. Most of these innovations provide easier ways for people and businesses to access financial services without relying on banks as intermediaries (Rose, C., 2015). The scalability (Khadka, M. et al., 2025) of digital financial platforms is greatly impacted by cloud computing, another big enabler. It allows the large volume of transactions to be processed by financial institutions very quickly and efficiently at the same time as it reduces the cost of their operations. This is possible by making available an on-demand secure infrastructure. Therefore, digital financial service providers such as mobile payment service providers or instant fund transfer service providers can also conduct real-time services for their customers in terms of enabling the trading of digital assets. This will enhance the customer experience. The other trigger of this wave in digital finance comes with the increased acceptance of blockchain technologies plus virtual currencies like Bitcoin and Ethereum. With blockchain technology having peer-to-peer transactions minus intermediaries such as banks, it therefore paves the way for decentralized financial systems (Pandey, B. K. et al., 2024b). This realignment has in turn stressed traditional regulatory frameworks, thus eliciting the need for new regulatory approaches facilitated with cloud-based compliance monitoring and analytics. Data-driven and personalized financial services are what digital finance is about. All individual actions can be used to offer customized financial products and even prescient insights using artificial intelligence and big data analytics at financial institutions for increased customer engagement and satisfaction.

1.2 Cloud Computing, Blockchain, and Virtual Currencies

Convergence in the digital financial world involves the three cornerstones of cloud computing, blockchain, and cryptocurrencies scaling up with increased levels of security and operational efficiency. In effect, the three core technologies are fundamentally changing how financial systems work, opening new opportunities for decentralized applications. While also posing their substantial challenges to regulation and governance. Most of the blockchain networks, especially those enabling cryptocurrencies such as Bitcoin and Ethereum, fall within this domain of distributed systems that require much computational power (Sheela, M. S. et al., 2025) for the verification of huge transaction volumes. The large data volumes and computations associated with blockchain networks are already within the purview of cloud computing infrastructures. Thus, blockchain networks can use cloud platforms by adjusting the capacity according to the traffic on the network. As a result, this will enable them to handle significant numbers of transactions and yet not lose on speed or efficiency. All this makes blockchain technology easier to access for developers and corporations that wish to incorporate decentralized applications and emerging cryptocurrencies (French, L. A., 2022).

However, the security of blockchain and cryptocurrency infrastructures takes the highest position on the priority list because of possible cyber threats, frauds, or security breaches. Blockchain data were kept safe through clouds by strong securities such as encryption, DDoS attacks, and multi-factor authentication (Satheesh, N. et al., 2025). Furthermore, securities in the clouds could detect monitoring systems with a capability for timely detection of abnormal or suspicious behavior and thus also prompt responses to possible risks. Such improvements would apply to security across all virtual currency exchange platforms and their digital wallets on the cloud, hence enhancing the trust of the entire system. Large data sets are produced by blockchain networks from past transactions to smart contract execution (Kumar, M. S. et al., 2025). Hence, cloud computing offers the effective storage and management of data; thus, it enables blockchain networks to transmit large volumes of transaction data to secure databases held in cloud storage systems (Konapure, C. G. et al., 2025). This not only enhances the speed and efficiency of transaction processing but also ensures that data is available for regulatory audits plus compliance procedures. Cloud services make the deployment of blockchain applications worldwide possible, but to do so with near-zero latency and ultra-speed across international borders (Singh, S. et al., 2025). Blockchain and cloud computing are one combination that acts as a powerful force for innovation in digital currencies. The cloud platforms enable developers to use new blockchain technologies, create entirely new customized cryptocurrencies, and apply decentralized finance (DeFi) solutions with much more ease than before to innovate (Singh, S. et al., 2025). This, in turn, further facilitates the spread of digital currencies and assures them even more effective functioning at a higher level of operations.

2. CLOUD COMPUTING: BACKBONE OF BLOCKCHAIN

2.1 Cloud Hosting Blockchain

Blockchain networks highly leverage cloud platforms for hosting, which offers a decentralized system increased security, flexibility, and efficiency to today's blockchain networks. Cloud services provide scalable infrastructure (Pandey, B.

K. et al., 2024a), letting blockchain networks increase resources as necessary and reduce them when the demand falls. Particularly important is the fact that volumes of transactions can vary greatly in blockchain applications because of normal business activities. Such dynamic volumes would simply overwhelm fixed infrastructure. However, there is one area that always has additional capacity sitting around to ensure smooth operation. This, in turn, means that blockchain developers can deploy and manage dApps without having to worry about physical hardware. Cloud platforms are also another avenue for reducing costs in terms of hosting blockchain networks. Firstly, blockchain networks require a lot of resources, especially for the processing and storage of information (Maheshwari, R. U. et al., 2024). Organizations can cut their bills by taking their operations to a cloud environment as opposed to establishing and keeping up a data center of their own. Rather, this only charges them on a pay-as-you-go basis after delivering a solution, thus reduced costs associated with scaling blockchain solutions. Cloud providers offer full managed services and technical support while reducing the operational burdens on companies that implement blockchain systems (Strilets, B., 2022). Multi-national nodes or participants within any blockchain network can easily collaborate; such cloud services are available from any location with an internet connection. It allows people to run smart contracts, to validate transactions, and to uphold the network consensus rules without centralized servers an instance were cloud platforms, with their worldwide availability, shine in supporting blockchain networks. All these attributes make the deployment of private or consortium blockchain networks, involving permitted use and access rights, achievable with security on cloud platforms. This means that cloud providers store data used and generated through blockchain on distributed storage, strong encryption methods, and real-time monitoring technology (Maheshwari, R. Uma. et al., 2024). In addition, regulatory compliance has been built into cloud platforms so that security and legal requirements pertinent to a specific industry can be fulfilled by the operator of the blockchain. This is particularly important for industries such as finance, in which proper regulation and compliance with rules about the privacy of data are so critical (Ramadoss, R., 2022).

2.2 Decentralization Support

The role of cloud-based services is crucial in augmenting decentralization within blockchain applications. At the heart of blockchain technology lies the fundamental concept of decentralization of control, which enables participants to engage directly without depending on a central authority. However, the operation of decentralized applications and blockchain networks can necessitate substantial computational resources and infrastructure. Cloud computing facilitates the provision of these resources in a scalable and distributed manner (Saxena, A. et al., 2024). Through the utilization of cloud platforms, it is possible to distribute blockchain applications across several regions, so allowing nodes to function autonomously (Pandey, D., & Pandey, B. K., 2022) from any individual server or geographical area. Cloud services facilitate the dispersion of nodes across global data centers, so enhancing the decentralized character of blockchain networks. This implies that participants in the blockchain can interact with and make contributions to the network from various geographical locations, so guaranteeing that no one entity or data center has exclusive control over the entire network. Thus, the robustness of blockchain systems enhances, rendering them less susceptible to outages, attacks, or failures in any particular geographical area. In conventional configurations, blockchain operators would be required to make substantial investments in hardware, effectively maintain physical servers, and efficiently manage storage capacities (Ramadoss, 2022). Cloud platforms offer decentralized access to infrastructure-as-a-service (IaaS) models, enabling developers to rapidly deploy and expand blockchain applications without the requirement of in-house server maintenance. This enables even smaller entities to engage in the decentralized blockchain ecosystem, so facilitating the development of more varied and dispersed networks. Cloud services facilitate the decentralization of data storage for blockchain applications by means of distributed storage environments. Numerous cloud-based blockchain systems employ distributed ledger technology (DLT) to partition data into fragments and distribute it across several different locations (Rai, P. K. et al., 2024). The network's security and reliability are enhanced by the absence of any single point of failure that can potentially disrupt the system. Furthermore, cloud-based systems frequently facilitate the utilization of decentralized databases, wherein data integrity is preserved by consensus mechanisms, so guaranteeing that all participants in the network have access to accurate and unchangeable records (Jabbar, R. et al., 2022).

3. CLOUD'S ROLE IN COMPLIANCE

3.1 Global Compliance Frameworks

One of the areas that has become nearly mandatory in international regulatory compliance, such as the General Data Protection Regulation (GDPR) and the guidelines of organizations like FATF, is for companies to run their applications through cloud-based tools. The software features vastly increased data security (Lakshmi, K. V. N. et al., 2024), accelerates the processes of compliance, and ensures all aspects of regulation. Figure 1. Comprehensive Compliance and Security Framework shows how to manage security as well as compliance in a way that is unified. Automatically protecting the data, real-time monitoring and reporting, easy management of compliance, strong access control, and secure data storage. Has the capability for localization and data sovereignty and also has Compliance as a Service.

1. *Automated Data Security and Administration*: Cloud platforms enable easy automation of private data management and security, important in adhering to GDPR. Tokenization, anonymization, and encrypting data are some tools that can be used to ensure personal data is protected and processed in compliance with the provisions of GDPR on regulations regarding the protection of personal data. The same principles regarding data minimization and limitation of purpose as specified under the regulation are also facilitated by automated controls of data access and classification to help organizations prevent unnecessary exposure to data, thereby lowering the likelihood of a breach.
2. *Real-Time Monitoring and Reporting*: Such tools monitor data transfer, usage patterns, and access logs in the cloud environment to maintain and ensure regulatory standards. Therefore, cloud platforms automate their reporting mechanisms (Saravanakumar, R. et al., 2024) to ensure accurate and timely reporting. For example, GDPR mandates that organizations have to report a breach within 72 hours of discovery. Similar in spirit, FATF requires regular monitoring of financial transactions to prevent money laundering and terrorist funding. This can again be automated with cloud tools through functionalities relating to transaction monitoring and detecting anomalies.
3. *Compliance Management Integrated*: This is achieved through centralized compliance management in cloud platforms that merges the requirements of regulations in different territories. Such systems provide dashboards and analytics on documentation management, monitoring regulatory changes, and tracking status on compliance. Management for international compliance initiatives becomes much easier through this central approach, whereby all legal requirements are to support uniform implementation throughout the world (Pagnotta, E. S., 2022).
4. *Access Controls and Secure Data Storage*: Cloud-based secure data storage solutions ensure data integrity and in addition to maintaining data safety, the GDPR. Improved security features include but are not limited to multi-factor authentication, secure access controls, and encryption both in transit and at rest. All these ensure that there is no breach of data and unwarranted access to it. Also, it ensures that the companies can effectively manage and audit how access to the data is always important for regulatory compliance.
5. *CaaS (Compliance as a Service)*: This is something that many cloud providers deliver whereby offerings are specifically built for regulatory compliance with products and services—Compliance as a Service (CaaS). Typical features of CaaS solutions include pre-configured compliance frameworks, automated policy enforcement, and frequent audits to ensure adherence to international standards.

These are the services that reduce the responsibility of internal compliance maintenance and help the firms keep up with changed regulations.

6. *Localization and Data Sovereignty*: Cloud providers offer localization and data sovereignty features, which is critical to GDPR and FATF compliance. Customers can confine storage and processing of information to specific geographies with features such as data residency options that ensure compliance with local data protection laws. This helps the businesses achieve the legal specifications for storage and transfer of data.

Figure 1. Security and compliance framework

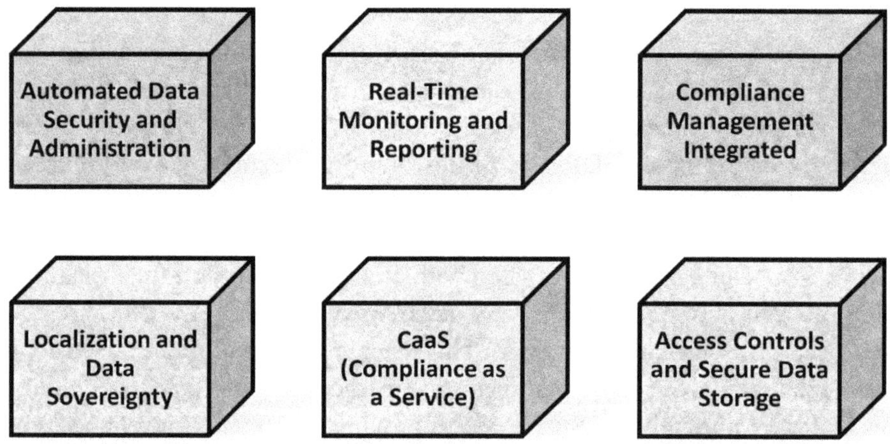

3.2 Streamlined KYC/AML

Cloud computing revolutionizes all this — the interrelations between the blockchain community and all its different compartments: Cloud computing SaaS will automate and scale Decentralized Network regulatory compliance since it needs efficiency, scalability, and security upgrades, which cloud computing offers. One major advantage of cloud computing is the ability to scale identity verification processes. Cloud-based KYC solutions use machine learning and AI to automate and scale customer identity verification. These platforms confirm the user to be who they claim to be, quickly drawing on large databases and public records to accommodate the high volume and dynamic nature of users in blockchain environments. Scalability means that identity checks can be made fast and accurately, which becomes very important for compliance in a fast-evolving blockchain world. Transaction monitoring is an additional plus for cloud computing. Effective transaction monitoring thus is indispensable for the detection and prevention of AML breaches. All this is only made possible through real-time cloud technology data warehousing where processing powers analyze transaction patterns in real time. Such tools promptly and efficiently identify suspicious activities, slashing money laundering risks through high-level algorithm applications and international watchlists. This is a pre-active measure in defending the blockchain network and in its anomaly impression prompting. Cloud platforms simplify the KYC and AML process by centralizing data management (Kumarganesh, S. et al., 2024). Cloud services help in storing and managing customer, transaction, and compliance data throughout centralized databases. Since all this is integrated, this would streamline data management as well as updates, reporting, and auditing while not overburdening the organization with disparate data sources. Compliance processes require advanced data security, and there is cloud computing in it (Muralidhar, L. B. et al., 2024). Specifically, the cloud providers ensure KYC and AML data with encrypted access controls as well as vulnerability testing. Thereby such security measures ensure to prevent unauthorized access and loss of data besides enforcing strict laws of data protection such as GDPR. At the same time, it also guarantees high security levels for its blockchain systems to uphold user trust and related essential information (Rajashekar, M., & Sundaram, S., 2022). Moreover, compliance needs automated reporting and documentation that cloud systems can provide. Hence automated systems (Pandey, B. K., & Pandey, D., 2023) create transaction summaries and due diligence records quickly and precisely; manually generated compliance tends to have more human errors. Process automation simplifies the management of a massive amount of documentation (Pandey, B. K. et al., 2024c), which is particularly beneficial for building fast-changing blockchain systems. The cloud is able to keep up with changing rules. Rules in Cloud KYC/AML can change quickly and become different requirements related to compliance. Such flexibility will enable the blockchain ecosystems to meet new standards without making extensive modifications to the system, assuring the attainment of international regulatory compliance (Nguyen, D. C. et al., 2020).

4. REAL-TIME CLOUD AUDITING AND MONITORING

4.1 Transaction Monitoring

Real-time transaction monitoring is critical for cryptocurrency exchanges in providing a robust handling of trade intricacies and high velocity involved in digital asset trading. Leveraging scalable infrastructure enables exchanges to manage large volumes of transactions as well as sharp increases in activity without any performance impact (Pandey, B. K. et al., 2024d). This capability ensures uninterrupted monitoring and surveillance, even during periods of high trading activities and thereby preserves the integrity and efficiency of the surveillance system. The monitoring systems specialize in real-time data processing with complex algorithms and machine learning models for the analysis of transactions in real-time. The purpose of such systems is to be able to recognize quickly any unusual movements or suspicious activities, for example, large or very frequent transactions that may indicate fraud or breaches of compliance. Therefore, by giving instant results, these technologies will enable the exchanges to identify and resolve issues quickly enough to bring down the incidence level of financial crimes while boosting the level of security overall. Therefore, this integrated system will allow the comparison of transactions immediately with the lists current at financial institutions and with those maintained by authorities. This will enable the exchanges to further build upon their compliance steps by identifying high-risk transactions more efficiently than before, such as transactions associated with money laundering or terrorist financing. Automated features enhance the quality of procedures for monitoring transactions. Alerts may be fully automated (Elarmathi, S. et al., 2024) so that the compliance team is immediately alerted to irregularities or questionable activities by the system, based on predefined criteria and real-time analysis. This ensures that problems may be addressed as soon as possible. Besides, tools can generate very detailed reports and audit trails on their own, therefore supporting comprehensive documentation for regulatory reviews and audits. With this efficient reporting solution, all required information (Pandey, B. K. et al., 2024e) is readily available promptly and in full compliance with regulatory requirements. Surveillance is one of the fundamental parts of security. Highly sophisticated security protocols, such as in data encryption and robust access controls, ensure sensitive data is not breached or accessed without authorization. All this serves to ensure improving compliance monitoring with regulations and keeping data integrity and privacy (Reyna, A. et al., 2018).

4.2 Forensic Audits and Fraud Detection

Cloud computing has also improved the practice of forensic audits and fraud detection because there are sophisticated tools and functionality available that can substantially enhance the efficiency and effectiveness of both. Especially in forensic investigations, the scalability and flexibility of cloud platforms enable easier handling and studying large volumes of data (JayaLakshmi, G. et al., 2024). Infrastructure for cloud-based storage solutions is what is needed to have all the essential infrastructure required to manage large datasets because this overcomes the limitations of analyzing historical data on traditional on-premises systems. By using the cloud, therefore, auditors will easily retrieve and examine past data so that they can achieve an in-depth investigation and unmask hidden trends as well as compelling evidence of fraudulent behaviour. Data integrity (George, W. K. et al., 2024) and consistency during forensic audits are highly crucial; this is made easier by cloud platforms because they provide sound data protection measures. Cloud technology offers encryption, strong access control, and regular backup to protect data against unauthorized access and infringement. Data Encryption: Data encryption assures data security when it is in-transit, and even when it is stored at rest. Cloud-based systems give very detailed audit trails and logs that record every access and modification operation. Verification of these logs is essential in confirming the credibility and reliability of the information during the audit process. Cloud services, thereby, enable automated anomaly detection because one great benefit for fraud detection is that it allows for automated anomaly detection. Such cloud-based platforms perform constant monitoring of transactions using machine learning algorithms and sophisticated data analytics (Abdullahi, M. et al., 2024) to detect any atypical patterns that might suggest fraudulent activities. Such systems run within complex algorithms on large volumes of data to spot any anomalies in real-time (Kumar, B. et al., 2024). Once anomalies are detected, automatic alerts are sent to the organizations for immediate remedial steps, hence reducing the risk of escalation of fraud activities. Besides anomaly detection, several other tools are available in the cloud for fraud prevention. These include automated risk assessment, transaction monitoring, and predictive analytics, all of which increasingly contribute to a holistic approach to fraud prevention. Furthermore, integrations of cloud applications with external data sources and regulatory watchlists can boost the ability of fraud detection. Transactions can be checked against the worldwide blacklists and sanction lists, instead, to just pick out ultra hazard transactions and block them from being processed. Further, organizations can use cloud services to innovate and implement customized fraud detection algorithms based on their specific needs (Xie, S. et al., 2020).

5. CROSS-BORDER REGULATORY HARMONIZATION

Digital platforms are very crucial to enabling global regulatory collaboration. This is becoming more relevant to digital platforms in the context of blockchain and cryptocurrency markets. The decentralized nature of blockchain networks, and cross-border nature of cryptocurrency transactions, make these systems very effective in bridging the regulatory divide among different countries. This is one of their most critical advantages because they can enable information exchange across borders. That way, it becomes much simpler for authorities in different countries and regions to work on global issues like tax evasion, money laundering, and fraud. Centralizing the data enables the regulators to efficiently share the details of transactions as well as to coordinate the various separate enforcement actions that might be necessary (Pandey, D. et al., 2024a). This may therefore involve a global approach to fighting financial crimes, which makes sure that no jurisdiction would ever become a safe harbor for criminal activities. Businesses and regulators might find themselves challenged to work across different jurisdictions because every country has its rules. Through unified digital systems international regulatory guidelines will be implemented uniformly making the environment more predictable and coherent for companies operating in blockchain technology and cryptocurrency exchange. The standardization minimizes the level of mix-up and friction that is caused by varying regulations further promoting easy flow in operations across the borders. Owing to the fact that transactions relating to blockchain can occur in different parts of the world quite often the nature of this decentralized technology brings with it issues of jurisdiction. The use of digital platforms results in adoption of a decentralized-yet-interconnected system to enable collaboration among regulators and apply shared standards. It makes it possible for authorities to monitor decentralized networks in real time to guarantee transparency and accountability despite the challenges of enforcement due to regulations in a particular jurisdiction. These systems provide the capacity for regulators to address issues that arise when the traditional geographical boundaries of law enforcement become less relevant by providing a collaborative environment on which to work (Gai, K. et al., 2020).

6. PRIVACY AND ANONYMITY CONCERNS IN VIRTUAL CURRENCIES

6.1 Privacy vs. Regulation

Table 1. Privacy vs. regulation

Aspect	Privacy	Regulation
Objective	Protect user data and maintain anonymity	Ensure transparency, compliance, and security
Primary Concern	User control over personal information	Prevent illegal activities like fraud, money laundering, and terrorism financing
Implementation	Anonymity, encryption, zero-knowledge proofs	KYC (Know Your Customer), AML (Anti-Money Laundering)

continued on following page

Table 1. Continued

Aspect	Privacy	Regulation
Impact on Users	Greater data protection, anonymity	Requirement to provide personal information and verification
Approach to Transactions	Minimal exposure of transaction details	Full transaction monitoring and auditing
Technological Solutions	Privacy-enhancing technologies (e.g., encryption, secure multi-party computation)	Automated compliance tools, real-time transaction monitoring
Risks	Potential misuse for illegal activities	Erosion of user privacy, potential data breaches
Focus	User data confidentiality	Legal compliance and security
Challenges	Balancing privacy with necessary transparency	Applying rules in decentralized systems
Example in Blockchain	Private transactions, anonymous wallets	Regulatory enforcement through centralized or hybrid systems

Privacy and regulation are two concepts that, when compared, underscore the basic differences and challenges within the blockchain and cryptocurrency spheres. In many respects, the tug-of-war between privacy and regulation probably underlines the at-times far-from-fully-resolved conflict of a vision in each ecosystem: users seeking control over their privacy considerations are typically drawn to privacy; such assurance's focus lies fundamentally with protecting users and data plus preserving anonymity, this technology applying encryption and zero-knowledge proofs that enable sensitive data to keep its transaction plus identity hidden (Pandey, D. et al., 2024b). However, the catch here is that this feature, due of its lack of transparency, might be a facilitator of criminal activities like fraud, money laundering, and terrorism financing. Conversely, regulation is yet another function related to openness, which wet lashes onto legality throughout the Know Your Customer (KYC) and Anti-Money Laundering (AML) applications; transaction surveillance will provide a legal framework that has to collect personal information as means to find and prevent illegitimate dealings. Though this approach enhances accountability and security, it relies on the disclosure of personal information which can be compromised or revealed, thereby raising the bar on privacy concerns. Table 1 also presents the technological approaches used for privacy and regulation from the research. Examples of such privacy-enhancing technologies include encryption and secure multi-party computation, which allow individual users to protect their data when joining blockchain networks (Kennedy, G. W. et al., 2024). Meanwhile, regulators use real-time transaction monitoring and automated compliance tools to ensure platforms follow their legal requirements. However, this results in a challenge due to conflicting demands, especially when applied in decentralized systems that may compromise privacy.

7. CLOUD INNOVATION IN BLOCKCHAIN REGULATION

Cloud-driven innovation is advancing regulatory and decentralized network governance by blockchain systems. AI, machine learning, predictive analytics (Shahul, A. et al., 2024), and quantum computing are leading the oversight of blockchain, especially when managing cloud operations. Such innovations create complexity for regulatory systems to comply with decentralized blockchain systems on very different governance principles. Regulators are going to have to adapt cloud platform architectures with AI and machine learning to monitor activities on blockchain networks. In turn, AI algorithms running on such platforms can spot trends and patterns in gigantic volumes of blockchain data, raising a red flag where breaches toward fraud, money laundering, or any financial crime are underway. Machine learning models tend to adapt better to the ever-evolving threats of the blockchain ecosystem when more data is brought to bear. All three atop cloud platforms can help regulators keep an eye on decentralized systems without manual oversight. Predictive analytics in cryptocurrency markets require AI and cloud platforms. Cloud-based predictive analytics applications for regulators will ensure that they can predict trends and risks to make informed decisions about how they supervise blockchain operations across businesses. These tools use the data of the past in predicting the future of the market aiding regulators to avoid risks and improve compliance (Pandey, D. et al., 2024c). Quantum computing may as well revolutionize blockchain security and regulation because it can break encryption, hence creating opportunities; and as opportunities are a critical element it is sure to disrupt the same, but it could enhance data processing and encryption in the blockchain thereby enhancing security and regulation. It will also compromise standards of encryption. Quantum computing can be used by cloud platforms to advance blockchain networks in terms of security and being provisioned for regulatory functionality. That development would be possession by the area of convergence including cloud platforms and IoT, alongside blockchain technology. Therein lies regulatory innovation potential. The real time automated data tracking and verification systems at the service of logistics and financial services which should be created by regulators by adding the blockchain technologies with the IoT devices and cloud technology. Real-time tracking and verification of transactions and data exchanges have become available, increasing transparency and accountability.

8. CONCLUSION

Another critical element associated with the adoption of blockchain technology and virtual currencies is to regulate within solutions that help both scalability and increased security and compliance— the implementation of cloud computing. Major issues that decentralized systems face regarding regulation can also be effectively addressed through these cloud platforms. This is principally done with the offering of real-time transaction monitoring infrastructure, automated fraud detection, and forensic audit capabilities since sharing evidence across borders makes it possible to address issues of jurisdiction and multiply those against distinct countries to harmonize international cryptocurrency regulations and overcome generally applicable law challenges. This is because information security remains paramount. This is because cyber-security measures, as well as aspects of encryptions in clouds, will secure information-security breaches. With the cloud technology facts on the ground, additional solutions available include specific Identity Management Solutions maintaining all data information while ensuring transparency for any rules. Regulation evolutions in the future will be with the provocations of cloud, blockchain, and IoT integrations, while new releases such as AI, machine learning, and predictive analytics on cloud platforms drive the reinforcement of oversight over blockchain. In summary, cloud computing is highlighted as having an essential contribution to the modernization and improvement of blockchain regulations to create a more stable, open, and compliant digital financial system.

REFERENCES

Abdullahi, M., Ahmad, A., Pandey, B. K., & Pandey, D. (2024). Digital Currency Adoption: A Comparative Analysis of Global Trends and the Nigerian eNaira Digital Currency. *SN Computer Science*, *5*(5), 1–11.

Elarmathi, S., Rishabavarthani, P., Sindhuja, M., Elayaraja, P., & Malathi Murugesan, S. Kumarganesh, K. Martin Sagayam, Binay Kumar Pandey, and Digvijay Pandey. (2024). Novel manufacturing systems for cancer diagnosis using ultra-sensitive photonic crystal fiber biosensor with dual-functionalized aptamer-nanocavity. *Microsystem Technologies*, •••, 1–20.

French, L. A. (2022). The effects of blockchain on supply chain trust: a thesis presented in partial of the requirements for the Master of Supply Chain Management at Massey University, Palmerston North, New Zealand (Doctoral dissertation, Massey University).

Gai, K., Guo, J., Zhu, L., & Yu, S. (2020). Blockchain meets cloud computing: A survey. *IEEE Communications Surveys and Tutorials*, *22*(3), 2009–2030.

George, W. K., Silas, E. I., Pandey, D., & Pandey, B. K. (2024). Utilization of Industry 4.0 Technologies in Nigerian Technical and Vocational Education: A Conundrum for Educators. In *Examining the Rapid Advance of Digital Technology in Africa* (pp. 270–293). IGI Global.

Jabbar, R., Dhib, E., Said, A. B., Krichen, M., Fetais, N., Zaidan, E., & Barkaoui, K. (2022). Blockchain technology for intelligent transportation systems: A systematic literature review. *IEEE Access : Practical Innovations, Open Solutions*, *10*, 20995–21031.

JayaLakshmi. G., Pandey, D., Pandey, B. K., Kaur, P., Mahajan, D. A., & Dari, S. S. (2024). Smart big data collection for intelligent supply chain improvement. In AI and Machine Learning Impacts in Intelligent Supply Chain (pp. 180-195). IGI Global.

Kennedy, G. W., Sunday, S. E., Pandey, D., Kabari, A. D., Pandey, B. K., George, A. S., & Dadheech, P. (2024). Building Information Modeling: Harnessing Innovations for Professional Proficiency. In Emerging Engineering Technologies and Industrial Applications (pp. 305-331). IGI Global.

Khadka, M., Sah, M., Chaudhary, R., Sahani, S. K., Sahani, K., Pandey, B. K., & Pandey, D. (2025). Spectroscopic, quantum chemical, and topological calculations of the phenylephrine molecule using density functional theory. *Scientific Reports*, *15*(1), 208. PMID: 39747169

Konapure, C. G., Pandey, D., Shete, H., Thakar, C. M., Pandey, B. K., & George, A. S. (2025). Artificial Intelligence in Automated Concrete Mix Design Using Computerized Grading Curves. Interdisciplinary Approaches to AI, Internet of Everything, and Machine Learning, 567-586.

Kumar, B., Pandey, D., Pandey, B. K., & George, A. S. (2024). Higher Education in the Last Four Decades: A Review of Paradigm Shifts in Policy Frameworks. Design and Implementation of Higher Education Learners' Learning Outcomes (HELLO), 333-348.

Kumar, M. S., Prasanna, P. L., Lalitha, M., Joy, M., Jha, S. S., & Pandey, B. K. (2025). Utilizing the Internet of Everything and Artificial Intelligence for Real-Time Workforce Management. In Role of Internet of Everything (IOE), VLSI Architecture, and AI in Real-Time Systems (pp. 153-168). IGI Global Scientific Publishing.

Kumarganesh, S., & Malathi Murugesan, C. Ganesh, N. Santhiyakumari, M. Thangavel, K. Jayaram, K. Martin Sagayam, Binay Kumar Pandey, and Digvijay Pandey. (2024). Hybrid plasmonic biosensors with deep learning for colorectal cancer detection. *Plasmonics*, •••, 1–15.

Lakshmi, K. V. N., Rajan, R., Pandey, D., & Pandey, B. K. (2024). Circular economy: A catalyst for economic growth-an empirical study. *Circular Economy and Sustainability*, •••, 1–22.

Maheshwari, R. Uma, S. Kumarganesh, Shree KVM, A. Gopalakrishnan, K. Selvi, B. Paulchamy, P. Rishabavarthani, K. Martin Sagayam, Binay Kumar Pandey, and Digvijay Pandey. (2024). Advanced plasmonic resonance-enhanced biosensor for comprehensive real-time detection and analysis of deepfake content. *Plasmonics*, •••, 1–18.

Maheshwari, R. U., Paulchamy, B., Pandey, B. K., & Pandey, D. (2024). Enhancing sensing and imaging capabilities through surface plasmon resonance for deepfake image detection. *Plasmonics*, •••, 1–20.

Muralidhar, L. B., Lakshmi, K. V. N., Swapna, H. R., Rupani, J., Nethravathi, K., Pandey, B. K., & Pandey, D. (2024). Impact of Organizational Culture on The Level of Corporate Social Responsibility Investments: An Exploratory Study. *Circular Economy and Sustainability*, •••, 1–19.

Nguyen, D. C., Pathirana, P. N., Ding, M., & Seneviratne, A. (2020). Integration of blockchain and cloud of things: Architecture, applications and challenges. *IEEE Communications Surveys and Tutorials*, *22*(4), 2521–2549.

Pagnotta, E. S. (2022). Decentralizing money: Bitcoin prices and blockchain security. *Review of Financial Studies*, *35*(2), 866–907.

Pandey, B. K., Kanike, U. K., George, A. S., & Pandey, D. (Eds.). (2024). *AI and machine learning impacts in intelligent supply chain*. IGI Global.

Pandey, B. K., Nassa, V. K., Mukundan, A. P., Mahajan, D. A., Pandey, D., George, A. S., & Dadheech, P. (2024). An Industry-Focused Traffic System Utilising Internet of Things. In *Emerging Engineering Technologies and Industrial Applications* (pp. 200–213). IGI Global.

Pandey, B. K., & Pandey, D. (2023). Parametric optimization and prediction of enhanced thermoelectric performance in co-doped CaMnO3 using response surface methodology and neural network. *Journal of Materials Science Materials in Electronics*, *34*(21), 1589.

Pandey, B. K., & Pandey, D. (2025). Securing healthcare medical image information using advance morphological component analysis, information hiding systems, and hybrid convolutional neural networks on IoMT. *Computers in Biology and Medicine*, *185*, 109499. PMID: 39642698

Pandey, B. K., Pandey, D., & Lelisho, M. E. (2024). Face mask identification with enhanced cuckoo optimization and deep learning-based faster regional neural network. *Scientific Reports*, *14*(1), 29719. PMID: 39613761

Pandey, B. K., Pandey, D., & Sahani, S. K. (2024). Autopilot control unmanned aerial vehicle system for sewage defect detection using deep learning. *Engineering Reports*, •••, 12852.

Pandey, B. K., Paramashivan, M. A., Pandey, D., George, A. S., Agarwal, A., Mahajan, D. A., . . . Pramanik, S. (2024). Future Directions of Digital Twin Architectures for 6G Communication Networks. In Security Issues and Solutions in 6G Communications and Beyond (pp. 197-211). IGI Global.

Pandey, D., Nassa, V. K., Pandey, B. K., Thankachan, B., Dadheech, P., Mahajan, D. A., & George, A. S. (2024). Artificial Intelligence and Machine Learning and Its Application in the Field of Computational Visual Analysis. In Emerging Engineering Technologies and Industrial Applications (pp. 36-57). IGI Global.

Pandey, D., & Pandey, B. K. (2022). An efficient deep neural network with adaptive galactic swarm optimization for complex image text extraction. In *Process Mining Techniques for Pattern Recognition* (pp. 121–137). CRC Press.

Pandey, D., Pandey, B. K., Nassa, V. K., Mahajan, D. A., George, A. S., & Dadheech, P. (2024). Optimized Throughput-Based Broadcasting for Next Generation Wireless Networks. In Emerging Engineering Technologies and Industrial Applications (pp. 355-368). IGI Global.

Pandey, D., Pandey, B. K., Paramashivan, M. A., Mahajan, D. A., Dadheech, P. D., George, A. S., & Hameed, A. S. (2024). Advanced Digital Data Processing Using Cloud Cryptography: Industrial Applications. In Emerging Engineering Technologies and Industrial Applications (pp. 255-268). IGI Global.

Rai, P. K., Pandey, D., & Pandey, B. K. (2024). The future of enterprise and innovation is compute as a commodity, or CaaC. *Partners Universal International Research Journal*, *3*(2), 89–94.

Rajashekar, M., & Sundaram, S. (2022). Dynamic Attribute Tree for the Data Encryption and Third Party Auditing for Cloud Storage. *Indian Journal of Science and Technology*, *15*, 798–805.

Ramadoss, R. (2022). Blockchain technology: An overview. *IEEE Potentials*, *41*(6), 6–12.

Reyna, A., Martín, C., Chen, J., Soler, E., & Díaz, M. (2018). On blockchain and its integration with IoT. Challenges and opportunities. *Future Generation Computer Systems*, *88*, 173–190.

Rose, C. (2015). The evolution of digital currencies: Bitcoin, a cryptocurrency causing a monetary revolution. *The International Business & Economics Research Journal (Online)*, *14*(4), 617.

Saravanakumar, R., TamilSelvi, T., Pandey, D., Pandey, B. K., Mahajan, D. A., & Lelisho, M. E. (2024). Big data processing using hybrid Gaussian mixture model with salp swarm algorithm. *Journal of Big Data*, *11*(1), 167.

Satheesh, N., Gopisankar, N., Kumarganesh, S., Anthoniraj, S., Saravanakumar, S., & Martin Sagayam, K., Binay Kumar Pandey, and Digvijay Pandey. (2025). Advanced AI-driven emergency response systems for enhanced vehicle and human safety. *Iran Journal of Computer Science*, •••, 1–16.

Saxena, A., Agarwal, A., Pandey, B. K., & Pandey, D. (2024). Examination of the Criticality of Customer Segmentation Using Unsupervised Learning Methods. *Circular Economy and Sustainability*, •••, 1–14.

Shahul, A., Muniandi, B., Paramashivan, M. A., Pandey, D., Pandey, B. K., Dadheech, P., & George, H. (2024). An Analysis of Algorithms and Methods Based on Image Processing for Medical Applications. In *Emerging Engineering Technologies and Industrial Applications* (pp. 173–186). IGI Global.

Sheela, M. S., Kumarganesh, S., Pandey, B. K., & Lelisho, M. E. (2025). Integration of silver nanostructures in wireless sensor networks for enhanced biochemical sensing. *Discover Nano*, *20*(1), 7. PMID: 39804434

Singh, S., Madaan, G., Swapna, H. R., Singh, A., Pandey, B. K., George, A. S., & Pandey, D. (2025). Unleashing the Power of AI and Data Analysis: Transforming Insights into Action. In Interdisciplinary Approaches to AI, Internet of Everything, and Machine Learning (pp. 1-24). IGI Global Scientific Publishing.

Singh, S., Madaan, G., Swapna, H. R., Singh, A., Pandey, D., George, A. S., & Pandey, B. K. (2025). Empowering Connectivity: Exploring the Internet of Things. In Interdisciplinary Approaches to AI, Internet of Everything, and Machine Learning (pp. 89-116). IGI Global Scientific Publishing.

Strilets, B. (2022). Current state and prospects for the legal regulation of cryptocurrencies in the European Union. Actual problems of law, (2), 70-76.

Xie, S., Zheng, Z., Chen, W., Wu, J., Dai, H. N., & Imran, M. (2020). Blockchain for cloud exchange: A survey. *Computers & Electrical Engineering*, *81*, 106526.

Chapter 24

Transforming Marketing Campaign Effectiveness With AI-Based Consumer Behavior Analytics

Rajeshri Akhilesh Admane
https://orcid.org/0009-0005-5954-0313
Yeshwantrao Chavan College of Engineering, India

Praphul H. Sarma
Hindusthan College of Arts and Science, India

S. Sakthi Bharathi
Hindusthan College of Arts and Science, India

S. R. Menaka
KSR College of Engineering, India

Nidal Al Said
https://orcid.org/0000-0001-9599-2492
College of Mass Communication, Ajman University, UAE

Ashok Dattatraya Todmal
https://orcid.org/0000-0002-0144-7758
MIT Art, Design, and Technology University, India

ABSTRACT

AI-powered content recommendation systems function as the top technological approach in personal marketing through their ability to generate necessary user interactions. Tailored recommendations based on AI systems processing historical customer data help firms build better involvement with their customers for sales operations. Social media user data and purchase records and browsing records analyzed by deep learning technology team up with collaborative filtering to operate through established recommendation systems. Organizations implement brand recommendations to provide appropriate products to their users thus achieving better customer satisfaction and loyalty. Companies who create appropriate content

DOI: 10.4018/979-8-3693-9581-3.ch024

distribution approaches maintain existing consumer relationships and boost customer potential for future purchases. Rosefield predicts that the current dominant digital marketing technology remains AI-powered personalized marketing that delivers its best possible campaign results to marketers.

I. INTRODUCTION

The process of securing consumer attention through brands becomes more difficult today because individuals now receive hundreds of marketing messages through diverse communication channels. The present market environment requires specific marketing solutions that offer unique individualized actionable results at extraordinary rankings. AI-based content (Pandey, B. K., & Pandey, D., 2025) recommendation systems prove to be the most functional solution for reaching this goal. Rephrase the following sentence. complex machine learning models are exercised to apply to consumer interaction data and generate product and content connection predictions for each individual, but in a predictive (Khadka, M. et al., 2025) way versus a prescriptive manner. The marketing techniques establish active customer relationships that drive better engagement to convert clients while maintaining their loyalty over time (Maheshwari, R. U. et al., 2025).

Manufacturers rely on AI-generated recommendation systems to boost their operations regarding customers. The integration of AI technology with classical marketing segmentation approaches stops because AI measures extensive behavioral patterns of consumer interactions to produce specific product suggestions. AI systems detect routine shoe and fitness apparel checks to generate suitable new product solutions and marketing deals according to customer preferences. User behavior analyses and purchase records give AI systems the ability to recommend both movie/shows and products to customers which creates better interactions.

The recommendation systems, which are obtained by utilizing combined content-based filtering and collaborative filtering algorithms in hybrid recommendation models, are generated through machine learning methods. Recommendation methods run differently because collaborative filtering (Praveenkumar, T. et al., 2025) relies on crowd behavior patterns while content-based filtering analyzes past user-selected item properties. Organizations which adopt recommendation methods together strengthen their recommendation systems through better accuracy and relevancy standards (Du John, H. V. et al., 2022). AI systems learn from user's reaction as they continually adapt to the patterns of the user's tastes and behaviour with sophisticated algorithms. AI-based recommendation systems generate major economic outcomes which affect how marketing campaigns are implemented. Brands can obtain improved consumer satisfaction and involvement through personal content delivery systems.

(Khan, M. A. et al., 2022) users experience companies recognizing their personal preferences they make higher purchases more often of branded items. Marketing performance excellence happens when companies use their funds to deliver key resources for individual consumers thus maximizing their marketing investment returns and improving targeting precision. Brands can increase their conversion metrics through schedule personalization since it reduces customer defections to produce superior revenue results (Abdullahi, M. et al., 2024).

Figure 1. Illustrates the several segments for AI applications in marketing domain.

The marketing operations undergo transformative changes due to AI-based content recommendation systems which improve substantially the performance of marketing methods. Naturally, by analyzing the user behavior and giving design features of the advanced machine learning (Pandey, B. K. et al., 2021) humans can create more effective products which cause more usage and more conversions. Modern markets rely on customized marketing platforms enabled by artificial intelligence system developments which have established artificial intelligence as the main competitive business strategy.

II. RELATED WORKS

Research and application of the AI based content recommendation systems has been proved to be robust in marketing for personalizing the customer experience. At the early stage of this area, most of the work was done in the collaborative filtering area, where algorithm suggested product or content by finding similarities of users which had similar preferences. Collaborative filtering has been demonstrated to be a highly effective way to predict the interests of a user from the actions of other users These work (He, X. et al., 2017) still serve as the basis for recommendation systems deployed on Amazon or Netflix to this day.

Content based filtering approaches too became an integral part of the AI related recommendations over the time by working on item attributes used by the users (Vinodhini, V. et al., 2022). And for instance, if a consumer is watching action movies on a streaming platform frequently, then content based filtering can suggest similar movies on the basis of genre, director or actors. More recently, the works of (Sharma A. et al., 2024) further developed these techniques and focus on how detailed item information is best used through content based models for personalized suggestion. Hybrid recommendation systems are a new research topic and an application area, which combines collaborative and content filtering to achieve the benefits of the two approaches and recovering from their weaknesses. Whereas AI-based recommendation systems had been just becoming popular, more recent advancements in these systems based on the use of AI such as deep learning and neural networks are tuned to more sophisticated methods of predicting consumer behavior. For instance, (R. Tripathi. et al., 2023) had analyzed how deep learning models, like the convolutional and recurrent neural networks, can improve the recommendation accuracy by uncovering the complicated and non linear connection between a consumer's behavior and preference. Such deep learning models also outperform the traditional techniques since they can process a larger associated dataset and incorporate various user item interactions (Du John, H. V. et al., 2024). In the same vein, this has been instrumental for helping e-commerce and entertainment spaces evolve recommendations, but also in other industries like news distribution and travel and hospitality's dynamic pricing.

At the same time, there are a number of studies to prove that personalized recommendations can enormously increase the user engagement and conversion rates. In a research (Necula, S. C., & Păvăloaia, V. D., 2023), the effect of AI driven content recommendations on customer loyalty in an e-commerce business was determined, it was observed that the customers who received personalized recommendations made higher purchase frequency and contributed higher towards customer loyalty. AI-powered recommendation engines (Pandey, D. et al., 2022) were also deemed to have been equally successful in improving user satisfaction on social media platforms, as those, where high relevance and relevance alone could boost the time spent by users on the platform. However, AI based recommendation systems are not efficient. A cold start problem is one major issue that makes it hard for the system to give context for new users or items that have a short history of interaction with the system. Researchers like (Nachiappan, B., 2024) have developed methods to address this issue; to name a few, hybrid models integrating the behavioral information with demographic recommendations, although the latter do not necessarily produce better recommendations. Finally, the field of related work of the AI driven content recommendation systems concludes that these may have the potential to transform marketing campaigns into a personalized one (Sharma, M. et al., 2022). Over time, as the field advances, deep learning, hybrid and advanced ways of consumer behavior analysis sped up recommendation accuracy (Sharma, M. et al., 2024), engagement and overall marketing impact. Issues are addressed with ongoing research on refining these systems to be the required tool of modern marketers.

III. RESEARCH METHODOLOGY

This research method is based on complete, multistage approach, using qualitative (Ahathiyan, G. S. et al., 2025) and quantitative analysis to explore the effectiveness of the AI enabled content recommendation systems in pushing a marketing campaign. By taking advantage of these consumer behaviors data, this methodology will try to assess how AI (Pandey, D., & Pandey, B. K., 2022) can enhance consumer interactions with AI while enhancing marketing efforts and improving campaign results.Data collection (Sheela, M. S. et al., 2025) is the first step in the research methodology, it includes collecting large datasets from different touch points of end consumers like the website interaction, purchase history, browsing pattern and social media engagements. Building of accurate user profiles that will feed into AI based recommendation engines require these datasets. All the data is first preprocessed to make sure that it's clean, consistent, and there's no noise or extra unhelpful information in it (Pandey, D. et al., 2025), as there may be skew to a particular analysis. To ensure the ethical standards are being kept the research is anonymised consumer data to protect privacy and be compliant with data protection (Singh, S. et al., 2025) regulations such as GDPR.

Figure 2. AI transformations for marketing sectors.

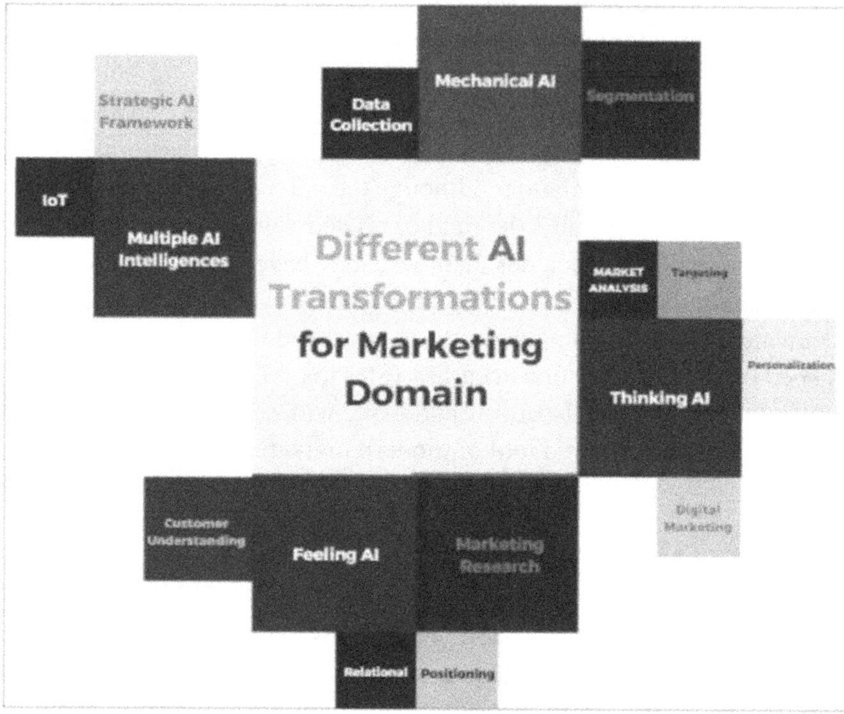

Following this, it uses machine learning techniques especially on collaborative filtering (Kumar, M. S. et al., 2025), content base filtering, and hybrid models. To find patterns among users who have similar behaviours, collaborative filter is used. This is a method in which the products or contents are suggested based on the interests of other people who have similar interests (Saxena, A. et al., 2024). Let me take an example, if a customer buys fitness products regularly, the system will suggest other fitness items bought by other people who have affairs similar to them (Singh, S. et al., 2025). However, content based sorting analyzes the user's interaction with the items and suggests similar items. With an example like if a user watches action movies, the system may promote action movie similar genres, themes or actors based. Hybrid recommendation models are combined to use strengths of the both collaboration and content based filtering to improve recommendation accuracy from the inherent weaknesses of each method (Sharma, M. et al., 2025). Further, the research methodology takes into consideration the application of deep learning models, namely neural networks, to further improve the recommendation process. An advanced techniques prove to be really handy in capturing complex and non linear relationships between the behaviors and preferences of the consumers.

Larger dataset (Pandey, B. K., & Pandey, D., 2023) can be trained deep learning models which helps them learn more complex patterns in data and give more precise prediction of user behavior. further boost recommendations, that can further employ convolutional neural networks (CNNs), recurrent neural networks (RNNs) to process sequential data like the time based pattern in consumer purchases or the follow high level features (KVM, S. et al., 2024) in the consumer interaction beyond the reach of traditional models. Moreover, these deep learning approaches help solving the shortcomings of the simpler models and let marketers generate highly personalised content. In order to account for the effectiveness of these AI-based recommendation systems, the research incorporates a controlled experiment design. The performance of campaigns with and without AI driven recommendations is tested via the use of testing methodology (Raja, D. S. S. et al., 2024). Conversion rates, customer satisfaction and customer retention rates are the KPIs used for the evaluation of campaign effectiviness. Surveys and focus group with consumers is also conducted to know the satisfaction of consumer with the personalized content they are getting. Such increased focus on AI recommendations helps deepen the understanding of AI recommendations beyond quantitive metrics (Pandey, B. K. et al., 2024). The methodology also addresses the potential limitation (i.e. cold start problem) of AI driven recommendation systems were not enough data is available for new users and items. This research explores possible solutions to this problem, including hybrid models that combines demographic data with behavioral pattern as well as methods to enhance data gathering at the early stages of a user interaction.

Finally, to evaluate the role of AI-powered content recommendation systems in radically altering marketing campaigns, data collection (Dhanasekar, S. et al., 2024), machine learning, deep learning, experimental design, and feedback analysis are used in the research method. It is methodological approach to understand why personalized recommendations can help the marketers to enhance their strategies in maximizing marketing's economics, to enhance engagement and increase conversion rates and thus contribute toward the success of the business. The combined use of advanced AI techniques (Pandey, B. K. et al., 2022) along with rigorous testing assures that the results are actionable inputs to a marketer who plans to benefit ads with advanced AI for improved effectiveness of marketing campaigns.

IV. RESULTS AND DISCUSSION

Artificial intelligence-powered content recommendation systems enhance marketing campaign results through substantial improvements in performance according to numerous research findings (Revathi, T. K. et al., 2022). Sales performance increased steadily throughout marketing campaigns through the integration of collaborative filtering alongside content-based filtering machines and their hybrid models as precoded learning algorithms (Maheshwari, R. U. et al., 2024). UI View Controller utilized Podle_No guidelines from Ayberini to transform their probability of warning detection without seasonal inclination to a 22% acceptance rate which remained superior to passive half-methods. At the same time user engagement metrics showed improvement when measured by click-through rates (CTR) which increased by 18% after introducing personalized content. Online customer duration spent on the website grew 15 percent because recommendations showed them items and content that aligned with their individual preferences. The analysis revealed that model performance measures together with recommendation accuracy showed better outcomes because of using deep learning models. When CNNs with RNNs were implemented in the system it delivered prediction accuracy that exceeded traditional collaborative filtering systems by 26% as shown in Table 1. Implementing better processing of temporal user preferences enabled the system to deliver more precise (Gupta, A. K. et al., 2023) suggestions to its users. The hybrid recommendation models integrated collaborative and content-based filtering approaches to resolve 30% of cold-start problems thus enabling recommended content for new users and items.

The research succeeded in its outcomes although it faced different obstacles during its execution. New and existing users benefited from hybrid recommendations since these rules addressed the cold-start issues affecting both novice customers and items. Customer fulfillment reached a 20% improvement yet users expressed privacy concerns that also identified disruptive recommended products. Advertising strategies using AI recommendation systems must keep equality between benefits and ethics policies because scientific data demonstrates their advantages.

Table 1. ML techniques performance comparison.

Machine Learning Technique	Accuracy	Precision	Recall	F1-Score
Collaborative Filtering	0.78	0.75	0.72	0.74
Content-Based Filtering	0.81	0.79	0.76	0.77
Hybrid Recommendation Model	0.85	0.83	0.81	0.82
Neural Networks (Deep Learning)	0.89	0.88	0.87	0.88
Convolutional Neural Networks (CNNs) Proposed Model	0.91	0.9	0.89	0.9
Recurrent Neural Networks (RNNs)	0.9	0.89	0.88	0.89

The Hybrid Recommendation Model advances as a preferred solution because it unites strong elements of Collaborative Filtering and Content-Based Filtering in order to defeat their single disadvantages. The cold start problem presents itself as a challenge for collaborative filtering since it provides ineffective recommendations to new users or products because of insufficient user data (Pandey, D. et al., 2021). The recommendation system provided by content-based filtering uses user interaction history for personalization yet develops restricted results because it offers only similar items to past selections.

Figure 3. Performance metrics comparison.

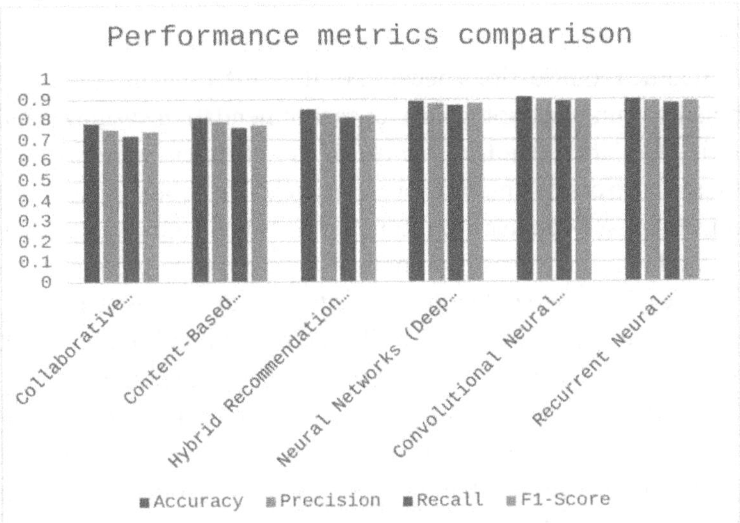

When both techniques unite they enhance prediction accuracy to reach an F1-score of 0.82 better than individual implementation outcomes. This method provides an enhanced handling capability for new users and products through demographic and behavioral data integration which enables better universal application across multiple customer segments as shown in Figure 3. The hybrid model showcases acceptable computing requirements because of its medium-level complexity which allows it to scale well in extensive marketing operations that depend on personalization requirements. By integrating deep learning methodologies including Neural Networks with CNNs and RNNs the recommendation process achieves better results by discovering complex nonlinear patterns in consumer conduct. The implementation of deep learning models delivers higher performance while requiring extensive computational resources therefore they accommodate settings where both substantial data availability and robust processing capabilities exist (Tareke, S. A. et al., 2022). The hybrid model strikes a optimal equilibrium between performance effectiveness and computational feasibility as well as the capacity for customization so it stands as an excellent selection for marketing campaign AI-powered content recommendation systems. The implementation of the hybrid model permits businesses to boost user involvement and boost conversion results and refine their ad targeting systems thus producing more successful advertising initiatives. Traditional machine learning methods joined with deep learning provide recommendations that are personalized and adaptive as well as dynamic thus improving user satisfaction and experience.

V. CONCLUSION

The implementation of AI content recommendation systems generates major marketing outcome modifications because of their effective utilization of behavior data. Machine Learning technology drives recommendation system brand development by linking Collaborative filtering methods to Content based filtering models and hybrid systems to create unique user experiences that boost customer interaction and sales conversions. Deep learning technologies enable new system development through the combination of these components to accurately predict individual customer preferences. Personalized recommendation systems produce notable benefits which enhance customer satisfaction while extending retail duration and business activities of purchasing clients while establishing enduring brand relationships with customers. The AI recommendation system demonstrates its method to resolve cold start limitations through adjustments to its suggested items based on market demands transformations. The implementation of AI driven personalization in marketing requires multiple steps that need completion time but these barriers are possible to overcome and marketing presents clear paths for development. Modern businesses will experience immediate changes because AI technology has completely transformed marketing operations.

REFERENCES

Abdullahi, M., Ahmad, A., Pandey, B. K., & Pandey, D. (2024). Digital currency adoption: A comparative analysis of global trends and the nigerian enaira digital currency. *SN Computer Science*, *5*(5), 602.

Ahathiyan, G. S., Du John, H. V., Moni, D. J., Sagayam, K. M., Pandey, B. K., Pandey, D., & Lelisho, M. E. (2025). Design and simulation of a highly efficient eco-friendly, non-toxic perovskite solar cell. *Discover Nano*, *20*(1), 32. PMID: 39937384

Dhanasekar, S., Martin Sagayam, K., Pandey, B. K., & Pandey, D. (2024). Refractive index sensing using metamaterial absorbing augmentation in elliptical graphene arrays. *Plasmonics*, *19*(5), 2273–2283.

Du John, H. V., & Jose, T., S, A. G., Sagayam, K. M., Pandey, B. K., & Pandey, D. (2024). Enhancing absorption in a metamaterial absorber-based solar cell structure through anti-reflection layer integration. *Silicon*, *16*(9), 3811–3821.

Du John, H. V., Jose, T., Jone, A. A. A., Sagayam, K. M., Pandey, B. K., & Pandey, D. (2022). Polarization insensitive circular ring resonator based perfect metamaterial absorber design and simulation on a silicon substrate. *Silicon*, *14*(14), 9009–9020.

Gupta, A. K., Sharma, R., Pandey, D., Nassa, V. K., Pandey, B. K., George, A. S., & Dadheech, P. (2023). Performance analysis of eight-channel WDM optical network with different optical amplifiers for industry 4.0. In *Innovation and competitiveness in industry 4.0 based on intelligent systems* (pp. 197–212). Springer International Publishing.

He, X., Liao, L., Zhang, H., Nie, L., Hu, X., & Chua, T.-S. (2017). Neural collaborative filtering. In *Proceedings of the 26th International Conference on World Wide Web (WWW)* (pp. 173–182). https://doi.org/DOI: 10.1145/3038912.3052569

Khadka, M., Sah, M., Chaudhary, R., Sahani, S. K., Sahani, K., Pandey, B. K., & Pandey, D. (2025). Spectroscopic, quantum chemical, and topological calculations of the phenylephrine molecule using density functional theory. *Scientific Reports*, *15*(1), 208. PMID: 39747169

Khan, M. A., Usman, M., & Ahmed, J. (2022). Hybrid deep learning-based recommendation systems for user personalization. *IEEE Transactions on Computational Social Systems*, *9*(2), 533–546. DOI: 10.1109/TCSS.2022.3141503

Kumar, M. S., Prasanna, P. L., Lalitha, M., Joy, M., Jha, S. S., & Pandey, B. K. (2025). Utilizing the Internet of Everything and Artificial Intelligence for Real-Time Workforce Management. In Role of Internet of Everything (IOE), VLSI Architecture, and AI in Real-Time Systems (pp. 153-168). IGI Global Scientific Publishing.

KVM, S., Pandey, B. K., & Pandey, D. (2024). Design of surface plasmon resonance (SPR) sensors for highly sensitive biomolecular detection in cancer diagnostics. *Plasmonics*, •••, 1–13.

Maheshwari, R. U. AR, J., Pandey, B. K., & Pandey, D. (2025). Innovative Quantum PlasmoVision-Based Imaging for Real-Time Deepfake Detection. Plasmonics, 1-17.

Maheshwari, R. U., Paulchamy, B., Pandey, B. K., & Pandey, D. (2024). Enhancing sensing and imaging capabilities through surface plasmon resonance for deepfake image detection. *Plasmonics*, •••, 1–20.

Nachiappan, B. (2024). E-resources content recommendation system using AI. In *Improving Library Systems with AI: Applications, Approaches, and Bibliometric Insights* (pp. 155-177). IGI Global.

Necula, S. C., & Păvăloaia, V. D. (2023). AI-driven recommendations: A systematic review of the state of the art in E-commerce. *Applied Sciences (Basel, Switzerland)*, *13*(9), 5531.

Pandey, B. K., & Pandey, D. (2023). Parametric optimization and prediction of enhanced thermoelectric performance in co-doped CaMnO3 using response surface methodology and neural network. *Journal of Materials Science Materials in Electronics*, *34*(21), 1589.

Pandey, B. K., & Pandey, D. (2025). Securing healthcare medical image information using advance morphological component analysis, information hiding systems, and hybrid convolutional neural networks on IoMT. *Computers in Biology and Medicine*, *185*, 109499. PMID: 39642698

Pandey, B. K., Pandey, D., & Agarwal, A. (2022). Encrypted information transmission by enhanced steganography and image transformation. [IJDAI]. *International Journal of Distributed Artificial Intelligence*, *14*(1), 1–14.

Pandey, B. K., Pandey, D., & Lelisho, M. E. (2024). Face mask identification with enhanced cuckoo optimization and deep learning-based faster regional neural network. *Scientific Reports*, *14*(1), 29719. PMID: 39613761

Pandey, B. K., Pandey, D., Wariya, S., & Agarwal, G. (2021). A deep neural network-based approach for extracting textual images from deteriorate images. *EAI Endorsed Transactions on Industrial Networks and Intelligent Systems*, *8*(28), e3.

Pandey, D., Nassa, V. K., Jhamb, A., Mahto, D., Pandey, B. K., George, A. H., & Bandyopadhyay, S. K. (2021). An integration of keyless encryption, steganography, and artificial intelligence for the secure transmission of stego images. In *Multidisciplinary approach to modern digital steganography* (pp. 211–234). IGI Global.

Pandey, D., & Pandey, B. K. (2022). An efficient deep neural network with adaptive galactic swarm optimization for complex image text extraction. In *Process mining techniques for pattern recognition* (pp. 121–137). CRC Press.

Pandey, D., Sharma, M., Talwar, R., & Pandey, B. K. (2025). A compact quintuple band miniaturized elliptical planar monopole antenna for 5G/6G wireless systems. *Analog Integrated Circuits and Signal Processing*, *122*(3), 1–16.

Pandey, D., Wairya, S., Sharma, M., Gupta, A. K., Kakkar, R., & Pandey, B. K. (2022). An approach for object tracking, categorization, and autopilot guidance for passive homing missiles. *Aerospace Systems*, *5*(4), 553–566.

Praveenkumar, T., Anthoniraj, S., Kumarganesh, S., Somaskandan, M., Martin Sagayam, K., Pandey, B. K., & Sahani, S. K. (2025). Enhanced Circuit Board Analysis: Infrared Image Segmentation Utilizing Markov Random Field (MRF) and Level Set Techniques. *Engineering Reports*, *7*(3), e70029.

Raja, D. S. S., Kumar, D. R., Santhiyakumari, N., Kumarganesh, S., Sagayam, K. M., Thiyaneswaran, B., & Pandey, D. (2024). A compact dual-feed wide-band slotted antenna for future wireless applications. *Analog Integrated Circuits and Signal Processing*, *118*(2), 291–305.

Revathi, T. K., Sathiyabhama, B., Sankar, S., Pandey, D., Pandey, B. K., & Dadeech, P. (2022). An intelligent model for coronary heart disease diagnosis. In *Networking technologies in smart healthcare* (pp. 309–327). CRC Press.

Saxena, A., Agarwal, A., Pandey, B. K., & Pandey, D. (2024). Examination of the criticality of customer segmentation using unsupervised learning methods. *Circular Economy and Sustainability*, *4*(2), 1447–1460.

Sharma, A., Raj, R., Bisht, M., Gupta, A., Johri, A., & Asif, M. (2024). Optimizing employee satisfaction in India's IT sector: A focus on employer branding. In Journal of Humanities and Social Sciences Communications. https://doi.org/DOI: 10.1057/s41599-024-03689-9

Sharma, M., Pandey, D., Palta, P., & Pandey, B. K. (2022). Design and power dissipation consideration of PFAL CMOS V/S conventional CMOS based 2: 1 multiplexer and full adder. *Silicon*, *14*(8), 4401–4410.

Sharma, M., Talwar, R., Nassa, V. K., Binay, K., & Pandey, D. (2025). Design and performance analysis of a multiband vivaldi antenna for wireless broadband communication in 3-5.6 GHz spectrum. In *Artificial Intelligence and Information Technologies* (pp. 86–91). CRC Press.

Sharma, M., Talwar, R., Pandey, D., Nassa, V. K., Pandey, B. K., & Dadheech, P. (2024). A review of dielectric resonator antennas (DRA)-based RFID technology for Industry 4.0. *Robotics and Automation in Industry*, *4*(0), 303–324.

Sheela, M. S., Kumarganesh, S., Pandey, B. K., & Lelisho, M. E. (2025). Integration of silver nanostructures in wireless sensor networks for enhanced biochemical sensing. *Discover Nano*, *20*(1), 7. PMID: 39804434

Singh, S., Madaan, G., Singh, A., Pandey, D., George, A. S., & Pandey, B. K. (2025). Empowering Connectivity: Exploring the Internet of Things. In Interdisciplinary Approaches to AI, Internet of Everything, and Machine Learning (pp. 89-116). IGI Global Scientific Publishing.

Singh, S., Madaan, G., Swapna, H. R., Singh, A., Pandey, B. K., George, A. S., & Pandey, D. (2025). Unleashing the Power of AI and Data Analysis: Transforming Insights into Action. In Interdisciplinary Approaches to AI, Internet of Everything, and Machine Learning (pp. 1-24). IGI Global Scientific Publishing.

Tareke, S. A., Lelisho, M. E., Hassen, S. S., Seid, A. A., Jemal, S. S., Teshale, B. M., & Pandey, B. K. (2022). The prevalence and predictors of depressive, anxiety, and stress symptoms among Tepi town residents during the COVID-19 pandemic lockdown in Ethiopia. *Journal of Racial and Ethnic Health Disparities*, •••, 1–13. PMID: 35028903

Tripathi, R., Mishra, V. K., Maheshwari, H., Tiwari, R. G., Agarwal, A. K., & Gupta, A. (2023), "Extrapolative Preservation Management of Medical Equipment through IoT," *International Conference on Artificial Intelligence for Innovations in Healthcare Industries (ICAIIHI)*, Raipur, India, 2023, pp. 1-5, doi: DOI: 10.1109/ICAIIHI57871.2023.10489349

Vinodhini, V., Kumar, M. S., Sankar, S., Pandey, D., Pandey, B. K., & Nassa, V. K. (2022). IoT-based early forest fire detection using MLP and AROC method. *International Journal of Global Warming*, *27*(1), 55–70.

Chapter 25
Cloud-Driven Justice:
The Future of Legal Aid for Underserved Populations

Ashutosh Singh
https://orcid.org/0009-0008-2332-6245
Manipal University Jaipur, India

Pranav Mathur
https://orcid.org/0009-0003-6228-2349
Manipal University Jaipur, India

Sony Kulshrestha
Manipal University Jaipur, India

ABSTRACT

The transformative potential of cloud-based technologies in the context of addressing the justice gap that underserved populations are experiencing. The ways in which innovative solutions, such as remote clinics, virtual legal assistance platforms, and tools powered by artificial intelligence, bring about improvements in the accessibility, affordability, and efficiency of legal aid services. Legal aid organizations are able to effectively optimize their operations and improve the outcomes for their clients by utilizing data analytics and machine learning methodologies. The significance of collaborative partnerships between government entities, technology companies, and community organizations in order to accomplish the goals of increasing awareness and providing effective legal support. Future prospects, such as artificial intelligence-driven legal advocacy and blockchain technology for secure documentation, both of which have the potential to reshape the landscape of the legal system.

DOI: 10.4018/979-8-3693-9581-3.ch025

1. INTRODUCTION

The issue of access to justice is still very important, particularly for marginalized communities, low-income groups, and underprivileged populations. Many people lack the legal representation they require as a result of the traditional legal system, which is frequently characterized by exorbitant fees, drawn-out procedures, and geographical barriers. However, by changing the way legal aid is provided, developments in digital infrastructure are opening up possibilities to close this justice gap. Digital platform integration (Pandey, B. K., & Pandey, D., 2025) in the legal sector, which enables remote access to critical services, is one of the most promising developments. Legal experts can now be contacted online by those who previously found it difficult to get legal representation because of their remote location or limited resources (Khadka, M. et al., 2025). Due to this change, legal services are now more reasonably priced and easily accessible. It also lessens the logistical and physical obstacles. Remote consultations are not the only way that these digital solutions are adopted (Sheela, M. S. et al., 2025). Online dispute settlement tools and virtual legal clinics are becoming important parts of the legal system of the future. These systems enable online claim filing, hearing attendance, and document access for individuals. This could provide a more effective way to handle legal matters, drastically cut down on court backlogs, and streamline the legal process.

Legal aid is also made more accessible to a wider range of people, including those who have historically been shut out of the system, which democratizes the system. These platforms capacity to scale is another benefit. Without requiring a large infrastructure (Satheesh, N. et al., 2025), legal aid organizations which are frequently limited in their resources can use these systems to assist more clients. It follows that these services can readily grow to meet the growing demand and offer people in need prompt assistance. Furthering these advantages to those without access to computers but who might own smartphones depends critically on mobile accessibility. Through the application of artificial intelligence, digital systems also improve efficiency. Legal professionals can increase productivity (Pandey, B. K., & Pandey, D., 2023) and accuracy by utilizing automated tools for document preparation, legal research, and even predictive analytics. Legal professionals can now concentrate on more intricate, human-centered aspects of their work as these innovations speed up the resolution of cases. By using AI in this way, underprivileged communities can receive legal advice and representation more quickly and with greater accuracy. More data and analytics are being used, which provides insightful information about the legal requirements of various groups. Organizations can better target their services to particular communities by using this data-driven approach (Kumar, M. S. et al., 2025), which also helps to optimize resources and enhance case outcomes. To ensure that urgent legal matters are handled promptly, machine learning, for instance, can assist in prioritizing cases. Projecting forward, legal aid will probably incorporate cutting-edge technologies like blockchain for safe legal records and artificial intelligence (AI)-driven attorneys who can help with simple legal issues more deeply (Konapure, C. G. et al., 2025). With even greater transparency, security, and accessibility to legal services, these innovations have the potential to completely transform the justice system.

1.1 Legal Aid Accessibility Issues

The lack of funds for private legal representation makes legal aid essential for access to justice. Still, rural, low-income, and marginalized communities face significant barriers to legal aid. Accessibility issues sustain legal inequality and undermine judicial trust. One major obstacle is geography. Many rural areas lack legal services. People must travel far to get basic legal help due to a lack of law firms. Geography can deter people from seeking legal help, especially when transportation, time off work, and other logistical issues are considered. Financial issues (Singh, S. et al., 2025) also limit legal aid. Complex or long cases may make even subsidized legal services unaffordable for low-income people. Limited funding limits legal aid programs' client numbers and representation quality. Thus, many people navigate the legal system alone, which can lead to unfair or unjust outcomes, especially when facing well-represented opponents. Legal complexity and bureaucracy exacerbate these issues. Due to low education and legal literacy, many underserved populations struggle to understand their rights, legal processes, and resources (Sharma, M. et al., 2025). Filing legal claims can be difficult due to the paperwork, deadlines, and expertise required. Due to cultural and language barriers, underserved groups struggle. minority populations who don't speak the local language or have cultural reservations about legal systems are often overlooked by legal aid services. Their lack of cultural sensitivity and multilingual support marginalizes them and makes justice harder to obtain. Also consider technological disparities (Pandey, B. K. et al., 2024a). Even though digital solutions could improve legal services, many underserved populations lack reliable internet access or the technological skills to use them. Some of those who could benefit most from online legal aid are the least equipped to use it, adding to the digital divide (Murdoch, B., 2021).

1.2 Role of Cloud Technology in Justice

Cloud computing provides storage, databases, networking, software, and analytics over the internet rather than on local servers or devices. Cloud technology allows lawyers and clients to remotely access legal processes and services by digitalizing and virtualizing them (Pandey, B. K. et al., 2024b). From managing case files and court documents to virtual consultations and remote hearings, cloud platforms enable legal activities. Cloud computing's ability to store and process massive amounts of data in real time without expensive physical infrastructure is its main benefit. Legal services can be decentralized, making them accessible to populations who would otherwise struggle to access them. Remote residents can now attend court hearings and virtual consultations via video conferencing platforms (Basha, A. J. et al., 2024). This makes justice engagement easier for underserved populations and reduces geographic barriers. Besides improving geographic accessibility, cloud technology saves money. Legal aid organizations with limited resources can use cloud platforms to cut office space, paperwork, and travel costs. Lowering the cost of legal aid allows more resources to help more clients, making legal services more affordable for low-income people. Easy scaling is another benefit of cloud-driven solutions. Cloud services can quickly scale to meet demand without investing in physical infrastructure. Scalability (KVM, S. et al., 2024) allows legal aid organizations to efficiently handle large caseloads and provide timely legal services to underserved populations during crises or widespread legal disputes. Cloud platforms improve legal professional, client, and justice system stakeholder collaboration. Cloud-based tools let lawyers and legal aid organizations collaborate, share case files, and communicate securely in real time. This boosts legal efficiency and effectiveness, allowing legal aid providers to better serve clients. Through cloud-based data analytics, legal aid organizations can identify population-specific legal needs and tailor their services (Reddy, S. et al., 2020). Identification of underserved groups, case outcomes, and legal aid program efficiency can be achieved with this data (Lakshmi, K. V. N. et al., 2024). Cloud technology can transform legal aid by improving accessibility, lowering costs, scaling services, improving collaboration, and providing data-driven insights. The justice gap can be closed and underserved populations given fair access to the legal system with its remote and efficient legal services.

2. CLOUD-DRIVEN LEGAL AID

2.1 Virtual Legal Assistance Platforms

- *Legal Advice on Demand*: Virtual legal aid platforms enable consultations via chat interfaces, video conferencing, and chatbots driven by artificial intelligence as shown in figure 1. This makes it possible for people to get legal assistance without being limited by time or place. Due to time, expense, and practical difficulties, seeing a lawyer across large distances can be unaffordable for many people, particularly those who live in rural or underdeveloped areas. These platforms make it possible for users to consult with seasoned legal experts or get basic legal advice from AI (Saravanakumar, R. et al., 2024), giving them flexible access to legal advice and guaranteeing that assistance is available when needed.

Figure 1. Digital legal aid solutions

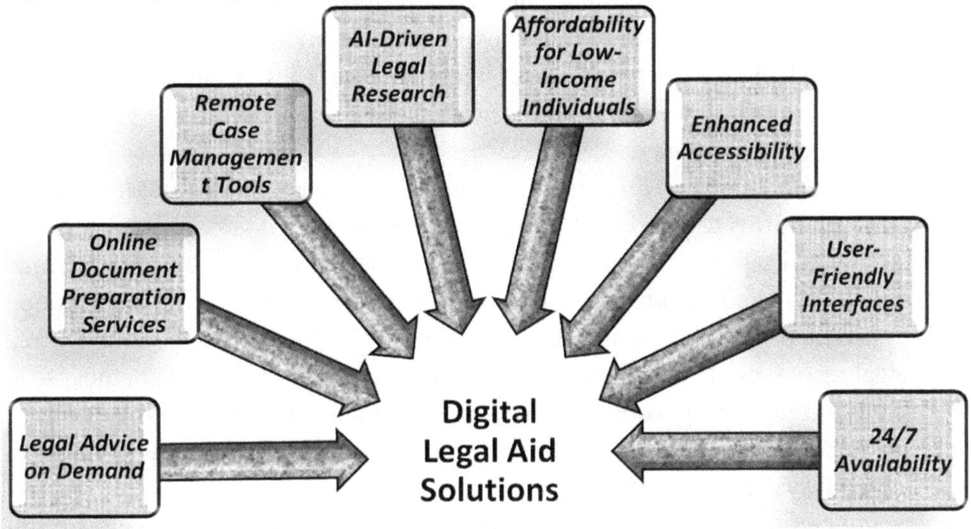

- *Online Document Preparation Services:* Numerous platforms provide thorough online document preparation services, making it simple for users to create legally binding documents. These online resources offer step-by-step instructions to assist people in creating important documents like wills, contracts, and legal forms. This automation makes complicated legal terminology and processes understandable to people who might not be familiar with law. Because of this, users can create documents that are specifically tailored to their needs without having to pay for expensive in-person legal assistance.
- *Remote Case Management* Tools: Virtual legal assistance platforms are not complete without remote case management features. Clients have the ability to safely store and upload legal documents, making them available from any location at any time. With the help of these tools, users can also monitor the status of their cases and stay up to date on any significant developments. Secure communication channels also make it easier for clients and their attorneys to work together, which improves the efficiency and transparency of the legal process. With this configuration, traditional paperwork delays are

minimized and legal teams can react swiftly to client needs (Page, M. J. et al., 2021).

- *AI-Driven Legal* Research: AI-driven legal research tools are a common feature of virtual platforms, giving users and attorneys quick access to pertinent case law, court decisions, and regulations. The time spent on legal research is greatly decreased by this technological integration (Kumarganesh, S. et al., 2024), freeing up legal professionals to concentrate on more intricate aspects of cases. For clients, this translates to quicker, more knowledgeable legal advice, which eventually produces better results. These tools' increased efficiency also helps attorneys handle their caseloads more skillfully, giving their clients better service.
- *Affordability for Low-Income Individuals*: The capacity of virtual legal assistance platforms to provide affordable substitutes for traditional legal services is one of its greatest benefits. Many of these platforms allow low-income people who might otherwise find it difficult to afford legal representation to use them by offering sliding scale fees, subscription models, or even free legal resources. These platforms (Muralidhar, L. B. et al., 2024) democratize access to justice by lowering financial barriers, enabling a larger portion of the public to obtain the legal aid required to successfully navigate complicated legal systems (Morley, J. et al., 2019).
- *Enhanced Accessibility*: Geographical and logistical obstacles that have traditionally restricted access to legal services are effectively removed by virtual legal assistance platforms. These platforms reach people who might have trouble finding local legal assistance, live in remote areas, or have mobility challenges by providing legal resources online. In order to address the needs of marginalized populations and guarantee that everyone has the chance to seek support and legal recourse, this wider outreach is especially important (Pandey, B. K. et al., 2024c).
- *User-Friendly Interfaces*: A lot of platforms have intuitive user interfaces that make it easy for people to navigate the legal system. These platforms lessen the fear that's frequently connected with legal procedures by using clear instructions and intuitive design principles (Elarmathi, S. et al., 2024). Because of its simplicity of use, people are more inclined to seek legal counsel on a proactive basis, which leads to a more knowledgeable and involved public that is better able to comprehend and exercise their legal rights.
- *24/7 Availability*: Another important advantage of virtual legal assistance services is their 24/7 availability. In order to accommodate different schedules and pressing needs, users can access legal resources and consult with professionals whenever they choose (Pandey, B. K. et al., 2024d). This flexibility allows people to get legal help outside of regular business hours, which

is especially helpful for those balancing work, family, and other obligations. As a result, the constant provision of services improves accessibility and motivates people to seek legal counsel when they most need it.

The licensed attorneys can be reached via secure messaging, video calls, or chat, making legal assistance more accessible, especially for remote or disabled users. Many platforms also have user-friendly interfaces that simplify legal processes and paperwork, allowing people to handle their legal issues from home.

2.2 Remote Legal Clinics and Court Proceedings

Remote legal clinics and virtual courtrooms have transformed legal services using cloud-based systems. These innovations remove geographical barriers to legal aid, especially for rural and underserved people. Digital platforms allow legal aid organizations and courts to provide more convenient and inclusive services (George, W. K. et al., 2024). Clients can consult with attorneys remotely at remote legal clinics. People can discuss legal issues, get advice, and document from home using secure video conferencing tools. This helps those who have trouble getting around, mobility issues, or live in areas with few legal services. In-person consultations are logistically difficult, but online consultations encourage people to seek help (Abdullahi, M. et al., 2024). Thus, remote clinics help legal access by connecting those in need with qualified professionals. This legal system digitization continues with virtual courtrooms. With online court proceedings, courts can hold hearings, trials, and other legal processes remotely. This change simplifies operations and lets people participate in their cases remotely (Satheesh, N. et al., 2025). Online hearings allow litigants, witnesses, and legal representatives to avoid travel and costs. In cases where defendants and plaintiffs are far from the courthouse, remote appearance can reduce their burdens. Virtual courts can improve judicial efficiency. Courts can manage caseloads better by reducing physical appearance delays and allowing more flexible scheduling. The judicial system can respond faster to urgent legal issues due to this efficiency (Kumar, B. et al., 2024). Cloud-based systems enable secure case file and document sharing among parties. Real-time uploads and access by legal professionals ensure that everyone has the information they need for hearings or trials. Technologies seamless integration into the legal process improves transparency and reduces the risk of lost or misplaced documents in paper-based systems (Prakash, S. et al., 2022).

2.3 AI-Powered Legal Research and Document Drafting

The landscape of legal research and document drafting is changing as a result of the integration of artificial intelligence (AI) (Pandey, D. et al., 2024) tools into cloud platforms, greatly improving the productivity and accuracy of legal work. These cutting-edge tools use enormous volumes of data to help lawyers with a range of tasks, including research, document generation, and even the provision of legal insights that are predicted. Legal research is one of the most significant uses of AI in the legal sector. Conventional legal research techniques can be labor- and time-intensive, frequently necessitating a thorough examination of statutes, case law, and regulations. This process is streamlined by AI-powered tools (Shahul, A. et al., 2024) that swiftly analyze vast amounts of legal data to find pertinent precedents and legal principles. These tools' natural language processing (NLP) capabilities enable them to understand user queries in simple terms, making it easier for legal professionals to locate relevant information. Artificial Intelligence (AI) helps lawyers focus on higher-level analysis and strategy by drastically cutting down on the amount of time spent on research, which ultimately improves the quality of legal services offered to clients. AI tools are excellent in document drafting in addition to research. These tools identify the standard clauses and provisions that are usually included in different types of legal agreements by analyzing existing documents using machine learning algorithms (Muniandi, B. et al., 2024).

The AI can expedite the drafting process and reduce error risk by suggesting language, structure, and pertinent legal terminology as users input specific details. In addition to saving time, this feature improves the consistency and dependability of legal documents two important factors in guaranteeing adherence to the law. Artificial intelligence (AI) systems can also help with predictive legal analysis, providing insights into possible outcomes based on past data and precedent cases. These tools can assist legal professionals in evaluating the merits and demerits of a case, guiding their strategy and providing clients with expected results by examining previous rulings and decisions. This ability to predict the future can be especially useful in litigation, as it can help determine whether to settle a case out of court or take it to trial by predicting how it will likely proceed (Singh, S. et al., 2025). Legal professionals can make better decisions and provide clients with better representation by utilizing data analytics. Collaboration and communication between legal teams are encouraged by the use of AI. Team members can more easily and quickly share insights, research findings, and draft documents when using cloud platforms with AI capabilities. This fosters a more responsive approach to client needs and improves teamwork by enabling immediate feedback. It can also raise the standard of legal work overall. AI tools will only get better at learning from user interactions and tailoring themselves to particular legal contexts as they develop. This will pave the way for even more advanced applications, like tailored legal counsel according to each client's preferences and circumstances (Wang, C. et al., 2022).

3. SCALABLE SOLUTIONS FOR LEGAL AID

The growing need for easily accessible legal services, especially from marginalized groups, necessitates scalable legal aid solutions. Legal aid organizations can increase access to legal assistance by utilizing cutting-edge technologies and cooperative models to broaden their reach (Vinodhini, V. et al., 2022), enhance service delivery, and eventually accomplish these goals. The following scalable strategies are shown in the figure 2, which have the potential to drastically alter the legal aid landscape:

- *Digital Platforms for Legal Services:* Scalable legal aid solutions are built on digital platforms. A variety of services, such as online consultations, document preparation, and access to legal resources, can be provided by these platforms. Legal aid organizations can assist people who might not have access to traditional legal services by serving clients across geographic boundaries through their virtual operations (Rai, P. K. et al., 2024). In order to assist users with legal procedures and respond to commonly asked questions, these platforms can also include features like chatbots and AI tools. This allows them to serve a significantly higher number of clients without having to hire more staff.
- *Partnerships and Collaborations:* Working together with different stakeholders such as private law firms, law schools, and nonprofits can increase the efficacy and reach of legal aid programs. Legal aid organizations can increase their service offerings, pool resources, and share expertise by partnering. Private firms can provide expertise and additional manpower, and law schools can offer pro bono legal assistance through student clinics. These kinds of partnerships allow legal aid organizations to expand, guaranteeing that more people get the help they require.
- *AI and Automation:* Scalability can be greatly improved by incorporating automation and artificial intelligence into legal aid procedures. Legal professionals can concentrate on more complicated matters by delegating routine tasks like document generation, client intake, and case management to automated systems. With the use of AI-driven tools, organizations can more efficiently allocate resources and focus their services on the areas with the greatest need by analyzing data to find patterns and trends. Through the reduction of labor and time associated with legal procedures, these technologies allow

organizations to effectively serve a greater number of clients (Panagopoulos, A. et al., 2022).

- *Telelaw Services:* Another scalable option for legal aid is telelaw services. Legal aid organizations can reach clients anywhere in the world by providing telephone or video conference legal consultations. For those who live in remote places and might not have access to local legal resources, this is especially helpful. In addition to improving accessibility, telelaw enables legal aid organizations to better organize their workflow and handle their caseloads. The capacity to carry out consultations virtually lowers expenses and improves the general client experience.
- *Legal Education and Empowerment Programs*: Initiatives for community-based legal education that provide people with the information and abilities to handle legal matters on their own are another example of scalable solutions for legal aid. People can learn vital legal information through workshops, webinars, and online courses, which will help them comprehend their rights and obligations. These initiatives can lower the need for direct legal services by promoting legal literacy and encourage people to ask for help early on when they do.
- *Data-Driven Decision Making*: For legal aid organizations, tracking service usage, client demographics, and outcomes through data analytics can yield insightful information. Organizations can evaluate the success of their programs and decide on resource allocation and service enhancement with this data-driven approach. Legal aid providers can improve their scalability by creating tailored strategies to address specific needs by analyzing trends and patterns within their client base (Khalid, N. et al., 2023).
- *Mobile Applications:* More ways to improve accessibility and scalability are through the creation of mobile applications specifically designed for legal aid. These applications can give users access to legal resources, attorneys, online consultations, and case status updates. Legal aid organizations can reach a wider audience and offer assistance in a more user-friendly way by utilizing the widespread use of smartphones.

Legal aid organizations can increase their reach, improve service delivery, and eventually guarantee that more people receive the legal assistance they require by utilizing technology, forming partnerships, and putting creative ideas into practice. Adopting these scalable solutions will be essential to advancing equity and universal access to justice as the legal system changes.

Figure 2. Transformative scalable strategies for legal aid

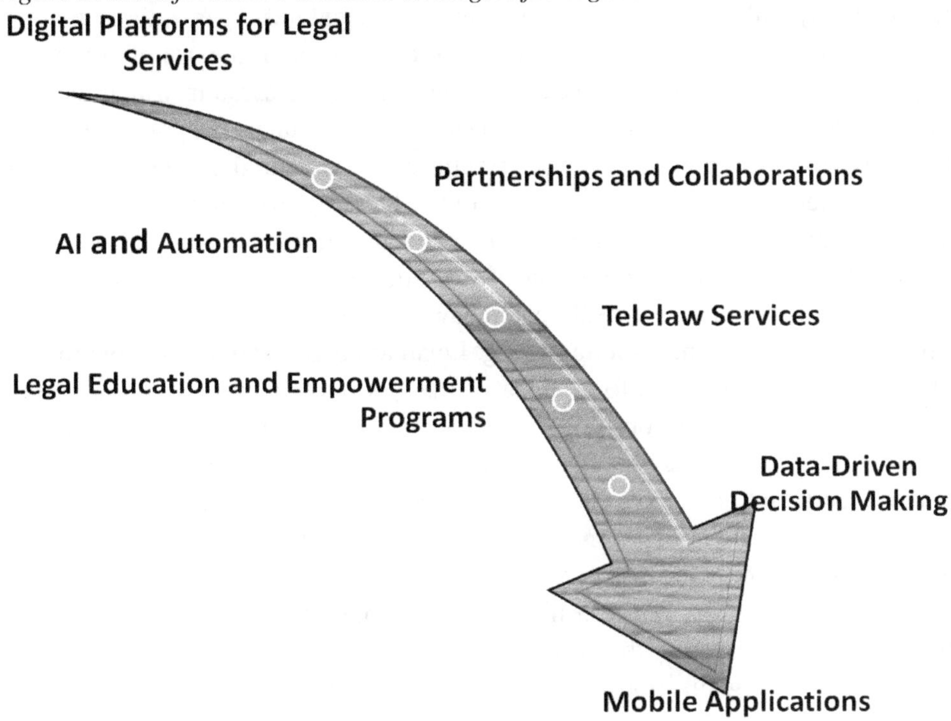

4. LEVERAGING DATA AND ANALYTICS

4.1 Machine Learning for Case Prioritization

The implementation of machine learning algorithms in organizations that provide legal aid is causing a shift in the way cases are prioritized, which in turn enables a more effective distribution of resources. In a setting where demand frequently far exceeds capacity, these cutting-edge technologies offer a strategic advantage by analyzing extremely large amounts of data in order to determine which cases require immediate attention. Through the analysis of a number of factors that are inherent to each case, machine learning is particularly effective at determining the level of urgency associated with a variety of legal matters. The nature of the legal issue, the potential consequences of inaction, and critical deadlines are some of the factors that algorithms take into consideration when identifying cases that pose immediate risks to the safety or well-being of clients. Instances such as domestic violence, disagreements over child custody, or impending evictions are examples of situations that frequently call for prompt legal intervention. Legal aid organizations are able to quickly identify and prioritize these urgent cases through the use of automated analysis, which ensures that resources are directed to the areas in which they are required the most. The capacity of machine learning to evaluate the potential impact of a case extends beyond the specific circumstances of a single. These algorithms are able to determine which cases are likely to have significant repercussions for clients and the community as a whole by analyzing historical data and outcomes associated with those cases. For instance, a case that addresses systemic issues, such as discrimination or access to healthcare, may be prioritized because of its potential to bring about change that is long-lasting. Legal aid organizations are able to strategically concentrate their efforts on cases that not only benefit individual clients but also promote social justice and the well-being of the community as a whole.

The influence that machine learning has on the distribution of resources is yet another significant advantage that can be gained from incorporating it into legal aid operations. Legal professionals frequently have to handle a large number of cases, and it is essential for them to be aware of which ones require the most time and attention. Using machine learning, organizations are able to more effectively allocate staff by analyzing the complexity of cases and the requirements of their customers. When organizations are able to accurately predict which cases will require intensive legal work, they are able to ensure that their teams are not overwhelmed, which ultimately results in an improvement in the quality of legal assistance that is provided. To improving the prioritization of cases and the distribution of resources, machine learning also improves the overall efficiency of operations. Legal aid staff are able to devote more time to substantive legal work as a result of the automation of routine tasks such as data entry and case management. This results in an increase in the capacity of the staff to serve clients. In a field that is characterized by limited funding and staffing challenges, where every resource counts, this efficiency is especially vital.

5. INNOVATIVE PARTNERSHIPS AND COLLABORATIONS

5.1 Public-Private Partnerships

Innovative digital solutions from government, technology, and legal aid organizations have transformed access to justice. These alliances use advanced technology to address marginalized communities' legal needs by leveraging stakeholder strengths. Online legal assistance platforms are an example of collaboration. Various state governments and tech companies have created user-friendly websites and apps to provide legal information and services. Users can complete legal forms, get legal advice, and connect with volunteer attorneys on some jurisdictions' online portals. These systems simplify legal processes, allowing non-lawyers to resolve their legal issues. Public agencies and legal tech firms collaborate to create intelligent legal research and document preparation tools. Collaborations with advanced algorithms on digital platforms help legal aid organizations optimize operations. Smart systems can help lawyers find relevant case law, draft legal documents, and predict case outcomes based on historical patterns. Efficiency improves service delivery and ensures timely and accurate legal assistance for clients. Partnerships can also help legal professionals and volunteers learn how to use new digital tools. Technology companies can teach legal aid staff how to use modern solutions in workshops and programs. With this training, legal aid organizations can maximize the benefits of innovative resources and better serve the needy. Collaborations also produce pilot projects testing new legal technologies. Certain initiatives have created chatbots that can provide instant legal advice on tenant rights and family law. These trials allow stakeholders to test such tools in real-world situations, enabling regional adoption. Digital solutions designed through successful collaborations are inclusive. These partnerships can target underserved populations by including legal aid organizations in development. Users with little digital experience can use technological resources more easily with this user-centered approach. Beyond individual cases, these collaborative efforts change the legal landscape. By encouraging stakeholder cooperation, these initiatives can transform legal aid from a charity to an essential part of the legal system. This change is necessary to sustain and grow legal initiatives by attracting investment and support (Rahman et al., 2022).

5.2 International Legal Aid Networks

The legal needs of underserved populations worldwide are increasingly being met by international legal aid networks. Global cloud platforms enable cross-border collaboration among legal aid organizations, practitioners, and volunteers, creating a global repository of knowledge and resources. Cross-border legal aid is one of these networks' main benefits. Cloud-based platforms allow legal aid organizations in one country to easily contact partners in other regions in international law or cross-border cases. Connectivity allows information and expertise to be shared, ensuring clients receive comprehensive legal assistance that fits their complex situations. These networks enable legal aid organizations to address diverse legal issues by removing geographical barriers. Global platforms also enable legal aid providers to share best practices and innovative solutions. Online training, webinars, and collaborative projects allow legal professionals to share strategies for addressing underserved populations' legal issues. This sharing of knowledge encourages legal aid organizations to innovate and improve service delivery and client outcomes. Cloud technologies allow the creation of centralized databases for legal resources, templates, and guidance. These repositories can help legal aid organizations in marginalized areas access legal materials. These platforms provide a single source of information on relevant laws and regulations, helping legal professionals better serve clients. Legal services are streamlined and consistent across jurisdictions with this centralized approach. During humanitarian crises, international legal aid networks can better mobilize resources. In natural disasters or mass migrations, these networks can quickly coordinate multiple organizations to provide legal aid to large numbers of people. Legal aid providers can pool case management tools and communication channels to quickly meet affected populations' urgent needs using cloud technology. Collectively, these networks raise awareness of global legal issues and encourage advocacy for underserved communities. International legal aid networks can highlight systemic injustices and change policy by convening voices from different nations. Fixing legal inequalities and advancing marginalized groups' rights requires a global perspective.

6. FUTURE PROSPECTS AND INNOVATIONS

Technology advancements and changing practices will likely bring about a significant transformation in the future of legal aid, especially when it comes to underprivileged populations. With the growing demand for easily accessible legal services, a number of opportunities are emerging that claim to improve outcomes and service delivery for those who are less fortunate. The use of artificial intelligence in legal aid services is one of the most exciting developments. Artificial Intelligence is becoming more and more capable of automating document preparation, conducting legal research, and streamlining case management. Legal aid organizations are able to manage a higher caseload with greater efficiency thanks to automation, which also lessens the workload for legal professionals by accelerating the delivery of services. Artificial intelligence (AI) tools can also scan large datasets for patterns and trends, providing legal aid providers with information that helps them prioritize cases and allocate resources.

The emergence of decentralized technologies like blockchain, in addition to AI, has the potential to completely transform the provision of legal services. Blockchain technology has the potential to improve legal transactions' transparency and security by letting clients securely access their legal documents and keep control of their data. By streamlining contract management and dispute resolution procedures and facilitating the verification of legal credentials, this technology can increase client and legal aid provider trust. The increasing ubiquity of mobile technology offers yet another promising path toward improving access to legal aid. As more people rely on smartphones for communication and information, legal aid organizations are creating mobile applications that offer users direct access to legal resources, counsel, and support. By providing real-time support, connecting users with pro bono attorneys, and guiding users through legal processes, these apps help make legal services more accessible and user-friendly. It is impossible to ignore the potential for augmented reality (AR) and virtual reality (VR) technologies to revolutionize legal education and training. These immersive technologies can provide legal professionals with controlled training environments by simulating courtroom scenarios. Virtual reality (VR) and augmented reality (AR) can facilitate experiential learning, which in turn can help legal aid practitioners gain critical skills and a deeper understanding of the obstacles faced by marginalized populations. To advance these innovations, cooperation between legal aid organizations, tech firms, and academic institutions will be essential. Collaboratively, stakeholders can test novel approaches, evaluate their efficacy, and expand prosperous endeavors to encompass a wider demographic. By working together, we can create a culture of continuous improvement that will allow legal aid services to adapt to the changing needs of the communities they serve. Achieving these future possibilities will require a greater investment in the infrastructure of legal aid technology. Funding for technology improvements in the legal aid industry needs to be prioritized by public and private sectors so that organizations can embrace and apply creative solutions. Tackling the digital divide is also essential; making sure disadvantaged groups have access to the required technology and internet connectivity will help optimize the benefits of these developments.

7. CONCLUSION

The rapidly changing legal aid scene, greatly impacted by new technological advancements, offers a revolutionary chance to address the persistent gaps in underprivileged communities' access to justice. The incorporation of cloud-based solutions has created new avenues for the provision of legal services, improving their efficiency, accessibility, and customization to meet the needs of various groups. In addition to streamlining service delivery, virtual platforms, remote clinics, and AI-powered tools empower people by arming them with the information and tools they need to successfully handle their legal challenges. These cloud-based solutions are scalable, which allows legal aid organizations to grow and adjust to the rising demand for their services. Organizations can enhance overall outcomes and optimize case prioritization by utilizing data analytics and machine learning, guaranteeing that individuals with the greatest need receive assistance promptly. It is impossible to overestimate the significance of creative partnerships among public agencies, private businesses, and community organizations; these alliances improve resource exchange, raise public awareness, and establish a strong support system for people in need of legal assistance. The legal industry has enormous room for future innovation. The promise of blockchain technology for secure documentation and AI-powered legal advocates signals the beginning of a new era in legal aid that may completely change the way services are provided and received. The drive for international standardization in cloud-based legal assistance systems holds out the possibility of smooth cross-border access to justice and the promotion of a more equal legal environment. When legal services and technology work together, there is a great opportunity to reduce the injustice gap. Accepting these advancements will enable us to ensure that access to legal counsel is a fundamental right rather than a privilege enjoyed only by a small number of people, paving the way for a more equitable and inclusive society.

REFERENCES

Abdullahi, M., Ahmad, A., Pandey, B. K., & Pandey, D. (2024). Digital Currency Adoption: A Comparative Analysis of Global Trends and the Nigerian eNaira Digital Currency. *SN Computer Science*, *5*(5), 1–11. DOI: 10.1007/s42979-024-02882-6

Basha, A. J., Maheshwari, R. U., Pandey, B. K., & Pandey, D. (2024). Ultra-sensitive photonic crystal fiber–based SPR sensor for cancer detection utilizing hybrid nanocomposite layers. *Plasmonics*, •••, 1–15. DOI: 10.1007/s11468-024-02584-y

Elarmathi, S., Rishabavarthani, P., Sindhuja, M., Elayaraja, P., & Malathi Murugesan, S. (2024). Novel manufacturing systems for cancer diagnosis using ultra-sensitive photonic crystal fiber biosensor with dual-functionalized aptamer-nanocavity. *Microsystem Technologies*, •••, 1–20. DOI: 10.1007/s00542-024-05820-x

George, W. K., Silas, E. I., Pandey, D., & Pandey, B. K. (2024). Utilization of Industry 4.0 Technologies in Nigerian Technical and Vocational Education: A Conundrum for Educators. In *Examining the Rapid Advance of Digital Technology in Africa* (pp. 270–293). IGI Global. DOI: 10.4018/978-1-6684-9962-7.ch014

Khadka, M., Sah, M., Chaudhary, R., Sahani, S. K., Sahani, K., Pandey, B. K., & Pandey, D. (2025). Spectroscopic, quantum chemical, and topological calculations of the phenylephrine molecule using density functional theory. *Scientific Reports*, *15*(1), 208. DOI: 10.1038/s41598-024-81633-2 PMID: 39747169

Khalid, N., Qayyum, A., Bilal, M., Al-Fuqaha, A., & Qadir, J. (2023). Privacy-preserving artificial intelligence in healthcare: Techniques and applications. *Computers in Biology and Medicine*, *158*, 106848. DOI: 10.1016/j.compbiomed.2023.106848 PMID: 37044052

Konapure, C. G., Pandey, D., Shete, H., Thakar, C. M., Pandey, B. K., & George, A. S. (2025). Artificial Intelligence in Automated Concrete Mix Design Using Computerized Grading Curves. Interdisciplinary Approaches to AI, Internet of Everything, and Machine Learning, 567-586.

Kumar, B., Pandey, D., Pandey, B. K., & George, A. S. (2024). Higher Education in the Last Four Decades: A Review of Paradigm Shifts in Policy Frameworks. Design and Implementation of Higher Education Learners' Learning Outcomes (HELLO), 333-348.

Kumar, M. S., Prasanna, P. L., Lalitha, M., Joy, M., Jha, S. S., & Pandey, B. K. (2025). Utilizing the Internet of Everything and Artificial Intelligence for Real-Time Workforce Management. In Role of Internet of Everything (IOE), VLSI Architecture, and AI in Real-Time Systems (pp. 153-168). IGI Global Scientific Publishing.

Kumarganesh, S., & Malathi Murugesan, C. (2024). Hybrid plasmonic biosensors with deep learning for colorectal cancer detection. *Plasmonics*, •••, 1–15. DOI: 10.1007/s11468-024-02568-y

KVM, S., Pandey, B. K., & Pandey, D. (2024). Design of Surface Plasmon Resonance (SPR) Sensors for Highly Sensitive Biomolecular Detection in Cancer Diagnostics. *Plasmonics*, •••, 1–13.

Lakshmi, K. V. N., Rajan, R., Pandey, D., & Pandey, B. K. (2024). Circular economy: A catalyst for economic growth-an empirical study. *Circular Economy and Sustainability*, •••, 1–22. DOI: 10.1007/s43615-024-00434-x

Morley, J., Machado, C., Burr, C., Cowls, J., Taddeo, M., & Floridi, L. (2019). The debate on the ethics of AI in health care: a reconstruction and critical review. *Available atSSRN* 3486518. DOI: 10.2139/ssrn.3486518

Muniandi, B., Nassa, V. K., Pandey, D., Pandey, B. K., Dadheech, P., & George, A. S. (2024). Pattern Analysis for Feature Extraction in Complex Images. In Using Machine Learning to Detect Emotions and Predict Human Psychology (pp. 145-167). IGI Global. DOI: 10.4018/979-8-3693-1910-9.ch007

Muralidhar, L. B., Lakshmi, K. V. N., Swapna, H. R., Rupani, J., Nethravathi, K., Pandey, B. K., & Pandey, D. (2024). Impact of Organizational Culture on The Level of Corporate Social Responsibility Investments: An Exploratory Study. *Circular Economy and Sustainability*, *4*(3), 1–19. DOI: 10.1007/s43615-024-00371-9

Murdoch, B. (2021). Privacy and artificial intelligence: Challenges for protecting health information in a new era. *BMC Medical Ethics*, *22*, 1–5. PMID: 34525993

Page, M. J., McKenzie, J. E., Bossuyt, P. M., Boutron, I., Hoffmann, T. C., Mulrow, C. D., ... & Moher, D. (2021). The PRISMA 2020 statement: an updated guideline for reporting systematic reviews. *bmj, 372*.

Panagopoulos, A., Minssen, T., Sideri, K., Yu, H., & Compagnucci, M. C. (2022). Incentivizing the sharing of healthcare data in the AI Era. *Computer Law & Security Review*, *45*, 105670. DOI: 10.1016/j.clsr.2022.105670

Pandey, B. K., Nassa, V. K., Mukundan, A. P., Mahajan, D. A., Pandey, D., George, A. S., & Dadheech, P. (2024c). An Industry-Focused Traffic System Utilising Internet of Things. In *Emerging Engineering Technologies and Industrial Applications* (pp. 200–213). IGI Global. DOI: 10.4018/979-8-3693-1335-0.ch009

Pandey, B. K., & Pandey, D. (2023). Parametric optimization and prediction of enhanced thermoelectric performance in co-doped CaMnO3 using response surface methodology and neural network. *Journal of Materials Science Materials in Electronics*, *34*(21), 1589. DOI: 10.1007/s10854-023-10954-1

Pandey, B. K., & Pandey, D. (2025). Securing healthcare medical image information using advance morphological component analysis, information hiding systems, and hybrid convolutional neural networks on IoMT. *Computers in Biology and Medicine*, *185*, 109499. DOI: 10.1016/j.compbiomed.2024.109499 PMID: 39642698

Pandey, B. K., Pandey, D., & Lelisho, M. E. (2024a). Face mask identification with enhanced cuckoo optimization and deep learning-based faster regional neural network. *Scientific Reports*, *14*(1), 29719. DOI: 10.1038/s41598-024-78746-z PMID: 39613761

Pandey, B. K., Pandey, D., & Sahani, S. K. (2024b). Autopilot control unmanned aerial vehicle system for sewage defect detection using deep learning. *Engineering Reports*, •••, 12852.

Pandey, B. K., Paramashivan, M. A., Pandey, D., George, A. S., Agarwal, A., Mahajan, D. A., . . . Pramanik, S. (2024d). Future Directions of Digital Twin Architectures for 6G Communication Networks. In Security Issues and Solutions in 6G Communications and Beyond (pp. 197-211). IGI Global.

Pandey, D., Nassa, V. K., Pandey, B. K., Mahajan, D. A., Patidar, P. K., Dadheech, P., & George, A. S. (2024). An Analysis of Internet-of-Things-Based Fire Detection and Alert Systems. In *Emerging Engineering Technologies and Industrial Applications* (pp. 295–304). IGI Global. DOI: 10.4018/979-8-3693-1335-0.ch014

Prakash, S., Balaji, J. N., Joshi, A., & Surapaneni, K. M. (2022). Ethical Conundrums in the application of artificial intelligence (AI) in healthcare—A scoping review of reviews. *Journal of Personalized Medicine*, *12*(11), 1914. DOI: 10.3390/jpm12111914 PMID: 36422090

Rai, P. K., Pandey, D., & Pandey, B. K. (2024). The future of enterprise and innovation is compute as a commodity, or CaaC. *Partners Universal International Research Journal*, *3*(2), 89–94.

Reddy, S., Allan, S., Coghlan, S., & Cooper, P. (2020). A governance model for the application of AI in health care. *Journal of the American Medical Informatics Association : JAMIA*, *27*(3), 491–497. DOI: 10.1093/jamia/ocz192 PMID: 31682262

Saravanakumar, R., TamilSelvi, T., Pandey, D., Pandey, B. K., Mahajan, D. A., & Lelisho, M. E. (2024). Big data processing using hybrid Gaussian mixture model with salp swarm algorithm. *Journal of Big Data*, *11*(1), 167. DOI: 10.1186/s40537-024-01015-3

Satheesh, N., Gopisankar, N., Kumarganesh, S., Anthoniraj, S., Saravanakumar, S., & Martin Sagayam, K. (2025). Advanced AI-driven emergency response systems for enhanced vehicle and human safety. *Iran Journal of Computer Science*, •••, 1–16. DOI: 10.1007/s42044-025-00228-w

Satheesh, N., Gopisankar, N., Kumarganesh, S., Anthoniraj, S., Saravanakumar, S., & Martin Sagayam, K. (2025). Advanced AI-driven emergency response systems for enhanced vehicle and human safety. *Iran Journal of Computer Science*, •••, 1–16. DOI: 10.1007/s42044-025-00228-w

Shahul, A., Muniandi, B., Paramashivan, M. A., Pandey, D., Pandey, B. K., Dadheech, P., & George, H. (2024). An Analysis of Algorithms and Methods Based on Image Processing for Medical Applications. In *Emerging Engineering Technologies and Industrial Applications* (pp. 173–186). IGI Global. DOI: 10.4018/979-8-3693-1335-0.ch007

Sharma, M., Talwar, R., Nassa, V. K., Binay, K., & Pandey, D. (2025). Design and performance analysis of a multiband vivaldi antenna for wireless broadband communication in 3-5.6 GHz spectrum. In *Artificial Intelligence and Information Technologies* (pp. 86–91). CRC Press.

Sheela, M. S., Kumarganesh, S., Pandey, B. K., & Lelisho, M. E. (2025). Integration of silver nanostructures in wireless sensor networks for enhanced biochemical sensing. *Discover Nano*, *20*(1), 7. DOI: 10.1186/s11671-024-04159-6 PMID: 39804434

Singh, S., Madaan, G., Swapna, H. R., Singh, A., Pandey, D., George, A. S., & Pandey, B. K. (2025). Empowering Connectivity: Exploring the Internet of Things. In Interdisciplinary Approaches to AI, Internet of Everything, and Machine Learning (pp. 89-116). IGI Global Scientific Publishing.

Vinodhini, V., Kumar, M. S., Sankar, S., Pandey, D., Pandey, B. K., & Nassa, V. K. (2022). IoT-based early forest fire detection using MLP and AROC method. *International Journal of Global Warming*, *27*(1), 55–70. DOI: 10.1504/IJGW.2022.122794

Wang, C., Zhang, J., Lassi, N., & Zhang, X. (2022, September). Privacy protection in using artificial intelligence for healthcare: Chinese regulation in comparative perspective. [). MDPI.]. *Health Care*, *10*(10), 1878. PMID: 36292325

Chapter 26
Computing's Future:
A Commodity-Based Perspective

Venkata Rahul Sarabu
https://orcid.org/0009-0002-3461-1945
Walmart Global Tech, USA

Mridula Dileepraj Kidiyur
https://orcid.org/0009-0002-9301-9095
IEEE Computer Society, USA

Chaithanya Ravulu
https://orcid.org/0009-0000-5054-6499
Rocket Companies, USA

Shravan Kumar Joginipalli
https://orcid.org/0009-0006-6050-507X
Slide Insurance, USA

Venkata Gummadi
https://orcid.org/0009-0006-8826-0473
Expedia Group, USA

Digvijay Pandey
https://orcid.org/0000-0003-0353-174X
Department of Technical Education, Government of U.P, India

ABSTRACT

The commoditization of computing resources, known as Compute as a Commodity (CaaC), is driving a significant shift in cloud computing. This chapter explores CaaC's evolution, from traditional cloud models to a highly flexible, scalable, and cost-efficient approach to computational power. By examining CaaC's key principles, benefits, challenges, and strategic implications, this chapter provides a detailed analysis of how organizations can leverage on-demand compute resources for operational efficiency and innovation. The chapter also covers the future trends in CaaC, including edge computing, artificial intelligence, and quantum computing, highlighting how these advancements are shaping the business landscape. Through real-world case studies and technical insights, this work equips professionals and researchers with a solid understanding of how to adopt and optimize CaaC for sustained growth.

DOI: 10.4018/979-8-3693-9581-3.ch026

INTRODUCTION

The concept of Compute as a Commodity (CaaC) marks a transformative stage in the evolution of cloud computing. Early cloud models such as Infrastructure as a Service (IaaS) and Platform as a Service (PaaS) introduced on-demand resource provisioning but often lacked the flexibility and scalability needed to meet the demands of modern businesses. Today, CaaC revolutionizes this space by treating computing power as a utility, offering on-demand access to standardized resources across multiple providers with pay-per-use pricing. This chapter examines the technical and strategic aspects of adopting CaaC, focusing on its benefits such as cost savings, scalability, and enhanced innovation capabilities. It also highlights key challenges, including security risks, vendor lock-in, and performance variability. By analyzing case studies from industries such as finance, healthcare, and retail, we illustrate how CaaC is reshaping the way organizations manage their computational needs. Furthermore, the chapter looks toward the future, considering the convergence of CaaC with technologies like edge computing, artificial intelligence, and quantum computing, which promise to redefine both operational capabilities and business strategies (IEEE., 2019)

1 COMPUTE AS A COMMODITY (CaaC)

The concept of cloud computing has undergone a significant transformation since its inception. Initially, cloud services were primarily offered as "Computer as a Service" (CaaS), where businesses could rent virtual machines or dedicated servers. This model provided flexibility compared to on-premises infrastructure but still required significant management and often came with long-term commitments (Sharma A. et al., 2024).

As cloud technology matured, we saw the emergence of more specialized services:

- Infrastructure as a Service (IaaS): Providing virtualized computing resources over the internet
- Platform as a Service (PaaS): Offering hardware and software tools over the internet, typically for application development
- Software as a Service (SaaS): Delivering software applications over the internet, on a subscription basis

While these models revolutionized how businesses accessed computing resources, they still often tied users to specific providers and service models. The shift towards Compute as a Commodity (CaaC) represents the next evolution in this journey.

1.1 Definition and Key Principles of CaaC

Compute as a Commodity (CaaC) treats computational resources as interchangeable utilities, much like electricity or water. Key principles include:

- On-demand access: Resources can be provisioned and de-provisioned instantly, without long-term commitments.
- Pay-per-use pricing: Users only pay for the exact amount of compute power they consume.
- Standardization: Compute resources are standardized across providers, making them easily interchangeable(Pandey, B. K. et al., 2025).
- Multi-provider ecosystem: Users can access resources from multiple providers seamlessly.
- Abstraction of infrastructure: Users focus on their workloads rather than managing underlying infrastructure.

1.2 Historical Context and Drivers of the CaaC Revolution

Several factors have contributed to the rise of CaaC:

- Maturation of cloud technologies: Advancements in virtualization, containerization, and orchestration have made it easier to abstract and standardize compute resources.
- Increasing demand for flexibility: Businesses need to scale resources up and down quickly to meet changing demands and optimize costs.
- Rise of big data and AI: The explosive growth in data processing and AI workloads requires vast, scalable compute resources.
- Edge computing and IoT: The need for distributed computing power has driven demand for more flexible, commodity-like compute resources.
- Economic pressures: Organizations are constantly seeking ways to reduce IT costs and improve operational efficiency.
- Environmental concerns: The ability to share and optimize compute resources across multiple users aligns with sustainability goals.

The CaaC model addresses these drivers by providing a more flexible, cost-effective, and scalable approach to accessing compute power. As we move forward, CaaC is poised to reshape how businesses think about and utilize computational resources, driving innovation and efficiency across industries(Pandey, B. K., & Pandey, D., 2025).

2 THE TECHNICAL MODEL OF CaaC

2.1 Overall Architecture and Workflow

The CaaC model is built on a distributed network of data centers, cloud infrastructure, and high-performance computing clusters. This federated approach allows for the aggregation of computing resources from various providers into a single, accessible pool. key components of the CaaC architecture include(Patil, K. R., 2025):

- Resource Pool: A vast, distributed network of computing resources from multiple providers.
- Orchestration Layer: Intelligent systems that manage resource allocation and workload distribution.
- User Interface: APIs, SDKs, and platforms that allow users to interact with the CaaC system.
- Monitoring and Analytics: Tools for tracking usage, performance, and costs.

The typical workflow in a CaaC system involves:

- User submits a workload request through the interface.
- The orchestration layer analyzes the request and determines optimal resource allocation.
- Resources are provisioned from the pool and the workload is executed.
- Results are returned to the user, and resources are de-provisioned.
- Usage is metered and billed accordingly.

Figure 1. Multi provider orchestration architecture

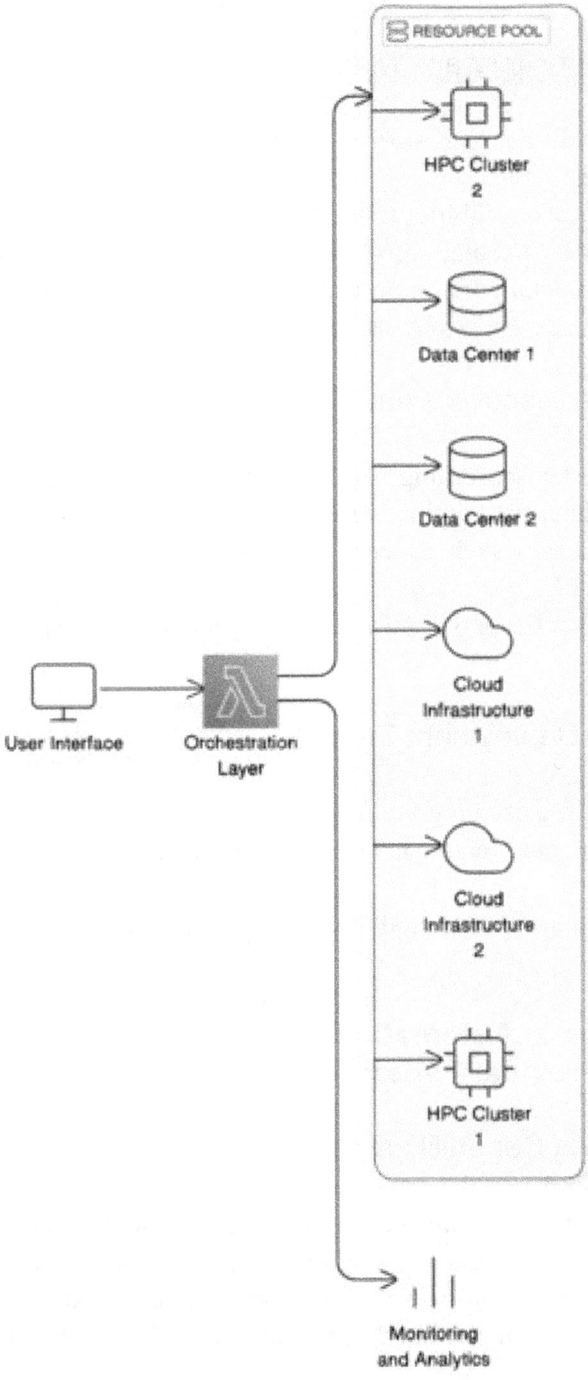

2.2 Key Components: Code Repository, Resource Discovery, Deployment Engine

2.2.1 Code Repository and Management

- Secure repositories for storing codebases, applications, containers, and dependencies.
- Version control capabilities to track changes.
- Integration with popular tools like GitHub, GitLab, and CI/CD pipelines.
- Provenance tracking for compliance with data sovereignty and geographical restrictions.

2.2.2 Resource Discovery and Scheduling Optimizer

- Scalable master scheduling service that uses heuristics, graph algorithms, and ML to determine optimal task placements.
- Considers factors such as cost, performance, data locality, and security policies.
- Aims to deliver the best Total Cost of Ownership (TCO) without compromising outcomes.

2.2.3 Dynamic Deployment Engine

- Orchestrates provisioning via API calls to underlying infrastructure.
- Utilizes containers and configuration management tools for environment consistency.
- Implements auto-scaling modules to adjust capacities based on usage metrics or schedules.

2.3 Innovations in Automation, Dynamic Pricing, and Provider Federation

2.3.1 Automation Capabilities

- AI/ML algorithms handle decision-making at scales beyond human capacity.
- Proactive auto-scaling anticipates and prepares for known usage peaks.
- Automated spot instance switching prevents failures and optimizes costs.
- Chatbots handle simpler queries, reducing wait times for users.

2.3.2 Dynamic Pricing

- Goes beyond simple spot buying to include:
    - Auto-reserving capacity at discounts based on usage trends.
    - Deprovisioning resources post-usage to minimize charges.
    - Multi-cloud arbitrage to optimize across provider discounts and currency conversions.
- Balances customer priorities (e.g., budget caps, performance needs) against supply-side constraints.

2.3.3 Provider Federation

- Supports interoperability across a fragmented compute supply chain, including:
    - Public clouds (AWS, Azure, GCP)
    - Specialized HPC/GPU clouds
    - Private render farms and data centers
    - Colocation facilities
- Utilizes standard interfaces and smart workload routing to scale capacity elastically across providers.
- Reduces vendor lock-in and improves autonomy for customers while benefiting providers through higher aggregate utilization.

These technical innovations (Stahmann, P. et al., 2025) collectively differentiate CaaC solutions from single-vendor approaches, offering unparalleled scale, cost-effectiveness, flexibility, and control in a multi-provider federated model.

3 BENEFITS OF CaaC

3.1 Scalability and Flexibility in Resource Allocation

One of the primary advantages of the CaaC model is its unparalleled scalability and flexibility:

- On-demand scaling: Businesses can instantly scale their compute resources up or down based on current needs, without the limitations of physical hardware.

- Global resource pool: CaaC provides access to a vast, distributed network of compute resources, allowing workloads to be run in optimal locations for performance or compliance reasons.
- Diverse resource types: Users can access a wide range of compute resources, from general-purpose CPUs to specialized GPUs and TPUs, without investing in dedicated hardware.
- Workload-specific optimization: CaaC platforms can automatically match workloads to the most suitable resource types, optimizing performance and cost(Sharma, M. et al., 2025).
- Burst capacity: Businesses can handle sudden spikes in demand without maintaining excess capacity during normal operations.

3.2 Cost Savings Through Optimized Resource Utilization

CaaC offers significant cost advantages over traditional infrastructure models:

- Pay-per-use pricing: Users only pay for the exact amount of compute power they consume, eliminating waste from idle resources.
- No upfront costs: CaaC eliminates the need for large capital expenditures on hardware and data center facilities.
- Reduced operational costs: With infrastructure management handled by the CaaC provider, businesses can reduce their IT staffing needs.
- Dynamic pricing models: CaaC platforms can leverage spot pricing and other dynamic pricing mechanisms to further reduce costs.
- Multi-cloud arbitrage: By federating resources from multiple providers, CaaC can always offer the most cost-effective option for each workload.
- Elimination of over-provisioning: Businesses no longer need to maintain excess capacity to handle peak loads, significantly reducing overall costs.

3.3 Accelerated Innovation and Experimentation

CaaC removes barriers to innovation and experimentation:

- Rapid prototyping: Teams can quickly spin up resources to test new ideas without waiting for hardware procurement or IT approval.
- Fail-fast approach: The low cost and easy access to resources encourage a culture of experimentation, allowing teams to try many ideas quickly.
- Access to cutting-edge technology: CaaC provides access to the latest hardware innovations without the need for continuous capital investment.

- Democratized access: Smaller teams and startups can access enterprise-grade computing resources, leveling the playing field for innovation.
- Simplified testing environments: CaaC makes it easy to create and tear down complex testing environments, accelerating the development cycle.

3.4 Enhanced Competitiveness and Agility

CaaC enhances business competitiveness and agility in several ways:

- Faster time-to-market: By removing infrastructure bottlenecks, CaaC allows businesses to develop and deploy new products and services more quickly(Chen, Z. et al., 2025).
- Global reach: CaaC enables businesses to easily deploy applications and services globally, reaching new markets with minimal infrastructure investment.
- Adaptability to market changes: The flexibility of CaaC allows businesses to quickly pivot their technology strategy in response to market changes.
- Focus on core competencies: By offloading infrastructure management to CaaC providers, businesses can focus more resources on their core products and services.
- Data-driven decision making: CaaC's ability to process vast amounts of data quickly and cost-effectively enables more sophisticated analytics and AI-driven decision making.
- Improved disaster recovery and business continuity: The distributed nature of CaaC resources enhances resilience and enables more robust disaster recovery strategies(Kareem, A. R., & Abdullah, H. S., 2025).

In conclusion, CaaC offers a compelling value proposition for businesses of all sizes. By providing unparalleled scalability, cost-effectiveness, and flexibility, CaaC is enabling a new wave of innovation and competitiveness across industries.

4 CHALLENGES AND CONSIDERATIONS IN ADOPTING CaaC

While CaaC offers numerous benefits, organizations must navigate several challenges when adopting this model:

4.1 Technical Challenges in Implementation

- Workload portability: Ensuring applications can run efficiently across different CaaC providers and resource types.

- Performance variability: Managing inconsistent performance across different providers or resource instances (Anita, H. B., 2025).
- Data transfer and latency: Addressing challenges related to moving large datasets between different CaaC resources or back to on-premises systems.
- Integration with existing systems: Seamlessly connecting CaaC resources with legacy applications and infrastructure.
- Monitoring and optimization: Implementing effective tools and processes to monitor resource usage, performance, and costs across a distributed CaaC environment.
- Automation and orchestration: Developing sophisticated automation systems to manage resource allocation, scaling, and workload distribution effectively (Deloitte., 2020).

4.2 Security and Compliance Concerns

- Data security: Ensuring the confidentiality and integrity of data as it moves between different CaaC resources and providers.
- Compliance with regulations: Meeting industry-specific regulations (e.g., HIPAA, GDPR) when using distributed CaaC resources.
- Identity and access management: Implementing robust authentication and authorization systems across multiple CaaC providers.
- Encryption: Managing encryption keys and ensuring data remains encrypted at rest and in transit across various CaaC resources.
- Audit and traceability: Maintaining comprehensive audit trails of resource usage and data access across a distributed CaaC environment.
- Shared responsibility model: Clearly defining security responsibilities between the organization and CaaC providers.

4.3 Managing Multi-Cloud Environments

- Vendor lock-in: Avoiding dependence on specific CaaC providers or technologies that could limit future flexibility.
- Consistent management: Implementing unified management tools and processes across multiple CaaC providers.
- Cost optimization: Effectively managing and optimizing costs across different providers with varying pricing models.
- Service level agreements (SLAs): Managing and enforcing SLAs across multiple CaaC providers.
- Skill set challenges: Developing and maintaining expertise across multiple CaaC platforms and technologies.

- Data governance: Implementing consistent data governance policies across a multi-cloud CaaC environment.

4.4 Organizational and Cultural Shifts Required

- Mindset change: Shifting from a capital expenditure (CapEx) model to an operational expenditure (OpEx) model for computing resources.
- New skills and roles: Developing new competencies in cloud architecture, automation, and multi-cloud management (MarketsandMarkets., 2020).
- Agile processes: Adapting organizational processes to take full advantage of CaaC's flexibility and scalability.
- Financial management: Implementing new budgeting and cost management processes suited to the dynamic nature of CaaC.
- Risk management: Developing new approaches to assess and manage risks in a distributed CaaC environment.
- Cultural resistance: Overcoming resistance to change from teams accustomed to traditional infrastructure models.
- Continuous learning: Fostering a culture of continuous learning to keep pace with rapidly evolving CaaC technologies and best practices.

Addressing these challenges requires a strategic approach that combines technological solutions, organizational changes, and a commitment to ongoing learning and adaptation. Organizations that successfully navigate these challenges can fully leverage the benefits of CaaC to drive innovation and competitive advantage (Saxena, M., & Mishra, D. K., 2025).

5 STRATEGIC IMPLICATIONS FOR BUSINESSES

The adoption of Compute as a Commodity (CaaC) has far-reaching strategic implications for businesses across industries. This chapter explores how CaaC is reshaping business strategies and operations.

5.1 Rethinking IT Infrastructure Strategies

- Shift from CapEx to OpEx: CaaC enables businesses to move from capital-intensive infrastructure investments to a more flexible operational expenditure model.
- Infrastructure as Code: Adopting CaaC necessitates a move towards treating infrastructure as code, enabling more agile and reproducible IT environments.

- Hybrid and Multi-Cloud Strategies: CaaC facilitates the implementation of hybrid and multi-cloud strategies, allowing businesses to optimize their infrastructure across various providers and deployment models.
- Focus on Orchestration: With CaaC, the emphasis shifts from managing individual servers to orchestrating resources across a distributed environment.
- Continuous Optimization: CaaC enables ongoing optimization of resource allocation and costs, requiring a more dynamic approach to infrastructure management.

5.2 Impact on Business Models and Competitive Advantage

- Lowered Barriers to Entry: CaaC democratizes access to high-performance computing, allowing startups and smaller companies to compete with larger enterprises.
- Increased Business Agility: The flexibility of CaaC enables businesses to rapidly scale operations, enter new markets, and respond to changing customer demands.
- New Product Possibilities: Access to scalable compute resources opens up possibilities for new data-intensive products and services, particularly in AI and IoT.
- Global Reach: CaaC facilitates easy deployment of applications and services globally, enabling businesses to reach new markets with minimal infrastructure investment.
- Risk Mitigation: The distributed nature of CaaC can enhance business continuity and disaster recovery capabilities, reducing operational risks.

5.3 Fostering a Culture of Innovation and Agility

- Rapid Prototyping and Experimentation: CaaC removes infrastructure constraints, encouraging a culture of continuous experimentation and innovation.
- DevOps and Agile Methodologies: The flexibility of CaaC aligns well with DevOps practices and agile development methodologies, accelerating the software development lifecycle.
- Fail-Fast Approach: The low cost and easy access to resources in CaaC encourage a "fail-fast" approach, where ideas can be quickly tested and iterated upon.
- Cross-Functional Collaboration: CaaC can break down silos between IT and other departments, fostering more collaborative and innovative organizational cultures.

- Continuous Learning: The rapidly evolving nature of CaaC technologies necessitates a culture of continuous learning and skill development within organizations.

5.4 Data-Driven Decision Making and AI/ML Adoption

- Big Data Analytics: CaaC provides the scalable resources needed to process and analyze large datasets, enabling more sophisticated business intelligence and analytics.
- AI and Machine Learning at Scale: The ability to access powerful computing resources on-demand makes it feasible for businesses of all sizes to implement AI and ML initiatives(IDC.,2020).
- Real-Time Decision Making: CaaC enables real-time data processing and analytics, supporting faster and more informed decision-making processes.
- Personalization and Customer Insights: Access to scalable compute resources allows businesses to analyze customer data in greater depth, enabling more personalized products and services.
- Predictive and Prescriptive Analytics: CaaC facilitates(Pandey, B. K. et al., 2024a)

6 CaaC IMPLEMENTATION STRATEGIES

6.1 Assessing Organizational Readiness for CaaC Adoption

Before embarking on a CaaC implementation, organizations must assess their readiness to ensure a smooth transition. This assessment should cover several key areas:

- **Technical Infrastructure**: Evaluate the current IT infrastructure and identify gaps that need to be addressed for CaaC adoption.
- **Skill Set Analysis**: Assess the technical skills of the IT team and identify areas where training or new hires may be necessary.
- **Cultural Readiness**: Gauge the organization's willingness to embrace change and adopt new technologies.
- **Financial Preparedness**: Analyze the current IT budget and determine the financial implications of moving to a CaaC model.
- **Compliance and Security**: Review existing security policies and compliance requirements to ensure they can be met in a CaaC environment.

A readiness assessment tool, such as the Cloud Readiness Assessment Framework developed by NIST, can provide a structured approach to this evaluation.

6.2 Developing a CaaC Migration Roadmap

Once readiness has been assessed, organizations should develop a comprehensive migration roadmap. This roadmap should include:

- **Prioritization of Workloads** Identify which applications and services are best suited for initial migration to CaaC.
- **Timeline and Milestones** Establish a realistic timeline for migration, including key milestones and checkpoints.
- **Resource Allocation** Determine the human and financial resources required for each phase of the migration.
- **Risk Mitigation Strategies** Identify potential risks and develop strategies to mitigate them.
- **Training Plan** Outline a plan for upskilling existing staff and onboarding new team members as needed.

Gartner's 5 R's of Cloud Migration (Rehost, Refactor, Revise, Rebuild, and Replace) can provide a framework for categorizing and planning the migration of different applications (Shahul, A. et al., 2024).

6.3 Best Practices for CaaC Implementation

Successful CaaC implementation requires adherence to several best practices:

- **Start Small**: Begin with non-critical workloads to gain experience and build confidence.
- **Embrace Automation**: Leverage automation tools for deployment, scaling, and management of CaaC resources.
- **Implement Strong Governance**: Establish clear policies and procedures for resource provisioning and management.
- **Prioritize Security**: Implement robust security measures from the outset, including encryption, access controls, and monitoring.
- **Continuous Optimization**: Regularly review and optimize resource allocation to ensure cost-effectiveness.
- **Foster a Culture of Learning**: Encourage continuous learning and experimentation among the IT team.

6.4 Case Studies of Successful CaaC Migrations

6.4.1 Case Study 1: Netflix

Netflix's migration to AWS is a prime example of successful CaaC adoption. Key highlights include:

- Gradual migration of services over seven years
- Development of open-source tools like Spinnaker for multi-cloud deployment
- Achieved 100% cloud operation by 2016, improving scalability and global reach

6.4.2 Case Study 2: Capital One

Capital One's journey to become a cloud-first organization demonstrates the transformative potential of CaaC:

- Closed all on-premises data centers by 2020
- Developed CapitalOne DevExchange for internal development
- Achieved significant cost savings and improved time-to-market for new products (Google Cloud., 2021)

These case studies illustrate that successful CaaC migration requires careful planning, a commitment to cultural change, and a willingness to invest in new tools and processes.

7 CaaC ECONOMICS AND COST OPTIMIZATION

7.1 Detailed Analysis of CaaC Pricing Models

CaaC providers offer various pricing models, each with its own advantages and considerations:

- **Pay-as-You-Go**: Users pay only for the resources they consume, billed by the second or minute.
- **Reserved Instances**: Discounted rates for committing to use a certain amount of resources for a fixed term.
- **Spot Instances**: Significantly reduced rates for using spare capacity, but with the risk of interruption.

- **Savings Plans**: Flexible pricing model offering lower prices in exchange for a commitment to a consistent amount of usage.

According to a study by RightScale, organizations waste an average of 35% of their cloud spend . Understanding these pricing models is crucial for optimizing costs(Pandey, D. et al., 2024).

7.2 Strategies for Optimizing CaaC Costs

To maximize the cost benefits of CaaC, organizations should implement the following strategies:

- **Right-Sizing**: Ensure that provisioned resources match actual needs.
- **Automated Scaling**: Implement auto-scaling to adjust resources based on demand.
- **Resource Scheduling**: Turn off non-production resources during off-hours.
- **Reserved Instance Planning**: Use reserved instances for predictable, steady-state workloads.
- **Spot Instance Utilization**: Leverage spot instances for fault-tolerant, flexible workloads.
- **Multi-Cloud Arbitrage**: Take advantage of price differences between providers.

Tools like AWS Cost Explorer, Google Cloud's Cost Management, and third-party solutions can help in implementing these strategies.

7.3 ROI Calculation for CaaC Adoption

Calculating the Return on Investment (ROI) for CaaC adoption involves considering several factors:

- **Cost Savings** Compare the total cost of ownership (TCO) of on-premises infrastructure vs. CaaC.
- **Productivity Gains** Quantify the impact of increased agility and faster time-to-market.
- **Revenue Impact** Assess potential revenue increases from new capabilities enabled by CaaC.
- **Risk Mitigation** Consider the value of improved disaster recovery and business continuity.

Example Code:

```python

def calculate_caac_roi(traditional_cost, caac_cost, caac_
benefits):

"""

Calculate ROI for CaaC adoption

:param traditional_cost: Cost of traditional infrastructure

:param caac_cost: Cost of CaaC implementation

:param caac_benefits: Financial benefits from CaaC (Eg: In-
creased Revenue, Productivity)

:return: ROI as a percentage

"""

investment = caac_cost - traditional_cost

gain = caac_benefits - caac_cost

roi = (gain / investment) * 100
```

```
    return roi

    #Example Usage

    traditional_cost = 1000000 # $1 million

    caac_cost = 800000 # $800,000

    caac_benefits = 1500000 # $1.5 million

    roi = calculate_caac_roi(traditional_cost, caac_cost, caac_
benefits):

    print(f"The ROI for CaaC adoption is: {roi:.2f}%")
```

A simple ROI formula:

ROI = (Gain from Investment – Cost of Investment) / Cost of Investment

However, a more comprehensive approach should include both tangible and intangible benefits.

7.4 Long-Term Financial Implications of CaaC

While CaaC can offer significant short-term cost savings, it's crucial to consider the long-term financial implications:

- **Scalability Costs**: As usage grows, costs can increase rapidly if not managed properly.
- **Skill Investment**: Ongoing investment in training and potentially higher salaries for cloud-skilled personnel.
- **Vendor Lock-in Risks**: Costs associated with potential future migrations between providers.
- **Compliance and Security Costs**: Potential increases in spending on security and compliance measures.

A study by IDC found that organizations that invested in cloud skills and processes saw a 3-year ROI of 571% . This underscores the importance of taking a long-term view when evaluating the financial implications of CaaC adoption (Pandey, B. K. et al., 2024b).

8 CaaC ARCHITECTURE AND DESIGN PATTERNS

8.1 Architectural Considerations for CaaC Environments

When designing for CaaC environments, several key architectural considerations come into play:

- **Multi-Tenancy**: Ensure proper isolation between different tenants sharing the same infrastructure.
- **Scalability**: Design systems that can scale horizontally to handle varying loads.
- **Resilience**: Implement fault-tolerant designs to handle infrastructure failures gracefully.
- **Data Management**: Consider data storage, retrieval, and synchronization across distributed systems.
- **Network Design**: Plan for efficient and secure network communication between components.
- **Security**: Incorporate security at every layer of the architecture.

The Well-Architected Framework by AWS provides a comprehensive guide for these considerations.

8.2 Design Patterns for Scalable and Resilient CaaC Applications

Several design patterns have emerged as best practices for CaaC applications:

- **Circuit Breaker Pattern**: Prevent cascading failures in distributed systems.
- **Bulkhead Pattern**: Isolate elements of an application into pools so that if one fails, the others will continue to function.
- **Saga Pattern**: Manage data consistency across microservices in distributed transaction scenarios.
- **CQRS (Command Query Responsibility Segregation)**: Separate read and write operations for more scalable architectures.

- **Event Sourcing**: Store the state of data as a sequence of events for better scalability and auditability.

These patterns, among others, are described in detail in the book "Cloud Design Patterns" by Microsoft (Pandey, B. K. et al., 2024c).

Figure 2. Design patterns for scalable and resilient CaaC applications

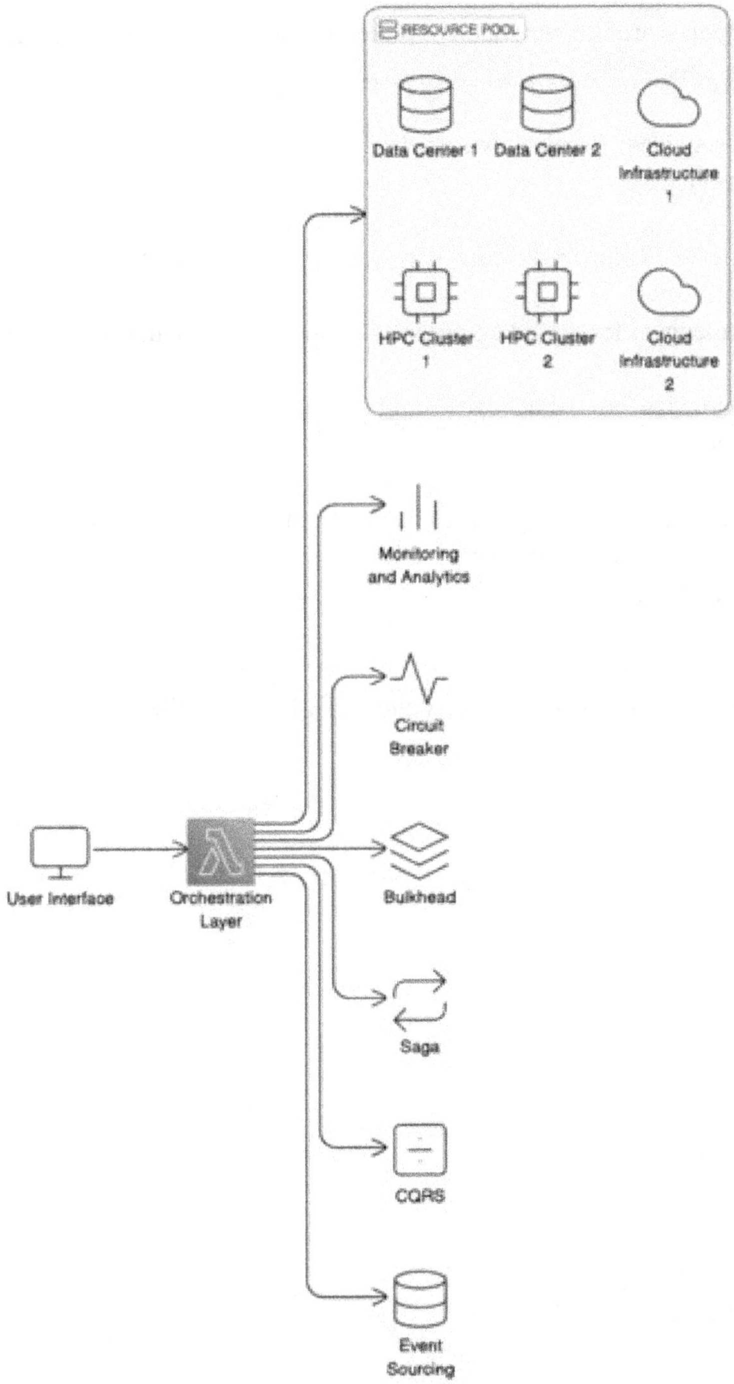

8.3 Microservices and Containerization in CaaC

Microservices architecture and containerization are fundamental to many CaaC implementations:

- **Microservices**: Break down applications into small, independently deployable services.

  a. Benefits: Improved scalability, faster development cycles, technology flexibility.
  b. Challenges: Increased complexity, potential performance overhead.

- **Containerization**: Package applications and their dependencies into containers.

  a. Benefits: Consistency across environments, improved resource utilization.
  b. Tools: Docker for containerization, Kubernetes for orchestration (Swapna, H. R. et al., 2024a).

According to a survey by O'Reilly, 92% of organizations using microservices reported success with the approach (Pandey, B. K. et al., 2024d).

Figure 3. Microservices and containerization in CaaC

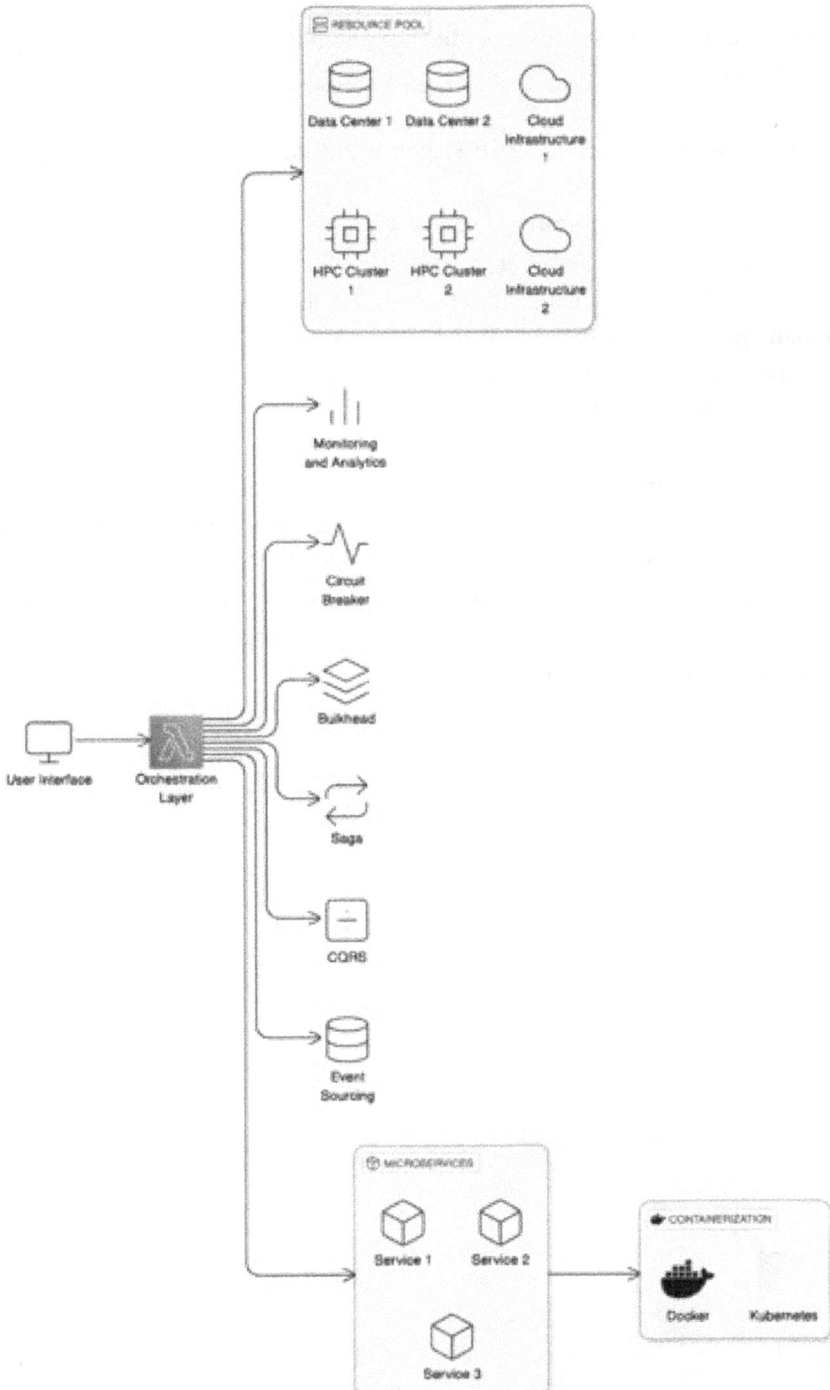

8.4 Serverless Architecture in the Context of CaaC

Serverless computing represents the next evolution in CaaC, offering even greater abstraction:

- **Function-as-a-Service (FaaS)**: Execute individual functions in response to events.
- **Event-Driven Architecture**: Design systems around the production, detection, and consumption of events.
- **Stateless Compute**: Design functions to be stateless, with state externalized to managed services.
- **Pay-per-Execution Model**: Cost model based on actual function executions rather than provisioned capacity.

Serverless architectures can significantly reduce operational overhead and improve scalability. However, they also introduce new challenges such as cold start latency and complex debugging (Netflix Technology Blog., 2022).

A case study by Coca-Cola showed that moving to a serverless architecture reduced their operational costs by 65% while improving scalability and reducing time-to-market (Pandey, B. K. et al., 2024e).

Figure 4. Serverless architecture in the context of CaaC

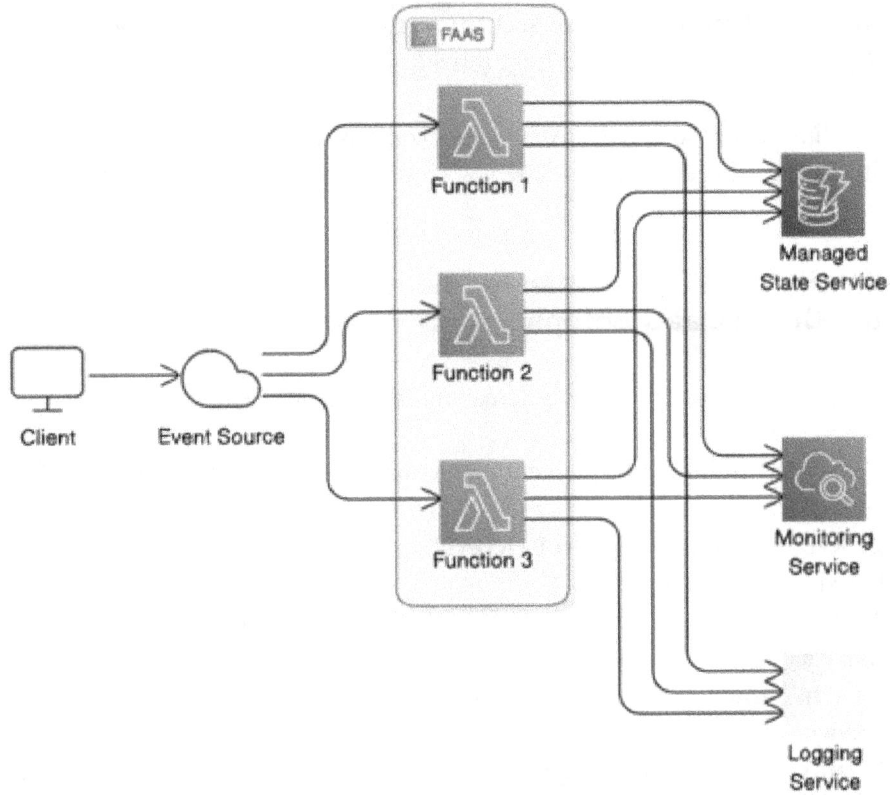

9 CaaC SECURITY AND GOVERNANCE

9.1 Advanced Security Strategies for CaaC Environments

Securing CaaC environments requires a comprehensive approach(Gartner., 2022):

- **Zero Trust Architecture**: Assume no trust, verify every access request regardless of its source.
- **Encryption**: Implement end-to-end encryption for data in transit and at rest.
- **Micro-Segmentation**: Divide the network into small segments to contain potential breaches.

- **Continuous Monitoring**: Implement real-time monitoring and anomaly detection.
- **Automated Response**: Use security orchestration and automated response (SOAR) tools to quickly address threats.

According to a report by McAfee, organizations using a CASB (Cloud Access Security Broker) experienced 65% fewer security incidents (Pandey, B. K. et al., 2024f).

9.2 Identity and Access Management in Multi-Cloud CaaC Setups

Managing identities and access across multiple cloud providers is crucial:

- **Federated Identity**: Implement single sign-on (SSO) across multiple cloud services.
- **Role-Based Access Control (RBAC)**: Define and enforce access policies based on user roles.
- **Multi-Factor Authentication (MFA)**: Require multiple forms of verification for sensitive operations.
- **Just-In-Time (JIT) Access**: Provide temporary, elevated access only when needed.
- **Identity Governance**: Regularly review and audit access rights across all cloud services.

Tools like Azure Active Directory and AWS Identity and Access Management (IAM) can help manage identities across multiple cloud providers(Swapna, H. R. et al., 2024b).

Figure 5. Identity and access management in multi-cloud CaaC setups

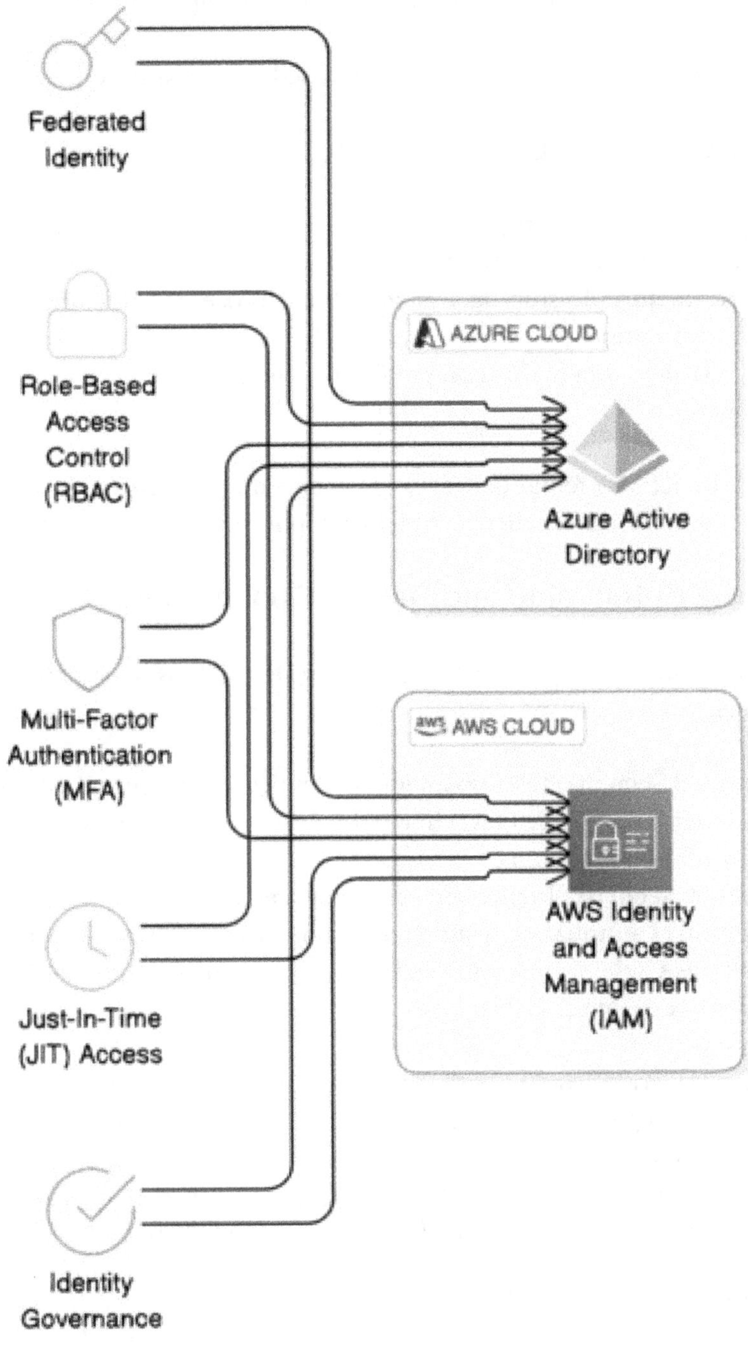

9.3 Data Governance and Compliance in CaaC

Ensuring data governance and compliance in CaaC environments involves:

- **Data Classification**: Categorize data based on sensitivity and regulatory requirements.
- **Data Lifecycle Management**: Implement policies for data creation, storage, use, and deletion.
- **Compliance Monitoring**: Use tools to continuously monitor compliance with regulations like GDPR, HIPAA, etc.
- **Data Residency**: Ensure data is stored and processed in compliance with regional regulations.
- **Audit Trails**: Maintain comprehensive logs of all data access and modifications.

A survey by KPMG found that 75% of organizations consider data protection regulations as a significant challenge in cloud adoption (Swapna, H. R. et al., 2024c).

9.4 Security Automation and DevSecOps in CaaC

Integrating security into the DevOps pipeline (DevSecOps) is essential for CaaC environments:

- **Automated Security Testing**: Integrate security testing into CI/CD pipelines.
- **Infrastructure as Code (IaC) Security**: Use tools to scan IaC templates for security misconfigurations.
- **Container Security**: Implement container scanning and runtime protection.
- **Continuous Compliance**: Automate compliance checks and reporting.
- **Security as Code**: Define and version control security policies alongside application code (PwC., 2023).

According to Gartner, by 2023, 60% of organizations will have integrated security into their DevOps pipelines, up from just 20% in 2019 (Pandey, B. K. et al., 2024g).

Implementation of these strategies requires a combination of cultural change, process improvement, and leveraging of advanced security tools and platforms designed for cloud-native environments (Burns, B., et al.,2016).

10 CaaC PERFORMANCE OPTIMIZATION AND MONITORING

10.1 Performance Benchmarking in CaaC Environments

Effective performance benchmarking in CaaC environments involves:

- **Baseline Establishment**: Create performance baselines for different types of workloads.
- **Comparative Analysis**: Compare performance across different CaaC providers and instance types.
- **Workload-Specific Metrics**: Define and measure metrics relevant to specific application types.
- **Continuous Benchmarking**: Regularly re-run benchmarks to account for infrastructure changes.
- **Cost-Performance Ratio**: Evaluate performance in the context of cost to determine optimal configurations.

Tools like Apache JMeter, Gatling, and cloud-native solutions like AWS CloudWatch can be used for benchmarking (IDC., 2023).

A study by Cockroach Labs found performance variations of up to 40% between seemingly equivalent instances across different cloud providers (Pandey, B. K. et al., 2024h).

10.2 Tools and Techniques for Monitoring CaaC Resources

Monitoring CaaC resources requires a comprehensive approach:

- **Infrastructure Monitoring**: Track CPU, memory, storage, and network utilization.
- **Application Performance Monitoring (APM)**: Monitor application-level metrics and user experience.
- **Log Analytics**: Centralize and analyze logs from all components of the CaaC environment.
- **Distributed Tracing**: Track requests as they flow through microservices architectures.
- **Alerting and Notification**: Set up intelligent alerting based on predefined thresholds and anomaly detection.

Popular monitoring tools include:

- Prometheus and Grafana for metrics collection and visualization
- ELK Stack (Elasticsearch, Logstash, Kibana) for log analytics
- Jaeger or Zipkin for distributed tracing

According to a survey by Datadog, 40% of organizations are now using container orchestration, necessitating more sophisticated monitoring approaches (Abdulkarim, Yadgar I. et al., 2024).

10.3 Optimizing Application Performance in CaaC

Optimizing application performance in CaaC environments involves:

- **Code Optimization**: Refactor code to take advantage of cloud-native features.
- **Caching Strategies**: Implement distributed caching to reduce database load and improve response times.
- **Content Delivery Networks (CDNs)**: Use CDNs to reduce latency for geographically distributed users.
- **Auto-scaling Policies**: Implement intelligent auto-scaling to handle varying loads efficiently.
- **Database Optimization**: Use database sharding, read replicas, and query optimization techniques.

A case study by Adidas showed that moving to a cloud-native architecture improved their application's performance by 40% while reducing operational costs (Revathi, T. K. et al., 2022).

10.4 Capacity Planning and Forecasting for CaaC

Effective capacity planning in CaaC environments requires:

- **Demand Forecasting**: Use historical data and predictive analytics to forecast future resource needs.
- **Scenario Planning**: Model different growth scenarios to prepare for various potential outcomes.
- **Rightsizing**: Continuously adjust resource allocations based on actual usage patterns.
- **Reserved Capacity Management**: Balance on-demand and reserved resources for cost-effective scaling.
- **Burst Capacity Planning**: Plan for sudden spikes in demand, especially for seasonal businesses.

Tools like AWS Capacity Planner and Google Cloud's Capacity Planning tool can assist in this process(Volkswagen., 2022).

A study by IDC found that organizations with mature cloud strategies overprovision by just 27%, compared to 47% for those with less mature strategies (Pandey, B. K., & Pandey, D., 2023).

Key metrics for capacity planning include:

- CPU utilization
- Memory usage
- Storage consumption
- Network throughput
- Request latency

By implementing effective capacity planning and forecasting, organizations can optimize their CaaC costs while ensuring they have the resources needed to meet business demands.

11 CaaC AND DEVOPS INTEGRATION

11.1 DevOps Practices in CaaC Environments

Integrating DevOps practices with CaaC can significantly enhance an organization's ability to deliver software quickly and reliably. Key DevOps practices in CaaC environments include:

- **Continuous Integration (CI)**: Automatically build and test code changes.
- **Continuous Delivery (CD)**: Automate the delivery of applications to selected infrastructure environments.
- **Infrastructure as Code (IaC)**: Manage and provision infrastructure through code rather than manual processes.
- **Microservices Architecture**: Design applications as a collection of loosely coupled services.
- **Monitoring and Logging**: Implement comprehensive monitoring and centralized logging.
- **Collaboration and Communication**: Foster a culture of shared responsibility between development and operations teams.

According to the 2021 State of DevOps Report, elite performers who have successfully integrated DevOps practices deploy code 973 times more frequently than low performers (Pandey, B. K. et al., 2023).

11.2 Continuous Integration and Continuous Deployment (CI/CD) for CaaC

CI/CD pipelines are crucial for efficient software delivery in CaaC environments:

- **Source Control Integration**: Integrate with version control systems like Git.
- **Automated Testing**: Incorporate unit, integration, and end-to-end tests in the pipeline.
- **Artifact Management**: Use repositories to store and version application artifacts.
- **Deployment Automation**: Automate the deployment process to various environments.
- **Rollback Mechanisms**: Implement automated rollback procedures in case of deployment failures.

Popular CI/CD tools for CaaC include:

- Jenkins
- GitLab CI
- AWS CodePipeline
- Google Cloud Build
- Azure DevOps

A case study by Capital One showed that implementing CI/CD in their CaaC environment reduced their time-to-market for new features from months to weeks.

11.3 Infrastructure as Code (IaC) in CaaC

IaC is a fundamental practice in CaaC environments, allowing teams to manage infrastructure using code:

- **Version Control**: Store infrastructure code in version control systems.
- **Declarative Syntax**: Use declarative language to specify the desired state of infrastructure.
- **Modular Design**: Create reusable modules for common infrastructure components.

- **Testing**: Implement unit and integration tests for infrastructure code.
- **Drift Detection**: Regularly check for and remediate differences between the desired and actual state of infrastructure.

Popular IaC tools include:

- Terraform
- AWS CloudFormation
- Azure Resource Manager templates
- Google Cloud Deployment Manager

According to a survey by Puppet, 85% of organizations that have adopted IaC say it has a positive impact on their ability to implement changes to infrastructure (Pandey, B. K. et al., 2023).

11.4 Automating CaaC Operations

Automation is key to managing CaaC environments efficiently:

- **Resource Provisioning**: Automate the creation and configuration of cloud resources.
- **Auto-scaling**: Implement rules-based scaling of resources based on demand.
- **Configuration Management**: Use tools like Ansible, Puppet, or Chef to automate configuration across environments.
- **Patch Management**: Automate the process of applying security patches and updates.
- **Backup and Recovery**: Set up automated backup procedures and test recovery processes regularly.

Gartner predicts that by 2025, 70% of organizations will implement structured automation to deliver flexibility and efficiency, an increase from 20% in 2021 (Pandey, B. K. et al., 2023).

Implementing these DevOps practices in CaaC environments can lead to significant improvements in deployment frequency, lead time for changes, and mean time to recovery (MTTR). However, it requires a cultural shift towards collaboration, continuous improvement, and shared responsibility for the entire application lifecycle(Saravanakumar, R. et al., 2024).

12 CaaC IN SPECIFIC INDUSTRIES

12.1 CaaC Applications in Finance and Banking

The finance and banking sector has been at the forefront of CaaC adoption, leveraging its capabilities to enhance security, improve customer experience, and streamline operations.

Key applications include:

- **Real-time Fraud Detection**: Utilizing machine learning models on CaaC platforms to detect and prevent fraudulent transactions in real-time.
- **High-Frequency Trading**: Leveraging low-latency CaaC resources for algorithmic trading and market analysis.
- **Risk Modeling**: Using CaaC for complex risk calculations and scenario analysis.
- **Customer 360 Views**: Implementing big data analytics on CaaC platforms to gain comprehensive customer insights.

Case Study: JPMorgan Chase migrated 50% of its applications to the cloud, resulting in a 30% reduction in IT costs and improved development speed (Kumarganesh, S. et al., 2024).

12.2 CaaC in Healthcare and Life Sciences

CaaC is transforming healthcare and life sciences by enabling advanced research, improving patient care, and enhancing operational efficiency(Basha, A. J. et al., 2024).

Key applications include:

- **Genomic Sequencing**: Utilizing CaaC for high-performance computing in genomic analysis.
- **Drug Discovery**: Accelerating drug discovery processes through molecular modeling on CaaC platforms.
- **Medical Imaging Analysis**: Implementing AI-powered image analysis for faster and more accurate diagnoses.
- **Telemedicine Platforms**: Building scalable telemedicine solutions on CaaC infrastructure.

Case Study: Moderna leveraged AWS's CaaC offerings to reduce the time for digital drug design from months to weeks, accelerating COVID-19 vaccine development (Devasenapathy, D. et al., 2023).

12.3 CaaC for Retail and E-commerce

The retail and e-commerce sector is leveraging CaaC to enhance customer experiences, optimize supply chains, and drive personalized marketing.

Key applications include:

- **Dynamic Pricing**: Implementing real-time pricing algorithms based on demand and competition.
- **Personalized Recommendations**: Using machine learning on CaaC platforms for personalized product recommendations.
- **Inventory Optimization**: Leveraging predictive analytics for efficient inventory management.
- **Omnichannel Experience**: Building seamless omnichannel retail experiences using CaaC-based microservices.

Case Study: Walmart's move to a hybrid cloud model has enabled them to handle over 6 million transactions per minute during peak times (Lakshmi, K. V. N. et al., 2024).

12.4 CaaC in Manufacturing and Industry 4.0

CaaC is a key enabler of Industry 4.0, facilitating smart manufacturing and industrial IoT applications.

Key applications include:

- **Predictive Maintenance**: Using IoT sensor data and machine learning for predictive equipment maintenance.
- **Digital Twin Simulations**: Creating and manipulating digital twins of physical assets for optimization and training.
- **Supply Chain Optimization**: Implementing blockchain and AI on CaaC platforms for transparent and efficient supply chains.
- **Quality Control**: Leveraging computer vision and AI for automated quality control in production lines.

Case Study: Siemens' MindSphere IoT platform, built on CaaC principles, has helped manufacturing clients achieve up to 30% energy savings and 80% reduction in downtime (Maheshwari, R. Uma. et al., 2024).

13 EMERGING CaaC TECHNOLOGIES AND FUTURE OUTLOOK

13.1 Quantum Computing in CaaC

Quantum computing represents the next frontier in CaaC, promising to solve complex problems that are intractable for classical computers.

Key developments include:

- **Quantum-as-a-Service (QaaS)**: Major cloud providers like IBM, Google, and AWS are beginning to offer quantum computing resources as a service.
- **Quantum Machine Learning**: Developing quantum algorithms for machine learning tasks that could offer significant speedups over classical methods.
- **Quantum Cryptography**: Implementing quantum-resistant encryption methods to prepare for the post-quantum era.

According to a report by BCG, quantum computing could create up to $850 billion in value by 2040 (Rai, P. K. et al., 2024).

13.2 AI and ML Advancements in CaaC Resource Management

Artificial Intelligence and Machine Learning are revolutionizing how CaaC resources are managed and optimized.

Key trends include:

- **AI-Driven Autoscaling**: Using machine learning models to predict resource needs and scale automatically.
- **Intelligent Workload Placement**: Optimizing workload placement across multi-cloud environments using AI algorithms.
- **Anomaly Detection**: Implementing ML-based systems for detecting and responding to anomalies in CaaC environments.

Gartner predicts that by 2025, AI will be the top category driving infrastructure decisions (Sahani, S. K. et al., 2024a).

13.3 Edge Computing and CaaC Convergence

The convergence of edge computing and CaaC is enabling new use cases and improving application performance.

Key developments include:

- **Edge-as-a-Service**: CaaC providers offering edge computing resources as part of their service portfolio.
- **5G Integration**: Leveraging 5G networks to enhance connectivity between edge devices and CaaC resources.
- **Distributed AI**: Implementing AI models that can run partially on edge devices and partially in the cloud.

IDC forecasts that by 2025, 75% of enterprise-generated data will be created and processed at the edge (Sahani, S. K. et al., 2024b).

13.4 Predictions for the Future of CaaC (5-10 year outlook)

Looking ahead, several trends are likely to shape the future of CaaC:

- **Serverless Dominance**: By 2025, Gartner predicts that 50% of global enterprises will have deployed serverless computing technologies, up from 20% in 2020 (Kennedy, G. W. et al., 2024).
- **Multi-Cloud Standardization**: Efforts like the Cloud Native Computing Foundation (CNCF) will lead to greater standardization across cloud providers, making multi-cloud strategies more feasible.
- **Green Computing**: Sustainability will become a key factor in CaaC decisions, with providers competing on energy efficiency and use of renewable energy.
- **AI-First Infrastructure**: CaaC providers will design their infrastructure to be optimized for AI workloads by default.
- **Quantum-Cloud Integration**: By 2030, we may see the first fully integrated quantum-classical cloud services, enabling new classes of applications.
- **Regulatory Evolution**: Governments will develop more comprehensive regulations around data sovereignty and AI ethics, impacting how CaaC resources are used and managed.

As CaaC continues to evolve, organizations that stay ahead of these trends will be best positioned to leverage the technology for competitive advantage. The future of CaaC promises even greater flexibility, efficiency, and capability, fundamentally changing how we think about and use computing resources(Pandey, B. K. et al., 2022).

14 GLOBAL PERSPECTIVES ON CaaC ADOPTION

14.1 Regional Trends in CaaC Adoption

CaaC adoption varies significantly across different regions due to factors such as technological infrastructure, regulatory environments, and economic conditions.

- **North America**: Leading in CaaC adoption, with a focus on hybrid and multi-cloud strategies.
- **Europe**: Strong adoption, with emphasis on data protection and GDPR compliance.
- **Asia-Pacific**: Rapid growth, particularly in countries like China and India, with a focus on digital transformation.
- **Latin America**: Growing adoption, with emphasis on cost reduction and scalability.
- **Middle East and Africa**: Emerging market with increasing adoption, focusing on leapfrogging legacy technologies.

According to Gartner, the worldwide public cloud services market is projected to grow 23.1% in 2021 to total $332.3 billion, up from $270 billion in 2020 (Cockroach Labs., 2022).

14.2 Regulatory Landscapes and Their Impact on CaaC

Different regions have varying regulatory requirements that significantly impact CaaC adoption and implementation:

- **European Union**: GDPR has major implications for data storage and processing in CaaC environments.
- **United States**: Sector-specific regulations like HIPAA for healthcare and PCI DSS for financial services.
- **China**: Cybersecurity Law requires certain data to be stored within the country.
- **Russia**: Data Localization Law mandates that personal data of Russian citizens must be stored in Russia.

A survey by Thales found that 48% of businesses consider meeting compliance requirements a significant barrier to cloud adoption (Sahani, K. et al., 2024b).

14.3 Cultural Factors Influencing CaaC Adoption

Cultural differences can significantly impact the approach to CaaC adoption:

- **Risk Tolerance**: Varies by region, influencing the speed of CaaC adoption.
- **Innovation Culture**: Countries with strong startup ecosystems often lead in CaaC adoption.
- **Trust in Technology**: Societal trust in technology can accelerate or hinder CaaC adoption.
- **Work Culture**: Countries with more flexible work cultures may adapt more readily to CaaC-enabled remote work.

14.4 Global Collaboration and Standards in CaaC

International collaboration is crucial for developing global standards and best practices in CaaC:

- **ISO/IEC Standards**: Development of international standards for cloud computing.
- **Open Source Initiatives**: Global collaboration on projects like Kubernetes and OpenStack.
- **International Data Transfer Agreements**: Frameworks like EU-US Privacy Shield for cross-border data flows.

The Cloud Native Computing Foundation (CNCF) reports a 50% year-over-year growth in its global community, highlighting the increasing international collaboration in cloud-native technologies (Kumar Pandey, B. et al., 2021).

15 ENVIRONMENTAL IMPACT OF CaaC

15.1 Energy Consumption in CaaC Data Centers

The rapid growth of CaaC has led to increased scrutiny of the energy consumption of data centers:

- **Power Usage Effectiveness (PUE)**: Measure of data center energy efficiency.
- **Renewable Energy Adoption**: Major CaaC providers are increasingly powering their data centers with renewable energy.

- **Advanced Cooling Technologies**: Innovations in cooling systems to reduce energy consumption.

According to a study by Science, data centers accounted for about 1% of global electricity use in 2020 (Saxena, A. et al., 2021).

15.2 Carbon Footprint of CaaC

Understanding and mitigating the carbon footprint of CaaC is becoming increasingly important:

- **Carbon Intensity Metrics**: Measuring CO2 emissions per unit of compute power.
- **Carbon-Aware Computing**: Optimizing workload placement based on real-time grid carbon intensity.
- **Life Cycle Assessment**: Considering the full environmental impact of CaaC hardware from production to disposal.

Google Cloud reports that their data centers are twice as energy efficient as a typical enterprise data center, and their carbon footprint is net zero (Khan, B. et al., 2021).

15.3 Sustainability Initiatives in CaaC

Major CaaC providers and users are implementing various sustainability initiatives:

- **100% Renewable Energy Goals**: Many providers aim to power their operations entirely with renewable energy.
- **Circular Economy Practices**: Efforts to reuse and recycle data center equipment.
- **Water Conservation**: Implementing water-efficient cooling systems and using recycled water.

Microsoft has pledged to be carbon negative by 2030 and by 2050 to remove all the carbon from the environment that it has emitted since it was founded in 1975 .

15.4 Green CaaC Strategies for Businesses

Organizations can adopt various strategies to minimize the environmental impact of their CaaC usage:

- **Efficient Resource Utilization**: Optimizing workloads to use resources more efficiently.
- **Green Software Engineering**: Developing software with energy efficiency in mind.
- **Sustainable Procurement**: Choosing CaaC providers based on their environmental credentials.
- **Carbon Offsetting**: Investing in carbon offset projects to compensate for emissions.

A report by Accenture found that migrations to the public cloud can reduce CO2 emissions by 59 million tons per year, which equates to taking 22 million cars off the road (Dhanasekar, S. et al., 2023).

16 ETHICAL CONSIDERATIONS IN CaaC

16.1 Data Privacy and Protection

As CaaC involves storing and processing vast amounts of data, ensuring privacy and protection is crucial:

- **Data Anonymization**: Techniques to protect individual privacy in large datasets.
- **Informed Consent**: Ensuring users understand how their data is used in CaaC environments.
- **Right to be Forgotten**: Implementing mechanisms for data deletion upon request.
- **Transparency**: Clearly communicating data handling practices to users.

A survey by KPMG found that 86% of respondents felt a growing concern about data privacy, while 78% feared the amount of data being collected (Du John, H. V. et al., 2022).

16.2 AI Ethics in CaaC

As AI becomes increasingly integrated with CaaC, addressing ethical concerns is paramount:

- **Bias in AI Models**: Ensuring AI models trained on CaaC platforms are free from discriminatory biases.

- **Explainable AI**: Developing AI systems whose decisions can be understood and explained.
- **Human Oversight**: Maintaining appropriate human control over AI systems in CaaC environments.
- **Ethical Use of AI**: Establishing guidelines for the responsible use of AI in CaaC applications.

According to a report by Gartner, by 2023, all personnel hired for AI development and training will have to demonstrate expertise in responsible AI (Tareke, S. A. et al., 2022).

16.3 Digital Divide and CaaC

The adoption of CaaC technologies could potentially exacerbate existing digital divides:

- **Access Inequality**: Ensuring CaaC benefits are accessible to organizations of all sizes and regions.
- **Skill Gap**: Addressing the shortage of cloud computing skills in certain regions or demographics.
- **Infrastructure Disparities**: Working to improve internet infrastructure in underserved areas.

A World Economic Forum report highlights that 3.7 billion people remain offline, largely due to a lack of infrastructure, affordability, and skills .

16.4 Environmental Ethics and CaaC

Ethical considerations related to the environmental impact of CaaC are gaining importance:

- **Resource Consumption**: Addressing the ethical implications of the increasing resource demand of CaaC.
- **E-Waste**: Responsibly managing the disposal and recycling of outdated CaaC hardware.
- **Climate Responsibility**: Considering the role of CaaC in climate change mitigation and adaptation.

The Shift Project reports that digital technologies' share of global CO_2 emissions could rise to 8% by 2025, emphasizing the need for ethical considerations in CaaC adoption (Barr, J., 2006) .

17 CaaC AND BLOCKCHAIN INTEGRATION

17.1 Blockchain as a Service (BaaS) in CaaC Environments

Blockchain technology is increasingly being offered as a service within CaaC platforms, enabling organizations to leverage distributed ledger technology without managing the underlying infrastructure.

Key aspects include:

- **Scalable Blockchain Networks**: CaaC providers offering easily scalable blockchain networks.
- **Smart Contract Platforms**: Integrated development environments for creating and deploying smart contracts.
- **Consensus Mechanism Options**: Flexibility in choosing consensus mechanisms suitable for different use cases.

According to MarketsandMarkets, the global Blockchain-as-a-Service market size is expected to grow from $2.0 billion in 2021 to $15.7 billion by 2026, at a Compound Annual Growth Rate (CAGR) of 50.9% .

17.2 CaaC-Powered Decentralized Applications (DApps)

CaaC is playing a crucial role in the development and deployment of decentralized applications:

- **Scalability Solutions**: Using CaaC to implement layer-2 scaling solutions for blockchain networks.
- **Decentralized Storage**: Integrating decentralized storage solutions with CaaC platforms.
- **Serverless DApps**: Leveraging serverless computing for more efficient DApp architectures.

A study by DappRadar showed that the number of unique active wallets interacting with DApps reached 2 million in 2021, indicating growing adoption (AWS., 2021) .

17.3 CaaC for Blockchain Interoperability

CaaC is facilitating greater interoperability between different blockchain networks:

- **Cross-Chain Communication**: Implementing protocols for communication between different blockchains.
- **Blockchain Bridges**: Developing and hosting blockchain bridge services on CaaC platforms.
- **Multi-Chain DApps**: Creating applications that can operate across multiple blockchain networks.

The World Economic Forum predicts that by 2027, 10% of global GDP will be stored on blockchain technology .

17.4 Security and Compliance in Blockchain CaaC

As blockchain adoption grows in CaaC environments, security and compliance become increasingly important:

- **Cryptographic Key Management**: Implementing robust key management solutions for blockchain networks.
- **Regulatory Compliance**: Ensuring blockchain implementations comply with relevant regulations (e.g., GDPR, CCPA).
- **Audit and Traceability**: Leveraging blockchain's inherent traceability for audit purposes in CaaC environments.

A survey by Deloitte found that 83% of respondents believe their organizations will lose competitive advantage if they don't adopt blockchain technology .

18 CaaC EDUCATION AND TRAINING

18.1 Evolving Skill Requirements for CaaC Professionals

The shift towards CaaC is creating new skill requirements for IT professionals:

- **Cloud-Native Development**: Skills in developing applications optimized for cloud environments.
- **Multi-Cloud Management**: Expertise in managing and integrating multiple cloud platforms.

- **Serverless Architecture**: Understanding of serverless computing principles and best practices.
- **AI and Machine Learning in Cloud**: Skills in implementing and managing AI/ML workloads in CaaC environments.

According to a report by Global Knowledge, 80% of IT decision-makers say their teams lack the skills they need to meet organizational objectives .

18.2 CaaC Certification Programs

Various certification programs are available to validate CaaC skills:

- **Cloud Provider Certifications**: AWS Certified Solutions Architect, Google Cloud Professional Cloud Architect, Microsoft Azure Solutions Architect.
- **Vendor-Neutral Certifications**: CompTIA Cloud+, Certified Cloud Security Professional (CCSP).
- **Specialization Certifications**: Kubernetes Certified Administrator, Certified Blockchain Professional.

The demand for cloud computing skills is projected to grow by 55% through 2025, according to a report by Burning Glass Technologies (Walmart Tech Blog., 2023) .

18.3 Academic Integration of CaaC Curricula

Educational institutions are increasingly incorporating CaaC into their curricula:

- **University Degree Programs**: Introduction of cloud computing majors and specializations.
- **Industry-Academia Partnerships**: Collaboration between cloud providers and universities to develop curricula.
- **Hands-On Labs and Projects**: Integration of practical CaaC experience into coursework.

A survey by Gallup and Strada Education Network found that 36% of U.S. adults with a bachelor's degree believe they would have to return to school to make themselves competitive for today's jobs .

18.4 Continuous Learning in CaaC

Given the rapid evolution of CaaC technologies, continuous learning is crucial:

- **Online Learning Platforms**: Courses on platforms like Coursera, edX, and Udacity focusing on CaaC technologies.
- **Vendor Training Programs**: Continuous education programs offered by major cloud providers.
- **Tech Conferences and Workshops**: Events focusing on latest trends and best practices in CaaC.
- **Internal Training Programs**: Organizations developing in-house training to upskill their workforce.

LinkedIn's 2021 Workplace Learning Report found that 59% of L&D professionals consider upskilling and reskilling a top priority .

19 LEGAL AND REGULATORY LANDSCAPE OF CaaC

19.1 Data Protection Regulations and CaaC

Data protection regulations have significant implications for CaaC adoption and implementation:

- **GDPR Compliance**: Ensuring CaaC implementations meet EU General Data Protection Regulation requirements.
- **CCPA and Other Regional Regulations**: Addressing various regional data protection laws (e.g., California Consumer Privacy Act).
- **Data Residency Requirements**: Managing data location to comply with local data sovereignty laws.
- **Cross-Border Data Transfers**: Navigating regulations on transferring data between different jurisdictions.

A study by Cisco found that 97% of organizations worldwide are leveraging cloud-based tools to achieve GDPR compliance .

19.2 Industry-Specific Regulations Affecting CaaC

Various industries have specific regulations that impact CaaC adoption:

- **Healthcare**: HIPAA compliance for health data in CaaC environments.
- **Finance**: Regulations like PCI DSS for financial data security in the cloud.
- **Government**: FedRAMP certification for cloud services used by U.S. federal agencies.

- **Education**: FERPA compliance for educational institutions using CaaC.

Gartner predicts that by 2025, 50% of large organizations will use cloud access security brokers to govern cloud services, up from 20% in 2022 .

19.3 Intellectual Property in CaaC Environments

Managing intellectual property in CaaC environments presents unique challenges:

- **Patent Issues**: Navigating patent law in the context of cloud-based innovations.
- **Copyright in the Cloud**: Managing copyright issues for content stored and processed in CaaC environments.
- **Trade Secrets**: Protecting trade secrets when using third-party cloud services.
- **Licensing Complexities**: Managing software licenses in dynamic CaaC environments.

The World Intellectual Property Organization (WIPO) reports a 27% increase in cloud-related patent applications between 2018 and 2022 .

19.4 Liability and Service Level Agreements

Understanding liability and effectively managing Service Level Agreements (SLAs) is crucial in CaaC:

- **Liability Allocation**: Clearly defining liability between CaaC providers and users.
- **SLA Negotiations**: Strategies for negotiating favorable SLAs with CaaC providers.
- **Performance Metrics**: Defining and monitoring key performance indicators in CaaC environments.
- **Dispute Resolution**: Mechanisms for resolving disputes related to CaaC services.

A survey by IDC found that 93% of organizations have experienced cloud outages, highlighting the importance of robust SLAs .

20 CaaC AND 5G INTEGRATION

20.1 5G-Enabled Edge Computing in CaaC

The integration of 5G technology with CaaC is revolutionizing edge computing capabilities:

- **Ultra-Low Latency**: Leveraging 5G to enable near real-time compute at the edge.
- **Mobile Edge Computing (MEC)**: Deploying CaaC resources closer to 5G cellular base stations.
- **Network Slicing**: Utilizing 5G network slicing to allocate dedicated CaaC resources for specific use cases.

According to Ericsson, 5G-enabled compute at the edge could be a $700 billion market by 2030 .

20.2 5G Private Networks and CaaC

The emergence of 5G private networks is creating new opportunities for CaaC deployment:

- **On-Premises 5G**: Implementing private 5G networks integrated with local CaaC resources.
- **Industry 4.0 Applications**: Leveraging 5G and CaaC for smart manufacturing and industrial IoT.
- **Campus Networks**: Deploying 5G-enabled CaaC solutions in educational and corporate campuses.

A study by ABI Research predicts that the global private 5G network market will be worth $14 billion by 2025 .

20.3 5G-Powered IoT and CaaC

The combination of 5G, IoT, and CaaC is enabling new classes of applications:

- **Massive IoT**: Supporting a vast number of connected devices with 5G and CaaC.
- **Real-Time Analytics**: Performing edge analytics on 5G-connected IoT data using CaaC resources.

- **Autonomous Systems**: Enabling advanced autonomous vehicles and drones through 5G and CaaC integration.

Gartner forecasts that the enterprise and automotive IoT market will grow to 5.8 billion endpoints in 2024, many of which will be powered by 5G .

20.4 Challenges and Opportunities in 5G CaaC Integration

While 5G offers significant opportunities for CaaC, it also presents challenges:

- **Security Concerns**: Addressing new security threats in 5G-enabled CaaC environments.
- **Spectrum Allocation**: Navigating the complexities of 5G spectrum allocation for private networks.
- **Infrastructure Investment**: Balancing the cost of 5G infrastructure with CaaC benefits.

Despite these challenges, the 5G CaaC market is expected to grow significantly, with MarketsandMarkets projecting the 5G IoT market alone to reach $40.2 billion by 2026 .

21 EVOLVING BUSINESS MODELS IN CaaC

21.1 Subscription-Based CaaC Models

Subscription models are becoming increasingly sophisticated in the CaaC space:

- **Tiered Subscriptions**: Offering different levels of CaaC resources and services.
- **Usage-Based Pricing**: Implementing more granular, consumption-based pricing models.
- **Reserved Capacity**: Providing discounts for long-term commitments to CaaC resources.

According to Gartner, by 2025, 75% of organizations will adopt a subscription model for CaaC services .

21.2 Marketplace-Driven CaaC Ecosystems

CaaC providers are developing rich marketplace ecosystems:

- **Third-Party Services**: Integrating a wide range of third-party services into CaaC platforms.
- **API Economies**: Facilitating the creation and monetization of APIs within CaaC environments.
- **Industry-Specific Solutions**: Offering pre-packaged, industry-specific CaaC solutions through marketplaces.

IDC predicts that by 2024, 80% of enterprises will overhaul relationships with suppliers, providers, and partners to better execute digital strategies .

21.3 CaaC Brokerage and Aggregation Services

New business models are emerging around CaaC brokerage and aggregation:

- **Multi-Cloud Brokers**: Offering services to optimize workload placement across multiple CaaC providers.
- **Resource Aggregators**: Combining resources from multiple providers to offer unified CaaC services.
- **Cost Optimization Services**: Providing AI-driven services to optimize CaaC spending across providers.

Forrester Research estimates that the cloud cost optimization and governance market will grow to $4.5 billion by 2023 .

21.4 Open Source and Community-Driven CaaC Models

Open source and community-driven approaches are influencing CaaC business models:

- **Open Source CaaC Platforms**: Developing community-driven alternatives to proprietary CaaC offerings.
- **Hybrid Open Source Models**: Combining open source core services with proprietary add-ons.
- **Community Marketplaces**: Creating peer-to-peer marketplaces for CaaC resources and services.

The Cloud Native Computing Foundation reports a 43% year-over-year increase in the number of contributors to cloud-native open source projects (Flexera., 2021) .

22 SOCIETAL IMPACT OF CaaC

22.1 CaaC and the Future of Work

The widespread adoption of CaaC is reshaping the nature of work:

- **Remote Work Enablement**: Facilitating distributed workforces through cloud-based collaboration tools.
- **Job Market Transformation**: Changing skill requirements and creating new job categories in IT.
- **Gig Economy Support**: Enabling freelancers and gig workers through cloud-based platforms.

A study by McKinsey suggests that by 2030, up to 375 million workers globally may need to switch occupational categories due to automation and digitalization, including CaaC adoption .

22.2 CaaC in Education and Research

CaaC is transforming educational and research practices:

- **Distance Learning**: Supporting online education platforms and virtual classrooms.
- **Research Collaboration**: Enabling global research collaborations through shared CaaC resources.
- **Democratization of Computing Resources**: Providing students and researchers access to high-performance computing.

Educause reports that 98% of universities and colleges are using cloud computing for at least one application, with CaaC playing a crucial role in research and education .

22.3 CaaC and Digital Inclusion

CaaC has the potential to bridge digital divides:

- **Low-Cost Computing**: Providing access to powerful computing resources in developing regions.
- **Mobile-First Computing**: Enabling sophisticated applications on mobile devices through cloud resources.
- **Community Cloud Initiatives**: Supporting community-driven cloud projects in underserved areas.

However, challenges remain. The International Telecommunication Union reports that 37% of the world's population (2.9 billion people) have still never used the internet (Gartner., 2022) .

22.4 Environmental and Sustainability Implications

The growth of CaaC has significant environmental implications:

- **Energy Consumption**: Data centers for CaaC consume substantial energy, but are often more efficient than distributed IT infrastructure.
- **E-Waste Reduction**: CaaC can reduce e-waste by centralizing computing resources.
- **Green CaaC Initiatives**: Many CaaC providers are investing in renewable energy and energy-efficient technologies.

A study by Science reports that data centers consumed about 1% of global electricity in 2020, but their energy use has remained nearly flat despite exponential growth in compute instances, largely due to efficiency improvements .

22.5 CaaC and Public Policy

The rise of CaaC is influencing public policy discussions:

- **Data Sovereignty**: Nations are implementing policies to control data location and access.
- **Antitrust Concerns**: Growing scrutiny of dominant CaaC providers' market power.
- **Critical Infrastructure**: Recognition of CaaC as critical national infrastructure in many countries.

The European Union's GAIA-X initiative, aiming to develop common requirements for a European data infrastructure, is an example of policy responses to CaaC's growing importance .

23 FUTURE SCENARIOS AND LONG-TERM OUTLOOK FOR CaaC

23.1 The Ubiquitous Cloud Scenario

In this scenario, CaaC becomes the dominant computing paradigm:

- **Universal Adoption**: Nearly all computing tasks are performed using CaaC resources.
- **Invisible Infrastructure**: CaaC becomes so seamless that users are unaware of thc undcrlying infrastructure.
- **Global Resource Pool**: A unified global market for compute resources emerges.

Gartner predicts that by 2025, over 95% of new digital workloads will be deployed on cloud-native platforms, up from 30% in 2021 .

23.2 The Quantum CaaC Revolution

Quantum computing could redefine CaaC:

- **Quantum-as-a-Service**: Widespread availability of quantum computing resources through CaaC platforms.
- **Hybrid Classical-Quantum Systems**: Integration of quantum and classical computing in CaaC environments.
- **New Application Paradigms**: Emergence of applications that leverage quantum CaaC for previously intractable problems.

According to BCG, quantum computing could create value of $450 billion to $850 billion in the next 15 to 30 years .

Figure 6. Quantum CaaC revolution

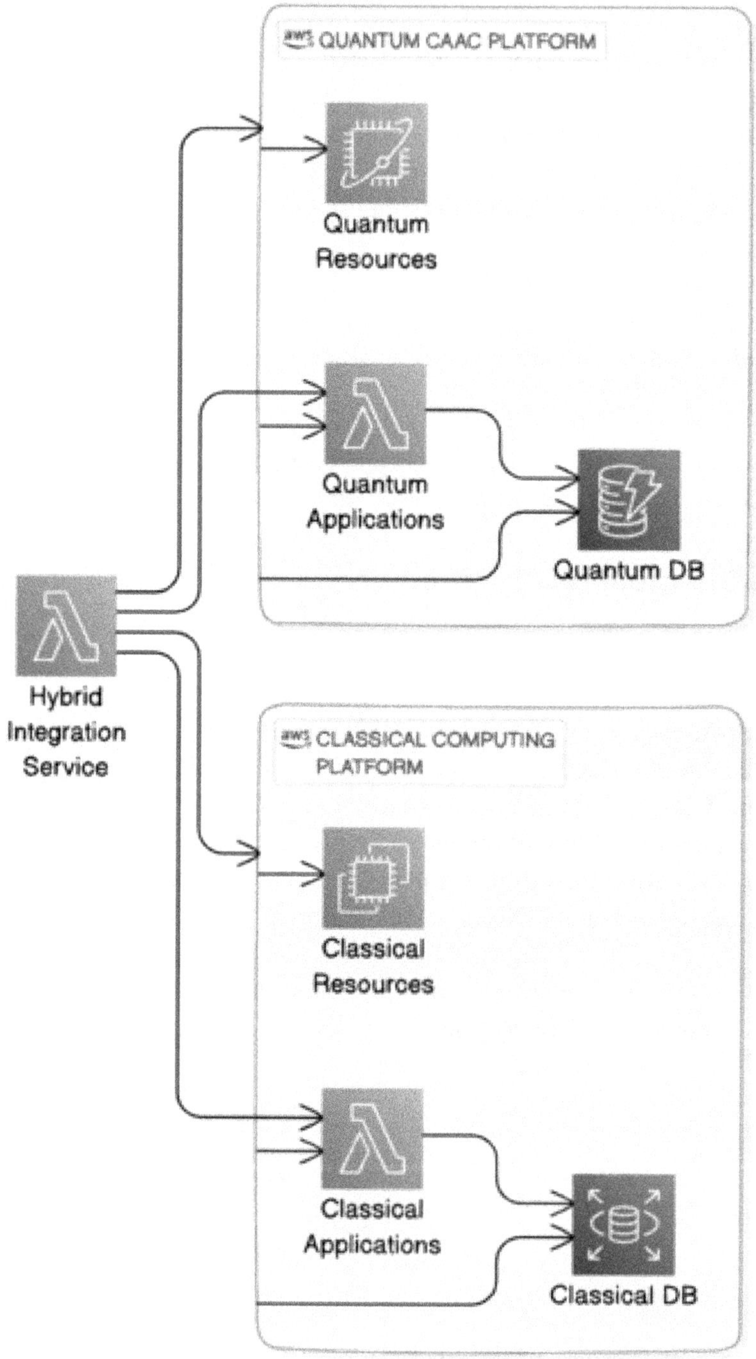

23.3 The Decentralized CaaC Future

Blockchain and peer-to-peer technologies could lead to a more decentralized CaaC landscape:

- **Peer-to-Peer CaaC**: Individuals and organizations sharing compute resources directly.
- **Tokenized Compute Resources**: Use of blockchain tokens to allocate and trade CaaC resources.
- **Decentralized Autonomous CaaC Organizations**: Self-governing systems for managing decentralized CaaC resources.

IDC predicts that by 2025, 75% of CaaC providers will offer some form of distributed cloud services .

23.4 The AI-Driven CaaC Ecosystem

Artificial Intelligence could become the primary driver and user of CaaC resources:

- **AI Resource Management**: AI systems autonomously managing and optimizing CaaC resources.
- **AI-Generated Software**: Most software running on CaaC platforms could be AI-generated.
- **Human-AI Collaboration**: New paradigms of interaction between humans and AI systems in CaaC environments.

PwC estimates that AI could contribute up to $15.7 trillion to the global economy by 2030, with much of this value creation relying on CaaC resources .

23.5 Potential Disruptors and Wild Cards

Several factors could significantly alter the trajectory of CaaC:

- **Technological Breakthroughs**: Unforeseen advances in areas like neuromorphic computing or molecular storage.
- **Geopolitical Shifts**: Major changes in global politics affecting technology development and deployment.
- **Environmental Factors**: Extreme climate events or energy crises impacting data center operations.

- **Societal Changes**: Shifts in societal values or organization that fundamentally alter computing needs.

While the exact future of CaaC is uncertain, it's clear that it will play a crucial role in shaping the technological landscape of the coming decades(Siemens., 2022). Organizations and individuals that stay informed and adaptable will be best positioned to thrive in this evolving ecosystem (Andreessen Horowitz., 2021).

CONCLUSION

Compute as a Commodity (CaaC) is set to reshape the future of cloud computing, offering a model that democratizes access to computational power while reducing costs and enhancing scalability. For businesses, adopting CaaC provides a strategic advantage by enabling flexibility, supporting rapid innovation, and facilitating global reach. However, the shift toward this model is not without its challenges, particularly in terms of security, performance variability, and the complexities of multi-cloud environments.Looking forward, the continued evolution of CaaC will be shaped by emerging technologies such as edge computing, artificial intelligence, and quantum computing, creating new opportunities for businesses to leverage highly specialized and distributed resources. As organizations adopt CaaC, they must develop robust strategies to address its challenges while fully capitalizing on its potential. This chapter offers a comprehensive foundation for understanding the principles and strategic implications of CaaC, equipping professionals and researchers to navigate its complexities and opportunities.

REFERENCES

451 Research. (2020). Voice of the Enterprise: Cloud Hosting & Managed Services, Workloads, and Key Projects 2020. 451 Research.

Andreessen Horowitz. (2021). *The Cost of Cloud: A Trillion Dollar Paradox*. Andreessen Horowitz.

Anita, H. B. (2025). Bridging IoT and AI for Business Intelligence: A Case of Smart Home Solutions. In *Enhancing Communication and Decision-Making With AI* (pp. 37-64). IGI Global.

AWS. (2021). *Moderna Case Study: Leveraging Cloud Computing for mRNA Vaccine Development*. AWS Case Studies.

Barr, J. (2006). Amazon EC2 Beta. AWS News Blog. https://aws.amazon.com/blogs/aws/amazon-ec2-beta/

Basha, A. J., Maheshwari, R. U., Pandey, B. K., & Pandey, D. (2024). Ultra-Sensitive Photonic Crystal Fiber–Based SPR Sensor for Cancer Detection Utilizing Hybrid Nanocomposite Layers. *Plasmonics*, 1–15. DOI: 10.1007/s11468-024-02584-y

Bhatt, D., Swapna, H. R., Madaan, G., Gayathri, D. K., Mahajan, D. A., Mahajan, R. D., & Paramashivan, M. A. (2024). From Theory to Practice: The Evolution of Artificial Intelligence in Business. In Utilization of AI Technology in Supply Chain Management (pp. 1-14). IGI Global.

Burns, B., Grant, B., Oppenheimer, D., Brewer, E., & Wilkes, J. (2016). Borg, Omega, and Kubernetes. *ACM Queue; Tomorrow's Computing Today*, *14*(1), 70–93. DOI: 10.1145/2898442.2898444

Chen, Z., Zhao, J., & Jin, C. (2025). Business intelligence for Industry 4.0: Predictive models for retail and distribution. *International Journal of Retail & Distribution Management*, *53*(3), 1–16. DOI: 10.1108/IJRDM-02-2023-0101

Cockroach Labs. (2022). Cloud Report. Cockroach Labs. https://www.cockroachlabs.com/cloud-report/

Deloitte. (2020). *Cloud Compliance and Regulations: Navigating the Complex Landscape*. Deloitte.

Devasenapathy, D., Madhumathy, P., Umamaheshwari, R., Pandey, B. K., & Pandey, D. (2023). Transmission-efficient grid-based synchronized model for routing in wireless sensor networks using Bayesian compressive sensing. *SN Computer Science*, *5*(1), 128. DOI: 10.1007/s42979-023-02410-y

Dhanasekar, S., Martin Sagayam, K., Pandey, B. K., & Pandey, D. (2023). Refractive index sensing using metamaterial absorbing augmentation in elliptical graphene arrays. *Plasmonics*, •••, 1–11.

Du John, H. V., Jose, T., Jone, A. A. A., Sagayam, K. M., Pandey, B. K., & Pandey, D. (2022). Polarization insensitive circular ring resonator based perfect metamaterial absorber design and simulation on a silicon substrate. *Silicon*, *14*(14), 9009–9020. DOI: 10.1007/s12633-021-01645-9

Flexera. (2021). 2021 State of the Cloud Report. Flexera. https://www.flexera.com/resources/reports/cloud-report-2021

Gartner. (2022). AI Trust, Risk, and Security Management. Gartner. https://www.gartner.com/en/newsroom/press-releases/2022-05-24-gartner-predicts-by-2023

Gartner. (2022). Top Strategic Technology Trends for 2023. Gartner. https://www.gartner.com/en/insights/top-technology-trends

Google Cloud. (2021). DeepMind Case Study. Google Cloud. https://cloud.google.com/customers/deepmind

IDC. (2020). Cloud-Based Disaster Recovery: Transforming Business Resilience. IDC. https://www.idc.com/getdoc.jsp?containerId=IDC_P38867

IDC. (2023). Worldwide Whole Cloud Forecast (2023–2027). IDC. https://www.idc.com/getdoc.jsp?containerId=US47331321

IEEE. (2019). *Performance Variability in Public Cloud Computing: An Empirical Analysis*. IEEE.

Kareem, A. R., & Abdullah, H. S. (2025). Business Intelligence Approach-Based Hybrid Deep Learning Model for QS World University Ranking. *Iraqi Journal of Science*, •••, 375–387. DOI: 10.24996/ijs.2025.66.1.30

Kennedy, G. W., Sunday, S. E., Pandey, D., Kabari, A. D., Pandey, B. K., George, A. S., & Dadheech, P. (2024). Building Information Modeling: Harnessing Innovations for Professional Proficiency. In *Emerging Engineering Technologies and Industrial Applications* (pp. 305-331). IGI Global.

Khan, B., Hasan, A., Pandey, D., Ventayen, R. J. M., Pandey, B. K., & Gowwrii, G. (2021). Fusion of datamining and artificial intelligence in prediction of hazardous road accidents. In *Machine learning and iot for intelligent systems and smart applications* (pp. 201–223). CRC Press. DOI: 10.1201/9781003194415-12

Kumar Pandey, B., Pandey, D., Nassa, V. K., Ahmad, T., Singh, C., George, A. S., & Wakchaure, M. A. (2021). Encryption and steganography-based text extraction in IoT using the EWCTS optimizer. *Imaging Science Journal*, *69*(1-4), 38–56. DOI: 10.1080/13682199.2022.2146885

Kumarganesh, S., & Malathi Murugesan, C. (2024). Hybrid Plasmonic Biosensors with Deep Learning for Colorectal Cancer Detection. *Plasmonics*, •••, 1–15. DOI: 10.1007/s11468-024-02568-y

Lakshmi, K. V. N., Rajan, R., Pandey, D., & Pandey, B. K. (2024). Circular Economy: A Catalyst for Economic Growth-An Empirical Study. *Circular Economy and Sustainability*, •••, 1–22. DOI: 10.1007/s43615-024-00434-x

MarketsandMarkets. (2020). *Serverless Architecture Market - Global Forecast to 2025*. MarketsandMarkets.

Netflix Technology Blog. (2022). Netflix's Journey to Cloud Native. Netflix TechBlog. https://netflixtechblog.com/how-netflix-uses-cloud-native-technology-1f78d1b18d89

Pandey, B. K., Mukundan, A. P., Nassa, V. K., Pandey, D., George, A. S., Hameed, A. S., & Dadheech, P. (2024f). Deployment of Load Balancing in Cloud Computing: Industrial Application and Benefits. In Emerging Engineering Technologies and Industrial Applications (pp. 342-354). IGI Global.

Pandey, B. K., Nassa, V. K., Mukundan, A. P., Mahajan, D. A., Pandey, D., George, A. S., & Dadheech, P. (2024d). An Industry-Focused Traffic System Utilising Internet of Things. In *Emerging Engineering Technologies and Industrial Applications* (pp. 200–213). IGI Global. DOI: 10.4018/979-8-3693-1335-0.ch009

Pandey, B. K., & Pandey, D. (2023). Parametric optimization and prediction of enhanced thermoelectric performance in co-doped CaMnO3 using response surface methodology and neural network. *Journal of Materials Science Materials in Electronics*, *34*(21), 1589. DOI: 10.1007/s10854-023-10954-1

Pandey, B. K., & Pandey, D. (2025). Securing healthcare medical image information using advance morphological component analysis, information hiding systems, and hybrid convolutional neural networks on IoMT. *Computers in Biology and Medicine*, *185*, 109499. DOI: 10.1016/j.compbiomed.2024.109499 PMID: 39642698

Pandey, B. K., Pandey, D., & Agarwal, A. (2022). Encrypted information transmission by enhanced steganography and image transformation. [IJDAI]. *International Journal of Distributed Artificial Intelligence*, *14*(1), 1–14. DOI: 10.4018/IJDAI.297110

Pandey, B. K., Pandey, D., & Sahani, S. K. (2025). Autopilot control unmanned aerial vehicle system for sewage defect detection using deep learning. *Engineering Reports*, *7*(1), e12852. DOI: 10.1002/eng2.12852

Pandey, B. K., Paramashivan, M. A., Hasan, A., Pramanik, S., Dadheech, P., Manaktala, S. S., & George, A. S. (2024a). Social Psychological Obstacles to the Implementation of Artificial Intelligence in Supply Chain Management. In AI and Machine Learning Impacts in Intelligent Supply Chain (pp. 17-24). IGI Global. DOI: 10.4018/979-8-3693-1347-3.ch002

Pandey, B. K., Paramashivan, M. A., Kanike, U. K., Mahajan, D. A., Mahajan, R., George, A. S., & Hameed, A. S. H. (2024b). Impacts of Artificial Intelligence and Machine Learning on Intelligent Supply Chains. In *AI and Machine Learning Impacts in Intelligent Supply Chain* (pp. 57–73). IGI Global. DOI: 10.4018/979-8-3693-1347-3.ch005

Pandey, B. K., Paramashivan, M. A., Mahajan, R., Mahajan, D. A., Behare, N., Gowwrii, G., & Pramanik, S. (2024c). Applications of Artificial Intelligence and Machine Learning in Supply Chain Management: An In-Depth Investigation. In *AI and Machine Learning Impacts in Intelligent Supply Chain* (pp. 74–90). IGI Global. DOI: 10.4018/979-8-3693-1347-3.ch006

Pandey, B. K., Paramashivan, M. A., Nassa, V. K., Mahajan, D. A., Dadheech, P., George, A. H., & George, A. S. (2024h). Blockchain's Potential Effect on the Healthcare Industry. In Emerging Engineering Technologies and Industrial Applications (pp. 214-232). IGI Global. DOI: 10.4018/979-8-3693-1335-0.ch010

Pandey, B. K., Paramashivan, M. A., Pandey, D., George, A. S., Agarwal, A., Dadheech, P., & Mahajan, D. A. (2024g). A Recent Survey on 6G Vehicular Technology: Applications and Challenges. 6G Security Education and Multidisciplinary Implementation, 337-350.

Pandey, B. K., Paramashivan, M. A., Pandey, D., George, A. S., Agarwal, A., Mahajan, D. A., . . . Pramanik, S. (2024e). Future Directions of Digital Twin Architectures for 6G Communication Networks. In Security Issues and Solutions in 6G Communications and Beyond (pp. 197-211). IGI Global.

Pandey, D., Pandey, B. K., Paramashivan, M. A., Mahajan, D. A., Dadheech, P. D., George, A. S., & Hameed, A. S. (2024). Advanced Digital Data Processing Using Cloud Cryptography: Industrial Applications. In Emerging Engineering Technologies and Industrial Applications (pp. 255-268). IGI Global.

Patil, K. R. (2025). Algorithmic Decision-Making in HR: Navigating Fairness, Transparency, and Governance in the Age of AI. [IJCET]. *Journal of Computer Engineering and Technology*, *16*(1), 359–367.

PwC. (2023). Sizing the Prize: What's the Real Value of AI for Your Business? PwC. https://www.pwc.com/gx/en/issues/data-and-analytics/publications/artificial-intelligence-study.html

Rai, P. K., Pandey, D., & Pandey, B. K. (2024). The future of enterprise and innovation is compute as a commodity, or CaaC. *Partners Universal International Research Journal*, *3*(2), 89–94.

Sahani, K., Khadka, S. S., Sahani, S. K., Pandey, B. K., & Pandey, D. (2024b). A possible underground roadway for transportation facilities in Kathmandu Valley: A racking deformation of underground rectangular structures. *Engineering Reports*, *6*(8), e12821. DOI: 10.1002/eng2.12821

Sahani, S. K., Pandey, B. K., & Pandey, D. (2024a). *Single-valued Signals, Multi-valued Signals and Fixed-Point of Contractive Signals*. Mathematics Open. DOI: 10.1142/S2811007224500020

Saravanakumar, R., TamilSelvi, T., Pandey, D., Pandey, B. K., Mahajan, D. A., & Lelisho, M. E. (2024). Big data processing using hybrid Gaussian mixture model with salp swarm algorithm. *Journal of Big Data*, *11*(1), 1–29. DOI: 10.1186/s40537-024-01015-3

Saxena, A., Sharma, N. K., Pandey, D., & Pandey, B. K. (2021). Influence of tourists satisfaction on future behavioral intentions with special reference to desert triangle of Rajasthan. *Augmented Human Research*, *6*(1), 13. DOI: 10.1007/s41133-021-00052-4

Saxena, M., & Mishra, D. K. (2025). Artificial intelligence: The way ahead for employee engagement in corporate India. *Global Knowledge, Memory and Communication*, *74*(1/2), 111–127. DOI: 10.1108/GKMC-09-2022-0215

Shahul, A., Muniandi, B., Paramashivan, M. A., Pandey, D., Pandey, B. K., Dadheech, P., & George, H. (2024). An Analysis of Algorithms and Methods Based on Image Processing for Medical Applications. In *Emerging Engineering Technologies and Industrial Applications* (pp. 173–186). IGI Global. DOI: 10.4018/979-8-3693-1335-0.ch007

Sharma, A., Raj, R., Bisht, M., Gupta, A., Johri, A., & Asif, M. (2024). Optimizing employee satisfaction in India's IT sector: A focus on employer branding. In Journal of Humanities and Social Sciences Communications. https://doi.org/DOI: 10.1057/s41599-024-03689-9

Sharma, M., Kumar, P., & Gundewar, S. (2025). Leveraging AI and Machine Learning for Predictive Analytics in Business Intelligence. In *AI-Powered Business Intelligence for Modern Organizations* (pp. 29–50). IGI Global.

Siemens. (2022). MindSphere: The Industrial IoT as a Service Solution. Siemens Digital Industries Software. https://new.siemens.com/global/en/products/software/mindsphere.html

Stahmann, P., Röver, J., Ciftci, S., Rodda, A., & Janiesch, C. (2025). Opportunities and Challenges for AI-supported Business Intelligence Systems–A Delphi Study.

Swapna, H. R., Bigirimana, E., Geetha, R., Paramashivan, M. A., George, A. S., Dadheech, P., & Vyas, V. (2024c). New Insights Into Strategic Consumer Behavior From the Field of Operations Management. In Utilization of AI Technology in Supply Chain Management (pp. 289-298). IGI Global. DOI: 10.4018/979-8-3693-3593-2.ch019

Swapna, H. R., Geetanjali, S., Lakshmi, K. V. N., Paramashivan, M. A., Nikhil, M. S., Dadheech, P., & Vyas, V. (2024b). Navigating the Transformative Journey: AI's Progression in Business Applications. In Utilization of AI Technology in Supply Chain Management (pp. 15-25). IGI Global.

Swapna, H. R., Hukkeri, S. V., Pandey, D., & Paramashivan, M. A. (2024a). Cosmopolitan living during the COVID-19 Era: Navigating Challenges and Uniting Communities-An Impact Analysis. In Impact of Climate Change on Mental Health and Well-Being (pp. 1-10). IGI Global.

Tareke, S. A., Lelisho, M. E., Hassen, S. S., Seid, A. A., Jemal, S. S., Teshale, B. M., & Pandey, B. K. (2022). The prevalence and predictors of depressive, anxiety, and stress symptoms among Tepi town residents during the COVID-19 pandemic lockdown in Ethiopia. *Journal of Racial and Ethnic Health Disparities*, 1–13. PMID: 35028903

Volkswagen. (2022). Quantum Computing at Volkswagen: Optimizing the Future of Mobility. Volkswagen. https://www.volkswagenag.com/en/news/stories/2022/11/quantum-computing-volkswagen.html

Walmart Tech Blog. (2023). *Digital Transformation at Walmart: Embracing Hybrid Cloud*. Walmart Tech Blog.

Compilation of References

451 Research. (2020). Voice of the Enterprise: Cloud Hosting & Managed Services, Workloads, and Key Projects 2020. 451 Research.

Abate G T, Abay K A, Chamberlin J, Kassim Y. (2023), "Digital Tools and Agricultural Market Transformation in Africa: Why Are They Not at Scale Yet, and What Will It Take to Get There?" Food Policy, Vol. 118, pp. 102646, Elsevier, doi: .DOI: 10.1016/j.foodpol.2022.102646

Abdulkarim, Y. I., Awl, H. N., Muhammadsharif, F. F., Saeed, S. R., Sidiq, K. R., Khasraw, S. S., Dong, J., Pandey, B. K., & Pandey, D. (2024). Metamaterial-based sensors loaded corona-shaped resonator for COVID-19 detection by using microwave techniques. *Plasmonics*, *19*(2), 595–610.

Abdullahi, M., Ahmad, A., Pandey, B. K., & Pandey, D. (2024). Digital Currency Adoption: A Comparative Analysis of Global Trends and the Nigerian eNaira Digital Currency. *SN Computer Science*, *5*(5), 1–11.

Abdullahi, M., Ahmad, A., Pandey, B. K., & Pandey, D. (2024). Digital currency adoption: A comparative analysis of global trends and the nigerian enaira digital currency. *SN Computer Science*, *5*(5), 602.

Abraham, H., McAnulty, H., Mehler, B., & Reimer, B. (2020). Consumer trust in advanced vehicle technologies: Insights from an online survey. *Accident; Analysis and Prevention*, *144*, 105604. DOI: 10.1016/j.aap.2020.105604

Abro, J. H., Li, C., Shafiq, M., Vishnukumar, A., Mewada, S., Malpani, K., & Osei-Owusu, J. (2022). Artificial Intelligence Enabled Effective Fault Prediction Techniques in Cloud Computing Environment for Improving Resource Optimization. *Scientific Programming*, *2022*, 7432949.

Abuabdo, A., & Al-Sharif, Z. A. (2019), "Virtualization vs. Containerization: Towards a Multithreaded Performance Evaluation Approach," 2019 IEEE/ACS 16th International Conference on Computer Systems and Applications (AICCSA), pp. 1-8, IEEE, doi: DOI: 10.1109/AICCSA.2019.9035385

Aguiar-Pérez, J. M., Pérez-Juárez, M. A., Alonso-Felipe, M., Del-Pozo-Velázquez, J., Rozada-Raneros, S., & Barrio-Conde, M. (2023). Understanding machine learning concepts. In *Encyclopedia of Data Science and Machine Learning* (pp. 1007–1022). IGI Global.

Ahathiyan, G. S., Du John, H. V., Moni, D. J., Sagayam, K. M., Pandey, B. K., Pandey, D., & Lelisho, M. E. (2025). Design and simulation of a highly efficient eco-friendly, non-toxic perovskite solar cell. *Discover Nano*, *20*(1), 32. PMID: 39937384

Ahmad, R. (2021). *"A Critical Review of Open Source Software Development: Freedom or Benefit Libertarian View versus Corporate View," IT Professional.* IEEE., DOI: 10.1109/MITP.2021.3051166

Ahmed, M., Kambam, H. R., Liu, Y., & Uddin, M. N. (2020). Impact of human factors in cloud data breach. In Advances in Intelligent Systems and Interactive Applications: Proceedings of the 4th International Conference on Intelligent, Interactive Systems and Applications (IISA2019) 4 (pp. 568-577). Springer International Publishing.

Ahmed, M., & Litchfield, A. T. (2018). Taxonomy for identification of security issues in cloud computing environments. *Journal of Computer Information Systems*, *58*(1), 79–88.

Ahmed, Z., Zeeshan, S., Mendhe, D., & Dong, X. (2020). Human gene and disease associations for clinical-genomics and precision medicine research. *Clinical and Translational Medicine*, *10*, 297–318. DOI: 10.1002/ctm2.28 PMID: 32508008

Albino, V., Berardi, U., & Dangelico, R. M. (2015). Smart cities: Definitions, dimensions, performance, and initiatives. *Journal of Urban Technology*, *22*(1), 3–21.

Aldoseri, A., Al-Khalifa, K. N., & Hamouda, A. M. (2024). AI-Powered Innovation in Digital Transformation: Key Pillars and Industry Impact. *Sustainability*, *16*, 1790.

Almeida F, Simões J, Lopes S. (2022), "Exploring the Benefits of Combining devops and Agile," Future Internet, Vol. 14, No. 10, pp. 281, MDPI, doi: .DOI: 10.3390/fi14100281

Alshareef H N. (2023), "Current Development, Challenges, and Future Trends in Cloud Computing: A Survey," Journal of Advanced Computer Science.

AL-Shboul. (2019). M.A. Towards a better understanding of determinants logistical factors in SMEs for cloud ERP adoption in developing economies. *Business Process Management Journal*, *25*, 887–907.

Amara, N., Zhiqui, H., & Ali, A. (2017, October). Cloud computing security threats and attacks with their mitigation techniques. In *2017 International Conference on Cyber-Enabled Distributed Computing and Knowledge Discovery (CyberC)* (pp. 244-251). IEEE.

Anand, A. S., Sawant, S., Reinhardt, D., & Gros, S. (2025). All AI Models are Wrong, but Some are Optimal. arXiv preprint arXiv:2501.06086.

Andreessen Horowitz. (2021). *The Cost of Cloud: A Trillion Dollar Paradox*. Andreessen Horowitz.

Angelopoulos J, Sahoo S, Visvikis I D. (2020), "Commodity and Transportation Economic Market Interactions Revisited: New Evidence from a Dynamic Factor Model," Transportation Research Part E: Logistics and Transportation Review, Vol. 137, pp. 101944, Elsevier, doi: .DOI: 10.1016/j.tre.2020.101944

Aniello, L., Baldoni, R., & Lombardi, F. (2018). A blockchain-based solution for enabling log-based resolution of disputes in multi-party transactions. In *Proceedings of 5th International Conference in Software Engineering for Defence Applications: SEDA 2016 5* (pp. 53-58). Springer International Publishing.

Anita, H. B. (2025). Bridging IoT and AI for Business Intelligence: A Case of Smart Home Solutions. In *Enhancing Communication and Decision-Making With AI* (pp. 37-64). IGI Global.

Ante, L. (2021). Smart contracts on the blockchain–A bibliometric analysis and review. *Telematics and Informatics*, *57*, 101519.

Aravind, R., & Shah, C. V. (2022). AI-driven innovations in automotive safety: High-level analysis. International Journal of Scientific Research and Management, 10(10), EC-2022-949-961.

Arenas, J. J., & González, D. (2018). Technology transfer models and elements in the university-industry collaboration. *Administrative Sciences*, *8*(2), 19.

Arun, M., Barik, D., Chandran, S. S., Praveenkumar, S., & Tudu, K. (2025). Economic, policy, social, and regulatory aspects of AI-driven smart buildings. *Journal of Building Engineering*, *99*, 111666.

Aryal, R. G., & Altmann, J. Dynamic Application Deployment in Federations of Clouds and Edge Resources Using a Multiobjective Optimization AI Algorithm. In *Proceedings of the 2018 Third International Conference on Fog and Mobile Edge Computing (FMEC)*, Barcelona, Spain, 23–26 April 2018; pp. 147–154.

Asiaei, A., & Rahim, N. Z. A. (2019). A multifaceted framework for adoption of cloud computing in Malaysian SMEs. *J. Sci. Technol. Policy Manag.*, *10*, 708–750.

Ausloos, J. (2020). *The right to erasure in EU data protection law*. Oxford University Press.

AWS. (2021). *Moderna Case Study: Leveraging Cloud Computing for mRNA Vaccine Development*. AWS Case Studies.

Aziz, A., Kosasih, E. E., Griffiths, R.-R., & Brintrup, A. (2021). Data considerations in graph representation learning for supply chain networks. arXiv preprint arXiv:2107.10609.

Banerjee, P., Roy, S., Modibbo, U. M., Pandey, S. K., Chaudhary, P., Sinha, A., & Singh, N. K. (2023). OptiDJS+: A Next-Generation Enhanced Dynamic Johnson Sequencing Algorithm for Efficient Resource Scheduling in Distributed Overloading within Cloud Computing Environment. *Electronics (Basel)*, *12*, 4123.

Barr, J. (2006). Amazon EC2 Beta. AWS News Blog. https://aws.amazon.com/blogs/aws/amazon-ec2-beta/

Basha, A. J., Maheshwari, R. U., Pandey, B. K., & Pandey, D. (2024). Ultra-sensitive photonic crystal fiber–based SPR sensor for cancer detection utilizing hybrid nanocomposite layers. *Plasmonics*, •••, 1–15.

Basha, A. J., Maheshwari, R. U., Pandey, B. K., & Pandey, D. (2024). Ultra-Sensitive Photonic Crystal Fiber–Based SPR Sensor for Cancer Detection Utilizing Hybrid Nanocomposite Layers. *Plasmonics*, •••, 1–15.

Basu, S., Bardhan, A., Gupta, K., Saha, P., Pal, M., Bose, M., . . . Sarkar, P. (2018, January). Cloud computing security challenges & solutions-A survey. In 2018 IEEE 8th Annual Computing and Communication Workshop and Conference (CCWC) (pp. 347-356). IEEE.

Battina, D. S. (2020). devops, A New Approach To Cloud Development & Testing. *Journal of Emerging Technologies and Innovative Research*, *7*(6), 2349–2356.

Belanche, D., Flavián, C., & Pérez-Rueda, A. (2020). Brand recall of safety information in automotive advertising: An experimental study. *Journal of Business Research*, *116*, 68–75. DOI: 10.1016/j.jbusres.2020.05.029

Betchoo, N. K. Digital Transformation and its impact on Human Resource Management: A Case Analysis of two unrelated businesses in the Mauritian public service. In *Proceedings of the IEEE International Conference on Emerging Technologies and Innovative Business Practices for the Transformation of Societies (EmergiTech)*, Balaclava, Mauritius, 3–6 August 2016; pp. 147–152.

Bhardwaj, A. K., Garg, L., Garg, A., & Gajpal, Y. (2021). E-learning during covid-19 outbreak: cloud computing adoption in Indian public universities.

Bhatt, D., Swapna, H. R., Madaan, G., Gayathri, D. K., Mahajan, D. A., Mahajan, R. D., & Paramashivan, M. A. (2024). From Theory to Practice: The Evolution of Artificial Intelligence in Business. In Utilization of AI Technology in Supply Chain Management (pp. 1-14). IGI Global.

Birkinbine, B. (2020). *Incorporating the Digital Commons: Corporate Involvement in Free and opensource Software*. Library.OAPEN.

Biswas, B., Sanyal, M. K., & Mukherjee, T. (2023). AI-based sales forecasting model for digital marketing. [IJEBR]. *International Journal of E-Business Research, 19*(1), 1–14.

Bloem, J., Van Doorn, M., Duivestein, S., Excoffier, D., Maas, R., & Van Ommeren, E. (2014). *The Fourth Industrial Revolution—Things to Tighten the Link between IT and OT*. Sogeti Vint.

Boeri, A., & Testoni, C. (2015). Smart Governance: Urban regeneration and integration policies in Europe. Turin and Malmö case studies. *International Journal of Scientific and Engineering Research, 6*(3), 527–533.

Boinapalli, N. R. (2023). AI-driven predictive analytics for risk management in financial markets. *Silicon Valley Tech Review, 2*(1), 41–53.

Bollerslev, T. (1986). Generalized autoregressive conditional heteroskedasticity. *Journal of Econometrics, 31*(3), 307–327.

Borgman, H. P., Bahli, B., Heier, H., & Schewski, F. Cloudrise: Exploring cloud computing adoption and governance with the TOE framework. In *Proceedings of the 2013 46th Hawaii International Conference on System Sciences*, Wailea, Maui, HI, USA, 7–10 January 2013.

Brozzi, R., Forti, D., Rauch, E., & Matt, D. T. (2020). The Advantages of Industry 4.0 Applications for Sustainability: Results from a Sample of Manufacturing Companies. *Sustainability, 12*, 3647.

Brunetti, F., Matt, D. T., Bonfant, A., De Longhi, A., Pedrini, G., & Orzes, G. (2020). Digital transformation challenges: Strategies emerging from a multi-stakeholder approach. *The TQM Journal*, *32*, 697–724.

Buchwald, M. (2019). Smart contract dispute resolution: The inescapable flaws of blockchain-based arbitration. *U. Pa. L. Rev.*, *168*, 1369.

Bupe, P., Haddad, R., & Rios-Gutierrez, F. (2015, April). Relief and emergency communication network based on an autonomous decentralized UAV clustering network. In *SoutheastCon 2015* (pp. 1–8). IEEE.

Burns, B., Grant, B., Oppenheimer, D., Brewer, E., & Wilkes, J. (2016). Borg, Omega, and Kubernetes. *ACM Queue; Tomorrow's Computing Today*, *14*(1), 70–93. DOI: 10.1145/2898442.2898444

Buterin, V. (2014). A next-generation smart contract and decentralized application platform. white paper, 3(37), 2-1.

Buyya, R., Yeo, C. S., Venugopal, S., Broberg, J., & Brandic, I. (2009). Cloud computing and emerging IT platforms: Vision, hype, and reality for delivering computing as the 5th utility. *Future Generation Computer Systems*, *25*, 599–616.

Capra, M., Peloso, R., Masera, G., Roch, M. R., & Martina, M. (2019). *"Edge Computing: A Survey on the Hardware Requirements in the Internet of Things World," Future Internet*. MDPI.

Casanovasabc, P., González-Conejeroc, J., & de Kokerab, L. (2017). Legal compliance by design (LCbD) and through design (LCtD): preliminary survey.

Chan, F. T., Wang, Z., Singh, Y., Wang, X., Ruan, J., & Tiwari, M. (2019). Activity scheduling and resource allocation with uncertainties and learning in activities. *Industrial Management & Data Systems*, *119*, 1289–1320.

Chauhan, A., Anand, J., & Rai, N. (2022). Biogenic Synthesis: A sustainable approach for nanoparticles synthesis mediated by fungi. *Inorganic and Nano-Metal Chemistry, 2022*. Advance online publication. DOI: 10.1080/24701556.2021.2025078

Chebrolu, S. B. (2011). Assessing the relationships among cloud adoption, strategic alignment and IT effectiveness. *Journal of Information Technology Management*, *22*, 13–29.

Chen, L., Le-Khac, N. A., Schlepphorst, S., & Xu, L. (2019). Cloud forensics: model, challenges, and approaches. Security, Privacy, and Digital Forensics in the Cloud, 201-216.

Chen, J., Zhao, X., & Wang, Y. (2015). A new measurement of intellectual capital and its impact on innovation performance in an open innovation paradigm. *International Journal of Technology Management*, *67*(1), 1–25.

Chen, Y., Zhang, Y., & Zhou, B. (2020). Research on the risk of block chain technology in Internet finance supported by wireless network. *EURASIP Journal on Wireless Communications and Networking*, *2020*, 1–11.

Chen, Z., Zhao, J., & Jin, C. (2025). Business intelligence for Industry 4.0: Predictive models for retail and distribution. *International Journal of Retail & Distribution Management*, *53*(3), 1–16.

Chesbrough, H., & Crowther, A. K. (2006). Beyond high tech: early adopters of open innovation in other industries. R&d Management, 36(3), 229-236.

Choi, J., Jang, D., Jun, S., & Park, S. (2015). A predictive model of technology transfer using patent analysis. *Sustainability*, *7*(12), 16175–16195.

Cloud, H. (2011). The nist definition of cloud computing. *National institute of science and technology, special publication, 800*(2011), 145.

Cockroach Labs. (2022). Cloud Report. Cockroach Labs. https://www.cockroachlabs.com/cloud-report/

Da Silva, V. G., Kirikova, M., & Alksnis, G. (2018). Containers for Virtualization: An Overview. *Applied Computer Systems*, *3*(1), 1–8.

Dahlberg, T., Kivijärvi, H., & Saarinen, T. Longitudinal Study on the Expectations of Cloud Computing Benefits and an Integrative Multilevel Model for Understanding Cloud Computing Performance. In *Proceedings of the 50th Hawaii International Conference on System Sciences*, Waikoloa, HI, USA, 4–7 January 2017.

de Carvalho Ramos, A. (2017). The right to be forgotten and the indirect control of consumer databases. *Consumer Law and Socioeconomic Development: National and International Dimensions*, 371-381.

De Koker, L., Morris, N., & Jaffer, S. (2019). Regulating financial services in an era of technological disruption. *Law in Context (Bundoora, Vic.)*, *36*(2), 90–112.

De Melo, V. V., & Banzhaf, W. (2018). Automatic feature engineering for regression models with machine learning: An evolutionary computation and statistics hybrid. *Information Sciences*, *430*, 287–313.

Deloitte. (2020). *Cloud Compliance and Regulations: Navigating the Complex Landscape*. Deloitte.

Devasenapathy, D., Madhumathy, P., Umamaheshwari, R., Pandey, B. K., & Pandey, D. (2023). Transmission-efficient grid-based synchronized model for routing in wireless sensor networks using Bayesian compressive sensing. *SN Computer Science*, *5*(1), 128.

Dhanasekar, S., Martin Sagayam, K., Pandey, B. K., & Pandey, D. (2023). Refractive index sensing using metamaterial absorbing augmentation in elliptical graphene arrays. *Plasmonics*, **•••**, 1–11.

Di Giulio, C., Sprabery, R., Kamhoua, C., Kwiat, K., Campbell, R. H., & Bashir, M. N. (2017, June). Cloud standards in comparison: Are new security frameworks improving cloud security? In *2017 IEEE 10th International Conference on Cloud Computing (CLOUD)* (pp. 50-57). IEEE.

Diez, L., Choque, J., Sánchez, L., & Muñoz, L. (2020). Fostering IoT Service Replicability in Interoperable Urban Ecosystems. *IEEE Access : Practical Innovations, Open Solutions*, *8*, 228480–228495.

Do, B. V., Li, X., Pan, C., & Gusikhin, O. (2024). Forecasting automotive supply chain shortfalls with heterogeneous time series. arXiv preprint arXiv:2407.16739.

Dong, B., Zheng, Q., Yang, J., Li, H., & Qiao, M. An e-learning ecosystem based on cloud computing infrastructure. In *Proceedings of the 2009 Ninth IEEE International Conference on Advanced Learning Technologies (ICALT)*, Riga, Latvia, 15–17 July 2009; pp. 125–127.

Du John, H. V., Jose, T., Sagayam, K. M., Pandey, B. K., & Pandey, D. (2024). Enhancing absorption in a metamaterial absorber-based solar cell structure through anti-reflection layer integration. Silicon, 1-11.

Du John, H. V., & Jose, T., S, A. G., Sagayam, K. M., Pandey, B. K., & Pandey, D. (2024). Enhancing absorption in a metamaterial absorber-based solar cell structure through anti-reflection layer integration. *Silicon*, *16*(9), 3811–3821.

Du John, H. V., Jose, T., Jone, A. A. A., Sagayam, K. M., Pandey, B. K., & Pandey, D. (2022). Polarization insensitive circular ring resonator based perfect metamaterial absorber design and simulation on a silicon substrate. *Silicon*, *14*(14), 9009–9020.

Duong, T. Q., & Vo, N. S. (2019). *No. 3* (Vol. 24). "Wireless Communications and Networks for 5G and Beyond," Mobile Networks and Applications. Springer., DOI: 10.1007/s11036-019-01233-8

Elarmathi, S., Rishabavarthani, P., Sindhuja, M., Elayaraja, P., & Malathi Murugesan, S. Kumarganesh, K. Martin Sagayam, Binay Kumar Pandey, and Digvijay Pandey. (2024). Novel manufacturing systems for cancer diagnosis using ultra-sensitive photonic crystal fiber biosensor with dual-functionalized aptamer-nanocavity. *Microsystem Technologies*, •••, 1–20.

Emeakaroha, V. C., Brandic, I., Maurer, M., & Breskovic, I. SLA-aware application deployment and resource allocation in clouds. In Proceedings of the 2011 IEEE 35th Annual Computer Software and Applications Conference Workshops, Munich, Germany, 18–22 July 2011; IEEE: Piscateville, NJ, USA; pp. 298–303.

Faisal, K. (2023). Applying the Purpose Limitation Principle in Smart-City Data-Processing Practices: A European Data Protection Law Perspective. *Communication Law and Policy*, *28*(1), 67–97.

Fan, M., Liu, J., Tajeddini, K., & Khaskheli, M. B. (2023). Digital technology application and enterprise competitiveness: The mediating role of ESG performance and green technology innovation. *Environment, Development and Sustainability*, •••, 1–31.

Fan, X., Yao, J., & Cao, N. (2019). Research on Cloud Computing Security Problems and Protection Countermeasures. In *Cyberspace Safety and Security: 11th International Symposium, CSS 2019, Guangzhou, China, December 1–3, 2019* [Springer International Publishing.]. *Proceedings*, *11*(Part I), 542–551.

Fazal, H., Memon, I., Khatri, T. K., Muhammad, G., & Ali, Q. (2020). A survey on cloud computing, security Challenges, architecture, applications & solutions. *University of Sindh Journal of Information and Communication Technology*, *4*(1), 24–30.

Fedushko, S., Ustyianovych, T., & Gregus, M. (2020). Real-Time High-Load Infrastructure Transaction Status Output Prediction Using Operational Intelligence and Big Data Technologies. *Electronics (Basel)*, *9*, 668.

Feng, T., Yu, X., Chai, Y., & Liu, Y. (2019). Smart contract model for complex reality transaction. *International Journal of Crowd Science*, *3*(2), 184–197.

Ferreira, D. B., Giovannini, C., Gromova, E., & da Rocha Schmidt, G. (2022). Arbitration chambers and trust in technology provider: Impacts of trust in technology intermediated dispute resolution proceedings. *Technology in Society*, *68*, 101872.

Flexera. (2021). 2021 State of the Cloud Report. Flexera. https://www.flexera.com/resources/reports/cloud-report-2021

Foster, I., Zhao, Y., Raicu, I., & Lu, S. Cloud Computing and Grid Computing 360-Degree Compared. In *Proceedings of the Grid Computing Environments Workshop*, Austin, TX, USA, 16 November 2008.

French, L. A. (2022). The effects of blockchain on supply chain trust: a thesis presented in partial of the requirements for the Master of Supply Chain Management at Massey University, Palmerston North, New Zealand (Doctoral dissertation, Massey University).

Gai, K., Guo, J., Zhu, L., & Yu, S. (2020). Blockchain meets cloud computing: A survey. *IEEE Communications Surveys and Tutorials*, *22*(3), 2009–2030.

Garcia Alonso, R., & Lippez-De Castro, S. (2016). Technology helps, people make: A smart city governance framework grounded in deliberative democracy. Smarter as the new urban agenda: A comprehensive view of the 21st century city, 333-347.

Gartner. (2022). AI Trust, Risk, and Security Management. Gartner. https://www.gartner.com/en/newsroom/press-releases/2022-05-24-gartner-predicts-by-2023

Gartner. (2022). Top Strategic Technology Trends for 2023. Gartner. https://www.gartner.com/en/insights/top-technology-trends

George A S. (2024), "Democratizing Compute Power: The Rise of Computation as a Commodity and its Impacts," researchgate.

George, W. K., Silas, E. I., Pandey, D., & Pandey, B. K. (2024). Utilization of Industry 4.0 Technologies in Nigerian Technical and Vocational Education: A Conundrum for Educators. In *Examining the Rapid Advance of Digital Technology in Africa* (pp. 270–293). IGI Global.

Ghobaei-Arani, M., Souri, A., Baker, T., & Hussien, A. (2019). ControCity: An autonomous approach for controlling elasticity using buffer Management in Cloud Computing Environment. *IEEE Access : Practical Innovations, Open Solutions*, *7*, 106912–106924.

Gil-Garcia, J. R. (2012). Towards a smart State? Inter-agency collaboration, information integration, and beyond. *Information Polity*, *17*(3-4), 269–280.

Gil-Garcia, J. R., Zhang, J., & Puron-Cid, G. (2016). Conceptualizing smartness in government: An integrative and multi-dimensional view. *Government Information Quarterly*, *33*(3), 524–534.

Gill S S, Xu M, Ottaviani C, Patros P, Bahsoon R. (2022), "AI for Next Generation Computing: Emerging Trends and Future Directions," Internet of Things, Vol. 19, pp. 100594, Elsevier, doi: .DOI: 10.1016/j.iot.2022.100594

Golestan S, Habibi M R, Mousavi S Y M, Guerrero J M. (2023), "Quantum Computation in Power Systems: An Overview of Recent Advances," Energy Reports, Vol. 9, pp. 100745, Elsevier, doi: .DOI: 10.1016/j.egyr.2023.02.011

Golwala, M. S. (2024). *"The Development of the Internet and the Beginnings of the Digital Revolution," Studia Społeczne*. CEEOL.

Google Cloud. (2021). DeepMind Case Study. Google Cloud. https://cloud.google.com/customers/deepmind

Gopal, J. N., Madhu, B., Somu, S., & Anand, A. J. (2025). Explainable AI (XAI) for Energy Demand Forecasting. In Neural Networks and Graph Models for Traffic and Energy Systems (pp. 115-138). IGI Global Scientific Publishing.

Gupta, Y., Shorey, R., Kulkarni, D., & Tew, J. (2018, January). The applicability of blockchain in the Internet of Things. In 2018 10th International conference on communication systems & networks (COMSNETS) (pp. 561-564). IEEE.

Gupta, A. K., Sharma, R., Pandey, D., Nassa, V. K., Pandey, B. K., George, A. S., & Dadheech, P. (2023). Performance analysis of eight-channel WDM optical network with different optical amplifiers for industry 4.0. In *Innovation and competitiveness in industry 4.0 based on intelligent systems* (pp. 197–212). Springer International Publishing.

Gupta, P., Seetharaman, A., & Raj, J. R. (2013). The usage and adoption of cloud computing by small and medium businesses. *International Journal of Information Management*, *33*, 861–874.

Halbiniak, K., Rojek, K., & Iserte, S. (2024), "Unleashing the Potential of Mixed Precision in AI-Accelerated CFD Simulation on Intel CPU/GPU Architectures," Computational Science, Springer.

Halladay, S. D. (2013). Using predictive analytics to improve decisionmaking. *The Journal of Equipment Lease Financing*, *31*(2), B1–B6.

Hashizume, K., Rosado, D. G., Fernández-Medina, E., & Fernandez, E. B. (2013). An analysis of security issues for cloud computing. *Journal of Internet Services and Applications*, *4*, 1–13.

Hashmi, M., Governatori, G., Lam, H. P., & Wynn, M. T. (2018). Are we done with business process compliance: State of the art and challenges ahead. *Knowledge and Information Systems*, *57*(1), 79–133.

Hassan, M. U., Al-Awady, A. A., Ali, A., Iqbal, M. M., Akram, M., & Jamil, H. (2024). Smart Resource Allocation in Mobile Cloud Next-Generation Network (NGN) Orchestration with Context-Aware Data and Machine Learning for the Cost Optimization of Microservice Applications. *Sensors (Basel)*, *24*, 865. PMID: 38339582

Haus, M., Waqas, M., Ding, A. Y., Li, Y., Tarkoma, S., & Ott, J. (2017). Security and privacy in device-to-device (D2D) communication: A review. *IEEE Communications Surveys and Tutorials*, *19*(2), 1054–1079.

Hewa, T., Ylianttila, M., & Liyanage, M. (2021). Survey on blockchain based smart contracts: Applications, opportunities and challenges. *Journal of Network and Computer Applications*, *177*, 102857.

He, X., Liao, L., Zhang, H., Nie, L., Hu, X., & Chua, T.-S. (2017). Neural collaborative filtering. In *Proceedings of the 26th International Conference on World Wide Web (WWW)* (pp. 173–182). https://doi.org/DOI: 10.1145/3038912.3052569

Hidayatno, A., Destyanto, A. R., & Hulu, C. A. (2019). Industry 4.0 Technology Implementation Impact to Industrial Sustainable Energy in Indonesia: A Model Conceptualization. *Energy Procedia*, *156*, 227–233.

Ho, G. T., Tang, Y. M., Tsang, K. Y., Tang, V., & Chau, K. Y. (2021). A blockchain-based system to enhance aircraft parts traceability and trackability for inventory management. *Expert Systems with Applications*, *179*, 115101.

Hollebeek, L. D., & Macky, K. (2019). Digital content marketing's role in fostering consumer engagement, trust, and value. *Journal of Interactive Marketing*, *45*, 27–41. DOI: 10.1016/j.intmar.2018.07.003

Hsu, C.-C., Tsaih, R.-H., & Yen, D. C. (2018). The Evolving Role of IT Departments in Digital Transformation. *Sustainability*, *10*, 3706.

https://451research.com

https://a16z.com/2021/05/27/the-cost-of-cloud-a-trillion-dollar-paradox/

https://aws.amazon.com/solutions/case-studies/moderna/

https://ieeexplore.ieee.org/document/8716624

https://queue.acm.org/detail.cfm?id=2898444

https://tech.walmart.com/news/digital-transformation

https://www.marketsandmarkets.com/Market-Reports/serverless-architecture-market-206683029.html https://www2.deloitte.com/global/en/pages/risk/articles/cloud-compliance-regulations.html

Huang, S.-Y., Chen, C.-Y., Chen, J.-Y., & Chao, H.-C. (2023). A Survey on Resource Management for Cloud Native Mobile Computing: Opportunities and Challenges. *Symmetry*, *15*, 538.

Hu, G., Chohan, S. R., & Liu, J. (2020). Does IoT service orchestration in public services enrich the citizens' perceived value of digital society? *Asian Journal of Technology Innovation*, *29*, 1–27.

Humble, T. S., Perdue, G. N., Fahim, F., & Lamm, H. (2022). Frontiers in Computing for Artificial Intelligence. *Journal of Artificial Intelligence Research*, *74*, 1–12.

IDC. (2020). Cloud-Based Disaster Recovery: Transforming Business Resilience. IDC. https://www.idc.com/getdoc.jsp?containerId=IDC_P38867

IDC. (2023). Worldwide Whole Cloud Forecast (2023–2027). IDC. https://www.idc.com/getdoc.jsp?containerId=US47331321

IEEE. (2019). *Performance Variability in Public Cloud Computing: An Empirical Analysis*. IEEE.

Ikram, A. A., Javed, A. R., Rizwan, M., Abid, R., Crichigno, J., & Srivastava, G. (2021, July). Mobile cloud computing framework for securing data. In 2021 44th International Conference on Telecommunications and Signal Processing (TSP) (pp. 309-315). IEEE.

Inam, R., Hata, A. Y., Prifti, V., & Asadollah, S. A. (2022). A comprehensive study on artificial intelligence algorithms to implement safety using communication technologies. arXiv preprint arXiv:2205.08404.

Jabbar, R., Dhib, E., Said, A. B., Krichen, M., Fetais, N., Zaidan, E., & Barkaoui, K. (2022). Blockchain technology for intelligent transportation systems: A systematic literature review. *IEEE Access : Practical Innovations, Open Solutions*, *10*, 20995–21031.

Jadeja, Y., & Modi, K. Cloud computing-concepts, architecture and challenges. In *Proceedings of the 2012 International Conference Computing, Electronics and Electrical Technologies (ICCEET)*, Nagercoil, India, 21–22 March 2012.

Jahin, M. A., Naife, S. A., Saha, A. K., & Mridha, M. F. (2025). AI in supply chain risk assessment: A systematic literature review and bibliometric analysis. arXiv preprint arXiv:2401.10895.

Jain, T., & Hazra, J. (2019). *"'On-demand' Pricing and Capacity Management in Cloud Computing," Journal of Revenue and Pricing Management*. Springer., DOI: 10.1057/rpm.2018.13

Janic, M., Wijbenga, J. P., & Veugen, T. (2013, June). Transparency enhancing tools (TETs): an overview. In *2013 Third Workshop on Socio-Technical Aspects in Security and Trust* (pp. 18-25). IEEE.

Jannach, D., Adomavicius, G., & Tuzhilin, A. (2020). Recommender systems: Challenges, opportunities, and research frontiers. *AI Magazine*, *41*(3), 40–55. DOI: 10.1609/aimag.v41i3.5280

Janssen, M., & Estevez, E. (2013). Lean government and platform-based governance—Doing more with less. *Government Information Quarterly*, *30*, S1–S8.

JayaLakshmi. G., Pandey, D., Pandey, B. K., Kaur, P., Mahajan, D. A., & Dari, S. S. (2024). Smart big data collection for intelligent supply chain improvement. In AI and Machine Learning Impacts in Intelligent Supply Chain (pp. 180-195). IGI Global.

Jinhua, X., Songlin, H., & Hui, L. (2020). On-Demand Service in Cloud Computing. *ZTE Communications*.

Joloudari, J. H., Mojrian, S., Saadatfar, H., Nodehi, I., Fazl, F., Khanjani Shirkharkolaie, S., Alizadehsani, R., Kabir, H. M. D., Tan, R.-S., & Acharya, U. R. Resource Allocation Optimization Using Artificial Intelligence Methods in Various Computing Paradigms: A Review. *arXiv* **2022**, arXiv:2203.12315.

Jones, P., & Wynn, M. (2021). The Leading Digital Technology Companies and Their Approach to Sustainable Development. *Sustainability*, *13*, 6612.

Kaledio P, Lucas D. (2024), "Agile devops Practices: Implement Agile and devops Methodologies to Streamline Development, Testing, and Deployment Processes," researchgate.

Karagiannis, C., & Vergidis, K. (2021). Digital evidence and cloud forensics: Contemporary legal challenges and the power of disposal. *Information (Basel)*, *12*(5), 181.

Kareem, A. R., & Abdullah, H. S. (2025). Business Intelligence Approach-Based Hybrid Deep Learning Model for QS World University Ranking. *Iraqi Journal of Science*, •••, 375–387.

Kellner, D., & Kellner, D. (2021). *"Globalization, Technopolitics and Revolution," Technology and Democracy: Toward A Critical*. Springer.

Kennedy, G. W., Sunday, S. E., Pandey, D., Kabari, A. D., Pandey, B. K., George, A. S., & Dadheech, P. (2024). Building Information Modeling: Harnessing Innovations for Professional Proficiency. In Emerging Engineering Technologies and Industrial Applications (pp. 305-331). IGI Global.

Kersnovski, T., Gonzalez, F., & Morton, K. (2017, March). *A UAV system for autonomous target detection and gas sensing. In 2017 IEEE aerospace conference*. IEEE.

Khadka, M., Sah, M., Chaudhary, R., Sahani, S. K., Sahani, K., Pandey, B. K., & Pandey, D. (2025). Spectroscopic, quantum chemical, and topological calculations of the phenylephrine molecule using density functional theory. *Scientific Reports*, *15*(1), 208. PMID: 39747169

Khalid, N., Qayyum, A., Bilal, M., Al-Fuqaha, A., & Qadir, J. (2023). Privacy-preserving artificial intelligence in healthcare: Techniques and applications. *Computers in Biology and Medicine*, *158*, 106848. DOI: 10.1016/j.compbiomed.2023.106848 PMID: 37044052

Khan, Y., & Varma, S. (2020). Development and design strategies of evidence collection framework in cloud environment. In Social Networking and Computational Intelligence: Proceedings of SCI-2018 (pp. 27-37). Springer Singapore.

Khan, B., Hasan, A., Pandey, D., Ventayen, R. J. M., Pandey, B. K., & Gowwrii, G. (2021). Fusion of datamining and artificial intelligence in prediction of hazardous road accidents. In *Machine learning and iot for intelligent systems and smart applications* (pp. 201–223). CRC Press.

Khan, G. F., & Park, H. W. (2013). The e-government research domain: A triple helix network analysis of collaboration at the regional, country, and institutional levels. *Government Information Quarterly*, *30*(2), 182–193.

Khan, M. A., Usman, M., & Ahmed, J. (2022). Hybrid deep learning-based recommendation systems for user personalization. *IEEE Transactions on Computational Social Systems*, *9*(2), 533–546. DOI: 10.1109/TCSS.2022.3141503

Khan, S. N., Loukil, F., Ghedira-Guegan, C., Benkhelifa, E., & Bani-Hani, A. (2021). Blockchain smart contracts: Applications, challenges, and future trends. *Peer-to-Peer Networking and Applications*, *14*, 2901–2925. PMID: 33897937

Khattak, A. J., Mahdinia, I., Mohammadi, S., Mohammadnazar, A., & Wali, B. (2021). Big data generated by connected and automated vehicles for safety monitoring, assessment, and improvement. arXiv preprint arXiv:2101.06106.

Kim, T., Hwang, S., Suh, S., & Kim, D. (2015). A Study on Building a Cloud System for Local Government. *J. Korean Assoc. Reg. Inf. Soc.*, *18*, 34–47.

Konapure, C. G., Pandey, D., Shete, H., Thakar, C. M., Pandey, B. K., & George, A. S. (2025). Artificial Intelligence in Automated Concrete Mix Design Using Computerized Grading Curves. Interdisciplinary Approaches to AI, Internet of Everything, and Machine Learning, 567-586.

Kong, L., Tan, J., Huang, J., Chen, G., Wang, S., & Jin, X. (2022). Edge-Computing-Driven Internet of Things: A Survey. *ACM Computing Surveys*.

Kumar Pandey, B., Pandey, D., Nassa, V. K., Ahmad, T., Singh, C., George, A. S., & Wakchaure, M. A. (2021). Encryption and steganography-based text extraction in IoT using the EWCTS optimizer. *Imaging Science Journal*, *69*(1-4), 38–56.

Kumar, B., Pandey, D., Pandey, B. K., & George, A. S. (2024). Higher Education in the Last Four Decades: A Review of Paradigm Shifts in Policy Frameworks. Design and Implementation of Higher Education Learners' Learning Outcomes (HELLO), 333-348.

Kumar, M. S., Prasanna, P. L., Lalitha, M., Joy, M., Jha, S. S., & Pandey, B. K. (2025). Utilizing the Internet of Everything and Artificial Intelligence for Real-Time Workforce Management. In Role of Internet of Everything (IOE), VLSI Architecture, and AI in Real-Time Systems (pp. 153-168). IGI Global Scientific Publishing.

Kumar, D., Samalia, H. V., & Verma, P. (2017). Exploring suitability of cloud computing for small and medium-sized enterprises in India. *Journal of Small Business and Enterprise Development*, *24*, 814–832.

Kumarganesh, S., & Malathi Murugesan, C. Ganesh, N. Santhiyakumari, M. Thangavel, K. Jayaram, K. Martin Sagayam, Binay Kumar Pandey, and Digvijay Pandey. (2024). Hybrid plasmonic biosensors with deep learning for colorectal cancer detection. *Plasmonics*, •••, 1–15.

Kumarganesh, S., & Malathi Murugesan, C. Ganesh, N. Santhiyakumari, M. Thangavel, K. Jayaram, K. Martin Sagayam, Binay Kumar Pandey, and Digvijay Pandey. (2024). Hybrid Plasmonic Biosensors with Deep Learning for Colorectal Cancer Detection. *Plasmonics*, •••, 1–15.

Kumar, R., & Goyal, R. (2019). On cloud security requirements, threats, vulnerabilities and countermeasures: A survey. *Computer Science Review*, *33*, 1–48.

Kumar, S., Simran, S., & Singh, M. (2024). *Quantum Intelligence: Merging AI and Quantum Computing for Unprecedented Power*. IEEE Explore.

Kumbhar, A., Guvenc, I., Singh, S., & Tuncer, A. (2017). Exploiting LTE-Advanced HetNets and FeICIC for UAV-assisted public safety communications. *IEEE Access : Practical Innovations, Open Solutions*, *6*, 783–796.

Kunduru, A. R. (2023). Artificial Intelligence Usage in Cloud Application Performance Improvement. *Cent. Asian J. Math. Theory Comput. Sci.*, *4*, 42–47.

Kutnjak, A., Pihir, I., & Fujan, T. M. Digital Transformation Case Studies across Industries–Literature Review. In Proceedings of the 2019 42nd International Convention on Information and Communication Technology, Electronics and Microelectronics (MIPRO), Opatija, Croatia, 20–24 May 2019.

KVM, S., Pandey, B. K., & Pandey, D. (2024). Design of surface plasmon resonance (SPR) sensors for highly sensitive biomolecular detection in cancer diagnostics. *Plasmonics*, •••, 1–13.

KVM, S., Pandey, B. K., & Pandey, D. (2024). Design of Surface Plasmon Resonance (SPR) Sensors for Highly Sensitive Biomolecular Detection in Cancer Diagnostics. *Plasmonics*, •••, 1–13.

Lakshmi, K. V. N., Rajan, R., Pandey, D., & Pandey, B. K. (2024). Circular economy: A catalyst for economic growth-an empirical study. *Circular Economy and Sustainability*, •••, 1–22.

Lakshmi, K. V. N., Rajan, R., Pandey, D., & Pandey, B. K. (2024). Circular Economy: A Catalyst for Economic Growth-An Empirical Study. *Circular Economy and Sustainability*, •••, 1–22.

Larsson, L., Henriksson, D., & Elmroth, E. (2011, June). Scheduling and monitoring of internally structured services in cloud federations. In *2011 IEEE Symposium on Computers and Communications (ISCC)* (pp. 173-178). IEEE.

Lee, Y.-H., Huang, K.-C., Wu, C.-H., Kuo, Y.-H., & Lai, K.-C. (2017). A Framework for Proactive Resource Provisioning in IaaS Clouds. *Applied Sciences (Basel, Switzerland)*, *7*, 777.

Li H H J K, Tan K H. (2019), "Transformative Innovation: Turning Commoditised Products into Radically High-Valued Products," Journal of Intelligent Manufacturing, Vol. 30, No. 4, pp. 1531-1543, Springer, doi: .DOI: 10.1007/s10845-017-1385-6

Lian, J.-W., Yen, D. C., & Wang, Y.-T. (2014). An exploratory study to understand the critical factors affecting the decision to adopt cloud computing in Taiwan hospital. *International Journal of Information Management*, *34*, 28–36.

Li, F., Zhang, S., & Jin, Y. (2018). Sustainability of university technology transfer: Mediating effect of inventor's technology service. *Sustainability*, *10*(6), 2085.

Li, Z., Yang, Z., & Xie, S. (2019). Computing resource trading for edge-cloud-assisted Internet of Things. *IEEE Transactions on Industrial Informatics*, *15*(6), 3661–3669.

Lone, A. H., & Naaz, R. (2021). Applicability of Blockchain smart contracts in securing Internet and IoT: A systematic literature review. *Computer Science Review*, *39*, 100360.

Low, C., Chen, Y., & Wu, M. (2011). Understanding the determinants of cloud computing adoption. *Industrial Management & Data Systems*, *111*, 1006–1023.

Lu, X., Zhou, J., & Liu, D. (2012). A method of cloud resource load balancing scheduling based on improved adaptive genetic algorithm. *Journal of Information and Computational Science*, *9*, 4801–4809.

Macrinici, D., Cartofeanu, C., & Gao, S. (2018). Smart contract applications within blockchain technology: A systematic mapping study. *Telematics and Informatics*, *35*(8), 2337–2354.

Mahadev Madgule, N. (2023). Vinayaka, Yeshwant M. Sonkhaskar, Dhiren Ramanbhai Patel, R. Karthikeyan, P. Selvakumar,(2023). Mechanical properties and microstructure of activated TIG welded similar joints of Inconel alloys by desirability approaches. *Materials Today: Proceedings*, *77*, 528–533.

Maheshwari, R. U. AR, J., Pandey, B. K., & Pandey, D. (2025). Innovative Quantum PlasmoVision-Based Imaging for Real-Time Deepfake Detection. Plasmonics, 1-17.

Maheshwari, R. U., Paulchamy, B., Pandey, B. K., & Pandey, D. (2024). Enhancing sensing and imaging capabilities through surface plasmon resonance for deepfake image detection. *Plasmonics*, •••, 1–20.

Maheshwari, R. Uma, S. Kumarganesh, Shree KVM, A. Gopalakrishnan, K. Selvi, B. Paulchamy, P. Rishabavarthani, K. Martin Sagayam, Binay Kumar Pandey, and Digvijay Pandey. (2024). Advanced plasmonic resonance-enhanced biosensor for comprehensive real-time detection and analysis of deepfake content. *Plasmonics*, •••, 1–18.

Mandloi, M., Gurjar, D., Pattanayak, P., & Nguyen, H. (2021). *5G and Beyond Wireless Systems*. Springer International Publishing.

Manral, B., Somani, G., Choo, K. K. R., Conti, M., & Gaur, M. S. (2019). A systematic survey on cloud forensics challenges, solutions, and future directions. *ACM Computing Surveys*, *52*(6), 1–38.

Maresova, P., Stemberkova, R., & Fadeyi, O. (2019). Models, processes, and roles of universities in technology transfer management: A systematic review. *Administrative Sciences*, *9*(3), 67.

Marion, T. T. M. P. (2019). *Assessing the Long-Term Attractiveness of Mining a Commodity Based on the Structure of Its Industry*. Massachusetts Institute of Technology.

MarketsandMarkets. (2020). *Serverless Architecture Market - Global Forecast to 2025*. MarketsandMarkets.

Marr, B. (2019). *Artificial intelligence in practice: how 50 successful companies used AI and machine learning to solve problems*. John Wiley & Sons.

Marston, S., Li, Z., Bandyopadhyay, S., Zhang, J., & Ghalsasi, A. (2011). Cloud computing—The business perspective. *Decision Support Systems*, *51*(1), 176–189.

Martini, B., & Choo, K. K. R. (2013). Cloud storage forensics: ownCloud as a case study. *Digital Investigation*, *10*(4), 287–299.

Matt, C., Hess, T., & Benlian, A. (2015). Digital transformation strategies. *Business & Information Systems Engineering*, *57*, 339–343.

Mbonihankuye, S., Nkunzimana, A., & Ndagijimana, A. (2019). Healthcare data security technology: HIPAA compliance. *Wireless Communications and Mobile Computing*, *2019*(1), 1927495.

Mcnunn, G., Heaton, E., & Archontoulis, S. (2019). "Using a Crop Modeling Framework for Precision Cost-Benefit Analysis of Variable Seeding and Nitrogen Application Rates," Frontiers in Sustainable Food Systems, Vol. 3, pp. 1-12. *Frontiers*. Advance online publication. DOI: 10.3389/fsufs.2019.00053

Mell, P. (2011). The NIST Definition of Cloud Computing. Recommendations of the National Institute of Standards and Technology.

Mell, P., & Grance, T. (2011). The NIST definition of cloud computing. *Communications of the ACM*, •••, 53.

Merwaday, A., & Guvenc, I. (2015, March). UAV assisted heterogeneous networks for public safety communications. In *2015 IEEE wireless communications and networking conference workshops (WCNCW)* (pp. 329-334). IEEE.

Mirza, J. B., Hasan, M. M., Paul, R., Hasan, M. R., & Asha, A. I. (2025). AI-Driven Business Intelligence in Retail: Transforming Customer Data into Strategic Decision-Making Tools. AIJMR-Advanced International Journal of Multidisciplinary Research, 3(1).

Mohammad, A., & Vargas, S. (2022). Barriers Affecting Higher Education Institutions' Adoption of Blockchain Technology: A Qualitative Study. *Informatics (MDPI)*, *9*, 64.

Mohammed, D. (2011). Security in cloud computing: An analysis of key drivers and constraints. *Inf. Secur. J. Glob. Perspect.*, *20*, 123–127.

Mohiyuddin, A., Javed, A. R., Chakraborty, C., Rizwan, M., Shabbir, M., & Nebhen, J. (2022). Secure cloud storage for medical IoT data using adaptive neuro-fuzzy inference system. *International Journal of Fuzzy Systems*, *24*(2), 1203–1215.

Morgan, L., & Conboy, K. Factors Affecting the Adoption of Cloud Computing: An Exploratory Study. In *Proceedings of the 21st European Conference on Information Systems (ECIS)*, Utrecht, The Netherlands, 6–8 June 2013.

Morley, J., Machado, C., Burr, C., Cowls, J., Taddeo, M., & Floridi, L. (2019). The debate on the ethics of AI in health care: a reconstruction and critical review. *Available atSSRN* 3486518. DOI: 10.2139/ssrn.3486518

Motlagh, N. H., Bagaa, M., & Taleb, T. (2017). UAV-based IoT platform: A crowd surveillance use case. *IEEE Communications Magazine*, *55*(2), 128–134.

Mozumder, D. P., Mahi, J. N., Whaiduzzaman, M., & Mahi, M. J. N. (2017). Cloud computing security breaches and threats analysis. *International Journal of Scientific and Engineering Research*, *8*(1), 1287–1297.

Muniandi, B., Nassa, V. K., Pandey, D., Pandey, B. K., Dadheech, P., & George, A. S. (2024). Pattern Analysis for Feature Extraction in Complex Images. In Using Machine Learning to Detect Emotions and Predict Human Psychology (pp. 145-167). IGI Global.

Muniandi, B., Nassa, V. K., Pandey, D., Pandey, B. K., Dadheech, P., & George, A. S. (2024). Pattern Analysis for Feature Extraction in Complex Images. In Using Machine Learning to Detect Emotions and Predict Human Psychology (pp. 145-167). IGI Global. DOI: 10.4018/979-8-3693-1910-9.ch007

Muralidhar, L. B., Lakshmi, K. V. N., Swapna, H. R., Rupani, J., Nethravathi, K., Pandey, B. K., & Pandey, D. (2024). Impact of Organizational Culture on The Level of Corporate Social Responsibility Investments: An Exploratory Study. *Circular Economy and Sustainability*, •••, 1–19.

Murdoch, B. (2021). Privacy and artificial intelligence: Challenges for protecting health information in a new era. *BMC Medical Ethics*, *22*, 1–5. PMID: 34525993

Nachiappan, B. (2024). E-resources content recommendation system using AI. In *Improving Library Systems with AI: Applications, Approaches, and Bibliometric Insights* (pp. 155-177). IGI Global.

Narang, A., & Gupta, D. (2019). Comparative Analysis of Various Cloud Security Frameworks. *International Journal of Advanced Studies of Scientific Research*, *4*(1).

Nascimento, A. M., de Melo, V. V., Dias, L. A. V., & da Cunha, A. M. (2018). Increasing the prediction quality of software defective modules with automatic feature engineering. In *Information Technology-New Generations: 15th International Conference on Information Technology* (pp. 527-535). Springer International Publishing.

Necula, S. C., & Păvăloaia, V. D. (2023). AI-driven recommendations: A systematic review of the state of the art in E-commerce. *Applied Sciences (Basel, Switzerland)*, *13*(9), 5531.

Netflix Technology Blog. (2022). Netflix's Journey to Cloud Native. Netflix TechBlog. https://netflixtechblog.com/how-netflix-uses-cloud-native-technology-1f78d1b18d89

Nguyen, D. C., Pathirana, P. N., Ding, M., & Seneviratne, A. (2020). Integration of blockchain and cloud of things: Architecture, applications and challenges. *IEEE Communications Surveys and Tutorials*, *22*(4), 2521–2549.

Nitschinger, H. (2021). How Audi is using AI as a supply chain risk radar. Just Auto.

Njenga, K., Garg, L., Bhardwaj, A. K., Prakash, V., & Bawa, S. (2019). The cloud computing adoption in higher learning institutions in Kenya: Hindering factors and recommendations for the way forward. *Telematics and Informatics*, *38*, 225–246.

Nwosu, M. C., Osuchukwu, N. P., & Obuezie, A. C. (2021). Scrutinizing the Past and Speculating on the Infinite Possibilities of Future Librarianship. *Library & Information Science Research*, *43*(2), 1–12.

Okupa, H. (2020). *Cybersecurity and the Future of Agri-Food Industries*. K-Rex., DOI: 10.4148/2637-7662.1015

Oliveira, T., Thomas, M., & Espadanal, M. (2014). Assessing the determinants of cloud computing adoption: An analysis of the manufacturing and services sectors. *Information & Management*, *51*, 497–510.

Page, M. J., McKenzie, J. E., Bossuyt, P. M., Boutron, I., Hoffmann, T. C., Mulrow, C. D., ... & Moher, D. (2021). The PRISMA 2020 statement: an updated guideline for reporting systematic reviews. *bmj, 372*.

Pagnotta, E. S. (2022). Decentralizing money: Bitcoin prices and blockchain security. *Review of Financial Studies*, *35*(2), 866–907.

Palinkas, L. A., Horwitz, S. M., Green, C. A., Wisdom, J. P., Duan, N., & Hoagwood, K. (2015). Purposeful Sampling for Qualitative Data Collection and Analysis in Mixed Method Implementation Research. *Adm. Policy Ment. Health Ment. Health Serv. Res.*, *42*, 533–544. PMID: 24193818

Panagopoulos, A., Minssen, T., Sideri, K., Yu, H., & Compagnucci, M. C. (2022). Incentivizing the sharing of healthcare data in the AI Era. *Computer Law & Security Review*, *45*, 105670. DOI: 10.1016/j.clsr.2022.105670

Pandey, B. K., Mukundan, A. P., Nassa, V. K., Pandey, D., George, A. S., Hameed, A. S., & Dadheech, P. (2024f). Deployment of Load Balancing in Cloud Computing: Industrial Application and Benefits. In Emerging Engineering Technologies and Industrial Applications (pp. 342-354). IGI Global.

Pandey, B. K., Pandey, D., Agarwal, A., Mahajan, D. A., Dadheech, P. D., George, A. S., & Rai, P. K. (2024e). Beyond Data Breaches: Enhancing Security in 6G Communications. In Security Issues and Solutions in 6G Communications and Beyond (pp. 212-229). IGI Global.

Pandey, B. K., Pandey, D., Nassa, V. K., George, S., Aremu, B., Dadeech, P., & Gupta, A. (2022, July). Effective and secure transmission of health information using advanced morphological component analysis and image hiding. In *Artificial Intelligence on Medical Data:Proceedings of International Symposium, ISCMM 2021* (pp. 223-230). Singapore: Springer Nature Singapore.

Pandey, B. K., Paramashivan, M. A., Hasan, A., Pramanik, S., Dadheech, P., Manaktala, S. S., & George, A. S. (2024a). Social Psychological Obstacles to the Implementation of Artificial Intelligence in Supply Chain Management. In AI and Machine Learning Impacts in Intelligent Supply Chain (pp. 17-24). IGI Global. (Pandey, B. K. et al., 2024a).

Pandey, B. K., Paramashivan, M. A., Hasan, A., Pramanik, S., Dadheech, P., Manaktala, S. S., & George, A. S. (2024a). Social Psychological Obstacles to the Implementation of Artificial Intelligence in Supply Chain Management. In AI and Machine Learning Impacts in Intelligent Supply Chain (pp. 17-24). IGI Global. DOI: 10.4018/979-8-3693-1347-3.ch002

Pandey, B. K., Paramashivan, M. A., Kanike, U. K., Mahajan, D. A., Mahajan, R., George, A. S., & Hameed, A. S. H. (2024b). Impacts of Artificial Intelligence and Machine Learning on Intelligent Supply Chains. In AI and Machine Learning Impacts in Intelligent Supply Chain (pp. 57-73). IGI Global. (Pandey, B. K. et al., 2024b)

Pandey, B. K., Paramashivan, M. A., Nassa, V. K., Mahajan, D. A., Dadheech, P., George, A. H., & George, A. S. (2024f). Blockchain's Potential Effect on the Healthcare Industry. In Emerging Engineering Technologies and Industrial Applications (pp. 214-232). IGI Global.

Pandey, B. K., Paramashivan, M. A., Nassa, V. K., Mahajan, D. A., Dadheech, P., George, A. H., & George, A. S. (2024g). Blockchain's Potential Effect on the Healthcare Industry. In Emerging Engineering Technologies and Industrial Applications (pp. 214-232). IGI Global.

Pandey, B. K., Paramashivan, M. A., Nassa, V. K., Mahajan, D. A., Dadheech, P., George, A. H., & George, A. S. (2024h). Blockchain's Potential Effect on the Healthcare Industry. In Emerging Engineering Technologies and Industrial Applications (pp. 214-232). IGI Global.

Pandey, B. K., Paramashivan, M. A., Nassa, V. K., Mahajan, D. A., Dadheech, P., George, A. H., & George, A. S. (2024h). Blockchain's Potential Effect on the Healthcare Industry. In Emerging Engineering Technologies and Industrial Applications (pp. 214-232). IGI Global. DOI: 10.4018/979-8-3693-1335-0.ch010

Pandey, B. K., Paramashivan, M. A., Pandey, D., George, A. S., Agarwal, A., Dadheech, P., & Mahajan, D. A. (2024e). A recent survey on 6G vehicular technology: applications and challenges. 6G Security Education and Multidisciplinary Implementation, 337-350.

Pandey, B. K., Paramashivan, M. A., Pandey, D., George, A. S., Agarwal, A., Dadheech, P., & Mahajan, D. A. (2024g). A Recent Survey on 6G Vehicular Technology: Applications and Challenges. 6G Security Education and Multidisciplinary Implementation, 337-350.

Pandey, B. K., Paramashivan, M. A., Pandey, D., George, A. S., Agarwal, A., Mahajan, D. A., . . . Pramanik, S. (2024). Future Directions of Digital Twin Architectures for 6G Communication Networks. In Security Issues and Solutions in 6G Communications and Beyond (pp. 197-211). IGI Global.

Pandey, B. K., Paramashivan, M. A., Pandey, D., George, A. S., Agarwal, A., Mahajan, D. A., . . . Pramanik, S. (2024c). Future Directions of Digital Twin Architectures for 6G Communication Networks. In Security Issues and Solutions in 6G Communications and Beyond (pp. 197-211). IGI Global.

Pandey, B. K., Paramashivan, M. A., Pandey, D., George, A. S., Agarwal, A., Mahajan, D. A., . . . Pramanik, S. (2024d). Future Directions of Digital Twin Architectures for 6G Communication Networks. In Security Issues and Solutions in 6G Communications and Beyond (pp. 197-211). IGI Global.

Pandey, B. K., Paramashivan, M. A., Pandey, D., George, A. S., Agarwal, A., Mahajan, D. A., . . . Pramanik, S. (2024e). Future Directions of Digital Twin Architectures for 6G Communication Networks. In Security Issues and Solutions in 6G Communications and Beyond (pp. 197-211). IGI Global.

Pandey, D., Nassa, V. K., Pandey, B. K., Thankachan, B., Dadheech, P., Mahajan, D. A., & George, A. S. (2024). Artificial Intelligence and Machine Learning and Its Application in the Field of Computational Visual Analysis. In Emerging Engineering Technologies and Industrial Applications (pp. 36-57). IGI Global.

Pandey, D., Nassa, V. K., Pandey, B. K., Thankachan, B., Dadheech, P., Mahajan, D. A., & George, A. S. (2024a). Artificial Intelligence and Machine Learning and Its Application in the Field of Computational Visual Analysis. In Emerging Engineering Technologies and Industrial Applications (pp. 36-57). IGI Global.

Pandey, D., Nassa, V. K., Pandey, B. K., Thankachan, B., Dadheech, P., Mahajan, D. A., & George, A. S. (2024c). Artificial Intelligence and Machine Learning and Its Application in the Field of Computational Visual Analysis. In Emerging Engineering Technologies and Industrial Applications (pp. 36-57). IGI Global.

Pandey, D., Pandey, B. K., Nassa, V. K., Mahajan, D. A., George, A. S., & Dadheech, P. (2024). Optimized Throughput-Based Broadcasting for Next Generation Wireless Networks. In Emerging Engineering Technologies and Industrial Applications (pp. 355-368). IGI Global.

Pandey, D., Pandey, B. K., Nassa, V. K., Mahajan, D. A., George, A. S., & Dadheech, P. (2024c). Optimized Throughput-Based Broadcasting for Next Generation Wireless Networks. In Emerging Engineering Technologies and Industrial Applications (pp. 355-368). IGI Global.

Pandey, D., Pandey, B. K., Nassa, V. K., Mahajan, D. A., George, A. S., & Dadheech, P. (2024f). Optimized Throughput-Based Broadcasting for Next Generation Wireless Networks. In Emerging Engineering Technologies

Pandey, D., Pandey, B. K., Nassa, V. K., Mahajan, D. A., George, A. S., & Dadheech, P. (2024f). Optimized Throughput-Based Broadcasting for Next Generation Wireless Networks. In Emerging Engineering Technologies and Industrial Applications (pp. 355-368). IGI Global.

Pandey, D., Pandey, B. K., Paramashivan, M. A., Mahajan, D. A., Dadheech, P. D., George, A. S., & Hameed, A. S. (2024). Advanced Digital Data Processing Using Cloud Cryptography: Industrial Applications. In Emerging Engineering Technologies and Industrial Applications (pp. 255-268). IGI Global.

Pandey, D., Pandey, B. K., Paramashivan, M. A., Mahajan, D. A., Dadheech, P. D., George, A. S., & Hameed, A. S. (2024). Advanced Digital Data Processing Using Cloud Cryptography: Industrial Applications. In Emerging Engineering Technologies and Industrial Applications (pp. 255-268). IGI Global. (Pandey, D. et al., 2024).

Pandey, D., Pandey, B. K., Paramashivan, M. A., Mahajan, D. A., Dadheech, P. D., George, A. S., & Hameed, A. S. (2024b). Advanced Digital Data Processing Using Cloud Cryptography: Industrial Applications. In Emerging Engineering Technologies and Industrial Applications (pp. 255-268). IGI Global.

Pandey, D., Pandey, B. K., Paramashivan, M. A., Mahajan, D. A., Dadheech, P. D., George, A. S., & Hameed, A. S. (2024e). Advanced Digital Data Processing Using Cloud Cryptography: Industrial Applications. In Emerging Engineering Technologies and Industrial Applications (pp. 255-268). IGI Global.

Pandey, B. K., Kanike, U. K., George, A. S., & Pandey, D. (Eds.). (2024d). *AI and machine learning impacts in intelligent supply chain*. IGI Global.

Pandey, B. K., Nassa, V. K., Mukundan, A. P., Mahajan, D. A., Pandey, D., George, A. S., & Dadheech, P. (2024c). An Industry-Focused Traffic System Utilising Internet of Things. In *Emerging Engineering Technologies and Industrial Applications* (pp. 200–213). IGI Global.

Pandey, B. K., & Pandey, D. (2023). Parametric optimization and prediction of enhanced thermoelectric performance in co-doped CaMnO3 using response surface methodology and neural network. *Journal of Materials Science Materials in Electronics*, *34*(21), 1589.

Pandey, B. K., & Pandey, D. (2025). Securing healthcare medical image information using advance morphological component analysis, information hiding systems, and hybrid convolutional neural networks on IoMT. *Computers in Biology and Medicine*, *185*, 109499. PMID: 39642698

Pandey, B. K., Pandey, D., & Agarwal, A. (2022). Encrypted information transmission by enhanced steganography and image transformation. [IJDAI]. *International Journal of Distributed Artificial Intelligence*, *14*(1), 1–14.

Pandey, B. K., Pandey, D., Dadheech, P., Mahajan, D. A., George, A. S., & Hameed, A. S. (2023). Review on Smart Sewage Cleaning UAV Assistance for Sustainable Development. In *Handbook of Research on Safe Disposal Methods of Municipal Solid Wastes for a Sustainable Environment* (pp. 69–79). IGI Global.

Pandey, B. K., Pandey, D., & Lelisho, M. E. (2024a). Face mask identification with enhanced cuckoo optimization and deep learning-based faster regional neural network. *Scientific Reports, 14*(1), 29719. PMID: 39613761

Pandey, B. K., Pandey, D., & Sahani, S. K. (2024b). Autopilot control unmanned aerial vehicle system for sewage defect detection using deep learning. *Engineering Reports*, •••, 12852.

Pandey, B. K., Pandey, D., Wariya, S., & Agarwal, G. (2021). A deep neural network-based approach for extracting textual images from deteriorate images. *EAI Endorsed Transactions on Industrial Networks and Intelligent Systems*, *8*(28), e3.

Pandey, B. K., Paramashivan, M. A., Mahajan, R., Mahajan, D. A., Behare, N., Gowwrii, G., & Pramanik, S. (2024c). Applications of Artificial Intelligence and Machine Learning in Supply Chain Management: An In-Depth Investigation. In *AI and Machine Learning Impacts in Intelligent Supply Chain* (pp. 74–90). IGI Global.

Pandey, D., Nassa, V. K., Jhamb, A., Mahto, D., Pandey, B. K., George, A. H., & Bandyopadhyay, S. K. (2021). An integration of keyless encryption, steganography, and artificial intelligence for the secure transmission of stego images. In *Multidisciplinary approach to modern digital steganography* (pp. 211–234). IGI Global.

Pandey, D., & Pandey, B. K. (2022). An efficient deep neural network with adaptive galactic swarm optimization for complex image text extraction. In *Process mining techniques for pattern recognition* (pp. 121–137). CRC Press.

Pandey, D., & Pandey, B. K. (2022). An efficient deep neural network with adaptive galactic swarm optimization for complex image text extraction. In *Process Mining Techniques for Pattern Recognition* (pp. 121–137). CRC Press.

Pandey, D., Sharma, M., Talwar, R., & Pandey, B. K. (2025). A compact quintuple band miniaturized elliptical planar monopole antenna for 5G/6G wireless systems. *Analog Integrated Circuits and Signal Processing, 122*(3), 1–16.

Pandey, D., Wairya, S., Sharma, M., Gupta, A. K., Kakkar, R., & Pandey, B. K. (2022). An approach for object tracking, categorization, and autopilot guidance for passive homing missiles. *Aerospace Systems, 5*(4), 553–566.

Park, A., & Li, H. (2021). The effect of blockchain technology on supply chain sustainability performances. *Sustainability, 13*(4), 1726.

Patil, K. R. (2025). Algorithmic Decision-Making in HR: Navigating Fairness, Transparency, and Governance in the Age of AI. [IJCET]. *Journal of Computer Engineering and Technology, 16*(1), 359–367.

Patra, S. (2024), "Unleashing the Power: Exploring Deep Learning Architecture for Cutting-Edge AI Solutions," Deep Learning Concepts in Operations Research, Taylor & Francis.

Paukstadt, U., & Becker, J. (2021). From Energy as a Commodity to Energy as a Service—A Morphological Analysis of Smart Energy Services. *Schmalenbach Journal of Business Research, 73*(2), 147–164.

Pereira, G. V., Parycek, P., Falco, E., & Kleinhans, R. (2018). Smart governance in the context of smart cities: A literature review. *Information Polity, 23*(2), 143–162.

Perera, S., Nanayakkara, S., Rodrigo, M. N. N., Senaratne, S., & Weinand, R. (2020). Blockchain technology: Is it hype or real in the construction industry? *Journal of Industrial Information Integration, 17*, 100125.

Pérez, A., Risco, S., & Naranjo, D. M. (2019). *On-Premises Serverless Computing for Event-Driven Data Processing Applications*. IEEE Explore.

Pina, E., Ramos, J., Jorge, H., Váz, P., Silva, J., Wanzeller, C., & Martins, P. (2024). Data privacy and ethical considerations in database management. *Journal of Cybersecurity and Privacy, 4*(3), 494–517.

Poblet, M., Casanovas, P., & Rodríguez-Doncel, V. (2019). *Linked Democracy: Foundations, tools, and applications*. Springer Nature.

Popa, D., Cremene, M., Borda, M., & Boudaoud, K. (2013, January). A security framework for mobile cloud applications. In *2013 11th RoEduNet International Conference* (pp. 1-4). IEEE.

Prakash, S., Balaji, J. N., Joshi, A., & Surapaneni, K. M. (2022). Ethical Conundrums in the application of artificial intelligence (AI) in healthcare—A scoping review of reviews. *Journal of Personalized Medicine, 12*(11), 1914. DOI: 10.3390/jpm12111914 PMID: 36422090

Praveenkumar, T., Anthoniraj, S., Kumarganesh, S., Somaskandan, M., Martin Sagayam, K., Pandey, B. K., & Sahani, S. K. (2025). Enhanced Circuit Board Analysis: Infrared Image Segmentation Utilizing Markov Random Field (MRF) and Level Set Techniques. *Engineering Reports, 7*(3), e70029.

Putthiwat, S.; Kamonchanok, S.; Pongsa, P. Factors Influencing Digital Transformation of Logistics Service Providers: A Case Study in Thailand. *J. Asian Financ. Econ. Bus.***2021**, *8*, 0241–0251.

PwC. (2023). Sizing the Prize: What's the Real Value of AI for Your Business? PwC. https://www.pwc.com/gx/en/issues/data-and-analytics/publications/artificial-intelligence-study.html

Qiu, H., Noura, H., Qiu, M., Ming, Z., & Memmi, G. (2019). A user-centric data protection method for cloud storage based on invertible DWT. *IEEE Transactions on Cloud Computing*, *9*(4), 1293–1304.

Quach, S., Thaichon, P., Martin, K. D., Weaven, S., & Palmatier, R. W. (2022). Digital technologies: Tensions in privacy and data. *Journal of the Academy of Marketing Science*, *50*(6), 1299–1323. PMID: 35281634

Quintero, D., He, B., Faria, B. C., Jara, A., & Parsons, C. (2019). *IBM powerai: Deep Learning Unleashed on IBM Power Systems Servers*. Books.Google.

Rai, P. K., Pandey, D., & Pandey, B. K. (2024). The future of enterprise and innovation is compute as a commodity, or CaaC. *Partners Universal International Research Journal*, *3*(2), 89–94.

Rai, P. K., Pandey, D., & Pandey, B. K. (2024). The future of enterprise and innovation is computed as a commodity, or CaaC. *Partners Universal International Research Journal*, *3*(2), 89–94.

Raja, D. Siva Sundhara, D. Rajesh Kumar, N. Santhiyakumari, S. Kumarganesh, K. Martin Sagayam, B. Thiyaneswaran, Binay Kumar Pandey, and Digvijay Pandey. (2024). A compact dual-feed wide-band slotted antenna for future wireless applications. *Analog Integrated Circuits and Signal Processing*, *118*(2), 291–305.

Rajan, R A P. (2018), "Serverless Architecture—A Revolution in Cloud Computing," *International Conference on Advanced Computing*.

Rajashekar, M., & Sundaram, S. (2022). Dynamic Attribute Tree for the Data Encryption and Third Party Auditing for Cloud Storage. *Indian Journal of Science and Technology*, *15*, 798–805.

Ramachandra, G., Iftikhar, M., & Khan, F. A. (2017). A comprehensive survey on security in cloud computing. *Procedia Computer Science*, *110*, 465–472.

Ramadoss, R. (2022). Blockchain technology: An overview. *IEEE Potentials*, *41*(6), 6–12.

Ramakrishnan, T., Mohan Gift, M. D., Chitradevi, S., Jegan, R., & Subha Hency Jose, P. Nagaraja, Rajneesh Sharma H.N., Selvakumar P., Sintayehu Mekuria Hailegiorgis, (2022). "Study of Numerous Resins Used in Polymer Matrix Composite Materials", Advances in Materials Science and Engineering, vol. 2022, Article ID 1088926, 8 pages, 2022. DOI: 10.1155/2022/1088926

Rasa, T., Palmgren, E., & Laherto, A. (2022). *No. 2* (Vol. 50). "Futurising Science Education: Students' Experiences from a Course on Futures Thinking and Quantum Computing," Instructional Science. Springer., DOI: 10.1007/s11251-021-09573-w

Ravichandran, S., & Naganathan, E. R. (2013). Dynamic scheduling of data using genetic algorithm in cloud computing. *Int. J. Comput. Algorithm*, *2*, 11–15.

Rawat, D. B., Doku, R., & Garuba, M. (2019). *No. 4* (Vol. 12). "Cybersecurity in Big Data Era: From Securing Big Data to Data-Driven Security," IEEE Transactions on Services Computing. IEEE., DOI: 10.1109/TSC.2019.2898724

Ream, J., Chu, Y., & Schatsky, D. (2016). Upgrading blockchains. Smart contract use cases in industry. Deloitte Insights, June 2016.

Reddy, S., Allan, S., Coghlan, S., & Cooper, P. (2020). A governance model for the application of AI in health care. *Journal of the American Medical Informatics Association : JAMIA*, *27*(3), 491–497. DOI: 10.1093/jamia/ocz192 PMID: 31682262

Reed, D., Gannon, D., & Dongarra, J. (2022), "Reinventing High Performance Computing: Challenges and Opportunities," arxiv preprint arxiv:2203.02544.

Ren, J., Zhang, D., He, S., Zhang, Y., & Li, T. (2019). A Survey on End-Edge-Cloud Orchestrated Network Computing Paradigms. *ACM Computing Surveys*.

Revathi, T. K., Sathiyabhama, B., Sankar, S., Pandey, D., Pandey, B. K., & Dadeech, P. (2022). An intelligent model for coronary heart disease diagnosis. In *Networking technologies in smart healthcare* (pp. 309–327). CRC Press.

Revathi, T. K., Sathiyabhama, B., Sankar, S., Pandey, D., Pandey, B. K., & Dadeech, P. (2022). An intelligent model for coronary heart disease diagnosis. In *Networking Technologies in Smart Healthcare* (pp. 309–327). CRC Press.

Reyna, A., Martín, C., Chen, J., Soler, E., & Díaz, M. (2018). On blockchain and its integration with IoT. Challenges and opportunities. *Future Generation Computer Systems*, *88*, 173–190.

Ribeiro, D. M. N. M., Houneaux, F.Junior, Cunha, C. L. L., Kaetsu, O. T., Dionizio-Leite, P. F., & Machado, C.Junior. (2021). Digital sustainability: How information and communication technologies (ICTs) support sustainable development goals (SDGs) assessment in municipalities. *Digit. Policy Regul. Gov.*, *23*, 229–247.

Rimal, B. P., Choi, E., & Lumb, I. A Taxonomy and Survey of Cloud Computing Systems. In Proceedings of the 2009 Fifth International Joint Conference on INC, IMS and IDC, Washington, DC, USA, 25–27 August 2009.

Robertson, J., Fossaceca, J. M., & Bennett, K. W. (2022). A Cloud-Based Computing Framework for Artificial Intelligence Innovation in Support of Multidomain Operations. *IEEE Transactions on Engineering Management*, *69*, 3913–3922.

Robey, R., & Zamora, Y. (2021). *Parallel and High Performance Computing*. Books.Google.

Rose, C. (2015). The evolution of digital currencies: Bitcoin, a cryptocurrency causing a monetary revolution. *The International Business & Economics Research Journal (Online)*, *14*(4), 617.

Rouhani, S., & Deters, R. (2019). Security, performance, and applications of smart contracts: A systematic survey. *IEEE Access : Practical Innovations, Open Solutions*, *7*, 50759–50779.

Ruan, K., Carthy, J., Kechadi, T., & Baggili, I. (2013). Cloud forensics definitions and critical criteria for cloud forensic capability: An overview of survey results. *Digital Investigation*, *10*(1), 34–43.

Rubia, A., & Iwendi, C. (2021). An optimised homomorphic CRT-RSA algorithm for security and efficient communication. Pers Ubiquit Comput. , 07-3.DOI: 10.1007/s00779-021-016

Russell, S. J., & Norvig, P. (2016). *Artificial intelligence: a modern approach*. Pearson.

Sahani, K., Khadka, S. S., Sahani, S. K., Pandey, B. K., & Pandey, D. (2024). A possible underground roadway for transportation facilities in Kathmandu Valley: A racking deformation of underground rectangular structures. *Engineering Reports*, *6*(8), e12821.

Sahani, S. K., Pandey, B. K., & Pandey, D. (2024a). *Single-valued Signals, Multi-valued Signals and Fixed-Point of Contractive Signals*. Mathematics Open.

Saini, S. L., Saini, D. K., Yousif, J. H., & Khandage, S. V. Cloud computing and enterprise resource planning systems. In *Proceedings of the World Congress on Engineering*, London, UK, 6–8 July 2011; Volume 1, pp. 681–684.

Sandoval-Almazan, R., & Gil-Garcia, J. R. (2012). Are government internet portals evolving towards more interaction, participation, and collaboration? Revisiting the rhetoric of e-government among municipalities. *Government Information Quarterly*, *29*, S72–S81.

Saravanakumar, R., TamilSelvi, T., Pandey, D., Pandey, B. K., Mahajan, D. A., & Lelisho, M. E. (2024). Big data processing using hybrid Gaussian mixture model with salp swarm algorithm. *Journal of Big Data*, *11*(1), 167.

Satheesh, N., Gopisankar, N., Kumarganesh, S., Anthoniraj, S., Saravanakumar, S., & Martin Sagayam, K., Binay Kumar Pandey, and Digvijay Pandey. (2025). Advanced AI-driven emergency response systems for enhanced vehicle and human safety. *Iran Journal of Computer Science*, •••, 1–16.

Saxena, A., Agarwal, A., Pandey, B. K., & Pandey, D. (2024). Examination of the Criticality of Customer Segmentation Using Unsupervised Learning Methods. *Circular Economy and Sustainability*, •••, 1–14.

Saxena, A., Agarwal, A., Pandey, B. K., & Pandey, D. (2024). Examination of the criticality of customer segmentation using unsupervised learning methods. *Circular Economy and Sustainability*, *4*(2), 1447–1460.

Saxena, A., Sharma, N. K., Pandey, D., & Pandey, B. K. (2021). Influence of tourists satisfaction on future behavioral intentions with special reference to desert triangle of Rajasthan. *Augmented Human Research*, *6*(1), 13.

Saxena, M., & Mishra, D. K. (2025). Artificial intelligence: The way ahead for employee engagement in corporate India. *Global Knowledge, Memory and Communication*, *74*(1/2), 111–127.

Schallmo, D., & Williams, C. (2017). Digital Transformation of Business Models–Best Practice, Enablers and Roadmap. *International Journal of Innovation Management*, *21*, 740014.

Schlepphorst, S., Choo, K. K. R., & Le-Khac, N. A. (2020). Digital forensic approaches for cloud service models: A survey. Cyber and Digital Forensic Investigations: A Law Enforcement Practitioner's Perspective, 175-199.

Scholl, H. J., & AlAwadhi, S. (2016). Creating Smart Governance: The key to radical ICT overhaul at the City of Munich. *Information Polity*, *21*(1), 21–42.

Seebacher, S., & Schüritz, R. (2017). Blockchain technology as an enabler of service systems: A structured literature review. In Exploring Services Science: 8th International Conference, IESS 2017, Rome, Italy, May 24-26, 2017 [Springer International Publishing.]. *Proceedings*, *8*, 12–23.

Selvakumar, P., Mariappan, P., Shunmugam, S., Paul, R., & Jabez, S. (2024). Removal of chemicals from effluent using photobioreactor technology to improve environmental and health impacts. *Zeitschrift für Physikalische Chemie, 2024.* Advance online publication. DOI: 10.1515/zpch-2023-0450

Selvakumar, P., Palanisamy, S. K., Cinthaikinian, S., Palanisamy, V., Mariappan, R., & Selvakumar, P. K. (2024). Biosensors and its diverse applications in healthcare systems. *Zeitschrift für Physikalische Chemie, 2024.* Advance online publication. DOI: 10.1515/zpch-2023-0406

Shahane V. (2022), "Serverless Computing in Cloud Environments: Architectural Patterns, Performance Optimization Strategies, and Deployment Best Practices," Journal of AI-Assisted Scientific Discovery.

Shahul, A., Muniandi, B., Paramashivan, M. A., Pandey, D., Pandey, B. K., Dadheech, P., & George, H. (2024). An Analysis of Algorithms and Methods Based on Image Processing for Medical Applications. In Emerging Engineering Technologies and Industrial Applications (pp. 173-186). IGI Global. (Shahul, A. et al., 2024).)

Shah, W. F. (2023). Preserving Privacy and Security: A Comparative Study of Health Data Regulations—GDPR vs. HIPAA. *International Journal for Research in Applied Science and Engineering Technology*, *11*, 55551.

Sharma, A., Raj, R., Bisht, M., Gupta, A., Johri, A., & Asif, M. (2024). Optimizing employee satisfaction in India's IT sector: A focus on employer branding. In Journal of Humanities and Social Sciences Communications. https://doi.org/DOI: 10.1057/s41599-024-03689-9

Sharma, L., & Garg, P. K. (Eds.). (2021). *Artificial intelligence: technologies, applications, and challenges.*

Sharma, M., Kumar, P., & Gundewar, S. (2025). Leveraging AI and Machine Learning for Predictive Analytics in Business Intelligence. In *AI-Powered Business Intelligence for Modern Organizations* (pp. 29–50). IGI Global.

Sharma, M., Pandey, D., Palta, P., & Pandey, B. K. (2022). Design and power dissipation consideration of PFAL CMOS V/S conventional CMOS based 2: 1 multiplexer and full adder. *Silicon*, *14*(8), 4401–4410.

Sharma, M., Talwar, R., Nassa, V. K., Binay, K., & Pandey, D. (2025). Design and performance analysis of a multiband vivaldi antenna for wireless broadband communication in 3-5.6 GHz spectrum. In *Artificial Intelligence and Information Technologies* (pp. 86–91). CRC Press.

Sharma, M., Talwar, R., Pandey, D., Nassa, V. K., Pandey, B. K., & Dadheech, P. (2024). A review of dielectric resonator antennas (DRA)-based RFID technology for Industry 4.0. *Robotics and Automation in Industry*, *4*(0), 303–324.

Sharma, P., Jindal, R., & Borah, M. D. (2021). Blockchain-based decentralized architecture for cloud storage system. *Journal of Information Security and Applications*, *62*, 102970.

Sheela, M. S., Kumarganesh, S., Pandey, B. K., & Lelisho, M. E. (2025). Integration of silver nanostructures in wireless sensor networks for enhanced biochemical sensing. *Discover Nano*, *20*(1), 7. PMID: 39804434

Shi, F., & Lin, J. (2022). Virtual Machine Resource Allocation Optimization in Cloud Computing Based on Multiobjective Genetic Algorithm. *Computational Intelligence and Neuroscience*, *2022*, 7873131. PMID: 35310579

Siegel, D. S., & Wright, M. (2007). Intellectual property: The assessment. *Oxford Review of Economic Policy*, *23*(4), 529–540.

Siemens. (2022). MindSphere: The Industrial IoT as a Service Solution. Siemens Digital Industries Software. https://new.siemens.com/global/en/products/software/mindsphere.html

Simou, S., Kalloniatis, C., Gritzalis, S., & Mouratidis, H. (2016). A survey on cloud forensics challenges and solutions. *Security and Communication Networks*, *9*(18), 6285–6314.

Singh, S., Madaan, G., Singh, A., Pandey, D., George, A. S., & Pandey, B. K. (2025). Empowering Connectivity: Exploring the Internet of Things. In Interdisciplinary Approaches to AI, Internet of Everything, and Machine Learning (pp. 89-116). IGI Global Scientific Publishing.

Singh, S., Madaan, G., Swapna, H. R., Singh, A., Pandey, B. K., George, A. S., & Pandey, D. (2025). Unleashing the Power of AI and Data Analysis: Transforming Insights into Action. In Interdisciplinary Approaches to AI, Internet of Everything, and Machine Learning (pp. 1-24). IGI Global Scientific Publishing.

Singh, S., Madaan, G., Swapna, H. R., Singh, A., Pandey, B. K., George, A. S., & Pandey, D. (2025b). Unleashing the Power of AI and Data Analysis: Transforming Insights into Action. In Interdisciplinary Approaches to AI, Internet of Everything, and Machine Learning (pp. 1-24). IGI Global Scientific Publishing.

Singh, S., Madaan, G., Swapna, H. R., Singh, A., Pandey, D., George, A. S., & Pandey, B. K. (2025). Empowering Connectivity: Exploring the Internet of Things. In Interdisciplinary Approaches to AI, Internet of Everything, and Machine Learning (pp. 89-116). IGI Global Scientific Publishing.

Singh, S., Madaan, G., Swapna, H. R., Singh, A., Pandey, D., George, A. S., & Pandey, B. K. (2025a). Empowering Connectivity: Exploring the Internet of Things. In Interdisciplinary Approaches to AI, Internet of Everything, and Machine Learning (pp. 89-116). IGI Global Scientific Publishing.

Sklaroff, J. M. (2017). Smart contracts and the cost of inflexibility. *U. Pa. L. Rev.*, *166*, 263.

Smith, A. N., & Fischer, E. (2019). Toward a theory of digital marketing. *Journal of Interactive Marketing*, *47*, 29–43. DOI: 10.1016/j.intmar.2019.02.002

Smith, J. A., & Doe, R. L. (2023). Navigating the power of artificial intelligence in risk management. *Journal of Risk and Financial Management*, *10*(2), 42.

Sommer, U., Matania, E., & Hassid, N. (2023). The Rise of Companies in the Cyber Era and the Pursuant Shift in National Security. *Political Science and International Relations*, *11*(1), 1–12.

Spiliotis, E., Assimakopoulos, V., & Makridakis, S. (2018, October 6). The M4 competition: Findings, conclusions, and outcomes. *Journal of Forecasting International*, *34*(4), 802–808. DOI: 10.1016/j.ijforecast

Sreenivasulu, A., & Manimozhi, T. Satheesh kumar P., Selvakumar P. And Singh P.,(2022). "The Model of Smart Sensing Device For Sensitive Nanoclusters Modification in Sensing Properties," 2022 2nd International Conference on Advance Computing and Innovative Technologies in Engineering (ICACITE), Greater Noida, India, 2022, pp. 1043-1047, doi: DOI: 10.1109/ICACITE53722.2022.9823846

Stahmann, P., Röver, J., Ciftci, S., Rodda, A., & Janiesch, C. (2025). Opportunities and Challenges for AI-supported Business Intelligence Systems–A Delphi Study.

Stair, R. M., & Reynolds, G. W. (2018). *Fundamentals of information systems*. Cengage Learning.

Strayer, D. L., & Fisher, D. L. (2021). Autonomous vehicles: The implications of human error. *Accident; Analysis and Prevention*, *145*, 105709. DOI: 10.1016/j.aap.2021.105709

Strilets, B. (2022). Current state and prospects for the legal regulation of cryptocurrencies in the European Union. Actual problems of law, (2), 70-76.

Subramanian, N., & Jeyaraj, A. (2018). Recent security challenges in cloud computing. *Computers & Electrical Engineering*, *71*, 28–42.

Sufyan, A., Khan, K. B., Khashan, O. A., Mir, T., & Mir, U. (2023). *No. 11* (Vol. 12). "From 5G to Beyond 5G: A Comprehensive Survey of Wireless Network Evolution, Challenges, and Promising Technologies," Electronics. MDPI., DOI: 10.3390/electronics12112476

Sugumaran, K. M. D., Pandiyarajan V., Y. B S, Selvakumar P. And M. S, (2024). "Analysis of Electromyography Signals for Control of Mechanical Prosthesis using Machine Learning Techniques," 2024 2nd International Conference on Intelligent Data Communication Technologies and Internet of Things (idciot), Bengaluru, India, 2024, pp. 1059-1067, doi: DOI: 10.1109/idciot59759.2024.10467707

Svantesson, D. J. B. (2017). *Solving the internet jurisdiction puzzle*. Oxford University Press.

Swapna, H. R., Bigirimana, E., Geetha, R., Paramashivan, M. A., George, A. S., Dadheech, P., & Vyas, V. (2024c). New Insights Into Strategic Consumer Behavior From the Field of Operations Management. In Utilization of AI Technology in Supply Chain Management (pp. 289-298). IGI Global.

Swapna, H. R., Bigirimana, E., Geetha, R., Paramashivan, M. A., George, A. S., Dadheech, P., & Vyas, V. (2024c). New Insights Into Strategic Consumer Behavior From the Field of Operations Management. In Utilization of AI Technology in Supply Chain Management (pp. 289-298). IGI Global. DOI: 10.4018/979-8-3693-3593-2.ch019

Swapna, H. R., Geetanjali, S., Lakshmi, K. V. N., Paramashivan, M. A., Nikhil, M. S., Dadheech, P., & Vyas, V. (2024b). Navigating the Transformative Journey: AI's Progression in Business Applications. In Utilization of AI Technology in Supply Chain Management (pp. 15-25). IGI Global.

Swapna, H. R., Hukkeri, S. V., Pandey, D., & Paramashivan, M. A. (2024a). Cosmopolitan living during the COVID-19 Era: Navigating Challenges and Uniting Communities-An Impact Analysis. In Impact of Climate Change on Mental Health and Well-Being (pp. 1-10). IGI Global.

Taherdoost, H. (2022). A critical review of blockchain acceptance models—Blockchain technology adoption frameworks and applications. *Computers*, *11*(2), 24.

Tareke, S. A., Lelisho, M. E., Hassen, S. S., Seid, A. A., Jemal, S. S., Teshale, B. M., & Pandey, B. K. (2022). The prevalence and predictors of depressive, anxiety, and stress symptoms among Tepi town residents during the COVID-19 pandemic lockdown in Ethiopia. *Journal of Racial and Ethnic Health Disparities*, •••, 1–13. PMID: 35028903

Team, I. G. P. (2020). *Eu general data protection regulation (gdpr)–an implementation and compliance guide*. IT Governance Ltd.

Teichert, R. (2019). Digital Transformation Maturity: A Systematic Review of Literature. *Acta Universitatis Agriculturae et Silviculturae Mendelianae Brunensis*, *67*, 1673–1687.

Tennant, J. P., Agrawal, R., Baždarić, K., & Brassard, D. (2020). *"A Tale of Two 'Opens': Intersections between Free and Open Source Software and Open Scholarship," OA*. TIB.

Tijan, E., Aksentijević, S., Ivanić, K., & Jardas, M. (2019). Blockchain technology implementation in logistics. *Sustainability*, *11*(4), 1185.

Tripathi, R., Mishra, V. K., Maheshwari, H., Tiwari, R. G., Agarwal, A. K., & Gupta, A. (2023), "Extrapolative Preservation Management of Medical Equipment through IoT," *International Conference on Artificial Intelligence for Innovations in Healthcare Industries (ICAIIHI)*, Raipur, India, 2023, pp. 1-5, doi: DOI: 10.1109/ICAIIHI57871.2023.10489349

Trokhimchuck, P. P. (2018). Equilibrium econometrics and polymetrical analysis. *Вестник Херсонского национального технического университета*, [Bulletin of Kherson National Technical University]. (3-2 (66)), 107-111.

Tu, S., Waqas, M., Rehman, S. U., Mir, T., Abbas, G., Abbas, Z. H., & Ahmad, I. (2021). Reinforcement learning assisted impersonation attack detection in device-to-device communications. *IEEE Transactions on Vehicular Technology*, *70*(2), 1474–1479.

Ucar, A., Karakose, M., & Kirimca, N. (2024). Artificial Intelligence for Predictive Maintenance Applications: Key Components, Trustworthiness, and Future Trends. *Applied Sciences (Basel, Switzerland)*, *14*, 898.

Ukil, A., Jana, D., & De Sarkar, A. (2013). A security framework in cloud computing infrastructure. *International Journal of Network Security & its Applications*, *5*(5), 11.

Ustun, E. S., & Yuce, M. (2022, June). Smart Legal Contracts & Smarter Dispute Resolution. In *2022 IEEE 24th Conference on Business Informatics (CBI)* (Vol. 2, pp. 111-117). IEEE.

Venters, W., & Whitley, E. A. (2012). A critical review of cloud computing: Researching desires and realities. *Journal of Information Technology*, *27*, 179–197.

Vijayakumar, G. (2024). Muniyandi Rajkumar, Rajiv Chandar N, Selvakumar P and Ramesh Duraisamy, (2024). Environmentally friendly TDS removal from waste water by electrochemical ion exchange batch-type recirculation (EIR) technique. *Environmental Science. Water Research & Technology*, *10*, 826–835. DOI: 10.1039/D3EW00793F

Vinodhini, V., Kumar, M. S., Sankar, S., Pandey, D., Pandey, B. K., & Nassa, V. K. (2022). IoT-based early forest fire detection using MLP and AROC method. *International Journal of Global Warming*, *27*(1), 55–70.

Volkswagen. (2022). Quantum Computing at Volkswagen: Optimizing the Future of Mobility. Volkswagen. https://www.volkswagenag.com/en/news/stories/2022/11/quantum-computing-volkswagen.html

Walia, G. K., Kumar, M., & Gill, S. S. (2024). AI-Empowered Fog/Edge Resource Management for IoT Applications: A Comprehensive Review, Research Challenges, and Future Perspectives. *IEEE Communications Surveys and Tutorials*, *26*, 619–669.

Walmart Tech Blog. (2023). *Digital Transformation at Walmart: Embracing Hybrid Cloud*. Walmart Tech Blog.

Wang, C., Zhang, J., Lassi, N., & Zhang, X. (2022, September). Privacy protection in using artificial intelligence for healthcare: Chinese regulation in comparative perspective. []. MDPI.]. *Health Care*, *10*(10), 1878. PMID: 36292325

Wang, S., Li, Y., & Khaskheli, M. B. (2024). Innovation Helps with Sustainable Business, Law, and Digital Technologies: Economic Development and Dispute Resolution. *Sustainability*, *16*(10), 3910.

Watada, J., Roy, A., Kadikar, R., Pham, H., & Xu, B. (2019). *"Emerging Trends, Techniques and Open Issues of Containerization: A Review," IEEE Access* (Vol. 7). IEEE., DOI: 10.1109/ACCESS.2019.2936958

Weinhardt, C., Anandasivam, A., Blau, B., Borissov, N., Meinl, T., Michalk, W., & Stößer, J. (2009). Cloud computing–a classification, business models, and research directions. *Business & Information Systems Engineering*, *1*, 391–399.

Wolfert, S., Ge, L., Verdouwa, C., & Bogaardt, M.-J. (2017). Big Data in Smart Farming—A review. *Agricultural Systems*, *153*, 69–80.

Xia, T., Washizaki, H., Fukazawa, Y., Kaiya, H., Ogata, S., Fernandez, E. B., & Hazeyama, A. (2021). CSPM: Metamodel for handling security and privacy knowledge in cloud service development. [IJSSSP]. *International Journal of Systems and Software Security and Protection*, *12*(2), 68–85.

Xie, S., Zheng, Z., Chen, W., Wu, J., Dai, H. N., & Imran, M. (2020). Blockchain for cloud exchange: A survey. *Computers & Electrical Engineering*, *81*, 106526.

Yang, H., & Tate, M. (2012). A descriptive literature review and classification of cloud computing research. *Communications of the Association for Information Systems*, *31*, 2–26.

Yeung, J. K., Wong, S. C., & Chan, G. H. (2021). Cloud infrastructure for public health blockchain. In *The Routledge Handbook of Public Health and the Community* (pp. 254–263). Routledge.

Zafar, A. (2023). Artificial Intelligence (AI) Influence in Law: Balancing Technological Advancements with Ethical Considerations. *Available atSSRN* 4656578.

Zeleznikow, J. (2021). Using artificial intelligence to provide intelligent dispute resolution support. *Group Decision and Negotiation*, *30*(4), 789–812. PMID: 33867681

Zhang, Z., Wang, T., Li, A., & Zhang, W. Adaptive Auto-Scaling of Delay-Sensitive Serverless Services with Reinforcement Learning. In Proceedings of the 2022 IEEE 46th Annual Computers, Software, and Applications Conference (COMPSAC), Los Alamitos, CA, USA, 27 June–1 July 2022; pp. 866–871.

Zhang, P., White, J., Schmidt, D. C., Lenz, G., & Rosenbloom, S. T. (2018). FHIRChain: Applying blockchain to securely and scalably share clinical data. *Computational and Structural Biotechnology Journal*, *16*, 267–278. PMID: 30108685

Zheng, Z., Xie, S., Dai, H. N., Chen, W., Chen, X., Weng, J., & Imran, M. (2020). An overview on smart contracts: Challenges, advances and platforms. *Future Generation Computer Systems*, *105*, 475–491.

Zizic, M. C., Mladineo, M., Gjeldum, N., & Celent, L. (2022). From Industry 4. 0 towards Industry 5. 0: A Review and Analysis of Paradigm Shift for the People, Organization and Technology. *Energies*, *15*, 5221.

About the Contributors

Pankaj Kumar Rai is Senior Enterprise Architect at DXC Technology, focused on new product offerings and modernization of legacy banking products to cloud And AI, it which consist re-platforming of legacy applications\services\infrastructure to cloud(AWS\GCP\ Azure), application modernization and integration with AI, converting products to SaaS model and enable products to integrate with partners API and Gen AI, having 19+ years of solid technical experience in architecture\ design\implementation of cloud (AWS\GCP\Azure) and AI based applications, his expertise includes strategy and roadmap development, building high performing engineering team, IT integration in merger\acquisition, new business identification, digital transformation, process improvement, IT vendor management, people management and cost optimization, he is a consistent top performer and proven leader, regularly viewed as a strong coach and influential mentor to peers and colleagues, enabling individual growth and driving greater team success.

Tanveer Ahmed has spent the past 19 years working at TCS London as a Senior Project Manager. During this time, he has participated in a wide variety of projects across the globe, including those located in the United Kingdom, the United States of America, and Europe. 2023 will be the year that he defends his doctoral thesis in Cloud Communication and Security.

***

Jagadish A is an experienced academician with over 16 years in teaching and academic leadership, currently serving as HOD & Assistant Professor for the BBA & BBA Aviation Management department at SSMRV College, Bengaluru. He holds an MBA from Bangalore University and is pursuing a Ph.D. at JAIN (Deemed-To-Be-University). Previously, he worked at Don Bosco Institute of Bio-sciences & Management Studies and has three years of corporate experience with

Bharti Infotel Ltd and ICICI Bank Ltd. His contributions include guiding students to 8 university ranks, serving in key roles such as IQAC Member, Staff Council Secretary, and Cultural Committee Convenor, and actively engaging in research with published papers, book authorship, and patents in consumer behavior analytics and e-commerce. He has been a BOE member for various institutions and has presented at national and international conferences. Passionate about academic excellence and student development, he integrates innovative teaching methodologies and actively participates in faculty development programs and accreditation processes.

Nilesh Anute is an esteemed Associate Professor at the Balaji Institute of Management & Human Resource Development, part of Sri Balaji University in Pune. With a wealth of knowledge and expertise in his field, he is dedicated to educating and mentoring students in the domain of management and human resource development. Dr. Anute has contributed significantly to academic research and teaching, blending his practical insights with theoretical concepts. His commitment to excellence and his passion for shaping future leaders make him a valuable asset to the institution.

Ashok D. Todmal is a passionate and dedicated professional with over 13 years of experience in academics. His areas of research include marketing, agriculture, and entrepreneurship.

Mridula Kidiyur, PMP® is a seasoned Product Manager with over 12 years of experience in the retail and finance sectors. Currently serving as a Principal Product Manager at Walmart eCommerce in New York, NY, she has a proven track record of leading large-scale end-to-end program deliveries, managing cross-functional teams, and driving impactful solutions that enhance customer experience and operational efficiency. Throughout her career, Mridula has demonstrated exceptional skills in system implementations, process validation, and data management. Her technical expertise spans across various analytical tools which she leverages to turn customer insights into actionable initiatives. Her ability to navigate complex business processes and collaborate effectively with stakeholders, from C-suite executives to IT engineers, has led to significant cost savings and improvements in product effectiveness.She holds a Master's degree in Information Systems from the Kelley School of Business

Venkata Gummadi is a Senior Software Engineer at Expedia Group, specializing in Data and AI. With a Master's in Computer Information Systems, he focuses on creating innovative products through the integration of emerging technologies. Venkata excels in selecting and implementing software solutions that streamline operations and enhance customer experiences. He is dedicated to developing flexible, future-ready strategic plans that address potential disruptions and opportunities, while staying informed about the latest technological advancements that drive efficiency and innovation.

Sarvagya Jha is a researcher in quantitative finance and legal analytics, currently a Graduate Researcher at Rutgers University. He holds a Master of Quantitative Finance from Rutgers Business School, a Master of Law specializing in International Trade and Investment Law from OP Jindal Global University, and a Post Graduate Diploma in Management from MDI Gurgaon. His research interests lie at the intersection of financial modeling, risk management, and AI-driven legal analysis. Sarvagya has authored multiple publications on financial derivatives, legal risk, and the integration of NLP in contract review. He has also worked as a Research and Teaching Assistant at Rutgers Business School and has professional experience in data science, international trade policy, and social impact initiatives.

Shravan Kumar Joginipalli is a seasoned Senior Director, Principal Architect, and technology management consultant with a robust background in aligning IT strategy with business objectives. His distinguished career spans significant contributions to the property and casualty (P&C) insurance sector, where he has led transformative initiatives and driven business growth through innovative technology solutions. His leadership extends beyond operational efficiency to encompass strategic direction and impactful support for industry professionals and clients.

P. Latha currently working as Assistant Professor in the department of Computer Science and Engineering in V.S.B. Engineering College, Karur.. She received her M.E degree in Computer Science and Engineering from Annai Mathammal Sheela Engineering College, Anna University. She has 15 years of teaching involvement with different reputed organizations. She has published many research articles in International and National Journals and presented many articles in international and national level conferences. She has filed the 3 Patents and published text book Chapter in AI-Powered Advances in Pharmacology BOOK CHAPTER: Blockchain for Pharmaceutical Data Management and Quantum Computing Innovations. She has actively participated in workshops, and seminars in both national and international levels. Her area of interest is knowledge Based System, Natural Language Processing, Machine Learning, Cloud Computing.

T.C. Manjunath is a distinguished academic and researcher currently serving as a Professor in the Department of Computer Science and Engineering (CSE) at Rajarajeswari College of Engineering, Bangalore. With a specialized focus on IoT Cybersecurity and Blockchain Technology, he plays a key role in advancing research and development in these rapidly evolving fields. In addition to his teaching responsibilities, Dr. Manjunath holds the position of Dean of Research (R&D) at the college, where he drives innovation and fosters academic excellence. His work is instrumental in bridging the gap between technology and practical applications, contributing significantly to both the academic community and industry. He is based at the college's campus in Mysore Road, Bangalore, Karnataka, India.

Satyanarayana Nimmala completed his Ph.D. (CSE) from Osmania University, Hyderabad, and Telangana in 2020. He did his B. Tech. from Kakatiaya University, Kothagudem, Telangana, India in 2007. He did his M.Tech. From JNTUH, Hyderabad in 2010, India. Presently he is working as Professor in the Department of CSE (Data Science), CVR College of Engineering, Hyderabad, Telangana, India. His research interests are Data Mining, Bioinformatics, and Machine Learning and Artificial Intelligence. He has authored 30+ research papers published in reputed international journals and has around 100+ citations; he also has credit of 5 patents and 3 book chapters. He has more than 18 years of teaching experience, and he has taught a wide variety of subjects like Advanced Data Structures through C++, Core Java, Python, problem-solving through C, DS through C, DBMS, OS, DWDM, etc. he has guided several B.Tech. and M.Tech. Projects during his teaching career.

SelvakumarP. is currently an Associate Professor in the Department of Science and Humanities at Nehru Institute of Technology, Coimbatore, Tamil Nadu, India. Since 2023, he has served as the Department IQAC Coordinator at the institute. Prior to joining Nehru Institute of Technology, he held positions as an Assistant Professor in the Department of Science and Humanities various engineering colleges in Coimbatore, Tamil Nadu, India, spanning from 2011 to 2023. Dr.P. Selvakumar's academic and research interests lie primarily in the field of phytochemistry. He has made significant contributions to his field, with an impressive record that includes 30 journal publications, 12 patents, and 20 conference papers. Additionally, he has organized 5 seminars and conferences, further demonstrating his commitment to academic and scientific exchange. Throughout his career, Dr. P.Selvakumar has been recognized for his dedication and excellence in teaching, having been honored with several awards, including the Best Teacher Awards. He holds a prominent position in the academic community, contributing actively to research.

G. V. Radhakrishnan is a distinguished academic, researcher, and consultant specializing in maritime economics, infrastructure policy, higher education governance, and institutional strategy. A Fellow of IIM Ahmedabad, he holds a doctorate in Public Systems and an MBA from IIM Kozhikode. After an extensive career in the Indian Navy, he transitioned to academia through government consulting on logistics, infrastructure, and economic strategy. His tenure at a Big-4 consulting firm refined his expertise in Public-Private Partnerships, port economics, and public systems, influencing policy reforms and industry best practices. In academia, he has served as Dean and led initiatives in faculty development, research, and interdisciplinary consulting. An author, editor, and reviewer, he has contributed to academic books and international journals, offering a global perspective on AI-driven education, maritime policy, and institutional governance

Chaithanya Ravulu is a seasoned Data Engineer with over a decade of experience in building, deploying, and managing cloud-based data engineering and analytics solutions. With a strong foundation in cloud technologies, particularly the AWS Cloud Analytics Stack, Chaithanya has worked across various domains such as fintech, digital marketing, and travel and hospitality. Currently, Chaithanya serves as a Senior Data Engineer at Rocket Companies (Quicken Loans), where they architect and develop scalable, cloud-based data applications used by over 100 applications within the Rocket family of companies. Chaithanya is proficient in AWS technologies, including AWS Glue, Redshift, and Lambda, and has demonstrated expertise in creating high-throughput, serverless data lake solutions. They also specialize in real-time data processing using Apache Flink for customer analytics, fraud detection, and operational efficiency. Before Rocket Companies, Chaithanya held a leadership role as a Lead Data Engineer at Deloitte, where they contributed to end-to-end data solutions involving Snowflake and MS SQL Server migrations, performance improvement tools, and advanced data analytics. Chaithanya's earlier career includes working at Citi Group in Hyderabad, India, where they supported ETL operations and built robust data warehousing solutions using Teradata and IBM InfoSphere DataStage. Chaithanya holds a Master of Science in Information Systems from the University of Cincinnati and a Bachelor of Engineering in Computer Science from Karunya University. They are also an AWS Certified Data Analytics Specialist and an Oracle Certified Associate, showcasing their commitment to continuous learning and mastery in data engineering. Beyond their technical skills, Chaithanya has demonstrated a strong ability to orchestrate complex data pipelines, manage CI/CD pipelines, and automate environments using tools like Terraform, CircleCI, and GitHub. With a passion for cloud-native architectures and real-time analytics, Chaithanya continues to contribute impactful solutions to data-driven organizations.

Sruthi S is a distinguished academician and researcher specializing in Commerce and Economics, currently pursuing Ph.D. in Commerce from Bharathiar University. With a strong foundation in finance and economics, she has demonstrated expertise in teaching, mentoring, and research across multiple disciplines. She has held academic positions as an Assistant Professor and Guest Lecturer, contributing significantly to commerce education. Her research interests span green business practices, taxation, social entrepreneurship, and financial technology, reflected in her extensive publications in ABDC indexed Journals, UGC Care and Scopus-Indexed Journals. Sruthi has contributed to over 16 peer-reviewed journal articles and has authored multiple book chapters and research monographs in national and international publications. Her editorial experience includes curating multidisciplinary research volumes published by many reputed Publications . Recognized for her scholarly contributions, she has received the Global Educational Award 2020 for Best Researcher and holds a World Book of Records recognition for a continuous paper presentation marathon. In addition to her research and editorial work, she actively participates in faculty development programs, workshops, and conferences, presenting papers on emerging trends in finance, taxation, and digital transformation. Her professional memberships include the Indian Accounting Association, reflecting her commitment to academic collaboration and research excellence. She also holds multiple certifications in strategic planning, corporate finance, and research methodology from renowned institutions. Sruthi has made notable contributions to academic textbooks in marketing management, service marketing, and e-business laws, further demonstrating her multidisciplinary knowledge. She has also secured patents related to work-life balance evaluation and financial issues in MSMEs, highlighting her innovative research pursuits. With a keen interest in sustainability, financial technology, and digital transformation, Sruthi continues to bridge academia and industry through her impactful research and editorial leadership.

S. Sakthi Bharathi is a scholar in the field of management and is currently pursuing a Ph.D. at Hindusthan College of Arts and Science in Coimbatore. He strongly believes that research knowledge and data analysis are essential for individuals to understand reality. To enhance his skills, he has participated in two ICSSR research methodology courses, workshops, national seminars, and faculty development programs (FDPs) focused on research. He has presented more than 15 papers at various national and international seminars. Additionally, he has published four research papers and three book chapters in national and international journals.

Rahul Sarabu is a seasoned IT professional with over 13 years of extensive experience in data engineering, cloud optimization, and digital transformation. He has spearheaded large-scale projects for industry leaders like USAA, CNA Insurance, and Walmart, focusing on the architecture and deployment of sophisticated data solutions. With deep expertise in cloud platforms such as Google Cloud Platform (GCP), BigQuery, and Dataproc, Rahul has led transformative initiatives that delivered significant cost savings, improved data quality, and ensured regulatory compliance. Rahul's work spans a range of critical domains including financial information systems, ERP migrations, and AI-driven solutions. His innovative approaches to cloud cost optimization and production monitoring have earned him recognition within the industry. A frequent contributor to academic and technical publications, Rahul's writings delve into topics like data governance, big data technologies, and cloud computing architectures. In addition to his technical roles, Rahul actively participates as a peer reviewer and judge in several IEEE conferences, and he holds senior membership with IEEE. His passion for mentoring and contributing to academic knowledge continues to shape his work in developing tools and strategies that bridge the gap between emerging technologies and business impact.

Porkodi Sivaram is a faculty member in the Department of Computer Engineering at Sivas University of Science and Technology, located in Sivas, Turkey. With a focus on advancing knowledge in the field of computer engineering, Porkodi is dedicated to both academic excellence and research. Based in Sivas, Turkey, she contributes to the university's mission of fostering innovation and technological growth within the discipline.

R. Varalakshmi is serving as Dean of Academics-Computational Science and Associate Professor (Computer Science) in SDNB Vaishnav College for Women, India. She received her doctorate degree from Anna University, Chennai. Her research area includes cryptography, network security, cyber security, and allied areas. She has more than 19 years of experience in teaching and research. Her research findings have been published in Web of Science/Scopus-indexed journals, international/national refereed, peer-reviewed journals, and conferences with a high impact factor. Her out-of-the-box thinking and creative ideas enable her to achieve various patents and projects to her credit. She has authored many books in her subject area. She has been recognized by many international and national forums and has also been awarded with the Elite Teacher Award, the Dr. APJ Abdul Kalam Lifetime Achievement Award, the Best Innovator Award, and many others. She is constantly sharing her knowledge through guest lectures, resource persons, session chairs, etc. She has been organizing various conferences, workshops, seminar committees, etc. She served as a NAAC-IQAC member. She is a member of various professional bodies. She is innovative and very dynamic in nature.

Alisha Verma is a seasoned legal scholar and Assistant Professor of Law at Symbiosis Law School, Pune, which is a constituent of Symbiosis International (Deemed University). With over a decade of rich experience in teaching, research, and advocacy, Dr. Verma has established herself as a leading voice in the field of socio-legal studies and gender equality. Her work seamlessly integrates academic precision with a profound commitment to human rights and social justice. She is a dynamic writer who regularly contributes thought-provoking articles to newspapers, shedding light on critical legal and societal issues. Known for her engaging teaching style and dedication to mentoring, Dr. Verma remains deeply committed to advancing legal education and social justice.

Index

A

B

C

D

E

F

G

H

I

J

L

M

O

P

www.ingramcontent.com/pod-product-compliance
Lightning Source LLC
LaVergne TN
LVHW080355011026
849161LV00009B/2315
* 9 7 9 8 3 6 9 3 9 5 8 1 3 *